GALLANTRY

ITS PUBLIC RECOGNITION AND REWARD IN PEACE AND IN WAR AT HOME AND ABROAD

BY

Sir ARNOLD WILSON, M.P.

AND

Capt. J. H. F. McEWEN, M.P.

'All men of prudence, rede, and faith shall give
Applause to me—when I have ceased to live . . .'
Firdausi, Book XII
(Lee & Warner's Trans.).

'True glory's stainless victories,
 Won by the unambitious heart and hand
Of a proud, brotherly and civic band,
 All unbought champions.'
BYRON, *Childe Harold*, Canto III.

'It is the especial duty of an historian not to allow the memory of those men to sink into oblivion who by their deeds have merited an immortality of fame.' PLINY.

Dedicated to
THE CREW OF H.M. SUBMARINE *THETIS*
WHICH SANK OFF GREAT ORME HEAD
ON JUNE 1st, 1939
DURING ACCEPTANCE TRIALS, WITH A LOSS OF NINETY-NINE LIVES

'The bearing of the officers and men in His Majesty's Submarine *Thetis* during the terrible period from the time of the accident was of the highest order, and in accordance with the best traditions of the Service. The behaviour of all the civilians on board was of an equally high standard. The whole country has been moved by the heroic behaviour of their relatives.'

LORD STANHOPE
First Lord of the Admiralty.
House of Lords, June 6th, 1939.

I would like to make known the very gallant behaviour of all the men on board. I saw no signs of panic at any time. Whenever there was any work to be done men sprang to help. I heard men talking and joking until the Commander gave them orders to keep quiet. They showed a quiet bravery which, as a memory, will live with me for ever.

CAPT. H. P. K. ORAM, R.N.
Cmdg. 5th Submarine Flotilla,
in evidence before Tribunal of Inquiry, July 4th, 1939.

Ὦ ξεῖν' ἀγγέλλειν Λακεδαιμονίοις ὅτι τῇδε
κείμεθα, τοῖς κείνων ῥήμασι πειθόμενοι.
SIMONIDES OF CEOS.

Stranger! to Sparta say, her faithful band
Here lie in death, remembering her command.

'Deep and solid minds are improved and brightened by marks of distinction which serve, as a brisk gale, to drive them forward in the pursuit of glory. They do not so much think that they have received a reward as that they have given a pledge, which would make them blush to fall short of the expectations of the public, and therefore they endeavour by their actions to exceed them.'

PLUTARCH: *Life of Caius Marcius Coriolanus.*

INTRODUCTION

'The brave and intelligent expect to leave to their posterity the splendour of their public services, embodied in rank and honours. A country that prohibits such a legacy destroys one of the chief sources of its greatness, and blasts the vital principle of public virtue.'

A New Trend on an Old Subject. DALLAS, 1791

NO one who has faced death alone in the voluntary pursuit of some warlike aim, or in the attempt to save life in peace, would admit that the hope of honour or reward was present to his mind for, disregarding self-interest, at supreme moments the human will overleaps, sometimes instinctively, often deliberately, the bounds of prudence, rising superior to custom and obedience, colour and class. Yet few will deny that public recognition of noble deeds, accorded to those who survive, or to their dependants, helps to create an attitude of mind which is ultimately the deciding factor. That, indeed, is the basis of every system of honours and awards for civil and military merit in ancient and modern times. It is to this end that Orders of Knighthood exist, and that His Majesty from time to time, on the advice of His Ministers, bestows some mark of royal favour upon those of His servants and subjects who have served the State in any capacity. Those who, in the words of Ecclesiasticus, 'maintain the state of the world, for all their desire is in the work of their hands', merit, when from the marriage of opportunity with nobility of soul there springs a gallant deed, no less recognition at the hands of the Head of the State and of their fellows.

Lord Chancellor Bacon[1] observed truly that 'there is no passion in the mind of man so weak but it mates and masters the fear of death'. Carlyle[2] was on higher ground when he wrote: 'Valour is still value. The first duty of man is still that of subduing fear; ... true valour, different enough from ferocity, is the basis of all.' The consecration of valour, he adds, was sufficient religion for Norsemen, and no bad thing, for it was worship of the highest in man known to them. Courage is one of the few virtues which no cynic has sought to denigrate: it is a necessary virtue in war; it is not less valuable in peace. 'The people', said Emerson,[3] 'give it first rank; they forgive everything to it.'

In ancient Greece the word 'hero' was applied not only to warriors of extraordinary strength and courage, but to all who were distinguished from their fellows by superior moral, physical, or intellectual qualities.

---

[1] *Essays. Of Death.*   [2] *Heroes and Hero-Worship.*   [3] *On Courage.*

Six mighty men of valour are mentioned by name in the Old Testament.[1] In the *Iliad*, in *Beowulf*, in the classic writings of Greece and Rome, in the *Shahnamah* of the Persian epic poet Firdausi, in what survives of the work of the great Arabian poets, in the Scandinavian sagas, we see courage first recognized as such and holding, so to speak, a mirror to itself.

The first mention of cowardice in literature is the Dolon incident in the 10th book of the *Iliad*, where it appears as a sporadic abnormality scarcely conceivable to the average man, one of the symptoms of the dawn of civilization and of introspection. Almost as old, perhaps, is the reference in the 78th Psalm to the children of Ephraim who 'being harnessed and carrying bows turned themselves back in the day of battle'. Plato tends to connect or even identify courage with knowledge: it is the main topic of *Laches*, where Nicias distinguishes it from the fearlessness of ignorance. Here, as later in the *Laws*, physical courage and valour are regarded as military virtues but of the lower sort: of courage in civil life nothing is said. Men of valour should be rewarded, as in the *Iliad* (viii. 162), with 'seats of precedence and meats and full cups' and, if young, with kisses and with every encouragement to marry and have children,[2] that there may be more such. Yet Plato would award prizes for victors in the pursuit of the good life as well as of the enemy. A Roman, when he saved the life of a fellow countryman, was crowned with a chaplet of oak[3]—a distinction which carried with it State privileges, which he could share with his father and his father's father. In Greece, a citizen who saved or protected the lives of others was honoured by a crown and a suit of armour. Cowardice was severely dealt with; the only Spartan to escape from Thermopylae was branded, and his bravery and ultimate death at Plataea counted an act less of atonement than of despair.[4]

The classic type of moral courage is that of Christian martyrs from the earliest times, to which, among many other authentic records, *The Acts of the Martyrs of Lyons* and *Foxe's Book of Martyrs* bear witness. Such men and women, boys and girls, were not indeed wholly dis-

---

[1] Gideon (Judges vi. 12); Jephthah the Gileadite (Judges xi. 1); Jeroboam (1 Kings xi. 26); Naaman (2 Kings v. 1); Zadok (1 Chron. xii. 28); and Eliada (2 Chron. xvii. 17).

[2] *Republic* v. 468. The same idea is implicit in the chorus of Dryden's 'Alexander's Feast'—'None but the brave, none but the brave, none but the brave deserves the fair'. Cf. *Laws*, viii. 829 and xii. 943.

[3] Cf. Plutarch, *Life of Caius Marcius Coriolanus*. The following crowns were used by the Romans: *Corona obsidionis* (grass or wild flowers), *civica* (oak), *navalis* or *rostrata* (gold), *muralis* (gold), *castrensis* or *vallaris* (gold), *triumphalis* (laurel or gold), *oleagina* (olive).

[4] Ross of Bladensburg, 'Causes which have led to the Pre-eminence of Nations', *Journal R.U.S.I.*

INTRODUCTION ix

interested, for they looked beyond the physical world to the certainty of a reward beyond the grave. The greatest moral courage is that of men who suffer to the uttermost for absolutely impersonal ends. There are many such to-day, yet no courage ranks higher than that shown by men who, not 300 years ago, stood mute when tried for felony and suffered *peine forte et dure*, being very slowly pressed to death by great stones placed on boards over their naked bodies. They did so generally[1] in order to save associates in the crime with which they were charged.

In the ultimate resort, the repute—sometimes, indeed, the survival—of a nation depends upon the display by a nation's youth, in time of emergency, of those qualities of self-sacrifice and abnegation which go to make courage. To foster these qualities, coupled with presence of mind and the capacity for swift action, in time of peace should be, and of recent years has been, the care of civil governments, not only, or even principally, for military reasons, but for their own sake, as adding dignity and significance to human life. The investigations set forth in successive chapters of this work suggest that we fail in practice to give full weight to the spiritual value, to the society in which we live, of organized and public recognition of civil gallantry such as we accord, from time to time, though with sparing, almost niggardly hand, to military heroes. Dr. Johnson[2] said truly that 'courage is reckoned the greatest of all virtues because, unless a man has that virtue, he has no security for preserving any other'. On another occasion he said: 'Courage is a quality so necessary for maintaining virtue that it is always respected even when it is associated with vice.'[3] It is found at its best among men too humble-minded to know they possess it, too obscure for the world to discover it. Of virtues it is the most unequivocal, for it cannot be counterfeited with impunity: it is, in Sir Philip Sidney's words, 'the valliance of men despising death, but confident, as men unwonted to be overcome'.

Courage is the generosity of men who will freely offer what they hold dearest. In the minds of such men, as Virgil[4] said of bees, the thought of death has no place, and like bees they seek a noble death that the race may live. But here the likeness ends, for the act of self-sacrifice is less often instinctive than deliberate, undertaken not without but in spite of knowledge of the full consequences to the man and to his dependants.

No apology, therefore, is needed, and no justification required, for the attempt here made, we believe for the first time, to summarize the

---

[1] *Middlesex Sessions Records* (N.S.), vols. i, ii.
[2] Boswell's *Life of Johnson*, ed. Birkbeck Hill, vol. ii, p. 339 (April 5, 1775).
[3] Ibid., vol. iv, p. 297. [4] *Georgics*, IV.

INTRODUCTION

existing practice of the State and of public and other bodies in this and other countries in rewarding acts of gallantry whether in peace or in war. Military gallantry has been placed first because, in a world in which effective political influence cannot long be exercised apart from military force, awards for deeds of valour in the presence of the enemy necessarily have historical precedence[1] over the public recognition of heroism in civil life.

The reader will note that whilst every officer and man of all the armed forces of the Crown is eligible for the V.C., and every officer for the D.S.O., there are, with the exception of the Medal of the Order of the British Empire, for Gallantry, no lesser military decorations or awards for which all officers and men of the three arms are alike eligible. It is perhaps too late now to suggest that the Military Cross of the Army, the Distinguished Service Cross of the Navy, and the Distinguished Flying Cross of the Air Force should be amalgamated and replaced by a single decoration which might be called the Conspicuous Gallantry Cross, yet there is much to be said for a change which would emphasize the unity and solidarity of the three services.

For similar reasons of sentiment it is perhaps useless to urge the replacement of the Conspicuous Gallantry Medal of the Navy, the Military Medal of the Army, and the Distinguished Flying Medal of the Air Force by a single Conspicuous Gallantry Medal, for which all ranks below that of commissioned officer would be eligible, with a similar unified counterpart for service not in the face of the enemy—viz. a Distinguished Conduct Medal, to replace the Naval D.S.M., the Military D.C.M., and the Air Force A.F.M. These possibilities are here mentioned less in the hope that they will be adopted than to emphasize the importance of uniformity and to draw attention to the present disparity between the pecuniary awards for which recipients of these medals are eligible in their respective Services. But there is a strong case for making all rewards for gallantry in the three Services identical both for officers and for men and there is reason to believe that it would be welcomed in the Services.

The Medal of the Order of the British Empire, for Gallantry (E.G.M.), was instituted in 1922 to reward acts of gallantry warranting a mark of Royal appreciation performed by persons of whatever rank whether in the service of the Crown or not, in the British Empire, or elsewhere.[1] It met a very real need and filled a notable gap; for instance, previous to its institution, acts of gallantry in peace, or behind the lines in war, could be recognized in the Armed Forces of the Crown only by the Albert Medal.

[1] Military medals are said to have been awarded in China in the Han dynasty (A.D. 10). Tancred, *Historical Record of Medals and Honorary Distinctions*, 1891.

INTRODUCTION

The number of awards of the Empire Gallantry Medal up to the 1st December 1938 totals about 100, equally divided between the Military and the Civil Division, an average of about six a year. The Medal carries no gratuity or annuity such as is attached to the Meritorious Service Medal, which is awarded for good service in peace, *not* for gallantry at critical moments.

It seems clear that further steps should be taken to make this Medal better known and to ensure that all suitable acts of gallantry should be brought to notice and given wider publicity.

As to Civil Awards for gallantry it is perhaps premature to contemplate the entire cessation of the present system, whereunder a number of unofficial societies award medals, permission to wear which has, in some cases,[1] been given by the Sovereign, for deeds which, in almost every case, are fully worthy of public and official recognition. There can, however, be little doubt that more frequent awards of the Albert Medal (A.M.), the Edward Medal (E.M.), and the Empire Gallantry Medal (E.G.M.) would be amply justified. Only 22 Albert Medals have been awarded since 1930, of which 10 in India. Since 1921 only one Albert Medal has been awarded to a civilian for a deed of gallantry in Britain other than for sea service. The figures suggest that much more effective machinery than now exists is required to ensure that heroic deeds deserving of recognition at the hands of the Sovereign are brought to notice. As things are the Albert Medal is as seldom given to a British civilian as the Order of Merit.

Board of Trade Sea Gallantry Medals have been somewhat more liberally awarded, averaging 2 gold, 20 silver, and 10 bronze medals a year. This decoration has precedence over the Edward Medal.

A standard of merit so high that not even one person is awarded the Albert Medal in ten years and only four the Edward Medal annually for deeds of gallantry performed in these Islands defeats its own object. There would seem to be a strong case for the creation (as in the case of the S.G.M.) of a third class in each order, so that each medal would be available in gold, silver, and bronze, or, better still, for the restriction of each medal to one class only. Few persons have ever seen, many have never heard of, these medals or the Empire Gallantry Medal. Wherever the King's writ runs, magistrates, coroners, public bodies, employers, and trade unions should be encouraged to report gallant deeds. Occasions of extreme gallantry in civil life are far more frequent than is commonly supposed. The very fact that they are brought to notice and the recipients honoured serves as a stimulus to national self-respect and individual endeavour. As British subjects in every part of the

[1] Viz. the Royal Humane Society, the Royal National Lifeboat Institution, and the Order of St. John of Jerusalem.

Empire are eligible alike for the Albert, Edward, King's Police Gallantry, and Sea Gallantry Medals, it would appear proper on constitutional, and convenient on administrative, grounds that, as in the case of many other marks of His Majesty's favour, submissions should be made by (or, in the case of the Dominion Governments, through) the Prime Minister as First Lord of the Treasury.

A King's Fire Brigade Medal, on the analogy of the King's Police Medal, would be a valuable innovation and in harmony with the increasing importance of this force, especially in connexion with the Civil Defence Services. The two services are independent and deserve separate recognition.

The Board of Trade Sea Gallantry Medal (see Chapter XIX) might well be replaced by a King's Sea Gallantry Medal, to be established by Royal Warrant, for which seamen of this country, the Dominions, India, and the Colonies would be eligible.

Existing arrangements for placing on public record the acts of gallantry in respect of which official awards are made leave much to be desired. They are generally published in *The London Gazette*, are occasionally mentioned in the popular press and, very seldom, by the B.B.C., but they are nowhere subsequently available in accessible form. We are confident that an annual publication devoted to recording such acts, in adequate detail, accompanied where possible by a photograph of the recipient and some reference to his circumstances, would be assured of a wide sale. One such unpublished record, of recipients of an unofficial award,[1] has come under our notice and, though incomplete, it is as stirring and heartening a record as any in existence.

We can see no good reason why arrangements should not be made for the appropriate department to keep in touch with all recipients, maintaining a record of their addresses so long as they live, in order that they may receive invitations when occasion arises to attend local and national ceremonies. This would not be a difficult task, for there are fewer Albert and Edward Medallists than V.C.s living in the United Kingdom.

Action on such lines might be facilitated by the transfer of responsibility for maintaining registers of the various orders and medals from the respective Ministries[2] to a Central Chancery for the Orders and Medals of Knighthood and Gallantry. Such an office might well publish annually, as an official publication, a book containing the Royal Warrants, with nominal rolls of all living recipients of orders

---

[1] *The Daily Herald* Order of Industrial Heroism (see p. 48).
[2] Albert and Edward Medals—Home Office, Board of Trade, and Admiralty.
Sea Gallantry Medal—Board of Trade.
Empire Gallantry Medal—The Treasury.

and medals for civil and military gallantry, and full details of all awards during the previous year—in words that, as Kipling once said 'may come to life and walk up and down in the hearts of men'.

The Corporation of Glasgow has the unique distinction of conferring its own medal on those citizens who have performed deeds of gallantry in civil life within its civil boundaries, while the L.C.C. and the Corporations of Manchester and of West Ham among others have long awarded medals for gallantry to members of their own fire brigades. We doubt whether these precedents could advantageously be followed by other great municipalities, but they might well imitate the simple record of gallant deeds of Londoners, originally initiated by G. F. Watts, and maintained since by the Corporation of the City of London in the old churchyard of St. Botolph's, Aldersgate (see p. 76).

That the public at large admire heroism and earnestly desire that it should be recognized is shown by the enthusiasm of those who witness the presentation of Unofficial awards, to men who so often amply merit one of those Official awards for gallantry that the Sovereign can grant, for deeds which, whether by accident, indifference, or ignorance, have not been reported to the proper quarter. It is in the highest interest of the nation at large that such deeds should be recognized and applauded: a public dinner to holders of these three medals, such as was given in the House of Lords on the 9th November 1929 under the presidency of the Prince of Wales, would arouse no less enthusiasm than was evoked on that occasion. In the words of *The Times* of the 11th November:

'Military rank or social standing counted for nothing at this unprecedented and astonishing dinner. Seats had been allocated by the drawing of numbers. . . . The turn of the ballot brought to the top table privates and generals, a one-time drummer and an Admiral of the Fleet. The wearing of a little Maltese Cross of bronze placed all the guests possessing the decoration on an equal footing.'

A large crowd gathered outside the Houses of Parliament to see the arrival of the V.C.s and as the guests hurried shyly through the throng they were loudly cheered. In an after-dinner speech the Prince referred to the gathering as members of 'the most democratic and at the same time the most exclusive of all orders of chivalry'—the 'Most Enviable Order of the Victoria Cross'—recruited from 'that very limited circle of men who see what is needed to be done and do it at once at their own peril and, having done it, shut up like the proverbial oyster.'

Those happy words apply with equal justice to the holders of all the

The Admiralty, War Office, and Air Ministry keep the registers of various military decorations.
The Central Chancery for the Orders of Knighthood keeps the registers for the Order and Medal of the British Empire.

Albert and Edward Medals, the Sea Gallantry, Empire Gallantry and King's Police Gallantry Medals. No society can safely ignore the ethical and spiritual importance of public recognition of unselfish heroism in daily life. We have need of heroes, and we have many. We do well to remind ourselves of this fact: we cannot be on safer ground than in honouring such men and women as those whose names are recorded in this work.

ARNOLD WILSON.

CONTENTS

CHAPTER I. BRITISH ORDERS OF MILITARY GALLANTRY *pages 1–22*
Early Awards. Monetary Awards. The Duke of Wellington's views. Earl St. Vincent. Lord Nelson. Napoleon's observations. The wrecks of the *Sea Horse* and the *Birkenhead*. The Victoria Cross. Recent Awards. The Royal Red Cross. The Distinguished Service Order. The Military Cross. The Distinguished Service Cross. The Distinguished Flying Cross. The Air Force Cross. The Order of British India. The Indian Order of Merit. The Distinguished Conduct Medal. The Conspicuous Gallantry Medal. The Distinguished Service Medal. The Military Medal. The Indian D.S.M. The Distinguished Flying Medal. The Air Force Medal. The Medal of the Order of the British Empire, for Gallantry. The Meritorious Service Medal.

CHAPTER II. FOREIGN ORDERS OF MILITARY GALLANTRY *pages 23–5*
France. Germany. U.S.A.

CHAPTER III. AWARDS FOR CIVIL GALLANTRY IN FOREIGN COUNTRIES . . . . . . *pages 26–31*
Belgium. Czechoslovakia. France. Germany. Italy. Japan. Poland. Portugal. Spain. Sweden. U.S.A. U.S.S.R.

CHAPTER IV. AWARDS FOR CIVIL GALLANTRY IN GREAT BRITAIN AND THE EMPIRE. I. ON LAND . . . *pages 32–58*
Medal of Order of British Empire, for Gallantry and for Meritorious Service. Kaisar-i-Hind Gold Medal. St. John of Jerusalem. Royal Humane Society and branches. Civil Gallantry awards in Canada. Australia, New Zealand, and Sarawak. Corporation of Glasgow. L.C.C. Fire Brigade Medal. Society for Preservation of Life from Fire. Corporations of Manchester and West Ham. Boy Scouts and Girl Guides. R.S.P.C.A. 'Daily Herald' Order of Industrial Heroism. Individual Medals. Maharaja of Burdwan. 'Charlie the Gunner.' 'Joseph Hanson, The Weavers' Friend.' S.S. *Baltic* and *Republic*. Hong Kong Plague Medal.

CHAPTER V. AWARDS FOR CIVIL GALLANTRY IN GREAT BRITAIN AND THE EMPIRE. II. AT SEA . . . *pages 59–68*
Board of Trade Gold and Silver Medals for Foreign Services. Sea Gallantry Medal. Awards in India and the Dominions. Unofficial Awards for Gallantry at Sea. Royal National Lifeboat Institution. Shipwrecked Fishermen and Mariners' Society. Liverpool Shipwreck and Humane Society. Lloyds Medals. Order of St. John of Jerusalem.

CHAPTER VI. THE CARNEGIE HERO FUND . . *pages 69–75*
How founded. Conditions of Trust. Number of awards.

CONTENTS

CHAPTER VII. A MUNICIPAL VALHALLA . . . *pages* 76–81
Postmen's Park. G. F. Watts. List of deeds recorded.

CHAPTER VIII. THE ALBERT AND EDWARD AND KING'S POLICE MEDALS . . . . *pages* 82–91
Albert Medal instituted. Correspondence from Windsor Archives. Early Awards. Conditions. Number of Awards. The Edward Medal instituted. Conditions. Number of Awards. King's Police and Fire Brigade Medals. Conditions. Number of awards.

CHAPTER IX. AWARDS OF THE ALBERT MEDAL, 1877–1914 *pages* 92–119

CHAPTER X. AWARDS OF THE EDWARD MEDAL, JAN. 1908–DEC. 1914 . . . . *pages* 120–55

CHAPTER XI. AWARDS OF THE ALBERT MEDAL, JAN. 1915–DEC. 1919 . . . . . . *pages* 156–87

CHAPTER XII. AWARDS OF THE EDWARD MEDAL, JAN. 1915–DEC. 1919 . . . . . . *pages* 188–207

CHAPTER XIII. AWARDS OF THE ALBERT MEDAL, JAN. 1920–DEC. 1938 . . . . . . *pages* 209–23

CHAPTER XIV. AWARDS OF THE EDWARD MEDAL, JAN. 1920–DEC. 1938 . . . . . . *pages* 225–80

CHAPTER XV. MEDAL OF THE ORDER OF THE BRITISH EMPIRE, MILITARY DIVISION, FOR GALLANTRY . *pages* 281–92

CHAPTER XVI. MEDAL OF THE ORDER OF THE BRITISH EMPIRE, CIVIL DIVISION, FOR GALLANTRY . *pages* 293–308

CHAPTER XVII. AWARDS OF THE ALBERT MEDAL, FOR SEA SERVICE (ADMIRALTY), 1868–1938 . . *pages* 309–35

CHAPTER XVIII. AWARDS OF THE ALBERT MEDAL, FOR CIVILIAN SEA SERVICE (BOARD OF TRADE), 1866–1938 . *pages* 336–81

CHAPTER XIX. AWARDS OF BOARD OF TRADE MEDALS FOR GALLANTRY IN SAVING LIFE AT SEA, 1854–1921 . *pages* 382–400

CHAPTER XX. AWARDS OF THE BOARD OF TRADE MEDAL FOR GALLANTRY IN SAVING LIFE AT SEA, 1922–1938 . *pages* 401–32

APPENDIXES

APPENDIX I. Medals Granted by Special Act or Resolution of Congress. . . . . *pages* 433–9

APPENDIX II. Correspondence from the Windsor Archives relating to the Institution of the Distinguished Service Order. . *pages* 440–50

INDEX (Names, Places, General) . . . *pages* 451–98

BIBLIOGRAPHY

Army, Navy, and Air Force Lists.
Bacon, *Essays.*
Boswell's *Life of Johnson*, ed. Birbeck Hill, vols. ii, iv.
Carlyle, Thomas, *Heroes and Hero-Worship.*
Carnegie, Andrew, *The Trusts and their Work*, 1935.
—— *Autobiography.*
Firdausi, *Shahnamah.*
Foster, T. E., *Memoir of the Hartley Colliery Accident*, Reid and Co., Newcastle, 1912.
Gibson, *British Military and Naval Decorations*, 1880.
Hammond, J. L. and B., *The Skilled Labourer.*
Hanson, Joseph, *Defence of the Petitions for Peace*, 1808.
Irwin, D. Hastings, *War Medals and Decorations*, 1910.
Jocelyn, Capt. Arthur, *Orders, Decorations, and Medals of the World*—Vol. I. The British Empire, 1934.
Mayo, *Medals and Decorations of the British Army and Navy*, Constable, 1897.
O'Moore Creagh, Sir N., and Humphris, E. H., editors, *The V.C. and D.S.O.*, Standard Art Book Co., Ltd.
Plutarch, *Life of Caius Marcius Coriolanus.*
Prentice's *Manchester, 1792–1832.*
Proctor's *Memorials of Manchester Streets* and *Annual Register of 1809.*
Tancred, *Historical Record of Medals and Honorary Distinctions*, 1891.
Watts, M. S. (Mrs.), *George Frederick Watts, Annals of an Artist's Life*, Macmillan, 1912.
Yonge, C. M., *Book of Golden Deeds*, Macmillan's 'Treasury for Young People' Series.
Seamen's Torch, The Life Story of Captain Edward Tupper, 1938.
Colonial Report No. 148, Hong Kong, 1895.
Report of Chief Inspector of Mines, Parl. Papers, 1862.
Journal R.U.S.I. Ross of Bladensburg, 'Causes which have led to the Pre-eminence of Nations'.
Journ. of Soc. for Army Historical Research, vol. xvii, 1938.
Middlesex Sessions Record (N.S.), vols. i, ii.
Statistics of Military Effort of British Empire during the Great War 1914–20, War Office, March 1922.
U.S. Bureau of Mines Information Circular 6831.

CHAPTER I
BRITISH ORDERS OF MILITARY GALLANTRY

'"Macte virtute esto" sanguinolentis ex acie redeuntibus dicitur.
'It is to the bloodstained soldier back from the war that men cry "Well done".'
SENECA, *Ep.* lxvi. 51.

NAVAL and military decorations may be given—
(i) to individuals
 (*a*) for personal valour;
 (*b*) for meritorious conduct.
(ii) for participation in battles or campaigns,
 (*a*) to commanders and superior officers;
 (*b*) to officers and men alike.

In the first class are the Forlorn Hope Badge of Charles I, the medals and chains for captains of fireships, the Indian Order of Merit (most unsuitably named) dating from 1837, the Victoria Cross, and certain other decorations described below. In the second class are the Armada medals, those given by Parliament to Monk, Blake, and others, the gold medals and crosses given in the reign of George III, the Mutiny and earlier medals of the E.I. Company, medals given by private persons, such as Davison, Hardy, and Boulton, and lastly medals given by the Crown, beginning with the Waterloo medals. There are, of course, many others, a list of which is given in Mayo's classic volumes, and in Tancred's work, which fall into both categories. With collars, jewels, swords of honour, and plate presented for gallantry we are not here concerned.

There is much obscurity surrounding the honorary badges struck in the reigns of Queen Elizabeth and James I, though they seem to have been worn as decorations. The magnificent Star and Jewel given by Queen Elizabeth to Sir Francis Drake is one of the few that can be verified.

Charles I at Edgehill on the 23rd October 1642 knighted Robert Welch on the field of battle for conspicuous gallantry and afterwards presented him with a gold medal.

William III and Mary recompensed bravery even in defeat. After an engagement in 1689 off Bantry Bay, in which the French repulsed the English fleet, Admiral Herbert was created a peer, ten captains were knighted, and every seaman received ten shillings. After Russell's victory at La Hogue gold medals were presented to senior officers and £30,000 divided among the seamen. Civil gallantry did not go unrecognized, several seamen receiving gold medals and chains as a reward for gallantry, and Queen Anne sent gold medals to the senior officers of Admiral Dilke's squadron in recognition of the intrepid conduct of those under their command, a precedent not forgotten by George II.

The earliest record of awards in Britain for gallantry to individual naval ratings is a letter dated Admiralty Office the 13th March 1703, requesting

'authority to pay £240 to Isaac Newton, Esq., Master of the Mint for two medals and two chains, for Henry Gilber, the master and Elisha Dann, the boatswain of the "Torbay" respectively, as already awarded to Benjamin Bryer, the gunner of the same ship, for gallantry in extinguishing the fire on board the "Torbay" at Vigo October 11 1702 when the Captain was blown overboard.'[1]

To this period, too, belongs a circular silver medal with a chased border, bearing on the obverse the bust of Queen Anne in high relief and, on the reverse, the following inscription:

'Her Maj'ties reward to Robt Taylor, Boy of þe "Mary" Galley for his Zeal and Courage at þe taking of þe French Privateer "Jacques La Blonde" of Dunkirk.'

The earliest record extant of an award for saving life at sea is a large silver medal granted during the reign of George I, having on the obverse the bust of the King and on the reverse the inscription:

'Admiral Sir George Byng gave this medall to Seaman Willm Wright for his courage in saving the lives of two seamen from drowning during the action with the Spaniards off the Cape of Passaro þe 31st day of July 1718.'[2]

Monetary awards for officers were first definitely established in 1742,[3] when Lieutenant Green was awarded £50 by Order in Council for gallantry, when, in June 1742, Captain Collis, in the fireship *Duke*, burned five Spanish galleys anchored in the French port of St. Tropez.

The Duke of Wellington was responsible for the extended distribution of medals. He wrote to the Secretary of State on the 11th July 1811, after a full and lucid discussion of the subject, 'the principle of selection without reference to ranks ought to be adopted in every instance of the grant of medals to the Army', though 'a selection of those who have had any opportunity of distinguishing themselves in an action is a less objectionable mode of granting it than the grant of it by classes, whether the individuals composing those classes have distinguished themselves or not'.[4]

[1] D. Hastings Irwin, *War Medals and Decorations*, 1910, p. 15.   [2] Ibid., p. 15.
[3] Ibid., p. 17. The Order is dated 16th Dec. 1742. Captain Collis was promoted, and received a gold medal and chain at the hands of King George II. The same Order in Council established a like financial reward for lieutenants in similar circumstances thereafter. See also Mayo, *Medals and Decorations of the British Army and Navy*, vol. ii, p. lviii (Constable, 1897).   [4] *Despatches*, vol. viii, p. 98.

Shortly after Waterloo he wrote complaining of the invidious task thrust upon him of distributing foreign Orders. 'Nobody is pleased ... the taste for Orders is like that for colour, it is impossible to know what will suit everybody.'

In 1793 the 12th Light Dragoons were present at the attack on the island of Corsica. Part of the Regiment took part by land in the capture of Bastia; the remainder was stationed at Città Vecchia in Italy. As a mark of satisfaction with their conduct there, His Holiness Pope Pius VI presented gold medals to all the officers, accompanied by a letter couched in the warmest terms.[1]

Foreign sovereigns frequently made special awards of medals to officers of individual regiments. The Emperor of Germany presented a gold medal in 1798 to each of the eight officers of the 15th Light Dragoons who distinguished themselves by their spirited attack upon the enemy, with a very inferior force, near Cambrai. General Eliott presented a silver medal to the officers of the Hanoverian Brigade for their part in the defence of Gibraltar *'per tot discrimina rerum'* from 1779 to 1782, another medal being struck and presented by General Picton to officers present during the siege. Both bore on the reverse:

'By a zealous exertion of patience, perseverance and intrepidity after contending with an unparalleled succession of dangers and difficulties in the defence of Gibraltar during a blockade and siege of almost four years, the garrison, under the auspices of George III, triumphed over the combined powers of France and Spain.'[2]

Medals were not always issued in respect of military operations. After the mutiny at the Nore, a silver medal inscribed *'Loyal and true. Earl St. Vincent's testimony of approbation 1800'* was issued by the Admiral to the petty officers and seamen of the flagship *Ville de Paris* as a token of their loyalty,[3] and none was more greatly prized. Private individuals sometimes struck medals at their own cost and secured their distribution through official channels. Mr. Davison, Nelson's prize agent, presented medals in gold, silver, bronze gilt, and bronze, at a cost of £2,000, to all admirals and captains, lieutenants and warrant officers, petty officers, and seamen and marines respectively, who were present at the battle of the Nile in August 1798.[4] Mr. Boulton, of the

[1] Irwin, p. 27. The letter, dated 30th May 1794, was signed by De Zelada, the Cardinal Secretary of State. [2] Idem., p. 26. [3] Idem., p. 34.

[4] Another medal, for Trafalgar, is said to have been presented by Mr. Davison to the officers and crew of H.M.S. *Victory*. The obverse has a bust of Lord Nelson, with the inscription: 'Tria juncta in uno. Palmam qui meruit ferat. Admiral Lord Nelson, D. of Bronte, natus Sept. 29, 1758. Hoste devicto requievit Oct. 21, 1805. England expects every man will do his duty.' The reverse has a man-of-war with furled sails, and reads: 'The Lord is a man of war. Exodus c. 15. v. 3. Victory of Trafalgar over the combined fleets of France and Spain, Oct. 21, 1805.'

Soho Foundry in Birmingham, presented a medal at his own cost to every seaman present at the battle of Trafalgar, inscribed:

'England expects every man will do his duty. To the heroes of Trafalgar from M. Boulton.'

Though given by a private person, they were worn like service medals—surely the high-water mark of private enterprise. No other medals were issued by the Government, nor was any medal issued for Trafalgar until 1849, when the survivors of that victory and that of the Nile received the Naval General Service Medal.[1]

Another medal of this type is the Hardy medal, no. KK3 in the catalogue of the Medal Section of the National Maritime Museum at Greenwich. The description of it is as follows:

'Engraved on a circular plate within a laurel wreath a foul anchor, crowned, G.R. as supporters, inscription below/inscription within a laurel wreath.
    Inscr. Obverse, Wm. Adams, Or Mr Mte HMS Victory. Reverse, Reward of merit by order of Capt. T. Hardy. Metal from French Ship Redoubtable taken at Trafalgar Oct. 21st 1805 after having 300 killed and wounded. Fitted with a loop.'

The preface to the catalogue, by Lord Sandwich, who presented the majority of the medals in the Museum, says:

'The executors of the late Mr John H. Walter have lent a number of specimens relating to Lord Nelson, the most important being an iron medal, probably unique, given by Captain Hardy for bravery to one of his petty officers.'

An example of individual medals to officers for gallantry during the nineteenth century is the medal and gold chain awarded by George III to the commander of H.M.S. *Mediator* on the 11th April 1809, inscribed on the reverse:

'Captain James Wooldridge led the British Fireships when four French sails of the Line were burnt under their own batteries in Aix Roads.'

During the action he was blown out of a port, and after years of intense suffering fell a sacrifice to the injuries he received.[2]

Another individual medal which the recipient was authorized to wear by Royal Warrant, dated 4th January 1813, was purchased at a cost of £100 by the officers of the 3rd Foot (Buffs) for presentation to Lieutenant Latham, who, at the battle of Albuera, during the Peninsular War, prevented the King's Colour from falling into the hands of the enemy.[3]

---

[1] Irwin, p. 47.   [2] Tancred, p. 416.
[3] Irwin, p. 3. 'The colour was being carried by Ensign Walsh, and the colour party being all killed or wounded, Ensign Walsh was taken prisoner. At that moment Lt. Latham seized the flag, and, though surrounded by the enemy, clung with heroic tenacity to his

The gold medal bears a representation of this heroic action with the inscription on the obverse:

'Albuera May 16, 1811. I will surrender it only with my life.'

The reverse reads:

'To Lieut. Latham, 3rd Regt. (or the Buffs) as a testimonial from his brother officers of their high opinion of his distinguished conduct in defending the colours of the Regiment in the Battle of Albuera, in which he lost an arm and part of his face.'

It is recorded that when Napoleon I surrendered on board H.M.S. *Bellerophon* in July 1815, he was received by a captain's detachment of Royal Marines. After acknowledging the salute, the ex-Emperor minutely inspected the men and, having remarked that they were very fine and well-appointed, added, 'Are there none amongst them who have seen service?' Upon being told that nearly all of them were veterans, he exclaimed, 'What! and no marks of merit?' The officer in command explained that it was not customary to confer medals, except upon officers of the highest rank. 'Such is not the way to excite or cherish military virtues,' replied Napoleon; a bold remark, having regard to the circumstances which had brought him on board![1]

Medals were occasionally presented to individuals for gallantry in the field by commanding officers. A score of examples, from 1793 to 1851, are mentioned by Tancred. They show clearly how widespread was the desire to recognize gallantry. One of them relates to deeds of individual heroism performed by members of the British Legion in Spain under General de Lacy Evans (see Tancred, p. 467).

But the initiative was left to commanding officers, and the value of public recognition of gallantry and discipline in face of danger was not, and indeed is still not, appreciated.

A notable example of military discipline in such circumstances which was accorded no public recognition is that of the transport *Sea Horse* from Ramsgate for Ireland with 16 officers and 286 men of the 2nd/59th Foot, 33 women and 38 children, a naval lieutenant and the master and 18 sailors, wrecked on 28th January 1816, in a gale under the Brownstown Head on the east side of the Bay of Tramore, 7 miles south of Waterford.

precious charge. A French hussar seized the staff and, cutting at Lt. Latham's head, wounded him severely but failed to make him release his hold. A second sword cut severed his left arm from his body, but grasping the staff with his right hand, he exclaimed, "I will surrender it only with my life." Although defenceless he would not yield: he was knocked down and trampled on, but contrived to conceal the colour under his body. At this moment the advancing British cavalry compelled the French to retire. When the Fusilier Brigade advanced they found Lt. Latham apparently dead, with the colour still in his possession.'

[1] Irwin, p. 7.

'There was no hope for the soldiers. They stood firm on deck and the only sounds, besides the raging of the storm, were the cries of those who were washed off and the prayers of the rest. Between decks was noticed a sergeant's wife, holding her three children to her breast, resigned to her fate. Others, who could not save themselves, packed their children in chests and committed them to the sea, which washed them ashore....

'Quartermaster Baird, hoping against hope, kept coming up from the cabin where his wife was seated with a child in her lap, while Lieutenant Scott was gradually comforting the other child—a girl of eleven—who was frantic in the berth, while the sea water poured down the companion-way: so the end came to them—the young Ulster subaltern, the veteran of twenty years' service, his wife and two daughters.... Altogether only 4 subalterns and 24 soldiers (including 3 batmen of the 4 officers) and one sailor reached the Strand alive.

'There were drowned 364 souls—including 15 officers and 245 men of the 2nd/59th and 55 women and children of the Regiment. Everything was lost—including the Mess plate (valued at some £2,000) and spoils of war (chests of which were plundered by the peasantry). The women and the young officers, half of them Scots, were laid in the village churchyard, and the men were buried at the entrance to the sand-hills or rabbit burrow, above high water, two miles down the Great Strand, where it is almost surrounded by the sea.

'The surviving officers had an inscribed slab placed over their comrades' grave in Tramore churchyard, but subsequently, when they replaced it with a column (sculptured in Waterford with a brief Record of the Battalion), the slab was returned to Waterford and later placed at the sand-hills grave.'[1]

Thirty-six years later H.M. Steamship *Birkenhead* from Cork to India with troops was lost on the reefs off Point Danger in Simon's Bay, Cape of Good Hope, at about 2 a.m. on 26th February 1852, 438 seamen, soldiers, and boys out of 630 being lost; the women and children on board were saved.[2] The Report of the Naval Court-Martial proceedings laid before Parliament include the testimony of Captain Wright, 91st Regiment, one of the survivors, that 'the utmost order was observed on board by all; until the vessel disappeared there was

[1] *Journal of Soc. for Army Historical Research*, vol. xvii, p. 65, 1938.
Another transport, the *Lord Melville*, was wrecked off the Old Head of Kinsale the same day.
[2] Of this tragedy Mr. D. Joel, M.P., wrote in *The Times*, 16th June 1939:
'When I visited the lighthouse at Danger Point a couple of years ago there was a signed photograph of an elderly cavalry major or colonel hanging up. He, as a young lieutenant, was one of the few male survivors of the disaster and had reached shore by hanging on to the tail of a horse. The lighthouse-keeper told me that the photograph had been presented to a predecessor of his when the officer had revisited the scene many years later. He also said that he had recently had a visit from the grandson of the Boer owner of the surrounding land at the time of the wreck. The farmer and some members of his family happened to be sleeping in their wagon by the beach that fatal night, having come down to fish. They were awakened by the galloping of a grey horse for whose presence they were unable to account and knew nothing of the tragedy till daylight disclosed it. That so few survivors managed to swim ashore was no doubt due to the masses of seaweed around the reef as well as to the presence of sharks.'

not a cry or murmur from soldiers or sailors. It struck me as one of the most perfect instances of what discipline can effect.'

The Naval Court Martial on the survivors acquitted them of blame, and saw reason 'to admire and applaud the steadiness shown by all in most trying circumstances', but they received no official recognition of the fact that by their bearing in face of death they set an example to their countrymen, the memory of which is still kept alive by Yule's poem—which was once a favourite recitation piece in English schools—and in the thousands of humble homes in which may still be seen reproductions of Thomas M. M. Hemy's picture of the last moments of the *Birkenhead*.[1] We make no apology for discursiveness in here reproducing an extract from Henry Yule's poem, which will be found in full in *Lyra Heroica*[2]—a book which most schoolmasters and mistresses have long forgotten or laid aside :—

THE BIRKENHEAD
(*Wrecked off Danger Point, Cape of Good Hope, Feb. 28th, 1852.*)
... Europe, hear!
When they tell thee 'England is a fen,
Corrupt, a Kingdom tottering to decay,
Her nerveless burghers lying an easy prey
For the first comer,' tell how the other day
A crew of half a thousand Englishmen
Went down into the deep in Simon's Bay!

Not with the cheer of battle in the throat,
Or cannon-glare and din to stir their blood,
But, roused from dreams of home to find their ship
Fast sinking, mustered on the deck they stood,
Biding God's pleasure and their chief's command.

. . . .

Heroes! Who were those heroes? Veterans steeled
To face the King of Terrors mid the scaith
Of many a hurricane and trenchéd field?
Far other: weavers from the stocking-frame;
Boys from the plough; cornets with beardless chin,
But steeped in honour and in discipline!

Weep! Britain, . . .
. . . but as thou weepest thank
Heaven for those undegenerate sons who sank
Aboard the Birkenhead in Simon's Bay.   YULE.

[1] Painted in 1892 or 1893: photogravure published by Graves in 1893, now at Glanusk Park, Crickhowell, Breconshire, S. Wales, together with a picture by the same artist of the sinking of the *Lusitania*.
[2] First published in *Edinburgh Evening Courant*: republished in *Fragments of Unprofessional Papers* (Anon.), P.W.D. Press, Calcutta, 1862.

More than forty years after the close of the Napoleonic wars the *Victoria Cross* was instituted, on the termination of the Crimean War, by Royal Warrant dated the 20th January 1856, Field-Marshal the Prince Consort being, it was said, the originator and designer and responsible for selecting the inexpensive metal used—bronze from captured guns. But it was in the Crimea itself that the idea was born, and it was voiced by William Howard Russell, correspondent of *The Times*, who, in a letter dated the 13th December 1855, referred to the need for such a distinction, adding that—

'If it be established, it is hoped that it will bear the name of the Queen, with the significance of whose Royal *praenomen* it would so thoroughly harmonize.'

The Victoria Cross was long unique among British decorations for valour, in that it was given alike to all ranks, to men and women alike without distinction, and for valour only. With the exception of the Medal of the Order of the British Empire, Military Division, for Gallantry, which is given to all ranks, all other military decorations are awarded either to officers or to other ranks, a practice which was long ago abandoned in the case of war medals and was never universal.

The Victoria Cross carries an annuity of £10[1] (except for officers) and £5 for each bar or clasp, but may be forfeited for crime or cowardice. The essential qualification is conspicuous bravery or devotion to the country in presence of the enemy, but provision was made in 1858 for an award to officers and men of the armed forces 'who may perform acts of conspicuous courage and bravery in circumstances of extreme danger, such as the occurrence of fire on board ship, or the foundering of a vessel at sea, or in any other circumstances in which, through the courage or devotion displayed, life or public property might be saved'.[2] This provision was omitted when the amending and consolidated Warrant was issued in May 1920—a retrograde step which passed unnoticed at the time.[3] It was, in successive warrants, extended to civilians, to colonial forces, and, on the recommendation of Sir N. O'Moore Creagh, then C.-in-C. in India, it was extended in 1911 and 1916 to Indian troops. Posthumous grants to relatives were authorized in 1912.

---

[1] May be increased to £75 in special cases of need: Royal Warrants, 1898 and 1921. The number of British holders of the V.C. in receipt of this special annuity is nine, of whom three receive the maximum annuity. A special rate of annuity, on a higher scale, is provided for Indian recipients, of whom there are nine now living, and for a pension to the holder and to his widow, a form of recognition which should certainly be of general application to all holders.

[2] The only case on record is that of Private Timothy O'Hea, 1st Bn. The Rifle Brigade, for helping to extinguish a fire in an ammunition railway car during the Fenian Raid of 1866 in Canada. In 1876 he was lost in the Australian Bush and no trace of him was ever found.

[3] See *Debates* H.C., 14.6.39, col. 1303.

Different ribands were at one time prescribed for the Navy (blue) and Army (red) and for civilians (white), but the Royal (Amending) Warrant of the 20th March, 1931, prescribed a single type of red riband for all recipients. Provision is made, in cases of collective gallantry, for the selection of the recipients by secret ballot among those engaged.

Queen Victoria's letters show that she took a keen interest in the details of this decoration. On 5th January 1856, she wrote: 'The motto "For Valour" would be better than "For the Brave" as this would lead to the inference that only those are deemed brave who have got the Victoria Cross.' In June 1856 she handed the decorations personally to the first recipients and in the same month expressed the opinion that 'Persons decorated with the V.C. might very properly be allowed to bear some distinctive mark after their name. The warrant instituting the decoration does not style it an "Order" but merely a "Naval and Military Decoration" and a distinction; nor is it, properly speaking, an order, not being constituted. V.C. would not do. K.G. means *Knight* of the Garter, C.B. a *Companion* of the Bath, M.P. a *Member* of Parliament, M.D. a *Doctor* of Medicine, etc., etc., in all cases designating a person. No one could be called a Victoria Cross. V.C., moreover, means Vice Chancellor at present. D.V.C. (decorated with the Victoria Cross) or B.V.C. (Bearer of the Victoria Cross) might do: The Queen thinks the last the best.'

A full list of recipients of the Victoria Cross from 1856 up to the 31st December 1918, with details of the circumstances in which it was awarded and photographs of the recipients, is to be found in *The V.C. and D.S.O.*, edited by Sir N. O'Moore Creagh, V.C., and E. H. Humphris (Standard Art Book Co., Ltd., 1920).

Captain Arthur Jocelyn in his *Orders, Decorations, and Medals of the World—Vol. I. The British Empire*, 1934, gives the following analysis of awards by campaigns from 1856 to 1914 in order of frequency of awards:

Campaign	Year	Number awarded
Crimea and Baltic	1854–5	111
Indian Mutiny	1857–9	182
S. African War	1899–1902	78
Zululand	1879	23
Afghanistan	1878–80	16
New Zealand	1860–1, 1863–6	15
India—N.W.F.	1897–8	11
China	1860–2	8
Basutoland	1879–81	6
S. Africa—Boer War	1880–1	6
Somaliland	1902–5	6
Little Andaman Island	1867	5
Ashanti	1873–4	4

Sudan	1884	4
Omdurman	1898	4
Persia	1856–7	3
Japan—H.M.S. *Euryalus*	1864	3
Egypt	1882	3
N.W. India—Hunza Nagar	1891	3
Matabeleland	1896	3
N.E. India—Bhutan	1814–15	2
N.W. India—Umbeyla	1863	2
Abyssinia	1867–8	2
Burma	1889	2
Ashanti	1900	2
China	1900	2
Canada	1866	1
W. Africa—Gambia	1866	1
N.E. India—Luskai	1871–2	1
Perak	1875–6	1
Baluchistan	1877	1
S. Africa—Kaffir War	1879 80	1
India—Naga Hills	1879–80	1
Nile Expedition	1884–5	1
N.E. India—Manipur	1895(?)	1
W. Africa—Gambia	1892	1
Burma	1895	1
Chitral	1895	1
Khartum—Kassala	1898	1
Crete	1898	1
Nigeria	1903	1
Tibet	1903–4	1
		522

To this must be added 579[1] awards during the Great War, 1914–20, bringing the total awards to 1,101 up to 31st May 1920.

It will be noted that the total number awarded during the Indian Mutiny, in which only some 30,000 British troops were engaged for less than two years, was about one-fifth as great as that awarded for all ranks in all theatres of war during the six years 1914–20, a circumstance which suggests that the standard set is higher than was originally intended, and higher perhaps than is desirable. Probably less than 250 holders of the V.C. are now alive.

The first person to win the V.C. was Lt. (later Admiral) Charles Lucas, mate of H.M.S. *Hecla*, who threw overboard a live Russian shell on the point of exploding. This was on 21st June 1854, eighteen months before the Victoria Cross was instituted. The first military recipients won it at the Battle of the Alma—viz. Robert James Lindsay (later Lord

[1] *Statistics of Military Effort of British Empire during the Great War 1914–20*, p. 534, War Office, March 1922. Stationery Office, 10s. 6d. This gives a full list of all honours and awards from the outbreak of war to 31st May 1920.

Wantage), James McKechnie, John Simpson Knox, William Reynolds, Luke O'Connor, and Edward W. D. Bell.

The first to receive the Cross twice was Lt. A. Martin Leake, R.A.M.C., on the first occasion in S. Africa at Vlakfontein on 8th February 1902, and again near Zonnebecke in Belgium on 8th November 1914. The only other recipient of a bar was Capt. N. Chavasse, R.A.M.C., who gained the Cross at Guillemont in October 1916, and the Bar in September 1917.

The first airman to win the Cross was 2nd Lt. W. B. Rhodes-Moorhouse, who bombed Courtrai railway junction on 26th April 1915. It was awarded posthumously. The first Indian to receive it was Sepoy Khudadad of the 129th D.C.O. Baluchis, during the Great War.

The following awards of the V.C. have been made since 31st May 1920:

TEMP. CAPT. HENRY JOHN ANDREWS, M.B.E., I.M.S.[1] For most conspicuous bravery and devotion to duty on 22nd October 1919, when as Senior Medical Officer in charge of Khajuri Post (Waziristan) he heard that a convoy had been attacked in the vicinity of the post, and that men had been wounded.

He at once took out an Aid Post to the scene of action and, approaching under heavy fire, established an Aid Post under conditions which afforded some protection to the wounded but not to himself. Subsequently, he was compelled to move his Aid Post to another position, and continued most devotedly to attend to the wounded. Finally, when a Ford van was available to remove the wounded, he showed the utmost disregard of danger in collecting the wounded under fire and in placing them in the van, and was eventually killed whilst himself stepping into the van on the completion of his task.

LIEUTENANT WILLIAM DAVID KENNY,[1] 4/39th Garwhal Rifles, Indian Army For most conspicuous bravery and devotion to duty near Kot Kai (Waziristan) on the 2nd January 1920 when in command of a company holding an advanced covering position, which was repeatedly attacked by the Mahsuds in greatly superior numbers.

For over four hours this officer maintained his position, repulsing three determined attacks, being foremost in the hand-to-hand fighting which took place, and repeatedly engaging the enemy with bomb and bayonet. His gallant leadership undoubtedly saved the situation and kept intact the right flank, on which depended the success of the operations and the safety of the troops in rear. In the subsequent withdrawal, recognizing that a diversion was necessary to enable the withdrawal of the company, which was impeded by their wounded, with a handful of his men he turned back and counter-attacked the pursuing enemy, and, with

[1] Awarded posthumously.

the rest of his party, was killed fighting to the last. This very gallant act of self-sacrifice not only enabled the wounded to be withdrawn but also averted a situation which must have resulted in considerable loss of life. (9.9.20.)

CAPTAIN GEORGE STUART HENDERSON,[1] D.S.O., M.C., 2nd Bn. Manchester Regt.

For most conspicuous bravery and self-sacrifice. On the evening of the 24th July 1920, when about fifteen miles from Hillah (Mesopotamia), the Company under his command was ordered to retire.

After proceeding about 500 yards a large party of Arabs suddenly opened fire from the flank, causing the Company to split up and waver. Regardless of all danger, Capt. Henderson at once reorganized the Company, led them gallantly to the attack and drove off the enemy.

On two further occasions this officer led his men to charge the Arabs with the bayonet and forced them to retire. At one time, when the situation was extremely critical and the troops and transport were getting out of hand, Capt. Henderson, by sheer pluck and coolness, steadied his command, prevented the Company from being cut up, and saved the situation.

During the second charge, he fell wounded, but refused to leave his command and just as the Company reached the trench they were making for he was again wounded. Realizing that he could do no more, he asked one of his N.C.O.s to hold him up on the embankment, saying, 'I'm done now, don't let them beat you.' He died fighting. (29.10.20.)

No. 1012 SEPOY ISHAR SINGH, 28th Punjabis, Indian Army

For most conspicuous bravery and devotion to duty on the 10th April 1921, near Haidari Kach (Waziristan).

When the convoy protection troops were attacked, this Sepoy was No. 1 of a Lewis-gun Section. Early in the action he received a very severe gunshot wound in the chest, and fell beside his Lewis gun. Hand-to-hand fighting having commenced, the British officer, Indian officer, and all the havildars of his company were either killed or wounded, and his Lewis gun was seized by the enemy.

Calling up two other men, he got up, charged the enemy, recovered the Lewis gun, and, although bleeding profusely, again got the gun into action.

When his Jemadar arrived he took the gun from Sepoy Ishar Singh and ordered him to go back and have his wound dressed. Instead of doing this the Sepoy went to the medical officer, and was of great assistance in pointing out where the wounded were, and in carrying water to them. He made innumerable journeys to the river and back for this purpose. On one occasion, when the enemy fire was very heavy, he took the rifle of a wounded man and helped to keep down the fire. On another occasion he stood in front of the medical officer who was dressing a wounded man thus shielding him with his body. It was over three hours before he finally submitted to be evacuated, being then too weak from loss

---

[1] Awarded posthumously.

of blood to object. His gallantry and devotion to duty were beyond praise. His conduct inspired all who saw him. (25.11.21.)

CAPTAIN GODFREY MEYNELL, M.C.,[1] 5th Battalion (Queen Victoria's Own Corps of Guides), 12th Frontier Force Regt., Indian Army

For most conspicuous gallantry and extreme devotion to duty.

On the 29th September 1935, while operating against Mohmand tribesmen in the attack on Point 4080, Captain Meynell was Adjutant of the Battalion. In the final phase of the attack, the Battalion Commander·was unable to get information from his most forward troops. Captain Meynell went forward to ascertain the situation and found the forward troops on the objective, but involved in a struggle against an enemy vastly superior in numbers. Seeing the situation he at once took over command of the men in this area. The enemy, by this time, was closing in on the position from three sides.

Captain Meynell had at his disposal two Lewis guns and about thirty men. Although this party was maintaining heavy and accurate fire on the advancing enemy, the overwhelming numbers of the latter succeeded in reaching the position. Both the Lewis guns were damaged beyond repair and a fierce hand to hand struggle commenced. During the struggle Captain Meynell was mortally wounded and all his men were either killed or wounded.

Throughout the action Captain Meynell endeavoured by all means to communicate the situation to Headquarters, but determined to hold on at all costs, and encouraged his men to fight with him to the last.

By so doing he inflicted on the enemy very heavy casualties which prevented them from exploiting their success.

The fine example Captain Meynell set to his men, coupled with his determination to hold the position to the last, maintains the traditions of the Army and reflects the highest credit on the fallen officer and his comrades. (24.12.35.)

Next in seniority, dating from 1863, but in a special category, is the *Royal Red Cross* (R.R.C.). Alone of all decorations of its kind other than the Indian Order of Merit it has two classes:[2] it may be awarded, though rarely, for service in time of peace. It may be worn by the Queen Regnant, the Queen Consort, or the Queen Dowager, and may be conferred upon Princesses of the Royal Family as also upon queens and

---

[1] Awarded posthumously.
[2] The first class is for fully trained nurses belonging to officially recognized nursing services who have shown exceptional devotion and competence in the performance of actual nursing duties in the field or in auxiliary war hospitals over a continuous and long period, or who have performed some very exceptional act of bravery or devotion at their posts of duty. The second class is for fully trained nurses, assistant nurses, probationers, or nursing members of a voluntary aid detachment who belong to an officially recognized nursing service and who are otherwise qualified by service as defined above. The number of awards is limited to 2 per cent. of total establishment, but special provision is made for awards of either class to ladies overseas who have voluntarily undertaken nursing duties over a continuous and long period in hospitals specially established for the armed forces of the Crown.

princesses of foreign countries who may have specially exerted themselves in providing for the nursing of the sick and wounded of foreign armed forces.

Awards during the Great War were as follows:

R.R.C. 1st class: 456 (overseas)   465 (at home)
       2nd class: 1,506   „   1,506   „
Bars to 1st class: 37   „   37   „

We have dealt with the V.C., of all decorations the widest in scope, and with the R.R.C., which is less extensive in range, and for women only.[1] The remaining military orders, decorations, &c., which may be given for gallantry, vary greatly in scope, but are usually awarded only for deeds performed under active service conditions. Exceptions to this rule are the Air Force Cross, the Medal of the Order of the British Empire, Military Division, for Gallantry (E.G.M.), the Medal of the Order of the British Empire, Military Division, for Meritorious Service, and the Indian Distinguished Service Medal. Some are for officers, some for officers and warrant or petty officers, others for warrant or petty officers and men. Some are for the Army and Air Force only, others for the Navy, or for the Air Force only. In some cases, but not in others, an award is accompanied by extra pay or a monetary grant. The following table sets forth the position succinctly.

Date of first institution[2]	Ranks eligible	Navy and R.M.	Army	Air Force
September 1886	Commissioned officers	D.S.O.	D.S.O.	D.S.O.
October 1914	Officers and warrant officers	D.S.C.	..	..
December 1914	„ „ „	..	M.C.[3]	M.C.[3]
June 1918	„ „ „	..	..	D.F.C.
June 1918	„ „ „	..	..	A.F.C.
June 1918	Indian officers	..	O.B.I.[4]	..
June 1918	„ „	..	I.O.M.[4]	..
1922	All ranks	E.G.M.	E.G.M.	E.G.M.

The *Distinguished Service Order* (D.S.O.) is a military decoration for which only commissioned officers of the armed forces of the crown are eligible. Unlike most British Orders it has no motto.[5] It was instituted in December 1886; the Bar to the Order was added by an amend-

[1] In addition to the V.C. and R.R.C. women are eligible for the M.M.
[2] The text of the Warrants will be found in Debrett or in the January issue of the Half-Yearly Army List and in the Air Force List (but not in Navy List).
[3] Grants to warrant officers carry monetary awards.
[4] All awards carry extra pay and pension.
[5] The mottos of other orders are as follows: Garter—*Honi soit qui mal y pense*; Thistle—*Nemo me impune lacessit*; St. Patrick—*Quis separabit?*; Bath—*Tria juncta in uno*; Order of Merit—*For Merit*; Star of India—*Heaven's Light our Guide*; St. Michael and St.

ing Warrant in August 1916. The Order ranks next to and immediately after the Order of the British Empire. (The V.C. is not an Order, and holders are entitled to no precedence but that of public respect.) The D.S.O. was originally awarded for meritorious or distinguished service, not necessarily for gallantry, but the Royal Warrant of the 5th February 1931 now requires that no one shall be eligible whose services have not been marked by the special mention of his name in dispatches for *distinguished services under fire, or under conditions equivalent to service in actual combat with the enemy.* There were 'vintage years' before this alteration, and such will doubtless occur again, but the change is unquestionably for good. The correspondence of Her Majesty Queen Victoria with her advisers on the subject of this Order, printed in full in Appendix III with the permission of the Keeper of the King's Archives at Windsor, is of great interest as showing with what ripe wisdom and care Her Majesty considered the question in all its bearings. Her reference to the need for a Civil Branch is of particular interest.

Awards during the Great War were as follows:[1]

	Overseas	At home (air raids, &c.)
D.S.O.	8,981	21
1st Bar	708	1
2nd Bar	71	..
3rd Bar	7	..

The *Military Cross* (M.C.) is for officers and warrant officers of the Army and Air Force only (the Navy not being eligible), not above the substantive rank of major, *'for gallant and distinguished services in action'* whether in the air or on the ground. This definition in the amending warrant of the 5th February 1931 replaces that originally set forth when the decoration was first instituted in December 1914, which provided for awards 'in recognition of distinguished and meritorious services in time of war'. Future awards will therefore be for gallantry only. No annuity or extra pay is provided for officers and the receipt of the decoration confers no precedence, but warrant officers who hold it are entitled to receive a gratuity of £20 on discharge or promotion and, if pensioned, an extra 6*d.* a day (3*d.* for non-European or Maltese

George—Auspicium melioris aevi; Indian Empire—Imperatricis auspiciis; Victorian Order —Victoria; British Empire—For God and Empire; Companion of Honour—In action faithful and in honour clear; Imperial Service Order—For faithful service.

[1] A complete record of all awards of the D.S.O. from its institution in 1886 until 31st December 1919 is contained in *The V.C. and D.S.O.*, ed. by Sir N. O'Moore Creagh and E. H. Humphris (Standard Art Book Co., 1920, vols. ii and iii). The above-quoted figures are taken from *Statistics of British Military Effort during the Great War*, War Office, 1922.

holders). This is equivalent to £9 0s. 6d. a year, a sum almost equal to that enjoyed by the recipients of the V.C.

Within the Services, as in the case of the D.S.O., this decoration carries a repute which varies to some extent with the year and with the campaign and locality in which it was earned. The recent alteration in the statutes is generally welcomed. Awards during the Great War were as follows:

	Overseas	At home (air raids, &c.)
M.C.	37,081	23
1st Bar	2,983	1
2nd Bar	168	1
3rd Bar	4	..

The *Distinguished Service Cross* (D.S.C.) is, for the Royal Navy, the equivalent of the Military Cross. Officers and warrant officers below the rank of lieut.-commander are eligible, provided that their services have been marked by the special mention of their name in dispatches *for meritorious or distinguished services before the enemy*. It replaced the Conspicuous Service Cross (C.S.C.), instituted by Royal Warrant in June 1901. Awards of the D.S.C. from date of institution, 14th October 1914, to 31st December 1919 numbered 1,786: from 1st January 1920 to 31st December 1938, 39. This in addition to 8 awards of C.S.C.: these figures include 153 awards to foreign officers.

There seem to be good grounds for amalgamating the M.C. and the D.S.C. under the latter title, and for making members of all three Services eligible upon identical conditions. It is to the advantage of the Services that, when possible, equivalent distinctions should be awarded for like services and that the decorations should be readily recognizable. I have been assured that this was Lord Kitchener's original desire and intention. This decoration actually antedates the M.C. by three months.

The *Distinguished Flying Cross* (D.F.C.) is peculiar to the Royal Air Force[1] and is awarded to officers and warrant officers only, in recognition of acts of exceptional valour, courage, and devotion to duty *whilst flying in active operation against the enemy*. Up to 1st January 1920, 1,080 Distinguished Flying Crosses had been awarded. The number awarded up to the end of July 1937 was 1,187.

The *Air Force Cross* (A.F.C.) is also limited to the Royal Air Force[1] and is likewise awarded to officers and warrant officers only, for exceptional valour, courage, or devotion to duty *whilst flying though not in active operations against the enemy*. Up to 1st January 1920, 655 Air Force Crosses had been awarded. The number awarded up to the end of July 1937 was 803.

[1] Including the air forces of the self-governing Dominions.

Two Honours given in India may be mentioned here: the Order of British India and the Indian Order of Merit, which date from 1837.

The *Order of British India* (O.B.I.) is the senior and consists of two classes. The first class carries the title of 'Sirdar Bahadur' and consists of risaldar-majors, subadar-majors, risaldars, and subadars only. The second class carries the title of 'Bahadur' and consists of officers of all grades holding the Viceroy's Commission. All appointments to, and promotions in, the Order are made by the Viceroy for long, faithful, and honourable service. As a rule, Viceroy's commissioned officers, sub-assistant surgeons and veterinary assistant surgeons, Indian officers of the Indian State forces and Frontier Corps, and Militia and Military Police on the active list are alone eligible. Vacancies in the establishment are filled as they occur on the recommendation of unit commanders. Promotion from the second to the first class follows the same rule. A risaldar-major or subadar-major who is a member of the first class is granted on retirement the honorary rank of captain. A Viceroy's commissioned officer of other rank who is a member of the first class is granted on retirement the honorary rank of lieutenant. The numbers in each class are strictly limited and no military order is more highly prized. The number now on the roll in the first class is 306, and in the second 730. The Badge is worn round the neck and is inscribed 'Order of British India'; the riband is crimson.

Holders of the Order of British India are entitled to additional pay as follows:

		Per diem Rs.
To members of the First Class of the Order of British India	Allowance in addition to pay or pension for life unless forfeited for misconduct	2
To members of the Second Class of the Order of British India		1

The *Indian Order of Merit* (I.O.M.) consists of a military division and a civil division, both with three classes. Viceroy's commissioned officers, Indian officers, and soldiers are eligible for admission to and promotion in the military division for conspicuous personal bravery in the field and in aid of authority and the public safety. In submitting recommendations, the act of gallantry, which must be conspicuous, as distinguished from ordinary bravery in the performance of duty, shall be specified, and the testimony of eyewitnesses shall be given. The riband is dark blue with two narrow crimson lines at either end. The badge is inscribed 'Reward of Valour'.

A record of such acts of gallantry is kept, and is gazetted at the time of the award. Each class carries extra pay and pension. The allowance is continued for life or to the widow of a member of the Order who was in receipt thereof at the time of his death. The first wife married has the preference, and the allowance ceases on remarriage.

The numbers of members, according to the Supplement to the Indian Army List of January 1938, were: First Class, 22; Second Class, 1,156; Third Class, 9.

Military holders of the Indian Order of Merit receive extra pay as follows:

Rank or Equivalent Rank	First class per mensem Rs.	Second class per mensem Rs.
Risaldar, subadar, &c.	37	25
Jemadar	21	14
Warrant officer ranks	10	7
Squadron dafadar-major, dafadar, havildar	$7\frac{1}{2}$	5
Lance-dafadar, trumpeter, naik	6	4
Sowar, sepoy	$4\frac{1}{2}$	3

No money allowance accompanies the civil division of the Order unless specially sanctioned by the Government of India.

The position, though of long standing, is not wholly satisfactory. Both Orders are legacies of the East India Company[1] and no change was made when the Queen's Government took its place.

We now turn, from what are technically known as 'decorations', to 'medals' for which the rank and file of the three Services of or below the rank of warrant officer are eligible. These are as follows:

Date of first institution[2]	Ranks eligible	Navy and R.M.	Army	Air Force
September 1862 (1855)	Non-commissioned officers and men	..	D.C.M.	..
July 7 1874 (1855)	Warrant officers, petty officers, non-commissioned officers and men	C.G.M.	..	..
October 1914	,, ,, ,,	D.S.M.	..	..
March 1916	,, ,, ,,	..	M.M.	M.M.
June 1918	,, ,, ,,	..	..	D.F.M.
June 1918	,, ,, ,,	..	..	A.F.M.
June 1907	Indian non-commissioned officers and men and British troops and military police in India	..	I.D.S.M.	..
1917	N.C.O.s & men	B.E.M.	B.E.M.	B.E.M.[3]
1922	All ranks	E.G.M.	E.G.M.	E.G.M.
1922	N.C.O.s & men	B.E.M.	B.E.M.	B.E.M.[4]

[1] The correspondence which led to the institution of these Orders in 1837 is printed in full in Mayo, vol. ii, pp. 539 sqq.

[2] Honorary awards of all these decorations (but not of the Victoria Cross) may be made to foreign officers of appropriate rank who have been associated in military or naval operations. In every case bars or clasps may be awarded for further acts of gallantry. Forfeiture, in case of grave misconduct, and restitution, are provided for in the Royal Warrants in all cases. [3] Discontinued in 1922. [4] For Meritorious Service.

DISTINGUISHED CONDUCT AND CONSPICUOUS GALLANTRY 19

The *Medal for Distinguished Conduct in the Field*[1] (D.C.M.) dates from the Crimean War and is awarded to warrant officers, non-commissioned officers, and men of the Army for distinguished conduct in action in the field. It carries, like the M.C., a gratuity of £20 on discharge or an increased pension of 6*d*. a day (3*d*. a day for Maltese or non-Europeans). Awards during the Great War were as follows:

	Overseas	At home (air raids, &c.)
D.C.M.	24,591	29
1st Bar	472	..
2nd Bar	9	..

During the period 1st June 1920 to 31st May 1930, 25 D.C.M.s were awarded and 1 Bar to the D.C.M. From 1st June 1930 up to the end of July, 18 awards have been made.

The *Conspicuous Gallantry Medal*[2] (C.G.M.) was instituted in 1874 for petty officers and men of the Royal Navy[3] who may at any time distinguish themselves *by acts of pre-eminent bravery in action* with the enemy. This carries an annuity of £20 for chief and first-class petty officers of the Navy, and for naval ratings or marines, a single gratuity of £20 on discharge. Financially, therefore, it offers a smaller reward than the D.C.M. of which it is the counterpart. There are the usual provisions for Bars. There is no record of awards of the C.G.M. before 1914. From 1914 up to 1st January 1920, 108 naval ratings received the medal, of whom one received a bar. Since then two awards have been made.

The following statement shows the numbers of naval ratings and Royal Marine ranks at present in receipt of annuities of £20 and £10 as holders of the Conspicuous Gallantry Medal:[4]

	Total number		Number awarded the annuity since 1st June 1920		Number awarded the annuity since 1st June 1930	
	£20	£10	£20	£10	£20	£10
Naval ratings	5	54	Nil	3	Nil	Nil
Royal Marine ranks	1	12	Nil	3	Nil	1

The *Distinguished Service Medal* (D.S.M.) is for petty officers and men of the Royal Navy and non-commissioned officers and men of the Royal

[1] Instituted to replace the medal for meritorious service, first established in 1845.
[2] It was originally sanctioned for the Crimean War only, but was reinstated in 1874.
[3] Including non-commissioned officers and men of the Royal Marines, who rank respectively as petty officers and naval ratings.
[4] *Debates H.C.*, 15th June 1938.

Marines and all other persons holding corresponding positions in the naval forces who *'may at any time show themselves to the fore in action'*, and *'set an example of bravery and resource under fire'*, but without performing acts of such conspicuous bravery as would render them eligible for the Conspicuous Gallantry Medal. It carries no monetary award. There is no published list of holders. From 1914 up to January 1920, 5,513 awards were made; of these 67 received 1, and 2 received 2 bars. Since then, up to 1st July 1938, 10 awards have been made.[1]

The *Military Medal* (M.M.) is 'for individual or associated acts of bravery in the field' by warrant officers, non-commissioned officers, and men of the Army or Royal Air Force, and, in exceptional circumstances, by women, whether British subjects or foreigners, who have shown bravery and devotion *under fire*. It carries no addition to pension and no gratuity on discharge.

Awards during the Great War up to 31st May 1920 were as follows:

	Overseas	At home (air raids, &c.)
M.M.	115,577	12
M.M. 1st Bar	5,796	..
2nd Bar	180	..
3rd Bar	1	..

233 Military Medals and 16 first bars have been awarded since 31st May 1920. Of these, 81 medals were awarded since 1st January 1930.[2]

The *Indian Distinguished Service Medal* (I.D.S.M.) dating from 1907 is for Viceroy's commissioned officers, Indian officers (non-commissioned officers and men), and for the members of the military police and British troops when employed under the Government of India. The Royal Warrant implies that it may be given for distinguished services in peace as well as in war.

The Air Force, like the Navy, has two medals corresponding roughly to the D.C.M. and M.M. These are:

The *Distinguished Flying Medal* (D.F.M.) for non-commissioned officers and airmen for exceptional valour, courage, or devotion to duty whilst flying in *active operations against the enemy*. The medal bears the words 'For Courage'.

The *Air Force Medal* (A.F.M.) for exceptional valour, courage, or devotion to duty whilst flying *though not in active operations against the enemy*. Neither of these carries any monetary advantage to the recipient.

---

[1] *Debates H.C.*, 11th July 1938. [2] Ibid., 6th July 1938.

The following table[1] shows the total number of awards to date:

	Distinguished Flying Cross			Distinguished Flying Medal		
	Crosses	Bars	Total awards	Medals	Bars	Total awards
June 1918 to 5th July 1938 .	1,192	95	1,287	168	3	171
Jan. 1 1930 to Dec. 31 1938 .	33	4	37	30	1	31

	Air Force Cross			Air Force Medal		
	Crosses	Bars	Total awards	Medals	Bars	Total awards
June 1918 to 5th July 1938 .	804	16	820	185	5	190
Jan. 1 1930 to July 5 1938 .	70	6	76	35	..	35

It will be seen from the foregoing that all decorations which the rank and file of the Army can earn may be earned also by the Air Force, but that the Navy and the Air Force each have two decorations restricted to those Services. It will be noted that only two decorations, the V.C. and the E.G.M., can be earned alike by officers and by the rank and file and, further, that in no case can recipients, if commissioned officers, secure any pecuniary reward for themselves or their widows. The Victoria Cross may be, but seldom is, awarded to a civilian, and there is a Civil Division of the E.G.M. specially constituted as a reward for gallantry in civil life. The Victoria Cross and the Military Cross, however, carry monetary rewards for life and during service with the colours for other than commissioned officers, while Indian recipients of the V.C. earn in addition a pension for their widows (unless they remarry).

Until 1917 no soldier, sailor, or airman who, in peace-time or in time of war behind the lines, performed an act of heroism, however great, was eligible for a military award.

The *Medal of the Order of the British Empire*, instituted in 1917, and with a Military as well as a Civil Division, did something to fill this gap. One hundred and forty-five medals were awarded in the Military Division for service during the Great War overseas, and 260 for service at home.[2] In 1922 awards of this medal were discontinued and two new medals were instituted in its place: a *Medal of the Order of the British Empire, for Gallantry* (E.G.M.) which may be regarded as the equivalent of the Albert and Edward Medals, and a *Medal of the Order of the British Empire, for Meritorious Service*. Each of these has a Military and a Civil Division. There are two types of medal—in silver

[1] Ibid., 11th July 1938. [2] *Statistics of Military Effort*, p. 554.

(see Chapter IV), but the difference between the Military and Civil Divisions in each case is confined to the ribbon. There have been 95 grants of the Medal of the Order of the British Empire, for Gallantry. Of these there have been 40 awards of the Medal of the Order of the British Empire, Military Division, for Gallantry (E.G.M.), and 55 awards of the Medal of the Order of the British Empire, Civil Division, for Gallantry (E.G.M.). A list of these is given—up to 1st July 1938—in Chapter XV.

To these decorations should be added the *Meritorious Service Medal* (1845) for warrant officers, non-commissioned officers, and men who are recommended for the grant in respect of gallant conduct in the performance of military duty otherwise than in action against the enemy or in saving or attempting to save the life of an officer or soldier, or for devotion to duty in a theatre of war. The recipient is entitled to an annuity of £10. Awards during the Great War and up to 31st May 1920 were as follows:[1]

	Overseas	At home
M.S.M.	21,963	2,741
Bars	4	1

Since 1st June 1920, 1,447 awards have been made, of which 650 were made since 1st June 1930. Seven hundred and fifty ex-soldiers are in receipt of the Meritorious Service Annuity.[2] When one annuitant dies the annuity is re-allotted. New awards in 1938 average about eight a month.

[1] *Statistics of Military Effort*, p. 554.   [2] *Debates H.C.*, 29th June 1938.

CHAPTER II
FOREIGN ORDERS OF MILITARY GALLANTRY

> Disce, puer, virtutem ex me verumque laborem
> fortunam ex aliis, nunc te mea dextera bello
> defensum dabit et magna inter praemia ducet:
> tu facito, mox cum matura adoleverit aetas,
> sis memor et te animo repententem exempla tuorum
> et pater Aeneas et avunculus excitet Hector.
> <div align="right">VIRGIL, <i>Aeneid</i> xii. 435–40.</div>

> My Son, from my Example learn the War
> In Camps to suffer, and in Fields to dare
> But happier Chance than mine attend thy Care.
> This day my Hand thy tender Age shall shield
> And crown with Honour of the conquer'd Field.
> Thou, when thy riper Years shall send thee forth,
> To Toils of War, be mindful of my Worth:
> Assert thy Birthright; and in Arms be known
> For Hector's nephew and Aeneas' Son.
> <div align="right"><i>Trans.</i> DRYDEN, 644–52.</div>

FRANCE.

There are three military decorations for war service only, and they are for either sex and for all the fighting services, Army, Navy, and Air Force alike. The first is the *Légion d'Honneur*, reserved, in principle, for officers, but sometimes given in exceptional cases to other ranks. The second is the *Médaille Militaire*, reserved, in principle, for 'the troops', but sometimes awarded as a special distinction to officers of high rank who have held commands on active service, such as Marshals Joffre, Foch, and Pétain. The right to wear it is retained on promotion to commissioned rank. The third, the *Croix de Guerre*, for which all ranks (and civilians) are eligible, was instituted for the Great War. It must be regarded, like certain much-prized colonial decorations, as being in a special category. The *Croix de Guerre* is of two kinds, one for the Great War and one for foreign theatres of war. Minor but scarcely less coveted decorations are the *fourragère*, *chevrons*, the *Croix du Combattant*, the Medal for Escaped Prisoners (*Évadés*), the *Médaille de la Reconnaissance Française*, and the *Insigne des Blessés et Réformés*.

The medals are sometimes awarded to cities, towns, and other places which have been defended with courage or have endured much at enemy hands, and to institutions such as military colleges which have played a creditable part in war.

GERMANY.

President von Hindenburg founded, on the 13th July 1934, a Cross of Honour in memory of the Great War. The text of the decree is as follows:

'1. To the memory of the imperishable deeds of the German people in the World War I found a Cross of Honour for all participants as well as for the widows and parents of those who fell or died of wounds or as prisoners of war or were reported missing and have not since been traced.

'2. The Cross of Honour is of iron. The Cross of Honour for front fighters bears two swords.

'3. Every *Reichsdeutscher* (German citizen) who has rendered military services for the German cause or for the cause of the allies of Germany is qualified as a participant in the world war. A front fighter is a participant who was with the fighting forces in any engagement.

'4. The Cross of Honour will be worn on the left breast; the ribbon is to be black-white-red.

'5. Those on whom the Cross of Honour is conferred will receive a certificate; it must be applied for in due form.

'6. The Cross will not be conferred upon persons who have been found guilty of treason in any form, desertion or cowardice.

'7. The *Reichsminister* of the Interior is responsible for maintaining a roll of recipients.

'8. The Cross of Honour of a deceased person will remain with his relatives.'

The Great War, for the purpose of this enactment, started on the 1st August 1914 and ended on the 31st December 1918. A 'Widow' must have been married before the 18th December 1918. 'Parents' include step-parents or parents through adoption. 'Wounds' comprise all external or internal injuries by direct or indirect effects of means of warfare and ill effects on health, so far as they are caused by the war conditions. 'War service' implies that a *Reichsdeutscher* had been called to the Forces during the Great War, but it also comprises the staff of the voluntary nursing organizations, of the voluntary motor-car and motor-boat organizations in the war zone. 'Front fighting' includes naval services of all kinds, mine-sweeping, &c., accompanying U-boats to waters where mines have been laid. *Reichsdeutsche* includes Germans who have lost their German nationality by the treaty of Versailles. The Cross for front fighters is made of iron in a shade of bronze. The front part of the cross shows a shield with the inscription 1914–1918 and a laurel garland. Right through the shield pass two swords. These two swords are lacking in the Cross for war participants, and instead of laurel the garland shows oak leaves. The Cross for the widows and parents is of lacquered iron. The Crosses of Honour are only conferred upon application. The requisite inquiries laid a very heavy administrative burden upon military departments and upon the

Verleihungsbehörde, the authority conferring the decoration—in most cases the Police or the local authorities—having often to make many investigations in order to identify the claim made by the applicant. The Cross was conferred in the name of the *Reichspräsident*. A document of identification was added.

Apart from the Cross of Honour there is also the *Verwundeten-Abzeichen*, the Medal of the Wounded. The particular conditions relating to this decoration are laid down in the ordinance of the 30th January 1936. Here also are enumerated in fullest detail (§ 2, 2–3) the specific wounds which entitle a soldier to the decoration. The mark, which can be worn, is conferred on application. A *Berechtigungsausweis* (document of authorization) is issued and given to the applicant, who, however, has to procure the badge himself.

On the 16th March 1936, when compulsory military service was reintroduced, the Führer established a *Dienstauszeichnung* (Service Medal) to be conferred on all members of the military forces who were of good conduct and had served their full term on the 16th March 1935 or later, as follows.

This distinction is divided into four classes:

I. *Gold Cross* for 25 years' service.
II. *Silver Cross* for 18 years' service.
III. *Light Bronze Medal* for 12 years' service.
IV. *Frosted Silver Medal* for 4 years' service.

The riband in each case is the same—cornflower blue, which was always popular in Prussia as the favourite flower of the Emperor William I. The first class is awarded on the recommendation of the War Minister, the second by the head of the Army, Navy, and Air Departments respectively, the third by high military commanders, the fourth by departmental heads.

A lower class of the medal may be worn with a higher class which has been earned later.

UNITED STATES OF AMERICA.

Apart from the Badge of Military Merit already mentioned, and from other military decorations, many gold medals have been granted by Special Act or Resolution of Congress, and presented personally by the President to the recipient or his heirs. The list of these awards is of such historical interest that it is reproduced in Appendix I.

CHAPTER III

AWARDS FOR CIVIL GALLANTRY IN FOREIGN COUNTRIES

Fear is nothing else but a betraying of the succours which reason offereth.
And the expectation from within, being less, counteth the ignorance more than the cause which bringeth the torment.
Wisdom of Solomon xvii. 12–13.

A NUMBER of foreign countries have medals and decorations roughly corresponding in scope to our Albert and Edward Medals. Under the King's Regulations respecting foreign orders and medals, British subjects may accept and wear, without special permission, medals conferred for saving life.

BELGIUM.

In 1867 the '*Décoration Civique*' was instituted by King Leopold II for the purpose of rewarding 'acts of outstanding courage, devotion or humanity'. The decoration is divided into (1) the Cross (in two classes), (2) the Medal (in three classes). It can be awarded to foreigners.

DENMARK.

In the case of a death of a workman in an attempt to save human life the State pays compensation to the dependants under the Workmen's Compensation Law.

FRANCE.

In France there exist two decorations which may fairly be compared to the Albert or the Edward medals, or the Medal of the Order of the British Empire, Civil Division, for Gallantry.

(*a*) *La Médaille de Sauvetage ou de Dévouement* (1815). This decoration is divided into four grades of medals—namely, gold, enamel, silver (in two classes), and bronze: its riband is blue, white, and red, and bears a silver clasp in the case of the Silver Medal of the First Class, a gold clasp in the case of the Enamel Medal, and a tricolour rosette for the Gold Medal. It is given by the Ministers of the Interior, of the Marine, and of Foreign Affairs.

(*b*) *La Médaille des Épidémies* (1885) to reward those who had distinguished themselves during attacks of epidemic diseases or in the matter of public health generally, in France and in Algeria. This medal is in the gift of the following Ministers—Interior, Health, Commerce, War, and Colonies. The riband is red, white, and blue, the colours of equal breadth in vertical stripes.

In addition to these two decorations each ministry has at its disposal a medal which may be given at the discretion of the Minister concerned in cases of individual acts of exceptional devotion or bravery.[1] Such medals, however, are rarely conferred.

Mention should also here be made of the Prizes which bear the name of the Baron de Monthyon which are in a sense the forerunners of the Carnegie Bequests. By his will he bequeathed a sum of forty thousand francs to provide an annual prize of equal value for—

1. Whoever shall discover any mode of rendering any mechanical art less unhealthy.
2. Whoever shall invent any means of perfecting medical science or surgical art.
3. The French man or woman who shall have composed and published in France the book most beneficial to morals.
4. The poor French person who shall have performed in the course of the year the most virtuous action.

The first two were to be awarded by the Academy of Science, the two latter by the French Academy.

This *Prix de Vertu*, as it is called, has been frequently awarded for acts of individual heroism, for rescues from water, from fire, from wolves, and from any accidents to which human life is liable.[2]

GERMANY.

A very complete system of recognition of acts of civil gallantry is in force which may conveniently be considered under the following heads:

Red Cross Decoration for persons who have rendered notable services in voluntary hospital, sanitary or nursing work: conferred by the Führer and Chancellor on the recommendation of the President of the Red Cross Association—at present the Duke of Coburg.

Rettungsmedaillen—Life-Saving Medals—regulated by an Ordinance of President Hindenburg dated 22nd June 1933, under the law of 7th April 1933.

Reichsfeuerwehrabzeichen—State Fire Brigade Medals.

Reichsgrubenwehrabzeichen—State Mining Medals.

Rettungsmedaillen (Medals for Life Saving) corresponding roughly to our Albert Medal, are conferred upon persons who have successfully saved others from death or imminent peril at the risk of their own lives and have shown courage in so doing. There are two medals: that

---

[1] As an example of the sort of cases in which these medals are conferred the instance may be cited of the award in 1896 of a gold medal by the Minister of Foreign Affairs to M. de Margerie, afterwards French Ambassador in Berlin, then a Secretary of Embassy at Constantinople, for his services at the time of the Armenian massacres.

[2] For details see *The Book of Golden Deeds* (Golden Treasury Series), Macmillans.

of the first class is worn with a riband and is given in exceptional cases only; the other is not worn. In each case the medal can be awarded once only and there is no provision (as in England) for bars.

A special paragraph (3) requires that the recipient should have been in some measure personally responsible independently for the act of saving life, that it was successful, and that his character and personality are worthy of the distinction. Both medals are to be considered, according to § 4, as being conferred for saving life in conditions which show a general desire to make a sacrifice (*Rettungstaten allgemeiner Opferwilligkeit*). It follows that such medals should rarely be granted to persons to whose care the protection of lives of others is confided and who, by risking their lives for the protection of those entrusted to them, are doing their plain duty. Adolescents are not entitled to receive the first-class medal at once; but they receive a 'mention' or certificate (*Belobigung*) forthwith: the medal is conferred after they have reached their eighteenth birthday. The commemorative or second class of the medal may, however, be conferred irrespective of age. Both medals are to be conferred on the recommendation of the Minister of the Interior or of the Defence Services. The recipient of the medal is also given a certificate of honour signed, in the case of the first class, by the Führer and in the case of the second class by the appropriate Minister. The medals remain the property of the recipient and, after his death, of his family.

The *Reichsfeuerwehrabzeichen* (Reichs Fire Brigade Medal) includes two classes:
   I. Awarded to members of professional and voluntary Fire Brigades and to persons who have shown outstanding courage or special service in fire-fighting.
   II. For meritorious service of not less than twenty-five years as voluntary or professional members of such Brigades.

Foreigners are also eligible for the medals, which may be worn on the breast and are conferred with a certificate by the Minister of the Interior on the recommendation of the Chief of Police. Local Fire Brigade medals and certificates have now been abolished.

The *Ehrenzeichen* (Mark of Honour—Decoration) of the Red Cross and of Fire Brigades as now awarded are regularized forms of earlier decorations.

The *Reichsgrubenwehrabzeichen* or Mining Medal, established on 13th November 1936, is a new development, corresponding roughly to our Edward Medal. The following are eligible:
   1. Members of Mines Brigades who have performed meritorious service for fifteen years or, if they are obliged to quit the service through accident, for a lesser period.

2. Members who have rendered distinguished service in Mines Brigades, particularly if they have risked their lives.
3. Persons who have rendered distinguished service to the organization and development of mines Brigades.
4. Persons who have earned distinction in connexion with rescue work in mines at the risk of their own lives.

The medal is conferred by the Minister of the Interior and may be worn: it is accompanied by a certificate.

ITALY.

The following are the Italian decorations given in recognition of acts of heroism in civil life:

(a) A medal, in gold and silver, instituted in 1851, awarded for life-saving, for re-establishing public order in cases of grave disorder, and for arresting or helping to arrest criminals. In 1888 a third class (bronze medal) was added to the two classes already existing, to be awarded in slightly less meritorious cases. The medal is attached to a tricolour riband of the national colours and is conferred by the Minister of the Interior.

The bestowal of the medal was by a decree of 1934 extended to all persons who 'knowingly have risked their lives in the cause of science or in upholding, in civil life, the name and prestige of their country'.

(b) The medal of 1860 for acts of valour at sea.

The provisions of this decree were extended by a later decree of 1899 covering all acts of heroism at sea. The following were the decorations which were thereby instituted: a gold, a silver, and a bronze commemorative medal (the last two being for such meritorious acts as assistance given to other ships in distress).[1]

JAPAN.

The 'Medal with Red Riband' is awarded to a person who has saved a life in disregard of danger to his own. In addition to the medal a set of gold, silver, or wooden cups or a sum of money may also be awarded to such a person.

POLAND.

The 'Medal for Life Saving' is awarded to civilians, whether Polish or foreign, who save the lives of Poles in Poland or abroad at the risk of their own.

The decoration may be bestowed more than once upon the same individual.

[1] A special medal was struck by the King of Italy for issue to officers and men of the British man-of-war, and others, who assisted in succouring the injured after the great earthquake at Messina in December 1908. Officers and men of the Royal Navy were permitted to wear it in uniform.

Portugal.

The decoration usually conferred for acts of heroism in civil life is the *Medalha de Merito, Filantropia y Generosidad* which dates from 1839.

Spain.

There is no decoration reserved solely for cases of personal bravery in civilian life, but the '*Cruz de Beneficencia*' is conferred in such cases as well as to persons who carry out charitable enterprises.

Sweden.

The 'Medal for Deeds of Valour' was instituted in 1805 by His Majesty King Gustavus Adolphus IV. It is struck in gold and in silver and is awarded by the King in Council, mostly for acts of individual heroism. The medal originally bore the motto '*Sin memores alios fecere merendo*' but now bears only the Swedish motto: '*För berömliga gärninger*' (For Deeds of Valour).

United States of America.

An Act of 20th June 1874 instituted first- and second-class life-saving medals in gold and silver 'for persons who endanger their lives in endeavouring to save lives from perils of the sea'.

An Act of 18th June 1878 authorized the bestowal of a second-class life-saving medal on persons making 'signal exertions in rescuing and succouring the shipwrecked, and saving persons from drowning'.

An Act of 23rd February 1905 authorized the President to provide for the award of bronze medals of honour to persons who 'endanger their lives in endeavouring to prevent railroad accidents or save lives in such accidents'.

An Act of 4th March 1929 provided for an annual award of gold and silver medals for conspicuous service in the District of Columbia Police and Fire Departments.

Apart from the above, medals for bravery in various departments of civil life are awarded by many non-official agencies—viz. The Carnegie Hero Fund Commission, New York Fire Department, New York Police Department, Theodore N. Vail Fund (for telephone operators); A. N. Brady Memorial Fund; the Electric Institute, American Museum of Safety; Holmes Safety Awards (for safety in mines); and the Pennsylvania Railroad.

Of these, the awards of the Joseph A. Holmes Safety Association deserve special attention. It was founded in 1916 by twenty-four leading national organizations of the mining, metallurgical, and allied industries to commemorate the efforts of the first Director of the U.S. Bureau of Mines, whose name it bears, to reduce accidents and ill health in the mining and allied industries. It is thus a Federation of National Associations.

Apart from these activities it took power to award medals for personal heroism or distinguished service in the saving of life in the mining, quarrying, metallurgical, and mineral industries. Between 1919 and 1934 it issued 72 gold, 40 silver, and 40 bronze medals, and 34 certificates of honour, covering 84 separate occasions. Of these awards 86 went to foremen employed in the coal, 75 in the metal, and 22 in the petroleum, industry.[1]

U.S.S.R.

The Order of the Red Labour Banner (1920) is awarded for conspicuous achievement in the industrial field.

[1] These figures are taken from U.S. Bureau of Mines Information Circular 6831.

CHAPTER IV

AWARDS FOR CIVIL GALLANTRY IN GREAT BRITAIN AND THE EMPIRE

I. ON LAND

The material prosperity of a nation is not an abiding possession: the deeds of its people are.   G. F. WATTS, O.M., Letter to *The Times*, Sept. 5, 1887.

APART from the Albert and Edward Medals, the King's Police Medal, which is also given to members of Fire Brigades, and the Board of Trade Medals for Gallantry in Saving Life at Sea, the only official rewards in these Islands available for persons who have displayed gallantry in military life not in face of the enemy, or in civil life, are the Medals of the Order of the British Empire, for Gallantry (E.G.M.), already referred to in Chapter I. This decoration has two divisions, Military and Civil: awards to the end of December 1937 are 40 and 55 respectively. Instituted in 1922, it is of silver and bears on the obverse a representation of Britannia with the motto of the Order ('*For God and the Empire*'), and upon the exergue, the words '*For Gallantry*'; on the reverse the Royal and Imperial Cypher, and the words '*Instituted by King George V*'. The medal is worn on the left breast pendant to a rose-pink riband edged with pearl grey, $1\frac{1}{4}$ in. wide, with the addition, in the case of the Medal of the Military Division, of a vertical pearl-grey stripe about one-sixteenth of an inch wide in the centre of the riband. The clasp is ornamented with laurel-leaves and the riband of the medal '*For Gallantry*' is ornamented with a branch of laurel in silver.

Recipients of a Military or Civil Medal of the Order 'For Gallantry' may, on all occasions when the use of such letters is customary, place after his or her names the letters E.G.M. (Empire Gallantry Medal).

A few decorations are given either for gallantry or for meritorious service. The India Burma and Colonial Police Medals and the old King's Police Medal are in this category. Some appointments to the Fourth Class of the Civil Division of the Order of the British Empire (O.B.E.) and to the Fifth Class (M.B.E.) were made for services in connexion with the Quetta Earthquake of June 1935 in which some 30,000 persons lost their lives. The Medal of the Order of the British Empire, for Meritorious Service, is given quite frequently for gallantry, but the standard for the award of the Medal of the Order of the British Empire for Gallantry (E.G.M.) is higher.

The Medal of the Order of the British Empire, for Meritorious Service, is also divided into two divisions, Military and Civil. It differs from the Gallantry Medal, described above, in three ways. The words upon the exergue are *For Meritorious Service*, the clasp is ornamented with oak-leaves, and the riband bears no silver ornament. The ribands in the Military and Civil Divisions respectively are the same as for the Gallantry Medal. The grant of this Medal does not entitle the recipient to the use of letters after his name.

The Kaisar-i-Hind Gold Medal has also been given specifically for gallantry when Mrs. Starr and two Indian officers received it for rescuing Miss Ellis, a missionary, from Afridi tribesmen; and the Medal was given in connexion with the Quetta Earthquake, but in this case gallantry was incidental to the services rendered.

The principal medals awarded in Great Britain by unofficial agencies for civil gallantry on land are:

A. The Life Saving Medal of the Order of St. John of Jerusalem.
B. The Royal Humane Society's Medals, including the Stanhope Medal, which may also be worn by members of H.M. Forces in uniform, and those of local branches and independent societies in the Dominions and Colonies.
C. The L.C.C. Silver Medal for bravery at fires.
D. The Liverpool Shipwreck & Humane Society (p. 64) and Glasgow Corporation (p. 43) Medals.

THE GRAND PRIORY IN THE BRITISH REALM OF THE VENERABLE ORDER OF THE HOSPITAL OF SAINT JOHN OF JERUSALEM,[1]

whose Sovereign Head is the King, has power by its Statutes to award medals, badges or certificates of honour 'for special services in the cause of humanity, especially for saving life at imminent personal risk', whether by sea or land.

The award of medals is made in the name of the Sovereign Head by the Grand Prior on the recommendation of the Chapter-General.

The medals at present awarded by the Order are:

The Life-saving Medal, which may be bestowed on those who, in a conspicuous act of gallantry, have endangered their own lives in saving, or attempting to save, life. It is inscribed 'For service in the cause of humanity'. It may be presented either made of gold, silver, or bronze, as may be determined in each case by the Grand Prior on the recommendation of the Chapter-General. It is worn on the left breast suspended from a black watered silk riband 1½ inches broad.[2]

Certificates of Honour may be likewise awarded to those who in a conspicuous act of gallantry have endangered their own lives in saving, or attempting to save, life in cases where the circumstances are not deemed to have merited a medal.

[1] Offices at St. John's Gate, Clerkenwell, London, E.C. 4.
[2] It should not be confused with the *Service Medal*, bestowed on those who have rendered conspicuous services to the Order, which is of different pattern and riband but is also worn on the left breast.

The first mention of such awards is made in the Report of the Chapter-General for 1874, which reads as follows:

'Connected with the ambulance service, is a proposal to establish a system of rewards for bravery in saving life in accidents in mines and collieries. Sir E. Lechmere has offered the die for a suitable medal, and has consulted the Earl of Dudley, a large colliery proprietor, who highly approves of the ambulance system, and believes that when that is generally carried out, the plan for giving the honorary medal will very properly follow.'

The first presentation of medals took place at Whittington Moor on the 18th November 1875. Since the institution of the Medal, 10 gold, 129 silver, and 283 bronze medals, and 316 certificates have been issued. During 1933–8 1 silver and 5 bronze medals were issued, and 8 certificates. There is in the Library at St. John's Gate a list of all recipients of these medals and certificates, with a short account of the action for which the award was made.

THE ROYAL HUMANE SOCIETY

The *Royal Humane Society's Medals* are in silver and bronze, and are granted by the Society[1] to 'those who by their brave efforts and at personal risk to themselves have been the means of saving life from drowning, dangerous cliffs, mines, &c.' Testimonials on vellum, and in a lower grade on parchment, are also issued.

The Society was founded in 1774 by Drs. Cogan and Hawes to make known to the general public the art of resuscitating the apparently drowned, then quite unknown in England, and very little on the Continent. There was at that time a strong popular disbelief in the possibility of resuscitation, and the idea was ridiculed, by doctors as well as laymen, as hopeless and frowned upon in some quarters as impious. Dr. Hawes and those associated with him persevered, in spite of professional ridicule, and the truth of his theory having been demonstrated by a number of remarkable recoveries of apparently drowned persons, carried out under their direction, the Society received the support of the public and became firmly established. It gradually extended its sphere of usefulness, and increased in influence and prestige

[1] The Offices of the Society are at Watergate House, Adelphi, W.C. 2. Honorary rewards are granted by the Society to those who by their brave efforts, and at personal risk to themselves, have been the means of saving life from drowning, dangerous cliffs, mines where a fall of roof has occurred, or from the effects of foul gas in mines, &c., the number of such cases annually dealt with by the Society being about 700 and steadily increasing. These cases are forwarded from all parts of the Empire, and many individual acts of heroism that would otherwise be lost sight of are thus placed on record. Resuscitation Certificates are also awarded for the successful application of treatment to the apparently drowned or dead.

and has enjoyed royal patronage since 1783, though permission to wear the medal in uniform was given in 1869 when the smaller size was first issued. The three medals have each a distinctive riband: the bronze—dark blue; the silver—dark blue with a narrow yellow stripe in the centre, and a narrow white stripe at either end.

The obverse of the Royal Humane Society's medal represents a boy blowing an extinguished torch, in the hope that 'LATEAT SCINTILLVLA FORSAN', 'peradventure a little spark may yet lie hid'. Under the device is the following inscription abbreviated: 'SOCIETAS LONDINI IN RESUSCITATIONEM INTERMORTUORUM INSTITUTA, MDCCLXXIV'—'The [Royal Humane] Society, established in London for the recovery of persons in a state of suspended animation, 1774'.[1]

The reverse of the medal exhibits a Civic Wreath with the words 'HOC PRETIUM CIVE SERVATO TULIT'—'He has obtained this reward for having saved the life of a citizen', and with the wreath, 'VITAM OB SERVATAM DONO DEDIT SOCIETAS REGIA HUMANA'—'The Royal Humane Society presented this gift for saving life'. The riband of the bronze medal is dark blue; of the silver, blue, with a white vertical stripe at either end and a yellow stripe in the centre.

When the medal is presented to persons who have endeavoured to save the lives of others, at the risk of their own, but without success, the inscription reads instead: 'VITA PERICULO EXPOSITA DONO DEDIT SOCIETAS REGIA HUMANA'—'The Royal Humane Society presented this to . . . his life having been exposed to danger'.

Awards of the silver medal are about six, of the bronze about fifty, annually.

The Stanhope Gold Medal, founded in 1873 in memory of Capt. C. S. S. Stanhope, R.N., has been issued annually since 1873 for the most gallant act for which a silver medal has been awarded during the year. It is identical in design with the bronze and silver medals of the Society but carries a clasp inscribed 'Stanhope Medal'. The riband of the Stanhope Medal is blue in the centre, black at either side, with two thin vertical yellow stripes between the brown stripes and the blue centre.

Local branches of the Royal Humane Society, and of other Societies, at one time issued their own medals; but the parent Society is the only Society which has been granted the privilege of permitting recipients of its medals to wear them in uniform—on the right breast.[2] The only local branch is that of Brighton and Hove (1836).

Australia, Canada, and New Zealand started their own Societies at the latter end of the last century, and all rescues occurring in those

---

[1] The British Museum Collection includes specimens of this medal for the years 1774 (2), 1789, 1806, 1807, 1810.

[2] Another medal to be worn thus was the Medal of the India Total Abstinence Association founded in 1862. The Medal was earned by four years' total abstinence. See Gibson, *British Military and Naval Decorations*, 1880, p. 132.

Dominions, except those performed by officers of His Majesty's Fighting Forces, are dealt with by them direct. The parent Society gives awards in all other British Possessions, in India, and on the High Seas, as well as in the British Isles.

The Bristol Humane Society[1] was founded in 1775, a year after the Royal Humane Society. From 1794 to 1806 it was a branch of the Severn Humane Society, but in 1807 resumed its independent existence.

It gives certificates, accompanied by wrist watches, &c., and, especially when clothing has been damaged, cash, in approved cases: it has sometimes given medals (without ribbon) but not of recent years. The cost of awards for the past three years average £8 a year. Grants are made to encourage members of Boys' Clubs to learn swimming.

The Humane Society for the Hundred of Salford[2] was established in 1789 and, after some years in eclipse, was revived in 1824. The original object of the Society, which purchased and maintained life-saving apparatus at suitable points on rivers and canals in Manchester and Salford and the neighbourhood, was to reward persons who had shown courage and self-possession when life was endangered. Up to 1922 many gold and silver medals were awarded for bravery in saving life from drowning or from fire. Lack of public support necessitated the discontinuance after 1922 of awards for bravery, and the activities of the Society are now confined to the organization of life-saving swimming tests for children, for which silver medals are awarded annually. The awards for gallantry in saving life show a high standard of merit, equal at least to that of the parent Society. They include cases as far afield as Rochdale and Oldham, and cover deeds of courage in pits, and in boiler explosions, as well as rescues from canals and the foul waters of the Irwell.

It is little to the credit of Manchester and Salford that such a Society should lack funds.

The Glasgow Humane Society,[3] founded in 1790 as an offshoot of the Royal Humane Society of London, was the outcome of a European movement towards showing greater humanity to persons drowning or apparently drowned. Before then, in many countries, it was a crime to assist such persons, as they were looked upon as suicides and, therefore, as felons.

It does whatever is possible to recover bodies and to hand them to relatives.

---

[1] Hon. Treasurer (1937), C. H. Abbot, 2 Beaufort Road, Clifton, Bristol.

[2] Secretary, J. C. Daniels, 38 Barton Arcade, Manchester 3.

[3] Hon. Sec., David McKail, M.D., D.P.H., Glasgow Humane Society's House, Glasgow Green, C. 3.

During the past seventy years, 1,113 persons have been saved from drowning in the Glasgow Green area, of whom 762 were men and 351 women; while in the same area, 496 persons were drowned, 402 being men and 94 women. Nearly half of the occurrences among the men were suicidal, and of these about 60 per cent. were drowned; while among the women about three-fourths of the occurrences were classed as suicidal, but of these two-thirds were saved and one-third lost.

In addition to all these, 471 bodies were found at a later date, 342 being bodies of men and 129 of women, including many suicides. The combined total is 2,080 for the Green area alone. In the Harbour District the combined total for the same period, 1867–1936, was 5,612 occurrences, and in many of these the Society's Officer rendered assistance in recovering bodies among the 1,107 drowned and the 1,426 found drowned. Over and above the work in these two areas, calls from the outside areas are answered, and, though not so numerous, are sometimes very exacting in time and endurance.

The Society formerly awarded silver medals, as well as parchment certificates and monetary awards, but no medals have been issued for the past fifty years. Parchment certificates awarded average two or three per annum. The Society maintains close co-operation with the parent Society and with the Carnegie Hero Fund Trust.

The Bath Humane Society[1] was founded in 1805. Prior to 1872 it gave monetary awards and from 1872 onwards certificates but no medals. From 1872 to 1937 the number of certificates awarded was eighty-six.

The Southampton Humane Society[2] was founded in 1814 'after the plan of the Royal Humane Society in London' for the 'Preservation and Restoration of Human Life in Southampton and its neighbouring districts' and incorporated with the Southampton Charitable Dispensary in 1827 as a consequence of numerous fatal accidents in Southampton Water. Between 1829 and 1839 it distributed an average of about £5 a year in rewards for saving life. 'Honorary Certificates' for those who 'do not seek for any pecuniary recompense' were first given in 1862: the present custom is to give £2 2s. or an inscribed wrist-watch to the recipient of a certificate. The awards for the past forty years average two or three a year. Medals, if awarded, are given by the Royal Humane Society.

The Vale of Leven Humane Society[3] was founded in 1862 for the purpose of restoring to friends and relatives the bodies of victims of boating and bathing accidents in Loch Lomond and the River Leven. It gives

---

[1] Hon. Sec., F. G. Hamilton, 3 Miles's Buildings, Bath.
[2] Secretary (1937), W. C. Westlake, New Road, Southampton.
[3] Hon. Sec., C. Stevenson, 83 North St., Alexandria, N.B.

neither medals nor awards, preferring to leave this to the Royal Humane Society in London, to whom suitable cases are referred. The Society has taken part in about 300 organized searches and has recovered 132 bodies of victims of drowning fatalities. It keeps lifebuoys, poles, &c., suitable for protecting life at places where accidents are likely to occur.

The Jersey Humane Society[1] was instituted in 1865 and has up to the present awarded 1 gold cross, 2 gold medals, 38 silver medals, 68 bronze medals, and numerous certificates, mostly for rescues and attempted rescues from drowning. The type of deed for which awards are made is sufficiently indicated by the following, which relates to awards in 1937:

Mr. L. Bradford and Miss James were awarded the certificates of the Society, and Mr. K. Cawley the Bronze Medal for rescue at Anne Port on August 8th.

Miss James was bathing and got into a current; Mr. Bradford, a non-swimmer, went to her rescue, and himself got into difficulties. Miss James then tried to save him; both were eventually brought ashore by Mr. Cawley.

Mr. Renouf saw a girl fall into the water. He jumped on to a passing lorry, leapt off near the steps, vaulted the protective wire, dived into the water fully clothed and brought the exhausted child ashore.

Bronze Medals were awarded to Messrs. Herbert Edwardson and J. Pegge, holidaymakers, and Eric Dennis Spicer, for their part in the saving of Mr. Franklin and the bringing ashore of the body of another man in heavy seas in St. Ouen's Bay on September 3rd.

Franklin and Ellwood had been carried out by a very strong undertow while bathing. Messrs. Edwardson and Pegge made gallant and repeated attempts to get through the heavy breakers and strong undertow to their rescue. Franklin was brought in by the two former and was revived. Ellwood was brought ashore by Mr. Spicer but was found to be dead. Spicer himself collapsed after his gallant efforts, and was ill for some time. The rescue was described as one of the pluckiest seen for some time in view of the terrible sea conditions which prevailed.

Other Local Humane Societies,[2] such as formerly existed, e.g. in Bolton,[3] in Hull, and in Norfolk, have ceased to function, the responsibility for awards being assumed by the parent Society and the educational work in connexion with teaching swimming and life-saving being assumed by Local Education Committees.

The Annual Report for 1835 records the existence at that date of Humane Societies, the success attending which had exceeded the best hopes of their founders and supporters, in the following places or areas:

[1] Secretary, G. R. Langdon, 12 Coastlands, Grève d'Azette, Jersey, C.I.

[2] The British Museum Collection includes a medal awarded by the Rym Lynter and Tavy Humane Society in 1831.

[3] Hon. Sec., F. Lomax, 56 Rydal Road, Heaton, Bolton.

1. UNITED KINGDOM

Aberdeen.	Isle of Wight.	Reading.
Barnstaple.	Kingston-upon-Hull.	Rivers Wreak and Eye.
Bath.	Lancaster.[1]	Salford Hundred.
Chatham.	Leicester.	Scarborough.
Chester.	Leith.	Sheffield.
Cork.	Liverpool.	Shrewsbury.
Dublin.	Melton Mowbray.	Shropshire.
Eastern Coast.	Montrose.	Southampton.
Edinburgh.	Newcastle-upon-Tyne.	South Wales.
Exeter.	Northampton.	Stromness.
Falmouth.	Norwich.	Suffolk.
Forth & Clyde Navigation.	Orkney Isles.	Sunderland.
Glasgow.	Oxford.	Wisbech.
Greenock.	Plymouth.	Wooler.
Guernsey.	Portsmouth.	Worcester.
Holywell.		

2. BRITISH EMPIRE

Calcutta.	Madras.	
Jamaica.	Quebec.	

3. FOREIGN

Berlin.	Prague.	Boston.
Boulogne-sur-mer.	Copenhagen.	New York.
Calais.	St. Petersburg.	Baltimore.
Gorlitz.	Massachusetts.	Duchy of Nassau.
Hamburg.	Pennsylvania.	

THE DOMINION OF CANADA.

Monsieur Victor Morin, President of the Numismatic Society of Canada,[2] has been good enough to send the following details of a rare Canadian medal, which is included in the great collection at the Château de Ramezay. It is of oxidized silver, 1⅜ in. diameter, and bears on the obverse the inscription:

'Presented by the Corporation of Montreal to members of the Montreal Fire Brigade for gallantry.'

The medal[3] depicts a fireman saving a woman from a burning house. Below is a wreath surmounted by crossed axes and helmet. The riband top-brooch bears the arms of Montreal. The reverse is plain but for the name of the makers, Garb Frères, Montreal.

M. Morin, who was good enough to get in touch with the Archives Department of the City of Montreal, writes:

'Following the disastrous fire of *The Herald* Newspaper building in Montreal, the Fire Committee recommended to the City Council to award a medal to the

---

[1] The British Museum Collection includes a medal of the Lancashire Life-Saving Society which states that it was founded in 1789. [2] 57 St. James Street, Montreal, P.Q.
[3] An example of this medal is in the House of Commons Collection.

firemen who should distinguish themselves in saving human lives or other acts of gallantry. The same recommendation was made in connexion with the Police Department for acts of bravery, but it does not seem to have been followed by execution.

'The recommendation concerning firemen was adopted by the City Council, and the medal referred to was struck and distributed to 37 firemen whose names are recorded. The ceremony took place on the Champ de Mars, the 23rd of June, 1914, and the presentation was made by the Mayor of the City.

'The Archives do not show that any other presentation has ever been made, so that it appears that the presentation of such medals was restricted to the 37 distributed on that occasion.'

A further Canadian Medal,[1] also in the Château de Ramezay, issued in silver and bronze, is $1\frac{1}{2}$ in. diameter. The obverse shows a man holding on to the branch of a tree with one hand and rescuing a woman with the other from the surrounding flood, with the words 'COURAGE —HEROISM—HUMANITY'. The reverse bears only the words 'THE CANADIAN GOVERNMENT'. (Artist's name at base—P. Hebert.) This medal is unknown to the Public Archives of Canada, and to the Royal Mint.

The Royal Canadian Humane Association[2] for life-saving was instituted in 1894 under Royal Warrant from Queen Victoria, and is founded upon the same high principles as the Royal Humane Society of Great Britain. It has made during its existence some 2,800 awards including parchment certificates, bronze, silver, and gold medals. For the year 1935–6 the number of certificates issued totalled ninety-six, bronze medals, thirty-three.

THE DOMINION OF AUSTRALIA.

The Royal Humane Society of Australasia awards medals for saving life. Details are not available.

THE DOMINION OF NEW ZEALAND.

The Royal Humane Society of New Zealand was formed in Christchurch in 1898, Mr. John Joyce, M.H.R., being the first President. On the 30th December 1898 Her late Majesty Queen Victoria was pleased to give permission to add the word 'Royal' to the Society's title. His Excellency the Governor-General of New Zealand is the Patron, and the Rev. Canon W. S. Bean is the President of the Society. The Court of Directors, which is the adjudicating body of the Society, sits in Christchurch.

The objects of the Society are to investigate all cases reported of

---

[1] An example of this medal is in the House of Commons Collection.
[2] Office, 202 Imperial Building, Hamilton, Canada. Hon. Sec.–Treasurer (1927), H. E. McLaren.

efforts made to save life either on land or in water in New Zealand, its dependencies, and mandated territories, and to bestow awards upon all who have risked their lives in so doing.

Since the inception of the Society, 737 awards consisting of framed letters of commendation, framed certificates, and bronze, silver, and gold medals have been presented, after full investigation and consideration, for acts of bravery in saving, or in attempting to save, life. The medals awarded are similar to those of the parent Society. The usual procedure is for a coroner or other responsible person to forward in his reports to the Department of Justice any comments he may wish to make on outstanding acts of gallantry.

In the early days of the Society money collected locally and an annual government grant financed the work. It is apropos to point out that prior to the formation of the N.Z. Royal Humane Society, an annual sum of £100 was voted by the N.Z. Parliament to the Australasian Society. On the formation of the N.Z. Society the Government recognized that the latter Society had a claim for support and the grant was transferred, being paid to the N.Z. Society annually until 1915. Records then show that a period of rigid economy set in which seriously hindered the work of the Society, but subscriptions, mostly collected in and about Christchurch, together with a small reserve kept the work going until 1931, after which year subscriptions fell away. Various methods were tried to bring in money. Circular letters were sent out and these were followed by a personal canvass. Honorary Vice-Presidents and representatives of the Society throughout the Dominion were written to and urged to solicit contributions, but all this resulted in a poor response in the aggregate. The financial position was improved in 1934 when the N.Z. Government made another grant of £100, and during the time the grant was renewed, the work was carried on again with vigour. Additional representatives in populated districts were appointed until there were and are now fifty-seven from one end of New Zealand to the other. Applications for the recognition of courageous acts from the dependencies and mandated territories of New Zealand were also received and dealt with.

SARAWAK.

His Highness the Raja of Sarawak instituted a Medal for Conspicuous Bravery in 1926, and in the following year twenty-five silver medals were struck by the Mint in Birmingham.

The medal bears a likeness of H.H. with the inscription '*Vyner Brooke, Rajah*'. On the obverse are two palm leaves, below which are the words 'FOR CONSPICUOUS BRAVERY', and round the lower edge 'Sarawak Government'. The riband is black, yellow, and red, one inch in length. Presentations are made annually on the Raja's birthday (26th September). Fifteen medals have been issued to date, as follows:

(1) Jumari, Nakoda of the bandong *Kim Hiok*. When at sea off Pulau Burong he sighted the wreckage of the bandong *Burong Wali*. He approached in heavy weather, launched a small boat and picked up the juragan, four sailors and one woman passenger who had been clinging to the mast of the wrecked vessel for about one hour. The *Kim Hiok* suffered damage to rudder and several planks sprung. Jumari took the vessel to Sebangan, repaired the rudder and the stern planks, and then proceeded to Pusa with the survivors of the *Burong Wali*. (1928.)

(2) Sailor Kipli, of m.l. *Jean*. While lying off Kamong Patong Bahru (Samarahan River), he and engineer Undi went to fetch water in a small boat. Returning with a heavy load of water, the boat capsized. Undi, unable to swim, was carried away by a strong current, but Kipli swam to his rescue and brought him and the capsized boat to shore. But for Kipli's action Undi would almost certainly have been drowned. (1929.)

(3) Abang Haji Khalil, Datu Imam, seized Bong Vong, a leper, who was attacking his wife with a parang, thus saving her life. (1929.)

(4) Makbul Khan, watchman of the Monopolies Department, dived several times into Sungei Kuching to rescue a Chinese youth aged 18 who fell over a bridge with his bicycle into the river 15 feet deep. He eventually recovered both the youth and the bicycle. The youth was unfortunately dead. (1929.)

(5) Lau Khiok Kang, Chinese, at great personal risk intervened in a case of attempted murder of Ng Lai Kian by Eo Ng Seng. (1929.)

(6) Abang Ahmad at great personal risk apprehended Sumok, a dangerous Dayak lunatic, who had just chopped down another Dayak with an axe. (1930.)

(7) Jais, juragan of m.l. *Anne*. A Hylam Chinese aged about 25 years slipped into the river (Batang Lupar) whilst bathing off some steps. A Teochew Chinese named Ban Hee entered the water to try to find him.

Jais, seeing both men had disappeared, dived, fully clothed, into the river in which there was a strong current, grasped both men and saved their lives. (1930.)

(8) Usop bin Daud, Melanau, of Pandan, Bintulu River, was paddling a boat with his wife; they met a number of wild pig crossing the river. Usop stood up in the prow of the boat to spear a pig. As he did so his wife was snatched from the stern by a crocodile. Usop promptly jumped into the river where the crocodile had submerged; frightened by this disturbance the crocodile let go of the woman, whom Usop grasped and got back into the boat. His wife was badly mauled, but her life was saved by Usop's action. (1930.)

(9) Private Rian, Sarawak Ranger, whilst on orderly duty attached to the Pengkalan Batu Guard, entered the river fully clothed and rescued a Macao woman named Chiew Lia Kui who had thrown herself into the river in an attempt to commit suicide. (1932.)

(10) Police Constable Mamba, during an expedition against Dayak rebels under District Officer H. E. Cutfield's command, stood over some wounded members of the Government force; he was single-handed, but he kept the rebels at bay, thus preventing them from taking the heads of the wounded (a Dayak custom). (1932.)

(11) Sailor Spawi of m.l. *Joan*. Spawi's attention was drawn to a boat which

had just capsized at the mouth of the Bintulu river. Some members of the crew were trapped under the capsized boat; he entered the water and succeeded in dragging the trapped men from under the boat and landing them alive on the river bank.

(12) Police Sub-Inspector Wan Bujang personally arrested the murderer in an 'amok' case in the Sibu Bazaar. (1934.)

(13) Police Sub-Inspector Jemat, for capturing Langgi, a Dayak rebel. (1935.)

(14) Ong Kee Poh, a Chinese of Simanggang. A discharged Dayak leper, named Tingkau, suddenly attacked and severely wounded a Dayak and a Chinese. He then chased a Malay woman with a raised 'parang'. The woman fell down, and Ong Kee Poh hit the Dayak with a pole. The Dayak then turned on Ong Kee Poh, who managed to disarm him and overpowered him, thus enabling him to be apprehended. (1935.)

(15) Layang, Dayak, for conspicuous bravery displayed during an 'amok' at Nanga Meluan by a Chinese prisoner named Chin Sui Chai, who had already cut down a Dayak named Ubam. Layang was badly wounded and lost the use of his right hand.

THE CORPORATION OF GLASGOW.

The only Local Authority in Great Britain or the British Empire which at present issues a medal for bravery in saving or attempting to save life is the Corporation of Glasgow. This award dates from 1923 and is awarded both to the police and other officials and to private citizens for brave actions, on the recommendation of the Chief Constable.

One hundred and eighty-seven medals and two bars to medals have been awarded up to December 1938, together with cash payments to compensate persons involved in rescues from fire or water for damage done to clothing, &c.[1]

The cost of the medals and of the monetary payments is met from a fund at the disposal of the Corporation known as the 'Common Good', held by them on behalf of the community, in the disposal of which the discretion of the Corporation is not fettered by Statute.

It is perhaps permissible here to express regret that a similar fund is not at the disposal of other local authorities and surprise that they have not asked for powers to create one.

THE LONDON COUNTY COUNCIL FIRE BRIGADE.

This medal is awarded by the Council on the recommendation of the Chief Officer of the Brigade.

The obverse shows a female figure, with a mural crown, seated

[1] The 'Glasgow Bravery Medal' in the House of Commons Collection was issued to John Canavan for rescuing a boy from drowning in the Forth and Clyde Canal near Firhill Bridge on the 10th June 1932.

holding a chaplet of laurel, with the words below 'Awarded by the London County Council for bravery'. The reverse shows a two-horsed fire-engine. On the exergue are the words 'London Fire Brigade'. It replaced awards formerly made by the London Private Fire Brigade Association and the Metropolitan Fire Brigade; the latter was instituted in 1877 by the Metropolitan Board of Works, whose functions were taken over at the beginning of this century by the London County Council.

The regulation of the Council governing the award of the medal is as follows:

'A silver medal may be given to every man in the fire brigade who distinguishes himself by extraordinary bravery at fires.'

The number of awards to date is eighty-two,[1] of which nine are held by men still serving (1939). A record of the act of gallantry for which an award is made is published in the minutes of the Council meetings. The latest reward is thus recorded therein:

REPORT OF THE FIRE BRIGADE AND MAIN DRAINAGE
COMMITTEE (L.C.C.)

7th May, 1936.

Council's silver medal for extraordinary bravery.

Flames were coming from the windows of the upper four floors and window frames were falling out when the escape from the Soho fire station was pitched to a front room window on the second floor, where the head and arms of a woman could be seen above the window sill. Fireman J. W. Root ascended the escape through the flames and tried to make a rescue, but could not enter the window owing to the fierceness of the fire in the room and the flames coming from the window beneath, which scorched the escape. A jet of water was played on to Fireman Root in order to protect him, but he had the benefit of this water for only about ten seconds. He was burned on his hands, arms and face, and was forced to retreat down the escape. He was then taken to hospital, where he remained an in-patient for three weeks.

After Fireman Root had come down the escape, other firemen tried to ascend, but they could not, owing to the intense heat. Five lives were lost in this fire and, in addition to Fireman Root, three other firemen were injured, of whom two were removed to hospital.

At the inquest, the coroner, in his summing up, said:

'Fireman Root sustained injuries, and I must express my commendation of his brave conduct in the entering of what must have been a furnace in his efforts to save his fellow creatures.'

The chief officer recommends the award of the Council's silver medal to

---

[1] No account has here been taken of such lesser awards as testimonials, pecuniary awards, and so forth which do not come within the scope of the present survey.

Fireman Root for his extraordinary bravery and we cordially endorse his commendation. Under regulation 326 a sum of £10 is payable out of the Foot bequest to each member of the Brigade to whom the Council's silver medal is awarded. We recommend—

1. That the Council's silver medal be awarded to Fireman J. W. Root in recognition of the extraordinary bravery displayed by him on the occasion of the fire at 5 Peter Street, Soho, on the 29th February 1936. (*Agreed.*)

Resolved—that the report be received.

(1) Recommendation 1 moved, put, and agreed to.

Resolved—accordingly.

Presentation to Fireman.

The Chairman having ascertained that it was the pleasure of the Council that the silver medal awarded to Fireman J. W. Root in recognition of extraordinary bravery displayed by him should be presented forthwith, Fireman Root was admitted to the Council chamber, and was presented to the Chairman of the Council by the chief officer of the fire brigade (Major Morris).

The Chairman congratulated Fireman Root and presented to him the silver medal awarded by the Council for extraordinary bravery, and the sum of £10 paid under regulation 326.

One award, in 1915, related to a fire caused by an incendiary bomb from a Zeppelin. There have only been five awards in the last seven years. There seem to be good grounds for making such presentations in public, in presence of the recipients' comrades.

The Society for the Protection of Life from Fire[1] was established in 1836 when, according to contemporary statistics, fifty-seven persons were burned to death annually in London alone and a much larger number seriously injured, though the population did not exceed two millions. It was the successor of an earlier Society[2] which failed from lack of support. The protection of life and property against fire was left mainly to insurance companies. Their respective establishments were amalgamated in 1835 as the London Fire Brigade Establishment, which was taken over in 1866 by the Metropolitan Board of Works whose Brigade was transferred in 1889 to the London County Council. Queen Victoria became patron of the Society in 1837 and during her lifetime the word 'Royal' was prefixed to its present designation. Medals were awarded at the first meeting to policemen and others for gallantry in saving lives from fire. The type of medal both in silver and in bronze was changed in 1852 and again in 1892. This Society was the pioneer of fire-escapes and of a public fire service: it enjoyed prestige as such, and was unquestionably efficient within the narrow financial limits at its disposal. When the Metropolitan Fire Brigade Bill was introduced in 1865 the Society transferred all its equipment

---

[1] 96 New Bridge Street, London, E.C. 4. [2] See *The Times*, 20th Feb. 1829.

to the controlling Authority, on certain conditions, from the 1st July 1867, but continued its activities in the provinces.

The bestowal of awards for gallantry in saving life from fire continued to be a prominent feature of the Society's work which was well supported by the public, and in 1878 it took power not only to give medals, testimonials, and monetary awards in recognition of such deeds, but to make grants to their dependants. In 1878 the interest on the accumulated capital seemed enough to meet all probable demands. It was decided to cease to solicit subscriptions, and in 1881 the Charity Commissioners established an agreed scheme for the future Regulation of the Society, which was thereafter limited to the bestowal of awards as mentioned above.

During the years 1937–8 it made cash awards in Great Britain averaging about £150.

The presentations of rewards for cases in London and suburbs were made by the stipendiary magistrates presiding at the several Metropolitan police courts, or by other persons holding responsible positions. In the country the awards were in most instances presented to the recipients by the Mayor or other authorities in the district where the fire happened. The obverse has two branches of oak encircling the legend 'The Society for the Protection of Life from Fire. 1845'. The reverse depicts a rescue from a fire.

About twenty bronze medals and (for chief officers of Fire Brigades) two or three silver medals are issued annually, but there is no public record of the deed for which the medals are awarded. Silver watches and certificates are also awarded.

The West Ham Corporation have, since 1899, awarded medals for bravery on fifteen occasions to their servants, who have twice earned bars. Such a medal is that in the House of Commons Collection, given to Fireman Henry Chapple. *The Times* of the 21st November 1899 gives details of the deed which earned it. Soon after midnight on the 19th November a fire broke out at 22 Watson St., Plaistow, where a man with his wife and five children slept. Three children, sleeping upstairs, were cut off. Chapple entered the burning house and climbed to the first floor and rescued two children successively. One was dead—the flesh coming away in Chapple's hands; the other died a few hours later in hospital. The medal bears a bar marked 19th January 1917—the occasion of the Silvertown disaster in which a munitions factory exploded, killing hundreds of persons.

The Corporation of Manchester instituted in 1894 a medal for courageous conduct which has been awarded on 65 occasions up to December 1938, to police officers and members of the City Fire Brigade. A specimen is in the House of Commons Collection.

The National Fire Brigades Association (1 Montague St., London, W.C. 1) established in 1929 a conspicuous gallantry medal. The design is a seven-pointed bronze star with the badge of the Association (an eight-pointed star and Union Jack) in the centre surrounded by the words 'Conspicuous Gallantry'.

The London Private Fire Brigades Association[1] with a membership of some sixty firms was instituted in 1899. It issues silver and bronze medals for long service and has recently instituted a medal for gallantry, but no award has as yet (1938) been made.

The Boy Scouts Association[2] has its own system of awards for gallantry. The Cornwell Scout Badge was instituted after the war in memory of the heroism displayed by a naval rating, Boy Jack Cornwell, R.N., of H.M.S. *Chester*, who was awarded the V.C. posthumously for heroic conduct at the Battle of Jutland.

The essential conditions of the award are that the person recommended

(a) Must be specially recommended by a recognized body of Scouts for pre-eminently high character, devotion to duty, *and specific acts of physical courage*;

or (b) Hold an award for *bravery* for having saved life under exceptional circumstances;

or (c) Have undergone great *suffering* in a heroic manner.

Awards during the past five years average about eight a year.

Apart from the Cornwell Scout Badge the following awards for gallantry are made:

	Average annual awards during past five years
Bronze Cross. Red riband.	
The highest possible award for gallantry granted only for special heroism or extraordinary risk	4
Silver Cross. Blue riband.	
For gallantry with considerable risk	33
Gilt Cross. Riband with blue and red vertical stripes.	
For gallantry with moderate risk	37

There is the usual provision for bars and certificates.

The Girl Guides Association[3] makes the following awards for gallantry on roughly parallel lines with those for the Boy Scouts, viz.:

Bronze Cross (Red riband), as above.
Silver Cross (Blue riband), as above.
Medal of Merit (Green enamel laurel wreath, with Silver Tenderfoot in centre —White riband). For duty exceptionally well done, though without great personal risk.

---

[1] Secretary, W. A. Stillwell, 27 Old Park Road, N. 13.
[2] Imperial H.-Q., 25 Buckingham Palace Road, S.W. 1.
[3] 17–19 Buckingham Palace Road, S.W. 1.

The Royal Society for the Prevention of Cruelty to Animals[1] makes awards for courage shown by individuals in rescuing animals as follows:

The Margaret Wheatley Cross, instituted in 1936. (The highest award.)

Silver and Bronze Medals inscribed 'For Animal Life Saving' (since 1909), and Certificates of Merit.

Other animal protection societies make analogous awards.

In a special category of its own is the *Daily Herald* 'ORDER OF INDUSTRIAL HEROISM' instituted in 1923, since when some 130 awards have been made of the medal which bears on the obverse a modernized representation of Saint Christopher bearing the Christ Child on his shoulders with the letters D.I.H. and on the reverse 'A garden of roses in Jericho'. The explanation of the medal, given to each recipient, reads as follows:

Christopher was a man of great strength and simpleness. He had given his strength to a king, thinking he ought to serve one who feared no one. But the king feared the Devil. So Christopher left him and hired himself to Satan. But Satan feared Christ! So Christopher left him and sought to find Christ. At last he was taught by a wise man that in the service of Christ he might give his strength to his fellow men. So he became a ferryman and carried people across a river. In the course of this employment he once carried a small child across the river in a night of flood and storm. The burden seemed to grow heavier and heavier—at last it seemed to Christopher that he carried the whole world on his shoulder and he needed all his great strength to reach the farther shore. 'What child are you,' said Christopher, 'that are as heavy as the world?' 'I am He who made you and the whole world also,' said the Child.

Thus Christopher stands as the type of 'Industrial' hero. For his employment is the occasion of his heroism, as God is the cause of it.

'As long as you did it to one of these My least brethren, *you did it to Me*' (*mihi fecisti*). Matt. xxv. 40.

'A garden of roses in Jericho' is the symbol of Holy Wisdom as opposed to the Power and Riches of the world which are the idol of the Industrial system.

The dated certificate which accompanies each medal reads as follows:

'Order of Industrial Heroism: instituted by *The Daily Herald*. Presented as a mark of respect and admiration to . . . a brave man who in a moment of peril thought more of others than of himself.'

The presentations are usually made by Labour M.P.s and trade-union leaders.[2]

The critic of this example of journalistic and political enterprise is silenced and abashed by the recital of the deeds which have thus been recognized, and of which the following are typical:

---

[1] Offices at 105 Jermyn Street, London, S.W. 1.

[2] *Vide* Mr. Hannen Swaffer, in the *Daily Herald*, 5th Sept. 1936.

Alfred Gardiner, while driving a train from Holborn to Brixton, found his clothes on fire. Yet, before leaving the footplate, he calmly did all that was wanted to save the train and the passengers. He stopped it, and then leapt on the line. Two days later he died in hospital. 'A splendid example of bravery and of devotion to duty', said the South London Coroner.

William Jackson, a deputy of Swindon, near Doncaster, lost his life in April 1936 trying to save two miners from gas.

Four dockers were on duty in 1923 on the bank of the Mersey when a steam crane collapsed. The boiler fires fell under some railway wagons laden with 120 tons of picric acid. Instead of rushing away to save themselves, *Joseph Sloss*, *Michael Lavan*, *Joshua Bamber*, and *Thomas Pinnington* went right into the heart of the danger zone and extinguished the flames just in time. Had they not done so, the resulting explosion must have caused vast loss of life and property.

J. W. Shippey of Bridlington was in a motor fishing-boat off Spurn Point when the ship caught fire. He seized a burst and blazing tin of petrol in the engine-room and rushed with it on deck. Although so terribly burned that his right hand was maimed for life, he saved the ship and his comrades (1923).

Fred Davies was a fireman on an express train from London to Liverpool. A rod broke; steam escaped, scalding the driver badly. He stuck to his post, in great pain and danger, and brought the train to rest. The presentation was made by Mr. George Lansbury at Swindon. It was a memorable scene. Engine-drivers and firemen and their wives and friends were present by the hundred. Half the town would have been there had there been room in the hall. So it is, often, when these medals are given.

Nicholas A. Nugent, a Southampton shipwright's apprentice, saved a man from drowning by diving through a port-hole (1924). *William Forrester*, a tram-driver of Stoke-on-Trent, stuck to his post on a run-away car (1924).

A youth named David Scourfield was stripping off the roof of a high building at a Llanelly copper works when it gave way. As he fell, he grabbed a joist and hung suspended in mid-air. There was a drop of 40 feet and then, beneath, machinery in motion. But for *Harold Acton*, a young man of 22, Scourfield would have fallen and then been mangled to death. Aston made for the roof. Then he had to spring from joist to joist, which were 4 feet apart. A slip would have meant certain death. He reached the suspended man when he was nearly exhausted and carried him to safety. That, however, was not the end. A moment later, there was another crash. When the dust was cleared away, Acton was seen himself to be in peril, hanging by one hand. Happily, he was able to draw himself up. Then other men went up to save him (1924).

An engine on a circular track ran away at Vickers' works at Sheffield. *A. H. Sutton*, an engine-driver, tried to mount the runaway at great risk to his life. After failing, he had the presence of mind to conceive the idea of driving another engine in front of the runaway and by gradually reducing its speed, made it act as a moving brake against the runaway engine (1924).

There was a shortage of hewers in the Harvey seam of the Bishop Auckland Collieries. So *Edward Thompson*, who was not really a hewer, took on the job. Within a few hours he had received fatal injuries. Suddenly a tub became detached from the rest and started running down a steep gradient. At the same time, a boy driver with an empty tub and pony was coming towards the detached tub. Without hesitation, Thompson ran after the tub and, by an almost superhuman effort, succeeded in dragging it from the lines. Then a second tub became detached, and before Thompson had time to get clear, it dashed into him. When comrades came, Thompson said, simply, 'If I had not done it, the driver and his pony would have been killed.' Three days afterwards, he himself died.

Ben Tanner and *Gilbert Klee* went down into a manhole at Barry to rescue five men imprisoned in foul air (1926).

Ernest Johnson was working in a deep trench at Manchester when his mate, David Inglis, was buried in quicksand. Johnson stood supporting a great load of debris for eight hours, and kept his mate's chin above the earth. 'I owe my life to my pal Johnson, who supported a great load of earth on his back', said Inglis. 'He could have moved, but refused, for fear the earth would fall and crush me. He cracked jokes and laughingly told me we should be out in time for the pictures!' (1920.)

W. Taylor, a Newcastle crane-driver, figures in it (1930); *J. W. Sutton*, a Barnsley bus-driver; *Patrick Troy*, a Southampton shipyard worker; *C. Tomlinson*, a Bradford lorry-driver; and *James Crumpton*, a Walkden engineer; and Councillor *James Fletcher*, chairman of the Sunderland Labour Party and a bus-inspector (1930).

J. R. Hughes of Port Talbot climbed down single-handed into a blast-furnace bell full of gas to rescue two of his workmates, at the British Iron and Steel Company works.

A fitter and his helper had climbed to the top of the skip and were standing on the coke trying to fix the hook of the hoist, when the skip tilted and flung them, with the coke, into the main bell.

Hughes, who was watching to signal the hoist driver, realized there was no time to lose, and went to their help.

Lowering himself as far as he dared into the skip, he succeeded, by superhuman efforts, in bringing both men out before the gas had completely overcome them. Both men would have died had he waited to get assistance (1938).

Had this man been injured or killed, and had breach of a statutory regulation, or negligence by his employer, been proved, he might not have succeeded in an action at Common Law, as the insurance company concerned would probably have pleaded the 'Defence of Common Employment'—which would apply to several, if not most, of the above-mentioned cases. This particular case was put up to the Home Office, and rejected as unworthy of reward!

In every one of these, and hundreds of other cases dealt with by voluntary societies every year, public recognition is richly merited.

The existence of these unofficial tokens of public esteem, which may not be worn on official occasions and, if worn, are seldom recognized, so rare are they and so seldom seen, is a proof of the widespread public desire that deeds of heroism should be rewarded.

Surely the time has come for an extension of the Albert and Edward

Medals by constituting three classes, in gold, silver, and bronze, respectively in each Order (at present there are only two), and by increasing the number awarded, by taking steps to ensure that suitable cases are reported. The total number of Albert Medals in gold awarded in 60 years is only 69; of Edward Medals in silver 82. Awards of all classes of these medals for the past three years in the United Kingdom total only 3 and 8 respectively. Alternatively, if steps were taken to ensure that cases were reported, an increasing number of the Medals of the Order of the British Empire might be awarded, either for Gallantry or for Meritorious Service.

There are some 500 living holders of the Victoria Cross: there are not half as many holders of the Albert and Edward Medals combined. Only one civilian has been awarded the Albert Medal for a gallant deed on land in Britain since 1st January 1921!

Individual Medals

Medals are occasionally presented by private persons or companies or by public subscription to one or several persons to commemorate deeds of individual or collective heroism or gallantry in civil life.

In 1804 a gold medal was awarded to Mr. Lys, Edward Touzel,[1] and Ponteney (a soldier) who entered a burning powder magazine at St. Helier in Jersey, and, in face of almost certain death, extinguished it.[2]

In 1876 the Maharaja of Burdwan wrote to *The Times* (22nd February 1876) expressing his desire to present a medal, through the Lord Mayor of London, to boys who had distinguished themselves when the training ship *Goliath* was destroyed by fire on 22nd December 1875. His letter, dated 28th January 1876, reads as follows:

The Palace, Burdwan, India, Jan. 28, 1876.

To the Editor of *The Times*.

Sir,—Having read with the greatest admiration the account of the heroic conduct displayed by some of the boys of the training ship *Goliath* on the occasion of the recent destruction by fire of that ill-fated vessel, I have felt a strong wish to present a silver medal to each of those who signally distinguished themselves on that occasion.

I may have been forestalled in this wish, but I trust that I may be allowed to do something of the kind, as, coming from India, it will prove to the boys

---

[1] The medal awarded to E. Touzel, inscribed 'Fire at St. Helier 1804', is in the British Museum Collection.

[2] C. M. Yonge, *Book of Golden Deeds*, p. 281. The continued popularity of this book, first published in 1864, as a Treasury for Young People, suggests that this generation is not less ready than its predecessors to pay a tribute to the golden deeds of young and old, of our own and other countries, of the present or of earlier ages.

that deeds like theirs have not merely a local fame, but are marked and appreciated by their fellow subjects in the most distant parts of Her Majesty's Empire.

I have taken the liberty of addressing you upon the subject, as I have been unable to ascertain the name of the society to which the ship belonged. I should have written direct to its offices had I been able to discover it, and I have, therefore, to beg that, while pardoning me for the trouble I am giving you, you will do me the further favour of forwarding to the proper authorities the enclosed draft to cover the cost of the medals, and of intimating that, if necessary, I shall be happy to remit a further sum.

The training-ship *Goliath* was of wood: it was moored off Gravesend and held some 500 boys, pauper children from various unions.

The fire started in the lamp-room, and spread so rapidly that some boys were forced to take to the water to escape the flames and not all being able to swim a number were drowned. The Coroner said (*The Times*, 1st January 1876): 'Every boy behaved himself like a man. Had they not been well disciplined, calamity would have been widespread, but they were free from all panic and tumult. The 14-year-old boy who dropped the lighted lamp in the lamp-room gave his evidence in an honest and manly way, as did all concerned.' Several boys received the medal, which is of silver. The obverse shows the Head of the Queen, crowned, with veil thrown back, '*Victoria Regina*'. On the reverse is '*The gift of the Maharajah of Burdwan*.[1] Presented by the Lord Mayor of London for gallant conduct at the burning of H.M.S. *Goliath*, Dec. 22, 1875.' One boy, Bolton, was awarded the sum of £10 in addition and a watch to replace one that he had lost,[2] but he had already emigrated.

The sort of life led by pauper boys in Poor Law Institutions at this time is indicated by a remark in *The Times* that a few boys ran away and hid after the catastrophe, 'the boys having a great horror of returning to the workhouses whence they came'. On learning that they would not be so dealt with they were overjoyed and at once reported themselves for duty.

The British Museum and House of Commons Collections also include a medal awarded to rescuers in the colliery disaster at Hartley, Northumberland, on 10th January 1862. One gold and thirty silver medals were issued: an unspecified number were struck in bronze. Two hundred and four miners perished on this occasion, of whom 199 died in the pit. There were eight persons in the cage which was

[1] The present Maharaja, who succeeded in 1909, received the Indian Order of Merit, Civil Division, 3rd Class, in 1909 for gallantly shielding with his body, against a would-be assassin, the person of Sir Andrew Fraser, Lt. Governor of Bengal. The father would have been proud of his adopted son!

[2] Tancred, vol. ii, p. 403.

being drawn up when the pumping-engine beam, weighing over 40 tons, broke and half fell down the shaft carrying with it a mass of machinery and debris. Much of it came to rest 138 yards from the surface on the massive oak buntons on which stood the middle set of pumps in the shaft.

Among this wreck and upon it fell masses of stone from the unwalled sides of the shaft, closing it completely. Most strenuous efforts to reach the men were unavailing, for debris continued to fall. It was six days before the men were reached, and all were found dead. 'It appears to be certain from the date of the entry in the book found on the person of the overman Armour that all had died not later than the afternoon of the day following the accident, having fallen victims to the noxious gases generated in the pit. The death of the sufferers occurred early and appears not to have been attended by much pain.' (Report of Chief Inspector of Mines, Parliamentary Papers, 1862.)

While the Relief Fund was being raised it was decided to raise a special fund to recognize the sinkers and others who had risked their lives in unsuccessful attempts to rescue the men in the pit. £1,587 was raised, and the balance remaining after the cost of the medal by Wyon had been met was divided among them. Thirty-eight silver medals and one in gold (for Mr. William Coulson) were struck and presented at a public meeting in the Town Hall, Newcastle, on 28th May 1862.[1]

Another silver medal privately issued in recognition of gallantry displayed by rescuers was struck in connexion with a fire which occurred at Hamstead Colliery, five miles north-west of Birmingham, on 4th March 1908 resulting in the loss of twenty-five lives, including one of the rescuers.[2] Some of the recipients were officials and others who had not risked their lives.

A later example in the House of Commons Collection is a medal 'presented in 1904 to Charles Fitzpatrick by the public of the east portion of Hewarth parish in recognition of his gallantry in having brought 21 persons out of the water, 19 of whom survived'.

The medal is of 9 carat gold, 2 inches in diameter, with three heavy gold clasps one of which reads '*Wardley Colliery*,[3] *Bill Quay, Pelaw Main*'.

---

[1] T. E. Forster, *Memoir of the Hartley Colliery Accident*, Reid & Co., Newcastle, 1912, gives full details and a list of recipients.

[2] Parliamentary Report Cd. 4231, 1908. The collection in the House of Commons includes one presented to John Summerton 'for conspicuous bravery in attempting to rescue the entombed miners' and one in gold inscribed with the name of H. R. Makepeace.

[3] This colliery was closed in 1912.

'CHARLIE THE GUNNER'

In repy to an editorial note of inquiry, *Heslop's Local Advertiser and Monthly Record*, of Felling, on Tyneside, published on 15th July 1938 the following letter concerning Fitzpatrick from Mr. R. Bell of Wingrove, Hewarth:

I am sorry that I cannot give any particulars concerning Charles Fitzpatrick prior to tragic circumstances in the loss of our own little son, Robert Bell, aged 6 years, who was accidentally drowned in the reservoir at Wardley Colliery, on July 16th, 1904.

He was a native of Bill Quay, known to everybody as 'Charlie the Gunner'. On July 16th, 1904, the Water Company, owing to some necessary repairs to their water-main pipes, had cut off the water during the early part of the day; the whole village was without water, and the residents of the Colliery had to secure water from any source available. The reservoir being handy, people flocked there for their requirements. Our little boy Robert accompanied by his eldest sister was amongst the many seeking water, when he fell into the water. There was no one there able to swim; he was never seen to rise after he had fallen into the water.

The news spread round the district and large crowds gathered round from Pelaw and Bill Quay and Wardley. There were several young men engaged in diving and swimming about, but failed to find the body.

Police-Sergeant Sanderson, then stationed at Pelaw, took a great interest in the case, and I think it was he who had sent word to Charlie to hasten to the spot.

When Fitzpatrick arrived he was not long in getting to work, diving and swimming about under the water until he was compelled to rise for breathing space. It was an awful experience, as he came out of the water time after time without result.

At last he found the body lying some considerable distance away from where Robert had fallen in.

This incident prompted the idea of some public recognition. Sergeant Sanderson and myself organized a small committee and solicited public subscriptions and raised £10 with which we purchased the medal. It was presented to him at the Wesleyan Hall, Bill Quay.

The members of the Bill Quay and Wardley Social Club, of which Charlie was a member, presented him with a foy-boat on behalf of the members. He was a foy-boatman for several years down at Pelaw Main Staiths.

R. BELL, Old Timer.

Charles Fitzpatrick died at the early age of 34, and the *Weekly Dispatch*, on the 1st November 1908, told of his death and recorded his life-saving services in the following terms, here reproduced from a newspaper cutting in the possession of his widow, who (1938) still resides at Bill Quay:[1]

'Tyneside has lost by death, at a comparatively early age, one of those heroes in humble life whose valour is too rarely recognized.

---

[1] Mrs. Hussler, 19 Reay St., Bill Quay.

'Charles Fitzpatrick had long been known on the water-side of the mid-Tyne district as a man who could always be relied upon to risk his life for a drowning fellow creature, and his death was due to complications following on asthma, which was produced through the deceased not taking sufficient care of himself in getting into dry clothing after his immersions.

'His career as a life saver commenced early, for it was while still a boy on the *Wellesley* training ship at the mouth of the Tyne that he sprang into Shields Harbour and brought a companion to safety. While still on the *Wellesley*, Fitzpatrick was the hero of a daring escapade only made possible by his swimming abilities. Refused permission to go home for some festivity, he swam ashore to the north bank of the river, walked the five miles up to Bill Quay, and then swam across the Tyne at one of its broadest parts.

'Later he was a sailor, and then settled down by the water-side as a wherry-man and gained the sobriquet of "Charlie the Gunner". When any one was known to be in danger on the river "Charlie the Gunner" was always sent for, but he came into public prominence for the first time about five years ago, when one of Justice Grantham's retinue was rescued by him. A man had jumped overboard from a vessel on which the judge was proceeding down the river, and the man who was subsequently saved by Fitzpatrick jumped in after him, but was in turn overwhelmed, and it fell to the lot of Fitzpatrick to rescue them both.

'The judge sent for the hero, and in his rooms at Newcastle congratulated him, and the matter being brought to the notice of Deputy-Coroner Shepherd, the police and the foreman of the coroner's jury investigated his record. Representations were made which resulted in Fitzpatrick receiving the Humane Society's medal and certificate in recognition of his having saved twenty-three lives from drowning. A gold medal was also presented by the people in the district. The deceased's rescues included two women.'

Another of Charlie's friends wrote on the 13th June 1938 from Rotherham, Yorks.:

'The last time I saw him was just thirty years ago, bringing a boy out of Wardley Reservoir one Saturday afternoon. I think it was his last great deed. He was a wonderful swimmer and his name will never die to the people of Bill Quay, Pelaw, Wardley, and Hewarth, if I know them. Long after he was dead men used to go about with banjoes singing about his deeds.'

He lies buried in Hewarth Churchyard.

The British Museum Collection also contains a medal presented 'To William Pearse; for saving twelve fellow creatures from a watery grave (1806).'

A different type of gallantry is exemplified by a bronze medal, of which a number of examples were struck, bearing on the obverse a fine bust of Jo$^{h.}$ (Joseph) Hanson, The Weavers' Friend, of Strangeways, Manchester, 1810, and on the reverse a reproduction of a loom of that period, with the words 'Printing–Weaving–Spinning' on three sides, on the fourth, a weaver's shuttle bearing the figure 39600—a reference to the number of pennies contributed to the fund referred to below.

Joseph Hanson, born in Manchester in 1774, was Colonel of the Loyal Masonic Rifle Corps, which drilled and practised shooting in the grounds of Strangeways Hall, where he lived, but is better known as the author of a *Defence of the Petitions for Peace*, 1808, although he was once arrested on Kersal Moor when about to fight a duel with Colonel Phillips. It is said that he was told by George III to appear at Court with his hat on and in the uniform of the regiment of which he was commander.

Although greatly admired by his regiment and the recipient of handsome presents from them, it is as 'The Weavers' Friend' that he is remembered. He was vastly popular with the working men of his day, whose cause he often championed. He suffered six months' imprisonment for taking sides with the weavers in a dispute with their employers. There were great rejoicings on his release from prison and a 'Penny Subscription' was raised to which there were about 40,000 contributors, and this medal was struck in honour of the occasion.

He died in 1811; his grave may still be seen in the old Unitarian graveyard at Stand, near Whitefield, with the weaver's shuttle and the title by which he was known to his own generation at least.[1] The original monument over his grave fell into decay and was demolished in 1877. It is now marked by a flat stone which bears his name and a commemorative inscription added in November 1908.

Another example is a medal bearing on the reverse 'From the saloon passengers of R.M.S. *Baltic* and R.M.S. *Republic* to the officers and crews of the s.s. *Republic*, *Baltic*, and *Florida* for gallantry; commemorating the rescue of 1,700 souls. Jan. 21. 1909.' The obverse shows a ship, the s.s. *Republic*, sending out a wireless message, the letters C Q D above.

This medal commemorates an occurrence which in its day aroused intense excitement. The Italian steamship *Florida* came into collision in heavy fog with the White Star Liner *Republic* on Saturday, 21st January, 175 miles east of the Ambrose Lightship at 5.30 a.m. The passengers of the *Republic* were first transferred to the *Florida* and then to the *Baltic* which went to the rescue, arriving twelve hours after the accident owing to the heavy fog. The *Florida*'s passengers later joined

---

[1] Readers who wish to extend their acquaintance with the 'Weavers' Friend' and his period may be referred to *The Skilled Labourer*, by the Hammonds, Prentice's *Manchester, 1792–1832*, Proctor's *Memorials of Manchester Streets*, and the *Annual Register* of 1809, which on p. 325 gives an account of Hanson's trial at Lancaster Assizes.

THE HONG KONG PLAGUE MEDAL

them. Two passengers in the *Republic* were killed and four of the crew of the *Florida*. The *Republic* had a crew of 300 and 460 passengers. The *Florida* had 800 Italian emigrants. The wireless operators of the *Republic*, Jack Binns, and of the *Baltic*, H. G. Tattersall, were acclaimed equally with Capt. Ransom of the *Baltic*, Capt. Sealby of the *Republic* and Capt. Rospiri of the *Florida*, and their respective crews, as heroes.

Crowds marched out to the ship blowing steamship trumpets and carried the embarrassed Capt. Sealby and Jack Binns on their shoulders to the offices of the Company. The *Republic* sank in forty-five fathoms while being towed to New York.

The incident gave a great stimulus to the demand for universal compulsory use of Wireless Telegraphy, and the letters C Q D by which the *Republic* notified her need became proverbial until replaced for technical reasons by S O S.

The Hong Kong Plague Medal deserves special mention. In April 1894 a severe epidemic of bubonic plague broke out near Canton, and in May gained a strong foothold in Hong Kong. We know to-day that it is spread exclusively by rat-fleas: at that time the virulence of the attack was ascribed by doctors to 'the increasing moisture of the atmosphere and the stirring up of the soil caused by the flow of storm water'. Deaths reached the figure of 100 a day in June. An attempt was made to cope with the epidemic by segregation of individual cases: the Chinese strongly objected, preferring to die among friends and dreading, above all, pit burial. The vast majority preferred to be treated by Chinese doctors.[1]

Attempts to keep the epidemic within bounds, to remove the sick, and to destroy the infected huts were bitterly resented. Many members of the mercantile community in Hong Kong played their part as volunteers in assisting the Government of the colony, but the greatest burden fell upon the British garrison, including some Royal Engineers and a battalion of the Shropshire Light Infantry. A medal was also given to the nursing sisters and to several civilians: officers received gold medals without ribands; N.C.O.s and men silver medals with riband, but authority was never given for it to be worn. The obverse shows a sick man on a trestle bed, his head supported by the arms of a soldier who, with his left arm, is warding off the Angel of Death. At the other side of the bed stands a European nurse. On the reverse is 'Hong Kong' graven in Chinese characters. A tar-brush and pail and a whitewashing brush in the foreground signify the means used to repel the plague.

The reverse bears the inscription 'Presented by the Hong Kong

[1] Colonial Report No. 148, Hong Kong, 1895.

Community' with, in the exergue, the words 'For services rendered during the plague of 1894'. The medal was designed by Frank Bowcher (who died in 1938), and was executed by A. Wyon: the riband is yellow with one broad and two narrow scarlet stripes.

CHAPTER V

AWARDS FOR CIVIL GALLANTRY IN GREAT BRITAIN AND THE EMPIRE

II. AT SEA

'The medals for troops in general (given by the East India Company) are a new and doubtful thing, and now it is proposed to reward even a special case of personal distinction by the *Company's* conferring a mark of honour. Lord Grey will agree with the Queen that it will be better not to establish two fountains of honour in the Realm.'   QUEEN VICTORIA to EARL GREY, 26th Oct. 1848.

APART from the occasional awards to civilians mentioned in Chapter I, the first official medal for gallantry displayed at sea by civilians was the Board of Trade Medal for Saving Life at Sea (S.G.M.) in silver and bronze awarded to British subjects, or to foreigners serving in British ships. Foreigners who have displayed gallantry in foreign ships in saving the lives of British subjects are eligible for *Board of Trade Gold and Silver Medals 'for Foreign Services'*. In all cases these awards are made by His Majesty on the recommendation of the President of the Board of Trade. They carry no pecuniary grant: there is no published list of persons who have received them, though awards to British subjects are notified in *The London Gazette*. The riband and medal are worn on the left breast, and holders are entitled to append the letters S.G.M. after their names. These letters stand for Sea Gallantry Medal.

The Board of Trade's authority to issue such medals for gallantry at sea in British ships is derived not from Royal Warrant but from the Merchant Shipping Acts of 1854 and 1894, 677 (*i*) (L). They are the only medals now current which are issued under the authority of Parliament. When first struck in 1855, from the design of W. Wyon, Engraver to the Royal Mint, they were not intended to be worn, but in 1903 they were reduced in size and made wearable and since then, when awarded to British subjects in the United Kingdom, have as a rule been personally presented by His Majesty at Investitures. The obverse of the medal gives the effigy of the reigning sovereign and the Royal Cypher with the words 'Awarded by the Board of Trade for gallantry in saving life'. The reverse shows a man clinging to a spar and beckoning to a life-boat; also a man supporting a rescued seaman and a woman and child on a raft. The riband is scarlet with two narrow white vertical stripes.

In the nine years 1914–22, apart from 194 awards of plate, the awards of Board of Trade medals, for British and foreign seamen, were:

gold, 8; silver, 349; and bronze, 116. The total cost of the medals in nine years was about £250, and of the plate about £1,708, and there were monetary awards of £1,153.

Awards of the S.G.M. from 1st January 1920 to 31st December 1938 were: silver, 107; bronze, 172 (see Chapter XIX).

The Medal for Foreign Services dates from 1839. At first it was made of large size by Pistrucci,[1] Engraver to the Royal Mint, and was not intended to be worn. In 1854 they were reduced in size and made wearable. After the creation of the Marine Department of the Board of Trade in 1850 the Foreign Services medals were still granted by the Foreign Office, but paid for out of the Civil Contingencies Fund. In 1872 the Lords Commissioners of His Majesty's Treasury raised the question as to the payment of Mr. Wyon's account for making and engraving the medals and suggested payment of the account out of the Board of Trade Vote for the Relief of Distressed British Seamen. This course was ultimately adopted, but the Board of Trade suggested that, on the grounds of economy, the medals should in future be struck at the Royal Mint. The Foreign Office agreed to the proposal that the Mint should take charge of the dies, and promised that, in future, the Board of Trade would not be called upon to pay for any medals, other than such as might be ordered at their own request. This arrangement was continued down to 1882, when the Foreign Office suggested that the Board of Trade should order these medals without consulting them, except in rare cases where a doubt existed as to the propriety of conferring a medal. It was, however, decided that the medals should still be sent to the Foreign Office for presentation in the same manner as was done in regard to other awards granted by the Board of Trade to foreigners. Since that time (1882) the Board of Trade have ordered the medals from the Royal Mint, and the entire cost is borne upon the Board of Trade Vote.

The Four Classes of Medals. The medals are struck in gold and silver, and are reserved to foreigners or British seamen serving in foreign ships who render services to British ships and British seamen. Four impressions are issued, each of which bears the head of the Sovereign on the obverse side, whilst on the reverse side appears an inscription indicating the nature of the services rendered; viz. 'Presented by the British Government for saving the life of a British subject,' or 'for saving the lives of British subjects', or 'for gallantry and humanity',

---

[1] Benedetto Pistrucci, b. in Rome 1784, came to London in 1815 and in 1828 was appointed Chief Medallist under William Wyon (see p. 66, footnote) at the Royal Mint. He is best remembered as the designer (1816) of the St. George and the Dragon which has been the accepted reverse type on our gold coinage ever since. He died near Windsor in 1855.

or 'assisting a British vessel in distress'. These medals, when they became wearable, were originally suspended by a crimson riband, but the riband is now identical with that worn with the Board of Trade Gallantry Medal for Saving Life at Sea.

The medal 'for Gallantry and Humanity' is frequently given, and it is awarded in cases where some degree of personal risk is incurred. A gold medal with this inscription is very rarely awarded. Medals bearing the inscription 'For Humanity' are reserved for cases in which a life or lives are saved without risk to the person rendering the service. There is a third type, inscribed 'for assisting a British subject in distress', for occasions on which assistance has been rendered primarily to the vessel, the crew having remained on board. These are usually of bronze. Rewards of plate or money are usually given in cases of foreigners saving life without risk, except where a medal is more likely to be appreciated, as in the case of the *Drummond Castle* disaster in 1896, for which 'Special Commemorative Silver Medals' were struck and issued with the approval of Her Majesty Queen Victoria.[1] At one time the practice adopted appears to have been to award gold medals to officers and silver medals to seamen, &c. Since 1903 the medals have been awarded by the Sovereign on the recommendation of the President of the Board of Trade. Since 1st January 1920, up to 31st December 1938, 36 gold and 241 silver medals 'for foreign services' have been issued.

As will be seen from Chapters XIX and XX the S.G.M. is awarded in practice only to seamen serving in ships with British registry. In no case for many years has any award been made to seamen on ships with Indian, Colonial, or Foreign registry. For such men there appears to be no provision.

The only other official award specifically for gallantry at sea for which civilians are eligible is the Albert Medal, which is dealt with elsewhere. It ranks before the Sea Gallantry Medal.

The Medal of the Order of the British Empire, in the Military or Civil Division, for Gallantry (E.G.M.) may also be awarded for gallantry at sea (*vide* Chapter XV).

---

[1] The Castle liner S.S. *Drummond Castle* homeward bound from Natal and Capetown struck a reef off Ushant in a fog at 11 p.m. on the night of 16th June 1896. Of 143 passengers and 104 officers and crew only three escaped. The grant of a medal was foreshadowed in *The Times* of 30th June 1896: 'Her Majesty's Government propose to give some tangible recognition of the humanity and sympathetic kindness shown by the inhabitants of Molène and Ushant and the mainland in connexion with the loss of the *Drummond Castle* and the burial of the dead. It may be that a medal commemorative of the nation's gratitude would be most highly appreciated.' For a full description of the wreck by a survivor, see *The English Illustrated Magazine* for August 1896.

INDIA AND THE DOMINIONS.

Apart from the Indian Order of Merit, Civil Division, the Government of India has no medal or order of its own for gallantry in civil life, and though the Indian subjects of His Majesty perform deeds of the greatest heroism almost daily, the only form of official recognition utilized by the Government, besides the Medal of the Order of the British Empire, for Gallantry or for Meritorious Service, is the Albert or the Edward Medal, ten of which have in each case been awarded during the past eighteen years on the recommendation of the Government of India. The presentation of the Albert and Edward Medals has often taken place two years after the date of the deed thus recognized.

The Government of Bengal have issued, on two occasions, a medal in silver (and bronze) 'for bravery in saving life at sea'. Eleven such medals were issued to the master (Mr. G. T. Knox) and crew of s.s. *Nubia* in 1894 for gallantry displayed by the crew of that vessel in rescuing the crew of the British Indian brig *Shah-in-Shah* on 22nd May 1893. The Bengal Government on that occasion were authorized by the Governor-General, with the approval of the Secretary of State for India, to reward British crews who saved the lives of Indian crews in the same way as foreigners were rewarded by the Board of Trade for saving the lives of British subjects[1] and in such manner as was deemed suitable. This authority extended to all local governments, including Burma, but has not been acted on except by the Bengal Government.

In 1901 the Bengal Government awarded a similar medal to an Indian ferryman employed by the East Indian Railway Company, named Bhattu, 'for gallant conduct in trying to save a man from drowning at Manharighat on the Ganges on 25th July 1900'. He also received Rs. 50 in cash. This award remains unique!

In 1923 medals were issued by the Government of Bengal to the officers and crew of the s.s. *Lady Blake* for gallantry shown by them in saving 111 lives at sea off the Chittagong coast. Two specimens of this medal were issued in 1933 in connexion with a collection of medals exhibited in Canada.[2]

UNOFFICIAL AWARDS FOR GALLANTRY AT SEA.

The oldest of unofficial awards are the medals of the *Royal National Life-Boat Institution*,[3] in three classes: gold (1824), silver (1824), and bronze (1917), given to persons 'whose humane and intrepid exertions

[1] Resolution 5350 S.R. of 19th Oct. 1894, Govt. of India, Finance and Commerce Dept.
[2] D.O. Letter 11th March and 13th Sept. 1938 from Asst. Sec. to Governor of Bengal.
[3] Life Boat House, 42 Grosvenor Gardens, S.W. 1. The British Museum Collection includes a medal of this Society dated 1824 in which it is described as the Royal National Institution for the preservation of life from shipwreck.

in saving life from shipwrecks on our coasts are deemed sufficiently conspicuous to merit those honourable distinctions'.

Since the foundation of the Institution in 1824, 118 gold, 1,390 silver, and 198 bronze medals have been awarded. From the beginning of 1927 up to date 7 gold, 19 silver, and 82 bronze medals have been awarded. There is the usual provision for clasps.

During the year 1936 the Institution gave rewards for the rescue of 491 lives, 385 by life-boats and 180 by shore-boats. The total number of rewards in the 114 years of the Society's existence covers the rescue from shipwreck of over 65,000 lives, an average of 11 a week.

Previous to 1913 there was in existence the *Tayleur Fund*, founded from the surplus of subscriptions raised for the benefit of the survivors of the wreck of the emigrant ship *Tayleur* on 24th Jan. 1854, in Bantry Bay, from which awards of medals for gallantry were sometimes made. The Trustees, residents of Dublin, proposed to the Life Boat Institution that they should hand over the Fund, amounting to nearly £1,200, in return for an undertaking that a motor life-boat should be placed at Kingstown. The undertaking was given and the funds transferred in Dec. 1913 with the assent of the Court of Chancery.

The obverse of the medal shows the bust of King George V with the double legend, 'Royal Life-Boat Institution. Founded 1824. Incorporated 1860. George V Patron.' The reverse shows three seamen in a life-boat, one of whom is seen in the act of rescuing an exhausted mariner from the waves, with the words 'Let not the deep swallow me up' (W. Wyon. Mint). The Medal is worn on the right breast.

Next comes the *Shipwrecked Fishermen and Mariners' Society*[1] founded in 1839 and incorporated by Act of Parliament in 1850. This Society's medal is in gold and silver, and is given for 'heroic or praiseworthy exertions to save life from shipwreck, etc., on the High Seas or coasts of India and the Colonies'.

Both medals have the same design. In the centre of the obverse are two oval medallions, the left of which bears the bust of Horatio Lord Nelson, and the right has a three-masted ship. The medallions are surmounted by sprays of laurel and a crown with the Union Jack and the Society's flag on either side. On the left is a figure standing by a capstan looking at a vessel through a spy-glass; on the right another capstan, and in the distance a vessel; below, a vessel sinking with two men on a raft. The clasp represents two dolphins. The reverse bears the words 'England expects every man to do his duty', and in the centre 'Presented for heroic exertions for saving life from drowning. Job xxix. 13' (viz. 'The blessing of him that was ready to perish came upon me: and I caused the widow's heart to sing for joy').

The Institution has awarded up to date 39 gold and 532 silver medals and 72 aneroid barometers, besides pecuniary awards totalling over £5,000.

[1] Carlton House, Regent Street, London, S.W. 1.

This Society also administers the 'Émile Robin' Trust.[1] Fifty-four awards have been made since it was instituted in 1881.

The Liverpool Shipwreck and Humane Society[2] was called into existence by the great hurricane which swept over the Irish Channel on the 7th and 8th of January 1839. Public feeling was wrought to the highest pitch by the shipwrecks that followed and by the heroism displayed in rescuing crews and passengers. A public meeting was held to raise funds, and in the course of a few days £5,000 was subscribed. After having afforded ample relief to the sufferers, and rewards to all those who had distinguished themselves in saving life on this occasion, a balance of £3,291 remained and was made the nucleus of a fund, to be administered by a permanent society to be formed for the purpose of saving human life, particularly in cases of shipwreck in the neighbourhood of Liverpool, to hold out inducements to render immediate assistance to vessels of all nations in distress near that port, and to reward persons instrumental in rescuing human life from danger. Relief was also granted to the widows and families of those who might have perished in the attempt to save others. The immediate necessities of those saved were to be relieved, regardless of nationality, and assistance afforded to enable them to return to their homes.

The awards of the Society are as follows:

1. The Society's Medal in silver and bronze for heroism in saving life at sea, with a blue riband. The obverse shows a man on a raft rescuing two drowning persons surmounted by the words '*Lord, save us we perish*'. The reverse shows a gull in flight holding a laurel sprig surmounted by the name of the society and the date 1839.
2. The Society's General Medal in silver and bronze dates from 1894. The riband consists of two white and three red vertical stripes. The medal shows a cross pattée in relief with a crown in the centre, and the words '*For Bravery in Saving Life*'.
3. The Society's Fire Medal in gold, silver, and bronze dates from 1882. The riband is red. The obverse shows a fireman descending the stairs of a burning house with one child on his back and another under his right arm. Below the fireman kneels the figure of a woman with arms extended towards the children. In the exergue are the words '*For Bravery in Saving Life*'.

[1] The more important terms of this Trust are the following: 'At each Annual General Meeting of the Society, the Society shall pay the income of the Trust Fund, for the year preceding, to the captain and chief officer (being natural born or naturalized British subjects) as, in the opinion of the Committee, shall during such year have saved the crew of a vessel, whether British or foreign, from imminent peril ... The said income to be paid as to four equal fifth parts thereof (£16) to such captain and as to the remaining one equal fifth part (£4) to such chief officer.'   [2] 5 Chapel Street, Liverpool, 3.

4. The Camp and Villaverde Medal: no riband: the design on the obverse is that of other medals of the Society. Words on the reverse '*Camp and Villaverde Medal for Saving Life*'.[1]

Honorary and other Awards granted by the Society from 1839 to 1937 include:

Society's Gold Medals and Medallions	65
,, Silver Medals and Medallions	2,293
,, Bronze Medals	1,058
,, Gold Bars	7
,, Silver Bars	223
,, Bronze Bars	22
Fire Gold Medal	1
,, Silver Medals	156
,, Bronze Medals	205
,, Bronze Bars	2
,, Silver Bar	1
General Gold Medal	1
,, Silver Medals and Medallions	369
,, Bronze Medals	495
,, Silver Bars	73
,, Bronze Bars	12
Camp and Villaverde Silver Medals	25
,, ,, Bronze Medals	23
Bramley-Moore Gold Medal	1
,, Silver Medals	24
,, Bronze Medals	2

as well as Framed Certificates of Votes of Thanks, and other Honorary Awards.

The Pecuniary Awards, Annuities, Sick Allowances, to persons who received injuries while engaged in rescuing others, Relief to Sufferers from Shipwreck and other Disasters, and the Special Funds raised from time to time for the widows and orphans of brave men who have laid down their lives in attempting to save the lives of others, would together amount to many thousands of pounds.

The latest awards are for deeds which well merit national recognition: unlike the Albert and Edward Medal, the awards include, when necessary, pecuniary aid to the dependants.

'*LLOYDS*' established in 1836 a *Medal for Saving Life at Sea*. The riband

---

[1] In 1847 a subscription was opened at Liverpool for a testimonial to Captain Bernardino Camp, of the Spanish brig *Emilio*, and his mate, Mr. Villaverde, for having rescued survivors of the passengers and crew from the wreck of the Royal Mail Steamship *Tweed*, lost on the Alacran Shoal, Gulf of Mexico, in February of that year. The idea of presenting a testimonial having been abandoned, the amount collected was used to found a medal for saving life at sea.

has one red stripe, two white and two red at the edges. The medal, by Wyon,[1] is inscribed on the reverse 'Presented by Lloyds, for life saving'.

The medal was not actually cast till 1839. In its original design it had a diameter of 72 mm. (about 2⅞ in.). The obverse of the medal depicts Odysseus (Ulysses) clinging to a floating spar; Leucothoe hovers about him and renders aid. The legend reads: LEUCOTHOE NAUFRAGO SUCCURRIT. The subject is taken from the *Odyssey* (V. 334), where Ulysses, after various adventures during his return to his native Ithaca, subsequent to the fall of Troy, is described as being rescued from the perils of a storm by Ino Leucothea,

'A mortal once, . . .
But now an azure sister of the main.' (*Pope*)

The words addressed by her to the shipwrecked hero represented the action of this side of the medal:

'This sacred girdle round thy bosom bind,
Live on, and cast thy terrors to the wind.'

The reverse is taken from a medal of Augustus; a crown of oak-leaves within which is inscribed OB CIVES SERVATOS, 'for saving citizens', such being the reward given by the Romans to one who saved the life of a citizen. For sixty years the medal was awarded as originally cast, but in 1896 it was decided to substitute a smaller medal with a riband attached for suspension.

The first award of Lloyds Medal for Saving Life at Sea was made on the 10th May 1837, to Martin Walsh, master of the Wexford schooner *Alicia*, for his gallantry in saving over fifty passengers and crew of the *Glasgow*, while on a voyage from Liverpool to New York. The medal was struck in silver. In the following December six awards were made for various acts of bravery, and these included the first medal to be bestowed on a foreigner, Otto Reinhold Spowf, mate of the Russian ship *Lygden*, receiving the medal in bronze. One example of the medal has been struck in gold, this being in 1921, when it was awarded to Captain (later Admiral Sir) E. R. G. R. Evans, of H.M.S. *Carlisle*, in the case of the *Hong Moh*. On three occasions the medal has been awarded to women: Miss Kate Gillmour, stewardess of the s.s. *Sardinia*, received a silver medal in recognition of her bravery when the vessel was on fire off Malta in 1908, and Madame Matelot, widow of the keeper of Kerdonis Lighthouse, was awarded a bronze medal in

---

[1] The production of the medal is still entrusted to the Wyon family, the present representative of which is the Rev. Allan Gairdner Wyon. The family is of German origin, and George Wyon (1710–44), its first member to come to England, was a native of Cologne, and formed one of the suite of George II, from whom he held the appointment of Chief Goldsmith. William Wyon, who executed the design for the medal, was the son of Peter Wyon, the second son of George Wyon the Younger (son of the first George Wyon). William was born in Birmingham in 1795. He came to London in 1815, and in the following year was appointed Assistant Engraver to the Royal Mint, becoming Chief Engraver in 1828. He died in 1851.

1911. The third recipient was Miss Ethel Langton, who received the silver medal in 1926. She maintained St. Helen's Fort lighthouse lamp in perfect order in the absence of her father and mother, who could not return owing to the weather for three days, during which she was without food (20th–23rd March 1926). Two clergymen have received the decoration, the Rev. A. H. Synge, in 1853, and the Rev. C. A. W. Robins, of Lydd, in 1891.

In the course of a hundred years Lloyds Medal for Saving Life at Sea has been awarded in connexion with nearly 300 sea disasters;[1] the small number of awards in itself testifies to the rarity of the distinction. Many of the disasters, famous as they were in their day, have been forgotten, but among the major events within recent years for which medals were awarded are the following:

1899—*The Vindobala, Gallina, Glendower, Brilliant, Bulgaria, Silver Spray*; 1906—*British King*; 1914—*Volturno*; 1922—*Hammonia*; 1923—*Travessa*; 1926—*Antinoe*; 1929—*Volumnia*; 1930—*Casmona*; 1935—*Usworth*.

The years mentioned are those in which the medals were awarded; the events were in some cases of earlier date.

There is also a Lloyds medal in silver and bronze, dating from 1893, for meritorious service, bestowed on ships' officers and others who by extraordinary exertions have contributed to the preservation of vessels and cargoes from perils of all kinds.

The bronze star, with blue and red riband, originally adopted, was changed to a silver oval, with blue and silver riband, in July 1900; and ordered to be made circular in shape, and struck both in silver and bronze, April 1913. In June 1936 the Committee of Lloyds approved a new design for this medal, with riband in blue and silver.[2]

The Life-Saving Medal of the Order of Saint John of Jerusalem (see p. 33) is also occasionally awarded for saving life at sea.

The Mercantile Marine Service Association[3] from 1880 onwards issued silver medals for gallantry by their members in saving life at sea,[4] but have not done so since 1909. A medal composed of alloys was

[1] A list of recipients of Lloyds medals is printed by Lloyds from time to time. The latest is dated April 1930.

[2] This should not be confused with the 'Lloyds Medal for Services to Lloyds' which dates from 1913, and is struck in gold and silver and bronze. The obverse is Neptune in his chariot, and the reverse similar to Lloyds Medal for Meritorious Service, with the same blue and silver riband. It is presented to Captains and Navigating Officers of the Merchant Navy, incorporated by private Act of Parliament in 1863.

[3] Secretary's address, Tower Building, Water St., Liverpool, 3.

[4] The example in the House of Commons Collection is inscribed as follows:
To Mr. Michael Tallant 2nd Officer of the s.s. *Tudor Prince*
Who gallantly took charge of a boat's crew and in a heavy sea rescued the crew of the dismasted German brig *Sirius*.
Lat. 37 N. Long. 70 W. on the 10 Sept. 1889.

also issued, and replicas in gold have from time to time been awarded not for gallantry but for general proficiency to the best boy on H.M.S. *Conway*.

The British Museum Collection includes an (undated) medal. On the obverse is a view of Tynemouth with a boat going out to a wreck and the legend '*Palmam qui meruit*. Awarded to —— for bravery in saving life at sea.' The donor stated that it had been 'founded by a U.S. citizen for bravery in saving life at sea'. It has not been identified.

CHAPTER VI
THE CARNEGIE HERO FUND[1]

'We live in a heroic age: not seldom are we thrilled by deeds of heroism where men or women are injured or lose their lives in attempting to preserve or rescue their fellows. Such are the heroes of civilization.'

ANDREW CARNEGIE, 1908.

THE Carnegie Hero Fund Trust of Great Britain was instituted in 1908 by Mr. Carnegie, who in 1904 had inaugurated a similar Hero Fund for the North American Continent. The idea was entirely his own[2] and was suggested by a serious accident in a coal-mine near Pittsburg, U.S.A. The superintendent of the pit drove instantly to the scene and, gathering round him volunteers, he led them down the pit to rescue those below. In so doing he lost his life.

This incident so impressed Mr. Carnegie that he forthwith established a fund to support the families of heroes who perish in an effort to serve or save their fellows, and to reward heroes for outstanding bravery.

The steps taken to this end in America evoked protests in the U.S.A. under the misconception that the purpose of the Fund was to stimulate heroic action, and that men were to be induced to play their heroic parts for the sake of reward. This thought had certainly not entered Mr. Carnegie's mind, as he intended that the primary purpose of the Fund should be to assist dependants of those who might perish in an attempt to save the lives of others. At later dates similar Trusts were established in France, Germany, Italy, Belgium, Holland, Norway, Sweden, Switzerland, and Denmark.

Before establishing the Trust in Great Britain, Mr. Carnegie consulted His Majesty King Edward VII, who, when its provisions had been fully explained to him, warmly commended the idea, and personally expressed his appreciation of the proposal.

The administration of the British Hero Fund Trust was undertaken by the Trustees of the Carnegie Dunfermline Trust, constituted in exactly the same way, viz. sixteen Life Members, six members of the Corporation of Dunfermline, and three members of the Educational Authority for the Burgh of Dunfermline.

[1] (From *Andrew Carnegie. The Trusts and their work*, 1935.) The office of the Secretary, Carnegie Hero Fund Trust, is in Abbot St., Dunfermline, Scotland.

[2] In his *Autobiography*, Mr. Carnegie states regarding the Hero Fund established in America: 'I cherish a fatherly regard for it, since no one suggested it to me. As far as I know, it never had been thought of; hence it is emphatically "My ain bairn".'

As in the case of the Carnegie Dunfermline Trust, Mr. Carnegie wrote an Explanatory Letter placing at the disposal of the Trustees 1,250,000 dollars in 5 per cent. Bonds, yielding £12,500 per annum.

Judging from our experience, this sum is ample to administer the Trust; meeting the cost of maintaining injured heroes and their families during disability of the heroes; the widows and children of heroes who may lose their lives in the United Kingdom, and still leave a surplus for emergencies and contributions.

The interest of the Fund is to be used as follows:—

First: To place those following peaceful vocations, who have been injured in heroic effort to save human life, in somewhat better positions pecuniarily than before until again able to work. In case of death, the widow and children to be provided for until the widow re-marries, and the children until they reach self-supporting age. If there be any other immediate dependants, the Trustees in their discretion may provide for them also. For exceptional children exceptional grants may be made for advanced education. Grants in money or in other forms may also be made to heroes or heroines as the Trustees deem advisable—each case to be judged upon its merits. As a rule grants should be paid monthly.

Second: No grant is to be continued unless it is being soberly and properly used, and the recipients remain respectable, well-behaved members of the community. No exception will be made to this rule; but heroes and heroines are to be given at first a fair trial, no matter what their antecedents. They deserve pardon and a fresh start.

Third: Many cities provide pensions for policemen, firemen, and others, and some may give rewards for acts of heroism. All these and other facts the Trustees will take into account and act accordingly in making grants. Nothing could be further from my intention than to deaden or interfere with these most creditable provisions, doubly precious as showing public and municipal appreciation of faithful and heroic service. I ask from the Trustees most careful guard against this danger. Whether something cannot judiciously be done in cases of heroism by policemen and firemen or others, at the request, or with the approval, of the city authorities, the Trustees shall determine. I hope there can be.

Fourth: For many years claims upon the income will not exhaust it. In course of time, however, the number of pensioners will increase. Should the Trustees find, after allowing liberally for this, that a surplus will still remain, they have power to make grants from such surplus to those injured in case of accidents, preferably where a hero has appeared. They should not act, however, until employers and communities have done their parts, for their contributions benefit both givers and recipients. Widows with children are to be your first care.

Fifth: The field embraced by the Fund is the British Islands and the waters thereof. The sea is the scene of many heroic acts.

Sixth: No action is more heroic than that of doctors and nurses volunteering their services in the case of epidemics. Railroad employees are remarkable for their heroism. All these and similar cases are embraced. Whenever heroism is displayed by man or woman in saving human life in peaceful pursuits the Fund applies.

Seventh: When the King presents medals for heroism in peaceful pursuits in the United Kingdom, you will make immediate and careful inquiries into the circumstances of the recipients, and wherever needed, make provision for their wants, or those of their families, in accordance with the requirements in paragraphs 1st, 2nd, and 3rd. If His Majesty ever chooses to express a wish in these cases, it is to be your law. I am glad to inform you that the purpose and general plan of this Fund have been honoured by His Majesty's gracious approval.

Eighth: You will give instructions for the preparation of a formal Trust-Deed to be signed by me, giving legal effect to the arrangements made in this letter, and containing the powers of the Trustees, and granting them the same immunities as are expressed in the Trust-Deed creating the Carnegie Dunfermline Trust, and providing also that the Trustees are to be the sole judges of the proper action to be taken in each case.

Ninth: An Annual Report, including a detailed statement of sums granted, and to whom, and the reasons therefor, shall be made and widely published each year. A finely executed roll of the heroes and heroines shall be kept displayed in the office at Dunfermline.

At our recent conference here I stated that it was your admirable administration of the Dunfermline Fund 'for bringing into the lives of the toilers more of sweetness and light' that induced me to appeal to you to take this Fund also into your wise keeping. Your prompt and unanimous response was only what I expected from such a body of men.

That I am privileged to know you well, and also the Trustees of my Scottish Universities' Fund, and your worthy compeers of similar Funds across the Atlantic, who labour as you do, is one of the chief pleasures of my life.

While I only give money, many of you are giving yourselves freely to service for your fellows without compensation other than that all-sufficient reward of knowing you are thus performing a holy duty, since the highest worship of God is service to man.

With deep and abiding gratitude,
Always yours,
(Signed) ANDREW CARNEGIE.

Investigation. When a case of heroism is reported to the Trust or the accounts of a heroic effort to save human life are noticed in newspapers, a communication is sent to the Chief Constable of the area or the town in which the case has occurred. The Chief Constable is asked to complete a form giving full particulars of the names and addresses of the rescuer and rescued, the locality, the nature of the incident, and other details. Statements and signatures of eyewitnesses of the occurrence are also invited.

Types of Cases. Reported cases considered suitable for submission to the Trustees fall into several categories, e.g. rescues from drowning and shipwreck, runaway horses, motor-vehicles, coal-mines, fire, gas, &c.

The Fund particularly applies where, in performing heroic acts, loss of life or bodily injury has been sustained.[1] Where there has been no such injury a case must be one of outstanding heroism before it will be considered by the Trustees.

Cases involving consanguinity or near relationship of the rescuer to the rescued are not recognized, unless the person who attempted the rescue lost his life or was so severely injured as to impoverish his future circumstances or those of his family.

The act of heroism must have been voluntary, and have involved risk to the rescuer's life. In many occupations the ordinary discharge of duty involves risk, and such risks cannot in general be regarded as voluntary; but, where the ordinary requirements of duty are exceeded, the exceptional circumstances are considered.

Hero Fund Roll. The name of each rescuer recognized by the Trust is inscribed in an illuminated Roll of Heroes. The first volume of this Roll, which was executed in the School of Handicrafts, Dunfermline, is kept displayed in the Carnegie Birthplace Memorial.

Awards. Two forms of certificate are in use—(1) a Memorial Certificate awarded to the representatives of those who have lost their lives, and (2) an Honorary Certificate issued in other cases. The Trustees also had struck a Bronze Medallion, which they award very rarely, and only in cases of exceptional heroism. Honorary Certificates are accompanied by grants of money ranging from £10 to £25. In some instances silver watches are awarded, and where, owing to the circumstances of the rescuer, money is not required, gifts in kind capable of suitable inscription are made. These take the form of gold watches, clocks, canteens of cutlery, &c.

If a deceased rescuer happens to be a young lad who contributed, or was likely soon to contribute, to the family income, his parents are granted a sum ranging from £25 to £50.

An endeavour is made to have all awards presented publicly, so that

---

[1] For many years the Trustees considered their Charter sufficiently wide to permit of the recognition of cases where no injury had been suffered. Doubts, however, having been expressed as to the validity of such action, the Trustees in 1931 obtained a private Act of Parliament authorizing them at their discretion to apply any interest and income arising from the Fund in making provision for those who perform heroic acts within the scope of the Trust Deed although not injured in making such effort.

not only the act of the rescuer, but also the operations of the Trust, may be made widely known.

Annuitants. If a rescuer loses his life his widow and other dependants are granted an annuity according to their previous circumstances. Many of the Trust annuitants live in distressed areas, and were it not for the allowances made by the Trustees many of these families would have to depend on public assistance for a living.

Where a rescuer has been injured in performing a heroic act, an allowance to make up his income to the level of his previous earnings is granted until such time as he is certified fit to work. In some instances the rescuers suffer permanent partial incapacity, and permanent supplementary allowances are paid. Each family or person in receipt of an annuity from the Trust is visited biennially by a Trustee.

Other Recognizing Bodies. The Trustees endeavour so far as possible to guard against the duplication of awards and to avoid encroaching upon the activities of other recognizing bodies such as the Royal Humane Society, the Order of St. John of Jerusalem, the Royal National Life-Boat Institution, the Society for the Protection of Life from Fire, the Liverpool Shipwreck and Humane Society, and the Glasgow Humane Society. Close and friendly relations with these Societies are maintained.

Cases Recognized. Between the inception of the Trust and the end of 1934 the Trustees considered 6,029 cases. Of these, 2,879 were recognized and 3,150 rejected as not coming within the scope of the Trust or not being sufficiently outstanding. By the 31st December 1934 there were on the Hero Fund Roll 3,882 names. From 1908 to 1934 there were added to the Annuitant Register of the Trust 284 widows, 533 children, 163 other annuitants, and 73 injured heroes. During this period, however, widows died or remarried, children grew up, and other annuitants were removed from the Register for various reasons, so that on the 31st December 1934 there were on the Register 190 widows, 150 children, 37 other annuitants, and 21 injured heroes.

Finance. As in the case of the Carnegie Dunfermline Trust, the initial capital of the Trust, which amounted to £250,000, was converted during the War to War Loan, and at a later date to $3\frac{1}{2}$ per cent. Conversion Loan. The income at the beginning of the Trust was £12,500 per annum. To-day, the capital of the Trust is close on £500,000, and the annual income amounts to over £22,000. Pensions and allowances to widows and children amount to approximately £12,000 per annum, while pensions and allowances to other dependants and injured heroes amount to approximately £3,000 per annum. The number of single payments to heroes and dependants and the cost of watches, medallions, and certificates vary from year to year, but amount in all to approximately £2,000 per annum.

Up to the present the Trustees have been able each year, after allowing for the cost of administration, to carry a sum to reserve account. It is difficult to say whether the income of the Trust will continue to be adequate to meet all its provisions and to maintain the Trustees' scale of allowances on the existing basis.

On several occasions the Trustees have made large block grants to public funds raised in connexion with large colliery disasters.

In many cases a local fund is raised on behalf of the dependants of some one who has died in heroic circumstances. In the case of large disasters there is invariably a big public effort to raise a relief fund, but the number of annuitants on the Trust Register slowly but surely increases, and it is estimated that this will continue for some time. Indeed, it is almost impossible to say whether or not the Trust will ever reach a peak year.

It is apparent that, although the Trust has been in existence for twenty-seven years, its work is not yet fully understood or appreciated in some parts of the country. It is inevitable that a number of unsuitable cases should annually be reported, but, on the other hand, many cases which involve death or serious injury to the rescuer are not reported. A leaflet explanatory of the Trustees' powers has already been widely circulated throughout the British Isles, and a copy will gladly be sent to any one interested in the work.

The following is taken from the Annual Report of the Trust for 1936:

During the year 1936, 111 suitable and 162 unsuitable cases were reported to the Trust. Ten cases remained over for consideration from the previous year. Of those cases eligible for consideration, 114 have been investigated, submitted to the Trustees, and adjudicated upon, leaving 7 still in process of investigation.

Of those investigated, 81 were accepted for recognition, and 33 were rejected, some not being within the scope of the Trust and others having already been sufficiently recognized. In some cases more than one rescuer took part, with the result that 108 names were added to the Roll of Heroes, making 4,116 in all since the institution of the Trust in 1908.

Of the 108 rescuers whose names were inscribed on the Roll during 1936, 21 lost their lives as a result of heroism.

In one case in which the rescuer had lost his life, the financial resources were such that there was meantime no need for the Trustees to grant an award other than of an honorary nature. The case has, however, been placed on the Trust register, and will be further considered when the need arises for the provision of pecuniary aid.

The highest award of the Trust, the Bronze Medallion, is granted only for exceptional bravery. Three such awards were made during the past year.

The number of annuitants on the Trust register has steadily risen since the Trust was instituted and, at the end of 1936, totalled 421. This figure shows an increase compared with the previous year, and represents 272 individual cases, the highest total yet recorded.

Geographically, these 272 cases are distributed as follows:

Scotland 35, England 194, Wales 26, Ireland 15, New Zealand 1, and Canada 1. (These last two relate to Scottish widows who have emigrated since the heroes' deaths.)

CHAPTER VII

A MUNICIPAL VALHALLA

’Ω ξεῖν’, ἀγγέλλειν Λακεδαιμονίοις ὅτι τῇδε
κείμεθα τοῖς κείνων ῥήμασι πειθόμενοι.
'Go stranger, tell the Spartans, here we lie
Who to support their laws dared boldly die.'
SIMONIDES OF CEOS (HERODOTUS, vii. 228), and CIC. *Tusc. Disp.* i. 42.
'Sta, viator, heroem calcas.'
'Stay, traveller, a hero lies under your feet.'
*Inscription on tomb of Count de Mercy
killed in 1645 at the battle of Nördlingen.*

'POSTMEN'S PARK', as the old churchyard of St. Botolph's, in Aldersgate, close to the General Post Office, is often called, contains certainly the simplest, and perhaps the most moving and spontaneous, of privately executed memorials of individual heroism. As G. F. Watts, the artist and sculptor, who conceived the idea and executed it at his own cost, wrote at the time, it is 'a covered walk, not splendid as the deeds, but unaffected as the impulse'. Upon an old wall, beneath a penthouse-roof, are fifty-three memorial plaques of glazed Doulton ware tiles, harmonious in colour, dignified in design, recording the deeds of Londoners who died in attempting to save others. Carved into the beam supporting the roof are the words:

In Commemoration of Heroic Self-Sacrifice.

In the centre is a small wooden figure; below it this inscription:

In Memoriam
GEORGE FREDERIC WATTS
who desiring to honour heroic self-sacrifice
placed these records here

The plaques read thus:

SARAH SMITH. Pantomime artiste at Prince's Theatre. Died of terrible injuries when attempting in her inflammable dress to extinguish the flames which had enveloped her companion, January 24, 1863.

WILLIAM DRAKE. Lost his life in averting a serious accident to a lady in Hyde Park, April 2, 1869, whose horses were unmanageable through the breaking of the carriage pole.

JOSEPH ANDREW FORD, aged 30. Metropolitan Fire Brigade. Saved six persons from fire in Gray's Inn Road; but in his last heroic act he was scorched to death, October 7, 1871.

AMELIA KENNEDY, aged 19. Died in trying to save her sister from their burning house in Edward's Lane, Stoke Newington, October 18, 1871.

ELLEN DONOVAN, of Lincoln Court, Great Wild Street. Rushed into a burning house to save a neighbour's children and perished in the flames, July 28, 1873.

EDMUND EMERY, of 272, King's Road, Chelsea. Passenger. Leapt from a Thames steamboat to rescue a child and was drowned, July 31, 1874.

WILLIAM DONALD, of Bayswater, aged 19. Railway clerk. Was drowned in the Lea trying to save a lad from a dangerous entanglement of weed, July 16, 1876.

GEORGE LEE. Fireman. At a fire in Clerkenwell, carried an unconscious girl to the escape, falling six times, and died of his injuries, July 26, 1876.

FREDERICK ALFRED CROFT. Inspector, aged 31. Saved a lunatic woman from suicide at Woolwich Arsenal Station, but was himself run over by the train, January 11, 1878.

RICHARD FERRIS. Labourer. Was drowned in attempting to save a poor girl who had thrown herself into the canal at Globe Bridge, Peckham, May 20, 1878.

HARRY SISLEY, of Kilburn, aged 10. Drowned in attempting to save his brother after he himself had just been rescued, May 24, 1878.

JAMES HEWERS. On September 24, 1878, was killed by a train at Richmond in the endeavour to save another man.

WILLIAM GOODRUM. Signalman, aged 60. Lost his life at Kingsland Road Bridge in saving a workman from death under the approaching train from Kew, February 28, 1880.

GEORGE BLENCOWE, aged 16. When a friend bathing in the Lea cried for help, went to his rescue and was drowned, September 6, 1880.

HERBERT MACONOGHU. Schoolboy from Wimbledon, aged 13: his parents absent in India. Lost his life in vainly trying to rescue his two schoolfellows, who were drowned at Glover's Pool, Croyde, North Devon, August 28, 1882.

ERNEST BENNING. Compositor, aged 22. Upset from a boat one dark night off Pimlico Pier, grasped an oar with one hand, supporting a woman with the other, but sank as she was rescued, August 25, 1883.

SAMUEL RABBETH. Medical officer of the Royal Free Hospital, who tried to save a child suffering from diphtheria at the cost of his own life, October 26, 1884.

G. GARNISH. A young clergyman, who lost his life in endeavouring to rescue a stranger from drowning at Putney, January 7, 1885.

THOMAS SIMPSON. Died of exhaustion after saving many lives from the breaking ice at Highgate Ponds, January 25, 1885.

ALICE AYRES. Daughter of a bricklayer's labourer, who by intrepid conduct saved three children from a burning house in Union Street, Borough, at the cost of her own young life, April 24, 1885.

JOSEPH WILLIAM ONSLOW. Lighterman, who was drowned at Wapping on May 5, 1885, in trying to save a boy's life.

WILLIAM FISHER, aged 9. Lost his life on Rodney Road, Walworth, while trying to save his little brother from being run over, July 12, 1886.

DAVID SELVES, aged 12. Off Woolwich, supported his drowning playfellow, and sank with him clasped in his arms, September 12, 1886.

GEORGE FREDERICK SIMONDS, of Islington. Rushed into a burning house to save an aged widow, and died of his injuries, December 1, 1886.

SAMUEL LOWDELL. Bargeman. Drowned when rescuing a boy at Blackfriars, February 25, 1887. He had saved two other lives.

ELIZABETH BOXALL, aged 17, of Bethnal Green, who died of injuries received in trying to save a child from a runaway horse, June 20, 1888.

HERBERT PETER CAZALY. Stationer's clerk, who was drowned at Kew in endeavouring to save a man from drowning, April 21, 1889.

HENRY JAMES BRISTOW, aged 8. At Walthamstow, on December 30, 1890, saved his little sister's life by tearing off her flaming clothes, but caught fire himself and died of burns and shock.

ROBERT WRIGHT. Police constable of Croydon. Entered a burning house to save a woman knowing that there was petroleum stored in the cellar. An explosion took place. He was killed, April 30, 1893.

WILLIAM FREER LUCAS, M.R.C.S., LL.D. At Middlesex Hospital, risked poison for himself rather than lessen any chance of saving a child's life, and died October 8, 1893.

JOHN CLINTON, aged 10, who was drowned near London Bridge in trying to save a companion younger than himself, July 16, 1894.

EDWARD BLAKE. Drowned while skating at the Welsh Harp Waters, Hendon, in the attempt to rescue two unknown girls, February 5, 1895.

FREDERICK MILLS, A. RUTTER, ROBERT DURRANT, and F. D. JONES, who lost their lives in bravely striving to save a comrade at the Sewage Pumping Works, East Ham, July 1, 1895.

EDWARD MORRIS, aged 10. Bathing in the Grand Junction Canal, sacrificed his life to help his sinking companion, August 2, 1897.

WALTER PEART, driver, and HARRY DEAN, fireman, of the Windsor express. On July 18, 1898, whilst being scalded and burnt, sacrificed their lives in saving the train.

MARY ROGERS. Stewardess of the *Stella*. March 30, 1899, self-sacrificed by giving up her life-belt and voluntarily going down with the sinking ship.

THOMAS GRIFFIN. Fitter's labourer. April 12, 1899, in a boiler explosion at a Battersea sugar refinery, was fatally scalded in returning to search for his mate.

GEORGE STEPHEN FUNNELL. Police constable. December 22, 1899, in a fire at the Elephant and Castle, Wick Road, Hackney Wick, after rescuing two lives, went back into the flames, saving a barmaid at the risk of his own life.

MRS. YARMAN, wife of George Yarman, labourer. At Bermondsey, refusing to be deterred from making three attempts to climb a burning staircase to save her aged mother, died of the effects, March 26, 1900.

ALEXANDER STEWART BROWN, of Brockley, Fellow of the Royal College of Surgeons. Though suffering from severe spinal injury, the result of a recent accident, died from his brave efforts to rescue a drowning man and to restore his life, October 9, 1900.

GODFREY MAULE NICHOLSON, manager of a Stratford distillery, GEORGE ELLIOTT, and ROBERT UNDERHILL, workmen. Successively went down a well to rescue comrades, and were poisoned by gas, July 12, 1901.

JOHN CRANMER, Cambridge, aged 23. A clerk in the London County Council, who was drowned near Ostend whilst saving the life of a stranger and a foreigner, August 8, 1901.

SOLOMAN GALAMAN, aged 11. Died of injuries, September 6, 1901, after saving his little brother from being run over in Commercial Street: 'Mother, I saved him, but I could not save myself.'

JAMES BANNISTER, of Bow, aged 30. Rushed over when an opposite shop caught fire, and was suffocated in the attempt to save life, October 14, 1901.

ELIZABETH COGHLAM, aged 26, of Church Path, Stoke Newington. Died saving her family and house by carrying blazing paraffin to the yard, January 1, 1902.

ARTHUR REGELOUS, carman ('Little Peter'), aged 25, who with ALICE MAUD DENMAN, aged 27, died in trying to save her children from a burning house in Bethnal Green, April 20, 1902.

ARTHUR STRANGE, carman, of London, and MARK TOMLINSON. On a desperate venture to save two girls from a quicksand in Lincolnshire, were themselves engulfed, August 25, 1902.

JOHN SLADE. Private, 4th Batt. Royal Fusiliers, of Stepney. When his house caught fire, saved one man, and, dashing upstairs to rouse others, lost his life, December 26, 1902.

DANIEL PEMBERTON, aged 61. Foreman, L.S.W.R. Surprised by a train when gauging the line, hurled his mate out of the track, saving his life at the cost of his own, January 17, 1903.

HAROLD FRANK RICKETTS. Police constable, Metropolitan Police. Drowned at Teignmouth whilst trying to rescue a boy bathing and seen to be in difficulty, September 11, 1916.

EDWARD GEORGE BROWN GREENOFF. Police constable, Metropolitan Police. Many lives were saved by his devotion to duty at the terrible explosion at Silvertown, January 19, 1917.

ALFRED SMITH. Police constable, who was killed in an air raid while saving the lives of women and girls, June 13, 1917.

PERCY EDWIN COOK. Police constable, Metropolitan Police. Voluntarily descended high-tension chamber at Kensington to rescue two workmen overcome by poisonous gas, October 7, 1927.

Watts's biographer records[1] that the genesis of this inspiring memorial was the following letter to *The Times*:[2]

'Among other ways of commemorating this 50th year of Her Majesty's reign, it would surely be of national interest to collect a complete record of the stories of heroism in everyday life.

'The character of a nation as a people of great deeds is one, it appears to me, that should never be lost sight of. It must surely be a matter of regret when names worthy to be remembered and stories stimulating and instructive are allowed to be forgotten.

'The roll would be a long one, but I would cite as an example the name of Alice Ayres, the maid of all work at an oilmonger's in Gravel-lane, in April, 1885, who lost her life in saving those of her master's children.

---

[1] *George Frederic Watts, Annals of an Artist's Life*, by M. S. Watts, vol. ii, pp. 102-4 (Macmillan, 1912).   [2] 5th Sept. 1887.

'The facts, in case your readers have forgotten them, were shortly these:—Roused by the cries of "Fire" and the heat of the fiercely advancing flames the girl is seen at the window of an upper storey, and the crowd, holding up some clothes to break her fall, entreat her to jump down at once for her life. Instead she goes back, and reappears dragging a feather bed after her, which, with great difficulty, she pushes through the window. . . . The bed caught and stretched, the girl is again at the window, a child of three in her arms, which with great care and skill she throws safely upon the mattress. Twice again with still older children she repeats the heroic feat. When her turn comes to jump, suffocated or too exhausted by her efforts, she cannot save herself. She jumps, but too feebly, falls upon the pavement, and is carried insensible to St. Thomas's Hospital, where she dies.

'It is not too much to say that the history of Her Majesty's reign would gain a lustre were the nation to erect a monument say, here in London, to record the names of these likely to be forgotten heroes. I cannot but believe a general response would be made to such a suggestion, and intelligent consideration and artistic power might combine to make London richer by a work that is beautiful, and our nation richer by a record that is infinitely honourable.

'*The material prosperity of a nation is not an abiding possession; the deeds of its people are.*'

Elsewhere he wrote, on the same subject:

'The facts it is proposed to record cannot be subject to opinion, as all art must be. No art can stand on a level with the sublime sacrifices, the memory of which it is the desire to rescue from forgetfulness. Art, which should be worthy of and demand recognition for its own sake, must not be presumptuously put forward in competition. A record of the event, date, and name is all I ever thought of or proposed. I have none of the means necessary for the carrying out of any great object. All I can attempt will amount to no more than something of the nature of a simple cutting of the first sod.'

Nothing was done, though many people were interested[1] and approved of the idea. Finally, in 1899 Watts did it himself at his own cost with the approval of the parish council, to whom, in a letter dated 3rd March 1904, Mrs. Watts wrote:

'The idea in Mr. Watts's mind was to create a permanent record of deeds for which no V.C. would be received and of which there would be no history except buried in the volumes of past newspapers, deeds solely prompted by generous impulse and of which the nation should be proud.'

In a further letter of 11th July 1904, Mrs. Watts stated that the memorial in St. Botolph's should be for London only, as it had been her husband's hope that similar records might be placed in other towns throughout the country.

---

[1] Mr. Passmore Edwards was inclined to give the necessary funds, but Watts was unaware of this till later.

Of the fifty-three tablets Watts himself put up thirteen and, after his death in 1904, his wife continued with the erection of further tablets at her own expense. The remainder have been put up from time to time by public subscription.

The memorial to G. F. Watts was unveiled by Sir William Richmond, R.A., on 13th December 1905. The present upkeep of the memorial and tablets is in the hands of the parish and churchwardens of St. Botolph's, Aldersgate, Mrs. Watts having been obliged to relinquish the care and maintenance of them more than ten years before her death in September 1938.

It is still fashionable in certain quarters to decry the outlook and even the deeds of our Victorian forebears. Let those who may still cherish the underlying illusion reflect upon the deeds recorded on these tablets, and upon the spirit which inspired them, and those to whom we are indebted for their rescue from oblivion.

CHAPTER VIII

THE ALBERT AND EDWARD AND KING'S POLICE MEDALS

> Vixere fortes ante Agamemnona
> Multi; sed omnes inlacrimabiles
> urgentur ignotique longa
> nocte, carent quia vate sacro.
> <div align="right">HORACE, <i>Odes</i>, IV. ix.</div>
>
> Ere Agamemnon, many a hero fell
> But all unwept in dark oblivion lie
> Because no bard arose their tale to tell.

TEN years after the institution of the Victoria Cross and five years after the death of the Prince Consort, the Albert Medal was instituted, by Royal Warrant in 1866,[1] for those endangering themselves in seeking to rescue others from the perils of the sea. In Queen Victoria's published letters there is no reference to this decoration, but the following correspondence in the Archives of Windsor Castle, here published by permission for the first time, sufficiently indicate the circumstances in which it was first instituted. It will be noted that no reference is made to the Board of Trade Medal for Sea Gallantry which was already in existence.

WINDSOR CASTLE,
10th December, 1864.

Sir Charles Phipps presents his humble duty to Your Majesty.

He has consulted with General Grey upon the enclosed submission.[1]

They are both of opinion that two new principles are involved in this proposition.

In the first place, up to the present time, all honours and decorations have been awarded by the Sovereign for acts performed by persons in the Royal Service, or for acts done in the Royal Service.

Secondly, the recommendation for such rewards have come from the Superior Officer in the particular branch of the Service, to which the recipients of these honours belonged, and the grounds for bestowing them rested upon an official chain of responsibility.

It is now proposed to give a peculiar decoration to private individuals, for acts of daring, which must probably be attested chiefly by persons of their own class, and whose recommendations would be guarded by no official responsibility.

It is not impossible that men who perform these gallant acts may be of irregular habits, and bad moral character.

Again—could such a distinction be limited to deeds of distinguished daring in

[1] From Mr. Milner Gibson, then Secretary of State for Home Affairs.

ALBERT MEDAL

one Service, or on one element alone?—and could the claims be disregarded of those who had saved human life, at the risk of their own, in the hundreds of accidents that constantly occur?

If it should be thought advisable that any such decoration should be given, it is humbly submitted that it would be better, in peculiar exceptional cases, *approved by the Sovereign*, to give the present Medal *of a smaller size* and more valuable metal—with a sanction to wear it, during pleasure, and an engagement to give it up in the event of the possessor subjecting it to disgrace by his bad conduct.

The conditions under which even this should be done would require careful consideration—and the honour could only be granted upon the responsible advice of a Minister.

OSBORNE,
January 18th, 1866.

Sir Charles Phipps presents his humble duty to Your Majesty.

Your Majesty may remember that in December 1864 Mr. Milner Gibson made a proposal for a *decoration for the reward of persons who risked their lives in gallant efforts to save the life of others found drowning in the sea.*

Sir Charles at the time wrote a letter, by Your Majesty's command, (a copy of which is enclosed) stating the objections Your Majesty entertained to the proposal, and the condition which Your Majesty thought absolutely necessary if it were sanctioned.

Mr. Milner Gibson has now sent to Sir Charles the papers contained in this box, by which it appears that the conditions which Your Majesty laid down have been embodied in the Order in Council.

The number of shipwrecks and the great loss of life in the late tempestuous weather have probably caused a pressure in favour of this decoration.

OSBORNE,
January 18th, 1866.

Sir Charles Phipps presents his humble duty to Your Majesty.

Since Sir Charles wrote to Mr. Milner Gibson this morning he has ascertained that the riband upon which the *Albert Medal* is hung is the same as that given for the Sutlej campaign. This, of course, is objectionable and Sir Charles proposes to write to Mr. Milner Gibson to-night requesting him to submit another riband for Your Majesty's approval.

OSBORNE,
January 10th, 1867.

Sir Stafford Northcote presents his humble duty to the Queen, and has the honour to submit to Her Majesty the accompanying memorandum upon the cases in which applications have been made for the Albert Medal.

Sir Stafford Northcote is desirous of being honoured with an expression of Her Majesty's pleasure with reference to the class or classes of cases in which the Medal ought to be awarded. He is more particularly anxious to receive Her Majesty's commands with respect to the case of Bombardier Rourke, mentioned in the accompanying letter from Sir Thomas Biddulph as one which has attracted Her Majesty's especial attention.

If the Albert Medal is to be awarded to Bombardier Rourke, it would probably be right that it should also be awarded to Mr. Hood (case 8), Mr. Barnard (case 9),

Mr. Veitch (case 15), Captain Lewis (case 16), and perhaps also to Messrs. Crane, Davies, Graves, and Steele (cases 10, 12, and 17), in all of which it has been refused upon the ground that the services rendered did not fall within the definition of the Warrant.

It would also be still more necessary that it should be awarded to Mr. Lawrence (case 11), whose service was performed on the high seas; and if medals were granted in these cases they certainly should be granted in the cases of Bartlett and Couth (case 3), of Sprankling (case 7), and of Salmon (case 14).

The only case in which the Medal has as yet been awarded is that of Mr. Popplestone (case 6), which appears to be distinguished from all the others by the cool and daring gallantry displayed under very difficult circumstances. Sir Stafford Northcote ventures to express a doubt whether it would be desirable to make so large an addition as 15 to the Medals granted in the first year of the Institution.

As the decision at which Her Majesty may arrive on this occasion will probably govern the distribution of Medals in future years, Sir Stafford Northcote ventures to submit for consideration the following suggestions:

1. That, as the Medal is given in substitution for the rewards provided by the Merchant Shipping Act, and as the expenses attending it are defrayed out of the Mercantile Marine Fund (a fund raised by the contributions of the Shipping interest), it ought not to be given in respect of gallantry displayed in saving life in inland waters, or on the sea coast, except in cases of shipwreck. Gallant actions, such as that of Bombardier Rourke, or that of Captain Barnard, may properly be rewarded by some special distinction or decoration, should such at any future time be instituted, applicable to other cases of courage displayed in civil life; but hardly by the Albert Medal.

2. That it might be well to establish a second-class distinction—which might perhaps consist of the riband without the Medal attached to it—to be granted in such cases as those of Bartlett, Sprankling, and Salmon (cases 3, 7, and 14), being cases within the definition of the 'perils of the sea', but in which the gallantry displayed and the risk incurred fall short of the high standard of Mr. Popplestone's service.

3. That in the numerous cases of good conduct and good service by the crews of life-boats, coastguards, and others, which cannot all be rewarded with decorations for fear of making the decoration too common, a certificate of merit might be given, as is suggested in the accompanying memorandum.

Sir Stafford Northcote takes the liberty of forwarding to Your Majesty a lithograph of the Medal.

Jan. 10th, 1867.

Maj.-Gen. Sir T. M. Biddulph's humble duty.

With regard to the cases for which the *Albert Medal* should be given, Sir T. M. Biddulph is clearly of opinion that the circumstance of its being paid for out of the Mercantile Marine Fund settles the question, and makes it almost impossible to grant it for any gallant acts except those originally contemplated.

BOARD OF TRADE.
March 7th, 1867.

Sir Stafford Northcote presents his humble duty to the Queen and has the honour to submit to Your Majesty the name of seven persons to whom he considers that the Albert Medal may properly be awarded, should such be Your Majesty's gracious pleasure.

The names are as follows:

1. Mr. S. Lake, of the Bombay Reclamation Company's Works;
2. Mr. W. H. Millett, third officer on board the Peninsular and Oriental Company's Steamship *Emeu*;
3. The Reverend Charles Cobb, Rector of Dymchurch in the county of Kent;
4. John Batist, a Coastguardsman stationed at Dymchurch;
5. John Donovan, Chief Boatman at the Kinsale Coast Guard Station;
6. Charles Sprankling, a Commissioned Boatman of the Burton Coast Guard Station;
7. Christopher Bartlett, a fisherman.

The details of the service rendered by these persons respectively are stated in the accompanying memorandum. Sir Stafford Northcote requests permission to represent to Your Majesty that, while all the seven persons whose names he has mentioned were distinguished for gallant and meritorious conduct, the conduct of the three first-named (Mr. Lake, Mr. Millett, and Mr. Cobb) appears to have been peculiarly praiseworthy.

Sir Stafford Northcote ventures humbly to submit for Your Majesty's gracious consideration whether it might not be desirable to establish a second-class of the Albert Medal, so that there might be a means of rewarding gallant services of different degrees of merit, without making the highest order of reward too common.

Sir Stafford Northcote has caused the accompanying draft of a warrant establishing two classes of decoration to be prepared for Your Majesty's gracious consideration. He has also caused two new medals to be made, which he sends herewith, together with the present Albert Medal.

It will be for Your Majesty's gracious consideration whether the present Albert Medal should be retained as the first-class of decoration, a plainer medal being added as a decoration of the second-class, or whether the present medal should be made the decoration of the second-class and a handsomer one be adopted as the decoration of the first-class. Should Your Majesty be of opinion that the present Medal should be made the decoration of the second-class a reduction might be made in its cost by the substitution of a less expensive material for the gold at the back.

The medals have been prepared by Mr. Phillips of Cockspur Street; and, should Your Majesty be pleased to honour him with a command to that effect, he will be ready to wait upon Your Majesty at any time in order to receive any further instructions.

The first awards for deeds on land were made in 1877 in connexion with a colliery disaster on Tyneside which deeply moved the public mind. As the result of a sudden flooding of a mine five men were cut off and little hope was entertained for their safety. They were rescued after heroic efforts, aided by divers and helped by the hewing through a coal barrier forty yards thick. The progress of events was followed with deepest interest by the public, and the story, when it became known, of the entombed men's prayers and hymns, as the water slowly rose round them, touched all hearts. The announcement of the award of the Albert Medal to Daniel Thomas, who headed the rescue party, and to his gallant companions was welcomed throughout the country.

The following correspondence, also from the archives of Windsor Castle, indicates the manner in which Lord Beaconsfield dealt with the matter:

2, Whitehall Gardens, S.W.
April 23rd, 1877.

Lord Beaconsfield with his humble duty to Your Majesty.

It seems quite clear that the Albert Medal, as at present constituted, could not be extended to gallantry on land.

What should be done? Should it be extended to land?

or

Should another medal for land, called the Victoria Medal, be struck?

If so, an announcement might be made, and, indeed, in any case, at once, of Her Majesty's gracious intention, and to confer, whether the Albert Medal extended, or the Victoria Medal, in the first instance, on the gallant Welsh miners who rescued their comrades.

10, Downing Street,
May 16th, 1877.

Lord Beaconsfield with his humble duty to Your Majesty:

He sends two specimens of the Albert Land Medal, 1st and 2nd Class, in their final state. He hopes Your Majesty will think that the gold and red enamel is effective.

The Albert Medal is the civilian's Victoria Cross, foremost among non-military British decorations for self-sacrifice in saving, or attempting to save, life by land or sea respectively. Following the precedent of the Victoria Cross, it is sometimes awarded posthumously, and is then presented by the Sovereign in person to the next of kin. Recommendations for awards are now made by the Home Secretary, the Admiralty (in the case of persons belonging to the Royal Navy or Royal Marines), and the President of the Board of Trade (in the case of members of the British Mercantile Marine). Each office keeps a separate register. This system replaced an earlier system whereunder (see p. 309) submissions were made only by the First Lord of the Treasury. There would appear to be good grounds to-day for a reversion to this practice. It carries the right to the letters 'A.M.' In August 1917 the first and second classes were abolished, the only distinction retained being a provision whereby outstanding cases of heroism may be distinguished by the award of the Albert Medal in gold. Ordinarily the medal is of bronze. In the case of a second act worthy of recommendation a bar or clasp may be added to the riband of the medal.

The Albert Medal for sea service is oval, and carries a representation of the crown of the Prince Consort. A monogram composed of the letters V and A appears against a dark blue enamelled background. A Garter surrounds the medal, inscribed with the words 'For gallantry in saving life at sea'.[1] The riband of the sea medal is dark blue, with two white longitudinal stripes; four white stripes indicates that the medal has been awarded in gold. The Albert Medal for Saving Life on Land has a crimson riband with similar white stripes and bears the words 'For gallantry in saving life on land'.

The chief criterion used to measure the standard of performance[2] of those whose gallant acts at sea have brought their names under consideration for the award of the Albert Medal is that the rescuer must seriously imperil his own life under conditions which make his survival unlikely. In the case of the Albert Medal in gold the act must have placed the recipient's own life at the extremest hazard, or the risk must have been incurred more than once on the same occasion. Men who gain the Albert Medal in gold must very nearly have laid down their lives for those whom they have saved or tried to save. There is nothing in the Royal Warrant to support this limitation; it is an official interpretation and, as such, subject to modification.[2]

Awards of the Albert Medal (both classes) to date are as follows:

	Land Service				Sea Service	Admiralty
	U.K.	Dominions	Colonies	India		
1866–9					15	8
1870–9	35				21	5
1880–9	29	1		2	18	5
1890–9	7			4	10	4
1900–9	20	3		5	6	5
1910–19	142	9		19	29	64
1920–9	7	5		9	9	14
1930–8	2	1	1	10	6	2

This table requires no comment, except that something is clearly amiss as regards awards for gallantry on land. Most of those shown under 'U.K.' were for deeds overseas. Few were awarded to civilians.

THE EDWARD MEDAL

On 13th July 1907, by Royal Warrant under the sign manual of King Edward VII, a new medal was instituted known as the Edward Medal for which Miners and Quarrymen alone were eligible. This medal, according to the intention of the original Warrant, was intended to distinguish 'the many heroic acts performed by miners and quarry-

---

[1] The example in the House of Commons Collection in bronze was awarded to Mr. Henry Wesley for gallantry in saving the lives of the crew of the ship *Harriet* of London, 3rd Aug. 1879.   [2] *Board of Trade Journal*, 8th Feb. 1933.

men and others who endanger their own lives in saving or endeavouring to save the lives of others from perils in mines or quarries within our Dominions and territories under our Protection or Jurisdiction'. This decision was probably the outcome of the deliberations of the Royal Commission on Mines, then sitting, which issued its Report a few months later, as Mr. Herbert Gladstone, then Home Secretary, linked his announcement of the institution of the Edward Medal in the House of Commons on 18th July 1907 with a reference thereto. Two years later, on 2nd December 1909, its scope was extended to all subjects 'who in course of Industrial Employment endanger their lives . . .', for though, as Robert Smillie was wont to say, 'there is blood on coal', there is blood also on wheels.[1]

The medal is worn on the left breast and bears the effigy of the Sovereign. It is in bronze but, when awarded for acts of such exceptional gallantry as to merit special recognition, may be awarded in silver. There is the usual provision for bars. The riband is dark blue, $1\frac{3}{8}$ inches in width, with a narrow yellow stripe on either side. It is awarded on the recommendation of the Home Secretary and was, until 1917, divided into a First and Second Class. These designations were later changed to 'The Edward Medal in Silver' and 'The Edward Medal'. Up to the end of 1938 the total number of awards of the Edward Medal of the First Class or in Silver was 82. These facts are not available in any official publication. The names of miners who have received the Edward Medal are indeed printed in the Annual Report of the Minister for Mines, but no details whatever are given.

The total number of awards of both classes (other than for quasi-military acts of gallantry during the War, in the case of the Albert Medal) is far less than of the Victoria Cross. About 250 men now living hold the latter: there are not half as many living holders of the Albert and Edward Medals. Their names are not to be found in any published lists: their addresses are not known and, when an invitation was extended by wireless announcement and through the press to holders of either medal to witness the Coronation procession from an official grand stand (proceeding to London, of course, at their own expense), few applied for tickets.

No pecuniary grant accompanies the award of either medal (the V.C. carries an annuity and, in the case of Indians only, a pension to the widow): holders are entitled (since 1918) to write A.M. or E.M. after their names, but, so rare is the decoration, few realize the significance of the letters. The B.B.C. seldom if ever mentions an award, and it is never referred to in *The Ministry of Labour Gazette*.

[1] A cog-wheel is appropriately embodied in the design, symbolical of Industry, of the German *Arbeitsfront*.

The rarity of awards has indeed had the effect of depriving the holders of some of the honour due to them; the medals are so seldom seen that few recognize the ribands. There would indeed seem to be good grounds in any case for adding a third class to each Order, so that the first class would in each case be in gold, the second in silver, and the third in bronze, the riband in each case being identical.

Awards of the Edward Medal up to date are as follows:

	United Kingdom	Dominions	Colonies	India
1907–9 . .	20	17	. .	. .
1910–19 .	291	13	4	12
1920–9 . .	74	9	2	8
1930–7 . .	67[1]	. .	1	1
1938 . .	8	. .	. .	1

The authors are so profoundly impressed with the importance of bringing to public notice the importance and value to society of the services for which the Albert and Edward Medals are awarded, that they have reproduced in this volume a full summary of all deeds, as recorded in *The London Gazette*, for which each medal has been given. They have added a full nominal and geographical index in order to facilitate its use by provincial newspapers and local authorities, in the hope that they, and perhaps other bodies such as the Miners' Welfare Fund, may be moved to institute local memorials, such as that in Postmen's Park (see Chapter VII), of past and future deeds of heroism.

THE KING'S POLICE MEDAL

The King's Police Medal was instituted by Royal Warrant of 7th July 1909.[2] It is of silver, with the effigy of the Sovereign on the obverse, and bears on the reverse a watchman leaning on a sword and bearing a shield inscribed 'To guard my people': in the background is a fortified city. Since 1933 the words 'For gallantry' or 'For distinguished service', as the case may be, have been added.

British subjects and others serving in recognized Police Forces or properly organized Fire Brigades in the United Kingdom of Great Britain and Northern Ireland, in India and in the Colonies, Protectorates and Mandated Territories, are eligible, as also those within any

---

[1] In the years 1929–38 sixty Edward Medals were awarded for bravery in mines.
[2] Amended 3rd Oct. 1916, 1st Oct. 1930, 12th Dec. 1933, 25th May and 15th Dec. 1936.

Dominion if its Government so desires. Awards are made on the recommendation of the Home Secretary.

The conditions of award are:

(a) Conspicuous gallantry in saving life and property, or in preventing crime or arresting criminals; the risks incurred to be estimated with due regard to the obligations and duties of the officer concerned.
(b) A specially distinguished record in administrative or detective service, or other police service of conspicuous merit.
(c) Success in organizing Police Forces or Fire Brigades or Departments, or in maintaining their organization under special difficulties.
(d) Special services in dealing with serious or widespread outbreaks of crime or public disorder, or of fire.
(e) Valuable political and secret services.
(f) Special services to Royalty and Heads of States.
(g) Prolonged service; but only when distinguished by very exceptional ability and merit.

The riband is dark blue with a narrow stripe on either side, and a similar silver stripe in the middle. When awarded for acts of exceptional courage, each silver stripe contains a thin red line down the centre.

The Royal Warrants contain the usual provision for bars and for forfeiture. Only 120 medals are usually awarded in any year. The awards in the last New Year Honours List included five for firemen.

Awards of the King's Police Medal to 31st Dec. 1938 are as follows:

	United Kingdom	Dominions	Colonies	India & Burma
1909	38	2	5	50
1910–19	396	54	82	483
1920–9	356	50	83	417
1930–6	201	43	90	312
1937	35	8	17	26
1938	43	5	13	23

As British subjects in every part of the Empire are eligible alike for the Albert, Edward, Sea Gallantry, and King's Police Gallantry Medals, it would appear proper on constitutional, and convenient on administrative grounds that, as in the case of many other marks of His Majesty's favour, submissions should be made by (or in the case of Dominion Governments through) the Prime Minister as First Lord of the Treasury.

APPENDIX TO CHAPTER VIII

Notice approved by the King and issued to the press in December 1909

GALLANTRY IN CIVIL LIFE

THE KING'S MEDALS

THE King has been graciously pleased to extend the scope of the Edward Medal, which was established by His Majesty in the year 1907 for rewarding acts of gallantry performed in saving life or attempting to save life in mines and quarries, to similar acts in the course of industrial employment.

Before 1907 conspicuous gallantry in civil life could be recognized by the high but rare distinction of the Albert Medal. There were, however, no means of rewarding acts of great courage on land—less conspicuous but perhaps equally meritorious—by decorations appropriate to particular vocations.

The King was therefore pleased to institute in the first instance the Edward Medal for gallantry in mines and quarries. His Majesty has now extended the qualification for the medal to acts of gallantry performed in the course of industrial employment other than in mines and quarries, and has established the King's Police Medal for merit or courage on the part of members of police forces and fire brigades in the discharge of their duties.

These medals, with distinct and appropriate designs, will be granted for conduct and service throughout the Empire; and, in conjunction with the Board of Trade medal for saving life at sea, cover the whole range of dangerous employment in civil life.

The Albert Medal remains the reward for acts of the highest devotion and courage in civil life. His Majesty's purpose in establishing the new medals is to provide recognition for actions of exceptional bravery in dangerous callings, which, owing to the rarity of the award of the Albert Medal, might otherwise have been unrecognized.

CHAPTER IX
AWARDS OF THE ALBERT MEDAL*
Land Service 1877-1914

* Awards in the 1st Class (in gold) are given in Old English type. The date of the actual deed is given in parentheses at the end. The dates at the top of the page are those on which the Gazette appeared.

The Tynewydd Colliery disaster

Daniel Thomas
Isaac Pride
John William Howell
William Beith

The Tynewydd Colliery, in the Rhondda Valley, was inundated with water from old workings of the Cymmer Colliery. Of 14 men in the pit, 4 were drowned, and 1 killed by compressed air, leaving 9 imprisoned by the water, of whom 4 were released after 18 hours and 5 after 9 days' imprisonment.

To rescue these five men it was necessary to pierce a barrier of coal 38 yards thick, which kept back a large quantity of water and compressed air. This task was carried on for 4 days, without any great danger, but about 1 p.m. on April 19, when only a few yards of barrier remained, the danger from an irruption of water, gas, and compressed air was so great as to cause the colliers to falter. These four men at once volunteered to resume the rescuing operations, the danger of which had been greatly increased by an outburst of inflammable gas under great pressure, and in such quantities as to extinguish the Davy lamps. The danger from gas continued at intervals until 3.30 a.m., and from that time the above four men at great peril to their own lives continued the rescuing operations until 3 p.m. on the 20th when the five imprisoned men were safely released. (7.8.77)

The Albert Medal (2nd Class) was conferred on the same occasion upon

George Ablett,[1] collier.
Charles Baynham,[2] collier.
Richard Hopkins,[3] collier.
Richards Howells,[1] collier.
Charles Oatridge,[1] collier.
John Williams,[4] collier.
Edward David,[5] collier.
William Morgan,[6] collier.
David Rees,[1] collier.
Rees Thomas,[7] fireman.
David Davies,[1] colliery owner.
Thomas Jones,[3] ,, ,,
Edmund Thomas,[8] colliery manager.
Thomas Thomas,[4] ,, ,,
Thomas Getrych Davies,[9] colliery manager.
David Evans,[10] colliery manager.
David Jones,[11] ,, ,,
Henry Lewis,[12] ,, ,,
Isaiah Thomas,[2] ,, ,,
William Thomas,[13] colliery manager.

[1] Tynewydd Colliery. [2] Brithwynydd Colliery. [3] Ynishir Colliery. [4] Pontypridd Colliery. [5] Dinas Isaf Colliery. [6] Harod Colliery. [7] Of Penriwfer, Rhondda. [8] Of Llwyncelyn, Rhondda. [9] Of Tylacoch, Rhondda. [10] Of Ferndale, Rhondda. [11] Of Cymmer Valley, Rhondda. [12] Of Energlyn Colliery. [13] Of Resolven, near Neath, Glam.

A Salford Waterman's bravery

Mark Addy At great risk to himself, owing to the violence of the river and the pestilential nature of its waters, in 25 years he saved 36 persons from drowning in the polluted River Irwell.

He received the Bronze Medal of the Royal Humane Society; the Gold and Silver Medals and an illuminated address from the Salford Humane Society; and a purse of 200 guineas.

The Abercarn Colliery disaster (Monmouthshire)

Henry Davies
John Harris
William Simons
Thomas Herbert
Miles Moseley
Charles Preen
William Walters
Lewis Harris
Charles Morgan

An explosion of firedamp occurred in the Abercarn colliery, whereby 260 persons perished; the greatest gallantry was exhibited in saving about 90 lives. The force of the explosion was terrific, doing great damage to the roadways and to the bottom of the shaft, and setting the coal and timber on fire. Into this state of confusion and danger these men descended without hesitation. Although they discovered that fires were raging in the mine, and the chances of another explosion considerable, they remained below, until satisfied that no one was left alive in the pit.

Henry Davies, after being down the Abercarn Pit all the afternoon, with the men mentioned above, volunteered to descend the Cwmcarn Pit, two miles distant, to tell the explorers who had attempted to enter the workings from that side to come out, as a second explosion was deemed inevitable, which, had it occurred, would have killed every man below ground. After being deserted by two men, who refused to accompany him farther, and when he must have felt that there was little or no chance of his coming alive out of the pit, he pursued his course alone for 500 or 600 yards and heroically accomplished his mission.

John Harris, a mason, also went down the pit with those mentioned above. Having descended about 295 yards, the cage stuck in the damaged shaft. Sliding down a guide-rope he reached the bottom where, although he knew well that any moment might be his last, he remained for many hours, until all who were alive (some of whom were badly burnt and otherwise injured) reached safety by his aid. (11.9.78)

Gallantry of doctors

Henry Grier Lieutenant Graham of the 10th Regiment was dying of diphtheria, when Surgeon Grier of the Army Medical Dept. performed upon him the operation of tracheotomy. Observing that no attempt at inspiration followed, he applied his lips to the wound and, at the imminent risk of his own life, restored to the patient the power of breathing. (20.8.80)

David Lowson Dr. Lowson of Huddersfield was called to attend the child of a Police Constable who was suffering from diphtheria, and he performed the operation of tracheotomy. Finding the child livid, and breathing with very great difficulty, he applied his lips to the wound, and, at the imminent risk to his own life, afforded relief by suction and continued to do so throughout the day. Dr. Lowson was seized a few days later with a severe attack of diphtheria which resulted in his retirement from a lucrative practice. (12.11.80)

Gallantry at Devizes

William Henry Burt A fire broke out on the premises of an Italian warehouseman in the Market Place at Devizes. After the fire had been raging for some time, and all the inmates of the house had effected their escape, it was reported that there was gunpowder stored in the shop. Mr. Burt volunteered to remove it. At this time a great body of flame was distinctly visible on the other side of the shop counter only a few feet distant from the spot where the gunpowder was deposited.

Mr. Burt made his way into the shop through the window and removed the gunpowder, thereby preventing an explosion which might have been attended with serious loss of life. (15.7.81)

Gallantry of a schoolmistress

Hannah Rosbotham The stone belfry of the Sutton National Schools was blown down during a violent gale of wind and fell through the roof into the Infants' Schoolroom where nearly two hundred children were assembled, killing one, and injuring many others, and filling the room with debris. Whilst others fled for safety, Miss Rosbotham, aged 23, entered the room and there remained until every child had been placed in safety. At the imminent risk of her own life, Miss Rosbotham extricated four infants and rescued a little girl who was completely buried and who must otherwise have been suffocated. (14.10.80)

Gallantry at Halesowen, Staffordshire

WILLIAM HINTON A fire occurred at Halesowen on an ironmonger's premises in the basement of which a large quantity of oil and explosives was deposited, and a large crowd had collected in front of the shop.

Mr. Hinton, an Inland Revenue Officer, at imminent risk to his life, at once entered the burning premises and succeeded in removing a quantity of gun- and blasting-powder, in canisters already hot and blistered by flames, which were then in actual contact with it.

Had not Mr. Hinton removed the canisters the resulting explosion would probably have destroyed a block of three buildings, and caused great loss of life.

HENRY KEMP   Superintendent of Police Kemp was also awarded the Albert Medal in connexion with this fire. (16.1.83)

Gallantry of a railway official

JAMES CARNEY   An Indian shunting porter was coupling up the wagon of a train that was moving slowly through the station at Dinapur. A sudden movement of the train knocked him down, and he fell half stunned between the rails and underneath the train.

The man's convulsive struggles threated every moment to throw him under the wheels of the moving wagon. Mr. James Carney, who was at the time on duty at the station, jumped down from the platform without hesitation, rushed under the train which was still in motion, and, grappling with the injured man, held him down until the train had passed, himself narrowly escaping. (10.7.81)

From January 1883 until the end of Queen Victoria's reign no details were given in *The London Gazette* of the acts of gallantry in respect of which the Albert Medal was awarded. Interest in such matters appears to have been at a very low ebb, and no records are available even at the Home Office. The following is a statement, in tabular form, of such awards as were made during this period.

Month and Year of Award	Name and Occupation of Recipient	Description of Deed
	The Baddesley Colliery Disaster, Staffs.	
Feb. 1883	P. C. James Dee, Swansea.	Saving life at a fire.
Jan. 1883	Reuben Smallman, Mining Engineer. Charles Day, Collier. Charles Chetwynd, Collier.	Gallantry in saving life on occasion of fire and explosion at Baddesley Colliery in May 1882.
	Samuel Spruce, Mining Engineer. Frederick Samuel Marsh, Certified Colliery Manager. Thomas Harry Mottram, Certified Colliery Manager. William Morris, Collier. William Pickering, Collier. Joseph Chetwynd, Collier.	

Month and Year of Award	Name and Occupation of Recipient	Description of Deed
	Fenian Outrages	
Jan. 1885	P.C. WILLIAM COLE, A Div., Metropolitan Police Force.	Gallantry at explosion in Westminster Hall on Jan. 24, 1885.
	Ireland. Gallantry of a doctor	
Aug. 1885	Surgeon EDWARD C. THOMPSON, Tyrone County Infirmary.	Heroism in endeavouring to save life of child suffering from diphtheria.
	Clifton Hall Colliery disaster	
Oct. 1885	Thomas Worrall, Underlooker. John Crook, Manager, Agecroft Colliery. CHARLES PARKINSON, Fireman. GEORGE HIGSON, Fireman. AARON MANLEY, Pit Carpenter. GEORGE HINDLEY, Blacksmith.	Gallantry on occasion of explosion at Clifton Hall Colliery in June 1885.
Oct. 1886	EDWARD SCULLION, chemical labourer.	Attempting rescue of two men and a boy overcome in the airshaft of an unused sewer, of Newcastle and Gateshead Chemical Company.
	Queensland, Australia. Gallantry of an accountant	
Feb. 1887	WILLIAM E. YALDWYN, Accountant of Queensland Nat. Bank at Charleville.	Rescuing 6 persons from a flood at Charleville on July 1886.
	Hull. A soldier saves a life	
April 1888	PTE. JAMES SPRING, 1st Vol. Bn. E. Yorks. Regiment.	Saving life of James Sharp in St. Andrew's Dock at Hull in Dec. 1887.
	India. An officer attempts to save a life	
Sept. 1888	LT. PULTENEY MALCOLM, 4th Gurkhas.	Attempting to save life of comrade who had fallen over a precipice at Dalhousie in India in June 1887.
	Cornwall. Saving life in a mine	
Aug. 1889	THOMAS C. PITMAN, Drakewalls Mine, Calstock, Cornwall.	Saving life in accident in that mine in February 1889.
	Sheffield. Attempt to save life in a factory	
Aug. 1889	JOHN SMITH.	Endeavouring to save life of Benjamin Stanley at Norfolk Works, Sheffield, in May 1889.
	Aldershot. Attempt to save life	
June 1890	DAVID DAVIS, 16th Lancers.	Attempting to save life at Aldershot in May 1890.

Month and Year of Award	Name and Occupation of Recipient	Description of Deed
	London. *Gallant conduct at Wellington Barracks*	
Dec. 1890	PIONEER DAVID T. DAVIS, 2nd Coldstreams. COLOUR-SERGEANTS HENRY PICKERSGILL and WILLIAM WILSON, 1st Scots Guards.	Gallantry at fire in Wellington Barracks in Nov. 1890.
	Rotherham. *Gallantry of mine sinkers*	
Aug. 1891	AMBROSE CLARK, foreman sinker, and ROBERT DRABBLE, sinker.	Gallantry at accident in course of sinking Rotherham Main in July 1891.
	Staffordshire. *Gallantry at Audley Colliery*	
March 1895	William Dodd, undermanager, Diglake Pit.	Great heroism in saving many lives at flooding of Audley Colliery in Staffordshire in Jan. 1895.
	India. *Gallantry in Chitral*	
Nov. 1898	RONALD HUME MACDONALD, R.E., LANCE-NAIK HABIB KHAN, S. & M., SAPPER SHEIKH ABDUL SAMAND, Miners, and SAPPER KALLAN KHAN, all of Bengal Sappers and Miners.	Gallantry in saving life of comrade who with others had been overwhelmed by avalanche on summit of Lowari Pass in India.
	India. *Gallantry at Darjeeling*	
Dec. 1900	FREDERICK W. TIMME	Gallantry in saving life during cyclone at Darjeeling, India, in Sept. 1899.
	Malta. *Gallantry in dockyard*	
Feb. 1902	GIOVANNI BILOCA, GIUSEPPE ZAMMIT, dockyard labourers.	Saving lives of comrades overcome by fumes in H.M. Dockyard at Malta.

Royal Navy. *Gallantry of a stoker*

Alfred Stickley H.M.S. *Success* was steaming towards Lamlash, when it became apparent from deck that something was wrong in the after stokehold. Alfred Stickley, Chief Stoker, R.N., went below to ascertain the cause and found that there was an escape of steam from the top drum of No. 4 Boiler, which shortly caused one of the furnace doors, which had been left unlatched, to be blown open. The stokehold was immediately filled with flame and steam, and the men present were burnt and scalded.

Stickley grasped the situation with promptness, showing the greatest presence of mind in the emergency, and ran great risks in endeavouring to minimize the consequences of the accident and prevent further injuries to the men.

In spite of the conditions in the stokehold, and his own severe exposure to the flames, he managed to open out the fans to their full extent, and made many gallant attempts to close the furnace door and open the drencher valve. Finding it was impossible to drive the flames back, he gave orders for the hatch to be opened, and himself remained below until the four men in the stokehold effected their escape. His face and neck were severely burned, and his hands and forearms very badly scalded. For over four months he was on the sick list suffering from his injuries. His lungs escaped injury, as he had the presence of mind to put cotton waste into his mouth while he was in the stokehold. (11.6.04)

Saving life at Finsbury Park Station

Albert Victor Hardwick A platform at Finsbury Park Station was crowded with people. An elderly lady fell from the platform just as an incoming train loomed out of the dense fog at a distance of a few yards. She had injured her ankle and could not save herself. Mr. Hardwick leapt on the line, and just succeeded in placing the lady and himself at full length on the ground between the rail and the wall supporting the platform, thus protecting her, when the train overtook them. (21.12.04)

W. Australia. Gallantry at Lake View Consols Mine

Edward Nicholls Nicholls (with two other miners, Bentley and King) was working in a 'stope' on the 1,200-foot level of the Lake View Consols Mine, at Kalgoorlie. He and his comrades had charged a round of holes with dynamite, had lit the fuses, and were retiring to the level below when one of the charges exploded. All lights were put out by the explosion and the mine was in complete darkness. Nicholls, hearing the groans of his comrade Bentley, groped his way back to the top of the rill (which is the name of the pyramid forming the floor of the 'stope'), in this case about 40 feet high. On the top of the rill he found Bentley, on whose body a big stone was resting. He had to roll this stone away before he could move him, but succeeded, at the peril of his own life, in getting his comrade down the rill. While they were at the foot of the rill the other holes exploded.

When Nicholls returned to aid his comrade the lighted fuses of four other charged holes were burning and other explosions were momentarily to be expected. The fuses averaged 6 feet in length, and the rate of burning was about 90 seconds per yard, that is to say, the explosions were timed to take place within 3 minutes of the lighting of the fuses. (18.4.05)

Gallantry of postman at Stirling

John Wardrop Thomson While Thomson, a postman, was on duty at Stirling Railway Station, he learned that a man was lying on the metals of the down main line.

An engine was approaching rapidly, and was not more than 30 yards distant when Thomson, without hesitation, sprang to the man's assistance, and dragged the man, who was drunk, unhurt on to the six-foot way just as another train passed in the opposite direction. (21.10.05)

Heroism of British Consul at Baku

Leslie Urquhart Four British workmen, during the outbreak which occasioned serious losses to the petroleum industry at Baku, were surrounded by the insurgents in an isolated position and were in imminent danger of losing their lives, a fate which, shortly after their rescue, befell all the persons remaining in the buildings where they had been shut up. The four Englishmen had already been isolated for some time when news of their perilous position reached the British Embassy at St. Petersburg, and Mr. Urquhart, British Vice-Consul at Baku, accompanied by two Cossacks and several Tartars from the village of Mushtagee, started to relieve the beleaguered men. The district was full of armed Tartars, and in such a state of unrest that when Mr. Urquhart started upon his expedition it was not expected by the remainder of the British colony in Baku that he would live to return.

On the night of his departure Mr. Urquhart proceeded to a farm which he possessed in the neighbourhood, where he hoped to be able to get help from his own farm hands, who were Tartars, and also to collect supplies, and notwithstanding that the party was stopped and fired on from time to time the supplies were collected and a start was made early next morning for Balachani.

Mr. Urquhart's courageous and spontaneous action was rewarded with success. He got through and found the four Englishmen in a dreadful condition, especially on account of want of water, and after feeding them he persuaded them to go with him in carts which he had brought, with as many Armenians as they could bring with them. Immediately afterwards the whole of the buildings were carried by storm and every one found therein put to death. (Sept. 1905)

Gallantry of Railwayman at Ennis

Patrick Cullinan While a special cattle train was running through Ennis Station from Limerick a woman fell between the rails in front of, and about 15 yards from, the approaching train. Inspector Cullinan, who was on the platform at the time, immediately jumped on the track, and just succeeded in dragging the woman into the six-foot way, though not before the guard of the engine had come in contact with her clothing. But for Inspector Cullinan's promptitude and great personal strength the woman's life would have been lost. (16.11.05)

Heroism of road labourer of Co. Elgin

Robert Munro Munro, a road foreman named Alexander Ross, and one William Morris, were crossing over the railway bridge over the Brodie Burn when they were overtaken by a train travelling on the line of rails next the south parapet of the bridge by which they were walking.

Morris was walking between the rails; Munro, who was ahead but beside the parapet of the bridge and clear of the rails, tried to drag his comrades from the railway track. He had grasped Morris's shoulder, when he was caught by the engine and thrown into a space about 5 feet wide between the near rail and the parapet of the bridge. Unhappily his brave act resulted in his being maimed for life. (28.4.06)

Heroism of officer and men in Chitral

Robert Walter Edmund Knollys
MUHAMMAD ALI
HASIL

Captain Knollys, Assistant Political Agent in Chitral, who was returning from Peshawar, left Dir in order to cross the Lowari Pass. Having reached a point beyond Mirgo, the snow was found to be too deep to allow of the Pass being crossed that day, and it was decided to stop at Gujar Levy Post, about 5 miles from the top of the Pass.

The snow was about 6 or 7 feet deep, and was still falling. About half a mile from Gujar Post the last four of the party, including Captain Knollys and the Subadar Major of the Dir Levies, were suddenly caught and buried by an avalanche. Captain Knollys's Chitrali orderly (Hasil) and a villager of Dir, named Muhammad Ali, rushed back and succeeded in pulling out Captain Knollys, who with their help set to work to find the other three men, who were completely buried.

After half an hour's hard work the three men were found and extricated from the snow, one unconscious, the others conscious but exhausted. During this half hour the three rescuers were in imminent peril of their lives, as the spot is notorious for the frequency of the avalanches which fall upon it, and it is, moreover, well known that when one avalanche has fallen at this place it is almost invariably followed in a very short time by a second. Muhammad Ali of Dir and Hasil of Chitral were also awarded the Albert Medal of the Second Class for their gallantry. (19.12.05)

Gallantry of Railwaymen at Newcastle, N.S.W.

William Henry Pearce While a passenger train was approaching Thornton Railway Station a boiler-plate of the engine collapsed, and steam and boiling water were ejected. Both the driver of the engine, James Pead, who died later, and the fireman, William Pearce, were severely scalded. Pead was still exposed to the full force of the escaping steam when Pearce, at great personal risk, lifted him to a place of safety.

Pearce, having vainly tried to close the throttle valve, climbed to the front of the engine, exposing himself again to the escaping water and steam, and, having reached the footplate of the engine, applied the automatic brake and brought the train to a standstill. (4.12.05)

A heroic diver of W. Australia

Frank Hughes A sudden downpour of rain in the Bonnievale District caused the inundation of the Westralia and East Extension Mine from the lower level (1,354 feet from the surface) to the No. 9 (900 feet) level. All the miners escaped, except an Italian named Modesto Varischetti, who was working by himself in a rise 28 feet above the No. 10 (1,000 feet) level, and was imprisoned by the flood waters.

It was at first thought that he must have lost his life, but after a time his signals were heard. It was at once decided to attempt his rescue by the aid of divers, and in less than eight hours from the time of the dispatch of the telegraphic message a special train was on its way to the Goldfields with two divers, Messrs. Curtis and Hearne, with their assistants and diving outfits. Meantime two other divers, Messrs. F. Hughes and Fox, of Kalgoorlie, who had lately followed the occupation of miners and were familiar with the local mining practice, had volunteered their services and had gone to the flooded mine.

Hughes led the way and after some difficulty reached the bottom of the pass, where he found the shoot into the level choked with about half a ton of ore; he cleared this out, took the door off the shoot, and got down into the level, but then had to return twice to No. 9 as the other diver did not come down to him. It proved that Fox had been unable to get down, and on making his second attempt he sustained an injury to his leg which caused him to retire from further participation in the work. Diver Hearne then took his place, and Hughes and he went down to the No. 10 level, but both had to return to arrange certain matters. They then descended again, and Hughes struggled along the level, knee-deep in sludge, to the rise, where he was able to find the air hosepipe leading to Varischetti's rock-drill, and after shaking it several times obtained a signal in reply from the imprisoned man. Hughes was then so exhausted that he had to return after fixing a guide-line for future use.

After a rest of $3\frac{1}{2}$ hours Hughes and Hearne again descended, the descent being the fifth that Hughes had made that day. He succeeded in reaching Varischetti, shook hands with him, and supplied him with an electric lamp, food, and other necessaries. Next day he again made a visit, Hearne as before staying at the angle at the foot of the ore-pass; and daily visits were repeated until the 28th March, when the water had been lowered sufficiently to make it just possible for a man to wade along the No. 10 level from the ore-pass with his head out of the water. Diver Hughes then went in twice without his diving-dress and talked to Varischetti, and then made a third trip and brought him out, carrying him a part of the way, the entombed man's strength having failed him. (19.3.07)

A gallant railway-crossing keeper

Arthur Hardiment While an express train was approaching the level crossing at Tivetshall (Norfolk), Hardiment and Bloomfield, the crossing-keepers, were standing near one of the gates when Bloomfield's little boy was seen to be making for the line from the opposite side of the track to join his father.

The cries of the men did not avail to stop the child, so Hardiment dashed across the line towards the child, knowing that the father who had lost a leg and an arm could do nothing.

Before he was clear of the track the footplate of the engine had struck his left forearm, fracturing it and hurling him into a hedge 9 feet away. Just before he was caught by the engine he had the satisfaction of knowing that the child had turned away from the approaching train and had escaped unhurt. (30.8.07)

A gallant Able Seaman

John Ramsay As a down mail train was approaching Temple Meads Station, Bristol, a Marine, W. Howat, belonging to H.M.S. *Donegal*, fell from the platform. Ramsay, Able Seaman, of H.M.S. *Vivid*, at once jumped down to his assistance and succeeded, at the imminent risk of his own life, in dragging the fallen man back to the platform as the train passed the spot. (7.1.08)

Heroism in the Potteries

Alfred Hunt Alfred and his brother Robert were employed at Messrs. Johnson Brothers' Pottery at Tunstall in cleaning out a tank, containing hot water and oil, when Robert Hunt, who was bending over the opening of the tank, fell in.

Alfred Hunt, who was working close by at the time, hearing his brother cry out as he fell, immediately jumped into the tank after him and succeeded in pulling him out. Robert Hunt was so badly scalded that he succumbed to his injuries. (7.8.08)

A brave railway porter in Staffordshire

Arthur Eccleshall Three children were making their way over the level crossing at Bushbury, in Staffordshire, Railway Station, where Eccleshall was employed as a porter. A light engine was approaching at the time and, seeing that the children's lives were endangered, Eccleshall shouted to them, when two of the children ran forward and got clear of the rails on which the engine was travelling, while the third, a little boy, tried to escape by running between the platform and the rails; the engine was almost upon him when Eccleshall jumped from the platform in front of the engine and lifted the child clear of the railway track. In so doing he was struck by the engine and thrown into the four-foot way, being rendered unconscious. (2.10.08)

A gallant rescue in Bedfordshire brick-kilns

George Henry Smith A workman at the Woburn Sands Brickworks, named Charles Griffin, fell to the bottom of one of the kilns owing to the roof collapsing, and was imprisoned by hot ballast and bricks, the upper part of his body alone being free. His comrade Smith, on hearing of the accident, at once went to his rescue, but to effect an entry proved to be a work of some difficulty, as the wicket through which the bricks were taken into and removed from the kiln was almost completely blocked. He succeeded, however, in reaching his comrade and in removing the bricks and ballast imprisoning the fallen man, who was eventually drawn up to the top of the kiln by means of a rope fastened under his armpits. Griffin subsequently died of the injuries he sustained. (24.10.08)

Life-saving in dry dock at Jarrow

JAMES KENNEDY CHAPMAN
THOMAS MCCORMACK
ARCHIBALD WILSON

Workmen were engaged in painting the inside of an iron tank in the stokehold of a steamer lying in dry dock at Jarrow.

Owing to the fact that very strong fumes were given off by the anticorrosive paint or solution used the men were working in relays, each squad of three men being relieved after 10 or 15 minutes had elapsed.

A workman named Graham was overcome by the fumes, and the chargeman, Archibald Wilson,[1] sacrificed his life in endeavouring to save Graham.

Thomas McCormack, who had already been affected by the fumes while at work in the tank, went to Wilson's assistance, but was himself rendered insensible, and was rescued by James Kennedy Chapman, Works Manager at the Dock, who, having pulled McCormack out, re-entered the tank and endeavoured to save Graham, but was himself overcome by fumes.

The rescue of Chapman and Graham was eventually effected from the top of the tank. (27.11.08)

Heroes of the Messina Earthquake

JAMES VIVIAN REED
HENRY SMITH

On the occasion of the earthquake at Messina on the 28th December 1908 the steamship *Afonwen*, of Cardiff, was lying at her moorings, having arrived at Messina on the 24th December.

The first intimation the master of the ship (Captain William Owen) had of the disaster was on being awakened in the early morning of the 28th December by the noise of the upheaval and the commotion caused by the tidal wave, but owing to the darkness and the dense clouds of dust the full extent of the disaster could not be realized for some time. The danger to shipping claimed the first attention of the Captain, but having satisfied himself as to the safety of his vessel he proceeded ashore with his crew, as the dawn broke, to render assistance, and soon reached a building of five stories, where children were noticed at a great height from the ground crying for help. The interior of the building had for the most part collapsed, and one of the walls had disappeared; the structure was therefore in a very dangerous condition.

The Captain having given the word, Henry Smith, Able Seaman, and shortly after, James Vivian Reed, Second Mate, swarmed up a rope to the rescue of the children, who had lowered string by means of which the rope was hauled up and made fast. The rescue of the children having been effected, three persons were lowered down from a story above. (28.12.08)

Gallantry at Kirkee

HUGHES LANCASTER LITHGOW
CHARLES STEPHENS

A violent explosion of blank gun cartridges occurred in the store of the 44th Battery, R.F.A., at Kirkee, in India,

---

[1] His widow, Mrs. Isabelle Wilson, received the medal which was accorded posthumously to him.

and while the building was full of smoke, and it was impossible to tell whether a further explosion might follow, Major Lithgow, R.F.A., and Sergeant-Major Stephens, hearing that Battery Quarter-Master Dennis was in the burning building, at once went to his rescue through the dense smoke, and succeeded in bringing him out, though unhappily he was so seriously hurt that he succumbed to the injuries sustained. (25.2.08)

A boy saves a navvy's life at Newport

THOMAS LEWIS   A heavily timbered trench, 238 feet long and about 50 feet deep and 35 feet wide, suddenly collapsed at the Alexandra Dock Extension Works, Newport. The sides fell in and killed between thirty and forty of the workmen who were engaged in excavating the trench, and seriously injured others. Determined efforts were immediately made by the workmen and others who happened to be close at hand to rescue the survivors.

At 2 a.m. a man was discovered alive, his left arm having been caught between the elbow and the wrist, and he could only be reached by means of a small hole between two struts. Lewis, a lad of 16, succeeded in getting down, and after two hours released the man, who was extricated alive.

While Lewis was among the timbers, from 10 to 12 feet below the surface, he was in imminent peril of losing his life, for the ground was slipping and settling and the debris moving. It appeared as if at any moment he might have been crushed by a further subsidence. (2.7.09)

Bravery at Malta

ANTONIO DINGLI   These men, among others, were engaged in
PAOLO BONNICI   emptying cess-pits at Zabbar, Malta. The foul air rendered any lengthened period of work impracticable and resulted in one of the men losing his life.

Antonio Dingli was the first man to descend, but he was compelled in a short time to return to the surface. The next man to descend had almost regained the surface after a short absence, when he fell back into the pit. Dingli descended at once, and succeeded in getting him to the pit opening when he himself lost consciousness, and both fell back into the pit.

Bonnici then tied a rope round his waist and descended to the rescue of his comrades. As he was unable to lift Dingli, a rope with a hook attached was lowered, and the rope having been made secure, Dingli was hauled up to the pithead in an apparently lifeless condition. Bonnici was rescued by means of the rope. The third man succumbed before he was brought to the surface. (31.5.09)

Children at Hove saved from burning house

CAROLINE HUGHES   A fire occurred at 129 Clarendon Road, Hove, where two children named Austen, aged 11 and 4 years respectively, had been left at home by their mother, who was out working. Mrs. Hughes, whose house was in the same street, ran to the house and on entering found a paraffin lamp in flames on the table, and the two children crouching in the far corner, too frightened to move. She led them out one at a time, and in shielding them from the flames her dress caught fire.

Mrs. Hughes afterwards carried out the blazing lamp, and while doing so sustained serious injuries to her face, chest, and arms, which eventually led to the amputation of her left arm two years later. (14.10.05)

A heroic conductor on the C.P.R. in Ontario

THOMAS REYNOLDS   An express train left Sudbury, Ontario, for Minneapolis, in charge of Conductor Thomas Reynolds. As it approached the bridge crossing the Spanish River, at a point where the stream is 250 feet wide and 30 feet deep, Conductor Reynolds and several passengers were seated at dinner in the dining-car. On reaching the bridge a part of the train left the track and plunged down the embankment.

Two of the vehicles, a first-class car and the dining-car, crashed through the ice, which is said to have been 18 inches thick, and sank to the river bed. The dining-car was almost completely submerged and but for the resourcefulness and heroic conduct of the conductor the disaster would have resulted in a much heavier death-roll.

The fore part of the car rapidly filled with water and the occupants, hurled to the end of the car, were in danger of drowning in 10 feet of water, their situation being made more perilous by the accumulation of debris. Reynolds, on coming to the surface, found daylight entering from the top of a window some 6 inches above the level of the water, and, grasping a hat rack, he smashed with his feet the heavy plate-glass windows. He then turned his attention to the imprisoned passengers, rescuing those in danger of drowning, and urging all to make use of the only means of support, namely, hat racks, lamps, &c. The passengers having been assisted in this way, he turned to effect an exit, only to find that the car had settled down, and that the opening made was submerged. After swimming about and locating the broken window with his feet, he dived and cautiously pushed himself through the window, using his feet to keep a hold on the window frame, in order that his body might not be swept away by the strong current.

With great difficulty he brought his body between the broken ice and the submerged car and succeeded in gaining a foothold on the top of the car. He at once commenced wrenching the fan-lights from the roof and succeeded in rescuing a lad and still another passenger through the small opening thus made. When, shortly after, an axe was brought to him, in response to his cries for help, he enlarged the opening sufficiently to allow of the rescue of the other imprisoned passengers. Reynolds was badly cut and injured and was for some time under medical care. (21.1.05)[1]

A gallant episode in the S. African War

CHARLES WAGNER
ALEXANDER JAMES STEWART

An armoured train which had been sent out on patrol was intercepted near Chieveley Station, in Natal, by Boers, and three carriages were thrown off the line. These vehicles lay between the rest of the train and the track over which it must travel on its homeward journey, and until they were removed the train, the engine, and its escort—about 150 men—were exposed to a severe converging fire of rifles and artillery from the surrounding hills.

The sole means by which the line could be cleared was the engine, which moving to and fro butted at the wreckage until after about 50 minutes' work it was heaved and pushed off the track. The part played by the driver of the engine, Charles Wagner, and by the fireman, Alexander James Stewart, was therefore indispensable to the rescue of the wounded with whom the engine and its tender became crowded.

The damage was exceptional. The heavy fire of shells and bullets inflicted many casualties, and more than one-quarter of all in the train were killed or wounded. The shells repeatedly struck the engine and at any moment might have exploded the boiler. The driver, a civilian, under no military code, was wounded severely in the scalp by a shell-splinter almost immediately. Although in great pain he did not fail during the whole of this affair to manage his engine skilfully, and by clearing the line saved from death and wounds a proportion at least of the fifty or sixty persons who effected their escape upon the engine and its tender. (15.11.99)[1]

Life-saving in Mysore

NICHOLAS BERNARD EDWIN DAWES

Captain Dawes, R.E., was engaged upon the difficult and dangerous task of reconstructing a large dam across the Canvery River at Krishnarajkatte, Mysore State, while the river was in full flood. Captain Dawes and a workman were on a raft towed by a boat consisting of two dugouts lashed together. Weighted barrels had been lowered to

---

[1] The great delay in making awards in these cases is notable, and unexplained. They were gazetted in June 1910.

the river bottom from the raft, which was then pulled towards the boat and allowed to drift towards a hawser for the purpose of being drawn to an island in the river. While the party were being hauled to land the strong current caused the dugouts to heel over, and the coolies becoming frightened matters were made worse, the occupants of the last boat and raft having to jump into the river.

Captain Dawes swam within about 10 feet of the island, and turned round and seemed to be counting the men to see that all were safe. He noticed one man being carried down mid-stream towards the breach, and swam out to help him. He was swept through the breach and must have been dashed against a rock, as there was no shout for help or other signal of distress. His body was not recovered until three days later. The Indian was washed ashore some 500 or 600 yards down stream in a badly bruised condition. The Medal was presented by the King to his widow. (30.7.09)

A brave sergeant-major in Jersey, Channel Islands

ALBERT JOSEPH KEMPSTER A carriage containing two ladies and two children was being driven near Pontac, in the Island of Jersey, when one of the horses stumbled and the driver was thrown into the road owing to the reins breaking when he tried to pull up. The horses became frightened and bolted at full speed past Sergeant-Major Kempster, of the R. Jersey Militia, who was cycling in the same direction. He promptly gave chase and, getting alongside the carriage, succeeded in transferring himself from his bicycle to the carriage.

Climbing along the pole of the carriage the Sergeant-Major managed to get hold of the broken reins and succeeded in bringing the frightened horses to a standstill. But for his presence of mind and courage the occupants of the carriage might have met with fatal injuries, for in about another minute the runaways would have reached the closed gates of a railway crossing. (20.9.10)

A schoolmaster in Clydach Vale saves many lives

Robert Ralph Williams Mr. Williams noticed a large volume of water rushing down towards his school—a dam having burst on the mountain side—and realizing that the girls' and infants' departments of the school were in great danger, he at once gave instructions for the boys to be dismissed, and rushed to give warning to the other departments, but not before the approach to the front of these schools was entirely cut off by an immense volume of water. His only route was through a doorway between the playground of the two departments. He unlocked this door and shouted to the children playing in the yard to make their escape to the boys' school yard, and one class escaped in this way. Mr. Williams afterwards opened the back doors of the girls' department, which all opened inwards, and closed the front door.

Mr. Williams then went to the infants' department, having to wade through a current up to his armpits. He satisfied himself that there was no imminent danger provided the walls of the girls' school could withstand the force of the water, and decided to take the girls to a slope near the back entrance of their school; but he found that the volume of water had greatly increased, and had burst in the front door and broken the lower parts of the windows. He succeeded, however, in entering the school and finally got all the children out safely, although the water inside the building was now fully 4 feet 6 inches in depth. While the last of the children were being rescued, a wall, 18 yards long, 10 feet high, and 2 feet 3 inches thick, which had formed a partial breakwater, was swept away, and the increased rush of water carried Mr. Williams out of the building, down a flight of steep steps, where he was severely bruised and narrowly escaped drowning. At the bottom of the steps he found about twenty girls struggling in 6 feet of water, and these he assisted to safety in the infants' school yard.

In the meantime, Mrs. Colville, an assistant teacher, and her class were caught in another corner of the yard, bounded by a high wall, which met the full force of the flood. She and the children were being whirled round by the torrent, but all were rescued by Mr. Williams, who, with a child in his arms, caught Mrs. Colville as she was sinking and being carried away.

Valuable assistance was rendered by Mr. Matthew Lewis and other members of the school staff. (11.3.10)

A mental patient rescued in Essex

Frank Diamond Diamond, an attendant at the Claybury Asylum, saw one of the patients climbing a stack-pipe at the asylum, and, realizing the man's danger, immediately followed him up the pipe. The man got on to the roof, at a height of about 37 feet, where Diamond reached him, and succeeded in supporting him until a rope and ladder were brought, and the patient was rescued unhurt. (7.6.10)

A gallant woman helps the Police

Frances Maude Wright Mrs. Wright had left her house to go to friends, when she saw a man running in her direction pursued by Police Constable Haytread. The man deliberately turned round—pausing to take aim—and fired at the constable; he then ran on, and again turned and fired a second shot. The constable was then close to his man, who fired a third time, before he was seized and a struggle ensued. Haytread called to Mrs. Wright to help and asked her to blow his whistle; she came up without hesitation and got hold of the man's collar and struck him in the face with her fist. She then broke the police whistle off its chain and blew it. A severe struggle now ensued between the officer and the burglar, through which Mrs. Wright still retained her hold on the latter. He, however, got his arm free and again fired; locked with the constable he then fell to the ground and pressed the revolver against Haytread's head and pulled the trigger, but the weapon missed fire. Mrs. Wright had in the meantime struck the man in the face and in so doing injured her left hand; her cries brought Seaman Barber to the spot. The burglar still had the revolver, but with further assistance he was overpowered.

Mrs. Wright was the wife of a newsagent's carman and had six children. But for her fearless action, the consequences might have been serious, and a most dangerous criminal (for he had previously attempted to shoot a constable) might have escaped. (26.12.10)[1]

A girl saves father and brother from a bull

AMY MADELINE JACQUES — Her brother, Francis Jacques, was suddenly attacked by a bull. A cowman who was with him shouted for help, and Mr. Jacques, sen., aged 74, came to the yard and struck the bull on the head with his stick. The animal turned and tossed the old man, and again attacked the son. Mr. Jacques, sen., was dragged out of the yard by the cowman, and Miss Jacques, who had been attracted to the scene by the shouting, went to the house for a gun, but she was afraid to use it as the bull had pinned her brother against a wall. With great presence of mind she got hold of the bull by its horns and pulled its head away, but was unable to release her brother. She ran to the house, and bringing back the cowman, who was helping her father indoors, she again held the bull's horns, while the cowman dragged Francis Jacques, who was insensible and severely injured, into safety. Happily, Miss Jacques escaped without injury, though narrowly, for the door-way through which she rushed on releasing her hold of the bull was immediately charged by the infuriated animal. (26.3.11)

Life-saving at Iffley Lock

PERCY HOPE MELLON — Mellon, a lock-keeper at Iffley, was called from his house one night and told that a woman was in the river: owing to the darkness he could find no trace of her. Returning towards the lock he saw in the water a dark object which

---

[1] Locality not stated in *The London Gazette*.

was being rapidly carried by the strong stream and high wind towards the partly opened weir. Swimming towards it he discovered that it was a woman floating on her side apparently lifeless, and aided by his son, who had pluckily swum out to his father's assistance, brought her safely to land. (24.2.11)

A nurse saves a mental patient from death

HILDA ELIZABETH WOLSEY A female patient at the Hanwell Asylum, while exercising in one of the airing courts, climbed over the wire covering of one of the fire-escape staircases, and, reaching the roof of the laundry ward, ran along the narrow guttering at the edge of the roof. Nurse Wolsey followed her over the wire covering of the escape, and along the narrow guttering, 25 feet above the ground, making her way by leaning with one hand against the sloping roof, and, reaching the patient, held her, at great personal risk, until ropes and ladders were procured and she was lowered to safety. (11.6.10)

A gallant engineer in Burma

ALGERNON EDWARD MANN When the S.S. *Leicestershire* of the Bibby Line was being brought alongside the Sule Pagoda Wharf, Rangoon, a Cingalese servant, who was leaning against a loose railing, fell overboard between the vessel and the wharf, striking his head against the edge of the wharf in falling, and was in imminent danger of being drowned or crushed to death between the incoming steamer and the wharf.

Mr. Mann, at great risk to his own life, for the moving vessel was only a few feet away at the time, immediately started to clamber down the stanchions of the wharf. He slipped and fell into the river, but was able to reach the drowning man, and swim with him to one of the stanchions, where he supported him until ropes were lowered, and both were rescued. (25.2.11)

A brave apprentice plumber

ALBERT SWAINSTON A boy, aged thirteen, while playing with a piece of wood in the water, overbalanced and fell into the river Tees which was running very high and about 12 feet deep. Albert Swainston, an apprentice plumber, being called to the spot by the cries of the boy's companions, jumped into the river, fully dressed, and swam towards the boy, who was then about 22 yards from the bank. He got hold of the boy, and struck out for the bank-side, but owing to a strong current of water, he lost his grip. He soon recovered the boy again, and, after considerable difficulty, brought him to the side of the bank, where he managed to get hold of a wall which projects from the bank-side. Owing, however, to his exhausted condition and the boy's continued struggles, he was unable to pull the boy up, and the current of water carried him away. The lad went under the water, and this time did not rise to the surface, and Swainston was too exhausted to attempt again to rescue him. (28.2.11)

A farmer saves a firework manufacturer

JAMES MOULDER Mr. Petty, aged 72, a manufacturer of fireworks, was at work in his factory at Barton Moss, near Manchester, charging bombs, when an explosion occurred, followed a few moments later by a second and more violent explosion. As a result of the explosions the shed was partially wrecked and set on fire, while Mr. Petty was hurled to the ground and pinned down among the burning debris. His son, who was approaching the shed at the time, was caught and knocked down by a second explosion. Mr. James Moulder, a farmer, was working in a field about 150 yards away, and on hearing the first explosion ran towards the shed. He had covered about 40 yards when the second explosion occurred, and he saw Mr. Petty's son knocked down, but, regardless of the risk of further explosions, he ran on, and entering the burning shed, brought Mr. Petty to safety from amongst the mass of burning wreckage and exploding fireworks. (12.7.11)

A gallant schoolboy at Goole

Jack Hewitt A boy friend of Hewitt's, named Drury, aged 9, was playing on the quay by the side of the River Ouse at Goole, when he overbalanced and fell into 10 feet of water. As the river at that point is broad and a strong tide was flowing, Drury, who could not swim, was in immediate danger of being swept away and drowned. Hewitt, a lad of 10 years of age, jumped fully dressed into the river and, though both were carried out some yards by the tide, succeeded in seizing Drury, and after skilfully controlling his struggles and turning him over on his back brought him in to the bank. (11.5.11)

The Hyderabad cordite explosions

Alfred Edwin Purkis On the 7th April 1906, and again on the 15th April, the cordite magazine at Hyderabad caught fire. On the first occasion Sub-Conductor Purkis entered the magazine with his Lascars while smoke was still issuing from the building, and extinguished the fire. Had he not succeeded in so doing the loss of life, both in the Fort and in the City, must have been very serious. On the second occasion the senior Officer ordered the evacuation of the Fort, and Purkis was the last person to leave after having done everything in his power to avert the explosion. Notwithstanding that the Fort was cleared and the City warned, lives were lost when the second fire occurred. On each occasion both gunpowder and cordite were involved. (7.4.06)[1]

The Ferozepore Explosion

Charles Creagh Donovan
Eglintoune Frederick Ross
CHARLES ALEXANDER ANDERSON, DAVID COLEY YOUNG, MALCOLM SYDENHAM CLARKE CAMPBELL, BASIL CONDON BATTYE, HUGH CLARKE, FREDERICK HANDLEY, HENRY PARGITER, ARTHUR JAMES ROBINSON, PATRICK JOHN FITZPATRICK, GEORGE SMITH, and ROBERT DUNN DOW

On the 30th August 1906, a fire broke out in one of the magazines of the Ferozepore Arsenal comprising five cells in which were stored cordite, small-arms ammunition, and gunpowder. At an early stage the ends of one of the outer cells (No. 10) were blown out by an explosion of cordite, while from cell No. 9, where small-arms ammunition was stored, smoke was seen to be issuing.

Major-General Anderson, who directed the subsequent operations from a roof at the edge of the magazine compound, at a distance of some 20 yards, having ordered all persons to be cleared out of the fort, and placed a cordon round it at 1,000 yards distance, a steam fire-engine was got to work, and the fire party which had been organized commenced their highly dangerous task of clearing cell No. 8 in which was stored some 19,000 lb. of gunpowder; they eventually succeeded in so doing, thereby cutting off the fire by the intervention of an empty cell. Had the powder in this cell exploded, the explosion must have been communicated to cells in an adjoining magazine where 300,000 lb. of gunpowder were stored.

Captain Donovan volunteered to clear cell No. 8, and led the fire party, and all concerned acted with the greatest coolness in circumstances calling for a high degree of courage. The door of the cell was opened and the fire-hose turned on. Major Campbell joined the party by the cell, and returned in a short while and reported to General Anderson that though the cell was full of smoke, and the barrels hot, there was no actual fire in the cell. As, however, the explosions in the ruined cell No. 10 were becoming more violent, General Anderson, fearing that the barrels of powder which were being removed from cell No. 8 would be ignited, ordered the discontinuance of efforts to clear the cell; the pumping-engine was, however, kept at work by Mr. Dow and some native assistants.

[1] Gazetted in Sept. 1911. The delay is unexplained.

A series of heavy explosions of cordite now took place and on the occurrence of a lull Captain Clarke went to reconnoitre, and reported that cell No. 9 was still apparently intact. Major Campbell and Mr. Pargiter subsequently went into the enclosure to investigate, and on their report being received a party including fifty Lascars was organized, and the removal of the powder barrels in cell No. 8 was recommenced under cover of the fire-hose. During their removal the last important explosion of cordite took place some 12 yards away. Eventually all the barrels were removed without accident.

Captain Ross discovered the fire, and with a detachment of his regiment entered the magazine compound with a small hand-engine fed from tanks in the magazine, and attempted to put out the fire. He also worked at getting the steam-engine into position.

Major Young, as General Anderson's Brigade-Major, was constantly with the General in positions of great danger. In particular he joined General Anderson at a critical moment by the door of No. 8 cell, from which the gunpowder was being removed, and remained with the General throughout the rest of the period of danger.

Captain Battye assisted in the removal of the gunpowder from No. 8 cell. He also, with Staff-Sergeant Fitzpatrick, directed the operation for piercing two holes through the masonry of the roof of cell No. 9 where the small-arms ammunition was burning and succeeded in getting the hose through these holes so as to play on the burning ammunition. By this means a check on the fire in No. 9 was effected. Both men were conspicuous throughout the day in the magazine enclosure. (30.8.06)[1]

Fire and Tornado in Ontario

EDWARD BELL   A disastrous forest fire broke out near the town of South Porcupine, Ontario, destroying the town and a mining camp, and the perilous position of the inhabitants was aggravated by a sudden tornado.

A party managed with great difficulty to pass through the smoke and flames to some water-barrels, but then collapsed from exhaustion, and were unable to use the water so as to keep their clothes from catching fire from the showers of sparks.

Mr. Bell, of the Canadian Copper Co., notwithstanding the dense smoke, which had incapacitated the party, went to their rescue, and stood by them for nearly two hours, damping their clothes, and by this and other means, preventing further injury by fire. By his courageous action he was instrumental in saving the lives of seven persons. (11.7.11)

[1] Gazetted in Sept. 1911.

An aboriginal prisoner saves his escort's life

'NEIGHBOUR'   Neighbour, an aboriginal native of the Roper River, Australia, who had been placed under arrest, was being conveyed in February 1911 to the Roper River Police Station by William F. Johns, a trooper of the Police Force of the Northern Territory. On the morning of the day in question the Wilton River—which was in full flood—had to be crossed, and Johns, who was on horseback, and was holding in his hand the neck-chain by which Neighbour was secured, set the prisoner to swim in front of him whilst he followed. The horse got into difficulties in mid-stream, and before the trooper could clear himself he was kicked in the face by the animal and carried off by the current. Neighbour, instead of using the opportunity of making his escape, went to Johns's assistance, and brought him ashore with great difficulty and at the risk of his own life. (1.2.11)

Heroism in Delhi Fort

JOHN WILLIAM HENDERSON   On the occasion of an explosion at the Laboratory, Delhi Fort, Colour-Sergt. Henderson, 1st K.O.S.B., entered the premises and rescued a Lascar, at imminent risk to his own life from further explosions, after which he returned to the danger zone to render further aid if possible. (24.4.12)

Life-Saving on the Yangtze River

ARTHUR HANSON   A number of houseboats containing foreign refugees from Szechuan were proceeding down the Yangtze River and in one of the gorges encountered a strong wind blowing against the current, with a result that several boats were caught in a dangerous whirlpool. With one exception the boats were brought out of the whirlpool by the strenuous efforts of those on board, but the remaining boat, which contained several women and children, was left drifting in the whirlpool in a perilous position, her rudder having been broken off. At great personal risk Mr. Hanson, who was on shore some considerable distance away, swam out with a rope tied round him, and succeeded in attaching this to the boat, which by this means was safely pulled to land. (10.11.11)

Nurse tries to save mental patient

ELIZABETH HOLLEY   Miss Holley, a nurse at Kingsdown House, Box, Wilts., endeavoured at great risk to her own life, to save the life of a lady patient who, while in her charge, was killed by an express train at Box Station.[1]

---

[1] No date given. Gazetted in Jan. 1913.

Heroes of Scott's Antarctic Expedition

WILLIAM LASHLEY
THOMAS CREAN

At the end of a journey of 1,500 miles on foot the final supporting party to the late Captain Scott's expedition towards the South Pole, consisting of Lieutenant Edward R. G. R. Evans, R.N. (later Admiral Sir Edward Evans, K.C.B.), Chief Stoker William Lashley, R.N., and Petty Officer (First Class) Thomas Crean, R.N., were 238 miles from the base when Lieutenant Evans was found to be suffering from scurvy. When 151 miles from the base he was unable to stand without support on his ski sticks, and after struggling onward on skis in great pain for 4 days, during which Lashley and Crean dragged their sledge 53 miles, he was unable to proceed farther.

At this point Lieutenant Evans requested his two companions to leave him, urging that unless they left him three lives would be lost instead of one. This, however, they refused to do, and insisted on carrying him forward on the sledge. Lashley and Crean dragged Lieutenant Evans on the sledge for 4 days, pulling 13 hours a day, until, on the evening of 17th February 1912, a point was reached 34 miles from a refuge hut, where it was thought possible that assistance might be obtained. During the following 12 hours, however, snow fell incessantly, and in the morning it was found impossible to proceed farther with the sledge.

As the party now had only sufficient food for three more meals, and both Lashley and Crean were becoming weaker daily, it was decided that they should separate, and that Crean should endeavour to walk to the refuge hut, while Lashley stayed to nurse Lieutenant Evans.

After a march of 18 hours in soft snow Crean made his way to the hut, arriving completely exhausted. Fortunately Surgeon Edward L. Atkinson, R.N., was at the hut with two dog teams and the dog attendant. His party, on 20th February, effected the rescue of Lieutenant Evans and Lashley.

But for the gallant conduct throughout of his two companions Lieutenant Evans would have undoubtedly lost his life. (Jan. 1913)

A brave cinema-proprietor

GEORGE EDWARD
BENNETT

During an exhibition at the Empire Cinema Palace, Slough, some cinematograph films, which a boy, aged 13 years, was rewinding, caught fire. In response to the boy's shouts an operator from the adjoining operating chamber tried without success to put out the fire with a blanket. Mr. Bennett, the proprietor, learning that the boy was in the rewinding room, at once climbed the vertical iron ladder leading to the trap-door of the room, from which volumes of flame and smoke were issuing. On entering the room he found the boy lying on the floor, and succeeded in dragging him to the trap-door and down the ladder into the hall, and thus saved the boy's life. Mr. Bennett was badly burnt. (28.12.12)

Gallantry at Redditch

GEORGE FREDERICK IRISH   While children were playing at Redditch, Worcestershire, on a piece of ground through which a sewer was being carried, a boy, one of their number, fell into the sewer and disappeared. Irish ran to the spot, where the sewer was open for some 30 or 40 yards. The boy was not to be seen, but the place where he had fallen in having been pointed out, Irish jumped into the sewer, which was $2\frac{1}{2}$ feet wide and 14 feet deep with perpendicular sides, and found the child in the water at the bottom. He lifted him out and found him to be insensible. The water was level with the rescuer's head, and owing to the narrowness of the sewer and the steepness of the sides he was unable to climb out, so he had to support the boy until assistance arrived. The child was apparently dead, but by the aid of artificial respiration he was brought round and recovered. (27.4.13)

Heroism on the Metropolitan Railway

Herbert Frederick Ewington   A fitter in the employment of the Metropolitan Railway, while crossing the permanent way at Aldersgate Street Station, slipped and fell across a live electric rail. Whilst a porter was fetching the insulating rubber gloves—without which it is very dangerous to touch any one who is in contact with a live rail—a train was seen entering the station on the same line. At that moment Ewington jumped on to the line and managed to pull the man's leg clear of the rail, receiving several shocks in doing so, and succeeded in getting the injured man into safety between the two sets of rails before the train pulled up a few feet away. The danger was increased by the fact that another train was approaching in the opposite direction. But for Ewington's exceptional bravery, there is little doubt that the fitter, who was unable to release himself, and whose leg was badly burned, would have lost his life. (1.7.13)

A brave Monmouthshire miner

JOHN JONES   As a passenger train, travelling about 7 miles an hour, was entering Pontypool Road Railway Station, a boy of 15 fell from the platform on to the rails, when the train was only 20 yards away. Jones, a miner, of Blackwood, Mon., at once jumped down, and, as there was not time to lift the boy on to the platform, lay down between the rails and the platform and held the boy on his breast until the train had passed. (15.5.13)

A brave labourer in a gasworks in Ireland

HUGH ADAMSON   The manager of the Banbridge Gasworks, County Down, was engaged in examining a gas exhauster which had become choked, when a loud explosion occurred, blowing out the window of the engine-house. Hugh Adamson, a labourer employed at the gasworks, had just left the engine-house on a message for the manager, and was thrown down by the force of the explosion. On getting up he saw the exhauster house in flames, and hearing the manager's call for help burst open the door which had jammed. He found the manager enveloped in flames, but managed to drag him outside and then collapsed. On recovering Adamson succeeded in turning the gas into another gasometer, thereby saving the premises from being blown up, though the engine-house was actually destroyed. Adamson was severely burned, and the manager succumbed to his injuries a few days later. (3.12.13)

A gallant Vice-Consul

WALTER RUSSELL BROWN   When fierce street fighting was raging in the city of Chungking, Mr. Brown, Acting British Vice-Consul at Chungking, assisted by his French colleague, Monsieur Bodard, in response to a message from the Chamber of Commerce, acted as intermediary between the two forces, and succeeded in bringing about a suspension of the hostilities. Both the officers ran great risk, as they were frequently exposed to the firing of the troops, and but for their prompt intervention it is probable that the fighting would have resulted in one body of troops being exterminated and the city, which contains a population of between 300,000 and 400,000 inhabitants, many of them British subjects, being pillaged and burnt to the ground. (21.9.13)

A brave brakesman on the C.P.R.

JAMES JULIAN CARTER   Carter was on the engine of a train running between Havelock and Smith's Falls in Ontario, which was rounding a curve near Tweed, when he saw a little girl named Violet Freeman trying to cross the line 200 feet ahead. He shouted to the driver to stop, and immediately made his way along the footboard to the 'pilot' on the front of the engine. Realizing that the train, the speed of which had been reduced to about 8 miles an hour, could not be pulled up in time, he jumped from the engine and rushing forward, just succeeded in rescuing the child, falling with her into the ditch at the side of the line. The train was stopped when the engine and 8 coaches had passed the spot where the child was rescued. (16.5.14)

Summary of Awards, 1877–1914 (36 years)
1st Class (in gold) . . . 51
2nd Class 99
150

In connexion with mining accidents 33 medals were awarded; to doctors, attendants, and nurses 6; to railwaymen 13; to schoolmasters and mistresses 2.

CHAPTER X
AWARDS OF THE EDWARD MEDAL
JAN. 1908—DEC. 1914

'Every one can reel off a list of the wives of Henry VIII, but who can give a list of the disciples of St. Francis of Assisi? It is the heroes of peace, both English and foreign, who must be celebrated on Humanity Day.'
EILEEN POWER, The Evolution of World Peace, 1921,
ed. by F. S. Marvin, p. 190.

Note. Silver medallists are printed in Old English type. The date of the deed is given in parentheses. The year of the Gazette notice is at the top of the page.

Hoyland Silkstone Colliery disaster

𝕱𝖗𝖆𝖓𝖈𝖎𝖘 𝕮𝖍𝖆𝖓𝖉𝖑𝖊𝖗   Chandler, a sixty-year-old miner, was engaged with five others in repairing an underground boiler house, when a fall of roof broke an iron girder, damaging the boiler, from which a rush of steam took place. All the men were scalded and hurt; one was killed on the spot and three others died afterwards. The lamps were extinguished. Although badly burnt and hurt, Chandler crept in the dark, at the risk of his own life, three times through the steam to the boiler top, to rescue others who could not move. Then, unable to do more alone, he signalled to the pit-top and was drawn up, but he again descended the pit to assist in the rescue, though almost exhausted. His son was one of the victims of the disaster. (23.11.07)

Canadian mine accident

𝕲𝖊𝖔𝖗𝖌𝖊 𝕳𝖚𝖉𝖉𝖑𝖊𝖘𝖙𝖔𝖓 𝕷𝖆𝖒𝖇   Lamb lost his life in endeavouring to save the lives of five men at a fire at the Strathcona Company's Mine, at Strathcona, Alberta, Canada.
There were two shafts in the mine, a hoisting shaft and an air shaft. The engineer of the mine woke Lamb at about 11.25 p.m., when the fire was discovered, and told him that there were five men in the mine. Lamb descended three times, once by the air shaft, and having found the men urged them to escape by the ladder, saying he would remain until they had ascended. One man made an attempt, but returned. Lamb himself then succeeded in reaching the surface, but his clothes were in flames, and he died from his injuries. (8.6.07)

Gallant rescue from a mine shaft

𝕳𝖊𝖓𝖗𝖞 𝕰𝖛𝖊𝖗𝖘𝖔𝖓   In the process of sinking the shaft of the Penallta Colliery, water was being raised from a depth of 345 feet, and a scaffold was suspended in the shaft for the purpose of walling the sides. The barrel containing the water came in contact with the scaffold and broke it from its chains, precipitating it with two men 30 feet into 12 feet of water. Henry Everson, who was at the top of the shaft, heard one of the men calling for help. He also called for assistance, but seeing the urgency of the case descended the shaft at once by a 4-inch pipe a distance of 270 feet. He then found the barrel, which he was able to pull towards him, got into it and was lowered till he found one of the men hanging on a thin wire, up to his neck in water and almost exhausted, his hands wounded. He jumped into the water, holding the barrel with one hand, and was able to grip the man by the collar and pull him into the barrel. They were then raised to the surface. The second man was drowned. (12.9.07)

Neath Colliery explosion

Morgan Howells   An explosion took place at the Neath Colliery, by which five men were killed and others injured. Morgan Howells and a boy, whose lamps were extinguished, began to make their way out. The boy, however, became almost insensible and Howells dragged and carried him 500 yards to a place of safety. (3.3.08)

Attempted rescue of entombed miners

James Hopwood
James Whittingham
James Cranswick
John Henry Thorne
Walter Clifford
Joseph Outram
John Welsby

Owing to an outbreak of fire at the Hemstead Colliery 24 miners were entombed. These six miners descended the mine at various times at great personal risk to rescue their comrades. They were provided with oxygen apparatus, but were unable to effect their object.

His Majesty graciously allowed the widow of John Welsby, who succumbed, to receive the Medal which would have been granted to her husband. (4.3.08)

A rescue from a Fife mine

James and George Dryburgh   A fire having broken out at Lockhead Colliery, Fife, it was feared that a fireman, who was known to be in the pit, was in danger. Two men descended to rescue him, but were overcome by poisonous gas. James and George Dryburgh, in spite of great risk, descended the shaft and rescued these two men. (29.12.07)

Two posthumous awards

Robert Pattinson
Matthew Hilliard

A miner named William Wharton was trapped by a heavy fall of roof which took place at the Roachburn Colliery, Cumberland. Robert Pattinson and Matthew Hilliard descended the mine in order to rescue him, but did not return. The medals were accordingly awarded to the widows of these two brave men. (28.1.08)

Rescue in Cadeby Colliery

HENRY BENTON   Three men, named John Churms, John Green, and Henry Benton, were at work in the Cadeby Main Colliery, when a very heavy fall of roof took place. Churms was completely buried, and Green partly so.

Benton, who was at some little distance, heard the fall, and, though the roof was obviously in a dangerous condition, rushed to their assistance and managed to pull out Green, who was fastened by the legs. All their lamps had been extinguished and the men were in the dark.

Benton placed Green, who was helpless from his injuries, in safety, and then ran for lights and assistance. On his return he found that a further heavy fall had taken place, and it was clear that there was no hope of getting Churms out alive.

By his prompt and brave action, Benton undoubtedly saved Green's life at the risk of his own. (27.10.08)

Gallant rescue work in Natal pit explosion

John Jones
William Dickson
T. Teasdale
William Nicol Muir

Owing to a series of destructive explosions which took place in the Glencoe Colliery, Natal, a large number of Europeans and natives lost their lives. The above-named showed most conspicuous gallantry in descending the shaft with various rescue parties, in accompanying which Inspector of Mines Muir lost his life. His widow, Mrs. Muir, received the medal which would have been presented to her husband. (13.2.08)

Accident in a gold-mine

John Jones   A native workman was overcome by gas at the bottom of the Witwatersrand Gold-mine, Johannesburg. Two men, named Owen and Griffiths, descended the mine to rescue him. With the help of Jones, who followed, the native was drawn up; but Owen, overcome by the gas, fell to the bottom of the shaft. Griffiths also was overcome, and Jones became unconscious on reaching the surface. Others went down, and one of them was unable to return. As soon as Jones regained consciousness, he insisted on again descending the mine, and succeeded in bringing up two of the men. He then descended the mine a third time and brought the last man, Griffiths, to the surface. Unfortunately Griffiths, Owen, and the native work-

Kimberley Diamond-mine accident

Arthur Torr Blakemore
Benjamin Kelly
James Brack Barnes
Thomas Menzies
Alfred Francis
Joseph Graham Richardson
MARTINUS, COCO,
THOMAS, ELIAS, AARON,
and ISAAC

man who first went down all succumbed later to the effects of the gas. (14.1.09)

In the Kimberley Diamond-mine owing to a mud-rush six natives were completely cut off by 65 feet of mud.

An attempt was made to clear the mud away but a second rush took place, and it was decided that the only possible method of reaching the men was by working over the top of the mud and passing it back in small quantities. The men concerned, after most arduous labour—they could only work stretched on planks—succeeded in rescuing the miners who had been entombed forty hours. There was great risk of a further rush, which would have overwhelmed the workers.

(30.1.09)

Accident in Hanham Colliery

Frederick Watts

Two miners, named Frederick Watts and Isaac Tanner, at work in the Hanham Colliery, had prepared four charges for blasting close to each other, and Tanner had just set fire to the fuses. He appears to have taken longer than he expected to light the fuses, and before he could get to a place of safety one of the shots exploded, and a falling stone broke his arm. He found himself unable to move, and called out to Watts to help him; whereupon Watts, who had left the dangerous spot, went back, and dragged him to a place of safety, although he knew that any of the three charges might explode at any moment.

Tanner unfortunately died subsequently from the effects of this injury. (29.5.08)

Gallant mine rescue in Queensland

Michael Lyons
John Shields

At the Mount Morgan Mine, Queensland, a subsidence of a mass of ore weighing about 12,000 tons occurred. Five men at work in the excavations were killed; two, Lyons and Banks, escaped, the latter being seriously injured in the head. Lyons called up the shaft for help. John Shields volunteered to descend, running very great risks while he was being lowered in consequence of falling debris. He reached the two men, and with the help of Lyons, who was unwilling to leave his wounded companion, Banks was securely fastened to the rope. Eventually all three were drawn up. (4.11.08)

Gallantry in an Australian gold-mine

Joseph Davis Three men, Davis, Darcey, and Allen, were employed at the bottom of a shaft in a gold-mine at Bendigo, Australia. They had prepared two holes for blasting, and the charges had been placed. Two of the men, Darcey and Davis, had retired to a place of safety; Allen, the third man, remained to set fire to the charges.

Having done this, he proceeded to climb up the ladder to safety; but, on reaching the top, he fell back to the bottom of the shaft. Davis at once descended the ladder, and found Allen lying across the two holes containing the charges. He seized him, dragged him to the east end of the shaft, and lay on the top of him to keep him still.

Both the charges exploded, and Allen, who had broken his leg, was hauled to the surface. Davis, refusing any assistance, climbed the ladder to the surface, changed his clothes, and went quietly home.

Davis's action was an exceptionally brave one, as he knew perfectly well that the explosion of the charges was imminent. (16.7.09)

Rescue of a steeplejack

David McWhirter
William McClelland

Two steeplejacks, with an assistant, were engaged in fixing new lightning conductors to a chimney, about 180 feet high, at the Coltness Iron Works, Newmains, Lanarkshire. The two steeplejacks, who were at the top of the chimney on a scaffold consisting of two planks, about 9 inches broad, were affected by gas fumes from the chimney. One of them lost consciousness and fell on the scaffold. The other, after tying his mate to the scaffold by a rope, was able to descend by a ladder to the ground, and received medical attention. Their assistant climbed the ladder, but was not sufficiently experienced to reach the scaffold.

There was not time to obtain the assistance of regular steeplejacks, but two men employed at the Iron Works volunteered—David McWhirter and William McClelland. They both ascended the ladder, got on to the narrow scaffold, and succeeded in placing the unconscious man in the 'boatswain's chair' used by the steeplejacks and in lowering him safely to the ground. Neither of them had previously had experience of climbing chimneys, and, in addition to climbing a vertical ladder 180 feet high, they had to deal with an unconscious man on a narrow open scaffold; they also ran the risk of being overcome by the gas fumes. (8.7.09)

A Girl of fifteen saves her mother's life

HANNAH HUGILL   Mrs. Hugill, on going into a field at Court House Farm, Great Busby, with her daughter to bring in some cows, was attacked by an infuriated bull. She defended herself with a pitchfork, but was knocked down by the bull, which began to gore her. Her daughter, Hannah, aged 15 years, who had been left at the gate, about a hundred yards from the place where her mother was attacked, came to her aid, and, recovering the fork from under the bull, used it to divert the animal's attention.

The mother and daughter then succeeded in making good their escape from the field, though the mother was again attacked while crossing the fence. The girl's action saved her mother from severe and, possibly, fatal injury. (11.9.09)

Darran Colliery explosion

EVAN OWENS
EDMUND DAVIES
WILLIAM EVANS
WILLIAM WAGNER TURNER

An explosion of coal-dust occurred at the Darran Colliery, Deri, in the Cardiff district by which twenty-seven persons lost their lives, five succumbing during the rescue operations.

Mr. Evan Owens, the Under-manager of the Colliery, Mr. Evans, Pit Carpenter, and Mr. Edmund Davies, the day fireman, were among the first to enter the mine, and made determined and continued attempts to succour the unfortunate men who had been affected by the explosion. They were all at times seriously affected by the noxious air and only desisted when their services were no longer of any avail.

Dr. Turner, who was the first medical man to reach the mine, displayed great courage by promptly going down the ladders in the upcast and pumping-shaft—an awkward descent to any one unacquainted with mining work. He rendered all the assistance he could, and nearly paid for his bravery with his life, as he was severely affected by afterdamp. (29.10.09)

Explosion in gold-mine

Harry Bennetts   On the 31st December 1909, an explosion occurred in the Randfontein South Gold-mine at Krugersdorp, through the firing of a packet of gelatine, giving rise to a suffusion of deadly gas. Four miners who were at work were killed by asphyxia due to the gas. Bennetts, with great courage and at imminent risk of his life, descended two winzes alone to the rescue of natives who had been overcome by the poisonous fumes of the gelatine. One of the winzes was 120 feet, the other 75 feet deep. (31.12.09)

Gallantry in Whitehaven Pit Fire
John Henry Thorne   James Littlewood

Richard Walker Moore
Robert Richmond Blair
Robert Steel
Samuel Turner
James Henry
Daniel Benn
John Whillans
James Dunlop
William John Henry
John Fearon
Matthew Walsh
John Graham
Thomas Graham
William Campbell
Thomas Swinburne
James Coulthard
David Devine
John Wilson
Matthew Wilson
John Pearson
John Quayle
James Knox
William Ball
James Wren
Charles Gibson
William Hoskin
Christopher Gregory
Robert McDonald
John Henry Parker
Ernest William Oswald
John Batty
John Smith
John Rothery
Wilson Graham
Thomas Cannon
James McKenzie
Samuel Birnie
Isaac Graham
Adam McKee
John Hanlon
John Thomas Mather
Archibald Thom, Jun.
Thomas Banks
Andrew Millar
Dr. Charles Joshua
Joseph Harris
John Graham
William James Mulholland
Joseph Lucas
James Taylor
Fletcher Young
Edward McKenzie, Sen.
Edward McKenzie, Jun.
George Henry
James Scawcroft
John McAllister
William Ginbey
Thomas Birkett
Thomas Donald
Joseph Cowan.
Hugh McKenzie
Allinson Mathers
John Hampson
Thomas Ferryman

A terrible fire occurred in the Wellington Pit, Whitehaven, at a point about 4,500 yards from the shafts. Various rescue parties, with great courage and self-devotion and at considerable risk, descended the mine and endeavoured to extinguish the fire and penetrate to the persons in the workings beyond. Thorne and Littlewood, fitted with breathing apparatus, reached within a distance of 150 yards of the fire, but were driven back by the great heat and effusion of gases. The others got to within about 300 yards of it, working in the thick smoke. It was found impossible to penetrate to where the fire was or to rescue any of the entombed miners.

Had an explosion occurred—a by no means unlikely eventuality, seeing that the mine is a very gassy one—they would undoubtedly all have been killed.

Special gallantry was shown by John Henry Thorne and James

Littlewood, to whom the Edward Medals of the First Class were awarded. (11.5.10)

Staffordshire Pit Fire

ARCHER CARTWRIGHT
SAMUEL SLATER
ISAIAH WALKER
ANTHONY WILLETS
EDWIN ARTHUR DANDO

An underground fire, in which the lives of two workmen were lost, occurred at the Russell Colliery, near Dudley, Staffs.—a district where the workings are peculiarly liable to spontaneous combustion.

The fire broke out at a point about 114 yards from the bottom of the downcast shaft, and when it was discovered by smoke issuing from the upcast shaft, the Manager of the mine, accompanied by several workmen, proceeded to the spot to try and put the fire out. After working for a considerable time in the heat and smoke, two of the party, Archer Cartwright (under-manager) and Anthony Willets, were sent to the surface for tools, leaving the Manager and two workmen to proceed with the work of fighting the fire. In their absence, both the Manager who, feeling the effects of the smoke, had walked back a short distance, and the two workmen were overcome by the fumes. Willets, on his return, found the Manager unconscious, and dragging him, in spite of his very heavy weight, to the bottom of the shaft, brought him safely to the surface. Willets and Cartwright, and a third man named Samuel Slater, then descended the shaft in order to try to rescue the two workmen who had succumbed. They found them, and attempted to carry them back; but Willets, who was already exhausted by previous efforts, showed signs of giving way, and Cartwright and Slater also feeling ill effects, they were all compelled to return and leave the two unfortunate workmen. On their way back, Willets fell down unconscious, and Cartwright and Slater, being unable to help him, made their way with difficulty to the surface. They were able, however, to tell Isaiah Walker of Willets's condition, and he volunteered to try to bring Willets out. Descending the mine alone, and crawling on his hands and knees under the smoke, Walker managed to reach Willets, whom he found lying on his face about 27 yards from the shaft. Seizing him by the shoulders, Walker managed to drag Willets to the shaft bottom, and then took him up in the cage. Walker again went down the shaft in the hope of reaching the two workmen left in the mine; but this time he was unsuccessful, and was forced to come back.

Dr. Dando, who was summoned to the mine when the fire broke out, also went down the pit and bravely assisted in the rescue work for several hours. He was at last overcome by poisonous gases and was brought to the surface unconscious. (17.4.10)

Shaft accident at Oulton

William Henry Pickering
George Handle Silkstone
Isaac Hodges
Albert Moore
James Hosey
Alfred Jones

A serious shaft accident occurred at the Water Haigh Mine, by which six men lost their lives. The mine, which is situated at Oulton, about five miles east of Leeds, consisted of four pits in course of sinking to develop a new mining area. Shaft No. 1 where the accident happened had been sunk to a depth of 109 yards, and the work of lining it with brickwork was being proceeded with. Skeleton iron rings are used to support the shaft during the process and it was necessary to remove these as the work of the bricking progressed.

At about 8 a.m. on the day mentioned, seven workmen, including a chargeman, were standing on a heavy scaffold, secured by bolts into the side of the shaft, engaged in the work of removing one of the iron rings. The chargeman, evidently having noticed some indication of danger, sent one of the men to the surface to call the master sinker, and, shortly after he had left, the scaffold gave way. Five of the men were hurled to the bottom of the shaft, and killed on the spot; but one of them, Patrick McCarthy, met with a less merciful death, being trapped by the legs between the heavy scaffold and the side of the shaft and partly buried by shale falling from the side, where he lingered in agony for over seven hours. Persistent efforts were made to rescue McCarthy from his perilous position.

Silkstone, Moore, Hosey, and Jones were among the first to descend the pit when it was known that an accident had happened. In response to McCarthy's cries for help, they tried to release him in spite of imminent danger from falling stones and bricks, but they were obliged to return to the surface for tools. Mr. Hodges, who had by this time reached the mine, immediately went down the pit and decided to build a temporary scaffold. Moore was given charge of this work and carried it out with admirable coolness and resource.

Mr. Pickering, His Majesty's Inspector of Mines, arrived on the scene just when this was completed, and accompanied by Mr. Hodges and Silkstone, Moore and Hosey, he entered the pit and reached the place where McCarthy was held a prisoner. In this descent Silkstone's head was severely injured by a falling stone, and Mr. Hodges and Hosey were also slightly injured. They found McCarthy still alive but the water was rising fast in the shaft and had reached his shoulders. It was evident that he would soon be drowned and that nothing could be done further to rescue him unless the water were lowered. Mr. Pickering at once sent all his fellow rescuers to the surface to enable a larger 'bowk' to be put on and more men to be sent down to bale the water. In the meantime Mr. Pickering resolutely stayed by McCarthy—now almost delirious with his sufferings—and supporting his head and his arms and breast, he administered such comfort as he could to the dying man. Realizing that McCarthy could not live until the water was baled out, Mr. Pickering decided that the only hope was immediate amputation of the legs, and at his request Mr. Hodges brought down two doctors and a priest, but McCarthy's terrible sufferings came to an end just as they reached him.

Mr. Pickering ran imminent risk of losing his life during the time that he stayed with McCarthy. Silkstone descended the pit no less than four times and did not desist until he had been severely injured. Mr. Hodges went down with three separate parties and displayed great bravery and skill in directing the work of the attempted rescue. Moore and Hosey also made three descents and showed great courage and presence of mind in face of danger, while Jones who organized the first rescue party was only prevented from continuing his brave endeavours by being seriously injured. (7.5.10)

An act of courageous perseverance

HENRY EVANS
WILLIAM RICHARD PROTHEROE
GOMER JONES

John Isaac, a repairer, was engaged in inspecting the return airway of the Bwlffa Dare Colliery, near Aberdare, South Wales, and while he was going under a closely timbered bridge in the airway for the purpose of examining it, the bridge collapsed without warning and covered Isaac with about 40 tons of debris. Isaac would have been instantly killed if the mass of fallen material had not been partly supported by the timber in the roadway. Isaac's assistant at once ran for help, and the under manager, Mr. Protheroe, and Mr. Gomer Jones, assistant examiner, were soon on the spot, followed by Mr. Henry Evans, the manager. They found Isaac lying about 7 feet below them under the debris with only his head exposed. The roof and sides were in a very dangerous state, and there was a continual risk from 'dribbling falls'.

In spite of the imminent danger, the three men set to work with great courage and perseverance. Digging carefully with their hands and sawing off the timber as they went, they were able to make a narrow tunnel to the place where Isaac lay. After working steadily and cautiously for over nine hours, they cleared a space large enough to admit of Isaac being drawn out, and finally with a united effort they managed to drag him into a place of safety. As soon as Isaac was released from his perilous position the whole fabric collapsed.

The work of rescue was carried out with excellent coolness and skill, and, thanks to the efforts of the three rescuers, Isaac escaped without serious injury. (6.4.10)

A porter's gallant act

William Piercey As an express train from Bournemouth to Waterloo was entering Lyndhurst Road Station, a little boy, about four years old, fell from the up platform on to the line, a few yards in front of the approaching train. William Piercey, a porter, who was on duty on the platform, hearing the child scream, and seeing him lying on the line, at once sprang on to the permanent way, seized him, and jumped with him in his arms into the six-foot way. Both the little boy and the rescuer were uninjured, though they had a narrow escape from death. (19.6.10)

A brave L.M.S. stationmaster

George Cole Cole was Stationmaster at Stockingford Station, on the Midland Railway. A little child between two and three years old had wandered, unnoticed, on to the level crossing at the station just as an express train from Birmingham to Leicester was approaching. George Cole's attention was called to the child's danger by the whistle of the engine, and, rushing across the level crossing, he caught hold of the child's shoulders and swung it out of danger. The train was travelling very fast, and was only about 25 yards away from the child when the stationmaster saw it, and he showed great promptness and courage in risking his life to save that of the child. (12.5.10)

Indian railwayman's bravery

Ram Lal Bauri Ram Lal Bauri was a shunting porter in the employment of the East Indian Railway Company. He was sitting upon the brake of the first of eight empty wagons, which were being shunted upon a colliery siding. As the wagons went round a curve he noticed three children playing upon the line. He jumped off, ran forward, and picked up two of the children, and was trying to get hold of the third when the wagon reached and killed her. The rescuer was knocked down but escaped injury. (14.3.10)

A brave action

HUGH THOMAS HUGHES Mr. Samuel Needham, of Man Farm, Castleton, Derbyshire, was driving his cattle from a field to his farm when a bull attacked him, knocked him down, and began to gore him. Mr. H. T. Hughes, a District Surveyor, who lives at Chapel-en-le-frith, and happened to be passing at the time, at once went to Mr. Needham's help, and managed to drive off the bull by beating it about the head and eyes with his cap. If it had not been for Mr. Hughes's timely and courageous action, in all probability Mr. Needham would have been killed or seriously injured. (30.8.10)

An engine-driver's presence of mind

JOHN EVANS Evans was driving a locomotive with a set of empty trucks on the North Eastern Railway near Amble, in Northumberland, when he saw a child in the four-foot way in front of the train, which was moving at a good pace. He shut off the steam, and, jumping off his engine, managed to reach the child and fall back with her in his arms clear of the rails before the engine reached the spot. His prompt action in the face of danger undoubtedly saved the child's life. (17.10.10)

One man saves three

WILLIAM THOMAS OXENHAM Mr. Oxenham, a skipman employed in the Simmer and Jack Mine at Germiston, in the Transvaal, went to the rescue of a white man and three Kaffirs who were overcome by fumes of poisonous gases. He descended a winze 60 feet deep and 3,500 feet from the surface, and was successful in bringing all in safety to the surface with the exception of one Kaffir. (15.3.10)

Brave act of a Canadian railwayman

ALBERT H. ADCOCK A train from Montreal was entering the train shed at St. John, New Brunswick, when a little girl about five years old ran across the track in front of the engine. The engine-driver applied his brakes, but could not stop the train in time, and the child would have been killed had not Adcock with great quickness and presence of mind jumped at once to the centre of the track, seized the child, and swung her clear of the track. The engine brushed Adcock's coat as he saved the child, showing how narrow was his own escape. (25.8.09)

Courageous rescue at Ardeer Explosives Factory

KENNETH McNAB McNab was an assistant foreman fitter in the factory of Messrs. Nobel's Explosives Company at Ardeer, in Ayrshire. A man named Richard Morgan was repairing an electric wire on the top floor of a four-story building when he was overcome by poisonous fumes given off by an overflow of acid on the ground-floor. The fumes, which were dense and suffocating, soon filled the building, and McNab and two other workmen went up an outside staircase, provided for cases of emergency, in search of Morgan; but, receiving no reply to their shouts, descended. McNab then, learning from other workmen that Morgan was on the roof, went up the staircase again, but without success. On hearing the sound of breaking glass and shouts from the top floor, McNab went up for the third time, and succeeded in entering the room where Morgan was. Crawling in on his hands and knees, he managed to grasp Morgan's hand and drag him out to the landing, where he obtained assistance in carrying him downstairs. McNab showed persistent bravery in face of danger, but his efforts were unfortunately unavailing, as Morgan succumbed after some hours to the effects of the poisonous fumes. (11.11.10)

A miner's gallantry on the Gold Coast

WILLIAM JOHN SOPER   Owing to a fire which occurred in the Côte d'Or Mine at Obuassi, Gold Coast, a European named Penrose and eight natives lost their lives. The fire broke out about 1,500 feet from the entrance of one of the levels by which the workings were approached. Those who tried to put it out were overcome by the fumes. W. J. Soper, a miner, went in with two natives, and, crawling along through foul air which extinguished their candles, found three unconscious natives, all of whom they saved alive. Soper dragged one back to a place where the air was pure; the two natives brought another. Soper returned and fetched a third, and then was overpowered himself. He returned again, however, in company of a native, who lost his life, and followed by a European they recovered Penrose's body. Soper later made three more attempts to enter the mine and desisted only when he could no longer face the gas. (13.9.10)

An accident in a well

FRANK SMITH   John Wapplington and another labourer,
JOHN WAPPLINGTON   named Albert Templeman, were engaged in sinking a well at East Markham, in Nottinghamshire, and had fired a shot in order to blast the rock at the bottom. After an interval, during which they tested the air with a lighted lamp and found no gas, Templeman went down the well and struck the rock with a crowbar. Immediately afterwards he cried out that he was feeling dizzy, and asked Wapplington to lower a ladder and rope. He did not wait to fasten a rope round himself, but tried to mount the ladder, and fell back when he was half-way up. Wapplington, calling for help, went down to Templeman's assistance; but he found that he could not lift him, and came up in a dazed condition. After a rest of a quarter of an hour, he bravely made another attempt; but called out that he could

not attach the rope to Templeman, as he was overcome by the gas. He managed, however, to reach the top before becoming unconscious. Frank Smith, foreman, then came to the spot with other men, and, fastening the rope round his body, went down the well, and succeeded in getting the rope round Templeman, by which he was hauled up. Smith reached the surface in a state of collapse, though he soon recovered. Templeman was found to be dead. (30.9.10)

Rescue from colliery roof-fall

WILLIAM BIRCH Charles Marshall and William Birch were engaged at the Coleorton Mine, near Ashby-de-la-Zouch, on repairing work, when a fall took place. Birch quickly extricated himself and set about releasing Marshall. Whilst he was so engaged another fall took place, covering the two men nearly up to the armpits. Again Birch extricated himself, but Marshall, who was evidently pinned by some large stone or stones, could not do so, and again Birch endeavoured to release him at imminent risk to himself, as another fall might have taken place at any moment. He had nearly released Marshall when a third fall occurred, completely covering Marshall and partly pinning Birch by the legs. Birch called another workman (Witham), who was on his way from the coal face, and they both set about releasing Marshall, but a fourth fall taking place, Witham went for further help, whilst Birch still endeavoured to release Marshall. Witham and others returned about five minutes later, and, after about half an hour, Marshall was extricated dead. (14.12.10)

A rescue from an ale-vat

WILLIAM MOIR
HENRY MORLEY HAWKINS

A workman at the Romford Brewery descended a large ale-vat for the purpose of cleaning out the spent hops, and while so engaged was overcome by the carbonic acid gas collected at the bottom. William Moir, a foreman cooper, though a heavily built man, went down through the manhole, which was only 18 inches square, in order to try to bring the man up. He also was overcome by the gas, and was with great difficulty drawn out by a rope. Thereupon Hawkins, a clerk employed at the brewery, volunteered to go to the assistance of the workman, although he had never been accustomed to work in vats. The manhole was enlarged before his descent, and he succeeded in getting a rope round the workman before himself succumbing to the fumes. Both Moir and Hawkins displayed conspicuous courage and presence of mind, although their attempts to save the workman's life were unavailing. (8.2.11)

Brave attempt at rescue in Southern Rhodesia

Frederick Holcombe Edgelow

Two natives descended a shaft of the Psyche Mine, in Southern Rhodesia, and as no sign was given to haul up the bucket, the natives on the surface concluded that something was wrong below. As Mr. Walsh, the miner in charge, was absent, they called to Mr. Edgelow, a mining prospector, who happened to be staying at the camp. He looked down the shaft, which was 110 feet deep, and saw the two natives lying unconscious. Although he had little experience of mines, and had never been down lower than 40 feet, he immediately descended the shaft with a native; but, when they encountered gas, the native lost his presence of mind, and gave the signal to draw up. On reaching the surface Mr. Edgelow tied a wet towel round his face, and, lashing himself to a rope, descended by himself. He tried to lift one of the natives into the bucket, but before he succeeded in doing so, he felt the effects of the gas and was only just able to give the signal to draw up. He was raised to the surface unconscious, and, on being revived, sent a note to Mr. Walsh, and again prepared to descend. Mr. Edgelow made two more descents with a rope provided with a running loop, and by this means he succeeded in bringing both the natives to the surface, although life in them was found to be extinct. (30.9.10)

Accident in a Yorkshire mine

James Cannon
George Handle Silkstone
PERCY ASQUITH
JOSEPH ARTIS
HERBERT PICKERSGILL

A shaft was being sunk at the Water Haigh Colliery at Oulton, near Leeds. A depth of 255 yards had been reached and the shaft had been lined to a depth of 240 yards with brickwork, the end of which rested on a stout oak crib. Below this and suspended from the crib were iron rings securing the unbricked sides of the shaft. On the day of the accident ten men were at work on or about a scaffold near the bottom of the shaft, when a mass of shale fell out of the seam, the timbering collapsed, and the rings broke away. The chargeman, James Cannon, noticed shale falling, and with great presence of mind and promptitude shouted to all to make for the centre; he also signalled for means of ascent to be lowered. He and five others jumped into the centre and escaped; the other four were caught, either by earth or by rings of timber, one being killed on the spot, two trapped and seriously injured, and the fourth seriously injured but not trapped. Cannon went to the surface with the uninjured men and at once came back with Artis and others, to take up the work of rescue. The rescue operations were protracted, the woodwork of the stout oak crib having to be sawn through before the men who were trapped could be liberated, and, as shale and other material kept falling down the shaft, the lives of all the rescuers were in danger. Cannon was engaged in the work of rescue for six hours and Silkstone for about half an hour. Artis, after assisting for two hours, was struck by a piece of shale and had to return to the surface. Asquith and Pickersgill were also down the shaft for a long time and risked their lives, the former being hurt by debris.

Pickersgill had the misfortune to lose his life in a subsequent accident. The presentation of his medal was made to his widow.

(19.11.10)

A mine manager's heroism

CHARLES LAWSON   A fall of stone occurred at the Lyons colliery, Hotton-le-Hole, burying a miner named Shears and striking the under-manager, Mr. Lawson, who was fortunately knocked clear of the main body of the debris. Mr. Lawson found that Shears was beneath a large mass of stone, which was held up to some extent by displaced timber and rubbish, but which also rested in part on a prop which pinned down his foot. He obtained help and freed Shears's head, but a larger fall appeared imminent, and, to prevent further injury to Shears if a fall should occur, so much material had to be placed round him to serve as supports that the party could hardly get room to work. On three occasions the rescuers had to retreat owing to fresh falls, which considerably increased the danger in which they worked. All the time Shears was held fast, and the prop holding him down could not be sawn through without injuring him. Finally, after many attempts, Lawson managed to creep through to Shears's side, where he remained till he had chipped away enough of the stone to enable Shears to be liberated, nine hours after the fall. (24.3.11)

Explosion at Hulton Colliery

ALFRED JOSEPH TONGE
JAMES HENRY POLLEY
JAMES MOSS
JOHN HILTON
WILLIAM MARKLAND
JOHN HARDMAN
ROBERT ROBERTS
JOHN HERRING
JAMES HARTLEY
LLEWELYN WILLIAMS

A terrible explosion occurred at the No. 3 Bank Pit at the Hulton Colliery, near Atherton, by which a portion of the casting of the upcast shaft was wrecked. Various miners were shut off from escape by the fall of earth, and suffered from the effects of poisonous gas. Among the many who used their utmost endeavours to rescue their fellow workmen in circumstances of great danger, the men here mentioned showed conspicuous courage. (21.12.10)

Attempted rescue in fire-damp

WALTER CULLEN
THOMAS MACFARLANE

Mr. Robert Edgar, the under-manager of the Loanend Colliery, Cambuslang, went up a highly inclined road to tear down a screen so as to disperse an accumulation of fire-damp, and was overcome suddenly by fire-damp. Macfarlane at once went to his assistance, but was in turn overcome and rolled down the road. Cullen, a man of 60, then made two attempts to rescue the under-manager, and on both occasions was helped back by Macfarlane, who had partly recovered. The under-manager's body was not recovered until three and a half hours afterwards. (21.4.11)

An engine-driver's devotion

William McFall

A passenger train from Ottawa was approaching North Wakefield on the Canadian Pacific line when the driver, McFall, suddenly perceived a gap in the track between 50 and 100 feet wide and over 20 feet deep, caused by thaws and rain. The fireman jumped off the engine, but McFall put on the emergency brakes and sticking to his engine managed to bring the train to a standstill. The engine, however, fell into the gap, and McFall received terrible injuries, from which he died. There were forty passengers in the train, and had it not been for McFall's heroic devotion to his duty serious loss of life would probably have occurred. Mrs. McFall received the medal posthumously awarded to her gallant husband. (14.4.11)

A stationmaster's bravery

CHARLES SAMUEL VASSAR CUDBIRD

As the 9.30 train from Epping was about to enter the station at George Lane, Miss Tremlett accidentally fell on the line about 70 yards in front of the train, which usually enters the station at 30 or 40 miles an hour. Mr. Cudbird, the stationmaster, jumped down and pulled her clear on to the 6-foot way. Had not the driver seen what was happening and applied the brakes, both would certainly have been cut to pieces, and the risk involved in Mr. Cudbird's action was very great. (30.6.11)

Rescue from a sump-hole

WILLIAM BRANDON
HERBERT CARTER

Alfred Butterfield, a workman employed by the Luton Corporation, descended a sump-hole at the Luton Sewage Farm, and was overcome by foul gas which had accumulated there. William Brandon immediately went to his rescue and descended the hole, but was also overcome by the gas. In spite of the serious danger disclosed by the previous attempt at rescue, Herbert Carter decided to make the descent, and, placing a handkerchief over his mouth, was lowered by two ropes into the hole. There he found that Butterfield was dead and Brandon was unconscious. He placed a rope round Brandon, and they were both drawn to the surface. Carter then descended again, and attached a rope to the body of Butterfield. (23.6.11)

Colliery explosion at Northop

GEORGE JONES A serious explosion, causing the loss of two lives,
HUGH ROBERTS occurred at the Main Coal Colliery, Northop, near Flint, owing to the ignition of fire-damp by a shot fired to bring down coal. Jones, the fireman in charge at the time of the explosion, was severely injured; but, although a fire was known to be burning in the mine, he returned twice to the workings in search of one of the men under his charge who was believed to be missing. On the second occasion Jones was accompanied by Roberts, a timberman, who subsequently went again into the mine in order to extinguish the fire. (5.8.10)

A lift accident

THOMAS BARKER A bobbin carrier named Whitehead, employed at the Hawk Cotton-spinning Factory, Shaw, Lancashire, slipped while entering the hoist cage on the third floor and, clutching the starting chain, set the hoist in motion. Whitehead fell forward, and, the doors of the hoist having closed automatically, he became tightly wedged between the top of the doorway and the cage-floor. Barker, a spinner, seeing what had happened, rushed to Whitehead's assistance, but found he could neither open nor shut the hoist doors. Squeezing through the small opening between the doors, Barker stood on a very narrow ledge where he ran a grave risk of falling down the open hoist-well, a depth at this landing of 60 feet. He managed to get hold of the chains, and by exercise of all his strength to lower the hoist cage until, with the aid of other helpers, Whitehead could be lifted away. Whitehead afterwards succumbed to the serious injuries he had sustained. (3.7.11)

A posthumous award

GEORGE GROVES A workman named Berry was employed at the Standard Ammonia Company's Works, at East Greenwich, in cleaning an ammonia tower, which is a cylindrical iron vessel about 30 feet high and 5 feet in diameter, when he was overcome by an inrush of poisonous gas, due to an unsuspected defect in the plant. He fell unconscious to the bottom of the tower, and Groves immediately went to his rescue. He was lowered into the tower, and succeeded in reaching Berry, but, before the men could be raised to the top of the tower, Groves was himself overcome, and both fell back into the poisonous atmosphere and lost their lives. Mrs. Groves received the medal posthumously awarded to her gallant husband. (2.11.11)

Accident in a disused working

JAMES FREDERICK BOOTH   James F. Booth, Surveyor at the Felling Colliery, Durham, accompanied by two men named George Padbury and William Robson, was engaged in the exploration of some disused workings. The workings were not ventilated, and, with a view to obtaining experience in the practice of rescue apparatus under actual mining conditions, it was arranged that the men should wear the Draeger breathing-apparatus. Owing, it is supposed, to some defect in the supply of oxygen, Robson became affected by foul air about two hours after entering the workings, and became unconscious. Padbury, who had gone for assistance, leaving Robson under Booth's care, was also overcome. Booth returned to the surface, obtained a fresh supply of oxygen, and went alone to the rescue of his companions. He was joined after a time by the remainder of the Rescue Brigade belonging to the Colliery; but it was not until additional assistance had been obtained from Elswick that Padbury and Robson could be removed to a place of safety. Both were found to be dead.

(31.10.11)

Explosion in a washer-tank

George Henry Rhodes
SIDNEY DICKSON
HERBERT WOOD

Rhodes was working in an underground washer-tank belonging to the Sheffield Gas Company, at Effingham Street, Sheffield, with two men named Jenkinson and Foster, when a serious explosion of gas took place. As a result, Foster was severely burned and imprisoned at the far end of the tank, access to which was blocked by the explosion. Having given the alarm, Rhodes returned through the underground passage to the tank, risking the danger of a further explosion from escaping gas, and managed to reach Foster, whose cries he heard. He could not, however, release him until Dickson and Wood came to his assistance. These two men were not working in the tank, but heard Foster's cries, and immediately went to his assistance without knowing that Rhodes had preceded them. They got into the underground passage by another entrance, and their help enabled Rhodes to release Foster. (26.6.11)

Explosion in a factory at Cliffe

Herbert Dobinson A serious explosion took place at an Explosives Factory belonging to Messrs. Curtis & Harvey, Ltd., at Cliffe, in the county of Kent, resulting in the death of three men and serious injury to three others. The explosion took place in one of the nitro-glycerine washing and filtering houses a few minutes after Dobinson had left the building. He was knocked down by the force of the explosion, but heard a fellow workman named J. Wordley call for help. Wordley had been blown by the explosion under a gun-cotton truck, which had caught fire, and was quite unable to do anything to free himself. Dobinson returned to the shed, ran in at the imminent risk of being killed by a further explosion, and released Wordley from his perilous position. (26.7.11)

Gallant rescue at Camborne

Albert Opie
WILLIAM KEMP
Three men employed at the East Pool and Agar United Mines at Camborne were descending to their work and were accidentally lowered into an accumulation of water, which was known to exist, but had greatly increased during the previous night, without the knowledge of the management. Two of the men, who were on the outside of the skip, jumped off; but the man who was inside was drowned. One of the two survivors caught hold of a ladder and managed to climb up the shaft to safety, while the other held on to an air-pipe, but was afraid to jump across the intervening space to the ladder. On the alarm being given, Opie immediately came down the shaft to try to get this man out; but failed to reach him. Accompanied by Kemp, he then descended another shaft and travelled along a cross cut to the shaft where the man was hanging. This cross cut was nearly filled with water, which was constantly rising, and at one point actually touched the roof. Opie, at the risk of his life, plunged under the water, came up on the other side, and made his way to the shaft where the man was hanging. He succeeded in bringing him out by dragging him through the water in the cross cut. Kemp did not go under water, but stayed in a position of considerable danger to maintain a light while the man was being brought out. (26.4.11)

Fire in Cannock Chase Mine

Henry Merritt
Thomas Stokes
An underground fire broke out in the intake airway of the No. 9 Cannock Chase Colliery, which rendered necessary the withdrawal of all the workmen. Most of the men, including Merritt and Stokes, reached the shaft

safely, but it was found that five were still in the pit. Merritt went with Stokes to their rescue, and penetrated 800 yards along the return airway, in spite of the smoke, which was rapidly increasing in density, and found the men. One of them got out by holding on to Merritt, but the other four were suffocated, and Stokes also lost his life. Merritt did not at first discover that the other men had not followed him, and when he became aware of this he made two further attempts to reach them, but was finally driven back by the smoke, and reached the surface in an exhausted condition. Mrs. Stokes received the medal posthumously awarded to her gallant husband. (14.12.11)

Rescues from a flooded mine

John Mitchell
James Green

Water in large quantities had broken into the Bamfurlong Mine, near Wigan, and by a heavy fall of earth a party of thirteen was cut off from safety. Mitchell explored the roads in order to find a way of reaching these men, though his life was exposed to constant danger in consequence of the continued rise of the water. Finally he succeeded in boring a passage through the fall, thereby rescuing all the men who had been cut off. In another part of the workings Green, who had heard of the inundation, went down the dip to warn the men under his charge, although he met the water already rushing down the roads. In doing so, he acted at grave risk to his life, and it was two hours before he was out of danger. He extricated all his men.

James Green subsequently died, and the medal was given to his widow. (23.12.11)

A gallant workman in S. Africa

ROBERT GREENLEES

Greenlees, an employee of the British South Africa Explosives Works, Modderfontein, S. Africa, was engaged, along with a fellow workman named Greig, in destroying bags of collodian cotton when one of the bags ignited and both men were severely burnt. Greig's clothes had caught fire and he was helpless from the shock. Greenlees, in spite of the fact that he was himself suffering from severe pain, went to Greig's assistance and extinguished the flames in time to save his life for the moment, though he subsequently succumbed. (27.2.11)

A brave attempt at rescue

GEORGE EDWARDS

At the Bryncethin Colliery, near Bridgend, a road was being driven in order to release an accumulation of gas, which, in a sudden outburst, overwhelmed the manager and three men. Edwards was summoned from his home, and with a rope tied round his legs tried to reach the unconscious men. He was overpowered by gas, and had to be dragged out. On recovering he made further attempts and at last succeeded in attaching a rope to the bodies of two of the men, who were drawn up, but too late to save their lives. (22.7.11)

South Africa: attempted rescue of two natives

JAMES A. WRIGHT At the Rand Clip Mine, Bocksburg, S. Africa, a bailing-tank was accidentally lowered too far down a shaft. It broke the slings carrying a sinking pump, which fell into the water at the bottom of the shaft, and pinned two natives under water. Wright made repeated efforts to extricate them by diving. The water, though only $4\frac{1}{2}$ feet deep, was rising, and there was great danger that the pump and other wreckage would be shifted by Wright's attempts to pull out the natives, and would pin him down under water. He was unsuccessful in his attempted rescue, but the action showed a high degree of courage. (25.4.11)

A porter's presence of mind

DAVID WHEAL Wheal, a gate porter at St. Margaret's station on the Great Eastern Railway, had been collecting tickets, and was waiting near the gates at the level-crossing for a train to pass. He knew that a train was approaching from the other direction, and, after the last vehicle of the first train had passed, he saw an old lady, with her head bowed down, stepping in front of the oncoming train. He rushed forward and succeeded in forcing her back clear of the rails just as the locomotive was upon her. (15.5.12)

A workman's courage

RICHARD BROOKES A workman named Thomas Rogers was repairing the spouting of a building at a height of 40 feet from the ground at the brewery of Messrs. Charrington & Co., Burton-on-Trent, when without warning the ladder on which he was standing broke, and he fell head foremost. Brookes, a fitter in the employment of Messrs. Charrington, rushed forward with outstretched arms and caught him as he fell, thereby saving Rogers's life at considerable risk to his own. His action was rendered more difficult and dangerous by his having to evade the portion of the ladder to which Rogers continued to cling as he fell. (8.2.12)

Explosion at Markham Colliery, Tredegar

WILLIAM DOWNING WOOLEY
ARTHUR THOMAS WINBORN
JAMES JOSEPH LEACH
LLEWELYN HOWELLS

At one of the pits at the Markham Colliery, Tredegar, an explosion of fire-damp resulted in the death of five men. At the time of the explosion two men were down the shaft, which was then full of after-damp. A rescue party was organized, consisting of the men above mentioned, who descended the shaft, and after an hour's work reached the pump lodge room at a depth of 350 yards from the surface, where they found a man named Snashall, who was badly burnt. After some difficulty they managed to get Snashall into the bucket, in which he was safely raised to the surface. All the rescuers were equipped with breathing-apparatus, but Mr. Wooley had not previously worn it. (18.5.12)

Men's gallantry in a melting-furnace

LLEWELYN INCE
ARTHUR DARBY
SHADRACH SPEKE
SHADRACH JACKSON

On the 24th July 1912, a man named Heald descended into a melting-furnace 30 feet high at the Darlaston Green Furnaces in order to adjust a piece of scrap iron under which some coke had to be placed. Heald descended into the furnace by a chain, and was almost immediately overcome by noxious gas which had collected there owing to damp. A man standing at the top at once gave the alarm, and Shadrach Jackson and Ince came to his assistance. Jackson without hesitation slid down the chain, and a rope was thrown to him, which he tied round Heald, who was then pulled up, Jackson climbing up the chain after him. As Jackson, however, reached the door through which Heald was being pulled, he too was overcome by the gas and fell back to the bottom of the furnace. Ince then descended and placed a rope round Jackson's body, but unfortunately it slipped off before the man could be pulled out, though Ince, feeling that he was being overcome by the gas, climbed up the chain and escaped. On recovering Ince went down a second time, once more tied the rope round Jackson, but again failed to bring him to the surface, though he himself escaped by a ladder which had been brought. Arthur Darby then went down the ladder with a rope, which was attached to Jackson's belt, but unfortunately the belt gave way. On Darby coming out Speke went down, and, the rope having been more securely tied round Jackson's body, he was extricated, though unhappily it was found on reaching the surface that he was dead. The medal awarded to Shadrach Jackson was presented to his widow. (24.7.12)

Rescue from a gas-filled manhole

ERNEST THACKERAY   A workman named Lightowler, employed by the Frodingham Iron & Steel Co., Ltd., was overcome by gas in a manhole at the company's blast furnace at Scunthorpe. After several ineffectual attempts had been made to rescue the unfortunate man, Thackeray, a fellow workman, volunteered, and, tying a handkerchief over his mouth, entered the manhole and succeeded in raising Lightowler sufficiently for other workmen outside to get him out, but it was too late to restore him. Thackeray himself was overcome by the gas and did not recover entire consciousness until the following morning. (10.8.12)

Brave rescues from a gas flue

Harry Parsons
ERNEST CANNELL
THOMAS EVANS
JOHN ROBINSON
WILLIAM ACKRED
GEORGE BAGNALL

A gas flue, which is a thousand yards long and 6 feet in diameter, was in process of being cleaned at the Barrow Hematite Steel Company's works when a workman engaged in the operation entered the tube contrary to orders to recover a broken rake. He was immediately overcome by the gas, as were also two fellow workmen, William Ackred and George Bagnall, who went to his assistance. Harry Parsons twice entered the flue at great risk to his life, and, with the help of Ernest Cannell, Thomas Evans, and John Robinson, succeeded in bringing out the three men, who unfortunately were found to be dead. The Edward medals of the Second Class awarded to William Ackred and George Bagnall were presented to their widows. (4.8.12)

A railway-station incident

WALTER CHARLES SIMMONS   As an express passenger train was entering Bournemouth Station, a woman jumped from the platform in front of the engine. The driver promptly applied the brakes and sounded the whistle; but was unable to stop the train until the engine had passed the spot where the woman jumped down. Simmons's attention was attracted by the whistle when the engine was only about 12 yards away, and, without an instant's hesitation, he jumped off the platform on to the permanent way, and succeeded in lifting the woman clear of the rails and holding her against another train, which was stationary on an adjoining line, neither of them sustaining injury. There is no doubt whatever that the rescue was effected by Simmons at the risk of his life, and any delay or hesitation would, in all probability, have resulted in fatal consequences. (20.8.12)

Brave action of two miners

HENRY SAUNDERS
ALEXANDER GRIFFITHS

Thomas Richards and a man named Jones were repairing an air road by taking down a low portion of the roof, known to miners as a bridge. The bridge was about 10 feet long and nearly 12 feet thick, and at one end of it the road below was nearly blocked by fallen debris. In order to do his work, Richards made a small hole in the debris, and went through it; but, as he was returning, a piece fell and pinned his feet in the hole. His mate sent for the overman, Henry Saunders. Alexander Griffiths followed, and others were soon on the spot. Griffiths and Saunders went under the bridge and tried to take away the stone that was holding Richards; but a further fall of about 5 tramloads of debris completely buried him, and Griffiths and Saunders narrowly escaped the fall. Notwithstanding this indication of danger, the two men bravely went again under the bridge, working one behind the other in the small space available. Before they could get Richards out, signs of further movement of stone warned them to retreat, and the whole bridge, weighing about 20 tons, fell in. All present then started to work down through the fall to Richards, who was 9 feet away, and eventually they got him out alive. (30.9.12)

A gallant action

ALBERT BENSTEAD

Charles Jex was cleaning the roof over the smelting furnaces at Messrs. Bolckow, Vaughan & Company's steelworks, and, while he was making his way along an iron beam 32 feet from the ground and immediately above a 50-ton ladle, which was being filled with molten metal, a column of flame and smoke shot up from the ladle to a height of 30 or 40 feet. The flames enveloped Jex, burning him so badly that he was rendered helpless and barely able to retain his foothold on the beam. Had he slipped, he would have fallen into the ladle. Benstead was standing near the foot of an iron ladder, 25 feet long, leading to the beam, and immediately climbed up and took hold of Jex, whose hands were so badly burnt that he could not assist himself in descending the ladder. Benstead placed him across his back and carried him down to the floor, the iron ladder being so hot that he had to use his cap to take hold of it and so steady himself as he came down. There is no doubt that Benstead saved Jex from falling into the ladle, and that he ran a very serious risk of falling in himself. (14.1.13)

A fallen-in sewer trench

ROBERT WARD
JAMES JONES

Two workmen, named John Lloyd and Morris Edwards, were employed in excavating a deep sewer trench at Old Colwyn, when the sides of the trench suddenly gave way. There was a heavy fall of earth and timbering, and both men were buried at the bottom. Robert Ward and James Jones promptly set to work to rescue them. The trench was 14 feet deep, and the two men had been working separate sections 7 feet long by $3\frac{1}{2}$ wide. Soil and timber fell in to the depth of about 4 feet, and Ward and Jones had to begin their work of rescue at a depth of about 10 feet. They had to remove practically all the fallen material in order to reach the two men. The soil was sand and gravel, and the danger of working was largely increased by the presence of water at the bottom, and, as they dug farther down, the risk increased. They persisted in their efforts for $3\frac{1}{4}$ hours, and, though John Lloyd was dead when they reached his body, they succeeded in saving the life of Morris Edwards. The two men ran a great risk of being buried themselves by a further fall of earth and timber. (21.11.12)

Rescue from an oil tank

KENNETH BURTON
GURZEI AHOM

A native foreman, named Rulia, employed by the Assam Oil Company at Digboi, entered an oil tank 10 feet deep and containing 4 feet of oil. He was overcome by oil fumes, whereupon one of his workmen, named Gurzei Ahom, who had tried to dissuade him from entering the tank and was aware of the danger, went to his assistance and was himself overcome. Another workman gave the alarm to Mr. Kenneth Burton, Assistant Manager in charge of the tank, who was in his office some 70 yards away. Mr. Burton immediately obtained a rope, and, climbing into the tank, fastened it around Gurzei Ahom and succeeded in pulling him out. Mr. Burton then entered the tank again, and, attaching the rope to Rulia, hauled him to the top of the tank; but Mr. Burton was overcome and collapsed, and Rulia fell back into the oil. The tank was then emptied, but it was too late to save Rulia's life. (12.12.11)

A railway guard's bravery

ALBERT EDWARD
STROUD

Stroud, a guard on the East Indian Railway, was employed on special duty at Bukhtiarpur station, and was engaged in controlling a large crowd of pilgrims. Just as a passenger train was entering the station, an elderly Indian woman jumped on to the line, intending to cross. Stroud at once jumped after her, and, though she had fallen, succeeded in dragging her out of the way of the train. (11.7.12)

Doncaster colliery explosion

G. Fisher
H. Hulley
J. E. Chambers
W. H. Prince
Herbert Williamson

Two disastrous explosions had occurred in the south workings of the Cadeby Main Colliery, near Doncaster, originating at the coal face and spreading along the roads for distances of nearly half a mile.

H. Hulley and G. Fisher, colliery deputies, were among the first to explore the affected districts after each of the explosions. They assisted in attending to and removing the injured, and also in building stoppings to shut off the dangerous areas, in spite of the constant risk of further explosions and falls. Altogether Fisher was in the pit for about 12 hours and Hulley even longer, and, as both men were experienced pitmen, they were well aware of the imminent risk to their lives that they ran during the whole time. Their great courage and tenacity render their conduct conspicuous even among the many brave actions performed in connexion with the disaster.

J. E. Chambers, manager of the Cortonwood Colliery, went down into the pit after the second explosion, immediately explored one of the roads near the point of origin alone, and was the probable means of saving two lives; he afterwards went through the district to assist in withdrawing all men from the workings.

W. H. Prince, a colliery contractor, helped to organize rescue parties and assisted in saving life by the use of apparatus. With great presence of mind, and at much risk to himself, he personally extinguished a fire which occurred while he was so engaged, and afterwards he helped to build the stoppings.

Herbert Williamson, mechanical engineer, superintended the rescue work in some of the roads after the first explosion. A fall caused by the second explosion prevented him from making any progress for a time; but he got together a body of men to clear a way over it, and then continued the work of rescue. He also returned to the affected roads by himself after the third explosion.

Sergeant Winch, Instructor at the Wath Rescue Station, went with his brigade into the workings after the first explosion to help in the rescue work; he was knocked down by the second explosion, but proceeded inwards and assisted in saving lives by the use of his apparatus. He displayed great coolness in dealing with a fire, which broke out in one of the roads, and in keeping his men together to continue the work.

All these men displayed remarkable courage, and set a splendid example in the face of great risk. (9.7.12)

Attempted rescue from a gas-bound mine

THOMAS CHATTERTON
ALBERT SCHOFIELD

Two men named James English and Alfred Sykes lost their lives from poisoning by noxious gases in some old workings at the Lodge Mill Colliery, Lepton, Huddersfield, which had been gas-bound for a fortnight. They had penetrated into the workings in order to continue the recovery of some rails; and after about half an hour, Chatterton and Schofield, who were there to load up the rails, became alarmed at their absence, and went in search of them. They had to go on hands and knees in the dark, in a low road only 3 feet high, through a foul atmosphere. Chatterton succeeded in getting within call of Sykes, and Schofield succeeded in going a distance of 70 yards before becoming unconscious. Failing to reach Sykes, Chatterton managed with difficulty to make his way back, and to telephone for assistance, while Schofield remained unconscious in the workings till his subsequent rescue. There is no doubt that both men ran very serious risk to their own lives in attempting to rescue Sykes and English. (28.1.13)

A Yorkshire miner's gallantry

THOMAS THOMPSON

A heavy fall of roof occurred in a gateway at the Swinton Common Colliery, Yorkshire, shutting off the face of the coal. There were five men working at the face; one of them, owing to injuries, was unable to escape. The work of rescue was begun at once and, chiefly owing to the efforts of Thomas Thompson, a collier employed at the mine, who worked almost without cessation for ten hours in removing the debris, the man was extricated. The roof under which Thompson worked was in a very dangerous condition, and three falls of stone occurred while the work was in progress. There is no doubt that Thompson ran prolonged and serious risk to his own life in persevering till the rescue was effected. (3.4.13)

A Derbyshire pit accident

ALBERT HENRY COOPER
ARTHUR BERNARD HEWITT
GEORGE THOMPSON

The collapse of a steel girder in the Markham No. 2 Colliery, Staveley, Derbyshire, caused a fall of the roof. Mr. Cooper, the under-manager of the mine, at once took steps to repair the damage, but while the debris was being removed in tubs, a second fall occurred without warning and buried three men engaged in the work of removal. Though fragments of the roof were still falling, Mr. Cooper dashed over the heap of debris and, assisted later on by Mr. Hewitt, the manager, he succeeded in rescuing two of the men. They then proceeded to search for the third man and discovered him completely buried. George Thompson, a workman employed at the mine, came to help, and the three worked for about fifty minutes in order to extricate the unfortunate man. They had all but succeeded when a further heavy fall took place, killing him outright. Notwithstanding the risk of further falls, the work of rescue was continued for four hours, till the dead body was reached. (8.1.13)

A Cumberland miner's self-sacrifice

JOHN CAIRNS — Shortly after a number of men had descended the pit-shaft to their work, an inrush of water from old workings occurred at the Townhead Iron Ore Mine, Egremont, Cumberland. As soon as the alarm was raised all men made for the shaft bottom, with the exception of James Ward, who had gone alone to his usual working-place some distance from the others. Cairns was rushing to the shaft to escape, when he recollected that Ward, who was working alone, would be unaware of the danger till too late. He promptly turned back to find Ward and hurry him out of the working. By the time he had reached him the water had risen and the two men found it impossible to get back to the shaft. Luckily, they reached a stone drift above the water-level which happened to be connected with the surface by a 6-inch bore-hole. Through this bore-hole communications were made to them from above and food was sent down. They remained imprisoned for $5\frac{1}{2}$ days until they were rescued after the mine had been cleared of water.

There is no doubt that Cairns imperilled his own life by his plucky action in going back into the mine to give warning to Ward. (13.3.13)

Double attempted rescue

THOMAS WAGSTAFF
ALLAN HOLLIDAY

At the Burton Brewery Company's Works, Burton-on-Trent, a number of men were lime-washing the ceiling of a hop-press room. On the wall, about 2 or 3 feet above the scaffolding on which the men were standing, a shaft was running, driving two cog-wheels. One of the men, named Arbon, was leaning over the shaft when he was suddenly caught and dragged into the machinery. Holliday, who was standing near, at once seized hold of him and became entangled in the gear-wheels himself. The clothes of both men were torn from them, and they were in imminent peril. With great presence of mind Wagstaff seized hold of Holliday, succeeding himself only with difficulty in keeping clear of the cog-wheels. Holliday escaped with very serious injuries, but Arbon unfortunately lost his life. There can be no doubt that by their plucky action both Holliday and Wagstaff incurred the gravest risk to their own lives. (20.2.13)

A foreman's pluck

THOMAS AITKEN Mr. George Lowthian, Consulting Engineer to the Tilehurst, Pangbourne and District Water Company, Ltd., descended a well at the pumping-station at Tilehurst to examine a set of pumps while they were working, accompanied by Aitken, the foreman. The engineer was standing on a staging nearly in the centre of the well, about 80 feet below the surface, when a plank suddenly broke, and he fell about 34 feet. He crashed through an old pump staging, shattering his left foot and ankle, but managed to get hold of an iron bar about 4 feet below the old staging and 6 feet above water. Aitken, who had almost crossed the plank when it broke, caught hold of a beam and crawled round the pump to a ladder. He was in darkness, for the light had fallen with the engineer, but he groped his way down the slippery ladder to the second staging. He obtained a light, and found the engineer clinging to the girder below the staging. He reached him, and, with great difficulty, as the engineer weighed 14 stone and the whole place was very slippery, succeeded in dragging him to the top of the girder and thence to a place of safety on a ledge of brickwork. Then, ascending to the surface, he arranged for tackle to be let down into the well, and going down again, managed to bring the man safely to the top. The engineer's strength was nearly exhausted when Aitken reached him, and he undoubtedly owes his life to Aitken's prompt and courageous action. (3.10.12)

Gas in a barge's hold

ALLAN MURDOCH On the 10th May the barge *Arctic*, belonging to the Liverpool Grain Storage and Transit Company, was taken alongside the S.S. *Monarch*, in the Harrington Dock, Liverpool, to transfer some damaged corn from the ship to the barge. On the 12th May the captain of the barge and the mate went on board and removed several of the hatch-covers to put in more grain. The mate, noticing a dead rat lying in the hatch, went down, but collapsed on reaching the bottom. Murdoch, seeing that something was wrong through the conduct of the captain, who ran up and down the deck calling for help, rushed on board and descended the hold, accompanied by William Brown, the mate of another vessel. On reaching the bottom of the ladder, 12 feet long, both Brown and Murdoch were affected by the gas. Murdoch climbed out again, but Brown, in spite of his endeavours, failed to do so. In the meantime other men had arrived on board the barge, and Murdoch, with a life-line attached to him, went down again into the hatch. He succeeded in bringing out the mate (Weedell), who was 6 feet away from the bottom of the ladder. He went down a second time, and managed to attach the rope to

Brown, but then himself collapsed, and the two men were drawn out together. Weedell's life was saved; but Brown unfortunately succumbed to the effects of the gas. It is clear that Murdoch ran a very serious risk to his own life in descending twice into the hold, after being overcome by the gas in his first descent, and that his gallant action in all probability saved the mate from death. (10.5.13)

A Glamorganshire pit mechanic's bravery

THOMAS THOMAS   Walling was in progress in a shaft, over 500 yards deep and 20 feet wide, in the Llewelyn Sinking Pit, belonging to the Britannic Merthyr Coal Company, Ltd., Gilfach Goch, Glamorganshire. Seven men were working on a stage suspended by ropes, about 10 yards from the bottom of the shaft, when a heavy fall occurred, smashing the stage and precipitating the seven men to the bottom of the shaft. As the winding rope had become entangled in the debris it was impossible to descend the shaft directly from the surface. Thomas, a mechanic employed at the colliery, and others accordingly descended another shaft to a seam where there was an inset from the Llewelyn shaft, about 70 yards from the bottom. Thomas volunteered to go down the shaft from that point and was let down by a rope with a loop at the end, although small falls were occurring at intervals and there was a risk of a larger fall at any moment. Successfully reaching the bottom, he found three men alive. He tied them to the rope and they were drawn up separately, after which he himself was drawn up. (27.4.13)

Rescue from a roof-fall

MATTHEW WITHERS   William Broughton, a dataller[1] at the Annesley Colliery, near Nottingham, was working under the directions of Withers, a deputy, when a fall of roof took place and buried him. Withers, who was near at hand, heard the noise of the fall, and, being unable to reach the place, went round to the opposite side of the fall and managed to clear away the dirt with his hands until he reached Broughton's head, which he protected by placing a piece of timber across large stones. Another fall of roof then occurred, burying both men and extinguishing the lamp. Withers's arms, fortunately, were free, and, being able to extricate himself, he started again to rescue Broughton. Though help had arrived in the meantime, there was only room for one man to work. Withers persisted in his efforts, in spite of the injuries he had himself received, and did not stop until he had uncovered his fellow workman sufficiently to admit of his being hauled to a place of safety.

Withers was engaged in the work of rescue for about three-quarters

[1] Dataller or datal man = day labourer.

of an hour, during which he ran great risk of being killed or severely injured by falls of roof. Had it not been for his courage and determination, Broughton would probably have lost his life. (19.8.13)

Heroism in a Natal colliery

John Hepburn
DAVID EASTON
ROBERT HENDERSON

A number of native 'boys' were engaged in building up the ends of old roads in No. 2 North Main Haulage of the Hatting Spruit Colliery, Natal, in order to prevent the fumes of a gob-fire from coming out into the haulage. A brattice cloth screen had been placed across the road to keep back the fumes at one point while work was proceeding at other points. The air was quite pure outside the screen, but very poisonous on the inside. In the absence of Hepburn, who was in charge of the party, two of the 'boys' went through the screen, contrary to orders, to get a shovel, and, on their way back, first one and then the other fell unconscious. Hepburn was informed, and with another 'boy' went in search of the two. His first search of the workings had no result, and he returned through the screen thinking that he had been misinformed. On being assured that there was no mistake, he went in a second time accompanied by a native, Mbuzimaceba, and an Indian named Munian, and found the missing 'boys'. They dragged one for 6 or 7 yards, when Hepburn collapsed. Mbuzimaceba then carried Hepburn on his shoulder almost as far as the screen, a distance of at least 100 yards. The attention of those outside the screen was attracted, and assistance arrived to carry Hepburn into safety. Mbuzimaceba became unconscious. Munian in the meantime remained behind with the missing 'boys'. Hepburn, though suffering from the effects of gas, managed to tell Easton what had happened. Easton shouted for Henderson, who was near at hand, and both penetrated into the danger area and succeeded in bringing out the missing 'boys', one of whom unfortunately died from the effects of the gas. They were able while in the working to discover a shorter way back to the screen, otherwise in all probability they would have lost their lives.

The native Mbuzimaceba and the Indian Munian showed great bravery, and a letter of appreciation, together with a suitable present, was sent to them by the Governor-General. (11.1.13)

Fire-damp explosion at Larkhall Colliery

Joseph Campbell
ALEXANDER FARQUHARSON

An explosion of fire-damp occurred in an old road at the Swinhill Colliery, Larkhall. A fireman was known to have been at the place of the explosion and, on hearing of the accident, Campbell, a fireman, and Farquharson, a miner, rushed to the spot in the hope of rescuing him. Both men attempted to penetrate the road, but were driven back by after-damp. Campbell made a second and third attempt, but without success. Then, remembering that a line of compressed-air pipes led into the roadway and that there was a blank flange on the end of them some distance away, the two men crawled into the blank flange and unscrewed the bolts, holding it in position. The after-damp had not been cleared away, and Campbell's hands and legs became numbed by its effect; but he courageously stuck to his work till the flange was removed. A length of hose piping was then given to the men by others near, and air was passed through the pipes to clear away the after-damp. Campbell then ran forward with the free end of the hose to the place where the fireman was supposed to be. He was, however, completely overcome, and had to be carried out.

The unfortunate fireman succumbed to the accident, but Campbell and Farquharson displayed very great courage in their gallant attempt to rescue their fellow workman under very dangerous conditions. (7.2.13)

Gallantry in a Leeds gas-holder

HERBERT BRIGGS
CHRISTOPHER BYWATER
THOMAS VINTERS

Repairs were being carried out at Lower Wortley, Leeds, on a large gas-holder 105 feet high by 117 feet in diameter. At the bottom of the holder was water 30 feet deep, and on this was placed a raft for the workmen to stand upon. The holder was entered at the top by means of an air-lock; 9 feet below was a small unrailed platform, about 6 feet by 5 feet, from which was suspended a rope ladder, 70 feet long, descending to the raft on the water below. The holder had been emptied of gas and two men were at work on the raft testing the rivets of the holder. Feeling the effects of gas given off by the water when disturbed, they decided to climb out, and the foreman outside, thinking that something was wrong, entered the holder and descended to the raft. Bywater, who was stationed at the air-lock, followed to the platform, taking with him a rope, and by means of this one of the three men was brought up from the raft below. Briggs and Vinters then made their way into the holder and on to the platform. Bywater had lowered the rope again to the raft; but, though the foreman had attached it to the second workman, the three men on the platform were unable to pull him up. At length all three began to feel the effects of the gas, and had to climb out of the holder. Briggs became unconscious, and Vinters descended to the ground for help; but, being unsuccessful, he climbed back and returned inside to the platform with Bywater. Unable to do anything, they were again forced to come out, Bywater beginning to lose consciousness. Further assistance then arriving, steps were taken to lower the holder and to revive the men suffering from gas, Vinters helping in the task. When the holder had fallen nearly to the ground-level a number of men entered, and succeeded in bringing out the two men remaining within, but attempts to resuscitate them were unavailing. (12.8.13)

Plucky rescue at a level crossing

Percy Norwood A blacksmith named Harry Rasell was driving downhill towards the London and South-Western Railway Station, Liss, when his pony bolted and dashed into the gates of a level crossing, which were already closed owing to the approach of a train only 80 to 120 yards away. Rasell was pitched over the gates and lay stunned across the inside rail on which the train was approaching. The driver of the train put on his brakes and reversed the engine, but was unable to pull up until he had run over the level crossing. Just as the train came up, Norwood jumped down from the station platform and tried to pull Rasell clear by his legs; failing to do so, he went in front of the engine, grasped Rasell by the shoulder, and tried to roll him over. Norwood just succeeded in getting Rasell clear, but was struck on the head by the front of the engine, which came to a standstill a few yards farther on.

If the driver had not reversed his engine, both Rasell and Norwood must have been killed. The injuries to Norwood's head were serious, and he is stated by the doctor who attended him to have had a miraculous escape from death. His intention to effect the rescue at all hazards is shown by his changing his hold on Rasell, and by his maintaining his hold after being struck by the engine. (27.11.13)

A Scottish miner's presence of mind

ROBERT DUNBAR A fire occurred at the Cadder Colliery, Lanarkshire, and, on the alarm being raised, a panic ensued. Most of the men, not knowing where the fire had originated, turned into the main airway down which the smoke was being carried, and were overcome by the fumes. Robert Dunbar, a miner, however, by presence of mind and by utilizing his knowledge of the workings, succeeded in bringing two of his fellow workmen into fresh air by another route, after having courageously waited for and revived one of them who had collapsed. After returning to the surface, Dunbar again descended underground to assist in the work of rescue, and, in the course of the subsequent operations, succeeded in saving one of the rescue party who was overcome. The Commissioner, who conducted the public inquiry into the disaster, made special mention of Dunbar's sustained courage and coolness. (3.8.13)

Accident at a blast furnace

WILLIAM BROOMHALL   William Broomhall, a workman employed by the Clay Cross Coal, Lime, and Iron Company, and Edwin William Birkumshaw were charging blast furnaces on a platform 75 feet above the ground when a severe explosion took place in one of the furnaces, accompanied by an outburst of flaming gases at a high temperature. Birkumshaw was standing about 10 feet away from the furnace; his clothing caught fire, and he was severely burnt. Broomhall was at the far end of the platform near the other furnace, about 50 feet away. A gale of wind carrying the gases was blowing almost straight down the platform, and he was burnt about the face and hands. In attempting to escape, he fell into the hopper of the other furnace. On regaining the platform he heard a cry for assistance. In the teeth of the gale and the flaming hot gases which were still escaping he made his way, at the risk of his life, to Birkumshaw, and succeeded in pulling off his burning clothes. In doing so he sustained further injuries. To add to his danger a wooden cabin and some timber near which he had to pass caught fire, and he also ran the risk of a further explosion in the furnace.

In all probability Broomhall, by his prompt and courageous action, saved the life of his fellow workman. (26.3.14)

A Lanarkshire miner's devotion

JAMES KENNEDY   A miner named Neil McKillop was engaged in the Earnoch Colliery, Lanark, in taking down head coal when the coal fell, pinning down his foot. Kennedy at once went to his assistance and continued to make every effort to release him, notwithstanding two further falls, which occurring at short intervals completely smothered McKillop. Others having come to his assistance, they managed after three hours' work to release the imprisoned man, who was unfortunately found to be dead.

Kennedy in his endeavour, at first unaided, to save McKillop's life ran grave risk of being himself smothered. (2.6.14)

Brave action of a Durham miner

JOSEPH COOK   Cook was underground in the Blackhouse Colliery, Durham, near the bottom of an old shaft filled with rubbish. Water had accumulated in it, and the weight of the debris burst out the pack walls at the shaft bottom. Seeing the danger, he rushed in-by to warn two shifters named Wilson and Coates, who were working there; they had no way of egress except past the bottom of this shaft. Before the three could get out, the debris filled up the road from floor to roof for a distance of 35 yards, completely cutting off their escape. The three men were eventually released after 22 hours' confinement.

By his action Cook ran the risk not merely of a long imprisonment, but of suffocation, which must have resulted had the debris proceeded much farther. (31.1.14)

CHAPTER XI

AWARDS OF THE ALBERT MEDAL
Land Service
JAN. 1915—DEC. 1919

Heroic deeds at Imbros

MICHAEL SULLIVAN KEOGH[1] An aeroplane, piloted by the late Capt. C. H. Collett, D.S.O., R.M.A., was ascending from Imbros Aerodrome, and had reached a height of 150 feet when the engine stopped. The machine was upset by the powerful air currents from the cliffs, and fell vertically to the ground, while the petrol carried burst into flames which immediately enveloped the aeroplane and pilot.

Chief Petty Officer Keogh, of H.M.S. *Ark Royal*, at once attempted to save Capt. Collett by dashing into the midst of the wreckage, which was a mass of flames. He had succeeded in dragging the fatally injured officer nearly clear of the flames when he was himself overcome by the burns which he had received from the blazing petrol. (19.8.15)

Heroic deeds at Boulogne

Arthur Richard Shaw Warden
EDWARD GIMBLE

Lt.-Cmdr. Warden, R.N., was informed that a fire had broken out in the after hold of the s.s. *Maine*, ammunition ship, in which a quantity of high explosives was stowed.

In the meantime the ship, then lying in the Loubet Basin at Boulogne, was abandoned by her officers and crew, and steps were taken by the local fire brigade to rig the shore fire-hose.

Lt.-Cmdr. Warden immediately proceeded on board. He went down into the hold, lifted up one of the cases, and called for the fire-hose, which was passed to him by Private Edward Gimble, 1st Batt. Middlesex Regiment, who had followed him on board.

This case and the one next to it were alight on their adjacent sides. Lt.-Cmdr. Warden played the hose on them and extinguished the fire. Subsequent investigation showed that the fire was in all probability due

[1] During the years of the Great War—1914 to 1918—a great number of awards of the Albert Medal were made to officers and men of H.M. Forces while on active service for actions which in many cases might appear at first sight to have been equally suited to the award of a V.C. or M.C. It should be remembered, however, that military decorations are only given for services rendered in the face of the enemy (which applies certainly to the V.C. and at any rate in theory to the M.C.), whereas the Albert Medal awards were all given in respect of acts committed, or services rendered, behind the lines or at least not by persons at the time in action with the enemy.

to the ignition by friction or spontaneous combustion of amorphous phosphorus, which had leaked from boxes containing that substance stowed above the cases containing the high explosives.

There is little doubt that the prompt and gallant action of Lt.-Cmdr. Warden prevented an explosion which would have had serious and possibly disastrous results with almost certain loss of life. (26.10.15)

A gallant bombing-officer

Charles Edward Cox Bartlett One of the men under instruction at a bombing-class at St. Peter's Barracks, Jersey, of which Lt. Bartlett, M.C., S. Staffs. Regt., was in charge, was practising with a catapult bomb-thrower, and had removed the safety-pin of a bomb, holding back the lever with his finger. In placing the bomb in the sling he dropped it, and in a fright ran backwards, colliding with Lt. Bartlett, who had started to pick up the bomb. Lt. Bartlett, however, succeeded in reaching the bomb in time to throw it over the parapet into the air, where it exploded harmlessly. The bomb was timed to explode five seconds after the lever was released. (2.2.16)

A lance-corporal gives his life to save others

George Alderson L.-Corp. Alderson, 10th D.L.I., with two other N.C.O.s, was moving some bombs into a room in a farm-house where they were to be stored. While the bombs were being stacked, one of them fell to the floor and the percussion cap was fired. Alderson, knowing that the bomb would explode in four seconds, and that to throw it out of the window would endanger the men who were outside, picked it up and tried to reach the door. Before he could get out of the door the bomb exploded, blowing off his hand and inflicting other serious wounds, from which he shortly died.

By his prompt action in picking up and carrying the bomb he probably saved the lives of the three men who were in the room with him, and by his presence of mind in not throwing it out of the window he certainly saved the lives of those standing outside. This act was the more meritorious as Alderson was fully aware of the deadly nature of the bomb and the danger to himself that his act involved. (14.10.15)

Gallantry in a bomb-store

Cyril Louis Norton Newall
HENRY HEARNE
HARRIE STEPHEN HARWOOD
ALFRED EDWARD SIMMS

A fire broke out inside a large bomb-store belonging to the Royal Flying Corps, which contained nearly 2,000 high explosive bombs, some of which had very large charges, and a number of incendiary bombs which were burning freely. Major Newall,[1] 2nd

---
[1] Later Air Marshal Sir Cyril Newall.

Gurkha Rifles, at once took all necessary precautions, and then, assisted by Air Mechanic Simms, poured water into the shed through a hole made by the flames. He sent for the key of the store, and with Corp. Hearne, Harwood, and Simms (all R.F.C.) entered the building and succeeded in putting out the flames. The wooden cases containing the bombs were burnt, and some of them were charred to a cinder.

A gallant Instructor

Thomas Barnard Hankey Second Lt. Hankey, 12th K.R.R.C., was in charge of a party under instruction in throwing live grenades.
A man who was throwing a grenade with a patent lighter became nervous when the lighter went off and dropped the grenade at his feet. Second Lt. Hankey at once picked up the grenade and threw it out of the trench. There were four men in this section of the trench.

Three months later, while Second Lt. Hankey was in charge of a party under instruction in throwing live grenades, a man pulled a pin from a grenade and threw the grenade straight into the parapet. Second Lt. Hankey at once picked up the grenade and threw it over the parapet. There were four men in the throwing-pit at the time.

Two days later Second Lt. Hankey was in charge of a party under instruction in throwing live grenades from a catapult. A live grenade was placed in the pocket of the catapult, the fuse was lighted, and the lever released. The grenade for some reason was not thrown by the catapult, and fell out of the pocket on to the ground. Second Lt. Hankey, who was standing on the other side of the catapult to that on which the grenade lay, rushed at the grenade, seized it and threw it away. The fuse was a short five-seconds fuse, and the grenade exploded on hitting the ground 15 yards away. There were eight men near the catapult at the time, and ten others not far away. (3.1.16)

Heroism at bombing-practice

WILLIAM MARYCHURCH MORGAN During grenade instruction in a trench, a man let fall a grenade, which sank in the mud, so that only the smoke from the burning fuse could be seen. Lt. Morgan, 15th R. Welch Fus., who was outside the danger zone, at once sprang forward and groped in the mud for the grenade. The difficulty of finding it added greatly to the danger. He picked up the grenade and threw it over the parapet just in time, thereby saving several men from death or serious injury. (14.2.16)

Soldiers save French civilians

JAMES WEBB
RICHARD FOLEY
During a heavy bombardment, Corp. Webb, R.A.M.C., and Driver Foley, R.F.A., acting entirely on their own initiative, left a place where they were safe and ran out to bring two wounded French civilians into a dug-out. They got both men into a cellar. During this operation heavy shells were falling all around them, and a motor-cyclist, who was assisting to bring in the second man, was killed. (2.1.16)

Heroism at bombing-practice

ALFRED GEORGE TEHAN
Whilst at bomb practice, one of the bomb-throwers detonated the cap of his bomb, thus lighting the fuse, preparatory to throwing it. The fuse was damp, and as he thought it had gone out he placed this bomb on the ground and went on bomb-throwing. Pte. Tehan, 12th Lancers, who was also in the trench, suddenly heard a fizzing noise, and saw that the fuse of the bomb was burning. He seized it, though the fuse was already half burnt through, and threw it out of the trench, thereby probably saving the lives of himself and four other men in the traverse with him. The bomb burst just before reaching the ground. (11.12.15)

George Broadhurst
A member of a class which was being instructed in bombing dropped a live bomb, picked it up again and threw it to a corner of the room. Corp. Broadhurst, 10th S. Wales Borderers, immediately placed his foot on the bomb with a view to minimizing the effect of the explosion. He was severely wounded in both feet. By his brave action he undoubtedly safeguarded his comrades. (10.2.16)

WALTER HOWDEN LYALL
One of the men in a party undergoing instruction threw a grenade on to the parapet directly in front of the party, thus placing them in great danger. Lt. Lyell, 3rd Batt. Gordon Highlanders, at once ran up, and, picking up the bomb, threw it over the parapet, when it at once exploded. (4.5.16)

PERCY WARWICK
A class of men attached to the Grenade Company of the 3rd Guards Brigade was being instructed in throwing live bombs from a sap-head into a small trench 25 yards away. One of the men when his turn came was nervous and, after igniting his bomb, dropped it behind him. L.-Corp. Warwick, 1st Grenadier Gds., at once, with great presence of mind, picked the bomb from between the legs of several men and threw it out of the trench, when it at once exploded. (10.9.15)

A.S.C. men's heroism

SIDNEY ALBERT ROWLANDSON
THOMAS MICHAEL WALTON
ALEXANDER ANDERSON
JOSEPH THOMAS LAWRENCE

Whilst a German 21-centimetre shell, in which several holes had been bored, was being 'steamed' in a laboratory in France for the purpose of investigation, the box of shavings in which it was packed caught fire. The officer in charge of the laboratory at once sent for help to the nearest Army Service Corps fire station, ordered all persons to leave the building, and warned the inhabitants of the neighbouring houses that a serious explosion was imminent.

On receipt of the request for help, Lt. Rowlandson, with Walton, Anderson, and Lawrence, all of the Army Service Corps, at once collected fire extinguishers and proceeded by motor to the laboratory. They entered the building, played on the fire (which had spread considerably), and after about two minutes were able to reach the burning shell, which they dragged into the yard and extinguished there.

At any moment after the fire broke out the shell might have exploded with disastrous results. (21.5.16)

Bombing-officer's bravery

NEIL MACKINNON One of the men under instruction in bombing failed to clear the parapet with his bomb, which rolled down into the mud at the bottom of the trench. Lt. Mackinnon, 14th H.L.I., at once sprang forward to seize the bomb, but was impeded by the thrower, who was endeavouring to get clear; he succeeded, however, in securing the bomb after groping for it in the mud, and in throwing it clear of the trench just before it exploded.

There were two men in the trench at the time besides the thrower and Lt. Mackinnon whose courage and coolness undoubtedly averted a serious accident. (27.5.16)

An officer's gallantry

Henry Joseph Higgs Whilst instruction in the use of bombs was being given to a class of non-commissioned officers and men at Newark, two members of the class dropped their bombs through nervousness. Lt. Higgs picked up the bombs, the fuses being more than half burnt at the time, and threw them over the parapet. The bombs exploded when just clear of the parapet.

Some weeks later an officers' class was being practised in the throwing of live grenades from behind a breastwork. One officer, when throwing a grenade, struck his arm against another officer, who was standing too close to him, so that the grenade was jerked out of his hand and fell between the class (numbering 30 officers) and the breastwork. Lt. Higgs dashed forward, seized the bomb, and threw it over the breastwork; it exploded in the air in front of the breastwork. In addition, on several other occasions, ten or twelve in all, men when being practised in throwing the live grenades had dropped them, through nervousness, and Lt. Higgs had picked them up and thrown them over the parapet, thus avoiding serious accidents. (17.2.16 and 11.4.16)

A pilot's bravery

OLIVER CAMPBELL BRYSON

Capt. (then Lt.) Bryson, with Second Lt. Hillebrandt as passenger, was piloting an aeroplane at Wye Aerodrome when, owing to a sideslip, the machine crashed to the ground and burst into flames. On disentangling himself from the burning wreckage Capt. Bryson at once went back into the flames, dragged his passenger from the machine and, notwithstanding his own serious injuries, which were aggravated by his gallant efforts to rescue his brother officer from the fire, endeavoured to extinguish the fire on his passenger's clothing.

Lt. Hillebrandt succumbed to his injuries a few days later. (15.3.17)

Gallantry at a fire

ROBERT JOHN FORBES

A fire broke out at the works of the Low Moor Munition Company, Ltd. Three motor fire-engines answered the alarm, one of which, in charge of the Chief Officer, drove into the yard of the premises, where a violent explosion had already taken place, while the other two remained outside. Another explosion took place almost immediately, injuring the Chief Officer and his chauffeur, and stunning Superintendent Forbes, of the Bradford City Fire Brigade. On recovery Forbes went to the assistance of the Chief Officer and chauffeur, when a still more violent explosion occurred, killing seven firemen and seriously injuring twelve others, including Forbes. Forbes nevertheless brought the Chief Officer to a place of safety and returned and rescued two other injured firemen, who would otherwise have lost their lives. After driving the engine away from the yard, and thus saving it from damage, he collapsed. (21.8.16)

A heroic lance-corporal

Charles Henry Anderson

L.-Corp. Anderson, the London Regt., was in a hut in France with eleven other men when the safety-pin was accidentally withdrawn from a bomb. In the semi-darkness he shouted a warning to the men, rushed to the door, and endeavoured to open it so as to throw the bomb into a field. Failing to do this, when he judged that the five seconds during which the fuse was timed to burn had elapsed, he held the bomb as close to his body as possible with both hands in order to screen the other men in the hut. Anderson himself and one other man were mortally wounded by the explosion, and five men were injured. The remaining five escaped unhurt. He sacrificed his life to save his comrades. (28.11.16)

Brave action in the trenches

WILLIAM LESLIE COUTTS RATHBONE
Corporal FELDWICK

As a working party under Second Lt. Rathbone, 15th London Regt., was proceeding down a communication trench by night, they were fired upon from close quarters. Second Lt. Rathbone ascertained that the shots came from a soldier who had run amok, and had posted himself with loaded rifle and fixed bayonet farther down the trench. Second Lt. Rathbone borrowed a rifle and, accompanied by Corporal Feldwick, advanced along the trench until in view of the mentally deranged man. They then advanced with rifles at the ready; the officer calling upon the man to surrender. Receiving no reply, they then dropped their rifles and rushed him, and after disarming him took him to the nearest dressing-station. Corp. Feldwick, who was afterwards a prisoner of war, was also awarded the Albert Medal. (6.5.16)

Officer's heroism in France

Douglas Wood

While a class of thirty men was under instruction at Warley in France, in bomb-throwing, one of the men threw a live bomb, which failed to clear the bank behind which the throwers were sheltering, and started to roll down the bank towards the class. Lt. Wood sprang forward and tried to seize the bomb while it was falling. He failed to do so, but picked it up from the bottom of the trench, and was in the act of throwing it away when it exploded, blowing off his right hand and severely injuring his back.

But for the officer's prompt and gallant conduct, there is no doubt that several lives would have been lost. (17.8.16)

A rescue from a burning aeroplane

JOHN PITTS CAMPBELL

A British aeroplane fell to the ground in the Rutoire Plain, near Loos, and turned completely over, throwing out the pilot and bursting into flames. The machine-gun and ammunition caught fire, with the result that bullets were flying in all directions. Lt. Campbell, R.F.A., ran up and at great personal risk dragged the pilot, who was wounded, out of danger. He then placed him in a neighbouring dug-out, sent for medical assistance and organized a party of stretcher-bearers to carry him to a dressing-station. (9.3.17)

Heroism at bombing-practice

WILLIAM DONALD CHESHIRE
While practice with live grenades was being carried out at Neuve Chapelle, one of the class, in attempting to throw a grenade from which the safety-pin had been withdrawn, struck his hand against the parados, so that the grenade was knocked out of his hand and fell into the trench, in which about twenty men were collected.

Capt. Cheshire, Lancashire Fusiliers, rushed forward, but was hampered and delayed by the men, who were trying to get clear. Nevertheless, he seized the grenade and threw it over the parapet. It exploded immediately after leaving his hand. (1.5.16)

A sergeant's bravery

ALBERT FORD
While a class of men was under instruction in bombing at Gorre in France, a member of the class hit with his bomb the traverse in front of him, so that the smoking bomb fell into the trench. The man immediately ran away, knocking down Sergeant Ford, R. Welch Fusiliers, who was acting as instructor. Ford at once recovered his feet, pushed past the man, and managed to pick up the bomb and throw it clear; it exploded immediately it left his hand. (30.5.16)

Children's fight with a cougar

DOREEN ASHBURNHAM
ANTHONY FARRER
Two children, Doreen, aged 11, and Anthony, aged 8, left their homes at Cowichan Lake, Vancouver Island, for the purpose of catching their ponies and, when half a mile from home, they were attacked by a large cougar. They were almost upon the animal before they saw it crouching in a path at a corner. The little girl was first attacked; the cougar sprang upon her, and she was knocked down with her face to the ground, the animal being on her back. The boy at once attacked the cougar with his fists and riding-bridle, and drove the animal off the girl; it then attacked him, and his companion, getting to her feet, came to his rescue, fighting with her clenched hands and bridle, and even putting her arm into the cougar's mouth, to try to prevent it from biting Anthony. She succeeded in getting it off the boy and it stood on its hind quarters and fought with her, but evidently it was disturbed by some sound, for presently it slunk away and ran under a log, where it was afterwards killed. The children, though both badly injured, were able to make their way home. (23.9.16)

Anglo-Persian Oil Company official's gallantry

Robert Leiper Lindsay
James Still

One of the oil-pipe valves at the Tembi pumping-station of the Anglo-Persian Oil Company burst. The pressure at this point was 700 lb. to the square inch, so that a great fountain of oil was thrown in all directions to a great height. The burst occurred within 30 yards of the open and glowing furnaces of the boilers, and it was obvious that a disastrous fire, involving the whole station and compound, which was populated by nearly 300 natives, was a question of seconds.

The only means of averting a disaster was to turn off the oil-fuel supply to the furnaces, thus extinguishing them, and to stop the pumps, thus cutting off the shower of oil.

Mr. Lindsay was near the furnaces; but to reach them it was necessary to pass through the oil shower, and thus arrive at the furnace doors soaked and dripping with oil. To do so meant almost certainly a terrible death, but Mr. Lindsay did not hesitate. Shouting to his assistant, Mr. Still, to turn off the pumps, he dashed through the oil, and had succeeded in turning off the first oil-cock, when the whole atmosphere burst into flame. He staggered away, but died from his injuries some hours later.

Meanwhile Mr. Still had succeeded in turning off most of the pumps when the fire burst out. He was cut off from all doors, but managed to escape by a window, stupefied by heat and smoke. He then sought for and found Mr. Lindsay, and having removed him returned to do what he could to limit the damage. Thanks largely to his efforts a new pumping-house, which had just been established, was saved.

Mr. James Still, Lindsay's assistant, was also awarded the Albert Medal for the courage and devotion to duty displayed by him on this occasion. (9.7.17)

An officer's self-sacrifice

Grey de Leche Leach

Lt. Leach, Scots Gds., was examining bombs in a building in France in which two non-commissioned officers were also at work, when the fuse of one of the bombs ignited. Shouting a warning, he made for the door, carrying the bomb pressed close to his body, but on reaching the door he found other men outside, so that he could not throw the bomb away without exposing others to grave danger. He continued, therefore, to press the bomb to his body until it exploded, mortally wounding him.

Lt. Leach might easily have saved his life by throwing the bomb away or dropping it on the ground and seeking shelter, but either course would have endangered the lives of those in or around the building. He sacrificed his own life to save the lives of others. (3.9.16)

Gallant rescue from a Poulsen mast

Nicholas Rath
Richard Knoulton
George Faucett Pitts Abbott

A seaplane collided with a Poulsen mast and remained wedged in it, the pilot (Acting Flight Commander E. A. de Ville) being rendered unconscious and thrown out of his seat on to one of the wings.

The three men above mentioned, Rath, a seaman, R.N.R., Knoulton, an ordinary seaman, R.N., and Abbott, a deck hand, R.N.R., at once climbed up the mast for 100 feet, when Rath, making use of the boatswain's chair, which moves on the inside of the mast, was hoisted up by men at the foot of the mast to the place, over 500 feet from the ground, where the seaplane was fixed. He then climbed out on the 'plane, and held the pilot until the arrival of Knoulton and Abbott, who passed the masthead gantline out to him.

Having secured the pilot with the gantline, Rath, with the assistance of Knoulton and Abbott, lifted him from the 'plane to the inside of the mast and lowered him to the ground.

The three men were very well aware of the damaged and insecure condition of the mast, which was bent to an angle where the seaplane had become wedged. One of the three supports of the mast was fractured, and, so far as the men knew, the mast or seaplane might at any time have collapsed. (14.9.17)

A railway goods inspector's brave action

CHARLES JOHN CARNE

A train loaded with ammunition was running to the coast when, on reaching a point near a town, a truck loaded with fuses was seen to be on fire. The train was stopped and the burning truck was detached, but in the meantime two other trucks containing large loaded shells became ignited. Carne, who had been summoned to the spot when the trucks had been burning for a considerable time, and had been warned of the great danger of an explosion, mounted one of the trucks and then took steps to put out the fire with the help of the engine-driver, fireman, and guard, thus averting an explosion with loss of life and valuable material. (22.9.17)

An officer's self-sacrifice

Arthur Halstead A bomb was accidentally dropped during instruction. Lt. Halstead, M.C., W. Riding Regt., placed himself between the bomb and the soldier who had dropped it in order to screen him, and tried to kick the bomb away, but it exploded, fatally wounding him. The soldier was slightly wounded, and

A R.A.M.C. private's bravery

James Collins A lunatic soldier escaped from his escort near an advanced dressing-station in France, and ran away along a trench. Pte. Collins, R.A.M.C., ran after him, and when he got near him the man threatened to throw a bomb at him. Collins closed with the man, who then withdrew the pin from the bomb and let it fall in the trench. In an endeavour to save the patient and two other soldiers who were near, Collins put his foot upon the bomb, which exploded, killing the lunatic and injuring Collins severely; fortunately the two soldiers were not hurt. Collins, who could easily have got out of the way, ran the gravest risk of losing his life in order to save others. (11.11.17)

A petty officer's bravery

ALFRED PLACE During grenade practice at Blandford, a live bomb thrown by one of the men under instruction fell back into the trench. Petty Officer Place, R.N., rushed forward, pulled back two men who were in front of him, and attempted to reach the grenade with the intention of throwing it over the parapet. Unfortunately the bomb exploded before he could reach it and inflicted fatal injuries on him. By his coolness and self-sacrifice Petty Officer Place probably saved the lives of three other men. (16.6.16)

A.S.C. officer and private's gallantry

LEWIS COLLINGWOOD BEARNE
ALBERT EDWARD USHER

A French motor-lorry loaded with 3,000 lb. of aeroplane bombs caught fire in the middle of a camp of the Serbian Army. Efforts to beat out the flames with earth proved ineffectual, and, after the fire had been burning for seven or eight minutes, and the bomb-cases were already involved, Major Bearne, D.S.O., and Private Usher, both of the A.S.C., ran up with extinguishers. Both immediately crawled underneath the lorry, and eventually succeeded in extinguishing the flames, thus averting a serious disaster at the risk of their own lives. Major Bearne was severely burned about the hands and arms. (22.10.16)

Bombing officer's gallantry

THOMAS CHARLES FITZHERBERT An instructional party was throwing live bombs from separate pits. A volley was ordered. All the bombs were thrown successfully except one, which hit the parapet and stuck in the mud. For three or four seconds the accident was unnoticed, as every one was watching the bombs in the air, and the man who threw the bomb was too frightened to call out or to move. Suddenly Capt. the Hon. T. Fitzherbert, Lancs. Hussars, noticed smoke issuing from the parapet and saw the bomb. He might have placed himself in safety by throwing himself on the bottom of his pit; but, seeing that the man would be exposed to the full force of the explosion, he picked the bomb out of the mud and threw it clear just as it exploded. By his courage and presence of mind he undoubtedly saved the man's life, while risking his own. (10.7.16)

Army doctor's brave action

CHARLES REGINALD HOSKYN As a result of a serious railway accident in France, a man was pinned down by the legs under some heavy girders. The wreckage was on fire, and the flames had already reached the man's ankles. Capt. Hoskyn, R.A.M.C., crawled into a cavity in the flaming wreckage, and after releasing one of the man's legs, amputated the other, whereupon the man was drawn out alive, Capt. Hoskyn retaining hold of the main artery until a tourniquet could be put on. (24.1.16)

An officer's presence of mind

ANDREW BERGHANS MCCREATH During an inspection of grenades, one of the grenades fell on the ground and detonated, and Lt. McCreath, Northumberland Fusiliers, hearing warning shouts, ran up and picked up the bomb. In order to get rid of it without endangering others, he had to run until he found an empty dug-out into which to throw it. As he was about to throw it away the detonator exploded, seriously injuring him. (26.7.17)

Bombing officer's bravery

ERIC ARNOLD SHACKLADY During bombing-practice at Cleethorpes, a live grenade which was thrown by one of the men under instruction failed to clear the parapet. The bomb was picked up and thrown a second time, but again failed to clear the parapet. By this time the fuse had burnt nearly to the end, but Lt. Shacklady, Manchester Regt., ran forward, picked up the grenade, and was about to throw it away when it exploded and blew off his hand. By this gallant action, in which he risked his life, Lt. Shacklady undoubtedly saved the life of the man who had thrown the grenade. (5.12.16)

Gallant rescue after an aerodrome explosion

FREDERICK STUART SMITH At an aerodrome in France a bomb
WILLIAM ERNEST RHOADES accidentally exploded in the mouth of
a dug-out forming a bomb store, which contained a large number of bombs packed in wooden cases and a quantity of rockets. Two men were killed by the explosion, and another man, who was severely injured, was thrown down into the store. Dense volumes of smoke issued from the dug-out, and there was great risk of a further explosion. Lt. Smith, on hearing a call for help, immediately entered the dug-out, followed by Sergeant Rhoades, and succeeded in rescuing the wounded man, who would otherwise have been suffocated. (14.10.16)

Bombing officer's brave action

FREDERICK LEONARD A bomb hit the parapet during bombing in-
HOUGHTON struction and fell back into the trench which was occupied by Lt. Houghton, R. Warwickshire Regt., a non-commissioned officer, and the man who had thrown the bomb. The non-commissioned officer shouted to the man to seek cover, which he could easily have done, but the man remained crouching near the bomb. Lt. Houghton had already placed himself in safety; but on hearing the shouts of the non-commissioned officer, he ran back into the trench, seized the bomb, and threw it over the parapet, where it at once exploded. Had not Lt. Houghton returned from safety into danger, the man would almost certainly have been killed. (27.7.17)

A sergeant's brave action

MICHAEL HEALY During bombing-practice in France, a live bomb failed to clear the parapet, and rolled back into the trench, which was occupied by the thrower, an officer, and Sergeant Healy, R. Munster Fusiliers. All three ran for shelter, but Sergeant Healy, fearing that the others would not reach shelter in time, ran back and picked up the bomb, which exploded, and mortally wounded him.

Sergeant Healy had previously performed other acts of distinguished gallantry, for which he had been awarded the Distinguished Conduct Medal, the Military Medal, and a bar to the Military Medal. (1.3.17)

Officer's bravery at burning ammunition dump

CHARLES HERBERT A party of men were loading trucks alongside an
WADE ammunition dump when the ammunition ignited and began to explode in all directions. The men rushed for shelter, but one of them was caught in the trucks. Lt. Wade,

88th Lab. Company, at once ran forward into the blazing ammunition and released the man, and then called for volunteers to save the trucks which, with their assistance, he succeeded in doing. (15.6.17)

Bombing officer's double act of gallantry

ALBERT NEVITT   A man under instruction threw a bomb which hit the parapet, and fell back into the trench, where it was deeply embedded in mud and water. Lt. Nevitt, M.C., R. Welch Fusiliers, at once groped for the bomb. He failed to find it at the first attempt, but made a second and successful attempt, seized the bomb, and threw it over the parapet, where it at once exploded.

On the 24th September 1916, bombing instruction was taking place under the command of Lt. Nevitt. Another officer and three men were present in the trench. A bomb fell back from the parapet into the trench, whereupon the men rushed for the entrance, nearly knocking Lt. Nevitt down. In the confusion Lt. Nevitt lost sight of the bomb, but he searched for it, and, having found it, threw it clear, when it at once exploded. Only one of the men had succeeded in escaping from the trench when the bomb exploded.

On both occasions Lt. Nevitt's courage and presence of mind undoubtedly saved the lives of others. (4.9.16)

Bombing officer's gallantry

THOMAS JOHNSTONE DICKSON   One of the bombs thrown during instruction failed to clear the parapet and fell back into the breastwork. Lt. Dickson, Yorkshire Regt., told the man to run to safety, and himself did so. On reaching shelter he found that the man had not followed. He at once ran back into the breastwork, and saw the man crouching in a corner on the far side of the bomb. He ran past the bomb, seized the man, and dragged him back past the bomb into safety just before the bomb exploded. Had not Lt. Dickson deliberately returned into the danger zone, the man would almost certainly have been killed. (26.6.17)

Officer's brave act

HERBERT WILLIAM SEWELL   During a fire at Calais, Lt. Sewell, R.E., broke through the roof of an engine-house which was in flames, and removed the weights of the safety valves. But for the officer's gallant action a serious explosion would have occurred, and he ran grave risk of being fatally scalded by the steam released by the removal of the weights. (6.6.17)

An officer's gallant action

RICHARD LESLIE BROWN
Lt. Brown, R. Lancaster Regt., was instructing a class in France in firing rifle grenades. Owing to the defective cartridge one of the grenades was lifted only about two inches, and then fell back into the cup. The safety catch had been released and the grenade was fusing. Lt. Brown at once ordered the men to clear and, running forward, picked up the rifle, seized it between his legs, grasped the grenade in his hands, and endeavoured to throw it away. While he was doing so it exploded, blowing off his right hand and inflicting other wounds. Had not Lt. Brown seized the grenade in his hand, thus sheltering the men, there can be little doubt that several of them would have been killed or severely injured. (27.3.17)

A company sergeant-major's bravery

WILLIAM SHOOTER
While bombing instruction was being given in a trench occupied by two officers, Sergeant-Major Shooter, Cheshire Regt., and a private, the private, who was about to throw a bomb from which he had withdrawn the safety-pin, dropped it. Without giving any warning of what had occurred, he ran away. After about two seconds had elapsed, Sergeant-Major Shooter saw the bomb. He could easily have escaped round the traverse, but, in order to save the others, he seized the bomb and threw it away. It exploded in the air before Sergeant-Major Shooter could take cover, wounding him. By risking his life he undoubtedly saved the two officers who were with him in the trench from serious or fatal injury. (8.4.16)

A sergeant's presence of mind

ALBERT HUTCHINSON
During bombing-practice at the Curragh Camp a live grenade hit the parapet of the trench and fell back at the feet of the man who had thrown it. The man was too terrified to move, and obstructed the efforts of Sergeant Hutchinson, M.L.I., to pick up the bomb. After the fuse had been burning for three seconds, Sergeant Hutchinson managed to push the man away, pick up the bomb, and throw it over the parapet, where it immediately exploded. But for the sergeant's coolness and gallantry the man would undoubtedly have been killed or severely injured. (2.4.17)

A Canadian corporal's bravery

PERCY FAIRBORN ANNIS
Corp. Annis, Canadian Infantry, was instructing a class in the use of the trench catapult, when a lighted bomb fell from the catapult into the trench. Annis at once picked up the bomb and threw it away.

On the 11th February 1916, on a similar occasion, the catapult failed to act properly, with the result that the bomb was thrown only a short distance, and fell close to another party under instruction. Annis at once ran out to pick up the bomb. The bomb exploded just as he reached it and wounded him. (23.12.16)

A gallant action

JOHN NEALE   Lt. Neale, R.N.V.R., was conducting certain experiments at Esher which involved the projection from a Stokes Mortar of a tube containing flare powder. An accident occurred rendering imminent the explosion of the tube before leaving the mortar which would almost certainly have resulted in the bursting of the mortar with loss of life to bystanders. Lt. Neale at once attempted to lift the tube from the mortar. It exploded while he was doing so, with the result that he was severely injured, but owing to the fact that he had partly withdrawn the tube from the mortar no injury was caused to others. (25.8.16)

A heroic officer

IAN FORBES CLARK BADENOCH   A live bomb thrown by one of the party during bombing-practice in France failed to clear the parapet and fell back into the bombing-pit. Lt. Badenoch, R. Fusiliers, at once rushed to pick up the bomb and throw it out of the pit. He collided with the man who had thrown it, but persisted in his attempt, and was in the act of throwing the bomb when it exploded, and he was mortally wounded.

Lt. Badenoch's prompt and courageous action undoubtedly saved the man who threw the bomb from death or severe injury. (19.3.17)

Bombing officer's gallant action

CHARLES WILLIAM FISKE   While bombing-practice was being carried out at Margate under the supervision of Capt. Fiske, 5th E. Kent Regt., a man threw a live bomb which failed to clear the parapet and fell back into the pit. Capt. Fiske at once placed himself under cover expecting that the man would do likewise. On finding, however, that the man had lost his head and was unable to move, Capt. Fiske ran back into the pit, seized the man, forced him into a corner and covered him with his own body. In the subsequent explosion Capt. Fiske was wounded in both thighs. (14.12.17)

Bombing officer's repeated acts of gallantry

CLIFFORD FOY   While bombing-practice was being carried out under the supervision of Lt. Foy, The Manchester Regt., one of the party withdrew the pin from a live bomb and, when in the act of throwing it, dropped the bomb and fainted, falling upon the bomb. Lt. Foy at once lifted the man off the bomb and carried him to a place of safety.

A short time afterwards another man threw a bomb which hit the parapet and fell back into the pit. He made no endeavour to run out of the pit, whereupon Lt. Foy entered the pit and dragged him out.

On the same occasion a third man threw a live bomb which hit the parapet and rolled to the side. He was running out to throw the bomb farther away when Lt. Foy stopped him by tripping him up and dragged him into safety.

By these repeated acts of gallantry Lt. Foy undoubtedly saved the men concerned from serious injury or death. (7.9.17)

A brave officer

FRED KELLY At a camp in England where rifle-grenade practice was being carried out, one of the men struck the loophole with his bayonet and caused the fuse of the grenade to ignite. Lt. Kelly, 6th D. of Wellington's (W. Riding) Regt., who was in charge, shouted to the man to drop his rifle and get clear, but he lost his nerve and remained in the trench gripping the rifle. Lt. Kelly then seized the rifle, and with much difficulty got it out of the man's hands and threw it away. He then tried to push the man out of the emplacement, but before he could get him clear the bomb exploded, and they were both slightly wounded. But for Lt. Kelly's courage and resource the soldier would probably have been killed. (30.1.18)

A gallant rescue

ALBERT EDGAR WARNE
HORACE CANNON

While flying in England, a pilot when attempting to land lost control of his machine, which crashed to the ground from a height of about 150 feet, and burst into flames. Flight Sergeants Warne and Cannon of the 24th Wing Aeroplane Repair Section and No. 50 Training Squadron, respectively, went to the rescue of the pilot at great personal risk, as one tank of petrol blew up and another was on fire; moreover, the machine was equipped with a belt of live cartridges, which they dragged out of the flames. They managed to extricate the pilot, who was strapped to the burning 'plane, but he died shortly afterwards from his injuries and burns. (21.1.18)

A runaway tram

WALTER GEORGE GUNNER A tramcar full of passengers was descending a hill at Dover, and got out of control. The driver, finding that the brakes would not act, jumped off the front platform, and Pte. Gunner, 1st D. Gds., promptly took the driver's place on the platform and made every effort to stop the car by the application of the brakes. Unfortunately, in spite of Pte. Gunner's courage and presence of mind, he was unsuccessful in stopping the car, which ran to the bottom of the hill at great speed and overturned. Pte. Gunner lost both his feet as a result of the accident. (10.8.17)

Gallant rescue in an air raid

FREDERICK WRIGHT   On the occasion of an enemy air raid a bomb fell on two adjoining houses, killing ten persons and imprisoning eighteen under the wreckage. When helpers arrived it was found that some of the persons who were imprisoned in the basement of one of the houses were alive, but the work of rescue was exceedingly dangerous, for escaping gas in the basement became ignited and set fire to the debris above. Inspector Wright, of the Metropolitan Police Force, with an axe, made a small opening in the floor over the basement, which was in a slanting and tottering condition, the joists which supported it being broken, and through this opening, though with much difficulty, thirteen persons were rescued. It was then ascertained that two children were left in the basement, and Inspector Wright, with Police Constables Robert Melton and Jesse Christmas, dropped into the basement through the opening and searched for the children under very dangerous conditions. In addition to the fumes from the escaping gas, which were suffocating, and the fire raging above, there was a possibility of a further movement of wreckage, which might have proved fatal to all below. The space was so confined that they were barely able to reach the back of the premises. The children were found to be dead.

Inspector Wright, on reaching the open air, collapsed, overcome by the fumes and by his exertions: but, after medical care, he recovered sufficiently to be sent home. He returned to the scene of the disaster shortly after, and continued his work of rescue throughout the night. Police Constables Robert Melton and Jesse Christmas were awarded the King's Police Medal in respect of the same occasion. (19.10.17)

Gallantry in airship accidents

Harold Victor Robinson
VICTOR ALBERT WATSON
ERIC EDWARD STEERE

On the occasion of an accident to one of His Majesty's airships, which resulted in a fire breaking out on board, Flight Lt. Watson, R.N., who was the senior officer on the spot, immediately rushed up to the car of the airship under the impression that one of the crew was still in it, although he was well aware that there were heavy bombs attached to the airship which it was impossible to remove owing to the nearness of the fire, and which were almost certain to explode at any moment on account of the heat. Having satisfied himself that there was in fact no one in the car, he turned away to render assistance elsewhere, and at that moment one of the bombs exploded, a portion of it shattering Lt. Watson's right arm at the elbow. The arm had to be amputated almost immediately.

Air Mechanic H. V. Robinson and Boy Mechanic E. E. Steere, on the occasion of another accident to an airship which caused a fire to break out on board, approached the burning airship without hesitation, extricated the pilot and two members of the crew, all of whom were seriously injured, and then unclipped the bombs from the burning car and carried them out of reach of the fire. As the bombs were surrounded by flames, and were so hot that they scorched the men's hands as they carried them, they must have expected the bombs to explode.[1]

A corporal's heroic action

James McCarthy Corporal McCarthy, 1st Batt. R. Irish Regt., was cleaning grenades in his quarters in Palestine, when the fuse of one became ignited. He carried it out to throw it into a safe place, but, finding a number of men standing round, he realized that he could not throw it anywhere without injuring his comrades. He clasped the grenade in both hands and held it close to his side. The grenade exploded, killing Corporal McCarthy, who by his devoted courage saved his comrades from serious injury. (24.1.18)

A Machine Gun Corps officer's heroism

Harry Thorner Lt. Thorner, 90th Co., M.G.C., was examining some Mills hand grenades in a small concrete dug-out in France prior to taking them up to his machine-gun position during an expected enemy raid. One of the grenades began to fizz when taken out of the box. There were twelve men in the dug-out at the moment, and there was no possible means of disposing of the bomb. Realizing what had happened Lt. Thorner shouted to his men to clear out whilst he himself held the bomb in his hand close to his body until it exploded and killed him. By this magnificent act of courage Lt. Thorner deliberately sacrificed his own life for others. Of the twelve men who were in the dug-out all but two escaped without injury—they were slightly wounded. (30.12.17)

A flight sergeant's bravery

THOMAS NICHOLL Two bombs exploded under an aeroplane in France, burning the machine entirely and causing considerable loss of life. Owing to the explosion a phosphorus bomb

---

[1] Date not gazetted.

attached to another machine standing near to it was ignited. Flight Sergeant Nicholl, R.F.C., with great presence of mind, and regardless of the danger to himself, unhooked the burning bomb and carried it to a place of safety. By his prompt action Flight Sergeant Nicholl, whose hands were badly burnt, saved the second machine and prevented further serious damage and loss of life which would probably have been caused. (26.2.18)

A gallant attempted rescue

PAUL DOUGLAS ROBERTSON A seaplane got out of control and spun to the ground. Acting Flight Commander Robertson, R.N.A.S., the observer, jumped from the machine just before it reached the ground and landed safely, as the ground was marshy. The pilot, Flight Lieutenant H. C. Lemon, was imprisoned in the seaplane, which, on striking the ground, immediately burst into flames; and notwithstanding that the vicinity of the seaplane was quickly a furnace of blazing petrol, and that heavy bombs, a number of rounds of ammunition, and the reserve petrol-tank were all likely to explode, Acting Flight Commander Robertson returned and endeavoured to extricate the pilot, and only desisted when he had been so severely burnt in the face, hands, and leg that his recovery was for some time in doubt.

He displayed the greatest gallantry, self-sacrifice, and disregard of danger in his efforts to extricate the pilot. (28.2.18)

Bombing officer's bravery

WILLIAM NEILSON Capt. Neilson, 7th Batt. Scottish Rifles, was superintending men of his company at grenade-throwing at a brigade grenade school in France. A man threw a grenade from a trench while Capt. Neilson was standing out of the trench behind him. The man slipped in the mud, and the grenade fell in the trench, in which several other men were standing. Capt. Neilson jumped down, picked up the grenade out of the mud, and threw it over the parapet. The grenade exploded just after leaving his hand, and wounded him slightly in several places. By his promptitude and courage he undoubtedly saved his men from injury. (24.2.17)

Bombing officer's bravery

GUY MADDISON VAISEY During bomb-throwing practice at a Divisional Bomb School in France, one of the men under instruction, having extracted the pin from a Mills grenade, allowed the grenade to slip out of his hand. Lt. Vaisey, 3rd Batt. Gloucestershire Regt., seeing what had happened, dashed round a traverse in the trench from which the practice was being conducted, picked up the grenade and threw it clear of the trench; it exploded almost immediately.

The action was performed at great personal risk, as the thrower was in his way and was dazed with fright. Lt. Vaisey by his courage and prompt action undoubtedly prevented a fatal accident. (6.4.17)

Attempted rescue from burning aeroplane

RICHARD WALKER BUSWELL   Capt. Buswell, Cheshire Yeomanry, att. to R.A.F., was flying at Yatesbury, when he saw another machine sideslip to the ground and burst into flames. He flew to the spot and landed; and seeing that the pilot, who was enveloped in flames, was still living, he dashed into the fire and endeavoured to rescue him. Several attempts had already been made to reach the pilot, but owing to the very intense heat they were unsuccessful. Capt. Buswell, however, managed to get hold of the pilot's clothes, which, being in flames, came away in his hand. He then procured a belt and succeeded in extricating the pilot, but was too late to save his life. (31.5.18)

Bombing officer's gallantry

ARTHUR RICHARD WADDAMS   In November last, Lt. Waddams, Indian Army, R. of O., was instructing a class in firing rifle grenades in Mesopotamia. While a private of the 85th Burmans was under instruction, the rifle missed fire and the detonator of the grenade started working without the grenade leaving the rifle. Lt. Waddams, realizing the danger, rushed forward, and, pushing back the soldier, seized his rifle with one hand and the grenade with the other, and tried to throw it over the wall before it exploded. Unfortunately, the grenade exploded in his hand and he received fatal injuries. The soldier whose life Lt. Waddams saved was only slightly injured. (Nov. 1918)

Gallantry at burning ammunition train

JOHN EDWARD BIGLAND
THOMAS HENRY WOODMAN
ALFRED HENRY FURLONGER
JOSEPH COLLINGTON FARREN
GEORGE EDWARD JOHNSTON

A train of ammunition had been placed at an ammunition refilling point in Flanders, and after the engine had been detached, and was being run off the train, the second truck suddenly burst into flames. Sergt.-Major Furlonger, D.C.M., immediately ordered L.-Corp. Bigland, the driver, to move the engine back on to the train for the purpose of pulling away the two trucks nearest the engine. Bigland did so without hesitation, and the engine was coupled up by Furlonger, assisted by Sapper Farren, while the burning truck was uncoupled from the remainder of the train by Sapper Woodman. The two trucks were then drawn away clear of the ammunition dump, it being the intention to uncouple the burning wagon from the engine and the first wagon, and so isolate it, with the object of localizing the fire as far as possible. The uncoupling was about to be done when the ammunition exploded, completely wrecking the engine and both trucks, killing Furlonger, Farren, and Sapper Johnston (a member of the train crew), and seriously wounding Bigland. Had it not been for the prompt and courageous action of these men, whereby three of them lost their lives, and one was seriously injured, there is not the slightest doubt that the whole dump would have been destroyed and many lives lost. (30.4.18)

A gallant rescue

SIDNEY WILLIAMS A soldier dropped a lighted match in a dug-out in France which had been used as a store for gunpowder. Although most of the gunpowder had been removed, there was a considerable amount scattered on the floor, which caught fire. The soldier was overcome by the fumes, and in spite of the volumes of smoke issuing from the dug-out, L.-Corp. Williams, 1/6 Batt. London Regt., entered the dug-out and rescued the soldier, who was then badly burnt and unconscious. Williams, who was severely burnt, had to carry the man up twenty steps, and, if it had not been for his prompt action, the man would have lost his life. (4.1.18)

A burning ammunition train

JAMES DUNN Several trucks, at a railhead in France, loaded with heavy ammunition caught fire, causing an explosion. Several men were wounded and some lay underneath the burning trucks. Pte. Dunn, Coldstream Guards, at once rushed forward, regardless of his own safety, and carried two of the wounded men to a shelter trench close by, where he rendered them first aid. He then returned to the assistance of the other wounded men, when a second explosion took place. Notwithstanding this, and also the very grave danger of further explosions, he continued to assist the wounded and to help to rescue those who were lying helpless under the burning trucks. His bravery, coolness, and prompt action undoubtedly saved several men from being burnt to death. (16.6.18)

An explosives factory accident

LEONARD HARPER   A melting-pot, used for refining high explosives at an explosives factory, was being freed from a deposit of sediment which had accumulated. During the absence of Lt. Harper (Cheshire Regt. T.F.R., one of the managers of the factory) a foreman attempted to break away the sediment, which was of a highly explosive nature, with an iron bar. The mixture fused, giving off fierce flames and thick fumes. On his arrival Lt. Harper at once crawled with a hose underneath the pot, which was raised about 3 feet from the ground, and directed water at the flames immediately above him.

It was not until five or six hoses had been brought to bear on the pot for some time that the burning mixture was cooled down. Meanwhile there was imminent risk of an explosion, which would certainly have killed Lt. Harper, and must have involved other buildings near by where 25 tons of high explosives were stored. Had such an explosion occurred, great loss of life and material damage must inevitably have resulted. (5.8.17)

A brave rescue

GEORGE BENNETT   A woman who was crossing the line in front of a troop train at a railway station in France, to reach a passenger train, was caught by the buffer of the engine. Pte. Bennett, 12th Lancers, hearing the woman's screams, and seeing her position, rushed to help her and pulled her into the six-foot way between the two trains. Unfortunately a basket which the woman was carrying was struck by the troop train and knocked Bennett against the passenger train, with the result that he was badly injured and suffered the amputation of both his legs. Had it not been for his presence of mind and courage the woman probably would have been killed. (25.2.18)

A heroic Australian sergeant

David Emmitt Coyne   In order to test some Mills grenades, Sergeant Coyne, A.I.F., threw one of them, but it failed to clear the parapet and fell into the trench in which there were a number of other men. Sergeant Coyne shouted to them to run for their lives, and endeavoured to find the bomb in order to throw it away, but owing to the darkness he was unable to lay his hand on it in time and, the men not being clear of the trench, he deliberately threw himself on to the top of it and let it explode under him, receiving fatal injuries, but saving the lives of his comrades. (15.5.18)

Australian officer's gallantry

JOHN PATRICK TUNN
As some Australian troops were advancing to an attack in France, one of the men tripped on some wire and a rifle grenade fell from his rifle to the ground with the pin out. Second Lt. Tunn, A.I.F., who was about 10 yards away, saw what had happened, and ran back and picked up the grenade. In doing so he also tripped on the wire and the grenade fell from his hand. He picked it up again, and as he did so it exploded and blew off his right hand, besides wounding him in the head. The men were unhurt. (19.7.18)

Bombing officer's heroism

STANLEY MARTIN REEKIE
A bomb thrown during practice at Newmarket failed to clear the parapet and rolled back into the pit. The man who had thrown it lost his head, and instead of running out of the pit ran into a corner away from the entrance. Second Lt. Reekie, M.M., R. Fusiliers, the bombing officer, who was in a position of safety, saw that there was no time to get the man out of the pit, and deliberately entered the pit and stood between the man and the bomb, shielding him with his body. The bomb exploded and the officer was seriously wounded, but the man escaped injury. (19.7.18)

A brave action

JAMES McLAUGHLIN
Pte. McLaughlin (1/5 Batt. A. & S. Hrs., att. 157th T.M. Battery), in the course of his duty, was examining a Stokes mortar shell in a gunpit in which there were nine other men and about 150 Stokes shells, when the striker of the shell gave way and ignited the fuse, timed to explode in thirteen seconds. McLaughlin warned the others, and, taking the shell with him, ran from the pit by the narrow rear exit and along a sap which he had difficulty in reaching, as the ground was slippery. It was necessary to traverse this sap for some distance to ensure that the inevitable explosion did not affect the men or the shells in the gunpit. The shell exploded as McLaughlin was throwing it clear and blew off his hand. His action undoubtedly saved the lives of all the men in the gunpit. (2.8.18)

R.E. officer's gallantry

FRANK HERBERT CALVERLEY
Lt. Calverley, R.E., was in charge of a party of men unloading 4-inch Stokes gas bombs from limbers in France, when he noticed that the safety lever on one of the bombs had been broken and that the fuse was burning. Regardless of personal danger, he at once rushed forward and

picked up the bomb, fully realizing the disaster that would inevitably occur should it explode amongst the men and horses. He carried it to leeward of the dump, where it burst, wounding him in several places. But for his prompt and gallant action there would have been numerous gas casualties, and in all probability loss of life. (19.7.18)

Attempted rescue from a gas-filled bomb-crater

ALFRED BURT
VICTOR BROOKS
ARTHUR JOHNSON
ALFRED HORNE

A corporal of the Royal Air Force, who had been lowered by a rope into a crater caused by a bomb which had been dropped by a hostile aeroplane, was overcome by carbon monoxide gas, which had accumulated in large quantities in the crater. Endeavours were made to haul him out, but his head became caught, and Pte. Johnson, A.S.C., volunteered to descend and readjust the rope, which he did successfully, and the corporal was rescued, but Johnson was himself overcome. Driver Horn, A.S.C., at once put on his respirator and lowered himself to the rescue, but was likewise overcome. Sergeant Brooks, Canadian Cav. Field Ambulance, then volunteered to attempt to rescue both men, but was also overcome by the gas; fortunately he was hauled out.

At this stage Brigadier-General Burt, D.S.O., refused to permit any one else to descend, but did so himself, and succeeded in dragging one of the unconscious men some way towards the rope; he, however, became unconscious and had to be pulled out.

There can be no doubt that all knew the risk that they were running, and willingly incurred it in the hope of saving life. (30.6.18)

An Australian officer's gallantry

WILLIAM HENRY
GREGORY GEAKE

An explosion occurred in the pressing-room of a munitions inventions experimental station. The room contained 25 lb. of thermit and 300 lb. of gunpowder, pressed into rocket heads. Lt. Geake, A.I.F., who was standing outside at the time, at once ran into the building, where explosions were still taking place, and helped one man out. He then ran back into the building, passed through the place where the thermit and powder were exploding, and carried out an injured man whom he found under a burning bench. Notwithstanding the fact that he was himself badly burnt, Lt. Geake entered the building a third time, under the mistaken impression that another man was still inside, but was eventually driven out by the fire and explosions.

Lt. Geake then worked for two hours to alleviate the injuries of the rescued men, one of whom was dying.

Unfortunately, at a demonstration on the following morning, which he attended, although unfit for duty, Lt. Geake suffered further injuries owing to a premature explosion, three fingers being blown off his right hand, and his right leg being broken and almost severed. (26.9.17)

Bombing officer's courageous acts

WALTER RICHARD BEARD
L.-Corp. Beard, R.E., was instructing recruits in throwing live bombs, when one of the men under instruction, as he was about to throw a bomb, dropped it in the trench. Beard at once ran out from cover, picked up the bomb, and threw it over the parapet, thereby undoubtedly saving the recruit from death or serious injury. The bomb exploded in the air before reaching the ground.

In almost exactly similar circumstances Beard repeated this gallant action on the 23rd August, thereby again saving the life of a man who had dropped a bomb in the trench. (16.8.18)

Mountaineering accident in New Zealand

ARTHUR HAMILTON AMBURY
Mr. Ambury, with his wife and two friends, were climbing on Mount Egmont, Taranaki, New Zealand, and had reached an altitude of about 5,500 feet when a call for help was heard from above.

Two members of Mr. Ambury's party immediately began to climb to render assistance, and Mr. Ambury, after putting his wife in a safe place, went up after them. At a height of about 7,300 feet they found two climbers, one of whom had been hurt. They took charge of the injured man, and his companion, who had an ice axe, proceeded higher up the mountain to assist a third member of the party.

The injured man had been assisted down some 1,000 feet and Mr. Ambury had nearly reached the party who were descending a steep ice slope in which they had to cut steps, when one of the two men in the rear slipped and slid down the slope at a terrific pace.

Mr. Ambury, who was about 60 feet lower down, braced himself and endeavoured to stop the falling man by seizing his alpenstock which was trailing behind him, but the alpenstock was jerked out of his hand and he was precipitated down the slope of the mountain. He was an experienced mountaineer and must have realized how terrible a risk he was running in endeavouring to save the falling man. (3.6.18)

An officer's brave action

GEOFFREY RACKHAM
A lorry (one of a convoy of seven) laden with shells and cartridges caught fire at Le Cateau. Lt. Rackham, A.S.C., who was awakened by the fire alarm, hurried to

the scene of the fire in his pyjamas to find that flames 3 to 4 feet high were issuing from the petrol tank. He put the cap on the petrol tank, jumped into the driver's seat, started up the blazing lorry, and drove it, while cartridges were exploding, to a place of safety, afterwards helping to extinguish the flames. By his prompt and courageous conduct, serious damage, and in all probability loss of life, was averted; for the other loaded lorries were close by, and some 130 men of the battery were only 30 yards distant. (27.10.18)

Nurses' bravery in hospital fire

GERTRUDE WALTERS CARLIN
HARRIET ELIZABETH FRASER
GLADYS WHITE

A serious fire occurred in No. 36 Casualty Clearing Station at Rousbrugge, in Belgium. At the time some of the patients were undergoing serious operations in the abdominal and general operating theatres, the walls of which were composed of wood. The first intimation of danger in the theatres was the extinction of the electric light, accompanied by volumes of smoke, and almost immediately the wooden walls burst into flames. Sister Carlin, of the T.F. Nursing Service, and Sister White, of the Brit. Red Cross Soc., and Staff Nurse Fraser, also of the T.F. Nursing Service, assisted in carrying the unconscious patients to safety, and returned to the burning wards to assist in carrying out other patients. During this time ether bottles and nitrous oxide cylinders were continually exploding, filling the air with fumes and flying fragments of steel. (1.10.18)

Bombing officer's presence of mind

GEORGE THOMAS
ROWLANDS

Corp. Rowlands was instructing a party at Clonmany, County Donegal, in the firing of live rifle grenades when a grenade, the fuse of which had been started, fell into the firing bay. Corp. Rowlands, D. of Cornwall's L. Inf., shouted to the party to take cover, and ran out of the trench, but the man from whose rifle the grenade had fallen did not move, and Rowlands thereupon returned to the trench, picked up the grenade, and threw it over the parapet, when it immediately exploded. He undoubtedly saved the man's life at the risk of his own. (21.10.18)

Bombing officer's bravery

WILLIAM HERBERT
MEREDITH

L.-Corp. Meredith, late Grenadier Gds., was instructing a class in the firing of live rifle grenades. One of the party fired a grenade, but the charge was insufficient to project the grenade, which fell back, with ignited fuse, into the barrel of the rifle. The man held on to the rifle, instead of throwing it down, whereupon Meredith threw himself forward in front of the man and attempted to remove the grenade, but it exploded, blowing off three fingers of his right hand, and wounding him in other places.

Meredith received the full force of the explosion, and undoubtedly saved the other man, who was only slightly wounded, from severe injury or death. (5.11.18)

An officer's bravery

EDWARD ARTHUR SIMMONS   A platoon was engaged in attack practice at Wouldham, in the course of which the rifle sections advanced under cover of a rifle bomb barrage. The riflemen had reached a point some 20 yards in advance of the bombers, when, owing to a defective cartridge, one of the bombs fired from the right flank, where Lt. Simmons, Middlesex Regt., was stationed as bombing officer, fell about 4 yards in the rear of the riflemen. Lt. Simmons, who was behind the bombers, at once rushed forward, and, as there was no time to pick up the bomb and throw it away, he kicked it away. It exploded immediately, and he received severe wounds.

Lt. Simmons undoubtedly saved some of the men from injury or death at the cost of injury to himself and at the risk of his own life. (1.11.18)

A brave V.A.D.

ALICE BATT   A fire broke out at No. 36 Casualty Clearing Station at Rousbrugge, Belgium, and quickly reached the operating theatre, where the surgeon was performing an abdominal operation. The lights went out, and the theatre was quickly filled with smoke and flames, but the operation was continued by the light of an electric torch, Miss Batt, V.A.D., continuing her work of handing instruments and threading needles with steadfast calmness, thereby enabling the surgeon to complete the operation. Miss Batt afterwards did splendid work in helping to carry men from the burning wards to places of safety. (1.10.18)

Bombing officer's gallantry

JAMES EDWARD MADDOX   Lt. Maddox, M.M., 24th Batt. Cheshire Regt., was instructing a class in throwing live bombs. One of the men, after withdrawing the pin from a Mills No. V Mark 1 Grenade, accidentally dropped the grenade in the trench, and then, apparently through fright, fell on it. Lt. Maddox, with great presence of mind, immediately pulled the man off the grenade, seized it, and threw it over the parapet, where it exploded almost immediately.

By his prompt and courageous action Lt. Maddox undoubtedly saved the man's life. (27.9.18)

A soldier's rescue from drowning

WILLIAM WHITEHEAD L.-Corp. Whitehead, 9th Batt. Manchester Regt., was in command of a guard on the River Meuse. One of the guard, in crossing a plank gangway from a barge where the guardroom was situated to relieve a sentry on the river bank, missed his footing and fell into the river, which was in flood. L.-Corp. Whitehead immediately jumped into the river, but in the pitch darkness missed the drowning man. He swam to the shore, climbed out, and ran down the bank until he reached the spot where the man had been carried by the swift-running stream, and again jumping in he succeeded in rescuing him.

Both rescuer and rescued were wearing equipment and greatcoats at the time, and L.-Corp. Whitehead undoubtedly risked his life in saving the life of his comrade who, when brought to the bank, was unconscious. (5.1.19)

Gallant attempted rescue in France

WILLIAM REVELL SMITH
ALEXANDER GIBSON
JAMES SMITH

A fire occurred at the brewery at Wizernes. In the engine-room a Frenchman, whose cries for help could be heard, had been entombed by a fall of masonry which completely blocked the entrance. The upper part of the building was blazing fiercely, and the only entrance to the engine-room was by a small hole in the wall which carried the machinery belting. Major Smith, M.C., R.F.A., Sergeant Gibson, R.E., and Corporal Smith, Military Mounted Police, succeeded in making their way through this hole into the room, and worked for three quarters of an hour before they exposed the head and shoulders of the entombed man, who was found to be dead.

They undoubtedly risked their lives in endeavouring to save life, for a further collapse of masonry (which appeared imminent) would have completely cut off their exit. (17.1.19)

A stationmaster's brave action

THOMAS WILLIAMS As a train was entering Pembroke Station, an elderly clergyman, Canon Bowen, of Pembroke, in stepping aside to avoid a luggage barrow, fell off the platform on to the rails. The train was not more than 30 yards away from him when he fell, and was travelling fast. The stationmaster, who was close by, at once jumped down in front of the engine and just succeeded in rolling Canon Bowen off the track, and held him down alongside the rails until it was safe to allow him to get up.

Although the brakes were applied it was found impossible to bring the train to a standstill until the engine and two coaches had passed the spot where rescued and rescuer were lying. Had it not been for Mr. Williams's presence of mind and courage Canon Bowen could hardly have escaped instant death. (13.3.19)

Heroic rescue work in India

DAVID ATKINSON MACMILLAN A serious fire broke out in the residential quarter of the town of Keonjhar Garh, in the Feudatory State of Keonjhar, India. Nearly all the men were absent at work, and a panic arose among the women and children. Mr. MacMillan, Superintendent, at once hastened to the scene of the fire, organized parties for fighting it, and by his personal efforts and direction brought it under control. When his work was nearly finished a burning roof fell in upon four men who were assisting to extinguish the fire. Regardless of his own safety, Mr. MacMillan at once entered the building, which was full of smoke and flame, and rescued all four men, one of whom was severely burnt. Mr. MacMillan was seriously injured, and died on the 19th September following. (9.4.18)

A gallant soldier

EDWARD MCCARTHY Two horses harnessed to a limber, having been left unattended at Wermels-Kirchen, took fright and ran away. While they were going at great speed down the village street Pte. McCarthy, M.M., R. Canadians, rushed forward and seized the reins. He would doubtless have succeeded in stopping the horses had the reins held, but they broke, and he was thrown under the limber, which passed over his body, inflicting injuries from which he subsequently died. He succeeded, however, in diverting the limber from two children, who would otherwise undoubtedly have been killed. (8.1.19)

Bombing officer's prompt courage

BERNARD GEORGE ELLIS Lt. Ellis, The Buffs, was with a party at Shahraban, in Mesopotamia, under instruction in the firing of rifle grenades. A volley was fired, but one of the grenades, owing to a defective cartridge, did not leave the rifle, but fell back into the barrel with the fuse burning. The firer lost his head and dropped the rifle and grenade in the trench, but Lt. Ellis, who was separated from the man by four other men in a narrow trench, at once forced his way past them and seized the rifle. Failing to extract the grenade, he dropped the rifle and placed his steel helmet over the grenade, which at once exploded, severely injuring him. There can be no doubt that his prompt and courageous action greatly minimized the force of the explosion and saved several men from death or severe injury. (21.8.18)

A bombing officer's heroism

DOUGLAS WILLIAM WRIGHT Lt. Wright, R. Fusiliers, was in charge of a rifle-grenade practice at St. Pol. One of the party accidentally released the safety lever of his grenade before he was ready to fire, and thereupon threw his rifle on the ground, calling to Lt. Wright to escape. The officer, however, fearing that the man would be unable to get away in time, rushed past him, seized the rifle, and held it to his body in order to minimize the force of the explosion. He was so severely injured as to necessitate the amputation of both legs and one arm. The man who was firing escaped from the trench by another exit.

Lt. Wright undoubtedly risked his life in endeavouring to save the life of another. (April 1917)

New Zealand bombing officer's gallantry

RANDOLPH GORDON RIDLING At Brocton Camp, Stafford, a recruit who was under instruction in bombing dropped a live Mills grenade in the throwing-bay after pulling out the pin. Lacking the presence of mind to attempt to escape, he kicked the bomb towards the entrance and retreated to the inner end of the bay. Lt. Ridling, N.Z. Rifle Brigade, the bombing officer, seeing the man's danger, went to his rescue. Seizing him in his arms, he started to carry him out, but the bomb exploded before he could get clear of the bay, and he was wounded severely in the groin. But for Lt. Ridling's coolness and bravery the man, who was only slightly wounded, would, in all probability, have lost his life. (19.4.18)

Heroic rescue from a burning hotel

WALTER CLEALL A fire broke out at the top of the Royal Hotel, Cardiff, and it was not until the sixth floor of the building was burning fiercely that one of the maids was seen to come to a window on that floor and gesticulate for help. Cleall, a demobilized soldier, who was in the crowd below watching the fire, at once entered the building without a smoke helmet, and eventually succeeded in getting to the sixth floor and into a room from which he could see the girl. From the window of that room he climbed along a narrow parapet, and reached the window where the girl was.

Above the ledge which afforded him foothold was a stone balcony for a part of the intervening space, but a very dangerous corner had to be negotiated with a sheer drop to the street of fully 100 feet. The risk of falling was very great, but he succeeded in carrying the girl back along the parapet, and into the room from which he started. A portion of the roof collapsed as the girl was assisted from the room. (11.8.19)

CHAPTER XII

AWARDS OF THE EDWARD MEDAL

JAN. 1915—DEC. 1919

A gallant plumber

JOHN GEORGE HINGE Hinge was engaged with another man, at the Borstal Institution, Feltham, in removing an obstruction which had occurred in a gas main, when an explosion occurred, hurling Hinge out of the door of the building where they were working. The other man was thrown against the opposite wall, and his escape jeopardized by the flaming gas between him and the door. Hinge pluckily returned to his rescue, and succeeded in helping him out. He then, although badly burnt and nearly collapsing, took steps to cut off the pressure of the gas, thereby preventing the possibility of further explosions, which might have caused very serious loss of life. (1.10.14)

A railway porter's pluck

DAVID HUMPHREY A woman, standing on the platform of Murton Railway Station, fell on to the line in an epileptic fit about 80 yards in front of a train, which was approaching at 15 miles an hour. Humphrey, a porter, who was standing some 15 yards away, ran up and jumped on the line. The train at this moment was only a little over 20 yards off, and he was unable to remove the woman; but he succeeded in holding her down between the rails until the train came to a standstill, after the engine and one wagon had passed above them. By this brave action he saved the woman's life at great risk to himself. (8.12.14)

Brave attempt at rescue in Co. Durham

GEORGE LOFTHOUSE Blasting operations were in progress at the bottom of a pit at Wingate, County Durham, 21 feet deep. The morning shift had fired three charges of gunpowder (between 30 and 40 lb.) at the bottom of the pit, and, when a man belonging to the afternoon shift was let down in a kibble or tub at 12.30, he was overcome by the fumes. His mate at the top shouted for assistance, and Lofthouse, who was not concerned in the operations in the pit, but was working some distance away, immediately ran to the pit and went down the rope to attempt a rescue. He got hold of the man and signalled to be raised, but, almost as soon as the kibble was lifted, both men fell out. Those at the top swung the kibble to and fro in order to clear away the fumes, and eventually, about 1.15, both men were brought out. Artificial respiration was resorted to; Lofthouse did not regain consciousness until two hours later, and the other man could not be revived.

Lofthouse was experienced in the use of explosives and knew the danger of descending into the fumes, and his action was, therefore, extremely courageous. (4.8.14)

A brother's devotion

JOHN LODGE John and Edward Lodge, two brothers employed in the Dunkerton Colliery, had drilled and charged eight shot-holes in the face of a stone drift, the fuse in each succeeding hole being 4 inches longer than that in the preceding one. The tools were then collected and carried some distance back, and Edward Lodge returned to light up the fuses. When he had lighted seven of the fuses, a charge in one of the holes exploded. John Lodge immediately went into the face and finding Edward lying on the floor conscious, but with the right thigh broken, dragged him away, though other charges were still exploding, thus, in all probability, saving his life. He himself was injured in the head from stones projected by shots that went off during the rescue, and his action was courageous to the highest degree. (21.11.13)

Accident on a Viaduct

JAMES DALLY Two workmen were engaged in painting the Crumlin Viaduct on the Great Western Railway, on a staging 175 feet above the ground, when a piece of timber forming one of the horizontal supports of the staging broke. One of the men fell to the ground and was killed on the spot; the second man succeeded in gripping an iron stretcher forming part of the bridge. Dally, who was standing on the gangway of the bridge at the time of the accident, went to the man's assistance, and, crawling along the diagonal bracings between the booms of the girders, persuaded him to swing his legs until they came within reach. He then instructed the man to move his hands gradually nearer, and in the end succeeded in drawing him into safety on the gangway. The man would probably have lost his life had it not been for the courage and presence of mind shown by Dally. (28.10.14)

South African miner saves five lives

JAMES WAGENAAR Wagenaar was working in the City Deep Gold Mine, Witwatersrand, South Africa, when he was informed by a native that five other natives down a winze, or steep incline, had been overcome by the fumes from explosives used in blasting. Wagenaar, tying a wet cloth round his mouth, immediately descended the winze to the place where the natives were lying in various stages of collapse, and, without assistance, brought out four of them in succession. He proceeded down the winze for the fifth time to bring out the last native, but was unable to carry him up more than a few yards, as he was fast being overcome by the fumes, and had himself to be helped out of the winze. Three men, who subsequently brought out the fifth native, also collapsed from the effects of the gas. It is probable that but for Wagenaar's brave action all the natives would have succumbed to the effects of the fumes. Wagenaar and the five natives were all in hospital for some days. (29.10.13)

A miner's gallant attempt at rescue

SAMUEL STOPPARD A miner named Haslam was hewing coal at the face of his stall, at the Clay Cross No. 2 Pit, near Chesterfield, when a fall of roof occurred and buried him all but his head. Stoppard ran to the spot and tried to get him out, but failed, and, as the roof was very weak and a further fall imminent, he set catch props to it and erected a metal plate to protect Haslam's head. He then made further attempts to liberate Haslam, and, while he was doing so, a further fall occurred, burying Stoppard himself up to his waist. He managed to free himself, and worked at the fall until Haslam was liberated; but unfortunately Haslam was by this time dead.

The place at which the fall occurred was difficult to get at, and only one man could work at a time there. During the whole of the rescue operations Stoppard ran great risk from a further fall of roof, and he was well aware of this. (8.6.15)

Brave rescue from drowning in the Bow River, Alberta

JOHN RODERICK MCDONALD While the Bow River, Calgary, Alberta, was in flood, a hundred-foot steel span was washed loose from a bridge in course of construction. A man named Garden was upon this span, and was precipitated into the water, which was icy cold. He managed to get hold of a baulk of timber, to which he clung. McDonald and Powell put off to the rescue in a small boat, which was used in connexion with the building of the bridge. No other boats were available, as the river is too dangerous for boats, even when not in flood. They had to cross a dangerous rapid, and also to avoid collision with logs which were coming down the river in large numbers, and timber from the broken bridge. Had they been capsized they would almost certainly have been drowned, as they wore heavy hip rubber boots. They reached Garden, though he had been washed nearly a quarter of a mile down the river. He was at that time nearly unconscious owing to the coldness of the water. It was too dangerous to take him aboard the boat, and they therefore tied a rope round him and secured it to the boat. All three were carried about a mile and a quarter down the river, when McDonald and Powell managed to steer the boat to an island. (26.6.15)

The Ardeer explosions

James Burt
Arthur Frankland
DUNCAN McPOLLAND

These awards to Sergeant Burt, Mr. Frankland, and Pte. McPolland, were made in connexion with the explosion at Messrs. Nobel's Factory at Ardeer in July 1915, but were not gazetted, it not being thought convenient at the time in the public interest to publish the fact that the accident in question had occurred. (30.7.15)

Black damp in a Derbyshire Mine

ARTHUR WOODHOUSE
JOSEPH PEAT

John Orrill, the manager of the Wood Lane Colliery, Horsley, nr. Derby, ordered a man named David Aldread to fetch a shovel from a point some 200 yards distant. As Aldread did not return Orrill ordered another man, William Peat, to fetch an electric lamp from the surface, and meanwhile Orrill himself went in search of the missing man. On his return with the lamp, William Peat followed Orrill and found both Orrill and Aldread lying unconscious on the ground, while he himself was nearly overcome by black damp. He at once summoned help, and guided his son, Joseph Peat, and Arthur Woodhouse to a spot about 12 yards distant from the bodies. By this time the air was so bad that a flame would not burn, and the only light by which the men could work was an electric hand lamp of one candle-power. In spite of the difficulty and danger, Woodhouse and Peat by successive rushes forward over an obstacle created by a fall of roof, into an atmosphere fatal to life, succeeded in attaching their belts round the bodies, first of Orrill and then of Aldread, fastening a long strap from some adjacent machinery to the belts and pulling them out over the fall. Had either man stumbled or fallen when near the bodies the result would in all probability have been fatal. The rescue lasted from 60 to 90 minutes. Both Orrill and Aldread were dead when their bodies were recovered. (24.12.15)

An under-manager's bravery

FREDERICK GEORGE
STEPHENS

A fireman of the Aberaman Colliery, on examining the pit at noon, found some timbers breaking owing to roof weighting, and instructed a workman named Gamble to set props beneath the collars of the timbers.

As Gamble was approaching the spot six pairs of timbers gave way causing a fall of about 16 tons of roof and sides, by which Gamble was caught. He was buried by about 4 feet of rubbish, his head and feet pinned tight; but his body protected by some fallen timber. Efforts were made to get him free, but were frustrated by the further falls, which were continually taking place. Stephens, the under-manager, arrived about half an hour after the accident, by which time the roof and one side had become so dangerous that no one would venture near Gamble in spite of his cries for help. Stephens, however, immediately placed himself over Gamble, so as to protect him, and called for volunteers. Four men responded and, under Stephens's instructions, began to pull down the overhanging stones, which Stephens, who is a strong man, diverted from falling on to Gamble, and by so doing was himself injured. After two hours' exertion Stephens succeeded in freeing Gamble, whose injuries were fortunately not very serious. There can be little doubt that, had not Stephens been able to divert the falling stones, Gamble would have been in great danger of being crushed or suffocated, and it was Stephens's example which prompted the other men to renew their attempt at rescue, from which they had desisted owing to the danger of falling stones. (10.9.15)

Gallant rescue of entombed miner

HAROLD GREGORY
CHARLES BENJAMIN FRANKLIN
CHARLES WILLIAM HUDSON
EDWARD NURSE
THOMAS SMITH

A fall of roof occurred at the Ireland Colliery, Staveley, Derbyshire, by which a filler named John William Fieldsend was imprisoned. Gregory, Franklin, Hudson, Nurse, and Smith at once set to work to open a passage through the fallen roof in order to rescue their fellow workman. The roof was everywhere very uneasy and a further fall was liable to occur at any moment. Owing to the narrowness of the place, only one man could work at the head of the passage (the most dangerous place), while the remaining four, one behind the other, passed out the material removed, the men taking by turns the post of danger. After about 3 hours' work, at 10 a.m. a further fall occurred, closing the passage which had been made for 3 yards. Fortunately the workers escaped without injury. Work was at once resumed, and Fieldsend was reached. As soon, however, as an attempt was made to remove him from under a piece of timber, by which he was pinned down, a third fall occurred, blocking up the passage for about 4 yards, and displacing much of the timber which had been used to prop up the roof and walls of the passage as it was made. Finally, at 5 p.m., after 10 hours' continuous work, Fieldsend was reached and taken out of the pit. He was not much injured. All five men ran continuous risk, during the whole 10 hours, of serious injury or death from falls of roof. (28.2.16)

Gallantry of a South African miner

JOSEPH JOHANNES VENTER

Thomas Reardon and Joseph Johannes Venter were carrying out blasting operations at the Government Gold Mining Areas (Modderfontein) Consolidated Mine, South Africa. Each man was working in a separate drive, and it was their practice to charge their shot-holes (13 in number) and await the signal of a 'boy' stationed at a point where the two drives joined, whereupon they lit their fuses and withdrew to the junction of the drives.

On this occasion Venter duly received the signal and lit his fuses. On reaching the junction of the drives he heard a report in Reardon's drive and was told by the 'boy' that Reardon was still at his working-place. He at once rushed down Reardon's drive, through heavy fumes, and, after travelling about 250 feet, fell over Reardon's body. He picked him up and carried him about 78 feet when two further shots exploded, knocking Venter down. Venter then dragged Reardon to the shelter of the wall and ran for help, returning in about 2 minutes with two or three men. As they entered the drive, further shots exploded. They went through the fumes and carried Reardon clear, but he died four days later.

In entering Reardon's drive for the purpose of rescuing him, when only one shot out of thirteen had exploded, and knowing that the remaining shots might (as in fact some of them did) explode at any moment, Venter undoubtedly risked his life to save Reardon. (19.4.15)

Rescue from a roof-fall at Harton Colliery

CHRISTOPHER DEVENPORT
WILLIAM WALKER

A large fall of roof occurred at Harton Colliery. Eight men, under the supervision of Walker, were engaged in clearing away the fallen stone when a further and heavier fall occurred, whereby one of the men, named Hall, was caught and apparently buried beneath the stone. Devenport was at once sent for and, on arrival, crawled through a small opening, which was left between the fallen stone and the side, until he reached Hall. He found him pinned by the legs, but otherwise safe. He put in two props to keep the roof, which was still very uneasy, from falling on him, and returned. Walker and Devenport then both crept into Hall, and, while Devenport lifted the stones from his legs, Walker dragged him out. Hall was a very heavy man, weighing 17 stone.

The rescue occupied 1 hour and 5 minutes, during the whole of which time the roof was working and threatening to fall into the small opening by which the rescue was effected. Half an hour after the rescue it did so fall in. (27.4.16)

Rescue of girls from an explosives factory

William Alexander Morrison
George Sang
Archibald Young

A small explosion occurred at 10 a.m. in a building at the Roslin Explosives Factory. Morrison and Sang, who were aware that four girls were in the building, which had caught fire, and that the building was full of explosives, at once ran towards it. As they approached two of the girls came out and fell unconscious on the grass. The building was now blazing furiously; but Morrison and Sang, who knew the position of the explosives within, used the fire buckets so as to allay the flames in the dangerous quarter, and to enable Morrison to dash in. He groped through the smoke, which was dense white, found one girl and passed her out to Young, who had arrived meanwhile; he then returned for the second girl, and eventually brought her out, while Young placed the first girl on a bogey, which he thrust along the line out of danger, and then returned for the second. Sang meanwhile kept the fire down as far as possible with water-buckets.

During the whole of this time small explosions were continually taking place within the building, and immediately after the second rescue a heavy explosion occurred, which destroyed part of it. Twelve minutes after the original explosion the whole building blew up. (20.6.16)

A miner's courage

Charles Slack A fall of roof occurred at the Woodland Colliery, Durham, completely burying a hewer named Richardson. Slack immediately sent for help, and himself started to remove the stone from Richardson, although the roof was still obviously very dangerous. Almost immediately a further fall occurred, burying Slack except for his legs. He was pulled out by two hewers, and, after recovering himself, returned to Richardson's assistance. He worked for about 10 minutes, and then told the other helpers to get clear, as another fall was about to occur. He attempted to prop the falling stone up with his back, and by so doing succeeded in canting it off Richardson's head, which was now exposed, but he himself was again buried. Both men were finally extricated after about one and a half hours' work. (2.11.16)

Presence of mind in a munitions factory

ROBERT JOHN KIRKHAM

Kirkham, a Munitions Dept. Examiner, who was working in a filling-shed at Watford, noticed smoke issuing from a filled 4-inch Stokes bomb. With most commendable presence of mind and courage he picked up the bomb, threw it out of the shed and shut the door. The bomb exploded in the open with sufficient violence to project the steel head, weighing 20 ounces, a distance of 120 yards. The steel propellant container flew 50 yards in the opposite direction. But for Kirkham's action the explosion would have occurred inside the filling-shed, in which about 50 persons were working and a quantity of explosives was stored, and it is probable that loss of life would have resulted. Kirkham was well aware of the nature of the bomb and of the destructive qualities of the explosives with which it was filled. (6.2.17)

Bravery of a Chief of Police

THOMAS LUTHER BURT

An outbreak of fire occurred at H.M. Explosives Factory, Watford. Burt, Chief of Police in the factory, who was on his round of inspection at the time, at once rushed into the building, which was burning fiercely and full of suffocating smoke. He carried out Mixer Price, and immediately returned to rescue Mixer Morecroft, the smoke being then so dense and the heat so great that he was compelled to crawl along on his hands and knees before he could reach Morecroft. Afterwards he worked hard in assisting in the removal of explosives from the building. (13.2.17)

Two posthumous awards

Andrea Angel
George Wenborne

Dr. Angel and Mr. Wenborne lost their lives in endeavouring to save the lives of others on the occasion of a fire which broke out at the Silvertown Chemical Works on the 19th January 1917. (19.1.17)

A pit-shaft accident

PERCY ROBERTS HAVERCROFT
ALBERT HENRY TOMLINSON
JOHN WALKER
EDWARD WINGFIELD

A descending cage containing ten men collided about half-way down one of the shafts of the Waleswood Colliery, near Sheffield, with an empty ascending cage. The impact was extremely violent, severely injuring all the men and breaking the winding-ropes. Both cages were, however, wedged together in the shaft, so that, fortunately, neither of them fell to the bottom, though there was serious danger that they might do so at any moment.

A hoppit manned by Tomlinson, Havercroft, and Walker was at once sent down to effect the rescue of the imprisoned men. All the men were carried from the damaged car along a girder to the hoppit, which made five descents altogether, the rescue occupying about 2 hours. During the whole of this time Tomlinson, Havercroft, and Walker were exposed to great danger either from the hoppit being upset by the winding ropes swinging in the shaft, or from the damaged cage breaking loose and falling down the shaft.

Wingfield, who was one of the occupants of the descending cage, had both legs fractured, and received a severe wound on the thigh and a wound on the head. He seized hold of another man who had fallen half-way through the bottom of the cage, and held him up until he was rescued. During the whole time he displayed the greatest coolness and bravery, despite his very severe injuries, and insisted on all his fellow workmen being removed to a place of safety before allowing himself to be taken to the surface. (27.8.15)

A courageous action

Alfred John Henney A bucket containing detonators was discovered to be on fire at the factory at which Henney was employed. He ran to the building, which was full of smoke, crawled through the smoke on his hands and knees until he found the burning bucket. The rope handle was in flames; but he seized it by the rim and carried it outside, where he extinguished the contents. His promptitude and courage averted a most serious disaster. (14.3.17)

Timely assistance rendered in pit-shaft

HERBERT JOHN GOLLEDGE   George Weeks, under-manager of the Braysdown Colliery, near Bath, was ascending the shaft when the cage struck a water-pipe which had become unfastened and was projecting from the shaft. The pipe pierced the roof of the cage and severely injured Weeks, at the same time preventing the cage from ascending. Golledge was working at a level about half-way down the shaft, which is 608 yards in depth, and about 80 yards above the point at which the accident occurred. Hearing Weeks's moans, he at once got into the shaft and climbed down to the cage by means of the buntons, or girders, which run horizontally round the shaft. Golledge lowered himself from one bunton to the next, the distance between the buntons being on an average 5 feet, or in some cases 6 feet.

On reaching the cage, Golledge rendered first aid to Weeks, and remained with him until the cage could be liberated and brought to the surface, a period of about 2 hours. (25.2.17)

The Faversham explosion

GEORGE EVETTS
WILLIAM EDMUND BETHNELL
URBANE CHARLES BEACH
JOHN HARRISON
JOHN SEARS
WILLIAM WALLACE
GEORGE GILHAM
WILLIAM JAMES WILTSHIRE
JOHN MORLEY STEBBINGS
CHARLES ASHLEY
BERT DUGDALE
CHARLES THOMAS HARRIS
ARTHUR FREDERICK EDWARDS

Awards given on account of their gallant action on the occasion of an explosion which occurred at Faversham. (2.4.16)

An Indian's bravery

NEWARTI KUSHABA While a brick plug was being removed from an outfall sewer-pipe at the Bombay Municipal Sewage Works, a coolie was overcome by gas. Two other coolies at once went down the man-hole, shaking off their fellow workmen who attempted to restrain them, and refusing to wait until they could be roped. They fastened their fellow workman to a rope and sent him up, but were then overcome themselves. Newarti then went down. He found one of the coolies with difficulty and sent him up, and was then ordered to the surface. He at once went down again, but failed to find the other, whose body was not recovered until hours later. Both the rescued men died shortly after their rescue.

Although the atmosphere was less foul when Newarti first descended, and was probably almost clear at his second descent, he was not aware that this was so, and undoubtedly risked his life in endeavouring to save the lives of others. (3.11.16)

Fife miners' gallantry

George Shearer Christie
James Erskine
David Baird
Andrew Scott
Edward McCafferty
John Boyle

At about 10 a.m. on the day in question, while operations were being conducted for the widening of a shaft at the Cowdenbeath Colliery, Fife, a portion of the side of the shaft collapsed, throwing a workman named Newton down the mine to a scaffold about 90 feet below.

Scott, McCafferty, and Baird at once descended in a large bucket or kettle to attempt a rescue. The whole of the shaft below the point at which the fall had occurred was in a highly dangerous condition: stones and rubbish were continually falling, and there was constant danger of a further collapse. Newton was found, alive and conscious, buried beneath about 12 feet of debris and pinned by some fallen timber. The men worked continuously from 10.45 a.m. until 7 p.m. They were joined at 11 a.m. by Christie, and at 1.30 p.m. by Erskine, both of whom remained at work with the others until 7 p.m. During the whole of this period all five men were in serious danger.

At 12.45 Boyle descended in the kettle with two other men. While the kettle was descending a fall occurred, killing one of his companions and injuring another. Boyle drew the kettle to the side of the shaft until the fall was over, and then took the kettle again to the surface. He subsequently remained in charge of the kettle, exposed to constant danger, until 7 p.m.

At 7 p.m., after 9 hours' continuous and highly dangerous labour, the rescue party were relieved by other men. Unfortunately Newton died at 8.30 p.m. Attempts to recover his body were then postponed until the shaft could be worked with greater safety. (20.1.17)

Northumberland miner's devotion

WILLIAM FISH   A heavy fall of roof occurred at the Hartford Mine, Northumberland, at a spot where two men were working, instantly killing one man and injuring and pinning down the other. Fish at once set to work to release the injured man, although there was constant danger of a further fall by which he himself might be killed or injured. After more than half an hour's work he succeeded in his attempt.

There can be little doubt that, but for Fish's gallant action, the injured man would have died. (19.1.17)

Brave conduct of Nottinghamshire miners

DANIEL FOULDS
JAMES HADDON
WILLIAM HEATHCOTE
JAMES SHORT
ALFRED SMITH

A heavy fall of roof occurred at the pye Hill Colliery, Nottinghamshire, by which three men were buried. Foulds, Haddon, Heathcote, Short, and Smith quickly arrived, and attempted to rescue the buried men by digging out the fallen roof and setting props as they progressed. The roof was still extremely dangerous and stones were constantly falling. Three times heavy falls occurred breaking the props which had been set up, but, on each of these occasions, the rescuers were fortunate in having sufficient warning to enable them to escape. They remained at work for 7 hours until all three buried men were reached and taken out; unfortunately all were found to be dead.

During the entire period the rescuers were in continuous danger of serious injury or death from a further sudden fall. (28.11.16)

An instance of resource and courage

WILBY BOOTH
WILLIAM JEFFELLS
At the North Gawber Colliery, Yorkshire, a train of empty tubs was being hauled towards the face while at the same time a train of 36 tubs, containing the day shift of over 100 men, who were leaving work, was being hauled away from the face. Both trains were being hauled at about 6 miles an hour. Shortly before the trains met the incoming empty train ran off the rails, knocking down the roof supports and bringing a heavy fall of roof on to the tubs, which were piled in confusion. Both lines were completely blocked, and the signalling apparatus was injured, so that it was impossible to stop the outgoing train. After rapid consultation with Booth, Jeffells jumped on to the hauling rope and, after it had travelled about 25 yards, succeeded in drawing the bolt which secured the pin fastening the rope to the train. Booth, meanwhile, mounted the first tub, and, as soon as Jeffells had drawn the bolt, succeeded, after the rope had travelled a farther 70 yards, in drawing out the pin, thus detaching the train from the rope. The train came to a standstill within 30 yards of the fall. As soon as the train was detached from the rope, the hauling engine accelerated to such a degree that Booth was jerked from the tub before he could leave hold of the rope, injuring both knees. The resource and courage of both men undoubtedly avoided a serious accident in which many lives must have been lost. Both men risked their lives, as had Jeffells slipped from the rope, as he might easily have done, he would certainly have been crushed by the train, while had Booth failed in the very difficult task of drawing the pin while the train was in motion he would have been the first to have been killed when the train crashed into the fall. (2.6.17)

A Welsh miner's devotion

ARTHUR MORRIS
A timberman named William Henry Dixon was drawing out timber in a part of the Llanhilleth mine, Monmouth, which it had been decided to abandon, and Morris was assisting him in this work. They had been at work for an hour when, owing to the collapse of a pair of timbers, a fall of roof and sides occurred. Dixon was caught by the fall and fell in a sitting position, being buried up to the neck with rubbish and timber, about 8 tons of which had fallen.

Morris was 8 yards away when the fall occurred, and at once responded to Dixon's call for help, and, although heavy stones were still falling from the roof, and Morris was urged by Dixon to stand back, he persisted in his efforts to release his fellow workman.

A large stone was then seen to be in imminent danger of falling on their heads, and with commendable presence of mind, Morris ran back 20 yards for a piece of timber, which he fixed in a slanting position over Dixon to support the stone temporarily. Morris then restarted uncovering Dixon, and succeeded in releasing him in about 25 minutes after the accident occurred.

Dixon was badly bruised and cut all over his body, and while his injuries were being attended to by Morris, who himself suffered from cuts, the stone, which had been supported temporarily and which weighed about 2 tons, fell to the ground on the place where the men had been, and would undoubtedly have killed them both had the rescue been effected less expeditiously.

Morris displayed coolness, intelligence, and initiative. He was 600 yards from the nearest man working in the mine, and if, as is the usual custom, he had gone for help, Dixon would have been buried by the falling debris and have lost his life. (30.3.17)

Gallantry in a Yorkshire mine

George Henry Taylor
Thomas Stokes
Thomas James White
Eli Purser

By an accident which occurred at the Askern Main Colliery, Yorkshire, two men were trapped by a fall of roof weighing about 30 tons, and extending over an area of about 160 square feet—one of them completely buried near the edge of the fall, and the other partially buried and severely injured. Eight of their fellow workmen were soon on the spot, and after working bravely for 2 hours succeeded in releasing both men alive. All the four men above mentioned ran considerable risk, for a space of 2 hours, of being buried by further falls, and had it not been for their presence of mind and self-sacrifice, their two comrades would certainly have lost their lives. Taylor and Stokes were exposed to the greatest danger, and displayed special initiative. (31.5.17)

Three posthumous awards

Thomas Anderson
James Edward Tierney
George Gale

During salvage operations on board the steamship *Great City*, the holds of which were known to be heavily charged with gas arising from decomposing grain, one of the stevedore's men noticed some pieces of wood floating towards the pump and, contrary to strict orders, went down in order to pick the wood up so as to prevent the pump from choking. While in the act of doing this, he was overcome by gas and fell into the water. Anderson, who had some time previously suffered from gas poisoning, and, therefore, knew the gravity of the risk, at once went to his assistance and succeeded in holding him up while a rope was being sent down to him, but before this could reach him he was also overcome and fell into the water. Tierney and Gale then went to the rescue, but both were also overcome.

Anderson, Tierney, and Gale undoubtedly lost their lives in an endeavour to save the life of their fellow workman. (31.8.17)

Five men's courage averts major disaster

Steven Arthur Rubythorn
Alfred Hamilton
John Harrison
Ernest Charles Allen
Henry Butcher

A large shell exploded in the Melt House of the National Shell Filling Factory, killing two men and filling the place with thick smoke. At the time of the explosion more than 4,000 filled shells were in the Melt House, and several trucks of shells caught fire. Regardless of the great danger to which they were exposed, the men, whose names are given above, seized extinguishers, and, rushing through the smoke, played them on the fire, and, with the help of other men, put it out. By their presence of mind and courage these men probably averted a great disaster. (5.10.17)

Gallantry in a munitions factory fire

Thomas Coppard   Thomas Kew
Abraham Clarke Graham   Thomas Tattersall

On account of their gallant conduct on the occasion of a fire which occurred at a munitions factory. (1.10.17)

A gallant attempt to save life

THOMAS JONES   A fall of roof occurred at the Cwm Cynon Colliery, Glamorganshire, as a result of which a boy was pinned down by a stone weighing 1½ cwt. It was obvious that another fall was imminent; but, notwithstanding this, Jones at once stood over the boy, and with his back supported a stone which was about to fall on the boy, and would have killed him. A further fall occurred, fortunately without injuring Jones. Jones supported the stone as long as possible; but as he weakened, it fell, seriously injuring him, but missing the boy.

The boy, after being extricated, died of his injuries. (19.11.17)

Bravery in a gas-filled mine

ROBERT FARRINGTON
HENRY FOSTER
THOMAS PICKERING

A fireman at the Deep Pit, St. Helen's Collieries, named Peter Anders, was inspecting a place where a level was being driven to cut off a brow, and he went round the brow to test the progress of the work by knocking on the coal. Unfortunately, gas had accumulated in the brow owing to the brattice-cloth by which it was ventilated being broken down by a fall of coal. Anders was overcome by the gas, and his groanings brought several men to the place where he lay, which was in complete darkness, as it was dangerous to use any light. Thomas Pickering, a jigger, first tried to rescue the fireman, but, though he succeeded in getting hold of Anders, he could not release the fireman's legs, which were fastened round a prop, and he was overcome with gas, though he managed to roll clear. Henry Foster, a collier, then tried to rescue Anders, but was in turn overcome by the gas and fell senseless. Pickering made a second attempt, without success. In the meantime, Robert Farrington, the under-manager, arrived and immediately went into the gas, but fell unconscious after two attempts, though he managed to grasp Foster's legs. Pickering then succeeded in grasping Farrington, who had kept his hold on Foster, with the result that both were rescued. Foster was brought round by artificial respiration. The position of Anders was ascertained with the help of an electric lamp, and, as soon as the ventilation was restored, Anders was also brought out, but life was, unfortunately, extinct. (26.2.18)

An act of courageous perseverance

JOHN THOMSON
PETER CUMMINGS

While engaged on repair work at the Giffnock Colliery, a fireman entered a place which was known to be dangerous owing to fire-damp, and was overcome. Three men attempted, without taking any precautions, to rescue him, and were themselves rendered unconscious. Thomson and Cummings then crawled on hands and knees into the dangerous space, and succeeded in rescuing three of the unconscious men in three separate journeys. They then entered a fourth time, followed by two others; but on reaching the body of the fourth victim they found that the two who had followed them were themselves partly overcome, and had to be removed. They then entered a fifth time, and recovered the body of the remaining man, who, however, was dead. (10.12.17)

Heroism in an Indian coal-mine

Cecil Herbert Whiffen   Sirdar Bideshi Kol
RUPAI KOL   SUKU KOL   BHUDU KOL

For gallantry in rescuing two men imprisoned through an accident in the Gorangdih Colliery in India belonging to the Burraker Coal Company. (3.3.17)

Boiler-house explosion at Rugby

JOHN GARNER   One of seven boilers in the boiler-house of the factory of the British Thomson-Houston Co., Ltd., at Rugby, exploded. Garner, a stoker, at once entered the house, which was filled with steam and boiling water, in the hope of rescuing any person who might be injured. Large masses of masonry were threatening to fall, and either of the remaining two boilers under steam was likely to explode at any moment. The only light available was a hand lamp carried by Garner. After searching some five minutes, Garner discovered an injured man lodged on a projecting beam; but was unable to reach him. He stood by him, however, until the beam canted and the injured man fell to the ground without further hurt. No other persons were injured by the accident. Garner undoubtedly risked his life to save a fellow workman. (29.4.18)

A Fife miner's bravery

James Simpson A repairer at Glencraig Colliery, Fife, whilst engaged with two other workmen in carrying out repairs, was killed by a fall of roof. The two workmen were both caught and held by the fall. Simpson, who arrived half an hour later, found the men imprisoned and realized that if he went for help they would be suffocated before it could arrive. He immediately set to work unaided and worked for three hours without relaxation, though exposed to danger from the falling roof. At last he succeeded in releasing one of the men. Simpson was then so exhausted that he could not release the second man; but he protected him with timber before going for help. Had it not been for Simpson's presence of mind and devotion the two men would have lost their lives. (21.5.18)

Successful rescue at Barnsley

CHARLES SELLARS
LAURENCE WISEMAN

A collier at the Grimthorpe Colliery, Barnsley, was buried by a fall of roof. Sellars was soon on the spot, and, after failing in an effort to get at the man by working under falling ground, he got on to the fall and worked along with Wiseman. After two hours and a half of persistent effort they succeeded in rescuing the workman. Both Sellars and Wiseman ran the risk of being injured by further falls. (20.4.18)

A case of determined heroism

Frederick Holdway
GEORGE HENRY LAVER
THOMAS HARPER

Three miners were working at the face in the Ackton Hall Colliery, Featherstone, when a heavy fall of roof occurred, imprisoning one of the men. Holdway, who was soon on the spot, immediately began the work of rescue, and, with six others, including Harper and Laver, succeeded, after working hard for nearly 24 hours, in rescuing the imprisoned workman. The rescue was carried out with exceptional skill and determination under very dangerous conditions. Holdway specially distinguished himself and showed a fine example of courage and coolness. Harper and Laver were also specially mentioned for their resource and presence of mind. (6.5.18)

A miner's self-sacrifice[1]

JOHN JOHNSON A heavy fall of roof occurred at the Newdigate Colliery, Nuneaton, by which a man named Pacey was buried. Johnson ran at once to the spot, where others were already at work, and, finding that the roof was still very uneasy, ordered props to be set. Leaving the men at work, he found his way to the other side of the fall, where the roof was also very uneasy. Estimating correctly, however, that it was from this side Pacey could most easily be reached, he decided to carry on the work, and himself started to set props. Almost immediately, however, a further heavy fall occurred, burying and severely injuring him. The roof then ceased to be uneasy, and Johnson and Pacey were rescued alive. Pacey unfortunately died in hospital. Johnson was in and out of hospital for nearly two years, and had to undergo many operations as a result of his injuries. (29.7.15)

Gallant rescue from a high chimney

EDWARD COLWELL Three men were ascending a steel chimney
FREDERICK LINDLEY 175 feet high at Vickers' River Don Works, Sheffield, for the purpose of fixing a scaffold in order to paint the exterior of the chimney. They ascended by means of iron rungs permanently bolted to the chimney, at distances of 12 inches throughout its height, by rivets bolted through the exterior casing of the chimney. The men were about 10 feet apart. When the topmost had reached a height of about 100 feet, one of the rungs supporting the second man broke away and he fell, in his fall breaking ten other rungs beneath him and striking the third man, who, fortunately, managed to retain his hold and descend to the ground. The man who fell was killed instantaneously.

The topmost man was left on the upper part of the ladder, 100 feet from the ground, with a gap of 10 feet below him preventing his descent. Although it was likely that many of the rungs below him were defective, Colwell and Lindley at once volunteered to rescue him. They ascended the rungs bearing the weight of a long wooden ladder with lifting and lashing tackle. In the course of the ascent they discovered another defective rung which they easily wrenched out and threw to the ground. They nevertheless proceeded and lashed the wooden ladder against the chimney and across the gap, thus enabling the man who was cut off by the gap to descend to the ground. (17.7.18)

[1] The delay of over three years in gazetting (in Nov. 1918) is unexplained.

Filling-factory disaster at Chilwell

ARTHUR HILARY BRISTOWE
This award to Lt. Bristowe, Works Manager, was made on account of the great courage and presence of mind which he had displayed on the occasion of an explosion which occurred at the National Filling Factory at Chilwell. (1.7.18)

Two brave Hindus

MARUTI VITHOBA
KRISHNA PARBATI
A masonry tank 9 feet square by $12\frac{1}{2}$ deep at the Simplex Mills in Bombay was being cleaned out by six Hindu workmen by means of buckets lowered through a man-hole, when one of the men fell through the man-hole into the tank and was at once rendered unconscious by poisonous gas. One of the other men went to his assistance, and immediately lost consciousness. The other four all attempted to rescue the two unconscious men, and were all likewise overcome. Maruti Vithoba then volunteered to rescue the men, and was lowered by a rope; he endeavoured to save one who appeared still living; but, before he could do so, was overpowered by the fumes, and had to be pulled up. Krishna Parbati at once volunteered to make a further attempt, and had nearly completed fastening a rope round one of the victims when he also had to be pulled out in an unconscious state. The six bodies were eventually recovered by the Fire Brigade, who were wearing smoke-helmets; one was still living, but died a few minutes after being rescued.

In view of the fact that it was obvious that the gas was highly poisonous and its action extremely rapid, Maruti Vithoba and Krishna Parbati undoubtedly risked their lives in endeavouring to save the lives of others. (2.2.18)

Bravery in a Cumberland mine

JOHN JOSEPH NEVIN
ALFRED HORN
Two miners were buried by a fall of ground in the Margaret Iron Ore Mine, Frizington, Cumberland. The fall swept out all the timber and left exposed a dangerous roof, in parts 20 feet high and fully 20 feet wide, from which masses of rock were liable to fall at any moment. As the place could not be made safe by means of timber in any reasonable time, several men took the risk of working under the exposed and dangerous roof in order to release the two imprisoned miners who were buried amongst a mixed mass of timber, stone, and iron ore, while others stood on the fall and watched the roof, thereby inspiring confidence amongst the men engaged immediately underneath. Fortunately no fall took place during the work, which lasted about $1\frac{3}{4}$ hours, or the

rescuers could hardly have escaped injury. One of the men rescued succumbed afterwards to his injuries.

Eight men were engaged in the work of rescue. Horn and Nevin specially distinguished themselves. (22.7.18)

Two Brisbane miners risk their lives for fellow workman

MICHAEL FOGARTY
FRANK DULLER

Fogarty and another miner named Fred Joga were blasting in the Mount Morgan Mine, Brisbane. Having inserted the charges, Joga lit the fuses, the last of which, however, did not light properly. Fogarty had already gone to a place of safety, but Joga remained behind attempting to light the last fuse. Fogarty was not aware of this until the first charge exploded. He then at once called to Duller, and both men went back to the face, where, as they knew, two charges were still unexploded, to rescue Joga. They found him about 6 feet from the face, and just succeeded in dragging him clear when the second charge exploded. Joga, unfortunately, died from the injuries he had received by the explosion of the first charge. Both men undoubtedly risked their lives in the attempt to save Joga's life. (12.7.18)

A colliery manager's bravery

RICHARD EDWARD FINCH

At the Park Lane Colliery, Wigan, two men named Shaw and Rimmer were replacing some timber near a self-acting haulage rope. At 4.30 p.m. the roof crashed down over their heads, burying both men. Nothing was done to rescue them until Finch, the Manager, arrived at 5 p.m. He shouted, and Shaw answered in a feeble voice. Finch crept over the fallen bars and was able to touch him. By dint of effort he was able to scrape the dirt from Shaw's mouth and saved him from suffocation. He called for volunteers to assist in digging out the men and three men came to his assistance. Stones and dirt continued to fall from the roof, and on several occasions Finch ordered his assistants back; though during the whole time he himself continued his exertions. Shaw was rescued at 5.30 p.m. Finch then endeavoured to rescue Rimmer, but he was found to be dead. His body was recovered at 6.30 p.m. Finch underwent great danger, and took risks no one else was willing to take. (29.1.19)

A boy's courageous action

JOHN MCCABE

An inrush of moss into the workings occurred at the Stanriff Colliery, Airdrie. McCabe, with two other drawers and three miners, was at the bottom of No. 3 shaft when they were told that the moss had broken in. The two other boys and the three men at once ascended the shaft and escaped. McCabe, a drawer, aged 17, however, knowing that there were men at the face who might be cut off, returned for a quarter of a mile and warned the men. He and the men he had warned were ultimately collected and raised by another shaft. When he returned to the face, McCabe did not know where the break had occurred, or whether the moss might not at any moment fill the workings through which he returned, as in fact it soon afterwards did. He faced a grave and unknown danger, which might have been fatal, in order to enable others to escape. (9.7.18)

A foundryman's gallantry

HARRY DENNY   Joseph Reynolds, a foreman in Messrs. Josiah Guest & Sons' foundry at West Bromwich, while superintending the filling of a series of pig-iron moulds, stumbled and fell on to the still molten metal. No one was near, but Denny, a labourer, hearing his cries, ran up and tried to pull him away by his clothes, but these were burned through and came away in his hands. Denny then thrust his arms into the molten metal under Reynolds, caught him round the body and lifted him clear. He then ran for assistance. Unfortunately Reynolds was so seriously injured that he died a few days afterwards.

Denny's burns were very severe, and he knowingly risked his life in endeavouring to save Reynolds. (27.3.19)

Twenty-five lives saved by boy of 14

GEORGE HOYLE   A fire broke out on the third floor of the cotton-factory of Nahum's Union Mills Company, Halifax, and at once spread with very great rapidity. Hoyle, a boy of 14 years of age, was working in the basement. As soon as he heard of the fire, he took a chemical extinguisher and ran up to the third floor. He then warned the women employed on the upper floors. By this time both staircases were burning, so that retreat by this means was impossible. He at once opened the crane door, and after seeing that the chain was run out to its full length, drew it in, and assisted about 25 women to descend by it. He remained until the last, and then descended himself without injury. Fifteen minutes after the fire broke out, the roof of the factory fell in.

By his coolness and courage Hoyle undoubtedly saved upwards of twenty lives at the risk of his own. (27.11.18)

CHAPTER XIII
AWARDS OF THE ALBERT MEDAL
Land Service
JAN. 1920—DEC. 1938

Note—The average interval between the date of the deed here recorded and the announcement of an award in *The London Gazette* is about 9 months. Minimum delay 26 days, maximum over 15 months. The date of the Gazette is shown in parentheses.

AWARDS OF THE ALBERT MEDAL
JAN. 1920—DEC. 1938

Awards of the Albert Medal in gold are in Old English type.

Two heroic dockyard workmen

MATTHEW RONALD MATHER
JOSEPH BOWMAN

Able Seaman Brewer had descended into the Wet Provision Room of H.M.S. *Tiger* at Rosyth in company with J. H. Anderson, a shipwright, on 27th August when he was overcome by poisonous gases and collapsed. Anderson, himself feeling the effect of the gases, left the compartment as quickly as possible to obtain assistance, and Mather and Bowman, dockyard workmen, who were near to the scene, descended without hesitation to endeavour to rescue Brewer. They did not wait for further assistance or for safety appliances, though they were fully aware of the cause of Brewer's collapse and of the risk they ran. They were at once fatally gassed. (21.5.20)

A burning munitions ship

ARTHUR STEDMAN COTTON

An ammunition dump exploded at Novorossisk, South Russia, on 14th October 1919, setting fire to s.s. *War Pike*, which was carrying a cargo of munitions, including shells. Colonel Cotton, C.M.G., D.S.O., as explosions were taking place both on the quay and on board the ship, cleared the bystanders from the neighbourhood, and assisted in casting off the hawsers from the vessel. He then organized a small party to follow the steamer in a tug, when it was towed out to sea, in order to render all possible assistance, and, although the vessel was burning fiercely, the hold and bunkers being well alight, he boarded her and endeavoured to get the fire under control. It was not until the fore part of the ship began to settle down that he and his party left the vessel. (16.7.20)

An Indian waterman's bravery

GHARIB SHAH

A Religious Fair was being held in India at Nariana, on the 3rd June 1919, on the right bank of the River Beas, and many pilgrims were being ferried across the river. Two boatloads had been taken over successfully, and the boat was crossing a third time when it got out of control. The river was in flood and the rapids very dangerous; the boat, filled to its utmost capacity, entered the rapids and was swamped. Gharib Shah, a young waterman, 25 years of age, in charge of a timber raft some 30 yards away, took his raft close to the overturned boat, and set to work to save the passengers as they were carried past him. Again and again he plunged into the river, and rescued 15 persons. Others in the water who had struggled to the raft were pulled on to it by him.

It is estimated that 150 passengers were on board when it started, and most of the 45 saved owed their lives to Gharib Shah, who had previously saved 5 persons from drowning in 1914 at great risk. (27.7.20)

A wife's gallantry

MRS. EMMETT On the 7th December 1919, Mrs. Emmett, wife of the Stationmaster at Peshawar, and her children were sitting with her husband, who was in bed with fever, when the eldest boy, aged 17, went into the sitting-room and found an Indian coming in from the garden who attacked him with an axe, breaking the boy's forearm. The boy closed with his assailant, and on his mother coming into the room she found that the man, who had dropped the axe, was stabbing her son with a dagger. She went to her son's assistance and seized the man, never relaxing her hold in spite of receiving a stab in her side. At this stage her husband came from his sick-bed to the rescue; the Indian wrenched himself free from Mrs. Emmett and stabbed Mr. Emmett in the thigh. Thereupon Mrs. Emmett again seized the man by the wrist, and in spite of receiving several more wounds on her hand and arm succeeded in getting hold of the handle of the dagger. Eventually, with the aid of servants, the assailant was overpowered. All three recovered; their assailant, a murderous fanatic, was tried and hanged. (17.8.20)

A fireman's gallantry

THOMAS WILLIAM BROWN A serious fire broke out on 23rd December 1919 in the basement of Cross House, Westgate Road, Newcastle-on-Tyne, where cinematograph films were stored.

The work of the Fire Brigade was performed under most difficult and dangerous conditions, owing to the great heat, noxious fumes, and explosions caused by the burning films. Flames were already shooting across the street on one side of the building when the Brigade arrived, and it was from the windows of the upper floors that a large number of the rescues were effected. The action of Fireman Thomas William Brown in reaching the top of the building by means of a hook ladder was a notable feature of the work of rescue.

A 50-foot fire-escape had been pitched on one side of the building, and Brown, having ascended the escape, fastened to a window on the fourth floor a 14-foot hook-ladder which he carried, and by this means enabled 13 persons to escape. He then threw up the hook-ladder to the main cornice above, which projected 2½ feet from the building, and with great coolness and daring ascended the parapet, where he effected the rescue of 3 other persons by making fast the hook-ladder in another position and attaching it to a 65-foot escape. There was great risk of the hook slipping while the fireman was ascending the ladder some 70 feet from the ground, seeing that by reason of the overhang of the cornice the ladder was clear of the wall.

Upwards of 100 persons were in the building when the fire broke out. Twelve deaths resulted, 57 were rescued, while 50 others effected their escape from the windows of the lower floors. (5.10.20)

Bravery in a Madras fire

IAN WILLIAM GALBRAITH
SUBADAR-MAJOR ELLAYA

A dangerous fire broke out on 18th June 1920, at the Arsenal at St. Thomas's Mount, Madras, and the flames, 20 feet high, had reached a spot within 5 yards of which a large quantity of aerial bombs were stacked. Lt. Galbraith, M.C., 19th Lancers, superintended the removal of the bombs for nearly three-quarters of an hour, remaining until the last bomb had been removed, and he set a splendid example to the troops by his gallantry and perseverance. Four thousand of these bombs were stored in the Arsenal, and an explosion would have resulted in heavy loss of life.

Subadar-Major Ellaya, 1/88 Carnatic Infantry, with 43 men of 'C' Company, took a prominent part in the work of removing the bombs which were lying close to the flames. He was the first member of his regiment to arrive on the scene, and he too set a fine example to the men under him by carrying away the bombs and continuing to do so until ordered to another duty by his Commanding Officer. The work he performed in moving the bombs exposed him to very great danger. (15.7.21)

A Sepoy's brave action

RAGHU NANDAN SINGH

Whilst moving the picquet bomb store on the 25th July 1920, near Piaza Raghza, on the NW. Frontier of India, Sepoy Raghu Nandan Singh, Indian Infantry, noticed that the fuse of a bomb was burning. He called to his comrades to take shelter and taking the bomb out of the box attempted to throw it clear of the picquet. The bomb hit the parapet and burst. By his prompt, clear-headed action, he undoubtedly saved the lives of his comrades by preventing the bomb exploding among and detonating the other bombs. (15.7.21)

Officer's brave action

GEORGE HUBERT BLAND
A Stokes mortar shell fused prematurely on 31st August 1921, at Moghal Kot, in India. Captain Bland, M.C., Mahratta L.I., with great presence of mind and disregard for his own safety—for a few seconds only would elapse before the shell exploded—at once rushed forward and threw the shell over the parapet. But for his courageous action there would in all probability have been loss of life, and it is unlikely that casualties would have been confined to the Trench Mortar Section, for many officers and men were in the near vicinity. (30.6.22)

Flying officer's gallantry

CHARLES CURTIS DARLEY
A Vickers-Vimy aeroplane, piloted by Captain Cecil Hill Darley, R.A.F., brother of Squadron Leader (then Flight Lieutenant) Darley, R.A.F., who was acting as Navigating Officer, made a false landing by Lake Bracciano, some 20 miles north of Rome, on the 27th September 1919, when on a flight from England to Egypt.

On the following morning, in taking off, the aeroplane failed to clear a telegraph pole, and crashed, immediately bursting into flames. Squadron Leader Darley was thrown clear, but at once rushed to the blazing wreckage and displayed very conspicuous bravery and devotion in persistent, but unavailing, attempts to rescue his brother, who was pinned in the pilot's seat. His efforts to release his brother were only brought to an end by his collapse. He sustained such severe burns that he was a patient in hospital for over eighteen months. (25.7.22)

A gallant attempted rescue in Waziristan

RUR SINGH
In the course of operations in Waziristan, a party of men were crossing the Shahur Tangi on 18th October 1921, and had reached some high ground in mid-stream, when they were cut off by a sudden rise of the water. The river rapidly became a roaring torrent; five of the men were swept away, and it seemed that the remainder were doomed. Havildar-Major Rur Singh, 48th Pioneers, made several attempts to swim out with a rope, and eventually succeeded in reaching the men, but they were then exhausted and, the river rising still higher, the whole party was swept away. One man to whom the rope was handed by Rur Singh was pulled to the bank, while Rur Singh himself was washed ashore some distance down the stream alive, but considerably battered. (22.12.22)

Flood rescues in New Zealand

CHARLES CHAPMAN Great destruction was caused by a severe flood which swept through the Paparoa Valley on 27th March 1920. An immense volume of water descended from the upper valley, and great loss of life ensued. Mr. Chapman, on receiving news of the disaster, put on a bathing-costume and at once set out for the Paparoa township, to find that the river which runs through the township had become a raging torrent, the water reaching almost to the top rail of the bridge spanning the river. Two men (one of whom could not swim) were clinging to timber in the middle of the river, while a crowd of terror-stricken people looked on helplessly from the bank.

After very strenuous efforts he rescued these men. He then heard that a woman and her child were in danger higher up the river. He found the woman clinging to a tree and swam out to her; to effect a rescue he had to return for a plank. A wooden form was available, and this he endeavoured to tow out to the woman and child. The rope broke, but his second effort, when a length of fencing wire had been procured, was successful, and he brought first the child, then the mother, to the bank. (16.2.23)

The Shackleton Trans-Antarctic Expedition

ERNEST EDWARD MILLS JOYCE
RICHARD WALTER RICHARDS
VICTOR GEORGE HAYWARD (deceased)
HARRY ERNEST WILD (deceased)

The Shackleton Trans-Antarctic Expedition of 1914–17 had for its object the crossing of the Antarctic Continent from the Weddell Sea to the Ross Sea, via the South Pole, a distance of about seventeen hundred miles. Sufficient supplies for the journey could not be carried, and it was therefore necessary to establish a chain of depots on the Ross Sea side as far southwards as possible. With this end in view the ship *Aurora* was sent to McMurdo Sound at the southern extremity of the Ross Sea, and, as it was intended that the vessel should winter there, a portion only of the stores and equipment were disembarked. McMurdo Sound was reached in January 1915, but during a blizzard in May the *Aurora* was blown out to sea and was unable to return, and the nine members of the Expedition who were on shore were left stranded. They recognized that failure to establish the depots would undoubtedly result in the loss of the main body and resolved, in spite of their grave shortage of equipment, to carry out the allotted programme.

For this purpose a party under the command of Sub-Lieutenant A. L. Mackintosh, R.N.R., and consisting of the Rev. A. P.

Spencer-Smith, Messrs. Joyce, R.N., Richards, Hayward, and Wild, R.N., and three other members who assisted for a part of the outward journey, left Hut Point, Ross Island, on 9th October. They took with them two sledges and four dogs, and 162 days elapsed before the surviving members of the party were back at Hut Point, the total distance covered being approximately 950 miles.

Mr. Spencer-Smith had to be dragged on a sledge for 42 days mainly by hand labour, the distance covered being over 350 miles. When more than 100 miles remained to be covered the collapse of Lieutenant Mackintosh imposed an additional burden on the active members of the party, who were all suffering from scurvy and snow blindness and were so enfeebled by their labours that at times they were unable to cover more than 2 or 3 miles in 15 hours.

Mr. Spencer-Smith died when only 19 miles remained to be covered, but Lieutenant Mackintosh was brought in safely to the base. (4.7.23)

An adventure with a man-eating tiger

VELADI SAMMAI   Mr. H. S. George, Deputy Conservator of Forests of the South Chanda Division of the Central Provinces, was returning to camp on 9th November 1924, along a jungle path, accompanied by Veladi Sammai, a Gond of Murvahi forest village. The latter, who was carrying Mr. George's gun, was walking in front. Suddenly and without warning a man-eating tiger jumped upon Mr. George's back, seized him by the neck, and proceeded to drag him into the jungle. Veladi Sammai, with extraordinary gallantry, rushed at the tiger, placed the muzzle of the gun against it and pulled the trigger, but was unable to discharge the weapon owing to the safety catch with which he was not familiar. He then shouted and waved his arms, thus driving the tiger off for a short distance. Mr. George was badly bitten in the neck and covered with blood, but with the Gond's assistance he managed to stagger slowly along and reached his camp which was about two miles away. The tiger followed them for some distance but was kept off by the shouts and demonstrations of the Gond.

It was known that a man-eating tiger was in the neighbourhood and had killed several villagers, but it had never attacked any one on the path used by the forest officer, and neither Mr. George nor the Gond had any suspicion of the tiger's presence until the attack was made. Veladi Sammai's action was an extremely brave one and he gravely imperilled his own life. He certainly saved Mr. George's life, as only his prompt and gallant action prevented the tiger dragging the forest officer into the jungle and eating him. (12.5.25)

A Gurkha's bravery

AIMANSING PUN On 16th May 1926, a party of men were washing their clothes on the banks of a wide river, which by reason of the strong converging currents was extremely dangerous to swimmers.

Contrary to orders, one of the party, Kishan Bahadur Thapa, entered the stream, swam out some 50 yards from the bank, was caught by the current and rendered helpless.

Although well acquainted with the danger involved, Rifleman Aimansing Pun, Gurkha Rifles, without hesitation went to the rescue of his comrade and succeeded in getting hold of the drowning man. He commenced to swim with him to the farther bank, but his efforts proved ineffectual owing to the violent struggles of Kishan Bahadur Thapa, who dragged his rescuer under water. On coming to the surface Pun, whose hold on the drowning man had been broken, could not see his comrade. He reached land only with great difficulty. (21.9.26)

An accident in the Himalayas

GEORGE STEWART BAIN SMITH Major Minchinton, with two Gurkha companions, was descending an ice slope on 3rd June 1927, when at a height of about 14,000 feet the party lost their foothold and slid or fell some 1,000 feet on to a snow slope below. Major Minchinton and one of his companions were so badly injured that they were unable to move, but the third managed to make his way to Lakka, some 3,000 feet lower, where he met and informed Mr. Bain Smith, R.A., of the accident. Mr. Bain Smith, though he had no experience of mountaineering, at once set out with an Indian to rescue Major Minchinton from his position which he reached at 4.30 p.m. after a climb of 3,000 feet. Mr. Bain Smith had no ice-axe and was wearing smooth-soled boots and he could only proceed across the snow-field by kicking foot-holes in the hard snow with stockinged feet. The coolie who had accompanied Mr. Bain Smith from Lakka was unable to cross the snow and remained behind. On reaching Major Minchinton Mr. Bain Smith made a sledge of his coat and, accompanied by the Gurkha who was just able to move, proceeded to drag the injured man over the then freezing snow to a point some 500 feet lower. Further progress without assistance was impossible, and Mr. Bain Smith therefore descended alone across the snow slope until he met with two shepherds who accompanied him back to where the injured man lay. Major Minchinton was lowered a further 500 feet until descent was checked by the roughness of the snow. Mr. Bain Smith sent one of the shepherds for more men, but he failed to return, and Mr. Bain Smith thereupon made a second journey and after great difficulty found four shepherds whom he sent back to Major Minchinton. He himself was by that time so exhausted that he could only proceed by crawling. He found Major Minchinton struggling and his struggles were such that, as the snow had frozen hard, he could not be moved. Mr. Bain Smith, after sending the injured Gurkha down with two of the men, made repeated but unsuccessful efforts to continue the descent. At sunset the remaining shepherds deserted him.

Mr. Bain Smith, who was clad only in a shirt, shorts, and stockings, stayed for half an hour with Major Minchinton, who was then unconscious, if not already dead. An ice-cold wind was blowing and there were occasional hailstorms and it was obvious that nobody left exposed on the slope would survive the night. Mr. Bain Smith, after covering Major Minchinton with his coat, descended to a fire that was burning below the glacier where he found Mrs. Minchinton and a party of men, none of whom were capable of tackling the mountain-side in the dark. The first rescue party arrived at 3 a.m. on the following morning and Mr. Bain Smith escorted them to a point whence Major Minchinton's body could be seen. He was then on the verge of collapse and both feet were frost-bitten. (30.9.27)

A gallant gunner

JOHN FAIRCLOUGH   A serious fire occurred in a petrol store in Ambala on 27th April 1927. Three Indian boys had gone to the store in a lorry to get petrol and they entered the building carrying a lantern. The naked light ignited the petrol vapour with which in the hot weather the building was filled and in a very short time the whole building was ablaze. On the outbreak of the fire the lorry-driver departed and before any organized aid could arise the boys were trapped in the burning building. Gunner Fairclough, R.A., who happened to be walking alone near by at once went to their assistance. In spite of the fact that the heat from the burning building was so intense as to keep onlookers at a considerable distance from the fire, he three times entered the building and rescued the three children. Gunner Fairclough was severely burned. The three Indian boys later died.

Gunner Fairclough, in entering on three separate occasions a burning building containing a highly inflammable and in certain circumstances a highly explosive substance, three times put his life in the gravest danger. To enter the building the first time was an act calling for great courage, but to enter it twice thereafter, knowing the full danger to be run, was an act of exceptional gallantry. (8.5.28)

Heroic attempted rescue from a fire

ALEXANDER DOCTOR CLARK   On 24th June 1929, a fire broke out at midnight in the premises at 89 Hylton Road, Sunderland, in which three children had been left alone by their parents. On hearing that children were in the building, Mr. Clark, a married man with three children, although he knew that previous attempts to effect the rescue had failed, broke a staircase window at the back of the premises, climbed through, and in spite of the intense heat and flames made his way to the assistance of the children. From the position in which the bodies were subsequently found it appears that Mr. Clark, on gaining entry, rushed up the burning stairway to an upper room and brought the youngest child down to the first floor, where unfortunately their escape must have been cut off.

It must have been plain to Mr. Clark that in attempting the rescue of the children he was placing his life in the gravest peril. (9.7.29)

The wreck of the R 101

HENRY JAMES LEECH   When the Airship R 101 was wrecked near Beauvais on 5th October 1930, despite terrifying experiences in extricating himself from the blazing wreckage, Mr. Leech, A.F.M., immediately at grave risk re-entered the burning mass and succeeded in disentangling a companion from the network of red-hot girders and hauled him into safety, himself sustaining burns in the process. (31.10.30)

Attempted rescue from a crocodile

LEONARD PEMBERTON   A number of children were bathing in the Zambesi River at Livingstone, Northern Rhodesia, on 14th November 1930, at a point where a wire enclosure, no longer crocodile-proof, had been made some time ago. One of the boys was seen suddenly to disappear. Mr. Pemberton, who was sitting on the bank, dived in fully clothed and made repeated but unsuccessful attempts to save the boy from a crocodile which was holding him under water. Mr. Pemberton was fully aware that he was close to a man-eating crocodile which might at any moment have turned and attacked him, and in acting as he did displayed the greatest courage. (6.3.31)

Soldier's bravery in Indian forest fire

WILLIAM HENRY FOSTER   A forest fire broke out in the neighbourhood of Sabathu, Simla Hills, on 14th June 1931, on a steep hill-side which was covered with highly inflammable pine-needles. A Company of the Leicestershire Regiment on fire picquet attempted to beat out the fire. The wind, however, fanned the flames, which became so fierce that the Company was withdrawn, but on the roll being called it was found that two men, Private A. L. Smith and Private Foster, were missing. Private Smith had been cut off by the fire and in endeavouring to escape he slipped on the hill-side where he lay with his clothing alight, surrounded by flames and unable to move. Private Foster was told by an Indian that one of his comrades was lying ablaze on the hill. He at once rushed down through 200 yards of flaring undergrowth and found Smith lying helpless in the fire. Foster picked Smith up and carried him some 300 yards to a place of safety, whence both men were taken to hospital. Smith died the same night.

Foster's action in endeavouring to save his comrade was an extremely brave one. He went into the fire at grave peril to his own life, and had he fallen on the slippery hill-side no one would have been there to go to his assistance. (27.11.31)

The Baluchistan earthquake, 1935

FLORENCE ALICE ALLEN At the risk of her own life, and at the cost of terrible injuries to her leg, Nurse Allen saved the life of the child in her charge by throwing herself across the cot. On subsequent occasions she displayed the highest courage.

JOHN GUISE COWLEY Lt. Cowley, R.E., and his party were the first to start relief work at the Civil Hospital, where the walls of all the wards had collapsed, bringing down the roofs intact on the inmates on whom the debris of the walls had already fallen. At first the men were too few in number to tear off the roofs. So they raised them up while Lt. Cowley crawled under and dragged out survivors from their beds. The survivors were hospital patients and mostly helpless. Lt. Cowley lifted many men in his arms regardless of the warning that they were suffering from all manner of diseases. But for him and his example many fewer would have been saved.

FIROZE KHAN On the morning of 31st May Lance-Naik Firoze Khan, 8th Punjab (Burma) Regt., was in charge of a party engaged in rescue work and fire-fighting in the city. Hearing cries for help from beneath the ruins near a fire, Lance-Naik Firoze Khan and his party commenced to dig and cut their way down into the building. After nearly two hours' work, the lance-naik was able to enter the building from above and discovered two people pinned down by beams and rubble. The fire had by this time spread to the building in question, which was full of smoke and fumes. In spite of this the lance-naik with pick and saw spent over half an hour beneath the ruins and finally released the injured people. He did this at great risk to his own life, as throughout there was grave danger of the ruins subsiding from the effect of the fire and further earthquake shocks.

HARRY FITZSIMMONS   Pte. Fitzsimmons, The W. Yorks. Regt., was on rescue duty in the area of Quetta City to the east of Sandeman Hall. He worked with conspicuous energy and devotion to duty throughout the period of rescue work, and in conjunction with others was responsible for saving several lives. On 1st June, in order to rescue an Indian whom he knew to be buried alive, Fitzsimmons, at great risk to his own life, made a passage under the debris of a house into which he was able to crawl. On reaching the man he discovered a woman lying dead across him, who was pinned down by a stout beam across her leg. In order to release the man, whom he eventually saved, he had to saw off the woman's leg with a carpenter's saw. The remains of the building, and the passage he made, were in imminent danger of collapse during the whole period he was working. Fitzsimmons's action was a very gallant one and worthy of special recognition.

HARKBIR THAPA   On the morning of the 31st May, Rifleman Harkbir Thapa, 8th Gurkhas, was detailed as part of a rescue party which was going to dig out some living people behind the Police Lines. On the way to the work he heard noises in a building and obtained permission from the N.C.O. to try to get these people out. At about 6.30 a.m. the Adjutant visited the area to ascertain how work was progressing. He found Rifleman Harkbir Thapa had worked his way with his hands through the debris under a tottering roof, and was nearing two people who were alive but buried. As there was clearly every chance of the roof collapsing on to him as he removed the debris, the Adjutant assisted him by propping up the roof as far as possible. Rifleman Harkbir Thapa continued his work and brought out two children alive. He undoubtedly saved those two children at the risk of his own life. On 2nd June this Rifleman's conduct was again brought to notice. On this occasion he formed part of a detachment working in Hudda Village. The upper story of a crumbling house was being cleared, part of the roof had fallen through the floor into a lower story, thus rendering the floor most dangerous. A living child was discovered in the lower story. This man and one other volunteered to dig through a corner of the floor opposite to where it had crumbled. They did so with khukries and their hands and got through to the lower story and rescued the child. They did this at considerable risk to their own lives, as the walls were in danger of falling and the floor might have collapsed at any moment.

HUKM DAD   While employed in rescue work in the city, Lance-Naik Hukm Dad, 8th Punjab (Burma) Regt., fought his way into the ruins of a burning house at considerable risk to his own life and rescued a woman who was imprisoned there. Two injured men had already perished in the flames, and it was only through the bravery and presence of mind of Hukm Dad that the woman was saved.

KABUL SINGH   Lance-Naik Kabul Singh, 19th Hyderabad Regt., at great risk and personal danger to his life entered the ruins of a burning house in Bruce Road and succeeded in rescuing two women and three children.

ROBERT SPOORS   Private Spoors, 1st W. Yorks. Regt., at very considerable risk to himself from falling debris entered Major O'Hanlon's house, which was in a dangerous condition. He was successful in clearing a path for Mrs. O'Hanlon, and was mainly responsible for saving her life. He then re-entered the house to save the nurse and baby, but was himself caught in the debris and was later rescued by two other men and brought out in an exhausted condition. He subsequently worked for long hours at the British Military Hospital. His action was reported by the Colonel Commanding the Hospital with a recommendation for special recognition; the facts being corroborated by Major O'Hanlon, R.A.M.C. Private Spoors's gallant behaviour and devotion to duty were most praiseworthy.

A doctor's bravery in Abyssinia[1]

André John Mesnard Melly   Mr. Melly, M.C., F.R.C.S., during the disorders in Addis Ababa in May 1936 displayed conspicuous gallantry in his efforts to rescue the British and other foreign nationals and wounded Abyssinians, in the course of which he received injuries from which he died. (23.6.36)

A R.A.F. corporal's bravery

ARCHIBALD CHARLES WOOD   Corp. Wood, of No. 60 (B) Squadron, R.A.F., Kohat, was the passenger in a R.A.F. machine that was wrecked on 21st February 1936 near Nidhauli, India. Uninjured, though dazed as a result of the crash, he re-entered the blazing wreckage in an endeavour to save the pilot. In doing so he received very severe burns in consequence of which his left hand had to be amputated. (15.1.37)

---

[1] It is difficult to understand why, having regard to the terms of the Royal Warrant, the Albert Medal should in this case have been awarded *in gold*—the only such award since 1920.

WILLIAM SIMPSON McALONEY	For conspicuous gallantry in attempting to rescue an officer from the burning wreckage of an aircraft at Hamilton, Victoria, on 31st August 1937.

Despite the fact that the aircraft was ablaze from nose to rudder, Aircraftsman McAloney dashed into the flames and continued his efforts at rescue until pulled away in an unconscious condition, having received very severe burns. (4.2.38)

CHAPTER XIV
AWARDS OF THE EDWARD MEDAL
JAN. 1920–DEC. 1938

Note.—The average interval between the date of the deed here recorded and the announcement of an award in *The London Gazette* is 2½ years. Minimum delay, 6 weeks; maximum, 33 months. The date of the Gazette is shown in parentheses. Of recent years, excluding the exceptional case of the Gresford awards, the average interval has not exceeded 6 months.

CHAPTER XIV
AWARDS OF THE EDWARD MEDAL
JAN. 1920–DEC. 1938

Awards of the Edward Medal in silver are given in Old English type.

Gallant rescue from a 150-foot chimney

Charles Whelpton
Edward Naylor
Horace Ball

Two steeplejacks were repointing the brickwork at the top of a chimney 150 feet high at the Atlas Works of Messrs. John Brown & Co., Ltd., at Sheffield on 26th August 1919. Before the work was completed, gas fumes were accidentally permitted to pass through the chimney. One of the men was overcome; his companion, a lad, was able to attract attention, but was unable to assist him.

Whelpton, Naylor, and Ball, who were not steeplejacks, at once ascended the ladder which, however, only reached a spot 7 feet from the summit. They then had to climb outwards over a projecting chimney crown by means of the steel straps which run round the shaft. On reaching the top, which was only 9 inches wide, they applied artificial respiration to the unconscious man for 20 minutes and then, with great difficulty, lowered him to the ground in a canvas ambulance sling, which had been passed up by means of a rope. (20.2.20)

Gallant conduct of a Monmouthshire miner

Geoffrey Fletcher A repairer named Jones was engaged on work in an air pit at the West Elliot Colliery in Monmouthshire on 2nd Jan. 1920 when a fall of rubbish occurred and Jones found himself entirely buried and tightly pinned down, though able to breathe owing to the looseness of the earth. His son, who was near by, heard his father's shouts and hurried for help. Fletcher, with other men, arrived on the scene and, for nearly three hours, in spite of the possibility of a further big fall, proceeded gradually to uncover Jones to below the shoulders, encouraging him by cheerful talk. No foundation could be obtained to put in supports to the rubbish which was constantly moving. Further falls occurred, and Jones was again buried up to the neck. After many attempts, lasting over a further three hours, during which time Fletcher fed Jones with stimulants, he found it possible to release the latter, and rescued him practically uninjured. (16.7.20)

Gallant rescue from a burning building

JAMES ROGERSON MANN A fire broke out on 5th December 1919, in one of the rooms on the middle floor of a five-story cotton mill belonging to Messrs. N. Pickering & Sons, Ltd., of Bolton. The fire spread to the floors above, and one of the firemen of the Bolton Fire Brigade on the top floor found himself cut off from the door-way and stairs, and from the fire-escape, by fire and smoke. He called for help from those below. Mann at once tied a rope round his waist and climbed the nearest water-spout to the windows of the top story where the fireman was seen. On reaching the level of the window he untied the rope and handed it to the fireman, who tied it inside the building and then descended by it. Mann descended by the water-spout, which was liable to break away at any moment. (16.7.20)

Gallant rescue by Kimberley miners

Isaac Barnard
John Barnard

A great rush of mud at the Wesselton Mine, Kimberley, on 25th September 1919, came from two places, 45 feet apart, and filled up two passes for about 100 feet.

Fourteen natives were found to be missing. It is customary after a mud-rush to leave the mud alone for two or three days before attempting to clear it away; but, as men were missing, clearing operations were started at once and after 24 hours' work sounds were heard which indicated that some one was alive in the mud. It was decided to try to reach the imprisoned men over the top of the mud, which was intensely hot, and the Barnard brothers, when a passage had been partly cleared, volunteered to make the attempt. The temperature inside the tunnel was stifling; but, with the aid of an air-hose, the Barnards managed to get forward a considerable distance. The manager of the mine considered that the heat was unbearable, and shouted to the Barnards to come back; but they declined to return, and eventually succeeded in getting through. They found two natives still alive, and managed to get them out while they themselves followed the natives, but both suffered severely from the effects of the intense heat, and, after crawling out with great difficulty, were unable to walk without assistance.

It was not until three days later that the bodies of the other twelve natives were recovered, and the two men rescued undoubtedly owed their lives to the action of the Barnards, who showed the greatest bravery and determination. (22.10.20)

A colliery manager's bravery.

Thomas William Elliott

A miner named Onley at the Hucknall Colliery was entombed on 19th August 1919 between the face at which he was working and the debris of a large fall of stones and rubbish from the roof. Several men at hand proceeded to clear the fall until a small gap was made between the fallen rubbish and the edge of the roof. These men had become exhausted when Elliott, the manager, reached the scene. Without waiting to consider the danger, he squeezed through, reached the wrists of the imprisoned man, and pulled him out. The roof gave way further immediately after the rescue. (16.11.20)

A miner's presence of mind

ALBERT EDWARD SMITH
Whilst timber at the Dinnington Main Colliery was being drawn from a part of the workings on 9th September 1919, a fall of material occurred, which struck a man named James Sharpe and pinned him by one foot. Some workmen from adjoining places went at once to try to rescue him, but they were unable to get him away. The fall of material had displaced some timber, and the roof was very unsettled. Albert E. Smith, one of the officials of the mine, quickly came to the spot, and, seeing that Sharpe was in grave danger of being buried by the unsafe and unsupported roof, arranged for a temporary chock to be set up. The chock had barely been erected when about two tons of material fell, which would but for the chock have killed Smith. The chock, however, protected him, and the men were able after the fall to continue the work for the liberation of Sharpe. Immediately afterwards the whole place collapsed. (16.11.20)

Woolwich foreman's bravery

DONALD ADOLPHUS BROWN
While a number of rockets and lights were being re-packed at the Royal Naval Ordnance Depot at Woolwich on 17th January 1919, one of the rockets ignited and exploded, thus causing other rockets in the same case to explode. Brown, a foreman in the Ordnance Depot, immediately threw water upon the flaming case, opened the doors of the storehouse, and dragged the case into the open. This he did single-handed, but as a result of his example, other employees came to his assistance, and the fire was eventually extinguished by the use of fire buckets and a portable pump. (4.3.21)

Brave action of a Staffordshire miner

Frank Halfpenny
An explosion of gas and coal-dust occurred on 12th January 1919 in the Minnie Pit of the Podmore Hall Colliery, Staffordshire. There was a great deal of noise caused by the reversal of the air current and a great deal of dust and smoke. Halfpenny was about 500 yards from the bottom of the pit at the top of the new haulage. When the explosion occurred he lay down on the floor, and then reaching the telephone he attempted to communicate with the top. He received no answer and, although enveloped in smoke, went

to the top of a dip about 800 yards away, where he telephoned to the mine manager. On his way he had found the bodies of two lads lying in the gutter; these he lifted out and placed by the side; one of them ultimately recovered. In all the circumstances Halfpenny's journey of 800 yards into the dip was a very brave act. Most men instead of making it would have at once rushed for the shaft, but Halfpenny, instead of doing this, went to see what aid he could render, quite regardless of the risk he himself ran in so doing. (1.3.21)

A workman's presence of mind at Oldham

FRANK PLATT On 10th May 1920, the walls of the Oak Mills at Shaw, near Oldham, were being pointed by three men. One man named Cavaghan was seated at the top of a wall in a cradle, which was controlled by means of pulleys and ropes. The latter were held by Platt and another labourer standing on the sloping roof of a low shed 50 feet below.

Owing to the displacement of one of the pulley-blocks the cradle swung round, and Cavaghan was precipitated head downwards. Platt's companion ran away, but Platt, standing firm, swung the rope he was holding so as to encircle Cavaghan, and succeeded in doing so. The rope tightening broke Cavaghan's fall, and when he was about 12 feet from Platt's standing-place, the latter, taking advantage of a projecting sill, managed to swing Cavaghan on to it. This broke his fall further, while as he recoiled from the window-sill Platt interposed himself so as to save him from injury so far as possible. Both men received injuries to the head, and there is no doubt whatever that Platt's action saved Cavaghan's life. Only wonderful presence of mind and lightning decision could have enabled him to do what he did, and but for his instantaneous action Cavaghan would have been dashed to the ground in two seconds.

This is the second occasion on which Platt has been instrumental in saving a man from injury by falling. (1.3.21)

Gallant rescue at Stratford railway station

GEORGE EDWARD PILGRIM While a number of passengers were waiting at Stratford Station on the Great Eastern Railway for a train to Liverpool Street on 23rd October 1920, it became known that the earliest train would start from another platform and many of them, instead of using the subway, proceeded to cross the metals. Three sets of rails separated the platforms, and among the last to cross was a woman with a child. As she was crossing, she saw an express train approaching on the line of rails on which she stood. (1.3.21)

Pilgrim, a railway porter, realized the dangers. The woman became terrified and clung to the edge of the platform. The train reached a point about 50 yards from the woman when Pilgrim leapt on to the line and dragged both out of danger by main force. The engine was not brought to a standstill until it had passed the place where the woman had been clinging to the platform. All three persons concerned had a very narrow escape. But for Pilgrim's prompt and courageous action they could not possibly have escaped. (1.3.21)

Gallantry in a Bulawayo mine

JACOBUS LOWIES VAN HEERDEN
MWENE

A European named Goode and two natives descended on 22nd November 1920 to the lowest level of the Lonely Mine, Bulawayo, too quickly after the conclusion of some shot-firing operations, and were overcome by carbon monoxide gas. Mr. van Heerden, who was at the next level, heard groans and, descending, found the two natives dead and Goode unconscious. After three attempts, during each of which he was partially overcome, Mr. van Heerden managed to rescue Goode, but himself collapsed.

In his last attempt he was assisted by two natives, one of whom (named Zamane) was affected by the gas and failed to return from the danger zone. Mwene, a native of Bulawayo, on his own initiative, though well aware of the danger, descended single-handed to the rescue of Zamane, whom he carried unconscious to safety. He then returned and endeavoured without success to recover the bodies of the other natives. (25.10.21)

Works fitter's bravery at Wandsworth

ARTHUR DENTON   On the 20th April 1921, an explosion of aluminium powder took place at the Wandsworth works of Metal Powders, Ltd. A Mrs. Draper was in the act of entering the room where the explosion took place, but became dazed and ran into the flames. Mr. Denton, the works fitter, entered the room, found Mrs. Draper on the floor enveloped in flames from the waist upwards, and carried her out, at the cost of severe burns, and at the risk of his life from a further explosion. (20.12.21)

Brave rescue from gas fumes

ROBERT EDWARD PADDOCK
JOSPEH THOMAS CHIDLEY

Chidley, with three other men, was pumping water on 20th April 1921 from old workings in the Bulthy Mine, in Shropshire, when the foreman became affected by fumes from a petrol engine, and ordered the men to leave. He became unconscious, and was carried out by Chidley, who was himself almost unconscious on arrival at the foot of the air-shaft. The two other men collapsed.

Paddock, while proceeding towards the working-place, met Chidley and the foreman and helped them into the open air. He then twice tried to reach the other two men, but was driven back by the gas. He returned to the surface, and after consultation with Chidley, who had now recovered, the two men determined to make a third attempt. They managed to reach one of the men and got him as far as the air-shaft, but were almost overcome, and had to leave him. This man was dead when brought to the surface, but the other man regained consciousness, and made his way to the surface. (20.12.21)

An engine-driver's bravery

JAMES WALSH   While a passenger train of the South African Railways Administration was proceeding on 1st October 1919 from Mafeking to Johannesburg, the engine developed a defect and a volume of scalding steam escaped. Walsh, the engine-driver, was severely scalded, but stuck to his engine and brought the train to a standstill. As a result of the injuries he sustained Walsh spent a long period in hospital, and will never again be able to follow his occupation of engine-driver. He displayed great bravery and presence of mind and, as the train was running downhill at the time, there is little doubt that, had he lost control of his engine, a serious accident would have resulted. (22.3.22)

Miners' endurance in Holmewood Colliery rescue

SAMUEL PETERS
JOSEPH HARRISON
HAROLD WEST
THOMAS CALLADINE

A heavy fall of earth occurred on 22nd September 1920 in a seam of the Holmewood Colliery, near Chesterfield, imprisoning two men who were working in the seam. It was ascertained that the men were uninjured, but, as it was obvious that the work of reaching them would occupy some days, the first necessity was to supply them with food. Peters, the under-manager, with great ingenuity passed food through a cycle tire enclosed in iron piping. Further falls occurred during the 48 hours following the original fall, but it then became possible to pass some timber through, although gas appeared in the cavity and began to give trouble. A small hole was made through to the imprisoned men, and they were eventually freed after four days in the seam.

Peters, West, Harrison, and Calladine all distinguished themselves greatly in the work of rescue, and were engaged for practically the whole time in a dangerous position at the face of the fall exposed to the risk of injury from falling stones. (24.3.22)

Lanarkshire miner's gallant conduct

JOHN SHIELDS While seven men were working on 12th August 1920 on a seam of the Darngavil Colliery, Lanarkshire, there was an inrush of surface water into the shafts. The pump at the bottom of the shaft was unable to cope with the water, and the men at work in the seam were likely to be cut off. The engineman at the surface ran to inform Shields, a miner living close by, who descended alone into the workings and brought out the men. The water was constantly rising, and Shields could have no idea as to when it would close the entrance to the seam. (5.5.22)

Welsh miner's conspicuous courage

ROBERT HANDFORD A fall of roof occurred on 25th October 1921 at the Llanbradach Colliery, Glamorgan, whereby a collier named Carter was partially buried. Some men working near by began to dig them out. Handford, the local fireman, arrived and immediately started to erect wooden sleepers as a protection for Carter's body. A second fall of about 30 tons took place almost immediately, but the few sleepers already erected prevented Carter being crushed. Handford then cleared the rubbish from Carter's head and had put up some more supports, when a third fall of about 45 tons took place and the rescue party had to jump clear. Handford persevered with the work of rescue; he gradually made his way over Carter's body, completely protecting it with timber, and succeeded eventually in freeing him from rubbish with the exception of his left leg, which was securely pinned down by a heavy weight of earth. Repeated attempts were made to pull Carter clear, but without success, and it was decided to amputate his leg. Handford, however, made further attempts, at great risk to himself, and Carter was eventually extricated without serious injury to his leg. Handford for four hours was continuously exposed to the danger of being buried; he displayed great promptitude in facing the situation, and his intelligence and bravery undoubtedly saved Carter's life. (30.5.22)

Gallant rescue in a Yorkshire mine

WILLIAM HUMPHRIES A workman named Creighton, employed in a
GEORGE SMITH seam of the South Kirkby Colliery, Yorkshire, was completely buried by a fall of roof on 11th February 1922. Several miners who were at work near the spot came to the rescue, among them Humphries and Smith. The imprisoned man's head and shoulders were soon freed, but owing to the pressure of debris on the lower part of his body and legs it was

impossible to pull him clear, while, so fast as earth was removed, more slipped down in its place. The rescue party placed sleepers across the body of the imprisoned man, thus preventing his being completely engulfed by the debris, and eventually a passage was made under the sleepers over Creighton's body, which was unhurt, with the exception of one foot, which was firmly pinned down by a large stone. The foot was eventually released and the man freed after $8\frac{1}{2}$ hours' work.

All the men who took part in the rescue were exposed to great risk for a prolonged period, and behaved with great gallantry and devotion to duty, but Humphries and Smith were unanimously selected by their comrades as having specially distinguished themselves. (22.6.22)

Attempted rescue in a Sunderland tar still

WILLIAM KING
THOMAS ATKINSON
WHITEHEAD

The stills used at the works of Messrs. Brotherton & Co., Ltd., Tar Distilleries, Wear Fuel Works, South Dock, Sunderland, were large cylinders 10 feet in diameter and 20 feet deep. While one of these stills stood empty and was thought to be disconnected from the adjoining stills, one Dougherty entered it through the small man-hole in the cover. When he reached the bottom he collapsed. His mate shouted for help and ran to get a rope. One George Rogers, without waiting for a rope, entered the still to rescue Dougherty, but was also overcome. William King at once entered the still with a handkerchief round his mouth and a rope attached to his body. He was overcome and had to be pulled out. Thereupon Whitehead made two attempts to reach the men at the bottom of the still, first equipped with a gauze respirator and then with a hood with oxygen pumped into it, but on both occasions he had to be pulled out. King then made a further attempt at rescue, and went in wearing a respirator and having a safety belt round his body. By this time other workmen had removed the pitch-pipe from the bottom of the still and begun to force air in, and in the second attempt King was successful in reaching the men who had been overcome. He attached ropes to the bodies and they were drawn out; artificial respiration was tried, but they were found to be dead. (No dates given in *The London Gazette*.)

The danger of gas in the still was well known in the works, and King and Whitehead were fully aware of the risks they ran. (5.9.22)

A Llanelly miner's gallantry

REES THOMAS

Thomas, a miner employed at the Castle Colliery, Llanelly, was engaged on 13th January with two other miners, named Meredith and Griffiths, in blasting operations with gelignite cartridges fired by time fuses. The fuses of the last three cartridges had been ignited, and the party was seeking safety when the cartridges fired by Meredith exploded prematurely, severely injuring him. Thomas, with entire disregard of the danger to himself, at once went to his comrade's assistance, and dragged him back some little distance, but the remaining charges then exploded, injuring Thomas in the face and body. Meredith unfortunately succumbed to his injuries. Thomas's action in going back to rescue him when one shot had exploded and the other two were certain to do so was an extremely brave one, and he undoubtedly risked his life. He had distinguished himself by gallantry on the occasion of a previous accident. (17.10.22)

Brave rescue in a Yorkshire mine

JAMES PARKIN
HARRY ASPINALL
JOSEPH MASON
ALBERT HENRY FOWLER
DAWSON

A miner named Bridges was removing timber in the Hickleton Main Mine, near Thurnscoe, Yorkshire, on 24th October 1922, when a fall of roof completely buried him. His workmates, Dawson and Mason, heard the fall, and went to his aid. They at once sent for Aspinall, the deputy in charge of the district, and for Parkin, the under-manager. They cleared the debris from Bridges's head, but further falls of roof occurred rendering the work of rescue very dangerous. The rescue party worked continuously throughout the night, sometimes shielding Bridges from the falling stones with their own bodies, and finally freed him after more than 16 hours' work, though he unfortunately died from the shock some hours later. (27.3.23)

Brave release of entombed miners

STEPHEN RICHARDS
JAMES BERESFORD

While two timbermen were at work in a deep seam of the Coppice Colliery, Derby, on 1st November 1922, a fall of about 60 tons of debris took place. Both men were buried and completely hidden, but help speedily came. Timber was erected over the imprisoned men to protect them from further falls, and they were eventually extricated after about three hours' work. Both Richards and Beresford took a leading part in the work of rescue at great risk to their own lives, as there were continuous falls of roof while the operations were in progress. (13.4.23)

Miner's heroic self-sacrifice

ARTHUR HATCHER

A workman named Burton at the Barnsley Main Colliery was seized with a fit on 10th October 1922 while guiding a tub down an inclined road; he was found insensible by Hatcher and two or three other men, who carried him towards the exit. Meanwhile, owing to Burton's absence, a tub which had been left at the top began to move and ran down the road towards the men. Hatcher heard it coming and, realizing that the lives of the other men were in danger, as there was no refuge for them, went up the track and threw himself down in front of the tub and brought it to a standstill. He was very severely injured about the spine and legs, and has not been able to work since. (29.5.23)

Miner's conspicuous gallantry

Bert Craig At Nixon's Navigation Colliery at Mountain Ash, Glamorganshire, a workman named Jones was completely buried on 14th November 1922 by a heavy fall of stones and rubbish. Four other men present tried to get him out, but further falls took place, and the four men, considering the risk too great, retreated under cover.

At this moment Bert Craig arrived and ran to where Jones was buried and began to remove the stones. In spite of his appeals for help, the other men present hung back until the falls ceased, but they then came to Craig's assistance, and Jones was extricated. All the time falls were taking place, and within two minutes of Jones being pulled out so large a fall took place that both he and Craig would certainly have been killed.

Craig's gallant action saved Jones's life. He was working under conditions of very great danger, and his conduct appears even more gallant in view of the fact that he suffers from the result of a severe bullet wound in the head, and any blow might have been fatal. (1.6.23)

Gallantry of a disabled ex-serviceman

GEORGE LIVERMORE Livermore served in the Royal Air Force during the War and was discharged in 1919 with a disability pension on account of a gun-shot wound in the foot. He was being trained in French-polishing at the Enham Village Centre, Andover, and on the day in question was, with other disabled men, in a room where some bees-wax mixed with turpentine, which was being heated on a stove, caught fire. Livermore, realizing the danger, lifted the blazing bucket on a stick and made for the door. His clothing was alight but, notwithstanding serious burns, he reached the door-way, when he was compelled to drop the bucket. When the fire occurred some of the men in the room escaped through the windows, but all were disabled and some unable to escape. As it was, some of the men were slightly burnt, while Livermore himself sustained severe injuries causing him intense suffering. He had to lose part of his left arm, while his right hand and arm were severely burnt. There is no doubt that Livermore realized the danger to his comrades if the building caught fire and without hesitation risked his life on their behalf. (3.8.23)

Indian railway porter's brave act

BEHARI DOME   A train with two engines in front was proceeding slowly on the Nayadih branch line of the East Indian Railway Company on 6th April 1923, when a little child was observed sitting in the centre of the line. It was impossible for the driver to stop the train in time, but Behari Dome, a shunting-porter on the leading engine, jumped off, ran ahead, and picked up the child. He stumbled but fell just clear of the track, though the child's fingers clutched the rails in the fall and were crushed by the approaching train. (7.12.23)

Gallant rescue of entombed miner in Co. Durham

WILFRID WESTOE   While some men were working in a seam on the South Garesfield Colliery, Co. Durham, on 27th October 1923, one of them named Mason was completely buried by a heavy fall of earth and stones about 5 tons in weight and received severe injuries to his head. The only means of reaching him was through a small opening and young Westoe alone felt equal to attempting a rescue. He squeezed his way through the opening to the injured man and after an hour and a half's work brought him to safety. Westoe had to work under a continuous hail of stones, while there was great danger of another large fall, and if this had occurred there would have been no possible means of escape. Westoe ran a very grave risk in effecting the rescue and but for him Mason would have lost his life. (21.12.23)

Rescues from a gas-filled tank

WILLIAM HENRY LEE   On 31st October 1923, while three men were cleaning a tank of the National Benzol Company at Cardiff they were overcome by benzol fumes. One near a man-hole escaped, the other two collapsed. The manager of the depot, Mr. Roberts, first attempted a rescue, but he and another workman named Simpson were forced by the fumes to withdraw. Lee, a labourer in the Company's employ, then entered the tank five times, coming out for short intervals to inhale fresh air. He eventually put a rope round the men and they were hauled out of the tank.

The rescuers from their previous experience were all well aware of the great risk they ran in entering the tank without a gas-mask or lifeline. Lee saved the life of one of the rescued men. The other, unfortunately, died. (29.2.24)

Man's brave action at Newport

JOHN JONES   Shortly after midnight on 2nd January, the steamship *Imanol* had finished unloading at a wharf in the River Usk at Newport (Mon.). As the last man of the unloading gang was coming ashore the ship swung from her moorings and lifted the gangway, throwing the man into the water, 15 feet below the wharf. Jones, a man of 50, who was one of the gang, had left the ship, but hearing the cry 'Man overboard', ran to the wharf's edge, and plunged into the water between the ship and the wharf but, after swimming for over ten minutes, became exhausted and had to be hauled out by a rope. The night was dark and cold and the tide ran strongly. (6.5.24)

Brave rescue of two boys at a dye-works

JAMES FREDERICK PORTER   During bleaching operations at the Smedley Bridge Dye Works, near Manchester, on 30th January 1924, two boys named Bamford and Marriott were plaiting down cloth running into a large two-ton 'kier' which was filled with a mixture of water, caustic soda solution, and tetralene. It was observed from the platform above the kier that the boys were not visible, being covered by the cloth, and, as a matter of fact, they had been overcome by the tetralene fumes. Two machine-minders and bleacher's assistants named Porter and Ingham were summoned. Porter entered the kier to look for the boys but could not see them and was forced by the fumes to return to the top. He recovered and again descended with Ingham and they brought out Marriott, who was unconscious. Porter, too, was badly gassed and both men were taken to hospital. The other boy Bamford was eventually pulled out by a rope but was found to be dead.

But for the efforts of Porter and Ingham, Marriott would also have lost his life. Both men behaved very gallantly, but Porter, who was only 18 years old, showed exceptional courage in twice entering the dark enclosed vessel. (16.5.24)

An accident in an Ashanti gold-mine

GEOFFREY WALTER CHARDIN
ERNEST ALFRED MORRIS   At Obuasi, Ashanti, on 29th May 1923, while a cyanide solution was being prepared in a vat of the Ashanti Goldfields Corporation a native named Robert, who was working in the vat contrary to orders, was overcome by the fumes. Two other natives, Sikeyena and Guruba, attempted to rescue him but were themselves overcome. The engineer, Mr. Chardin, realized the danger and without hesitation entered the vat by a ladder but was himself overpowered by the fumes. Mr. Morris, mill foreman, and Mr. Skinner, the shift engineer, arrived and between them dragged Mr. Chardin out. Skinner collapsed but Morris re-entered the vat and brought out the three natives alive. Mr. Chardin and the two natives Sikeyena and

Robert succumbed, but the conduct of Mr. Chardin and Mr. Morris was extremely gallant. (4.7.24)

Accident resulting from a bolting pit pony

WILLIAM SMITH
JAMES COLLINGWOOD

On 12th December 1923 a boy named Bacon, working in the Frickley Colliery in Yorkshire, was leading his pony drawing two empty tubs along a line of rails. One of the tubs became derailed. The pony bolted and displaced a prop, causing a heavy fall of roof. The pony was killed and Bacon was buried up to his waist. Smith and Collingwood, colliers working near by, heard the fall, went to the spot, and erected a temporary roof over him. A second fall took place a few minutes later; Bacon was unhurt, Smith and Collingwood just managed to jump clear. Bacon was eventually released after $3\frac{1}{2}$ hours' hard work.

Great credit is due to all the men engaged in the work of releasing Bacon, as pieces of the roof were continuously falling while the operation was in progress. It is, however, to Smith and Collingwood that Bacon owes his life. (11.7.24)

Intrepid rescue from a flooded mine

PALING BAKER
HARRY WILSON

An inrush of water took place on 10th March 1924 at the Harriseahead Colliery in Staffordshire. Most of the workmen had already left the mine, but one man named Booth, who had been working alone about 130 yards from the bottom of the shaft, was missing. Mr. Baker, the manager, was told that it was impossible to rescue him. The bottom of the pit was three parts full of water which was still rising.

Baker called for volunteers. Wilson was one of five men who responded and descended into the mine by a foot-rail. The rescue party reached a ventilation door which they dared not open owing to the pressure of water behind it and they therefore prepared to retire. Baker, who had followed, insisted that Booth could not be left. Wilson alone volunteered to continue, and with Baker forced the ventilation door, allowing the water to escape gradually. They then waded to Booth, reaching him after great difficulty, and all three men were eventually drawn to the surface.

Both Baker and Wilson ran a very great risk of being trapped. They could not tell to what height the water would rise and had it reached the roof all would have lost their lives. (22.8.24)

Quarryman's brave action

WILLIAM ROBERTS

Four men were clearing away debris on 15th January from a landslide blocking a road abutting on the Dorothea Slate Quarry in Carnarvonshire. A portion of the road suddenly slipped into the quarry carrying with it one of the men, who fell to the bottom and was killed. A second man named Robert Jones managed to clutch the edge of the road in his fall. Roberts went to his assistance, seized him by the wrists, and dragged him to safety.

The little firm ground left might have given way at any moment. But for the action of Roberts, Jones would certainly have lost his life, as he could hold on no longer when Roberts reached him and there is a clear drop of 240 feet to the bottom of the quarry. (12.9.24)

Conspicuous gallantry of two Durham miners

Vincent Elwick
George Wilson

Two men named McNally and Place were on 26th October 1924 filling debris into tubs at the Murton Colliery, Durham, when they were suddenly buried by a 200-ton fall of sandstone and shale. The roof was supported by iron bars and girders but the weight of the fall broke the bars and bent the girders, some of which fell and rested on the tubs. Elwick and Wilson had just left off work and were eating close by. They at once collected bandages and went to the spot. They found that owing to the tubs taking the weight of the fall McNally and Place were alive and, though stones were still falling, they began tunnelling towards the imprisoned men. They made a passage 12 feet long which Elwick entered, passing the stones back as he proceeded; Wilson followed him. After 20 minutes they reached the buried men and got out Place, but only after a struggle, as he had become hysterical. They then went back to McNally but found that he was held fast by three fingers. They built up stones to support some of the falling bars and attempted to cut off the top of the tub with a hammer and chisel. This proved impossible. McNally agreed that he must lose his fingers to save his life, so Elwick and Wilson applied tourniquets to his arm and tried to amputate the fingers with the only implements at hand—a knife, an axe, and a hammer. The operation was found impossible until a fellow workman arrived on the scene with a sharp chisel; this was passed up the tunnel and with it Elwick and Wilson managed to sever the three fingers. McNally was eventually extricated and taken to Sunderland Infirmary.

Elwick and Wilson knew well the risks they ran; there were continual further falls of roof during their 2 hours' work, during which time the spot where they were working gradually grew smaller. They never relaxed their efforts or suggested abandoning their task. Their passage back fell in shortly after the rescue was completed. Both Elwick and Wilson had been trained in ambulance work and had the good sense to apply tourniquets not only to prevent bleeding but also to stop the circulation so as to reduce the pain of the amputation. They saved McNally's life, and the story of their bravery and coolness is one of the most remarkable recorded in the history of rescue work. (2.1.25)

Rescues from a gas-filled shaft

JOHN KRULL
FREDERICK OLIVER

While workmen were engaged on 27th September 1924 in sinking shafts at the electrical engineering works of Messrs. Johnson & Phillips, at Charlton, one Timpson descended a 26-foot shaft. He was overcome by gas. Bass, a fellow worker, tried to reach him but was driven back by the gas. Oliver, a foreman, then tied a handkerchief over his mouth and went down, but was overcome on reaching the bottom and collapsed. Krull, knowing all this, dipped a muffler in water and tied it round his mouth and nostrils. With a rope round his body he went down and brought up first Timpson and then Oliver. Timpson died but Oliver recovered.

Both Krull and Oliver performed a very brave action. The former had been a miner and was well aware of the risk. (6.1.25)

Iron foundry accident in India

JOSEPH JOHN
D'SANTOS

While a cupola for melting pig-iron was being charged at the workshops of the East Indian Railway at Jamalpur on 23rd September 1924, a labourer named Tofi overbalanced and fell into the cupola. D'Santos, a chargeman who was working near by, immediately seized a rope and jumped into the cupola in order to effect a rescue. He found Tofi unconscious and suffering from burns, but tied a rope round him and then tried to climb back. D'Santos was affected by the fumes but other workers drew him out. He displayed great presence of mind in retaining his hold of the rope, thus making possible the rescue of Tofi, who died. D'Santos was badly gassed. (12.5.25)

Gallantry and strength in New South Wales

MATTHEW JAMES
CAMPBELL

Campbell, together with George Lawton and William Lambking, was working, on 27th October 1924, in a shaft of the Northern Suburbs Ocean Outfall Sewer at Sydney, New South Wales. A pile-driving hammer gave way and carried away most of the staging about 200 feet from the bottom of the shaft on which the men were working. Both Lawton and Lambking were injured, but Campbell, who was unhurt, managed to hold them one in each arm until his strength was exhausted and he had to loose his hold of Lawton, who fell to the bottom and was killed. He retained his hold of Lambking and placed him in a bucket, in which he was drawn to the surface. Campbell then went to the bottom of the shaft alone to render any help he could to Lawton, but, finding him dead, placed the body in the bucket and it was brought to the surface. Campbell then collapsed, but was extricated from the shaft by other workmen who came on the scene.

There is no doubt that in holding on to the two injured men while standing on a very narrow plank Campbell incurred a grave risk of falling to the bottom and of losing his life. (1.9.25)

Colliery accident in Australia: two posthumous awards

HUGH FREDERICK MOODIE
JOHN BORLAND BROWN

The fire started just after the afternoon shift had started work, one day in September 1923. Moodie, a deputy on the afternoon shift, entered the mine about 1 p.m. and was going to work when he met the day-shift deputies returning, who reported that all was in order. He continued on his way but soon encountered dense smoke. He went back to the day-shift deputies, told them what he had found, and then went forward alone to try to rescue his men. He was an experienced deputy and must have been fully aware of the risk he was taking. He was not seen alive again, but his body was later found in a position which showed that he must have travelled over a thousand yards in his efforts to save the men.

At about 2.30 p.m. on the same day Brown and other volunteers from neighbouring collieries entered the mine on rescue work. They found two unconscious men, but the air was so bad that the rescuers were forced to retreat. After two further attempts Brown reached the bodies and spent 20 minutes in a vain attempt to bring them round. He then, accompanied by another man, pushed on, but was driven back by foul air and returned to the surface to organize rescue parties. He descended with one party and recovered four bodies. He went down a third time and penetrated yet further, when an explosion occurred. Brown was seriously affected by the fumes and urged his companions to leave him and go on. His companions tried to help him, but at his urgent entreaty finally left him in the tunnel, where his body was later found. (1.9.25)

A brave woman

LILIAN PEYTO   Mrs. Lilian Peyto was employed at the flock factory of Messrs. Holdsworth Bros., at White Hart Lane, Plumstead. The flock is delivered from rag-grinding machines and falls to the floor in heaps to be packed by women into large sacks. A woman, Rose Wade, was working on 17th June 1925 at one of these machines in a corner, the woman being between the machine and the wall. The flock which was being delivered from the machine suddenly took fire, which spread to the heap of flock which was being bagged by Rose Wade. Her clothes, covered with small particles of flock, caught fire and there was fire all round the machine. She tried to run out from behind the machine but stumbled and fell. Mrs. Peyto, who was working on the other side of the machine, rushed to her assistance, caught hold of her and tried to drag her clear. A heavy sack of waste material which was suspended behind the machine, and which had itself caught fire, fell down on the girl and forced Mrs. Peyto to let go. She again, however, went to Rose Wade's assistance and this time was able to drag her out of the flames a good distance. All the other women working in the neighbourhood appear to have been too horror-stricken to render help. After Mrs. Peyto had dragged the burning woman away from the fire, a foreman came up and covered her with sacks, but Rose Wade died as a result of her injury.

Mrs. Peyto's attempt at rescue was attended with grave risks, as Rose Wade was surrounded with flames and the clothing of Mrs. Peyto herself might easily have caught fire. Her second and successful attempt to get the woman clear after the burning bag of material had fallen on her showed special courage. (22.8.25)

Stockport labourer's heroic self-sacrifice

ROBERT PEARSON   While two boys named Stothert and Bowden were working in a vat at the works of Messrs. H. Marsland, Ltd., at Stockport on 11th July 1925, there was a sudden inrush of scalding liquid and steam owing to a mistake made in opening the pipe of another vat. The screams of the scalded boys attracted the attention of other workers and attempts were made to extricate them through the manholes. Bowden was successfully drawn out, but Stothert, after reaching the manhole, fell back into the vat owing to the burnt flesh of his hand giving way. Pearson saw Bowden pulled out terribly scalded, and on hearing that Stothert was still in the vat he at once ran to it. He jumped down the manhole and, after groping about, found Stothert with some difficulty and hoisted him sufficiently to enable those outside to drag him to the surface. Pearson's feet were severely scalded during his efforts and he was practically unconscious on being drawn to the top.

Both boys died, but Pearson's effort to save Stothert's life was a very gallant one. Though the steam had been turned off when Pearson entered the vat he was unaware of this and so far as he could tell the vat might have been full of boiling liquid. He had never been inside one of these vats before; all he knew was that there was a boy inside and he faced the risk of attempting the rescue without any regard to his own safety, while neither the scalding he experienced nor the intense pain which he suffered deterred him from persisting in his efforts to get the lad out. (20.10.25)

A Derbyshire miner's gallant action

DONALD FLETCHER   A heavy fall of roof to a depth of 16 feet took place at the Creswell Colliery in Derbyshire, on 10th September 1925, completely burying a miner named Cooper. Some of the larger pieces of the roof became interlocked, affording him some protection from the full weight of the fall and thus preventing his being crushed to death. Efforts were made to discover where Cooper lay, and it was found that his head was near the edge of the fall so that it was possible to free it from debris. His shoulders were next freed, but his body and legs were held fast. The only way in which Cooper could be extricated was that some one should crawl under the debris and by working a passage alongside and over Cooper release him very gradually and stone by stone. Fletcher volunteered to do so and succeeded after two hours' continuous work. Great patience and skill were required, and in the course of the work Fletcher's body was completely under the fall, with his head close to Cooper's feet. Throughout the operation Fletcher was exposed to the risk of being crushed to death either by a second fall or by a settling down of the first fall, and he performed his task skilfully without regarding his own safety. (26.1.26)

An act of prompt courage

GEORGE LOCKE   Locke was erecting steel work for the re-building of the premises of Messrs. Bourne & Hollingsworth in Oxford Street on 8th October 1925. He and one Frederick Dowser were standing on parallel girders on the fourth-floor level when Dowser tripped and fell, striking his head in his fall and lying stunned on the girder. The girders on which the men were working were only 7 inches in width and 7 feet apart. Locke, seeing his comrade fall, leapt across and, throwing himself upon the legs of the fallen man, pinned him to the girder until help arrived. But for him Dowser would have fallen to his death. Locke's gallant action showed total disregard of his own safety. To spring from one girder to the other at a great height was no small feat, and he must have recognized in holding down his comrade that any struggle on the latter's part must endanger the lives of both. (2.3.26)

Brave rescue from an acid-vat

ALFRED WELDING   On 1st October 1925 a youth named Harper, employed at the works of the High Speed Steel Alloys, Ltd., at Widnes, fell into a vat $6\frac{1}{2}$ feet high and 8 feet in diameter, containing vanadic acid. The contents of the vat formed a jelly-like substance at a scalding temperature, and Harper, though his head was clear of the acid, was quickly sinking and would have been submerged in a few seconds. Welding, a fellow worker, heard Harper's shouts for help. He ran to his assistance and jumped into the vat and, by holding up Harper, prevented the latter's complete immersion. It was some 3 or 4 minutes before help arrived and both men were severely scalded before being dragged out. (2.3.26)

Rescue from a roof-fall in an Indian mine

JAMES KIPLING
JAMES JOHNSTON
NANI KHAN

On 7th January 1925 a very heavy fall of roof took place in the Mohpani Colliery of the G.I.P. Railway in India, killing one miner instantaneously and completely burying another named Nanoo Maora. On a report of the accident reaching Mr. Kipling, the under-manager of the mine, he went with Mr. Johnston, the senior European overseer, and Nani Khan, a native timber-drawer, and crawling through the fall of stone and earth, eventually got the man out.

Within 20 minutes of their extricating Nanoo 20 tons of rock fell on the very spot where he had been lying. (19.3.26)

Hydraulic packer's brave conduct

BERTIE TANNER Five men were in the lower chambers of one of the lock gates at the Barry Docks on 10th December 1925 when an explosion of gas occurred and they were overcome by fumes. The interior of the gate was wet and slimy; the only means of reaching the men was by a narrow iron ladder. Tanner, who was on watch at the top of the gate, went down and brought four men in succession to the surface. One man was left and Tanner again went down, but was forced to retire owing to the fumes. By this time other assistance had arrived and Tanner again descended and brought the fifth man's unconscious body to the surface.

Tanner showed great courage and perseverance in continuing at his work of rescue until all the men had been brought up. He descended no less than six times—on the first five occasions into utter darkness without any light. He did not know the nature of the explosion, and the danger of slipping on the slimy ironwork was considerable. Three of the men rescued were severely burnt and the last man brought to the surface died. (4.6.26)

Welsh miner's gallant rescue

George Coleman
JOHN GEORGE CORDEY
SAMUEL GRAHAM

At the North Celynen Colliery in Monmouthshire a fall of roof to the extent of 20 tons occurred on 8th March, almost completely burying two colliers. Efforts were made to erect timber supports over the buried men, but great care and skill were necessary in order to avoid further falls. A second fall of 5 tons took place while Coleman, the District Ambulance man, was fixing a timber, and he was himself pinned down by the fall. He was released after being buried for 10 minutes, whereupon a further fall of 10 tons occurred. Coleman, with the help of Graham, Cordey, and three other men, continued the work of rescue until Coleman was pinned down by a heap of earth, so badly bruised that he could continue his task no longer. Both the buried men were eventually extricated alive, but one of them died.

Coleman was undoubtedly the outstanding figure in the rescue work. His persistent courage certainly saved the life of one of the entombed men and contributed largely to the rescue of the other. He risked his own life for over 6 hours in the work of rescue and displayed exceptional skill and bravery in all he did. Graham and Cordey also exhibited courage of a very high order. (29.6.26)

Assam colliery rescues

BHIKAM SIRDAR
KRISTO KAMAR

Certain sections of a coal mine at the Tikak Colliery in Assam which had caught fire had been sealed off, but on 25th February 1926 fire broke out again. The European manager, with two European foremen and a gang of Indian colliers, proceeded to plaster the dams, but after 6 hours' work most of the men became affected by gas and were forced to withdraw. Early next morning the three Europeans, with forty Indian colliers, resumed the work, but all collapsed within an hour. Bhikam Sirdar, a contractor who had been engaged in the fire area on the previous day and was feeling the effects of the gas, came and brought three men into the fresh air. He then went to get more aid, and, meeting Kristo Kamar, the head Sirdar, told him to take two Indian colliers who were with him and to do what he could to get the men out. He himself collected twenty more and then went back to the fire area where Kristo Kamar had brought out the three Europeans and six Indians, all unconscious. Bhikam and Kristo then proceeded to bring out the rest, of whom one died. The men rescued had to be brought about 80 yards along narrow roadways into the fresh air and subsequently to the entrance of the mine some hundreds of yards away.

Both Bhikam Sirdar and Kristo Kamar behaved with great bravery, and but for their action there is no doubt that many lives would have been lost. (11.2.27)

Explosion in a shaft at Greenwich

GEORGE EDWARD THORPE
GEORGE GAUNT
THOMAS JOHN TAYLOR
JOHN HENRY PERKINS

A shaft 20 feet in diameter and 50 feet deep was being sunk at Greenwich. Six men, including George Thorpe, were working at the bottom under compressed air on 7th January, when an explosion occurred which blew off the top of the shaft and caused a heavy fall of timber and concrete. At the same time the water, which before the explosion was held back by the compressed air, began rapidly to fill the shaft. When the accident occurred, George Thorpe was partially sheltered from the falling material, but was rendered unconscious for a short time by the concussion. On regaining consciousness, he heard the cry of a companion, Martyn, who was pinned under fallen timber. Despite the fact that he was dazed by the explosion and by the sudden release of air-pressure, he left his shelter and held Martyn's head above the water until rescue came, preferring so to risk his life rather than to seek safety by climbing out of the shaft. He was all the time exposed to falling material and the water was rapidly flooding the shaft.

As soon as the explosion occurred, Gaunt, a foreman, Taylor, and Perkins at once sought means to descend the shaft and finally, by improvising a ladder 40 feet long, reached the bottom. They succeeded in freeing Martyn and bringing him and Thorpe to the surface. Further descents were made in a vain search for the other four workers who were held down by wreckage and were submerged in the rising water. Martyn subsequently died from his injuries.

During the time they were engaged on the work of rescue debris was continually falling, and as the cause of the disaster was unknown, so was it unknown whether the first explosion would not be followed by a second. (1.4.27)

A gallant rescuer

LEWIS MILLER The steamship *Endymion* was being unloaded in the City Docks, Bristol, on 7th September, and was lying 2 or 3 feet away from the quay-side. The cargo was being discharged by a crane which lifted the sacks from the ship to a platform about 20 feet above the quay-level. A man named Johns who was helping to pull the sacks inwards from the crane to the platform was struck by a sack and fell from the platform to the quay wall and then rolled into the water between the quay-side and the ship. Seeing him fall into the water, Miller jumped in and held him up by means of the chains at the water-level until a rope was lowered. Miller then fastened Johns to the rope and first Johns and then Miller was pulled out of the water. Miller knew the risk of being crushed between the wall and the ship, and the difficulty and danger of rescuing Johns, who died later. This is the sixteenth occasion on which Miller has rescued persons from the water. (28.10.27)

Gallant rescue of man overcome by benzine fumes

WILLIAM LLOYD
FRANK BOOT

On the night of 3rd October a man named Taylor was attending, at the works of Messrs. Quibell Brothers, Ltd., Newark-on-Trent, plant used for extracting grease from bones by means of petroleum benzine. Noticing that benzine vapour was escaping, he endeavoured, with the help of a fellow workman, to close a lid which had been incorrectly left open. His mate was affected by the fumes and on the suggestion of Taylor left the room. On recovering and finding later that Taylor had not followed him, he gave the alarm.

William Lloyd, a sub-foreman of the works, hearing that Taylor was in the building, put a scarf round his mouth and ran to the upper floor of the building, where he found Taylor lying unconscious near the lid of the extractor. He succeeded in dragging Taylor down three steps to a lower floor, but was himself overcome and collapsed, and was later taken out of the building by other men.

Frank Boot, the foreman of the works, who had been summoned from his home, meanwhile arrived at the works, and, having put a handkerchief round his mouth, went into the building and found Taylor where Lloyd had left him. Boot then dragged Taylor to a point where other men could reach him, but he himself became affected with the fumes.

Lloyd and Boot, in rescuing Taylor, displayed a high degree of courage. It was stated in evidence at the inquest on Taylor, who did not survive, that at the time of the rescue the building was full of benzine fumes and that a cloud of fume was also visible outside the building. Apart from the risk of suffocation, there was the serious risk of an explosion, and both men were well aware of these risks. (9.12.27)

Prompt action of S. African gold-miner

COERT HATTINGH VAN
STRAATE

On the 31st May 1927 a bag of explosives caught fire in one of the workings of a mine belonging to the Randfontein Estates Gold Mining Company. The miner in charge of the explosives told Mr. van Straate, who was working on the level below. Mr. van Straate at once realized that the air current proceeding up the stope would carry the poisonous fumes engendered by the fire through the working-places on the level above, and would thus endanger the lives of those working on the higher level. He ran up the stope past the burning explosives and up the raise for 170 feet to the level above. In passing through the raise he was enveloped in the poisonous fumes from the burning explosives.

The air current on reaching the higher level split into two—one current proceeeding up a south stope and one up a north stope. Mr. van Straate went first to the south stope and there warned a miner to leave at once, together with the other workers. He then proceeded towards the north stope and met the miner in charge of that stope on his way out. The miner was already overcome by the fumes and on the point of collapse. He was, however, able to tell Mr. van Straate that there were still two natives in the north stope and a third in another part of the workings who was in danger. Mr. van Straate continued to the north stope and fetched out the two natives. By this time he was feeling the effect of the fumes and instead of looking for the third native, with the chance that he himself might be overcome and unable to convey the warning, reported the native's danger to the shift boss.

Mr. van Straate then took personal charge of the rescued persons and conducted them to the surface.

Mr. van Straate's prompt and courageous action undoubtedly saved the lives of a number of persons. The Government Inspector of Mines for the district described the risk which Mr. van Straate took as appalling, and as Mr. van Straate was a man with many years' experience of mining, the risk must have been well known to him. (1.5.28)

A furnace accident

JAMES MARRON
JAMES MULLEN

While a furnace was being tapped at the Acklam Iron Works of Messrs. Dorman Long & Co., Middlesbrough, on 10th January, a portion of the brick flooring near the furnace was forced upwards by an explosion, and flames and several tons of molten metal belched forth, quickly covering all the ground near the furnace with molten metal. Flames were leaping into the air nearly 15 feet high and it was almost impossible to see on account of steam. A man named Davies, aged 76, employed as a cleaner, was partially overwhelmed and took refuge in a water-channel surrounding the furnace. Two attempts were made to rescue him by the foreman, but he was beaten back. Marron and Mullen, hearing that a man was believed to be trapped by the molten metal, ran to the scene of the explosion and jumped over the tapping channel which was then full of molten metal. At first they could see nothing on account of the steam and flames, but on the steam lifting for a few seconds they ran along the water-channel, where they saw Davies lying, and carried him away.

Davies later died from his injuries. (6.5.28)

A boy's gallantry in a fire

BERTIE FREDERICK CROSBY   A serious fire broke out on 9th September 1928 at the premises of the Film Waste Products Ltd., Redhill Street, Regent's Park. A quantity of cinematograph film in a drying-machine ignited; the fire immediately spread to other film on adjacent benches and in other containers.

Crosby, a boy of 16, was passing through the drying-room when the fire broke out. He at once ran to a door leading out into a yard, but on hearing a scream from near the drying machine he turned back into the room and made his way towards the machine, the contents of which were burning fiercely. He was unable to see any one and returned to the door leading into the yard. Here he met the foreman and together, Crosby leading, they re-entered the room. As they made their way in, Crosby saw a girl fall up against one of the work-tables, and he ran to her and half pulled and half carried her towards the door. Outside the door they both fell. Crosby was stupefied by the heat and the fumes, and did not recover full consciousness until he found himself out in the yard with his clothes alight. He extinguished his clothes by means of water from the canal which ran at the bottom of the yard, and was subsequently removed to hospital.

The fire, which spread to another factory and two workshops, was particularly violent and resulted unfortunately in the death of five persons. Crosby could easily have escaped from the building without injury, but on two separate occasions he re-entered the room where the fire originated, in an endeavour to save life. The girl whom he helped out of the building afterwards died, and the burns sustained by Crosby himself were such that at one time it was not thought that he would recover. (15.5.28)

Courageous behaviour of two men at Ebbw Vale steelworks

THOMAS BOURTON
THOMAS PHILLIP EVANS   The blast furnaces of the Ebbw Vale Steel & Iron Co. had been shut down in order that the gas mains of the blast-furnace plant might be cleaned out. The work proceeded normally for ten days, when two men engaged in cleaning a 3-foot pipe connecting two boilers were overcome on 17th December 1927 by carbon monoxide gas. The accident was not discovered until the relief entered the pipe and found the body of one of the workmen. This they drew to the manhole giving access to the pipe. Bourton and Evans then entered the pipe in

order to rescue the second workman, and after proceeding some 20 feet along the pipe they came upon the workman's body. With great difficulty and much distressed by gas, they dragged themselves and their fellow workman to the manhole through which they were assisted into the open air. Unfortunately the rescued workman died.

Bourton and Evans were both well aware that there was poisonous gas present in the pipe. One body had already been recovered and the two men who had entered it had been gassed.

Notwithstanding the grave and evident danger they both entered the pipe and proceeded for some distance away from the manhole where, if they were overcome, there was no chance of their receiving immediate aid. (1.6.28)

Staffordshire miner's brave action

ARCHIBALD BURTON Two miners, Burton and Gleaves, were engaged on 12th November 1927 in inserting timbers at the Burley Colliery, Apedale, Staffordshire, when a sudden fall of roof pinned Gleaves by the feet, and put out the lamps of both men. Burton found Gleaves but, finding that he was unable to release him, groped about for timber, and, having found it, erected a shield to protect his comrade from further falls. He then left to fetch lamps and assistance. As he was leaving a further fall occurred which buried Gleaves to the hips. Burton travelled some 150 yards, including some steep inclines, in complete darkness before he could get a lamp and send for assistance. Having secured a lamp, he returned to the scene of the fall and was soon joined by another miner, Moss. Together these two placed more timber in position to protect the imprisoned man. They were then joined by others who assisted in the work of clearing the fall. They had worked their way along under the protecting timber to Gleaves's feet when they had to withdraw on account of the imminence of another fall. This further fall was heavier than the previous two and completely buried Gleaves, breaking all the protecting timber except that originally erected by Burton. No further falls occurred and after four or five hours' work the imprisoned man was extricated.

Burton in waiting to erect a protection for his trapped comrade saved Gleaves's life and gravely imperilled his own. (12.6.28)

A Carmarthen miner's coolness in an emergency

HENRY BUTTERFIELD An outburst of fire-damp and small coal occurred in the main slant at the Ponthenry Colliery, Carmarthenshire, on 10th July. Butterfield, a fireman at the mine, heard the outburst and saw men running. He steadied them and started a pump to improve the ventilation. On being told that there were men lying unconscious in the main slant, he led others to their rescue. The air soon became so bad that his oil safety lamp would not remain alight, and he had to use an electric lamp. On reaching the main slant he found six men, of whom four were unconscious and one semi-conscious and struggling. These men were then helped to the surface. Butterfield then continued down the main slant where, in a side road, he found two men who were still conscious, and, a little farther on, three more who were unconscious. Assistance was summoned and the injured were taken to the surface. By this time Butterfield had himself been severely affected by the gas.

Similar sudden outbursts had occurred in these workings previously, several with fatal results, and Butterfield as a fireman would know what the danger was and the importance of prompt action. After doing what little he could quickly to reduce the danger he at once took the lead in the rescue operations, and his action in exposing himself to the effects of the foul atmosphere in order to ascertain whether it was possible to retain consciousness and carry out the work of rescue encouraged others to follow him in order to render assistance in removing the injured. Two of his helpers were themselves overcome. There is no doubt that Butterfield knowingly endangered his life in order to save the lives of his comrades. Two of those who were rescued died later. (10.10.28)

Indian railway employee's bravery

BABU LAKHAN RAM As a passenger train was approaching Najibabad Station on 1st May, a man threw himself on the track opposite the station building. Babu Lakhan Ram, an employee of the railway, heard the shouts of those who had witnessed the occurrence but were afraid to attempt a rescue, and running to the spot jumped on to the track although the train was then only 30 yards away. Despite the man's struggles Babu Lakhan Ram was just able to drag him clear of the lines and hold him down until the train came to a standstill.

The rescued man, who was strongly built, proved to be demented and bent on committing suicide. Had he succeeded in resisting Babu Lakhan Ram's efforts to drag him clear, Babu Lakhan Ram would undoubtedly have been killed. (13.11.28)

Lincoln man's brave attempted rescue at level crossing

ARTHUR WILLIAM LEWIN At about 8.45 p.m. on the 18th October 1928, Lewin was closing the gates at Pelham Street Level Crossing at Lincoln to permit an engine and two vans to cross. He had closed the large gates on the east side of the crossing and was moving to close the wicket gate on the same side when he saw an old man open the wicket gate and start to walk across the railway lines. The man disregarded the warning shouted by Lewin, who, seeing the danger, ran across the lines and tried to pull him clear of the engine, which was then moving at about five miles per hour. Unfortunately, Lewin, who is himself 67 years of age, was just too late, and not only was the old man knocked down and killed, but Lewin himself sustained serious injuries, which resulted in the amputation of one of his arms. (12.3.29)

A brother's devotion

HENRY CHARLES HAMBLIN
Henry Charles Hamblin and his brother, Arthur Albert Hamblin, colliers, were working in a seam at Mells Colliery, Somerset, on 10th November 1928, when the supporting timbers suddenly gave way and there was a fall of the roof. Arthur Hamblin was caught by the falling debris and was pinned by the right foot. In struggling to extricate himself a further fall occurred, burying him to the waist. Henry Hamblin, on hearing the fall, immediately ran to the scene of the accident and tried to free his brother, but could not do so. A further fall buried Arthur Hamblin up to his shoulders. Henry Hamblin shouted for help, but, being unable to make any one hear, he was forced to leave his brother and go for assistance. On his return he found his brother almost buried. As the roof continued to fall, Henry crouched over his brother's head to shield him and remained in that position for some twenty minutes until assistance came and a temporary covering of timber was erected over his brother's head. He knowingly exposed himself to considerable danger and himself received severe bruises while shielding his brother with his own body from the falling stones. His gallant conduct probably saved his brother's life. (23.4.29)

Gallantry in Durham pit accident

Robert Glendenning
JOHN THOMAS BAKER
SAMUEL HUGHFF
JOHN KENNY
JAMES SIDNEY PURVIS

A telephone message was received at the office of the South Garesfield Colliery, Durham, on 17th May, that Richard Lowes, one of the Colliery deputies, had been injured during blasting operations. Robert Glendenning, an over-man, 55 years of age, set off down the pit and, collecting two lads, James Sydney Purvis and John Thomas Baker, at the bottom of the shaft, and a tram and stretcher, went in search of Lowes. They were joined by two hewers, John Kenny and Samuel Hughff.

Meanwhile, five other men had been trying to rescue Lowes. Four of them were overcome by gas, while the fifth managed to crawl out just in time. It was on meeting this man some quarter of a mile from the scene of the accident that Glendenning realized the serious nature of the occurrence. He hurriedly organized his party and, by repeated efforts, they succeeded in extricating the five men who had been gassed, of whom three were dead.

The rescue party took such precautions as were possible at the time, but first Kenny and then Hughff were rendered unconscious. After they had, with difficulty, been removed from the danger area Glendenning sent Purvis for further help and continued the rescue work with the assistance of Baker. Baker was next overcome, and Glendenning was also affected by the fumes, but he continued his efforts until, when further help had arrived, he was able to bring out the last of the victims of the accident. He then collapsed and had to be carried out from the pit.

For an hour, during the whole of which time the atmosphere was thick with smoke and gas, Glendenning showed great courage and resource and displayed high qualities of organization in directing the rescue operations. He himself, and Baker, Hughff, Kenny, and Purvis under his leadership, knowingly and repeatedly risked their lives in determined and sustained efforts to save the lives of their fellows, and there is no doubt that but for their courageous action the death-roll would have been heavier than it was. (22.11.29)

A miner's brave conduct

JOSEPH WILSON   A fall occurred at the Murton Colliery of the South Hetton Coal Company on 10th April 1929, which resulted in the complete burial of one man, Ralph Chisholm, and the partial burial of another, David Stevenson. Hearing the fall, Joseph Wilson hurried to the place and protected Stevenson from further falls by standing over him and shielding him with his body, while others attempted to free the imprisoned man. Stevenson was liberated after 35 minutes, during which the whole roof in the locality was 'working' and further falls were continually taking place. When the rescue operations were completed, Wilson himself was buried above the knees and unable to move. Ralph Chisholm was unfortunately found to have died from suffocation.

Wilson's action in interposing his body between the falling debris and the imprisoned man almost certainly saved Stevenson's life, and gravely endangered his own. (11.2.30)

A workman's brave action at Jarrow

JOHN WILLIAM HENRY   John Shepherd and Hugh Black were told
SHEPHERD   on 16th October 1929 to clean a steam
                 boiler at Palmer's Shipbuilding & Iron Co.,
Ltd., Jarrow. Black entered the boiler and Shepherd was about to

follow when he detected traces of gas. In reply to a call, he received only a faint reply from Black, and immediately climbed inside to go to his help. He found Black half conscious some 25 feet from the boiler manhole. He endeavoured to drag him to the opening but had to abandon the attempt as he himself was succumbing to the action of the gas. He made his way out of the boiler, called for help and, though still seriously affected by the gas, returned with a rope, which he tried to fasten round his comrade, who was then unconscious. He collapsed, however, before being able to do so.

Further assistance was procured. Compressed air was used to clear the gas out of the boiler, and eventually a rescue party, wearing respirators, succeeded in extricating both Black and Shepherd. Black died a few hours later.

Twice during the course of the rescue operations Shepherd put his life in grave danger in a brave attempt to save the life of his fellow workman. (14.2.30)

A man's gallant attempted rescue of his father and brother

ALBERT TYLER   William Tyler and his two sons, Ernest and Albert, were engaged on 19th October 1929 in cleaning and enlarging the cess-pit of a factory at Burnham Green, near Welwyn, Hertfordshire. Ernest Tyler, who had been lowered to the bottom of the pit by means of a bucket attached to a rope, became affected by gas and was being drawn up, but fell out of the bucket when about 22 feet from the top of the pit. William Tyler at once went to the rescue of his son, but collapsed and became unconscious on reaching the bottom. In spite of the collapse of his father and his brother, Albert Tyler tried to descend the pit and rescue his relatives. He was driven back by the gas four times, but at the fifth attempt reached his father and brother and succeeded in passing a rope around them. They were hauled to the surface, but artificial respiration and the administration of oxygen failed to revive them.

Albert Tyler undoubtedly displayed great courage and determination in his attempts to save his father and brother. The rescue operations lasted over a period of about 40 minutes, and every time he entered the pit he must have been fully aware that he was endangering his own life. (14.2.30)

A gateman's brave action

MAHABIR DUBEY   On 3rd April 1929, a woman at a level crossing tried to pass in front of two moving wagons. Gateman Mahabir Dubey called out to warn her, but finding that she had taken no heed and had slipped and fallen on the track, he rushed forward and tried to drag her clear of the wagons. He was knocked over, receiving serious injuries; the woman was killed. (18.2.30)

Gallantry in a cordite factory fire

JOSEPH TURNER — An explosion accompanied by fire took place on 7th November 1929 in a press house of the Royal Naval Cordite Factory at Holton Heath. Turner went towards the press house and, as only one worker came out of the building, he knew that there would be others left inside. Regardless of his own safety, he entered the press house and found one man unconscious on the floor beneath burning debris. Despite the grave risk of further explosions he freed the injured man, extinguished so far as possible his burning clothing, and dragged him clear. The rescued man died later. (11.4.30)

A brother's devotion

GRANVILLE CHARLES WASTIE — At North Leigh, Oxfordshire, on 25th November 1929, Hector Wastie, a bricklayer, when descending a new well 30 feet deep and 3 feet wide, was overcome by gas half-way down and fell into 30 inches of water at the bottom. His brother Stanley went to his aid but he, too, collapsed. Another workman, George Broughton, attempted to descend the well, but when about half-way down he became faint and had to be pulled up by the rope which he had fastened round him. By this time Granville Wastie, a farmer, who had heard of the accident to his brothers, arrived. Tying a handkerchief over his face and roping himself, he went down and brought Stanley alive to the surface.

Granville then went down again and brought up Hector, who had been drowned whilst gassed. (6.6.30)

Gallant rescue of buried men in Derbyshire mine

SAMUEL CROFTS
JOHN INGRAM GOUGH — Two men, Redfern and Hardwick, were filling coal with other men at the Bretby Colliery, South Derbyshire, on 9th September 1929, and were warned to leave their work as a shot was about to be fired near them. As they were doing so about 10 tons of roof fell and buried them. Deputy Crofts and others tried, at great personal risk, to release the entrapped men. Although further falls were taking place, Crofts remained at work for 20 minutes trying to rescue Redfern until a further large fall of about 100 tons killed Redfern. Crofts was knocked down and bruised by this fall, but he only gave up the attempt when he had crawled under the fall and had found Redfern dead.

While Crofts was trying to release Redfern, Gough and others were attempting to free Hardwick. At great personal risk they removed the fallen coal from his head and shoulders and placed over his body some covering timber which saved his life when the second large fall occurred.

The rescuers were several times compelled to shelter from the falling material, and it was only after two hours' very dangerous work that they rescued Hardwick alive.

Although all the rescue party showed great bravery and disregard for their own safety Crofts and Gough were recognized by their comrades to have been the most prominent in risking their lives. (17.6.30)

Brave rescue from a 160-foot chimney

THOMAS PEARSON FLEMING
NICHOLAS WHITEHEAD

Thomas Brewis was engaged on 23rd April on painting a chimney 163 feet high at the Derwent Works of the United Steel Companies, Ltd., Workington, when he was seen to fall backwards, apparently unconscious, and hang head downwards 150 feet up. As he fell, his feet had become entangled and were held in the ropes of the bosun's chair in which he had ascended. The charge-hand, Fleming, who was on a gantry surrounding the chimney about 80 feet up, secured the rope on which Brewis's chair was suspended and, climbing a vertical iron ladder fixed to the chimney, supported the body of Brewis, who was still unconscious. Meanwhile, Whitehead, a painter's labourer aged 17 years, went up the ladder from the gantry and placed a safety belt around Brewis. Fleming and Whitehead then lifted Brewis into the bosun's chair and secured him there by the hook of the safety belt. In doing so, Fleming's body was inclined at an angle of about 60 degrees to the vertical ladder. Fleming and Whitehead then came down the ladder steadying and supporting Brewis while the chair was lowered by other workmen to the gantry. (25.7.30)

Colliery accident in co. Durham

ARCHBOLD HAWTHORN

A 20-ton fall of roof occurred on 12th May at the North Biddick Colliery, Washington, co. Durham, and buried Lawrence Taylor, a hewer, and Stewart Collins, a putter. An attempt was made by the Deputy to make a way over or through the fall by pulling away loose timber and stones. In jumping back to avoid a large falling stone the Deputy fell and struck his head against a rail, which rendered him semi-conscious.

Archbold Hawthorn, the fore-overman, arrived and, having first satisfied himself that the entombed men were unhurt, made a hole through the fall about 18 inches square and about 4 yards long. With conspicuous gallantry Hawthorn then crawled half-way through the tunnel and pulled both Collins and Taylor through the opening. Immediately after Taylor had been extricated, another extensive fall occurred and closed the tunnel completely. (24.10.30)

Brave rescue in Glamorganshire pit accident

EVAN ROSSER
ALWYN LEWIS
WYNDHAM EVANS

About 12 noon on 1st June, Herbert Clarke, surveyor, and Thomas William Rees, fireman, went down the Cicely Colliery, Tonyrefail, Glam., to make a survey. As they had not returned by 5 p.m. the banksman went down to look for them and found them entombed by a heavy fall in the workings. The alarm was given by the banksman and at about 6.30 p.m. rescue operations were begun by Henry Davies, overman, Thomas Harding and William R. Evans, firemen, and Alwyn Lewis, collier. They tried to remove the debris, but were unable to continue as the timbers supporting the lip of the cavity began to collapse. Temporary supports were erected and a second attempt at clearing the fall was made under the supervision of the under-manager. This resulted in a second fall in which Henry Davies and William Evans narrowly escaped injury, and the attempt had to be abandoned.

It was then decided to drive a small tunnel, by means of piles, through the fall and at 9.45 p.m. the rescuers were joined by Wyndham Evans, overman, and Evan Rosser, fireman. At midnight Henry Davies and William Evans retired exhausted. Harding, who was a night official, also had to leave to perform his normal duties of inspection, and the work was carried on by Lewis, Wyndham Evans, and Rosser, under the supervision of the under-manager. Water was conveyed to the entombed men by means of a 1-inch pipe and at 2.30 a.m. Rosser was able to pass some warm stimulants through the tunnel. From this time the place became very uneasy and the pressure on the supports in the tunnel was so great that a collapse appeared imminent. At 3.30 a.m. the tunnel was completed and Rosser got through to the entombed men. Wyndham Evans got hold of Clarke from Rosser and a human chain was formed and Clarke was drawn out through the tunnel. Rees was then rescued in the same way, Rosser being the last to come through the tunnel. He had scarcely got clear when the tunnel closed in and became completely impassable.

The rescue took 9 hours. Of the rescue party, Lewis was there throughout and Rosser and Wyndham Evans for the last $5\frac{3}{4}$ hours. All who took part in the rescue behaved with conspicuous bravery and incurred considerable risks; but the men exposed to the greatest danger were those who worked in the hastily constructed, lightly timbered tunnel through loose material and under constantly increasing pressure. This risk increased progressively as the tunnel reached completion and Rosser, Lewis, and Wyndham Evans (who worked in relays) were in constant danger of being buried by the total collapse of the passage. (31.10.30)

Man's gallant behaviour in ammonia works explosion

GEORGE TOLSON   One of a series of large tanks, about 18 inches apart, containing acetic acid exploded on 26th July 1930 at the works of Synthetic Ammonia and Nitrates, Ltd., Billingham, near Stockton-on-Tees. The explosion ignited the acetaldehyde vapour, burst the tank and allowed the acid to escape. The works Fire Squad, under George Tolson, immediately attacked the fire and in about 15 minutes had it under control. Tolson's attention was then called to a smouldering object lying between the burst tank and the next one. He at once directed a stream of water on to the object and, in order the better to direct the stream, he left the raised platform on which he was standing and went nearer to the object. As he did so it moved and he realized that it was a man. Although he must have fully realized the serious risk to which he was exposing himself, Tolson immediately drew his coat collar about his throat and rushed into the narrow space between the tanks in an attempt to rescue the burning man. On reaching him Tolson found that the man had been caught by the hand, and he was unable to release him without assistance. A second rescuer then joined Tolson, who was by this time so severely burned by the escaping acid and so overcome by the fumes that he was forced to leave the place and go into the fresh air. His place was taken by a third man, wearing breathing-apparatus, and the rescue was then completed.

It is estimated that Tolson was exposed to risk from escaping acid and fumes for about 5 minutes, and in that period he was severely burnt by the acid and was partially overcome by the fumes. (16.1.31)

Conspicuous gallantry of Metropolitan Railway employee

Arthur Devere Thomas   On the 14th January 1931, Ernest Percival, who was dismantling a wooden staging fixed across the track of the Metropolitan railway station at King's Cross, slipped and fell 20 feet to the permanent way. He was unconscious and lay face downwards across one running rail with his head close to the negative rail of the electrified system.

Thomas, a flagman, saw Percival fall and heard a down train approaching the station round the curve. Realizing that a signal could not be seen by the driver in time for him to stop the train, Thomas immediately jumped down from the platform to the up line, and, running across two positive and two negative rails carrying 600 volts, snatched Percival up from almost under the wheels of the approaching train, and held him, still unconscious, in a small recess in the wall whilst the train passed within a few inches of them. (31.3.31)

Gallantry at Yorkshire acid-mixing plant explosion

GEORGE HERBERT FRANK — A fire occurred on 4th July 1930 in the acid-mixing plant at the works of Messrs. Hickson & Partners, Castleford, Yorkshire. Mr. George Herbert Frank, the Works Manager, observing dense fumes arising from the vicinity of the plant, ran from the laboratory to the fire, at the same time ordering the fire appliances to be brought into action. Within a few minutes a very severe explosion occurred resulting in the death of 13 men and in injury to about 50 others. Mr. Frank took charge of the rescue operations and directed the fire brigade to the various points of danger.

Shortly afterwards the danger of a further explosion appeared to be so imminent that Mr. Frank withdrew all the employees to a place of safety and went alone into the danger area. On being satisfied that rescue operations were possible, he led a party into the devastated parts of the works and succeeded in rescuing one man who was still alive and in removing the bodies of two others.

After completing the rescues, Mr. Frank turned his attention to a neighbouring building which contained a store of benzol, and which had caught fire. Mr. Frank, with another helper, entered the building to satisfy themselves as to the conditions there, and it was not until after they had inspected the building and had satisfied themselves that a further explosion was unlikely to arise from that source that Mr. Frank allowed other persons to enter the danger zone. (3.6.31)

Kent miner's bravery

SYDNEY WILLIAM PADFIELD — Two youths, William Gazard and Frederick Crofts, were waiting in a junction on an auxiliary haulage roadway of the Tilmanstone Colliery, Kent, on 27th February, for a train of empty tubs to pass down the roadway. As the train came down, the front tub ran off the rails and crashed into the iron girders supporting the roof, knocking down five of them. Part of the roof collapsed and Gazard was pinned down by a falling girder. In response to a call for assistance from Crofts, who was unhurt, Padfield and others ran to the spot, and after removing some of the debris, were about to commence timbering the place to make it safe when they heard a cry from Gazard that he was being suffocated. Padfield promptly got down among the fallen debris, squeezed himself under the girder, and succeeded in raising Gazard's face, which was being pressed into the loose dirt on the ground. Padfield remained crouched in a small place under a heap of rubbish, which was supported by two props, and while protecting Gazard's face from the falling debris began to remove the rubbish from beneath him, while other men propped up one large stone and the girder with bricks until it was possible to release Gazard. This took about half an hour; Gazard was helpless as his spine was dislocated.

In carrying out this work Padfield was in imminent danger of being buried by a further collapse of the roof; two further falls actually took place and the whole roof might have fallen in at any moment. If this had happened, Padfield would have had no chance of getting away in safety. (12.6.31)

Accident at Hedley Pit, co. Durham

JOHN THOMAS AKERS
THOMAS BUCKLEY
PHILIP COX
JOHN DART
THOMAS DIXON
CHARLES JAMES BROOKFIELD FOX
ROBERT JOHNSTON

JAMES KENT
RICHARD HENRY KING
VICTOR KING
JOSEPH LEES
GEORGE FORSTER MASON
GEORGE NANCOLLAS

ROBERT REED
WALTER ROBERT SCOTT
WALTER HENRY SHELDRAKE
JOHN GEORGE TARN
THOMAS HENRY UREN
WILLIAM WAUGH

A fall of roof occurred in the Hedley Pit, South Moor, co. Durham, on 29th September 1930, partially burying a hewer, Frederick Beaumont. A chargeman, Victor King, was the first to come to the rescue. He found that a small passage-way remained open by which the buried man might be reached, and, with the assistance of his son Richard and John George Tarn, he immediately built two chocks of timber to keep it open. The passage was 7 yards long and about 2 feet square and the only practicable method of rescue was for three men to crawl along the passage-way and lie full length, two in the passage-way and one over Beaumont's body, and pass back, one at a time, the stones that were pinning him down.

This perilous and arduous work was carried on for nine hours by a team of miners (including Victor King) working in relays under the direction of the manager (Walter Robert Scott) and the under-manager (Robert Reed) until at last Beaumont was released, shaken but otherwise uninjured. During the whole nine hours the roof was shifting and 'trickling' and on four occasions Beaumont was almost free when a further fall buried him again. At one time the danger of a further fall appeared so great that the manager telephoned for a doctor

(Dr. Charles James Brookfield Fox) to come to the pit and amputate Beaumont's leg and so expedite his release. Fortunately—as it turned out—the doctor found it impossible to amputate in the restricted area in which Beaumont was confined, but he remained on the scene until Beaumont was rescued and examined and treated him before sending him to the surface.

Shortly after Beaumont was extricated the whole of the tunnel collapsed. (20.10.31)

Gallant rescue of a diver

William Davies A diver named Milton was working on 19th June, in a 12-foot cylinder which was being sunk in the Dagenham Dock, Essex. The water was standing considerably higher in the cylinder than in the river and suddenly at 9.30 a.m. a rush of water occurred, which carried Milton under the cutting edge of the cylinder and left him buried in the river bottom under mud and clay to a depth of about 16 feet. Fortunately, his life-line and air-pipes remained intact. Diver Scannell, who was on the spot, immediately went down inside the cylinder to try to reach Milton, but found it impossible. In the meantime Diver William Davies and Diver Smith had been summoned to assist in the work of rescue. Immediately they arrived Davies went down inside the cylinder and confirmed Scannell's view that there was no hope of a rescue from the inside. He then went down outside the cylinder with a high-pressure water-jet and weighted line. After several attempts he managed to get down about 12 feet into the mud, but the mud caved in on him, nearly burying him. He was forced to come up, but left the weighted line behind him. It was then decided to lift the cylinder slightly in the hope that the resulting inrush of mud under the cutting edge might bring Milton inside, but before the necessary gear could be obtained signals were felt on the weighted line. Davies immediately went down again with a water jet and after some very strenuous work succeeded in getting about 15 feet into the mud, and, following the line, at last reached Milton. With the help of the other divers, Milton was finally brought to the surface, practically unhurt, at 4.30 p.m., 7 hours after he was trapped. (10.10.31)

Charge-hand's brave conduct at Warrington

WILLIAM JAMES RUDD On the 14th October 1931, William James Rudd, a charge-hand in the ferrous metal department at the works of the White Cross Co., Ltd., at Warrington, instructed Albert Meakin, a labourer, to slack the fire of the furnace. Meakin, with one Nock, descended an eight-rung iron ladder to the furnace pit, which is 6 feet 6 inches below the floor-level and entirely covered by grating except at the point of descent. Meakin withdrew the fire-bars from the furnace before inserting dummy bars; this allowed the red-hot coke of the fire to fall into the water-sump under the furnace, filling the fire-pit with steam. Rudd heard screams from the furnace pit and running to the spot saw Nock on the ladder and clouds of steam issuing from the grating over the pit. He immediately went to the rescue, assisting Nock out and laid him on the grating. Then, wrapping his coat over his head, he descended the whole length of the ladder into the pit. His leg was grabbed by Meakin, who was apparently groping for the ladder, and Rudd managed to get hold of Meakin's arm only to find the skin come away in his hand. He succeeded, however, in getting Meakin up the ladder out of the pit and at once started first aid. Both Meakin and Nock were severely scalded and died as the result of their injuries.

Rudd's action in going to the rescue of Nock and then going down the ladder to rescue Meakin was a very gallant one. Although the danger was greatest immediately after the hot ashes fell into the water-sump and thereafter the risk to life in descending into the pit was not so great, Rudd, who had no knowledge of what had happened in the pit, had no means of estimating the danger he was incurring. He saw that Nock was badly burnt and he thought that a steam-pipe working an injector had burst or that molten metal had leaked into the fire-hold. Either of these occurrences would have involved serious risks, as the scalding steam would have been incessant, and Rudd faced what he thought were these risks and effected the rescue of both men single-handed without regard to his own safety. (12.12.31)

Gallant rescues at a Camden Town distillery

HAROLD HENRY HOSTLER
ALBERT JOHN MEADOWS

On the 18th September 1931, John Gale, an employee at the distillery of Messrs. W. A. Gilbey, Ltd., Camden Town, who was cleaning out with a hose-pipe the residue in an empty cherry-brandy vat, was discovered unconscious in the vat by his mate, Frederick Wormald, having apparently been gassed. Wormald went down the ladder and tried unsuccessfully to get Gale out. He then called Leonard Wright, one of the firm's analysts, and went down again but was slightly gassed and had to be assisted out by Wright. Wright then went down himself but fell unconscious in the bottom of the vat. In the meantime, the manager had sent for assistance, and Harold Hostler, a vatter, arrived on the scene and immediately emptied the vat. He succeeded in dragging Wright to a sitting position near the foot of the ladder, but feeling himself being overcome by the fumes he was forced to come out of the vat. He made a second attempt with a wet cloth round his mouth and at a third attempt, with a rope round his body, he succeeded in getting Gale to the foot of the ladder and part of the way up, when he was overcome by the gas and Gale slipped from his grasp. Hostler himself was drawn up by the rope.

Albert Meadows (assistant storekeeper) then volunteered to go into the vat, and at the second attempt, with a wet cloth round his mouth and a rope round his body, he succeeded in rescuing Wright. Although partially affected, he made a third but unsuccessful attempt to rescue Gale. He then asked for a length of rubber gas-piping and, placing it in his mouth to breathe through and taking a looped rope with him, he went down a fourth time. He managed to place the rope round Gale and he and Gale were both drawn up from the vat. Wright and Gale recovered consciousness after an hour.

Both Hostler and Meadows displayed great courage and resource in their attempts to rescue the two men. Both were aware of the risks they were incurring, as two of the rescuers had already been overcome by the gas, and both took precautions calculated to render their attempts at rescue successful. They showed great persistence in facing deliberately what was a considerable risk. Hostler entered the vat three times and Meadows four times and the periods occupied by their attempts at rescue were 10 to 15 minutes, and 15 to 20 minutes, respectively. (29.12.31)

A posthumous award

JOHN BIRKS Birks and another washerman, Harry Perkins, were changing their shoes in a mess-room on the premises of the Co-operative Laundries Association, Manchester, on 7th January. The mess-room was formed by two partitions in a corner of the boiler-room, and the floor was 3 feet below the general floor-level. Suddenly a large water-tank above the mess-room burst and volumes of scalding water cascaded through a skylight into the mess-room between the two men from the only door through which they could have escaped. The lights went out, and the room was dark and full of steam. Birks immediately placed himself between Perkins and the cascade of scalding water, and helped Perkins on to a table, whence he was helped over the partition by other men outside. Birks, who was probably unable to reach the top of the partition unaided, finally escaped from the mess-room through the door. Both men unfortunately died as a result of the scalds which they had sustained.

Perkins was only 18 years of age, and there can be no doubt that Birks, who was only 6 years older, deliberately gave up his own chance of escape in attempting to save Perkins. (6.5.32)

An engineer's gallantry at Walkden, near Manchester

JAMES CROMPTON   An explosion occurred on 18th April at the Park Mill of the Farnworth Cotton Spinning and Manufacturing Co., Ltd., at Walkden, near Manchester, wrecking the dividing wall between the boiler-house and the blowing-room as well as damaging the roof. The fires were not drawn at the time and the buildings, which were littered with debris from the wall and the roof, became full of smoke and escaping steam. Some 20 minutes after the explosion the chief engineer, Mr. James Crompton, learnt that Edith Jones, a woman worker in the blowing-room, was missing. He at once entered the room to search for her, crawling on his hands and knees among the machinery, but the steam was very dense and he failed to find the woman. He found his way back to the door and proceeded to make a second attempt but was again unsuccessful. He then entered the blowing-room at another point, through a broken window, and crawling through the steam among the debris he felt the woman's foot and ascertained that she was held down by fallen brickwork which partially covered her. Mr. Crompton called for assistance and with the help of two other men Miss Jones was released. She was carried out through the window and removed to hospital with a broken thigh.

Mr. Crompton is 65 years of age. His action was a very gallant one in that, as an experienced engineer, he must have been aware of the risk he ran, not only from further collapse of roof or wall but of scalding by steam and of being overcome by escaping gases. He showed great coolness and persistent bravery in thrice entering the steam-filled room with his sense of touch as his only guide in finding the injured woman. (22.7.32)

The Bentley Colliery disaster, Yorkshire

Ernest Allport
Edgar Hamilton Frazer
Samuel Jarrett Temperley
John Ward
RICHARD EDWARD DARKER
OLIVER SOULSBY
FRANK SYKES
PHILIP WILLIAM YATES

A violent explosion of fire-damp, followed by fires, occurred on 20th November 1931 in the north-east district of the Bentley Colliery, Yorkshire. Of some 47 persons working at or near the coal face, 45 were either killed or died later. A large number of persons rendered heroic assistance in the work of rescue; and after careful investigation it was decided that the eight persons named appeared to have displayed special gallantry.

Ward, a pony-driver, who was near an adjacent part of the coal face, was blown off his feet and enveloped in a thick cloud of dust, but as soon as he recovered himself went on his own initiative towards the face, guiding himself by rails and tubs, and assisted an injured man towards a place of safety. He repeatedly returned towards the face and helped to extricate injured men and bring them away; and he continued at rescue work for 3 hours, until completely exhausted. His bravery in groping his way towards danger, immediately after being knocked down by the blast, was outstanding. Darker, Soulsby, Sykes, and Yates also displayed great gallantry and perseverance in extricating the injured and conveying them to a place of safety. The atmosphere was hot and vitiated and there was evident risk of further explosions. One such explosion actually occurred at 10.30 p.m., injuring members of a rescue party, as mentioned below, and a third explosion occurred later.

Allport, Temperley, and Frazer were prominently concerned with rescues from the area of the fires, which was explored somewhat later and in which the danger was extreme.

Temperley, an assistant surveyor at the colliery, volunteered to lead a rescue brigade to the return air-way, where some men were still alive, by way of the face, there being a fire on the direct route. On the journey an explosion occurred severely injuring three members of the party. The party then returned, but Temperley, though not equipped with breathing-apparatus, went on, with one of the Mines Inspectors, as far as the entrance to the airway and subsequently helped to carry out an injured man past one of the fires and rendered other help. Allport, a member of the colliery Rescue Team, took a prominent part in the rescue operations, displaying energy, initiative, and bravery, and encouraging other rescue men. He was over 3 hours in breathing-apparatus and during part of the night, when his rescue apparatus required replenishing, he assisted in loading men on to stretchers. Subsequently, in answer to a call for volunteers after the second explosion, he seized a breathing-apparatus, and joined a rescue party which penetrated past a fire to rescue two other men. Frazer, one of H.M. Divisional Inspectors of Mines, explored much of the most dangerous area, displaying great gallantry in venturing among flames, smoke, and after-damp though not provided with a breathing-apparatus; on hearing moaning in the return air-way he ran back to summon a rescue party, but returned to the air-way without waiting for them. He subsequently remained in the most dangerous area assisting to organize rescue operations and helped to take out past a fire two rescued men from the airway; and although exhausted he continued his efforts, until all the men, dead or alive, who were reported to be in the district had been extricated. (30.9.32)

Durham miner's presence of mind

DAVID YORK A cage with four men on board was descending a shaft at Pelton Colliery, Pelton Fell, Durham, on 20th June when, just after leaving a platform at a seam 76 yards above the pit bottom, a corner of the cage caught a girder supporting the platform and the cage remained suspended about 7½ feet below the platform. Realizing the serious danger that any movement of the cage might send it crashing to the pit bottom, York, a master shifter, volunteered to try to obtain assistance. He climbed out of the cage into the shaft, and although he had only a few inches of clearance in which to work and although his only hand- or foothold was a 2-inch pipe, he succeeded in squeezing himself between the cage and the girder and reaching the platform. After telephoning for assistance he returned to the shaft, gave warning to the engineman to stop winding, and attempted to make the cage secure. He succeeded in attaching a cable to the cage chains, but before he was able to anchor it the cage fell to the shaft bottom, the other three occupants of the cage being killed. (4.10.32)

Brave rescues from fire-damp

FREDERICK RAYMOND CORDY
JOHN THOMAS BOWEN
ARIANFRYN HUGHES

An explosion of fire-damp took place in the Llwynpia Colliery, near Tonypandy, on 25th January, and caused poisonous gas to circulate round the ventilating system. Cordy at the time was working with a man named West at some distance from the point where the explosion occurred, but both were affected by the gas. West collapsed, and Cordy took him on his back for 30 yards before he too began to collapse. Leaving West, he made his way to the Main Heading where he found Bowen and Hughes attending to others who had been injured; he was too exhausted to do more than tell them of West's plight. Bowen and Hughes thereupon went to rescue West. Bowen's lamp went out indicating the presence of gas, but they pressed on and effected the rescue. Cordy, who had followed them as soon as he could, met them shortly after they started back. All three men deliberately endangered their lives in rescuing their comrade. (22.11.32)

A brave action in Sierra Leone

OSMOND WILLIAMS Mr. Williams, an electrical foreman in the Public Works Department, Sierra Leone, heard on 15th July that a distribution wire had fallen in a street in Freetown and went to investigate. He saw a woman approaching the broken wire and shouted to her to stop, but she continued on her way and became entangled in the wire. Mr. Williams immediately endeavoured to free the woman and, in spite of severe shocks, succeeded in doing so. He applied artificial respiration until the woman's breathing appeared to be normal and then drove her to hospital. Afterwards he returned and superintended the repair of the broken wire. The woman died later.

Mr. Williams was an experienced electrician and, in consequence, was fully aware of the danger which he incurred, especially as his clothing was wet with rain. (29.11.32)

A boy's rescue of a man from a bull

WILLIAM EDWARD GOFF On the 16th October 1933, Mr. A. R. Cooke, a farmer, of Pump Farm, Backford, Cheshire, was attacked by a bull in the yard behind his house. The farmer tried to hold the animal off, but became exhausted and was thrown to the ground and gored. Goff, who is employed by the farmer, is 16 years of age, but small for his age. He heard the farmer cry for help and ran to his master's assistance armed with a pikel. Goff rushed at the bull and by thrusting the pikel several times into the animal's head succeeded in driving it off for a short distance, while the farmer managed to get into safety. The farmer was seriously injured, and but for the boy's intervention, would almost certainly have been gored to death. (2.1.34)

A Welsh miner's bravery

THOMAS THOMAS An inrush of water occurred on 21st September 1933 in the Brass Vein Slant of the Brynamman Colliery, Glamorgan. Thomas, a young collier who was working underground at the time, assisted, at the risk of his own life, a youth who had lost his lamp and was unable, in the darkness and rush of water, to make his way to safety, to reach a part of the working where several of the colliers had gathered. The colliers then divided into two groups, one group seeking a way out by an air-way and another group by a roadway which was flooded and obstructed by a mass of timber and rails which had been washed down by the water. Thomas took up the rear in the group that took the roadway, and when they succeeded in reaching safety he returned, at great peril, to fetch the other group, who then escaped by the same route, Thomas being the last to leave. (6.2.34)

A workman's courage

PATRICK TORLEY On the 8th September 1933, at the United Steel Company's works at Workington, a man who was working in a bunker containing over 100 tons of iron ore was buried in ore up to his armpits, owing to the ore slipping. His cries attracted Torley who was working in the vicinity. Torley summoned help, and went into the bunker and supported the buried man by placing his arms round him and standing with his back against a pile of ore. More help was forthcoming in about 10 minutes; and Torley continued to support the man for a further period of 40 minutes while the ore was being shovelled from round the buried man. At any time the ore might have shifted and buried both men. (17.4.34)

A colliery manager's gallant action

DOUGLAS HUBERT ORMOND BISHOP
A heavy fall of roof took place on 5th February at a point in the workings at the Langwith Colliery, Derbyshire. A stallman was buried under the fallen material but was saved from fatal injury because he was beneath a girder, one end of which remained in position and the other on some of the fallen material. Mr. Bishop, who is the manager of the colliery, took charge of the rescue measures and undertook the most dangerous part of the work. He first raised one end of the girder with a coal-cutter's jack and then (largely with his hands) scraped away the ground from the imprisoned man's feet and hip. After a good deal of manœuvring the stallman, whose left leg had been fractured, was released. The release took a considerable time and Mr. Bishop was exposed to great risk for an hour and a half. (11.5.34)

Brave attempt at rescue in a Swansea pumping-station

JOHN SAMUEL MATHIAS
On the 18th March 1935, at the pumping-station of the National Oil Refineries at Queen's Dock, Swansea, a workman went down into a drainage chamber connected with pipes through which oil is pumped from ships to storage tanks on shore, and was overcome by fumes. He fell unconscious into oil which had collected to a depth of 2 feet at the bottom of the chamber. Mathias went down into the chamber without a gas-mask and tried to effect a rescue; but he had to return to fresh air when on the point of collapse. Mathias recovered sufficiently to go down a second time; but although he was able to catch hold of the workman, gas again forced him to give up the attempt at rescue. Had he succeeded, the life of the first workman, whose body was recovered somewhat later, might have been saved. (28.5.35)

Gallantry in N. Staffordshire colliery

ROWLAND BENNETT
ALBERT MALEY
A fall of roof occurred on 17th January at Hanley Deep Colliery, North Staffordshire. Tom Harrison, a collier, was knocked down and his legs and feet were fastened. He was saved from fatal injury in two

further falls by a steel prop and bar which were placed over him by another worker. After rescue operations had proceeded for some considerable time it was found that the only way to release the imprisoned man, apart from amputation, was for some one to work his way alongside him under the fall and scrape the debris away with his hands, passing it out piece by piece. The space was so small that only a man of slim build could undertake the task and in doing so he had to lie prone over the imprisoned man. Mr. Bennett, the colliery manager, and Albert Maley carried out this extremely dangerous work. Maley, with the aid of a pick, managed to set Harrison free after he had been imprisoned for about 6½ hours. Bennett was present most of the time and Maley for 4 hours. During the later stages the rescuer had to lie under the fall with his head beside Harrison's feet. Another fall while he was in such a position would probably have proved fatal to the rescuer. (23.8.35)

Belfast managing director's self-sacrifice

Ernest Reid Powell A fire broke out on 2nd August in the ground-floor premises of the building at 2 Amelia Street, Belfast, in which Mr. Powell was employed as managing director of a firm of handkerchief manufacturers. Instead of first giving an immediate alarm the staff on the ground floor endeavoured vainly to extinguish the flames, which had obtained a good hold before the workers on the upper floors became aware of the danger. When the danger became known, several women and girls escaped from the first and third floors by means of the main staircase and about forty women and female young persons on the second floor also proceeded to escape in the same way. A number succeeded, being assisted by Mr. Powell, who was in his office at the commencement of the outbreak and who was subsequently seen on two occasions assisting women down the stairs and out of the building.

In the meantime the heat and smoke had much increased and the remaining women were unable or unwilling to descend by the front stairway. Efforts were made to induce them to try the back stairway, but without success. A few were assisted through a window to the flat roof of an adjoining building, and the others, more or less panic-stricken, made for the front windows which the fire brigade officers were then preparing to enter.

Mr. Powell was in the street at this juncture, but observing the plight of the women at the windows, he again groped his way up the smoke-laden stairs to the second floor, endeavoured to calm them, and shepherded them one by one through the windows to the firemen, who, by means of a portable escape, conveyed them to the street.

During these rescue operations, Mr. Powell sustained very severe burns, from which he died two days later. (8.11.35)

South Kirkby Colliery explosions

GEORGE WILLIAM BEAMAN
NORMAN BASTER
JAMES POLLITT

Two explosions occurred on 22nd August 1935 at South Kirkby Colliery, Yorkshire, in a district about 1¾ miles from the shaft. It was thought that these were due to a gob-fire and it was decided to seal off a part of the district by erecting stoppings.

This work was undertaken, and there were twenty-one men in the district, some near to the face and the others, of whom Beaman was one, at distances varying up to some hundred yards away. A further explosion then took place, severely injuring a number of men. Beaman and two others, who had rescue apparatus, at once proceeded to look for and succour the injured, and with the assistance of others who followed shortly afterwards ten men were carried out of the district alive. One died almost immediately, eight within a few days, and one recovered. During the progress of these operations, which involved repeated journeys to and from the face, some of the rescuers who were not equipped with special apparatus were considerably affected by fumes.

It was found that every one had been accounted for except a man named Dale; and although there was an increasing risk of a further explosion owing to accumulations of gas, search for him was renewed by Baster, the colliery agent, with the manager and four rescue men, including one Ball. They located Dale but he was dead. They proceeded to remove his body, but while they were doing so a further explosion occurred and all six members of the party were burnt. This explosion was severe enough not only to cause injury to the rescue party, who were comparatively near the face, but to affect those nearer the shaft who were looking after the men first injured. Baster got back and did what was possible to reassure these men and then with three others (of whom Beaman was one) he went in and removed Dale's body and later went in again for a certain distance to look for Ball, one of the rescue party injured by the second explosion, who was said to be missing. Baster, who had no apparatus, was this time so much affected by fumes and fatigue that he had to retire, but Beaman and another man conducted some further search without success. It was then reported that Ball had reached the shaft.

Later in the evening, however, after the rescue parties had left the mine, it was found that Ball was still missing. There were reasons for fearing that a further explosion might shortly occur and that a fresh search might only swell the casualty roll; but volunteers were anxious to descend the mine and make a further attempt, and one of the rescue parties so formed found Ball and brought him out safe. In this final operation, which was conducted at once with determination and prudence, J. Pollitt acted as captain of the rescue party. (17.4.36)

Yorkshire mine manager's brave action

GEORGE CHRISTOPHER HESLOP   A fall of roof occurred on 17th December 1935 at the Loftus Ironstone Mine, Yorkshire, and two workmen, John Cooper Henry and Henry Murrell, were buried in the debris. Mr. Heslop, the agent and manager of the mine, arrived on the scene shortly afterwards, and although falls were still occurring and there was a considerable roof movement so that the workers in the mine had not ventured to go to the rescue of the two men, Mr. Heslop crawled for about 4 yards under the fall into a cavity of about 2 feet until he reached Henry, from whose face he removed stones, but whom he was unable to free as there was a baulk across his legs. He then instructed the men to pile a road through the fall to protect Henry from further falls and to expedite his release. Afterwards he again crawled under the fall, a distance of 3 to 4 yards, and located Murrell who was pinned by one of his feet. Mr. Heslop gave him a stimulant and then worked strenuously for 4 hours in a cavity so small that there was room for only one person, until he liberated him alive. Falls were frequent and workmen and officials repeatedly urged him to withdraw. After Murrell was released Mr. Heslop again crawled into the cavity to Henry and supervised the cutting of the runner bolt by which he was pinned, and was able to release him alive after he had been imprisoned for 8 hours. Shortly after there was a heavy fall and the whole of the piling which had been erected to assist in his release collapsed.

Both of the rescued men died later. (26.5.36)

Durham miner's courageous conduct

RALPH STOKER   A heavy fall of roof took place on 20th May in a coal-working at Eppleton Colliery, co. Durham, where three hewers, James Brown, Mark Summers, and William Moffatt, were removing the last loads of coal from a stook. Moffatt was trapped by the fall and his left hand pinned by large frames of stones to the top of a tub. Brown and Summers went to his help while the roof was still falling heavily but were unable to liberate him. With the assistance of two other hewers, Thomas Whitfield and David Wood, they erected supports over the tub to protect Moffatt from the large pieces of stone which were gradually moving down to him. About 10 minutes after the fall Ralph Stoker and George Storey (overmen) and John Tubby and Albert Simpson (deputies) arrived. Heavy falls were still occurring and it was difficult to maintain the supports, some of which were crushed as soon as erected. Stoker crawled into a narrow opening of about 20 inches between the tub and the coal side and in a working space of about 10 inches uncovered Moffatt, who was lying in a crouched position behind the tub, and erected additional supports to keep back the stones which were lowering towards him. This probably saved Moffatt from being crushed to death. Storey later relieved Stoker, the working-space being large enough to admit only one man. Stoker, helped by the deputies, tried to make the position less dangerous from the other side of the tub. Meanwhile the risk had increased and a larger roof-fall was expected. The deputies and hewers concentrated on erecting supports to maintain a means of access to Moffatt, who by this time was severely shocked and begging the rescuers to amputate his fingers and so release him. But for Stoker there is no doubt that this quick but dangerous method would have had to be adopted. Stoker and Storey continued their efforts to move the stone that was trapping Moffatt's fingers and by driving a wedge-piece on the top of the tub they were able at length to release the thumb and first and second fingers. The roof then started to 'weight' again. Stoker persisted in his efforts and by about 4.40 p.m. Moffatt was dragged through the narrow aperture to safety. (9.10.36)

The Gresford Colliery disaster, 22nd September 1934

JOHN EDWARD SAMUELS
The sole survivors of those working underground were six men, of whom Samuels, a coal-cutting machineman, was one. They had been working at the time in what was known as No. 29's District. The effect of the explosion was to close the normal means of access to this section of the mine and thereby to cut off those working there, but it seemed to a group of men who had got together that a way out might be found along a little-used road which served as a return air-way. This hope proved in the end to be justified, but the survivors had to fight their way for nearly half a mile through an atmosphere so laden with gas that at an early stage some of the party turned back to seek some other way out, only to meet their deaths. The worst place proved to be at a point where the road crossed a fault and it was necessary for a ladder to be climbed in order to reach the upper level. At various points, members of the party fell behind, and the temptation to leave them to their fate must have been very strong.

Throughout Samuels took a leading part in encouraging members of the party, in advising as to what should be done or attempted, and in giving other help, staying behind to render assistance at a time when any delay in escaping was fraught with grave danger. The Chief Inspector of Mines, in his Report, states that Samuels summed up the position and displayed qualities of leadership in a most terrifying situation, and there seems to be no doubt that some at least of the party owe their lives to his coolness and courage. (10.2.37)

Heroism in Kenya

LEONARD WILLIAM BANGLEY

On the 21st January 1936, Bangley, an employee in one of the Kimingini Company's gold-mines at Kakamega, Kenya, was firing the last of a round of nine holes, when one hole exploded prematurely. He was blown some little distance away, and his native assistant was struck by a rock and fell into the gutter with his face in the water, so that he was in danger of drowning. Bangley, although aware that the remaining fuses would shortly explode, returned in the darkness to search for the native and managed to carry him without assistance to a place of safety. The native assistant subsequently died of his injuries.

Bangley undoubtedly displayed great gallantry in his attempt to save the injured man. (24.6.37)

Rescue at Blaydon-on-Tyne

JOHN WRIGHT

A workman at the Ottovale Works, Blaydon-on-Tyne, was overcome by benzol fumes on 25th May 1937, when he was carrying out repairs at the top of a column. While steps were being taken to obtain ropes to lower the workman to the ground Wright immediately climbed up, without a gas-mask, with a view to preventing him from falling, pending the arrival of help. Finding it essential to remove him at once from the fumes he raised the unconscious man on to his back and crawled with him for about 14 feet along three 9-inch planks below which there was a drop of 44 feet. (7.9.37)

A gallant doctor in Southern Rhodesia

ROBERT BENJAMIN SAUNDERS

On the 4th January 1937 an accident occurred in the Tebekwe Mine, Salisbury, Southern Rhodesia, in which one of the miners—a man named Sheasby—was trapped underground by a fall of rock and completely buried.

Dr. Saunders arrived on the scene at 3.15 p.m., by which time the rescue party had succeeded in removing most of the spillage from the imprisoned man's body. It was found, however, that his left hand was firmly held between two timbers. He remained in this dangerous position until 12.30 p.m. the following day.

During the whole of this time (with the exception of a short interval when he went to the surface for some food) Dr. Saunders remained underground rendering every medical assistance under extremely difficult and dangerous conditions. The situation of the imprisoned man was such that, in order to attend his patient at all, the doctor had to lie on top of him with his back in close proximity to a dangerously shaky roof, any disturbance of which would have resulted in a fall sufficient to crush them both.

After a period of 16 hours, when all efforts to extricate the miner had failed, it was decided to amputate his arm. The conditions only allowed of left-handed work and the operation was therefore performed by a left-handed amputator under the personal supervision of Dr. Saunders. Sheasby was then transported to the surface, and has now completely recovered from the effects of his long ordeal.

Dr. Saunders displayed great devotion to duty in circumstances of grave danger, and his example undoubtedly inspired the injured man with fortitude and the rescuers with courage. (19.8.37)

Two gallant brothers in South Staffordshire

DAVID NOEL BOOKER
SAMUEL BOOKER

Three men were at work on 14th May dismantling the plant at a conveyor face in a gate, at a distance of some 70 to 80 yards from the main level, in the Littleton Colliery, South Staffordshire. Fire-damp appeared to be spreading in the gate, since, at about 8 p.m., a fireman set off from the level to see what the men were doing up the gate and found that his lamp was extinguished at about 20 yards from the level. Between this time and about midnight, when full rescue apparatus became available and the bodies were recovered, efforts at rescue were made by a succession of men, some of whom themselves collapsed and thereby added to the task of later rescuers: of these one, Mr. Walmsley, the under-manager, himself lost his life, thus bringing the death-roll to four. In these operations the brothers Booker were outstanding. Each of them forced his way up the gate on four or five separate occasions, and they were jointly or severally responsible for extricating four earlier rescuers who had succumbed to the gas; all of these survived except Mr. Walmsley, the under-manager. On all of these occasions the brothers Booker, who seem to have been men of high resisting-powers, displayed great courage, which is to be rated even more highly as it was reinforced by equal coolness and forethought. (22.1.38)

A gallant Englishman in Bihar

THEODORE GEORGE BARKER On the 20th October 1937, a roof in a part of the Kustore Colliery, Bihar, from which a pillar of coal was being extracted, began to 'weight' and the miners were withdrawn. It was decided to remove the props which supported the roof in order to allow it to 'cave' in. There were thirty-four props, and at about 10 p.m., when eight had been removed, a mass of roof stone suddenly collapsed, burying two men engaged in the work. The assistant manager, Mr. Barker, was informed of the accident, went to the scene, and organized rescue operations. While these operations were in progress a second fall occurred and two men, Bhima and Akal Tanti, were trapped. Bhima, who was completely covered by fairly small debris but was nearer the edge of the fall, was rescued within half an hour by Mr. Barker, working at such risk that the Agent who was also present had to pull him out twice because stone was falling where he was working. Akal Tanti was buried from the hips downwards and was firmly held by a large block of stone, whilst above him was a large mass of stone insecurely supported. Small pieces of stone were falling. Mr. Barker with the co-operation of the Agent and others put in additional props to support the roof and erected a timber cage round Tanti. Barker then, using wedges and a heavy hammer, broke up the large stone which was holding Tanti's feet and continued the work until he was released at about 4 a.m. The actual rescue of the two men took about $2\frac{3}{4}$ hours and Mr. Barker bore the brunt of the work. During the whole of the rescue operations, lasting about four hours, he was exposed to imminent risk of a further collapse of the roof, and this actually took place after the two men had been rescued. (28.3.38)

A heroic porter at Warrington

Harold Gleave At about 11 p.m. on 18th April 1938, at Bank Quay railway station, Warrington, a passenger named Gaughan fell from No. 1 platform and lay across the nearest rail in the path of an incoming train, then about 150 yards away and still travelling at a fair speed.

Gleave was then on No. 3 platform. Hearing shouts of persons on No. 1 he rushed to that platform, crossing some railway lines and No. 2 platform, a distance of about 35 yards. When he arrived, the train was only about 20 yards from where Gaughan was lying and it appeared obvious that it could not be stopped in that distance. It was then travelling at about 5 miles an hour, that is, at the rate of 22 yards in 9 seconds.

Another porter, James Topping, endeavoured to jump down on to the rails to rescue Gaughan, but was held back by passengers. Gleave, coming up behind him, jumped down, swung Gaughan's body on to the way between the rails so that the train might pass above him, and then endeavoured to scramble out of the path of the train, but was struck by it. Fortunately he was thrown clear; but he did not escape without some injuries. Gaughan was also injured.

After the train had come to a standstill Gleave, notwithstanding his injuries, assisted in the work of extricating Gaughan. (21.6.38)

Heroic rescue work in a pit

AZARIAH CLARKE   On the 2nd July 1937, at about 5.45 a.m., a fire started in the holing of the Four Feet Seam at Holditch Colliery, North Staffordshire. The fire spread rapidly, but of the 55 men employed in the affected area at the time all except two succeeded in withdrawing from the danger zone. As soon as it was found that the two men were missing, unsuccessful search was made for them. At 6.50 a.m. an explosion occurred and one of the search party was afterwards found to be missing.

Meanwhile a call for the Colliery Rescue Brigade had gone out, and by 7.30 a.m. Azariah Clarke had assembled three others at the pit-head and proceeded to lead them below ground. The party met the managing director of the colliery in the neighbourhood of the fire, and he instructed them to search for the man who had been lost after the explosion. They accordingly donned their breathing-apparatus and started on their search in the direction of the face. The atmosphere was hot, dusty, and foul with gas and smoke, and on reaching a fall which blocked the way into the face they retraced their steps, continuing meanwhile their search for the missing man, but without success.

The Rescue Brigade—now increased to five by the arrival of another member—next went to search for the two men who had been lost at the time of the original fire. Still using their breathing-apparatus, they stumbled in the smoke up a steep road, parts of which had a gradient of 1 in $2\frac{1}{2}$ to 1 in 3. Soon after 10 a.m., while they were thus engaged, a severe explosion occurred resulting in the deaths of 27 persons most of whom had been sent down for the purpose of erecting stoppings to seal off the fire. The Rescue Brigade were but slightly affected by this explosion and, having made their way to a telephone, they arranged to come out to secure fresh breathing-apparatus, since their supplies of oxygen were running low.

During the period of some two hours, during which the Brigade had been searching for the lost men under Clarke's leadership, they had survived two other explosions of lesser intensity (as well as the major explosion to which reference has been made) and had been working throughout in conditions of the greatest difficulty and danger with the realization, moreover, that further explosions might occur at any moment.

Having secured new apparatus, Clarke again led the Brigade into the danger zone. Travelling down the road over falls of ground and derailed tubs, and past other debris produced by the explosion, and extinguishing a fire encountered on the way, they came upon a number of badly injured men and dead bodies. They made the injured as comfortable as possible, and arranged for stretchers to be sent in.

On the arrival of further assistance some members of the Brigade helped in evacuating the injured and the dead, while Clarke and others made a further examination of the workings with a view to ensuring that no living person had been left behind. By 3.35 p.m. all the men known to be alive had been recovered, and as it was thought that there was a considerable risk of a further explosion all the men were withdrawn from the mine. The Rescue Brigade had worked almost continuously in breathing-apparatus since 7.30 a.m. Later on doubt arose as to whether there might still be some injured persons alive in the pit, and at 6 p.m. Clarke again led a brigade down the mine. After an exhaustive search they found no live men below, and returned to the surface at 8.30 p.m. (28.7.38)

Gallant quarry workers

WILLIAM WILLIAMS
BEN LITTLER JONES

Blasting was about to take place at the Llysfaen quarry, Caernarvonshire, on the morning of 21st May. All the men with the exception of three—Williams, Jones, and Roberts, whose duty it was to light the fuses—had been withdrawn from the danger zone.

Williams had lighted one fuse, Jones two, and Roberts three, when Roberts trod on a stone which tipped up and trapped his foot so that he could not move. The shots were timed to go off in 80 seconds, and Roberts was in imminent danger of being killed. Williams and Jones tried to release Roberts, and failing to do so, Williams shouted to the others to pull out the fuses and promptly pulled out four himself. Jones pulled out one and Roberts the other.

In doing so they ran considerable risk; had any one of the detonators exploded, it would certainly have had serious or even fatal results. (9.9.38)

Heroism in a sewer

JOHN HENRY MEARS On Monday, 25th July, two workmen making a sewer in Albion Street, Miles Platting, Manchester, discovered that the air at the bottom of the 50-foot shaft was bad. The bad air was removed partly by the primitive expedient of lowering and raising a skip with lighted waste and partly by using an air compressor. The same thing happened on the following day (Tuesday) but not on the Wednesday. On Thursday, 28th July, W. Bellingham, a tunnel miner, partly descended the shaft and found by candle test that the air was foul again. He returned to the surface and warned Mears and J. R. Byrnes who were trying in vain to get the air-compressor working. Byrnes, followed by P. Murphy, the foreman (who said he would go down and see how bad the gas was), started to descend the shaft by the ladder. On reaching the bottom Byrnes was seen to step off the ladder, but shortly afterwards collapsed. Meantime Murphy, presumably becoming aware of the foul air, but ignorant of Byrnes's collapse, had partly reclimbed the ladder but warned of Byrnes's plight by shouts from the workmen at the top of the shaft he turned back, and on reaching the shaft-bottom collapsed in turn while trying to raise Byrnes.

There were no life-lines, ropes, safety-belts, or breathing-apparatus available. Knowing this, Mears tied a wet handkerchief over his mouth, got into a skip, and was lowered to the bottom, although he was warned that the handkerchief was useless against sewer gas. At the bottom he got out of the skip, tried to raise Murphy but put him down again, then got back into the skip and signalled to be raised. Unfortunately, as the skip was being steadied prior to being raised Mears fell out of it. Nearly half an hour later the Fire Brigade arrived and extricated the three men, all of whom were dead. (13.12.38)

Repeated acts of heroism of London man

ERNEST WILLIAM KENT On the night of the 25th October 1938 gangs of workmen were engaged in concrete-piling work at the Hackney Wick Stadium. Metal cylinders about 15 inches in internal diameter were being sunk into the ground, the earth inside them being then removed. At about 2.30 a.m. a gang of three workmen under the charge of Herbert William Baker encountered an obstruction at the bottom of one of these cylinders, which had been sunk to a depth of some 18 feet. Baker, who was a small man, decided to have himself lowered down the cylinder, presumably with the idea of clearing the obstruction with his feet. He was advised against doing so by one of the workmen who said that he smelt gas, but Baker persisted and was lowered feet foremost into the shaft, hanging with outstretched arms on the hook of the winch rope. When he was about 12 feet down he shouted for help and the men began to pull him up, but before he reached the top he lost his grip on the hook and fell to the bottom.

Messages for help were sent, but in the meantime Kent, who was also a small man, volunteered to be lowered head first down the cylinder in an attempt to pull Baker up with his hands. His feet were lashed to the winch cable and he was lowered head first for some distance but then gave signs of distress and was hauled up in a state of semi-collapse and bleeding from the mouth. In the meantime the fire brigade and police had arrived, and an oxygen cylinder with the jet partially turned on was lowered to a position near Baker's head in an effort to improve the atmosphere until a rescue could be effected. The ground surrounding the cylinder was also dug away to enable the upper 3-foot section to be unscrewed, thus reducing the depth to about 15 feet. These operations had taken over an hour and it was realized that there was no chance of getting Baker out alive by these means. A call was made for a volunteer small enough to descend the shaft, and another workman volunteered and was lowered head first into the cylinder. A short distance from the top, however, a ridge round the inside of the tube jammed his shoulders and he had to be drawn up again. Kent, who had partially recovered, volunteered to make a further effort, and as there appeared to be no other chance of freeing Baker alive his offer was accepted and he was again lowered into the shaft. He succeeded in grasping Baker and as he was drawn up he was heard to be gasping for breath and called out 'Quick! Quick!' He just had sufficient strength to retain his grip until helpers round the shaft-top caught Baker's arms when he collapsed. Both men were taken to hospital, but it was found that Baker was dead. (20.12.38)

CHAPTER XV

MEDAL OF THE ORDER OF THE BRITISH EMPIRE, MILITARY DIVISION, FOR GALLANTRY (E.G.M.)

LIST OF RECIPIENTS UP TO 31st DECEMBER 1938

Note.—The average interval between the date of the deed here recorded and the announcement of an award in *The London Gazette* is 5 months. Minimum delay, 2 months; maximum delay, 14 months. The average and the maximum intervals have been lengthened by the necessary procedure in connexion with cases reported in India.
The date of the Gazette is shown in parentheses.

CHAPTER XV
MEDAL OF THE ORDER OF THE BRITISH EMPIRE, MILITARY DIVISION, FOR GALLANTRY (E.G.M.) LIST OF RECIPIENTS UP TO 31st DEC. 1938

Insurrection in Malabar

Pte. FREDERICK CHANT
Sgt. WILLIAM GEORGE HAND, M.M.
Pte. THOMAS MILLER
Pte. FREDERICK HENRY TROAKE
all of 2nd Bn. *The Dorsetshire Regiment*
Assistant Surgeon GEORGE DAVID RODRIQUES, *I.M.D.*

For services rendered in connexion with military operations in Malabar, 1921–2. (2.6.23)

Disturbances in China

Petty Officer ROBERT MILLS CHALMERS, *R.N.* — In recognition of his services on the 23rd June 1925, during disturbances in China. (18.6.26)

Gallantry in the Royal Navy

Stoker Petty Officer HERBERT JOHN MAHONEY, *R.N.* — H.M.S. *Taurus* was steaming at high speed when the supports to the starboard fore turbo fan fractured, causing the fan to drop; this in turn severed the main auxiliary exhaust steam pipe and several smaller exhaust pipes.

Mahoney ordered the boiler room to be cleared at once, but remained behind himself, at great personal danger, to close stop valves and take other necessary action.

The boiler room was enveloped in steam, and large pieces of metal were being hurled about by the turbo fan which was still running. (23.12.27)

Midshipman ANTHONY JOHN COBHAM, *R.N.*
Able Seaman GEORGE PATERSON NIVEN, *R.N.*
— On the 26th July 1929, H.M.S. *Devonshire* was carrying out full calibre firing, when at the first salvo there was a heavy explosion which blew off the roof of one of the turrets.

When the explosion occurred, Midshipman Cobham immediately took stretcher parties aft and ordered one crew to follow him and the other crews to rig hoses. On reaching the turret he assisted men who were coming out of it with their clothes on fire, and took charge of the work of extinguishing the flames, and getting the men into stretchers. He followed the gunnery officer into the turret when the latter first went in and remained in the gun-house until all necessary work was completed.

Niven entered the turret shortly after Cobham and helped to evacuate wounded. (1.1.30)

Able Seaman GEORGE WILLET HARRISON, *R.N.* At Portsmouth on the 15th February 1930, after a bad accident on H.M.S. *Hood*, Dockyard workmen were engaged in opening up for inspection the starboard after-bulge compartments. A shipwright named Langford entered through the man-hole into a compartment, was overcome by gas and collapsed.

As soon as the alarm was given a rescue party entered the bulge, but found great difficulty in locating Langford owing to gas, and the absence of effective lighting. Nevertheless Harrison made his way through successive compartments and, at great personal risk, with assistance, eventually rescued Langford who died later. (1.1.31)

Gallantry in Royal Air Force

Leading Aircraftman WALTER ARNOLD, *R.A.F.* On the 20th June 1928, at Digby Aerodrome, this airman was a passenger in a machine which was wrecked upon landing and immediately caught fire. Having extricated himself from the burning wreckage he re-entered the flames and succeeded in dragging the pilot, who was unconscious and very severely injured, to a position of safety. Arnold sustained burns to his face, neck, and hands, and his prompt and courageous action saved the pilot's life. (9.11.28)

Flying Officer WALTER ANDERSON, *R.A.F.* Corp. THOMAS PATRICK McTEAGUE, D.C.M., *R.A.F.* Pilot Officer H. A. Constantine while flying an aeroplane off Leysdown on the 10th December 1928 crashed into the sea, 200 yards from the shore. Corp. McTeague and F.O. Anderson swam to his assistance. The weather was bitterly cold; an on-shore wind was blowing, and the sea was rough. Constantine, fully clothed and suffering from injuries and shock, started to swim ashore, but was in a state of collapse when McTeague reached him. McTeague, though exhausted himself, supported him until the arrival of Anderson, and Constantine was then brought to safety by their efforts. (12.4.29)

Flight Cadet WILLIAM NEIL McKECHNIE, *R.A.F.* On the 20th June 1929, an aeroplane piloted by Flight Cadet C. J. Giles crashed on landing at Cranwell Aerodrome and burst into flames. The pilot was stunned but managed to release his safety-belt and fall out of the machine in a dazed condition. Flight Cadet McKechnie, who had landed in another aeroplane about the same time some 200 yards away, left his machine and ran at full speed towards the scene of the accident. The petrol had spread over an area of about 10 yards diameter in full blaze, with Giles lying in it, semi-conscious. McKechnie ran into the flames and pulled out Giles, who was badly burnt about the legs and face, with his clothes actually on fire. After dragging him clear of the flames, during the process of which he was scorched and burnt, McKechnie extinguished Giles's burning clothing. (18.10.29)

Pilot Officer SIDNEY NOEL WILTSHIRE, *R.A.F.* On 21st October 1929 this officer was flying with his instructor, F.O. H. E. Power, at Sleaford in an aeroplane that crashed on landing and at once caught fire. Having extricated himself from the wrecked machine, he found that his companion's foot was caught in the wreckage and that he could not get out.

Wiltshire re-entered the flames and helped Power to get clear, sustaining burns on his neck and face. Power's clothing was by this time well alight and he would undoubtedly have lost his life but for the prompt and courageous action taken by his pupil. As it was, he was badly burnt. (31.1.30)

Leading Aircraftman ROBERT EWING DOUGLAS, *R.A.F.* On the 13th June 1930, at Kohat, India, an aeroplane proceeding on patrol with a crew of two and a load of live bombs stalled shortly after leaving the ground and crashed on the edge of the aerodrome, immediately bursting into flames.

Douglas was the first to arrive on the scene of the accident and found the air gunner lying two yards from the wreckage, his clothes burning fiercely. These flames Douglas quenched with an extinguisher and, after disentangling part of the gun equipment from the injured man's person, dragged him clear of the machine with the assistance of another airman and got him on board the ambulance. He then turned his attention to the pilot in the burning machine and had approached to within 12 yards of the wreckage when the first of the bombs exploded.

In advancing so close to the flames this airman took a grave risk, as he was fully aware that the aircraft contained live bombs. (27.3.31)

Disturbances in Bengal

Sgt. ARNOLD BARRACLOUGH, *Assam-Bengal Railway Bn., Auxiliary Force, India* At Chittagong, Bengal, on the night of the 18th–19th April 1930, raids were simultaneously made on the armouries and the telephone exchange, the object being to seize all available arms and ammunition, destroy communications, and terrorize the population.

Whilst the raiders were engaged in burning the magazine at the police armoury, Sergeant Barraclough, of the Assam-Bengal Railway Battalion, who is an electrical engineer at the Pahartali Power House, was called out, took a Lewis gun and ammunition and accompanied the Superintendent of Police in order to try and get in contact with the raiders. Sergeant Barraclough brought the Lewis gun into action from a distance of about 200 yards, and although heavily fired on continued to work the gun and eventually dispersed the raiders who fled into the jungle. (25.11.30.)

Trooper CYRIL ANTHONY BAYLEY, *Surma Valley Light Horse, Auxiliary Force, India*

On the night of the 18th–19th April 1930, a party of insurgents attacked the armoury at Chittagong, Bengal, and subsequently fled into the hills. During the afternoon of the 22nd April, information was received as to their whereabouts and a troop of Surma Valley Light Horse and about twenty Eastern Frontier Rifles were dispatched at once to the village of Jijiriabahtali in motor-cars.

After this force had moved into the jungle for about three-quarters of a mile, the insurgents were found to be occupying a wooded hill. Bayley was in one of the two sections which were sent up on the left flank. Being the extreme left-hand man himself, he worked round under heavy fire through the thick jungle to within about 30 yards of the insurgents' position, and succeeded in killing three of them, including one of their leaders, besides wounding several others. Bayley himself was not hit though his helmet was shot off his head. (24.7.31)

Major DOUGLAS ALEXANDER BRETT, M.C., *1st Royal Bn. (Light Infantry) 9th Jat Regiment, Indian Army*
Captain RICHARD DEEDES, *The King's Shropshire Light Infantry, Adjutant, The Assam-Bengal Railway Bn., Auxiliary Force, India*

At Chittagong, Bengal, at about 5.30 p.m. on the 7th January 1934, an attack was made by four Hindu youths (terrorists) on a group of forty to fifty Europeans, including women and children, at the conclusion of a cricket match. The terrorists were armed between them with one revolver and seven bombs. The group of Europeans was collected under a shamiana on a hillock. Two of the assailants came out from behind a small bungalow and, running towards the Europeans, threw one bomb each. Both the bombs, fortunately, failed to explode. One of these assailants, who was armed with a revolver, ran on fast towards the Europeans, firing his revolver rapidly as he went. Major Brett, who at the time was unarmed, rushed at this man, grappled with him, and brought him to the ground, holding the man's right arm with the revolver firmly against the ground. Other Europeans came to his assistance, and the assailant was secured.

In the meanwhile the second terrorist ran down the slope towards the cricket ground, and across the road where some cars were parked. Capt. Deedes, seeing this man run away, dashed off in pursuit, and was close behind him when the latter was tripped up by a chauffeur. Capt. Deedes fell on the man, and held him until help came. (8.5.34)

Disturbances in China

Lance-Sergeant THOMAS EDWARD ALDER, *2nd Bn., The Green Howards*

On the 14th November 1930, Alder, of the 2nd Battalion, The Green Howards, in charge of a party of three other ranks of that Regiment, and employed on anti-piracy duties on the Yangtse-Kiang River, arrived at Hankow, and embarked on the S.S. *Wuhu*.

At 4.30 p.m. on the 16th, Alder and his party left the S.S. *Wuhu* in order to proceed to the assistance of the S.S. *Kiatung* which had run ashore and was being attacked by Communists in sampans. They proceeded $2\frac{1}{2}$ miles up river in an open sampan under rifle fire the whole time from both banks. Having arrived at the S.S. *Kiatung*, they boarded this vessel and disposed themselves for its defence. During the whole time that they were on the S.S. *Kiatung* until the S.S. *Kian* arrived to their assistance at 12.30 p.m. on the 17th November, Alder and his men were exposed to rifle and gun fire from both sides of the river. When they were relieved they had only forty-three rounds of small-arm ammunition left between them. (4.8.31)

The Earthquake in Baluchistan (30th May 1935)
(All dated 19.11.35)

Leading Aircraftman NORMAN GEORGE BREADON, *R.A.F.*

Though himself badly injured with cracked rib and collar-bone, Breadon remained until late in the day attending to injured airmen in the dressing-station.

Havildar AHMAD YAR, *24th Mountain Brigade, Royal Artillery*

In Sandeman Road, Quetta, Ahmad Yar for a period of $5\frac{1}{2}$ hours worked in a hole about 15 feet below a very unsafe wall, extricating a man who was eventually found to be unharmed. During the period there were several shocks of great intensity, and in any of these there was the grave risk of being buried. He was on continuous duty from the time of the earthquake until the Battery returned to its lines on the evening of 3rd June 1935, setting the highest standard of leadership.

Private ARTHUR BROOKS, *1st Bn., The Queen's Royal Regiment (West Surrey)* — Brooks at great personal risk rescued a man from beneath the debris of a building. A party of military policemen had located a man lying some 18 feet beneath debris and close to a wall in a very dangerous condition. They dug down with picks and shovels to a point within some 5 feet of the man, when from the imminent danger of the collapse of the wall and a broken beam that would have released further wreckage, they were unable to get any farther. Brooks then dug through the remainder of the wreckage with his hands, reached the man and removed him uninjured. Throughout the latter portion of the rescue Brooks was in imminent danger of being buried, and his action showed complete disregard for personal safety in undertaking a task that might have cost him his life.

Lance-Naik CHITRABAHADUR GURUNG, *1st Bn., 8th Gurkha Rifles, I.A.* — This non-commissioned officer, along with other men, was instrumental in saving the life of Mrs. Newington (wife of Superintendent Newington of the Railway Police). The family of Mr. and Mrs. Newington were buried in the ruins of their bungalow some 5 or 6 feet under the debris. The party started digging at about 7 a.m. on 31st May 1935. Through unceasing work carried out under very dangerous circumstances, as the work was carried out under the remaining wall of the bungalow, which would have fallen if another shock had taken place, the vicinity of the bodies was reached about 9.30. Great care and intelligence were required in order to avoid wounding the couple, whilst speed was essential if there was to be any hope of rescue. Soon after 9.30 Mrs. Newington was extricated alive and, shortly after, Mr. Newington, dead. Chitrabahadur Gurung showed initiative and courage which were undoubtedly instrumental in saving life.

Pte. ERNEST MATHEW ELSTON, *1st Bn., The West Yorkshire Regiment (The Prince of Wales' Own)* — Elston worked with untiring energy at rescue work and in the subsequent salvage operations 31st May–14th June 1935. He was personally responsible for saving the lives of several Indians buried under the debris in Quetta City; and on more than one occasion voluntarily endangered his own life in effecting a rescue. On 31st May 1935, in Quetta City, regardless of his own safety, he worked at great personal risk for 4 hours to effect the rescue of an Indian child entombed alive under a collapsed double-story building. In order to reach the child, whom he had heard crying, it was necessary to make a tunnel beneath the wreckage which was in a most unsafe condition. The dead bodies of other members of the family were encountered embedded in the debris; it was impracticable to extricate these, but the child was brought out unscathed.

Lance-Corporal GEORGE HENSHAW, *1st Bn., The Queen's Royal Regiment (West Surrey)* — Immediately after the earthquake Henshaw, together with other military policemen, went to carry out rescue work at Quetta Grammar School. During this period he showed an utter disregard for his own safety, and was most prominent in rescue operations in what was an extremely dangerous building. While employed in rescue work in St. John's Road, an Indian child was located below wreckage above which was a considerable amount of unsafe debris. Henshaw dug under the wreckage and at the risk of his life crawled in and dragged the child out alive.

Bombardier ALFRED LUNGLEY, *24th Mountain Brigade, R.A.* — In Bruce Road, Quetta, a survivor was located in a house on the east side of the road. In order to extricate him it was necessary to go to the bottom of a deep hole surrounded and overhung by tottering masonry. This was liable to collapse at any minor shocks, some of which occurred during the work. Bombardier Lungley showed the greatest zeal and disregard for his own safety, although he was already suffering from a severe injury to his foot. The survivor was extricated alive.

Lance-Naik MATA DIN, *4th Bn., 19th Hyderabad Regiment, I.A.* — He showed conspicuous devotion to duty by extricating a man who was buried in a very dangerous place and to rescue whom three parties had already made attempts.

Naik NANDLAL THAPA, *2nd Bn., 8th Gurkha Rifles, I.A.* — Nandlal Thapa formed part of the leading detachment of the battalion, which was conveyed by mechanical transport from the Lines to Quetta City. There was no time for the party to collect tools. On arrival in the City the detachment was split up into small parties and worked with their hands for 3 hours, prior to the distribution of tools, extricating injured men and women from the debris. The area in which they worked was one of the parts most damaged by the earthquake. During this period minor shocks frequently occurred, causing further falls of masonry in the houses in which they were digging. Working with the party this non-commissioned officer showed conspicuous bravery in the manner in which he entered tottering buildings in search of living people and in the work and initiative he displayed in removing them. As a result of his disregard of danger ten people were rescued alive at considerable risk. He fully realized the risks he ran, but was always ready to enter any building where there was any possibility of anybody remaining alive.

A forest fire

Pte. RICHARD BLACKBURN, 1st Bn., The Cheshire Regiment

During a forest fire at Kasauli on the 7th June 1935, a party of troops was threatened by the flames and had to retire. Captain Reed, who was in charge of this party, became separated from the remainder and failed to make his way to safety. Looking back, Pte. Blackburn saw Capt. Reed stumbling in a dazed condition with his clothing alight, and, returning to him, took him to a place which afforded some protection from the flames, and extinguished the burning clothing with his hands. But for Pte. Blackburn's action it seems certain that Capt. Reed would have perished in the flames. (23.6.36)

A gallant Sudanese captain

Yuzbashi (Captain) EL AMIN EFFENDI HEMEIDA, *Sudan Defence Force*

On the morning of 4th January 1936, in the Barracks at Omdurman, a part of the Sudan Defence Force was engaged in making explosive charges. El Amin Effendi Hemeida was in charge of a section of the working party, whose duty was to place the gun-cotton and primers in containers.

A charge which was being assembled in another part of the room accidentally exploded, killing one non-commissioned officer and injuring a native officer and eight non-commissioned officers. The building was extensively damaged and fire broke out in several places. El Yuzbashi El Amin Effendi Hemeida though uninjured was badly shaken and dazed. On recovering he immediately went to the assistance of the injured, and then took active steps to extinguish the fires and remove the unharmed charges to a place of safety.

His gallant behaviour was instrumental in saving at least one life among the injured, and his presence of mind prevented further explosions which must have resulted in greater loss of life. (23.6.36)

Operations in Palestine

L.-Corp. WILLIAM BARNETT, *1st Bn., The Royal Scots Fusiliers*

L.-Corp. Barnett rendered gallant and distinguished service in connexion with the emergency operations in Palestine, during the period 15th April to 14th September 1936. (27.11.36)

Gallantry in India

Pte. FRANK NAUGHTON, 10th Light Tank Company, Royal Tank Corps

On the 5th August 1936, when engaged in recovering an armoured car which had broken down on the Irish Bridge over the flooded river Indrayani, near Moshi, L.-Corp. S. J. Temple and Pte. R. A. S. Campbell were swept off the bridge into the water below, where there were very swift and dangerous currents.

Pte. Naughton, who was fully clothed except for his boots, immediately dived off the bridge to render assistance. He was drawn under the water several times, and it was only with the utmost difficulty that he was able to overcome the strong cross and under currents. He regained shallow water and was almost exhausted. Despite his personal fatigue, immediately he saw the body of one of the soldiers appear on the surface about 40 yards distant, he again heroically entered the water, and, swimming with the utmost difficulty, succeeded in bringing Temple, who was by this time unconscious, into shallow water, where both were assisted ashore, at a point about 100 yards down stream from the bridge.

By his courageous action Naughton saved Temple's life. (1.2.37)

Non-intervention off Spain

Lieutenant PATRICK NOEL HUMPHREYS, R.N.
Petty Officer JAMES SMAIL, R.N.

For gallant and distinguished services rendered by Lt. Humphreys and Petty Officer Smail when H.M.S. *Hunter* was mined off Almería on the coast of Spain on the 13th May 1937. (12.11.37)

Operations in Waziristan

Pilot Officer GERALD CHARLES NEIL CLOSE, R.A.F.

During the operations in Waziristan when an aircraft, laden with bombs, crashed and burst into flames on the Miranshah aerodrome this officer, who was duty pilot on the aerodrome, hastened to the scene of the accident and, in spite of the explosion of a bomb and small-arms ammunition, made persistent attempts to extinguish the flames and to rescue the crew until ordered by a superior officer to withdraw. (21.12.37)

A madman overcome in India

Naik BARKAT SINGH, 10th Bn., 2nd Punjab Regiment, I.A.

On 2nd May 1937, at Meerut, Sepoy Kanshi Ram, 2nd Punjab Regiment, ran amok, shot dead the Guard Commander and mortally wounded another sepoy of the Guard. Shouting out, 'If any Hindu comes near me I will shoot him', he went off to the lines with his rifle loaded and bayonet fixed, and with additional rounds in his pouches. While he was standing momentarily undecided looking around him, with his rifle at the 'high port' ready to shoot, he was grappled by Barkat Singh, also of the 2nd Punjab Regiment, who was an onlooker and unarmed, and who showed great promptitude and courage in seizing Kanshi Ram and pinioning his arms until others came and overpowered him. (1.1.38)

Disturbances in Palestine

Pte. JOSEPH EDWARD MOTT, *1st Bn., The Essex Regiment* — At about 8.20 p.m. on the 25th December 1937, a bomb was thrown into the Jordania Café, Haifa. The café was crowded with soldiers and civilians at the time. The bomb fell at the feet of Pte. Mott who was seated at a table with some other men of his Battalion. With the utmost coolness and presence of mind, Pte. Mott picked it up and hurled it through the window into the street, where it exploded with great violence. He thus saved many lives. (25.2.38)

Gallantry in Auxiliary Air Force

Pilot Officer GUY RAWSTRON BRANCH, *Auxiliary Air Force* — On 8th January 1938, an aircraft in which Pilot Officer Branch was a passenger crashed at Upavon, Wiltshire, and immediately burst into flames. Having extricated himself from the burning aircraft this officer found that the pilot was trapped in the cockpit by his legs. Despite the fact that there was grave danger of the petrol tank exploding, Pilot Officer Branch returned to the blazing wreckage and succeeded in extricating the pilot. (25.3.38)

Two cases of gallantry in Palestine

Rais RASHID ABDUL FATTAH, *Transjordan F.F.* — This officer by exceptionally cool leadership captured a village on 1st March 1938 by house-to-house leadership. Again on 4th March by exceptional resource and bold leadership he seized a hill commanding another village. He had shown great gallantry on previous occasions when leading troops against armed bands. (12.7.38)

Qaid YUSUF HUSAIN ALI BEY, *Transjordan F.F.* — On 5th July 1938 at Khirbat Samra he showed exceptional initiative. By his fine example under heavy fire, and when his men were nearly exhausted by heat, he was an inspiration to further efforts which resulted in the defeat of an enemy gang, and in the capture of prisoners and rifles.

In spite of his life being threatened he continues to produce most valuable intelligence.

He also did extremely well in the 1936 disturbances. (3.1.39)

CHAPTER XVI
MEDAL OF THE ORDER OF THE BRITISH EMPIRE, CIVIL DIVISION, FOR GALLANTRY (E.G.M.)
LIST OF RECIPIENTS UP TO 31st DECEMBER 1938

Note.—The average interval between the date of the deed here recorded and the announcement of an award in *The London Gazette* is about 4 months. Minimum delay, 15 days; maximum delay, over 8 months. The average and the maximum intervals have been lengthened by the formality in Indian cases of half-yearly submission by the Government of India. The date of the Gazette is shown in parentheses.

CHAPTER XVI
MEDAL OF THE ORDER OF THE BRITISH EMPIRE, CIVIL DIVISION, FOR GALLANTRY (E.G.M.)
LIST OF RECIPIENTS UP TO 31st DEC. 1938

Courage in Richmond Park

Park-Keeper ALBERT WATERFIELD, *Richmond Park, London* — Soon after midnight on 10th May 1921, Waterfield saw two young men in Spanker Hill Plantation, each carrying a rifle. They started to run off and he gave chase for about a mile, when they turned round and called out to him that if he would not halt they would fire. He advanced towards them, when one of the men, at a distance of about 50 yards, fired two shots, both of which missed. The two men then turned and ran. Waterfield borrowed a sporting gun and the men scaled a wall into Mount Clare, throwing down their rifles, and were caught at the end of Priory Lane, near the Upper Richmond Road, Putney. They were found to be carrying, between them, 76 cartridges. Waterfield showed great courage and it was due to his bravery in giving chase to these two armed men that their arrest was effected. (30.12.22)

Murderous attacks in Belfast

Constable FRANCIS AUSTIN MORTESHED, *Royal Ulster Constabulary* — For exceptional gallantry and devotion to duty in effecting the arrest, single-handed, of an armed criminal. In March 1924 an attempt was made by three armed men to carry out a robbery in an office in Belfast. During the course of the robbery, the raiders shot, and mortally wounded, the manager of the office. They then fled. They were pursued by Constable Morteshed, and though one of the criminals turned and, at close range, endeavoured to shoot the constable, the latter effected his arrest single-handed without drawing his revolver. The prisoner was subsequently sentenced to death for murder. (3.6.24)

Constable SAMUEL ORR, *Ulster Special Constabulary* — In 1922 he effected the capture of an armed criminal. Later in the same year, though unarmed, the constable endeavoured to effect the arrest of two armed robbers. He succeeded in grappling with one, but while doing so was severely wounded by the other. (3.6.24)

Veterans in life-saving service[1]

(All dated 30.6.24)

Captain THOMAS GERALD FITZGIBBON McCOMBIE, *Kingstown, Eire* — For life-saving service in Dublin Bay, in April 1874, and later in December 1895, for gallantly putting off in the boat with other members of the crew of S.S. *Tearaght*, of which he was master, and in two trips saving, at very great risk, the master, his wife and child, and the crew of the barque *Palme*, of Finland. The vessel had been wrecked two days previously, and the Kingstown No. 2 Life-Boat was totally wrecked while trying to effect a rescue, the whole of her gallant crew, fifteen in number, being drowned.

The Rev. JOHN MICHAEL O'SHEA, *Ardmore, Co. Waterford, Eire* — For his example and initiative in leading very gallant attempts, by means of a small boat, to save the lives of the crew of the schooner *Teaser*, which was lost, with her crew of three, in Ardmore Bay on the 18th March 1911, during a SE. gale and very heavy sea.

Major HERBERT EDGAR BURTON, O.B.E., Hon. Supt. *Tynemouth Motor Life-Boat* — For gallant conduct and fine seamanship in bringing the Tynemouth Motor Life-Boat 44 miles through the night and storm, unaided by coast lights, to Whitby and after all other efforts had failed rescuing, on 1st November 1914, fifty persons from the Government Hospital steamer *Rohilla*, wrecked at Whitby on 30th October.

Ex-Coxswain ROBERT SMITH, *Tynemouth Motor Life-Boat* — For his intrepid conduct and fine seamanship in conjunction with Major Burton when the life-boat under his command proceeded to Whitby and on 1st November 1914 saved fifty persons from the *Rohilla*, wrecked at Whitby on 30th October.

Coxswain HENRY GEORGE BLOGG, *Cromer Life-Boat* — For conspicuous gallantry, tenacity, and skilful seamanship in rescuing eleven of the crew of the S.S. *Fernebö* of Christinehaven, which was wrecked off Cromer on the 9th January 1917, during a strong NNE. gale and a very heavy sea.

[1] Recipients in each case of the R.N. Lifeboat Institution's gold or silver medal—for the services here recorded.

The work of rescue involved three trips to the wreck and occupied over 9 hours.

Ex-Coxswain JOHN HOWELLS, *Fishguard Motor Life-Boat* For rescuing, in circumstances of great peril, seven of the crew of the motor schooner *Hermina* of Rotterdam, which was wrecked in a NW. gale on Needle Rock, off Fishguard, on the night of 3rd December 1920. To effect the rescue involved taking the life-boat into a position of great danger among rocks.

Coxswain WILLIAM GEORGE FLEMING, *Gorleston No. 1 Life-Boat* For intrepid conduct and skilful seamanship in endeavouring to save the crew of twenty-four of the S.S. *Hopelyn*. After nearly 24 hours' efforts in the Gorleston life-boat he put off in the Lowestoft life-boat and assisted to save the men in circumstances of great peril on 21st October 1922.

Ex-Coxswain JOHN THOMPSON SWAN, *Lowestoft Motor Life-Boat* For intrepid conduct and skilful seamanship in rescuing the crew of twenty-four of the S.S. *Hopelyn* in circumstances of great peril. The vessel was wrecked on the Scroby Sands during a strong NE. gale on 19th October 1922, and the rescue was effected on 21st, after the Gorleston life-boat had made unavailing efforts to save the men.

Note.—In 1924 on the centenary of the R.N. Lifeboat Institution the above eight men received the Institution's gold medal.

Murder of Sir Lee Stack in Egypt

FREDERICK HAMILTON MARCH, *Chauffeur to the late Major-General Sir Lee Stack, G.B.E., C.M.G.* March was acting as chauffeur to Sir Lee Stack, Governor-General of the Sudan and Sirdar of the Egyptian Army, when on the 19th November 1924, near the Ministry of Public Instruction in Cairo, seven Egyptians opened fire simultaneously on the car from the pavement. The Sirdar and his Aide-de-Camp, who was in the car with him, were both wounded. Had it not been for the great gallantry and presence of mind displayed by March, who was himself also wounded but continued to drive the car, both passengers would, in all probability, have been killed outright. Sir Lee Stack died the next day from his wounds. The Aide-de-Camp and March both survived. (5.12.24)

Gallantry in Sudan

Nafar MUHAMMAD ABDULLA MUHAMMAD, *Khartoum Police Force*

Sol IBRAHIM NEGIB, *Khartoum Police Force*

Shawish JAK TAHA, *Khartoum Police Force*

Two platoons of the 11th Sudanese Regiment ran amok at Khartoum on the 27th November 1924. On that day and the next, three British officers and two Syrian medical officers were killed by the mutineers, and some nine other ranks were wounded.

Nafar Muhammad Abdulla Muhammad, Sol Ibrahim Negib, and Shawish Jak Taha were recommended for great gallantry displayed during the disturbances. (12.12.24)

Acting Shawish MUHAMMAD KHALIFA, *Berber Province Police*

For conspicuous gallantry and skill when in command of a patrol of three mounted police, in effecting the arrest of a murderer and three camel-thieves in the face of armed opposition and superior numbers at Wadi Adarowfie, Berber Province. It was entirely due to the personal courage of this non-commissioned officer that the object of the patrol was effected and the patrol itself was extricated without bloodshed from an exceedingly difficult and dangerous situation. (28.9.25)

Life-saving in India

Staff Sergeant REGINALD HARRY MALTBY, *11th Armoured Car Company, Lahore*

In recognition of the heroism he displayed in saving a child from drowning in a disused well. (3.7.26)

Gallant deeds in Lancashire

JAMES BURKE, *Manchester*

In recognition of his action in stopping runaway horses on two occasions at great personal risk. (3.6.25)

ROBERT WILD, *Rochdale*

In recognition of his gallantry in extinguishing with his bare hands the fiercely blazing clothing of a fellow workman which had become accidentally ignited. (22.10.26)

Gallantry of prison officers

CYRIL JAMES TUTTON, *Officer, Parkhurst Convict Prison*

On the 15th November 1926, he displayed outstanding gallantry in effecting, single-handed and at great personal risk, the arrest of an escaped convict on the ridge of the prison roof. (18.3.27)

JOHN STOVES, *Principal Officer, Pentonville Prison* — For services in connexion with the attempted escape of a prisoner from an express train. (23.10.28)

A gallant Londoner

HERBERT REUBEN HENDERSON, *London* — Although seriously burnt and in grave personal danger, Henderson succeeded in carrying to a place of safety a blazing cinematograph film, and in removing other films which were in danger of igniting, thereby preventing a disastrous fire and explosion at a film treatment works in London. (18.3.27)

Gallantry in Durham

JOHN BEATTIE, JOSEPH CLARK, *Trimdon Grange, Durham* — On the 19th November 1926, John Beattie and Joseph Clark, although in grave personal danger from falling debris, gas, and spontaneously generated heat, showed outstanding gallantry in making persistent attempts to rescue a miner imprisoned in a narrow tunnel. (3.5.27)

A vain search in China

Lt.-Col. JAMES ERNEST STEWART, M.C., *Late Royal Engineers* — In recognition of his gallantry in attempting to trace the whereabouts of Lt. T. S. Knowles, East Yorkshire Regiment, in the mountains north-west of Peking. (26.6.28)

Gallantry in a Gold Coast mine

JOHN FREDERICK BELL, *Underground Manager, Ariston Gold Mine, Prestea, Gold Coast* — John Frederick Bell showed great gallantry on the occasion of an accident in the mine on the 17th May 1930, when he was instrumental in saving the lives of several natives who would have otherwise been gassed. The two men who afterwards went in search of him lost their lives by gas in the attempt, and Bell himself would probably have shared their fate had he not, when he became unconscious, fallen with his mouth next to a leak in a compressed-air pipe. (2.12.30) (See also p. 305.)

Gallant police officers and men in India

Sgt. REGINALD RIMMER, *Police, Bombay, India* — Sergeant Rimmer showed on numerous occasions great courage and coolness. This officer's pluck and presence of mind evoked the highest praise from his superiors, and he has consistently set a fine example to the constabulary under him. (3.6.31)

JOSEPH BAPTISTA, This constable was orderly to the Excise Sub-
Excise Constable, Inspector, Sholapur, when, during the riots in
Sholapur District, May 1930, both the Sub-Inspector and the Con-
Bombay, India stable were completely surrounded by the mob,
severely beaten, and stoned. The Constable,
although ordered by the Sub-Inspector to seek safety, refused to leave
his post and protected the Sub-Inspector who had been rendered unconscious. He stood by the Sub-Inspector continually blowing his
whistle till police help arrived. His devotion to duty in the face of
great danger undoubtedly saved the Sub-Inspector's life. (3.6.31)

GHULAM MOHI-UD-DIN, This officer, who has enjoyed a reputation
Sub-Inspector of Police, for energy, courage, and strength of
Punjab, India character throughout his seventeen years'
service as a Sub-Inspector in the Punjab,
has been called upon, since the inception of the civil disobedience campaign, to deal with many very dangerous situations arising from the
presence of large and hostile crowds. On several occasions, while
behaving with commendable restraint, he has taken grave risks and he
has never been deterred from such steps as were necessary to maintain
law and order and the prestige of Government. (3.6.31)

BALDEV SINGH, This officer displayed great bravery in organizing
Sub-Inspector of and leading an attack under fire on a dangerous gang
Police, Punjab of offenders in the Ferozepore district in June 1931.
In July he narrowly escaped death in a raid on a
house occupied by persons in unlawful possession of arms. (1.1.32)

BHIM SINGH, For great courage and a total disregard of danger in
Sub-Inspector of effecting the capture of a native of the Jullundur
Police, Punjab district who had shot two persons dead and had
attacked another. (1.1.32)

A mad dog in the Sudan

YEHIA EL IMAM, For an act of conspicuous courage. This con-
Police Constable, stable, having failed to kill with his baton a rabid
Khartoum Province dog when it was attacking a man, strangled it with
Police his hands, being severely bitten in the struggle.
There is no doubt that by his prompt action and
bravery he saved many from infection. (1.1.32)

Conspicuous courage at Barton, England

Flt.-Sgt. ERIC WATT BONER, *Royal Air Force Reserve, Chief Pilot of Northern Air Transport, Limited*
For an act of conspicuous courage in rescuing the pilot of a burning aeroplane of the Royal Air Force at Barton in May 1932. Under the protection of an asbestos blanket Flt.-Sgt. Boner unfastened the straps binding the pilot, released him from his parachute harness, and with assistance dragged him from the burning wreckage. He gave first aid to the airman, who died later. (5.8.32)

Struggle with a murderer in Devon

EMMA JOSÉ TOWNSEND, *Portlemouth, Devon*
On the 9th May 1932, W. J. Yeoman, a farmer of Kingsbridge, South Devon, murdered one of his sons in the South Hams Cottage Hospital at Kingsbridge. The boy, aged 9, was an inmate under treatment at the hospital, and Yeoman attacked him as he lay in bed, first firing at him with a gun and then striking him with it several times. Miss Townsend, who was visiting her sister at the hospital, heard cries of 'Help!' and went into the ward. She showed great courage in trying to prevent the killing of the boy and behaved most gallantly. In the struggle Yeoman struck her with the barrel of the gun and cut her head open. (6.9.32)

Rescues from Nile

MIRGHANY AHMED MUHAMMAD, *Khartoum*
On 18th September 1932, at the height of the Nile flood, and at a point where the stream is particularly dangerous even for the strongest swimmer, Mirghany Ahmed rescued three girls, the eldest 15 years of age, from drowning. (2.1.33)

Rescue from the jaws of a lion

REGINALD HENRY MONTAGUE GRAY, *Clerk to the Magistrate in N'gamiland, Bechuanaland (Posthumous award)*
Whilst on an expedition in August 1932, Mr. Gray attempted to save a comrade from a wounded lion. Mr. Gray, who had as his only weapon an empty shot-gun, without hesitation clubbed the lion, which had attacked his companion, until the gun broke. He then tried, while kicking the animal, to pull it away with his hands. The lion was eventually shot by a third person. Mr. Gray died a few days later, as a result of shock. (31.3.33)

Explosion in an operating theatre

DOROTHY LOUISE THOMAS, *Sister, Middlesex Hospital*

Following on an explosion in the main theatre of the Middlesex Hospital the issuing oxygen caught fire and a stream of sparks and flames shot through the open door of the anaesthetic room across the theatre for a distance of about 15 feet. Onlookers described the burning cylinder as being most alarming, and there was a general fear that it would explode at any moment. The theatre was immediately vacated.

Sister Thomas stopped behind until all were clear and then removed the ether from the anaesthetic room and shut the doors with the idea of minimizing the effect of the explosion which she expected. After a moment's reflection, however, she decided that it was her duty to try to avert the wrecking of the theatre, re-entered the anaesthetic room, ran up to the cylinder, and turned it off. (2.3.34)

A man runs amok in the Sudan

Shawish TAHA IDRIS, *Blue Nile Province Police, Sudan*

Shawish Taha Idris showed conspicuous gallantry and devotion to duty in September 1933 in arresting an armed policeman. A native non-commissioned officer in charge of a police guard temporarily lost his self-control, and after loading his rifle with nine rounds of ball ammunition ran amok. The guard, not being able to deal with the situation themselves, sent word to Taha Idris who immediately came to their assistance. He was unable to approach without being seen. The non-commissioned officer aimed at Taha Idris at a few paces, distance and pulled the trigger, but for some reason the cartridge did not explode and Taha Idris eventually ran in and disarmed the man. (2.3.34)

A gallant landlord in Bombay

ABDUS SAMAD ABDUL WAHID GOLANDAZ, *Landlord, Property Owner, and Sand Contractor, Bombay*

Mr. Golandaz was the owner of a fleet of boats and trained boatmen which he placed at the disposal of the authorities whenever Surat, Rander, or the surrounding districts were threatened by floods, and on frequent occasions he risked his life in leading his men to works of rescue. He showed conspicuous personal bravery on several occasions. In particular on the 16th September 1933, when the Tapti River had swollen to such proportions that one of the sluices in the city wall had been damaged and water was pouring in through it, threatening to flood the city, he volunteered to dive into the flooded river and ascertain the nature and extent of the damage. He accomplished this brave feat successfully and blocked the sluice with sand-bags at considerable risk to his own life. In 1930 he had also performed an act of conspicuous bravery in rescuing the boys of the Government High School and the family of the Excise Inspector, whose bungalows had been cut off by the flood. (4.6.34)

Attempted assassination of Sir John Anderson

CHARLES WILLIAM TANDY GREEN, *Superintending Engineer, Public Works Department, Bengal*

BABU BHUPENDRA NARAYEN SINGH, *Zemindar Garh Barwari, Bhagalpur District, Bihar and Orissa*

At Lebong Race Course, Darjeeling, on the 8th May 1934, while the horses were being led in after the race for the Governor's Cup, an attempt was made by two Bengali youths to assassinate the Governor of Bengal.

Sir John Anderson was standing in his box facing the course. Mr. Tandy Green was on the judges' stand. Hearing a shot he looked round and observed a man pointing an automatic pistol at the Governor. He rushed at him immediately and brought him down. They rolled together to the bottom of the steps where Mr. Tandy Green pinned the assailant to the ground until others came to his assistance and disarmed and secured the man.

Mr. B. N. Singh was in the race-stand outside the Governor's box. On hearing a shot and observing that the other assailant was again taking aim with his revolver resting on the rail separating the stand from the Governor's box, he immediately grappled with him, endeavouring to pull him back and at the same time to divert the weapon, which was then pointed in the direction of the Governor. While the two were struggling, two shots were fired by the Governor's personal guard and the Superintendent of Police respectively.

These took effect on the assailant, but failed to hit any vital part. Both then fell to the ground and, others coming to Mr. Singh's assistance, the man was quickly overpowered, but not before at least one more shot had been fired at him from close quarters. (19.6.34)

A heroic Belgian

CAMIEL VAN HOVE, *a Belgian subject of St. Pietersveld Wyngene, Belgium*

On the 30th December 1933 the Imperial Airways aircraft *Apollo* crashed at Ruysselede in Belgium and was destroyed by fire. As soon as the machine fell a number of people rushed up to try to extricate the occupants from the wreckage. In their efforts various men received burns, some serious, and one of them, Camiel van Hove, who penetrated the cabin at grave personal risk, sustained such severe injuries to his face, hands, arms, and legs that he had to be removed to hospital with his life in jeopardy. (Not gazetted.)

A dangerous elephant

EDWARD OMARA, A Game Scout, who was anxious to punish a herd
Uganda of marauding elephants, had wounded two bulls when one of them charged him and pinned him to the ground. Omara, a native of the Chua District, Northern Province, Uganda, pulled out the Scout's rifle from between the elephant's feet and, being unable to reload, attacked the elephant with his spear. He drove it off and eventually killed it, and then carried the Scout, whose injuries unfortunately proved fatal, for 3 hours to Adilang.

In February 1934 an elephant which had been burnt in a bush fire and was consequently in a most dangerous temper took possession of a village water-hole and terrorized the local population. Omara at very great risk to himself and in the interests of his fellow villagers killed it with a heavy hunting-spear. (9.10.34)

Bandits in India

BABU RANJIT SINGH, When this Revenue Officer was one night in
Tahsildar, United the neighbourhood of the village of Jharwan in
Provinces, India the Saharanpur District he received information that a gang of twenty-five dacoits armed with short guns and lathis were attacking the house of a wealthy Bania. He collected four men and proceeded at once to the village and attacked the dacoits, his only weapon being a pistol. When two of his men had been wounded and his pistol had temporarily jammed, he continued to attack. Eventually, after wounding one of the dacoits, he succeeded in driving them off, and thus, by his prompt action and conspicuous bravery, was able to stop a very serious dacoity. (1.1.35)

A brave police inspector in Ceylon

ALBERT RIENZI DE LIVERA, For conspicuous courage in arresting a
Inspector, Mount Lavinia notorious criminal who, after assaulting
Police Station, Ceylon a man named Romiel Perera, had tied him to a tree and had threatened to stab any one attempting a rescue.

The criminal was armed with a chopper and, on seeing the police party approaching, advanced towards the Inspector but, changing his mind, cut Romiel Perera on the side of the neck. Before he could repeat the blow, Inspector de Livera was on him, and after a severe struggle disarmed him and took him into custody.

Romiel Perera was bleeding profusely from a gaping wound on the left side of the neck which had completely severed an artery. Inspector de Livera immediately applied digital pressure to the artery and took him in a motor-car to the Hospital, about four miles away. During the journey, with the assistance of a constable, he continued to apply the digital pressure necessary to arrest the bleeding. The injured man eventually recovered. (1.1.35)

A dockyard rescue

EDWIN CROSSLEY, *Yard Foreman, Admiralty Dockyard, Chatham*

In the course of their duty on board a vessel at Chatham in October 1935 two workmen who had descended into a compartment to recover tools and other articles were overcome with gas. When the information reached Crossley he made immediate arrangements to go to their rescue and, seizing a tackle which stood rigged above the hatch, descended into the compartment with two skilled labourers. The rescuers were successful in securing one of the two gassed workmen to the tackle and hoisting him through the hatchway to the open air. They were able to make fast the rope to the second man, but owing to the effects of the gas, could not help further, and he was hauled to safety by others on the deck above. (25.2.36)

Gallantry in a Gold Coast mine

WILLIAM JAMIESON, *Ariston Gold Mine, Prestea, Gold Coast*

Mr. William Jamieson, European Shift Superintendent, was being lowered underground in the service cage when one of the native workmen was found lying unconscious on the shaft station. As he appeared to have been gassed, Jamieson, with a companion, decided to investigate the cause of the trouble. On passing through the ventilation-door at the back of the shaft station they found three more 'boys' lying about 50 feet from the door, a few feet apart. It was evident that they had been seriously gassed and they were at once removed to the shaft station. At a point about 900 feet north of the shaft another 'boy' was found lying across the track, and Jamieson after sending back two 'boys' with this man continued on to the working-face of the drift, alone. There he found six boys lying about in a serious condition and he at once proceeded to drag them back out of the fumes. He had eventually himself to be helped out of the mine as he was then unable to walk without assistance. His prompt and gallant behaviour, carried out at great personal risk, undoubtedly saved the lives of these six Africans. (23.6.36) (See also p. 299.)

Gallant Frenchmen

JULIEN TANGUY
PAUL GRIEU,
Le Havre, France

Tanguy and Grieu, French citizens, at considerable personal risk rendered valuable assistance to the crew of the Royal Air Force aircraft K 4034, which crashed in the sea off Le Havre on the 19th February 1936. The aircraft alighted in the sea about a quarter of a mile off shore at about 4 a.m. and floated for a while before sinking: the crew, having shouted for help, started to swim for the shore. Tanguy, hearing the shouts, obtained the assistance of Grieu and together they put out in a small canoe in an endeavour to help the crew. They managed to find the pilot of the aircraft, Flying Officer Page, and to pass him a life-belt with the aid of which he eventually reached the shore. The canoe was not seaworthy and, becoming waterlogged, finally capsized during the repeated efforts of Tanguy and Grieu to find the remaining members of the crew. The current at this particular part of the coast is very strong indeed and it was only with difficulty that they finally managed to get ashore and save their own lives. (1936: not gazetted.)

A gallant rescue under water

Senior Shipwright Diver
CHARLES GODFREY DUFFIN,
H.M. Dockyard, Portsmouth

In August 1936 C. Gustar, a diver, was engaged under water in examining the launching-gear below H.M.S. *Aurora* at Portsmouth. Signals of distress were received, and his stand-by companion diver, G. Brown, went down and found Gustar jammed between the top of a dagger plank connecting the several launching-poppets and the bottom of the ship, presumably as the result of an unexpected movement of the poppets.

Duffin was immediately sent for, as an additional diver, to co-operate in the rescue work. Gustar was found to be securely wedged, with his head, arms, and breast weights hanging over the inboard side of the inside dagger planks, and his trunk and legs between the inner and outer planks.

In effecting the rescue, Duffin squeezed himself up between the two adjacent dagger planks which were holding Gustar, and with a handsaw cut through the plank (a piece of 15×4 in. Douglas fir) on one side of the man, while his companion, Brown, released the two 10-in. eye-headed screws joining the end of the plank to its succeeding length of plank. By this means the portion of the plank imprisoning Gustar was removed. Duffin next seized Gustar, straightened him and forced him down between his own body and the poppets, towards Brown, who dragged the man down and took him to the surface.

The risk to both Duffin and Brown in carrying out this rescue was a serious one, due to the possibility of the launching-poppets at any moment making a movement similar to that which had entrapped Gustar, and both men were regarded as worthy of commendation. The risk was increased because they had to work with all possible haste.

Duffin had displayed gallant conduct on a previous occasion. (1.2.37)

A British Consul in Ethiopia

ADRIAN SIDNEY GILBERT REGINALD TRAPMAN, Vice-Consul, Addis Ababa

Mr. Trapman played a prominent part in the incidents at Addis Ababa early in May following upon the flight of the Emperor, and was particularly concerned with the rescue of persons from the city, which was in the hands of a disorderly and uncontrolled mob. On the 2nd, 3rd, 4th, and 5th May 1936 he took part as a volunteer in repeated expeditions to rescue British and foreign men, women, and children from the town, and to bring them into the safety of the British Legation. Each expedition involved a drive of some ten miles in an open lorry exposed to dangerous rifle fire from the rioters, many of whom made a practice of discharging their firearms at every passing vehicle. (1.2.37)

Gallantry on the Hugli River, India

GEORGE JOHN ADAMSON, Inspector, River Traffic Police, Calcutta, Bengal
CECIL FRANCIS KELLY, Assistant River Surveyor, Port Commissioners, Calcutta, Bengal

In May 1936 Inspector Adamson, with Mr. Kelly as pilot, was in charge of two Port Police launches escorting a cargo of defective dynamite which was being taken for destruction up the Hugli in a barge in tow of a launch. The barge proved quite unseaworthy, and after a journey of about 15 miles up the river was in a sinking condition. Inspector Adamson and his assistants had no responsibility except for escorting the cargo, but in spite of this they tried at great personal risk to keep the barge afloat by bailing from 7 o'clock in the evening till midnight, when it was found necessary to beach the barge on the bank near a large jute-mill. In spite of the dynamite exuding nitroglycerine, Inspector Adamson with two sergeants worked indefatigably in the water and in the dark to help to guide the barge ashore by hand. The beaching took $5\frac{1}{2}$ hours. The barge was partially unloaded but it was found impossible to remove the $2\frac{1}{2}$ tons at the bottom owing to its dangerous condition, and the barge had to be refloated, towed into deep water, and sunk. Inspector Adamson rendered great assistance during the whole operation and stood by in a police launch in spite of grave danger. Mr. Kelly supervised the handling of the barge throughout, and without his skilled assistance the feat could not have been accomplished. A small accident would have resulted in practically certain death to those working, and a disaster of the first magnitude to the surrounding mills.

Though it was not his duty as pilot, Mr. Kelly remained in the barge while it was towed off the beach, and until it was safely sunk superintending its handling in the current by the aid of two launches. (1.2.37)

A heroic Indian lady

ASHRAF-UN-NISA BEGUM
Hyderabad, Deccan, India

A disastrous fire broke out in the Moti Mahal Cinema, Hyderabad City, and the building was practically razed to the ground, twelve women and two children being burnt to death. Ashraf-un-Nisa Begum, the wife of Lt. Muzaffaruddin, was responsible for saving the lives of several purdah women. She was sitting with the fourteen victims and some thirty more women in the purdah balcony, from which both exits were cut off by the fire.

Their plight was made the more terrifying by the smoke, darkness, and leaping flames which within a few minutes turned the whole building into one huge blaze. Ashraf-un-Nisa Begum, though a purdah lady, stripped herself of her sari, tied it to the balcony railing, and lowered five women to the lower floor, whence they escaped. Her own escape she left so late that she was unable to descend by the sari and had to jump, injuring herself in so doing. (1.2.37)

Gallantry on the Air Mail

Captain PATRICK GORDON TAYLOR, *Late Royal Air Force*

Capt. Taylor, on the occasion of the late Sir Charles Kingsford-Smith's attempted Australia–New Zealand Air Mail flight in 1935, showed great resource and courage of a high order in moving about outside the cockpit during the flight, carrying oil by means of a thermos cover from one engine to another, while clinging to the struts. He succeeded in enabling the party to reach the coast. (9.7.37)

A heroic attempt at rescue

EDWARD LETCH
JAMES LETCH
of 20 Dunholme Road, Edmonton

These brothers endeavoured, with the greatest courage, to rescue a R.A.F. Volunteer Reserve pilot who crashed into a private house at Edmonton on 4th September 1938. Both were burnt to death in the attempt.

CHAPTER XVII
AWARDS OF THE ALBERT MEDAL TO OFFICERS AND MEN OF THE ROYAL NAVY AND ROYAL MARINES, 1868–1938

WHEN first instituted, recommendations to the Sovereign for awards of the Albert Medal were made only by the President of the Board of Trade. When the terms of the Royal Warrant were enlarged to include acts of gallantry on land, provision was made for submissions to be made only by the First Lord of the Treasury (i.e. the Prime Minister). A few years later provision was made for separate submissions, and registers, by the Home Secretary and the President of the Board of Trade. Finally, provision was made for independent submissions, and the keeping of a separate register, by the Board of Admiralty also.

This chapter has been compiled from the Admiralty Register. Awards of the First Class, or in Gold, are printed in Old English type. A few of the entries are duplicated in the Home Office register, which has been summarized in previous chapters.

The following is a summary of awards by decades:

	1st class in gold	2nd class
1868–79	..	13
1880–99	1	7
1900–09	..	5
1910–19	7	57
1920–9	..	14
1930–8	..	2

The number of awards for the last decade is the smallest on record.

ALBERT MEDAL

*Lionel A. De Sausmarez	Sub-Lieut.	17.11.1868
*James B. Willoughby	Captain	22.7.1869
*William Balfour Forbes	Lieutenant	24.3.1871
R. B. Cay	Commander	15.3.1869
John Ricketts	Ldg. Seaman	21.12.1867
*James Crowden	Ch. Officer	15.4.1869
*William Simpson	Ch. Boatn.	7.2.1870
*John Batist	Boatman	21.6.1867

* For details see Chapter XVIII.

ALBERT MEDAL—continued

*John Donovan	Ch. Boatman	21.6.1867
*Charles Sprankling	Ch. Boatman	21.6.1867
*Hon. Francis Robert Sandilands	Lieutenant	15.3.1875
*Alfred Carpenter	Lieutenant	20.6.1876
*Robert A. J. Montgomerie	Act. Sub-Lt.	15.6.1877
George Oatley	Gunner's Mate, Gunnery Instructor, R.N. Reserve, Peterhead	26.4.1880

* For details see Chapter XVIII.

Seedie Tindal Farabani of H.M.S. Wild Swan   A fugitive slave boy, named Farajallah, jumped overboard on 3rd August and was seized by an enormous shark, which bit off his leg at the knee, dragging him under the water. When he rose to the surface, the shark again attacked him, tearing off his remaining leg. Farabani jumped into the water, and brought the unfortunate boy to the surface, and to a place of safety.

Farabani saw the whole of the horrible catastrophe from the first seizure of the boy, and when he jumped into the water not only the attacking shark but three others were close to the ship. (19.11.80)

GEORGE WILLIAMS
FREDERICK JAGGERS,[1]
*Boatmen, South Shields
Coast-guard Station*   The Norwegian schooner *Atlantic* was wrecked off the South Pier, at South Shields, on the 14th October 1881. As one of the crew was being hauled ashore by means of the rocket apparatus, the whip fouled the rocks. Frederick Jaggers, coastguard boatman, at the risk of his life, went into the surf with the view of clearing the line, but was washed off his feet by a heavy sea, and thrown against the rocks and rendered insensible. He was then hauled out of the sea.

On the 26th November 1881, six weeks after the wreck of the *Atlantic*, the ketch *Ida* of Ipswich ran ashore near the Pier, at South Shields. Between the *Ida* and the rocket apparatus was the wreck of a brig which made communication by rocket difficult. Jaggers volunteered to be hauled off to the brig, although cautioned of the danger, reached the brig safely, and from her forerigging succeeded in throwing a line on board the *Ida* by which the crew were saved. (21.1.82)

---

[1] Also received Board of Trade Bronze Medal for gallantry in saving life at sea.

JOHN BARBER, **H.M.S.** *Lily* was wrecked off Amour Point, Forteau
A.B. of H.M.S. Bay, coast of Labrador, on 16th September 1889,
Lily and seven of her crew were drowned. After her boats
had capsized, and although it was known that two
of the crew had been drowned in attempting to effect communication
with the shore, John Barber volunteered to swim with a line through
the surf, in a dense fog and heavy swell, enabling a 4-inch hawser to be
hauled ashore, whereby communication was established and the rest
of the crew saved. (7.12.89)

GEORGE HOARE, The schooner *Peggy* was wrecked during a severe
Boatman, Tynemouth gale on the night of 13th October 1891. After
Coast-guard Station four men had been rescued from the wreck by
the rocket apparatus, it was found that a disabled
man was still on board.

George Hoare volunteered to bring the man on shore, and was hauled off to the wreck through heavy seas but could not reach the man, owing to the hawser having been secured fourteen feet above the deck, where the man lay helpless and unconscious.

He then signalled to be hauled on shore again, to confer with the Chief Officer; and was then again hauled off. On reaching the wreck the hawser was eased, so as to allow him (in the breeches buoy) to reach the man on the deck. As the man was helpless, George Hoare, with his legs, seized the man round the body, and held him with both hands by his coat collar; the two men were thus safely hauled on shore through the sea.

LAWRENCE HENNESSEY On 11th November 1891, the French
Boatman, Hythe Coast- schooner *Eider* was wrecked on the sea-wall
guard Station at Seabrook; a heavy gale was blowing and
tremendous seas were sweeping the sea-wall.
Hennessey, who was on watch, obtained a heaving-line and cane, and unaided, at the risk of his life, saved the lives of four sailors belonging to the schooner, which broke up as she struck.

On the same day, a few hours later, Lawrence Hennessey, as coxswain of the lifeboat, attempted to go afloat from Sandgate, but the boat was thrown on to the beach.

Again at noon, a whole gale blowing at the time, Henessey went out in the lifeboat from Hythe; just as the breakers were cleared the lifeboat capsized, Hennessey (with the rest of the crew) being washed ashore in an exhausted condition, one man being drowned. Hennessey, though bruised and exhausted, ran into the surf and assisted in rescuing his comrades.

On the evening of the same day, at 9 p.m., Hennessey went out from Seabrook, as coxswain of the lifeboat, to the wreck of the *Bienvenue* and rescued the twenty-seven survivors. (8.2.92)

RICHARD WRIGHT TOMAN, *Engineer*, H.M.S. Foam
On the 3rd August 1898, whilst H.M.S. *Foam* was carrying out her full-speed trial at Malta, the mean-pressure cylinder burst without warning.

Mr. Toman at once ordered every one to leave the engine-room, and ran to the main throttle-valve and endeavoured to shut it off, being badly scalded as he did so. He then shut off the main stop-valves of boilers in the stokeholds.

He thus increased the chance of saving the life of any one left below.

After searching for any men left below, he tried to get on deck, but, owing to the excessive volume of steam, he twice fell half-way down the ladder. He eventually reached the deck, and at once turned on the fire-extinguishers to the boilers, his hands at the time being almost bare of skin. The valve wheel was heated to such an extent as to be almost unbearable to hands in an ordinary condition.

As the engines were flying round immediately after the accident there was every danger of the connecting-rod being driven through the bottom, but it was greatly lessened by the promptitude and pluck shown by Mr. Toman in shutting off the main stop-valves, and so reducing the risk of the ship being sunk or seriously damaged, and the lives of all on board being probably lost.

Mr. Toman, after having been driven out of the engine-room and severely scalded, again went below into the engine-room, which was filled with steam, to search for any one who might not have been able to escape, and only succeeded in finally getting out of the engine-room after two attempts. (15.11.98)

ARTHUR COLE LOWRY, *Lieutenant R.N.*
No details in Admiralty record. (18.12.1900)

HALTON STIRLING LECKY, *Lieutenant R.N.*
On the 25th August 1900, H.M.S. *Widgeon* anchored in Kosi Bay, 50 miles south of Delagoa Bay, in order to land stores and troops. The work of disembarkation was carried out, through heavy breakers, by surf-boats manned by Malays under the superintendence of Sub-Lt. Lecky, who had been sent on shore for the purpose.

One boat, loaded with stores and with Second Lt. Arnold Gray, Thorneycroft's Mounted Infantry, Trooper Frederick Trethowen,

Steinacker's Horse, and Pte. J. H. Forbes, Thorneycroft's Mounted Infantry, on board, capsized about 300 yards from the shore. The five Malays forming the boat's crew, and Pte. Forbes, by dint of hard swimming, with the assistance of the boat's oars, managed to reach the land after severe buffeting from the heavy seas. Lt. Gray was unable to swim, but, with Trooper Trethowen, clung to the boat, which drifted slowly keel upwards in a northerly direction almost parallel with the shore, carried by the set of a strong current. Huge breakers continually swept over the boat, and the men had great difficulty in retaining their hold. Sharks were observed near the boat both before and after the accident. Lecky plunged into the surf, and endeavoured to swim to their assistance. He was twice thrown back on the beach by the heavy seas, but succeeded in bringing first Gray and then the other, safe but unconscious, to the shore. Sub-Lt. Lecky and his servant, Pte. Botting, Royal Marine Light Infantry, then applied the usual methods for restoring animation, and both men eventually recovered. (28.6.01)

FREDERICK PAFFETT, *Chief Stoker* — On the evening of 10th June 1901, at about 9.30, H.M.S. *Daring*, torpedo-boat destroyer, was entering Portsmouth Harbour under easy steam, when an explosion suddenly took place in the after stokehold. A tube was blown out of the lower barrel of No. 2 boiler and the whole stokehold was filled with steam.

At the time of the accident there were five men in the stokehold—Chief Stoker Paffett and four stokers. Owing to the volume of steam it was impossible for them to see each other, but two men, though scalded and partly overcome by the great heat, managed to get up the ladder to the deck. Paffett, whose place of duty gave him the best chance to escape, was standing with his hand on the port side ladder. He remained, however, in the stokehold and endeavoured to avert the consequences of the explosion by opening the steam-valve of the starboard fan. With this object he went deliberately across the hold, groping for the valve, the steam from the boiler striking full on his left arm which was shielding his face. But he found it impossible to reach the valve and it was only with difficulty that he was able to regain the ladder, badly scalded. As he mounted the ladder he was able to save the life of Stoker Elliott, who was slipping down from above in a fainting condition. Paffett, being a very powerful man, raised him on his left shoulder and lifted him to the deck; then, reaching the deck himself, aided by those above, he fell down completely overcome. He was much disfigured by burns and scalds; and has almost lost the use of his left arm. (17.1.03)

JAMES SUTHERLAND, On the night of 2nd December 1901, H.M.S.
Leading Stoker T.B.D. *Salmon* was entering Harwich with the Chatham Instructional Flotilla, when a collision took place between her and the S.S. *Cambridge*.

It appeared that the *Salmon* was sinking from the injuries she had sustained, and the order was given for the men to go forward and leave the ship by ropes which had been passed over the bows of the *Cambridge*.

At the moment of the collision James Sutherland, Leading Stoker, was in the mess deck asleep. He went on deck but remained behind when the order was given, and went to the stokehold to open the hatches.

He opened one and was in the act of opening the other when it blew open in his face and a stoker named Scholfield was seen coming up.

Sutherland assisted him out. Scholfield tried to go back for Bartlett, a stoker who was afterwards discovered to have been killed by the steam which the shock of the collision had caused to escape in great quantities. He was prevented by Sutherland, who sent him on board the *Cambridge* and said he would look after Bartlett.

Sutherland then, by the aid of a light lowered from the *Cambridge*, went down into the stokehold. When he got down there was much steam, although the full force of it had gone. The chief danger, however, was from drowning, as it was full of water, and the ship was sinking.

Sutherland found Chief Stoker Church, got behind him and floated him along. A rope was passed down the hatchway, and Church, who was nearly unconscious, was got out.

Sutherland, after looking round to see if any one else was there, went on deck, searched the forward mess deck and stokers' mess deck, and then went on board the *Cambridge*. (19.1.03)

ALFRED STICKLEY, On 11th June 1904 H.M.S. T.B.D. *Success* was
Chief Stoker steaming towards Lamlash, when it became apparent from deck, owing to the issue of steam from the funnel, that something was wrong in the after stokehold. Stickley went below to ascertain the cause.

On reaching the stokehold he found that there was an escape of steam from the top drum of No. 4 Boiler, which shortly caused one of the furnace doors which had been left unlatched to be blown open. The stokehold was immediately filled with flame and steam, and the men present were burnt and scalded.

In spite of the conditions in the stokehold, and his own severe exposure to the flames, Stickley managed to open out the fans to their full extent, and made many gallant attempts to close the furnace door and open the drencher valve. Finding it was impossible to drive the flames back, he gave orders for the hatch to be opened, and himself remained below until the four men in the stokehold effected their escape. His face and neck were severely burnt, and his hands and forearms very badly scalded. For over four months he was on the sick-list suffering from his injuries. His lungs escaped injury, as he had the presence of mind to put cotton waste into his mouth while he was in the stokehold. (10.2.05)

JOHN RAMSAY,[1] *Able Seaman* — On 7th January 1900, when the 12.57 a.m. down mail train was approaching Temple Meads Station, Bristol, a Marine, W. Howat, of H.M.S. *Donegal*, fell from the platform.

Ramsay at once jumped down to his assistance, though the approaching train was only about sixty feet distant at the time, and succeeded in dragging Howat back to the platform as the train passed. (27.7.00)

JAMES CLAUDE SCOTT HENDRY, *P.O. Mechanic R.N.A.S.* — Gallantry displayed by him on the occasion of an accident to aeroplane 58 on 19th November 1914. Saved the life of the Pilot of No. 58 (who had been stunned by the premature explosion of a bomb) by extricating him from the sinking wreckage of the machine after both had fallen some 150 feet into the sea. (*Gazette* notice missing)

WILLIAM LASHLEY, *Chief Stoker*
THOMAS CREAN, *Petty Officer* — Gallantry in saving Commander Evans's life on the occasion of the return journey of the final supporting party to Captain Scott's expedition to the South Pole, February 1912. (*Gazette* notice missing)

FRDERICK GEORGE MARSHALL, *Mechanician* — For gallantry on occasion of bursting of boiler generator tubes of H.M.S. *Vengeance* on 27th February 1915. (*Gazette* notice missing)

JOHN SULLIVAN, *Chief Stoker* — Gallantry displayed at a fire in H.M.S. *Hope*, on 22nd March 1913.

Brought a stoker up from the lower mess deck through dense black smoke and suffocating fumes and returned to see if any one else was there. Afterwards went below once more to close bottom flap of the stove. (*Gazette* notice missing)

[1] Home Office award.

MICHAEL SULLIVAN KEOGH, See page 156. (12.1.16)
Chief Petty Officer

Arthur Richard Shaw Warden, See page 156. (14.4.16)
Temporary Lt.-Commander R.N.

ROBERT ARTHUR STARTIN, During a violent gale and snowstorm on
Lieutenant R.N. the night of the 28th March 1916, the whaler of H.M.S. *Melpomene*, with a crew of six men, was driven on to the mud three-quarters of a mile above Parkstone Jetty, Harwich. Lt. Startin set out alone to search along the river bed. After wading through deep mud, at times up to his armpits, for 300 yards, he eventually found the whaler, half full of water, aground on the mud, with her crew lying helpless in the boat, having given up all hope of being rescued. He only succeeded in rousing them by beating them with his stick, one man having to be forcibly dragged all the way to the shore, by Lt. Startin and the coxswain of the boat. After dragging him for about an hour, a distance of about 40 or 50 yards had been covered, when a light was seen moving inshore. Startin ordered the crew to remain where they were whilst he went to the light, which proved to be carried by a search party with a rope. This rope was taken backwards and forwards personally by Lt. Startin from the shore to the boat's crew until each one had been rescued, this exhausting and dangerous task in the deep mud being performed under the most trying weather conditions. All the crew were thus saved, though one afterwards died from exposure. (6.5.16)

Frederick Joseph Rutland, During the transhipment of the crew of
Lieutenant R.N. H.M.S. *Warrior* to H.M.S. *Engadine* on 1st June 1916, succeeding the naval battle off the coast of Jutland, one of the severely wounded, owing to the violent motion of the two ships, was accidentally dropped overboard from a stretcher and fell between the ships. As the ships were working most dangerously, the commanding officer of the *Warrior* had to forbid two of his officers from jumping overboard to the rescue of the wounded man, as he considered that it would mean their almost certain death. Before he could be observed, however, Lt. Rutland, of H.M.S. *Engadine*, went overboard from the forepart of that ship with a bowline and worked himself aft. He succeeded in putting the bowline around the wounded man and in getting him hauled on board, but it was then found that the man was dead, having been crushed between the two ships. Lt. Rutland's escape from a similar fate was miraculous. (11.8.16)

FREDERICK WILLIAM WEEKS, On the night of 18th January 1917, a
Acting Lieutenant R.N.R. member of the crew of one of H.M.
ships, returning from leave, fell into
the sea between the ship and the quay. The ship, which was kept clear
of the side of the quay by spar fenders of only nine inches in diameter,
was working to and fro with the slight swell entering the harbour. The
man was incapable of helping himself, was of heavy build, and was
wearing a uniform greatcoat. In view of the risk, Lt. Weeks decided
to go himself to the rescue with a line. He managed to obtain a hold
of the man's hair and kept him above water, whilst wedging himself
with his back against the quay with his knees against the ship's side.
During this time he was mostly under water. He succeeded in securing a line round the man, who was hauled on deck. (12.3.17)

MICHAEL JOYCE, H.M.S. *Zulu* was mined on the 8th November
Engine-Room Arti- 1916. The bottom of the after part of the engine-
ficer, 3rd Class room was blown out and the whole compartment
WALTER KIMBER, reduced to a mass of debris and broken steam and
Stoker Petty Officer water pipes.
Immediately after the explosion Joyce and
Kimber went to the engine-room, the former having just come off
watch. The latter had just left the boiler-room, after he had seen that
the oil-burners were shut off and everything was in order, and had
sent his hands on deck.

Hearing the sound of moans coming from inside the engine-room,
they both attempted to enter it by the foremost hatch and ladder.

As the heat in the engine-room was intense and volumes of steam
were coming up forward, they then lifted one of the square ventilating
hatches further aft on the top of the engine-room casing (port side) and
climbed into the rapidly flooding compartment over the steam pipes,
which were extremely hot.

Scrambling over the debris, they discovered well over on the starboard side Stoker Petty Officer Smith, with his head just out of the water.

A rope was lowered from the upper deck, and with great difficulty
Smith, who was entangled in fractured pipes and other wreckage, was
hauled up alive.

At the same time Stoker Petty Officer Powell was found floating in
the water on the port side of the engine-room. The rope was lowered
again and passed round Powell, who, however, was found to be dead
on reaching the deck.

The water was so high that further efforts to discover the remaining
Artificer left in the engine-room would have been useless, and the
attempt had to be abandoned. (4.5.17)

ERNEST A. POOLEY On the 22nd April a violent explosion occurred
HERBERT POWLEY   on board H.M. M.L. *No. 431* while she was
lying alongside the jetty at the Base, burying Sub-Lt. Charles W. Nash, R.N.V.R., beneath the wreckage in the after part of the vessel.

Chief Motor Mechanic Pooley and Deckhand Powley, who were on board their own vessel lying at the jetty fifty yards astern, hurried to the burning motor launch. The flames were every instant drawing nearer to the spot where Nash lay buried, and though it was clear that the after petrol tanks might explode at any moment, Powley and Pooley jumped on board the vessel and pulled out Nash from beneath the wreckage. Had they been delayed for another thirty seconds all three would have perished.

Deckhand Powley, who led the way on board the burning motor launch, suffered severely from the effect of burns. (3.7.17)

EDMUND JOHN PYSDEN   On the morning of the 27th February 1917, an auxiliary stop-valve in one of H.M. ships accidentally burst, the boiler-room immediately becoming filled with dense steam. As it was impossible to draw fires or at once to lift the safety-valves, a second and even worse accident was likely. Mr. Edmund John Pysden, Artificer Engineer R.N., gallantly entered the stokehold, brought out two men who were lying insensible, and helped to bring out others. He also succeeded in opening the safety-valve, which relieved the immediate danger of a further accident. Although he had a wet rag tied over his mouth, he swallowed a quantity of live steam, and was partially incapacitated by its effects. (3.9.17)

ALFRED PLACE, *Petty Officer, late R.N.* See p. 166. (Gazetted 28.12.17)

ROBERT SYDNEY STEELE SMITH   Surgeon Probationer R. S. S. Smith, R.N.V.R., was Medical Officer of one of H.M. ships which was torpedoed by an enemy submarine.

When the enemy torpedo struck the ship, Smith was in the wardroom aft with the 1st Lieutenant. The explosion wrecked the wardroom and rendered the 1st Lieutenant unconscious. All other exit being blocked, Surgeon Probationer Smith piled the wrecked furniture under the skylight, and got the 1st Lieutenant through this on deck. He then attended to a petty officer who was lying on deck with a broken arm and leg, adjusted and blew up his lifebelt, and after doing the same for the 1st Lieutenant got him overboard, as the ship was then foundering.

The 1st Lieutenant was by then partially conscious, but was again stunned owing to an explosion when the vessel foundered, and when he was picked up by the boat he was apparently dead. Smith applied artificial respiration with success. He afterwards attended to the injured in the boat, until they were picked up forty-three hours later. (20.11.17)

Nicholas Rath
Richard Knoulton } See p. 165. (Gazetted 12.12.17)
George Faucett Pitts Abbott

EDWARD PEVERALL MEGGS DAVIS   On the 3rd October, whilst carrying out a practice flight, a seaplane, piloted by Flight Sub-Lt. J. D. Grant, fell into the sea. The seaplane turned over and the pilot was enclosed in his seat under water.

Flight-Lt. Davis, R.N.A.S., immediately flew by seaplane to the spot, made fast to the wreck, and dived under the wreck in his uniform and endeavoured to extricate Grant.

To do this it was necessary for him to dive amongst and struggle through the mass of wires and broken parts of the wreck. Notwithstanding the imminent danger of being caught up amongst them, he continued his efforts to get Grant out, until the emergency boat arrived on the scene.

No other help was at hand until the arrival of this motor-boat, which at the time of the accident was about a mile and a half away. (18.12.17)

JOHN NEALE   On the 25th August 1916, Lt. Neale, R.N.V.R., was conducting certain experiments which involved the projection from a Stokes mortar of a tube containing flare powder. An accident occurred, rendering imminent the explosion of the tube before leaving the mortar, which would almost certainly have resulted in the bursting of the mortar with loss of life to bystanders. Lt. Neale, in order to safeguard the lives of the working party, at once attempted to lift the tube from the mortar. It exploded while he was doing so, with the result that he was severely injured, but owing to the fact that he had partly withdrawn the tube from the mortar no injury was caused to others. (23.1.18)

MAURICE MACMAHON   On the 8th November 1916 a series of fires and explosions occurred at Bakaritsa, Port of Archangel. After the merchant ships had been got away from the wharves, cries and moans were heard from the direction of a 100-ton floating crane moored between the s.s. *Earl of Forfar* and the quay.

The *Earl of Forfar* was on fire fore and aft, and it was obvious that any attempt to save life must be accompanied by the greatest risk, the ship having explosives on board and the quay abreast it burning furiously with intermittent explosions from small-arm ammunition.

In order to reach the floating crane, it was necessary to cross the *Earl of Forfar*, the after part of which had blown up, whilst the forepart was on fire and the forecastle was a mass of smouldering debris. Hearing moans from under the debris of the forecastle, Lt.-Commander MacMahon, R.N.R., with the aid of the crew of a tug, cleared away the wreckage and discovered the mate, with one arm, one leg, and collar-bone fractured. This man was extricated, and passed into the tug. MacMahon then proceeded on to the floating crane by means of a single plank and rescued from beneath the crane the carpenter of the *Earl of Forfar* and two Russian subjects, part of the crane's crew. (5.2.18) (See p. 323.)

ALFRED WILLIAM NEWMAN — On the 10th October 1917 an alarm of fire was given in the after magazine of one of H.M. ships. Mr. Newman, Acting Mate, R.N., who was on the upper deck, went to the magazine as soon as he heard the alarm and, seeing smoke issuing from a box of cordite, opened the lid and passed the cartridges on to the upper deck, where they were thrown overboard. One cartridge in the middle of the box was very hot, and smoke was issuing from the end. (1.3.18)

Harold Victor Robinson
ERIC EDWARD STEERE
VICTOR ALBERT WATSON
See p. 173. (Gazetted 6.3.18)

Francis Herbert Heaveningham Goodhart — Owing to an accident, one of H.M. submarines sank and became fast on the bottom in 38 **feet** of water, parts of the vessel becoming flooded. After several hours the only prospect of saving those remaining on board appeared to be for some one to escape from the submarine in order to concert measures with the rescuers, who were by this time present on the surface. Commander Goodhart, D.S.O., volunteered to make the attempt. After placing in his belt a small tin cylinder with instructions for the rescuers, he went into the conning tower with the commanding officer. The conning tower was flooded up to their waists, and the high-pressure air was turned on; the clips of the conning tower were knocked off and the conning-tower lid was soon wide open. Commander Goodhart then stood up in the dome, took a deep breath, and made his escape, but, unfortunately, was blown by the pressure of air against part of the superstructure, and was killed by the force of the blow.

The commanding officer, whose intention it had been to return inside the submarine after Commander Goodhart's escape, was involuntarily forced to the surface by the air pressure, and it was thus rendered possible for the plans for rescuing those still inside the submarine to be carried out.

Commander Goodhart displayed extreme and heroic daring in attempting to escape from the submarine in order to save the lives of those remaining on board, and thoroughly realized the forlorn nature of his act. His last remark to the commanding officer was: 'If I don't get up the tin cylinder will.' (23.4.18)

Tom Kenneth Triggs
WILLIAM BECKER
On the 6th December 1917 the French S.S. *Mont Blanc*, with a cargo of high explosives, and the Norwegian s.s. *Imo*, were in collision in Halifax Harbour, Nova Scotia. Fire broke out in the *Mont Blanc* immediately after the collision, and the flames very quickly rose to a height of over 100 feet. The crew abandoned their ship and pulled towards the shore.

The captain of H.M.S. *Highflyer*, which was about a mile away, at once sent off a boat to see if anything could be done to prevent loss of life, and Commander Triggs, volunteering for this duty, immediately got into the ship's whaler and pulled to the scene. A tug and the steamboat of H.M.C.S. *Niobe* were seen going there at the same time.

Triggs boarded the tug, and finding it was impossible to do anything for the *Mont Blanc*, decided to endeavour to get the *Imo* away, giving directions accordingly to the tug. He returned to the whaler, and was pulling towards the bows of the *Imo* which was about 300 yards from the *Mont Blanc*, to pass a line from her to the tug, when a tremendous explosion occurred.

Of the seven people in the whaler, one, Able Seaman Becker, was rescued alive on the Dartmouth shore, the remainder perished. (23.3.18) (See p. 327.)

THOMAS N. DAVIS
ROBERT STONES
On the 6th December 1917 the French s.s. *Mont Blanc*, with a cargo of high explosives, and the Norwegian s.s. *Imo* were in collision in Halifax Harbour, Nova Scotia. Fire then broke out on the *Mont Blanc*, whose crew abandoned their ship and pulled to the shore. A few minutes later a tremendous explosion took place, and the tug *Musquash* was seen to be on fire forward. The fire was increasing and there appeared to be a great danger of her getting adrift, and being carried down on to

another vessel. As the *Musquash* had a gun and ammunition on board there was danger of a further explosion and consequent loss of life.

The captain of H.M.S. *Highflyer* hailed a private tug and asked her to take the *Musquash* in tow, but as they were unwilling to board the *Musquash* to get her in tow, the tug was brought alongside H.M.S. *Highflyer*. Leading Seaman Davis and Able Seaman Stones immediately volunteered, and having been transferred by the tug to the burning *Musquash*, which had by this time broken adrift, they secured a line from her stern, by means of which she was towed into midstream. The line then parted, and Davis and Stones passed another line from the *Musquash* to the pumping-lighter *Lee*, which had now arrived. They then both went forward to the burning part, and succeeded in getting to the ammunition, which was by this time badly scorched, pulled it away from the flames and threw it overboard. They then broke open the door of the galley, which was on fire inside, to enable the *Lee* to play her hoses into it. They repeated the same thing with the cabin.

By their work they made it possible to subdue the fire and save further damage and loss of life. At any moment whilst they were on board the *Musquash* the ammunition might have exploded. (23.3.18)

JOHN GEORGE STANNERS On the 29th December 1917 some cotton
RUPERT WALTER BUGG waste, stored in a wooden cupboard in the magazine of H.M. M.L. *No. 289*, caught fire from an unknown cause. On the fire being discovered by the smell of burning and by the issue of smoke from the magazine hatch, when opened, Deckhand Stanners, without hesitation, went down into the magazine and brought up a quantity of the burning waste.

Leading Deckhand Bugg, who was in M.L. *No. 285*, alongside *No. 289*, smelt something burning, and on observing Deckhand Stanners coming up from the magazine with burning material, immediately went down and extinguished the remainder of the ignited cotton waste.

The high courage shown by these men in the face of very grave danger averted a serious fire, and saved the lives of those on board. (16.5.18)

PAUL DOUGLAS On the 28th February 1918 a seaplane got out of
ROBERTSON control and spun to the ground. Acting Flight Commander Robertson, R.N.A.S., the Observer, jumped from the machine just before it reached the ground and landed safely, as the ground was marshy. The Pilot, Flight-Lt. H. C. Lemon, was imprisoned in the seaplane which, on striking the ground, im-

mediately burst into flames. Though the seaplane was quickly a furnace of blazing petrol, and heavy bombs and the reserve petrol tank were likely to explode, Robertson returned and endeavoured to extricate the pilot, and only desisted when he had been so severely burnt in the face, hands, and leg that his recovery was for some time in doubt. (15.6.18)

GEORGE PARKER BEVAN On the 8th November 1916 a series of explosions and fires occurred at Bakaritsa, Port of Archangel, on merchant ships and on the wharves. The s.s. *Baron Driesen* had blown up at 1 p.m. and part of the s.s. *Earl of Forfar* forty minutes later, and fresh explosions were expected every instant. It was thought that all their crews had either escaped or been killed or rescued but, after dark, cries of distress were heard from the *Earl of Forfar*. The ship was a mass of flame at the time, and burning embers from the fire which was raging on shore were continually showered over her. She had a cargo of explosives on board and was abreast of the main conflagration. The flames were blown towards her by the wind, and the remaining portion of the ship was expected to be blown up at any moment. Captain Bevan, C.M.G., D.S.O., R.N., however, on hearing the cries, went on board, accompanied by Lt.-Commander MacMahon, and, hearing moans from under the smouldering debris of the forecastle, cleared away the wreckage and extricated the mate, who had an arm and a leg and his collar-bone broken, and passed him into a tug. (8.7.18) (See p. 319–20.)

EDWARD HENRY RICHARDSON
CHRISTOPHER WATSON
JAMES DIXON HENRY
MALCOLM THOMPSON
On the 8th November 1916, on the same occasion, Lt. Richardson, 2nd Engineer Watson, and Able Seamen Henry and Thompson, of the tug *Sunderland*, with the utmost gallantry volunteered to board the *Earl of Forfar* and effected the rescue of a considerable number of wounded and helpless men who would otherwise have perished. (8.7.18)

JAMES STARTIN An explosion occurred on board H.M. M.L. *No. 64* on the 10th June 1918. Immediately after the explosion Admiral Sir James Startin, K.C.B., then Commodore, proceeded alongside. On learning that the engineer was below, he sprang down the hatch and recovered the body practically unaided.

As the bulkhead between the engine-room and the forward tanks had been blown down by the force of the explosion, so that the fire was blazing upon the side and on the top of the forward tanks, which were liable to burst at any moment, the action of Commodore Startin showed the utmost possible gallantry and disregard of personal safety. (20.8.18)

KEITH ROBIN HOARE
ARTHUR GERALD BAGOT
On the 12th April 1918 an explosion took place in the engine-room of H.M. M.L. *No. 356*, and the forward tanks burst into flame. The officer and some of the crew were blown overboard by the explosion and the remainder were quickly driven aft by the flames, and were taken off in a skiff. By this time the flames were issuing from the cabin hatch aft, and there was much petrol burning on the surface of the water. It was then realized by the crews of adjacent vessels that the aft petrol tanks and the depth charge were being attacked by the fire, and might explode at any moment. At the moment when others were running away, Lt. Hoare, D.S.O., D.S.C., and Sub-Lt. Bagot, D.S.C., jumped into their dinghy, rowed to the wreck, got on board, and removed the depth charge, thereby preventing an explosion which might have caused serious loss of life among the crowd of English and French sailors on the quay. (20.8.18)

JOHN ALLAN
As the R.F.A. *Mixol* was dropping alongside to fuel one of H.M. battle cruisers on the 19th June 1918, an Able Seaman slipped and fell overboard between *Mixol* and the cruiser. *Mixol* was only about ten feet clear of the cruiser, and was closing at the time.

Donkeyman John Allan, standing on the fore well deck of *Mixol*, saw the man fall. Although it was clear that the man in the water was in imminent danger of being crushed between the two ships, Allan at once jumped overboard to save him. He assisted him to keep afloat until a rope was thrown, and the Able Seaman was hauled on board before Allan took the rope himself. (16.9.18)

WALTER HENRY CAL-
THROP CALTHROP
On the night of the 14th/15th April 1918 a fire broke out on board the S.S. *Proton*, an ammunition ship, at Port Said. Commander Calthrop, R.N., on being informed on the telephone that the ship was on fire, immediately proceeded to the scene. The ship had already been abandoned by her crew, and was ablaze in Nos. 1 and 2 holds. The forecastle was also alight, and it was impossible to get down to the fore well deck owing to the heat of the flames. Knowing that the *Proton* had 240 tons of ammunition on board, Commander Calthrop decided to endeavour to flood the ship, and for this purpose obtained assistance and went down into the engine-room and opened the sea

inlet. He also tried to break the main sea-valve cover, but was not successful in this. He accordingly sent for a gun-cotton charge for the purpose of sinking the ship, and warned all ships in the vicinity to get under way. He then returned to the *Proton*, which was now blazing fiercely forward, the sides being red-hot as far aft as the bridge, and the bridge screen alight. He again boarded her with the 1st and 2nd engineers and went below, trying to break the doors of the condenser with sledge hammers. After about five minutes this was found to be impossible, and they returned on deck. By this time a picket-boat had arrived with the gun-cotton charge, and it was decided that the ship ought to be sunk as soon as possible. This operation was accordingly carried out.

Commander Calthrop displayed the utmost gallantry. His efforts undoubtedly prevented serious loss of life. (28.9.18)

CHARLES DAVIE MILLAR On the 29th June 1918 an outbreak of fire occurred on board H.M. M.L. *No. 483* whilst refuelling in Pembroke Dock, the fire being caused by the ignition of an overflow of petrol from the hose.

Leading Seaman Millar, H.M.S. *P.C. 51*, who was walking up and down the forecastle of his ship, on seeing the flames break out on the upper deck of the motor launch, immediately slid over the bows of his craft on to the motor launch, rushed aft, and removed the primers of the depth charges. He then forced his way through the flames and kicked the hose overboard, getting his clothes ignited as he did so. Having extinguished his burning clothing by jumping overboard, he climbed inboard again and assisted in getting the motor launch in tow.

This man displayed initiative and disregard of danger, and by his prompt action he probably averted a serious accident. Had the depth charges detonated, very great damage would have been done and lives undoubtedly lost. (9.10.18)

WILLIAM FRYER HARVEY On the 28th June 1918 two of H.M. torpedo-boat destroyers were in collision, and Surg.-Lt. Harvey, R.N., was sent on board the more seriously damaged destroyer in order to render assistance to the injured. On hearing that a stoker petty officer was pinned by the arm in a damaged compartment, Harvey immediately went down and amputated the arm, this being the only means of freeing the petty officer. The boiler-room at the time was flooded, and full of fumes from the escaping oil. This alone constituted a great danger to any one in the compartment, and Surg.-Lt. Harvey collapsed from this cause after performing the operation, and had to be hauled out of the compartment. Moreover, at any time the ship might have broken in two and all hands were fallen in on deck, wearing lifebelts, at the time, in order to be ready for this eventuality. Harvey displayed the greatest gallantry and disregard of his personal safety in descending into the damaged compartment and continuing to work there amidst the oil fumes at a time when the ship was liable to sink. (29.10.18)

HARRY MELVILLE ARBUTHNOT DAY On the 9th November 1918 H.M.S. *Britannia* was torpedoed by an enemy submarine. The explosion of the torpedo was followed by another and more violent explosion of ammunition, and fires were started, resulting in the spread of smoke and fumes. Shortly after the explosion Acting Lt. Day, R.M.L.I., went down to the wardroom to search for wounded. He heard groaning forward of the wardroom, but found that the heavy wooden door leading forward had jammed and was immovable. He then burst open the trap hatch to the ward-room pantry and climbed through it. He discovered Engineer Lt. Stanley F. Weir, R.N., and a ward-room steward alive and conscious, but unable to move. Fearing that he would hurt them if he endeavoured to drag them through the trap hatch single-handed, he climbed back into the ward-room aft and up on to the quarter-deck and procured two or three stokers, with whom he returned to the wardroom, and eventually carried the dying officer and man on deck and to the forecastle. During his first visit to the ward-room Lt. Day was alone, in the dark, the ship with a list, and a fire close to the 12-in. magazine. Whilst carrying out this rescue work he inspected all scuttles and dead-lights in the ward-room (and cabins before it) and ascertained that all were properly closed before leaving. The cordite fumes were very strong, and his life was in danger throughout. (7.1.19)

GEORGE DEVEREUX BELBEN On the 16th September 1918 a serious
DAVID HYWEL EVANS explosion occurred amidships on board
ALBERT ERNEST STOKER H.M.S. *Glatton*, lying in Dover Harbour.
EDWARD NUNN This was followed immediately by an outbreak of fire, and the oil fuel burned furiously and spread fore and aft. Efforts were made to extinguish the fire by means of salvage tugs. The foremost magazines were flooded, but it was found impossible to get to the after magazine flooding positions. The explosion and fire cut off the after part of the ship, killing or seriously wounding all the officers, with one exception, who were on board. The ship might have blown up at any moment.

Lt. Belben, D.S.C., Sub-Lt. Evans, Petty Officer Stoker, and Able Seaman Nunn were in boats which were rescuing men who had been blown, or who had jumped, overboard. They proceeded on board H.M.S. *Glatton* on their own initiative, and entered the superstructure, which was full of dense smoke, and proceeded down to the deck below.

Behaving with the greatest gallantry and contempt of danger, they succeeded in rescuing seven or eight badly injured men from the mess deck, in addition to fifteen whom they found and brought out from inside the super-structure.

This work was carried out before the arrival of any gas-masks and, though at one time they were driven out by the fire, they proceeded down again after the hoses had been played on the flames. They continued until all chance of rescuing others had passed, and the ship was ordered to be abandoned, when she was sunk by torpedo, as the fire was spreading, and it was impossible to flood the after magazines. (31.1.19)

ALBERT CHARLES MATTISON
EDWARD S. BEARD

On the 6th December 1917 the French steamer *Mont Blanc*, with a cargo of high explosives, and the Norwegian steamer *Imo* were in collision in Halifax Harbour, N.S. Fire broke out on the *Mont Blanc* immediately after the collision. The commanding officer of H.M.C.S. *Niobe*, which was lying in the harbour, on perceiving what had happened, sent away a steam-boat to see what could be done. Mr. Mattison and six men of the Royal Naval Canadian Volunteer Reserve volunteered to form the crew of this boat, but just as the boat got alongside the *Mont Blanc* the ship blew up, and Mr. Mattison and the whole boat's crew lost their lives. The boat's crew were fully aware of the desperate nature of the work they were engaged on, and by their gallantry and devotion to duty they sacrificed their lives in the endeavour to save the lives of others. (18.2.19) (See p. 321.)

HENRY DE BEAUVOIR TUPPER
EDWARD THOMAS SPALDING

On the 4th August 1918 H.M.S. *Comet*, under the command of Commander Tupper, was seriously damaged in collision. The ship was badly holed on the starboard side, the deck and all compartments eventually filled with water as far as the engine-room bulkhead, and the stern was at any moment liable to fall off. On being informed that the hydraulic-release depth charge was set to 'fire', Commander Tupper sent away a man in a whaler to remove the primer. It was only possible to remove the primer from one of the charges, leaving the other depth charge about 15 feet under water, still at 'fire'. Commander Tupper then went away in a dinghy himself, and by repeated diving operations tried to render it safe. After a rest he returned to complete the operation, in which Able Seaman Spalding, who was a passenger on the ship at the time and was a good swimmer, volunteered to assist. Commander Tupper at first refused to allow Spalding to assist him, as the latter had no knowledge of depth charges, and Commander Tupper did not consider it safe for him to go down. Ultimately Commander Tupper and Able Seaman Spalding swam to the spot beneath which the depth charge was submerged, and alternately gave a turn to the iron bar which Commander Tupper had placed in the handle, until the primer was eventually unscrewed and taken out of the depth charge, thus rendering it safe. This operation was of the most dangerous nature, as at any moment the stern of the ship might have dropped off before the depth charge was removed and would have carried down both the officer and the man, who would inevitably have lost their lives. The explosion would also have destroyed the remaining portion of the ship, with loss of life to those of the crew who were on board. (21.2.19)

EDWARD LEICESTER ATKINSON   On the 16th September 1918 a serious explosion occurred amidships on board H.M.S. *Glatton*, lying in Dover Harbour. At the time of the explosion Surgeon Lt.-Commander Atkinson, D.S.O., was at work in his cabin. The first explosion rendered him unconscious. Recovering shortly, he found the flat outside his cabin filled with dense smoke and fumes. He made his way to the quarter-deck by means of the ladder in the Warrant Officers' flat, the only one still intact. During this time he brought two unconscious men on to the upper deck, he himself being uninjured.

He returned to the flat, and was bringing a third man up, when a smaller explosion occurred whilst he was on the ladder. This explosion blinded him and, at the same time, a piece of metal was driven into his left leg in such a manner that he was unable to move until he had himself extracted it. Placing the third man on the upper deck, he proceeded forward through the shelter deck. By feel, being totally unable to see, he here found two more unconscious men, both of whom he brought out.

He was found later on the upper deck in an almost unconscious condition, so wounded and burnt that his life was despaired of for some time. (20.5.19)

DAVID WAINWRIGHT   On the 4th February 1919 H.M.S. *Penarth* struck a mine and immediately began to sink. Lt. David Wainwright, R.N., taking command of the situation, at once superintended the manning and lowering of the starboard gig, and later the launching of the Carley floats. Hearing there was a stoker injured in one of the stokeholds, he called for volunteers to show him the way, and at once made his way forward. There was by now a heavy list on the ship, and it was apparent she would not remain afloat much longer, the upper deck on the starboard side being already awash. Lt. Wainwright made his way below unaided, and while he was in the stokehold the ship struck a second mine abaft of him. The forepart was blown off and sank, and he was forced to wait till the stokehold had filled before he could float to the surface up the escape.

He displayed the greatest gallantry and disregard of his own personal safety in going below at a time when the ship was liable to sink at any moment. (20.5.19)

RICHARD JAMES RODNEY SCOTT   On the 15th July 1919, during minesweeping operations in the Baltic, four mines were swept up which H.M.S. *Myrtle*, commanded by Lt.-Commander Scott, and another vessel were ordered to sink.

During the operations the two vessels were mined, and H.M.S. *Myrtle* immediately began to sink.

So great was the force of the explosion that all hands in the engine-room and boiler-room of the ship were killed with one exception, and many others of the crew were wounded.

After the wounded had been successfully transferred to another vessel, the forepart of H.M.S. *Myrtle* broke away and sank.

Lt.-Commander Scott, hearing that the fate of one of the crew of the *Myrtle* had not been definitely ascertained, gallantly returned alone to what was left of the ship, which was drifting through the mine-field, rolling heavily and burning fiercely, and regardless of the extreme risk which he ran, made a thorough search for the missing man, unfortunately without success. (12.3.20)

EDMUND GEOFFREY ABBOTT   On the 5th August 1919 an explosion occurred on board the ex-German battleship *Baden*, whilst in dry dock at Invergordon.

Lt. Abbott, R.N., immediately proceeded down the hatch to the main deck and saw that smoke was coming from the ladder-way tunnel leading down to the shaft passage and after room containing the cooling-plant.

Other methods proving ineffectual, he proceeded to the corresponding tunnel on the starboard side, to see whether it was possible to get below and work up to the scene of the explosion from that side.

The starboard tunnel was practically clear of smoke, so he proceeded to the upper deck, collected a party, and descended again through the tunnel to the room containing the cooling-plant. He made his way to the port side and found a dockyard workman lying unconscious. Assisted by the party which had accompanied him, Lt. Abbott got the body to the upper deck, but life was found to be extinct.

Although greatly affected by the fumes, Lt. Abbott called for further volunteers and again proceeded to the rescue of a second man whose groans had been heard, and succeeded in removing him out of danger.

Throughout the proceedings the officer showed an utter disregard for his own safety, and, in spite of the great difficulty occasioned by the absence of light, was the undoubted means of saving the second man's life. (12.3.20)

HENRY BUCKLE ALBERT VICTOR BAILEY While H.M.S. *Tiger* was undergoing repairs at Invergordon, on the 27th August 1919, two dockyard fitters and an able seaman were overcome by noxious gas in the hold of the ship, and Stoker Petty Officer Bailey, accompanied by a sick-berth attendant, made an unsuccessful attempt at rescue. Both he and his companion had put on respirators, but found them useless. Mr. Buckle, the officer of the watch, then arrived on the scene, and in spite of the grave risk of life, which it was now evident would be incurred by further attempts at rescue, immediately went down and succeeded in passing a rope round one of the men. This man was got out, but Mr. Buckle was considerably affected by the gas, and could do nothing further.

Stoker Petty Officer Bailey, though suffering from the effects of his previous attempts, repeated the operation, and succeeded in getting the other two men out, but all efforts to restore them were futile. (27.4.20)

HARRY SMITH On the 13th May 1920, while H.M. T.B.D. *Rob Roy* was proceeding at utmost speed on a full-power trial, a fire broke out in the forward boiler-room.

With entire disregard of his own safety, Mr. Smith (Commissioned Engineer R.N.) immediately went below to search for the two ratings who were still there, and to shut off the boilers, under extreme difficulties owing to the heat, escaping steam, and water, well knowing in doing so the danger he ran from the burning oil fuel and the unconsumed gases accentuated by the confined and congested space of a destroyer's boiler-room.

Owing to his prompt action and presence of mind, Mr. Smith localized the damage and saved the lives of all who were below. (5.10.20)

ERNEST EDWARD MILLS JOYCE
WILLIAM RAYMENT RICHARDS
VICTOR GEORGE HAYWARD
HARRY ERNEST WILD

The Shackleton Trans-Antarctic Expedition of 1914–17 had for its object the crossing of the Antarctic Continent from the Weddell Sea to the Ross Sea, via the South Pole, a distance of about 1,700 miles. Sufficient supplies for the journey could not be carried, and it was therefore necessary to establish a chain of depots on the Ross Sea side as far southwards as possible. With this end in view the ship *Aurora* was sent to McMurdo Sound at the southern extremity of the Ross Sea, and, as it was intended that the vessel should winter there, a portion only of the stores and equipment was disembarked. McMurdo Sound was reached in January 1915, but during a blizzard in May the *Aurora* was blown out to sea and was unable to return, and the nine members of the Expedition who were on shore were left stranded. They recognized that failure to establish the depots would undoubtedly result in the loss of the main body and resolved, in spite of their grave shortage of equipment, to carry out the allotted programme.

For this purpose a party under the command of Sub-Lt. A. L. Mackintosh, R.N.R., and consisting of the Rev. A. P. Spencer-Smith, Messrs. Joyce, Richards, Hayward, and Wild, and three other members who assisted for a part of the outward journey, left Hut Point, Ross Island, on 9th October. They took with them two sledges and four dogs, and 162 days elapsed before the surviving members of the party were back at Hut Point, the total distance covered being approximately 950 miles.

Mr. Spencer-Smith had to be dragged on a sledge for 42 days mainly by hand labour, the distance covered being over 350 miles. When more than 100 miles remained to be covered the collapse of Lt. Mackintosh imposed an additional burden on the active members of the party, who were all suffering from scurvy and snow-blindness and were so enfeebled by their labours that at times they were unable to cover more than 2 or 3 miles in 15 hours.

Mr. Spencer-Smith died when only 19 miles remained to be covered, but Lt. Mackintosh was brought in safety to the base. (4.7.23)

REGINALD WILLIAM
ARMYTAGE
DICK OLIVER

On the 23rd May 1928, whilst H.M.S. *Warspite* was lying alongside Parlatorio Wharf, Malta, an examination of the bulge compartments situated on the port side aft was being carried out. The manhole door of the lower bulge compartment was removed and the compartment tested. It was found that the air was foul and poisonous. A chief stoker attempted to enter the compartment, although aware that it was in a dangerous condition, and was immediately overcome by the gas and fell unconscious to the bottom of the compartment, a distance of about 20 feet.

The alarm was given and Lt. Armytage immediately fetched his gas mask and, with a life-line round him, entered the compartment and reached the bottom, when he was overcome and rendered unconscious. With great difficulty, owing to the small size of the manhole, he was hauled to the exit by means of the life-line. He was unconscious and had stopped breathing when hauled into the open air, and was eventually removed to the R.N. Hospital in a precarious condition. Lt. Armytage was aware that his gas-mask would afford no degree of protection against the CO or CO_2 gases likely to be present in the compartment. He realized that the delay incurred in passing a diver through the manholes would probably prove fatal to the chief stoker and appreciated to the fullest extent the grave risk he ran in entering the compartment.

As soon as Lt. Armytage had been withdrawn from the manhole of the upper bulge compartment Leading Seaman Oliver, who was in attendance with a shallow diving-helmet, volunteered to attempt the rescue of the chief stoker, despite the fact that he had witnessed the painful and distressing sights attendant on asphyxiation. After donning the helmet he was passed with considerable difficulty through the manholes of the upper and lower bulge compartments and he eventually succeeded in reaching the chief stoker and in passing a line round his body by means of which the latter was drawn up through the manhole to the pontoon abreast the ship. On emerging from the bulges Oliver was a very bad colour and suffering to some extent from the poisonous gases in the bulge compartments. Although a smoke-helmet provides a considerable degree of protection, it was obvious that any displacement would be attended by serious results, and further, having regard to the difficulty in passing Oliver through the manholes when equipped with the helmet, it was quite clear that his quick withdrawal in the event of being overcome was a matter of considerable conjecture, and the delay thus involved might have been attended with fatal results. (2.8.28)

ALBERT ERNEST RICHARDS On the 25th September 1928 blasting operations were in progress for the removal of rock on a site at St. Helena under the charge of No. Ply/14700 Sgt. Stewart Symons. Four charges had been laid, two in drilled holes and two in crevices in the rock. The drilled-hole fuses were each to be lit by a marine and the crevice fuses by Sgt. Symons. The hole fuses and the upper crevice fuse were lit simultaneously, and the sergeant was bending down to light the lower crevice fuse when the charge in the upper crevice exploded unexpectedly, blinding Sgt. Symons and knocking him helpless close to one of the drilled holes. The marines who had lit the other fuses had by this time run clear, but Marine Richards, seeing that the sergeant was disabled, turned back and helped him to his feet and dragged him clear of the subsequent explosions, from the effects of which he shielded him with his own body.

Marine Richards was well aware that at least two further charges were due to explode within some thirty seconds, and his presence of mind and disregard of personal danger undoubtedly saved Sgt. Symons from death. (10.4.29)

ALEXANDER HENRY MAXWELL-HYSLOP
ALBERT EDWARD STREAMS

H.M.S. *Devonshire* was carrying out full calibre firing on 26th July 1929, when at the first salvo there was a heavy explosion which blew off the roof of one of the turrets.

Marine Streams was the only man in the gun-house who was not either killed instantly or fatally injured. He was seriously shaken by the explosion and instinctively climbed to the top of the side plating to escape, but on arriving at the top he looked back and saw the conditions inside the turret, and deliberately climbed back into it amidst the smoke and fumes notwithstanding the grave risk of further explosions. He then helped to evacuate the one remaining man of the right gun's crew, and took charge and played a major part in evacuating the crew of the Fire Control cabinet. When all the wounded were out he collapsed. His bravery, initiative, and devotion to duty were beyond praise.

Lt.-Commander Maxwell-Hyslop, R.N., was in the fore control when the explosion occurred, and immediately proceeded to the turret and climbed inside. He made a general examination of the turret and descended the gun-well through most dangerous conditions of fumes and smoke, necessitating the use of a life-line, remaining in the turret until the emergency was over, directing operations for the safety of the magazine, and supervising the evacuation of the wounded. He was fully aware of the danger to himself from the results of cordite fumes, and the grave risk of further explosions.

At the time this officer and man entered the turret the fire produced by the explosion was still burning and it was impossible to estimate the real state of affairs due to the heavy smoke. They both were fully aware that there were other cordite charges in the hoist and handing room below which might ignite at any moment with almost certain fatal results to themselves, and they deliberately endangered their own lives to save the lives of others. (11.11.29)

PATRICK HENRY WILLIS   On the 9th June 1931 H.M. Submarine *Poseidon* collided with a merchant ship and eventually sank as a result of the severe damage sustained.

After the collision occurred and the order 'Close watertight doors' had been given, Petty Officer Willis took charge of the hands in the fore part, calling upon them to close the door of the torpedo compartment with those inside, as this step might mean the saving of the submarine. The operation was difficult, as the bulkhead had buckled, but by their united efforts the door was eventually closed, leaving only a slight leak. Whilst this work was in progress the ship lurched to starboard and sank with heavy inclination by the bows. The electric light leads were all cut at the moment of the collision, and from that time until the final evacuation the imprisoned men were working with the occasional illumination of an electric torch. Willis first said prayers for himself and his companions and then ordered them to put on their escape apparatus, making sure that they all knew how to use it. He then explained he was going to flood the compartment in order to equalize the pressure with that outside the submarine, and how it was to be done, telling off each man to his station. He also rigged up a wire hawser across the hatchway to form a support for men to stand on whilst the compartment was flooding. During the long period of waiting that ensued Willis kept his companions in good heart, while one able seaman passed the time in instructing a Chinese boy in the use of his apparatus. The other men worked cheerfully at the various valves and rigging the platform. After two hours and ten minutes, when the water was about up to the men's knees, Willis considered the pressure might be sufficient to open the hatch. With considerable difficulty the hatch was opened sufficiently to release two men, but the pressure then reclosed the hatch, and it was necessary to make the pressure more equal by further flooding before a second attempt could be made. After another hour, by which time the men in the compartment were nearly up to their necks in water and the air-lock was becoming very small, a second effort was made. This was successful and the hatch opened, and four other men came to the surface, including Petty Officer Willis.

It is abundantly clear that all the men imprisoned in the slowly flooding compartment, in almost total darkness, faced a situation more than desperate with courage and fortitude in accordance with the very highest traditions of the Service. The coolness, confidence, ability, and power of command shown by Petty Officer Willis, which no doubt were principally responsible for the saving of so many valuable lives, are deserving of the very highest praise. (24.7.31)

B. G. SCURFIELD   On the 13th May 1937 H.M.S. *Hunter* sustained serious damage in an explosion off Almería, Spain. Immediately the ship took on a heavy list, all lights were extinguished, and there was no steam. Apparently she was about to sink.

Lt.-Commander Scurfield, who was aft, rushed forward. Passing the galley he heard cries from Petty Officer Cook, who had fallen into the boiler-room. He jumped down through the smoke, oil fuel, steam, and debris, and by extraordinary feats of strength removed the wreckage pinning the man down. The rating was passed up on deck but did not long survive.

Lt.-Commander Scurfield then proceeded to the Torpedo-men's mess deck. This was flooded to a depth of $2\frac{1}{2}$ feet in oil fuel; also battery gas had escaped from the switchboard room. The ladder having been blown away, he jumped down into the mess deck, not knowing whether it was intact, and passed up two men. Calling for assistance, he was joined by Lt. Humphreys and A.B.s Collins, Thomas, and Abrahams.

After the mess deck had been cleared, he led the party into the Stoker Petty Officers' mess. The bulkhead had been shattered, and bedding and curtains were smouldering on top of the oil fuel. Bodies were pulled out from under the wreckage, and passed up on deck.

During the whole of this time, he might in the darkness have fallen into the oil-fuel tanks below or into the sea. By his gallant behaviour he saved five lives. (30.6.37)

CHAPTER XVIII

AWARDS OF THE ALBERT MEDAL FOR SEA SERVICE TO CIVILIANS
1866–1938

> Envy—ah! even to tears!—
> The fortune of their years
> Which, though so fair, yet so divinely ended.
>
> Scarce had they lifted up
> Life's full and fiery cup,
> Than they had set it down untouched before them.
> Before their day arose
> They beckoned it to close—
> Close in confusion and destruction o'er them.
>
> They did not stay to ask
> What prize should crown their task,
> Well sure that prize was such as no man strives for,
> But pressed into eclipse
>
> RUDYARD KIPLING, *The Queen's Men*.

WE have dealt in Chapter VIII with the circumstances in which the Albert Medal was first instituted—for services at sea only. It overlapped in scope the Board of Trade Medal for Sea Gallantry which, though it had been in existence for ten years, seems to have been ignored by Her Majesty's confidential advisers. It was from the first very sparingly awarded. Excluding the decade 1910–19, which covers the period of the Great War, awards of the Albert Medal for Sea Service from 1866 to the end of 1938 total 82; for Land Service 100. There is no record of the award of an Albert Medal in gold awarded to a civilian for Sea Service; yet the deeds recorded in this chapter constitute a record of heroism which few can read without a stirring of the pulse. Certainly no one can lay it down without experiencing at least a momentary feeling of exultation and of vicarious pride in the exploits of humble men, leading obscure lives, who, at a supreme moment, attained epic heights of selflessness which owed nothing to the excitement of battle and seldom anything to instinctive impulse. The Roll of Honour is long, for it covers three-quarters of a century; yet it includes but a tiny fraction of the heroic deeds performed at sea by subjects of Queen Victoria and her successors during that period, for, in the words of Ecclesiasticus (xliv. 9 sqq.):

'Some there be, which have no memorial; who are perished, as though they had never been; . . . But these were merciful men, whose righteousness hath not been forgotten. With their seed shall continually remain a good inheritance and their children are within the covenant.'

We of this generation are in a very real sense their children. In this record of the deeds of our forefathers and our contemporaries, men of our own flesh and blood, we are entitled to proclaim, in the words of Swinburne, that 'all our past proclaims our future'. The record is continuous, and if fewer awards have been made of recent years the cause is not only lack of worthy occasions, but the adoption in recent years of an artificial standard, not justified by the terms of the Royal Warrant (see p. 87), and perhaps to some lack of official interest in the matter.

The Order of the Garter, the Thistle, or of St. Patrick alone compare in rarity of award with the Albert Medal for Sea Service or, indeed, with the Albert Medals both for Sea and Land Service. The awards here summarized from *The London Gazette*, the date of which is shown in parentheses at the end of each entry, total 109 for a period (including the Great War) of 71 years, the first award being in 1867.

Awards of the Albert Medal of the first class, or in gold, are rarer than the Garter itself. The total number of awards in gold since 1866 is only 36, and none of them are for Sea Service other than a few awarded to naval officers or ratings. Another striking thing in this record is the inclusion therein of rescues of men of all nations, not only by men of British birth, but by foreigners serving on British ships. Space forbids the inclusion of a chapter devoted to gallant rescues of British subjects and ships by foreigners duly recognized by the award of the Board of Trade Medal for Foreign Services. It would constitute a record no less stirring.

The British Seamen's Union, alone of all Unions, voluntarily assumed, on the outbreak of war, some responsibility for the care of German seamen who, on the outbreak of war in August 1914, were arrested as a preliminary to internment.

With the funds of the Union the Secretary, Havelock Wilson, purchased Eastcote House, once the property of the Duke of Grafton, seven miles from Northampton, and took over some hundreds of Germans, many of whom had served for twenty years or more on British articles, and had wives and families in this country.

The Seamen's Union paid the whole cost of equipping the place for 900 men, receiving from Government only 10s. a week per head for food. It was an honest attempt at international goodwill—but it failed in circumstances, explained in *Seamen's Torch, The Life Story of Captain Edward Tupper*,[1] wholly creditable to the Union. They

[1] Hutchinson, 1938.

wanted to maintain the unwritten code of chivalry at sea, which this and the following chapter illustrate. The Germans abandoned it deliberately.

The Merchant Shipping Acts then provided but niggardly treatment for shipwrecked seamen. Pay stopped from the date of the wreck; in the case of ships under Charter to the Admiralty during the War shipwrecked men were given the fare to their home ports, and pay till their arrival home, or for a fortnight, whichever should be the shorter period.[1] Few shipowners made even this small concession until compelled to do so in 1917, and in those days seamen were not covered by the Unemployment or Health Insurance Acts.

'Mined and torpedoed men had to find their way home as best they could, from the sea, from open boats, from their port of landing—without pay from the day they met the disaster which robbed them of their belongings. It meant arriving home with a miserable balance of pay on which they and their dependants had to live until they were away at sea again.'[2]

Those men who were members of the Seamen's Union could insure their kit up to a maximum of £5—at their own cost, which meant that most of our men went to sea in war-time with insufficient gear to combat weather; carpenters, who lost their tool-chests, suffered particularly. Shipowners had special facilities to insure their ships and shippers their cargo, 80 per cent. being borne by the nation. Officers and seamen on ships chartered to Government were covered for loss of effects without payment of any premium; officers and seamen on other ships could insure through the shipping office at which articles were signed, at a premium much below usual rates, but with pre-War wages many merchant seamen had not the money to pay even a small premium.

A seaman's widow could look forward to a maximum pension of 12s. 4d. a week—only a small proportion of which was borne by shipowners, the mass of whom stood to the letter of the law and paid no more to their men, or to dependants, than the Statute required, though there were honourable exceptions.

Twenty thousand merchant seamen lost their lives while serving their country under such conditions. These pages afford the best insight into the character of the men who in fair and foul weather, in good and bad quarters, on great liners or in small craft, pursue a calling as essential to the daily life of this country as that of the miner, with whom and with the farm worker they have one thing in common—their work is worse paid on the average than that in any 'sheltered' industry.

[1] Since 1926 a wrecked seaman is normally entitled to two months' wages after the loss of his ship. [2] *Seamen's Torch*, p. 120.

The perils peculiar to sailing craft are matters of history; they have given place to risks, not less dreadful to contemplate, of agonizing death in the boiler- and engine-rooms. In tropical waters the shark is an ever present peril to the man who falls overboard and to his rescuers. But the spirit of man is dauntless, and, as these pages show, seldom fails to rise to the height of each new emergency.

A Man of Devon

SAMUEL POPPLESTONE, Farmer, Start Farm, Devon

The *Spirit of the Ocean*, a barque of 557 tons, with a crew of 18 and 24 passengers, was wrecked on the rocks 400 yards west of Start Point, Devon, on 23rd March 1866. The mate and one of the crew were saved by Samuel Popplestone, unaided and at the imminent risk of his own life, in the following circumstances:

The vessel, with a part of her crew sick, and the mates and passengers assisting in working her, was caught in a strong gale from the south-west. On 23rd March she was off the Start in a very dangerous position. Mr. Popplestone saw that, if she failed to weather the rocks, she must be lost with all hands failing assistance from the shore. He sent a man on one of his own horses to Tor Cross, to rouse the villagers, and another to tell the coast-guard. The vessel had by this time struck on the rocks and was breaking up.

Mr. Popplestone took a small coil of rope, and went alone over the shore from rock to rock, until he got near to the vessel. The wind was nearly equal to a hurricane; it was raining, and the sea was very heavy and dangerous. As he stood on the rock nearest to the vessel, he was washed off, but by the help of a returning sea regained his footing, and saved the lives of two persons. (12.6.66)

The wreck of a Pilgrim Ship near Bombay

SAMUEL LAKE, Bombay Reclamation Company's Works
W. H. MILLETT, Third Officer, P.&O. Company's S.S. Emeu

The *Diamond*, of Calcutta, from Jeddah for Calcutta, having on board the master, his wife, the mate, and another European, a crew of 47 Lascars, about 400 pilgrims, and a cargo of salt, met bad weather and, being dismasted, bore up for Bombay. On 20th June 1866 she was seen passing the Bombay lighthouse, but as it was blowing heavily, assistance could not be given and she drifted on to the rocks at Breach Candy, which were exposed to the full force of the south-west monsoon.

Attempts to render assistance were not at first successful; but on the two following days, by the unceasing exertions of rescuers, all those who remained on board (some having jumped overboard and swum ashore, or reached it by means of spars, &c., and some having lost their lives in the attempt) were, with much difficulty and danger, safely landed.

Amongst many who did much to help, two gentlemen, Messrs. S. Lake, of the Bombay Reclamation Company's Works, and W. H. Millett, Third Officer on board the P. & O. Co.'s S.S. *Emeu*, displayed conspicuous gallantry. Mr. Lake commanded the first boat that put off to the wreck on the 20th June. It was capsized, but the crew were saved by clinging to her. He was also one of the crew of another boat which made an attempt to board the wreck next day; it became waterlogged and unmanageable, and was driven on shore. It was at once repaired and Mr. Lake this time took her alongside the wreck, which he boarded, and thereupon assisted the almost helpless passengers into the boats. When night fell, he swam ashore, returning at daybreak in a surf-boat, and remained for some hours until all passengers had left the wreck.

Mr. Millett was in command of a lifeboat sent overland to the scene of the wreck by the Supt. of the P. & O. Co., at Bombay. Upon her arrival on the 21st June Mr. Millett, with Mr. H. B. Greaves, the Company's Deckmaster, and twelve Chinamen, went alongside, and in two trips brought ashore some of the passengers. Next day he made seven trips, and safely landed 120 people.

The sea was very heavy throughout, and the boat was continually filled with water. Twice Mr. Millett was washed out of the boat, and was with difficulty saved, but persevered till the last passenger was landed. (4.6.67)

A Wreck at Dymchurch

REV. CHARLES COBB, *Rector of Dymchurch*
JOHN BATIST, *Boatman, Dymchurch Coast-guard Station*

The French lugger *Courier de Dieppe*, 59 tons, with a crew of four persons in all, drove ashore at Dymchurch on the morning of 6th January 1867. On the evening of 5th January a strong gale arose, and the vessel was found to be off the English coast. Failing to get assistance, the master ran the vessel ashore. Attempts made to reach her by mortar apparatus were unsuccessful; the master, a cabin boy, and a seaman were washed overboard and drowned.

Soon the vessel parted, and the portion upon which the mate, the only survivor of the crew, had taken refuge, was driven within 50 or 60 feet of the shore.

John Batist, clad in a cork jacket, attempted to reach the vessel with a line but failed and was dragged ashore. The Rev. C. Cobb then entered the water, made for the bulwarks of the vessel and, after one or two attempts, reached a survivor who was in the rigging. Batist followed carrying a line with which the French sailor was dragged ashore, supported by Mr. Cobb and Batist. Mr. Cobb made this attempt in spite of the remonstrances of the people on the spot, and declined their assistance by refusing to take a line with him.

Gallantry at Kinsale Head

JOHN DONOVAN, Chief Boatman, Old Head Coast-guard Station, Kinsale

The Italian barque *Thetis*, 324 tons, with a crew of eleven, became embayed in Courtmacsherry Bay during a gale on 30th November 1866. She had anchored in a dangerous position surrounded by reefs, and had cut away her masts when she was observed by the coast-guard and fishermen on shore.

John Donovan, Chief Boatman in charge of the Old Head Coast-guard Station, Kinsale, endeavoured to prevail upon the fishermen, who lined the shore to the number of about 200, to launch one of their boats, well adapted for the service, and already on the strand, for the purpose of rendering assistance, but they refused.

Donovan then caused the coast-guard galley to be dragged across the land a distance of about $1\frac{1}{2}$ miles, and lowered over a perpendicular cliff about 50 feet in height. When this was done, he and four coast-guard men launched her and proceeded to the vessel. On getting alongside, the galley was capsized and partially stove, but by good management her crew, who had life-jackets on, got on board the barque, where they remained for some hours expecting that she would part her cables, owing to the heavy sea running and a gale blowing on shore. She, however, rode until the weather moderated, when the galley was repaired and the crews of the boat and vessel landed in her. (4.6.67)

CHARLES SPRANKLING, Chief Boatman, Burton Coast-guard Station

On the 11th June 1866 a fishing-boat containing five men ran for the beach at Burton. As she touched it, a heavy sea struck her and threw her upon the crew. Charles Sprankling, who was near by, managed, by great exertion and at some risk, to raise the side of the boat, which was washing backwards and forwards in a heavy surf, and thus freed three of the men.

The other two, who had been injured by the gear in the boat, drifted into deep water; Sprankling swam out and brought both in turn to land, apparently lifeless. He resuscitated them unaided and sent them to their homes. (4.6.67)

Two gallant men at Falmouth

JAMES HUDSON,
Apprentice, Maid of
Orleans, *Ardrossan*

THEOPHILUS JONES,
Falmouth

On the 17th March 1867 the *Marmion*, of North Shields, drove from her anchors and was stranded at Gylynvase, near Falmouth. The wind was blowing strong with squalls—the tide was first-quarter flood. At 10 a.m. the ship was in the midst of breakers, and often entirely covered with surf, and no communication with the shore appeared possible. The master and one of the crew died on board from exposure.

After an ineffectual attempt had been made to communicate with the shore by means of a line tied to a stool and flung overboard from the ship, James Hudson, an apprentice of 17 belonging to the *Maid of Orleans*, then lying at Falmouth, insisted on swimming off to the vessel; the coast-guards attached to him their life-lines and guided him afloat. He had neither jacket nor belt on. He was soon in the midst of a heavy sea, and in a short time got to the stern of the vessel, and after three attempts to reach the deck swung himself on board by the aid of a spar hanging over the side. The line attached to Hudson offered a communication between the ship and the shore, and six of the crew were thus rescued.

Hudson was compelled by his want of clothing to return when he had been about a quarter of an hour on board. His distress in returning was great. He expected to have been pulled on shore, but the running-gear had fouled and he was obliged to pull himself hand over hand along the hawser to the shore. He was very much exhausted, and without assistance would probably not have succeeded in landing himself upon the beach. There still remained one man alive on board, but he was too weak to fasten around himself the cork jacket with which he had been supplied. Theophilus Jones, who had a line but no jacket or belt on, threw himself into the sea, and after two or three attempts reached the vessel, and was lifted on board by the waves and by the aid of a spar.

He fastened a cork jacket round the seaman and pushed him overboard; this man, too, was saved. Jones was some time in the surf; he was very much benumbed and exhausted when he arrived on shore. (26.6.67)

A. T. SHUTTLEWORTH,
Deputy Conservator of Forests, Alibagh, Bombay

On the 22nd July 1866 the *Berwickshire* ran on Chaul Kadu Reef, near Alibagh. Mr. Shuttleworth went to her assistance in a fisherman's canoe and, after two days' exertions, succeeded in landing six men in one of the ship's boats. Mr.

Shuttleworth again proceeded to the ship, with the fishermen in another boat, in so dangerous a sea that some of the *Berwickshire*'s seamen, who had landed, and the coolies of Colaba, to whom a large reward was offered, declined to take a message to her. After rowing for three hours, the boat having twice filled to the thwarts, he reached the vessel and informed the captain of her true position and remained on board to give assistance.

On the 1st August 1866 the *Di Vernon* ran on the same reef. Mr. Shuttleworth put off in a boat with ten fishermen, and by his coolness averted a yet greater loss of life. The boat was dashed against the vessel's side and capsized, throwing all her crew into the water; while endeavouring to save some of these, Mr. Shuttleworth was washed overboard. He regained the vessel, and was for two hours lashed in the mizen rigging. He refused to forsake the captain and carpenter who were helpless, and saved the captain. The carpenter was drowned.

On the 18th July 1867 the ship *Terzah* was wrecked south-east of Kennery. Mr. Shuttleworth put off in a life-boat manned by fishermen and succeeded, in circumstances of great peril, in bringing off the captain and thirteen men out of a crew of thirty-one. Eight others came on shore on pieces of wreck. (21.12.67)

A gallant rescue on the coast of Mexico

JOHN RICKETT,
Able Seaman,
H.M.S. Clio

On the 24th May 1866, whilst H.M.S. *Clio* was lying at anchor off Ajiabampo (Mexico), a boy named Tom Walton fell from a stage outside the ship. He was sinking the third time when John Rickett jumped into the water, brought him to the surface, got him to the ship's cable, and there supported him for 10 or 15 minutes, when the ship's boat reached them.

The sea was heavy, and the port infested with sharks; just as the ship's boat came up Rickett, who was at the time still weak from a fever, relaxed his hold of the cable, and himself dropped into the water, from which he was picked up just in time to save his life. (21.12.67)

'*Let not England forget her precedence of teaching nations how to live*'[1]

A gallant Vice-Consul at San Sebastian

EDWARD B. MARCH,
British Vice-Consul,
San Sebastian

On the night of 7th December 1867 the French ship *Nouveau Caboteur* was cast on shore in the Bay of Zurriola on the north coast of Spain, during a gale of wind. The sea at the time was running so heavily that no boat would venture to put off.

[1] Milton, *To the Parliament of England*, 1643.

There was also a general belief that it was impossible for a boat to be of any service.

Mr. E. B. March, after unsuccessfully entreating some of the bystanders to accompany him, plunged into the sea, swam to the vessel, and succeeded in bringing a rope to land. The rope was then secured and one of the crew came safely to shore along it. The second, however (a lad), lost his hold, dropped into the sea, and sank. Mr. March, though benumbed with cold, at the greatest personal risk again swam to the vessel, dived under her keel, recovered the lad, and brought him safe to land. The remainder of the crew (six men in all) got safely to land.

Mr. March was for a time completely prostrated, but by care and attention was unexpectedly restored. (27.2.68)

A naval officer rescues an able seaman in the Congo

LIONEL AUDROZ DE SAUSMAREZ
Sub-Lieutenant, H.M.S.
Myrmidon

At about 10.30 p.m. on the 1st June 1868, while H.M.S. *Myrmidon* was lying in Banana Creek, River Congo, West Africa, William Torrance, an able seaman, fell overboard.

Mr. de Sausmarez was on watch, and although a strong current was running at the time, and the river infested with sharks, he jumped overboard, secured Torrance (who could not swim), swam with him to the pier, and supported him there until assistance came. (16.11.68)

Gallantry on the Kincardineshire coast

JAMES CROYDEN,
Chief Officer, 2nd Class,
Coast-guard Station,
Muchals

The schooner *Kinloss* was wrecked at Scatraw Creek, 1½ miles from Muchals, south of Aberdeen, on the coast of Kincardineshire, on the 21st December 1868.

Mr. James Crowden, the Chief Officer at Muchals Station, went to the spot and found the ship breaking up fast. The fishermen of the place had succeeded in getting a rope from the vessel, by which it was hoped that the lives of those on board would be saved.

Mr. Crowden ventured on to a rocky point and tried to fasten a lifebelt to the rope in order to send it out to the ship, but without success, being several times washed off into the sea. Once a heavy sea swept him off and carried him about 100 yards towards the wreck, and it was thought that he was lost; but after a few minutes' struggling he was carried round a point by a violent run of the sea, and thrown upon the rocks with such violence, however, that he was badly hurt and became insensible.

When he recovered his senses he succeeded in getting a coble launched in a very heavy sea and was the first to jump into it. He and his four men hauled off to the ship by the rope, took four men from the mast and brought them ashore.

On being informed that there was still another man on board Mr. Crowden and his crew hauled off again to the wreck, but the man was dead or dying, and could not be got at.

Mr. Crowden was fourteen days upon the sick-list in consequence of the injuries received by him.

This was the fourth time that Mr. Crowden had been instrumental in saving life from shipwreck, and, including the present instance, he had aided in the rescue of thirteen lives. (16.4.69)

A soldier rescued at Alexandria

JAMES BEAUTINE WILLOUGHBY, *Captain, Royal Navy, Principal Transport Officer in Egypt*

On the 3rd March 1869, whilst the 1st Battalion of the 21st Regiment was disembarking at Alexandria, one of the soldiers, who was fully accoutred, fell overboard in a fit and sank.

Capt. Willoughby at once dived and got hold of him and, after considerable difficulty, brought him out of the water.

The harbour was infested with sharks; but Capt. Willoughby, moreover, ran great risk from the fact that the soldier fell between the pier and the vessel and, owing to the swell in the harbour, both Capt. Willoughby and the soldier might have been crushed. (22.7.69)

Heroism of coastguardsmen on the cornish Coast

WILLIAM SIMPSON, *R.N., late Chief Boatman in charge of the Coast-guard Station, Bude, Cornwall*

During a heavy gale on the 13th September 1869, the ship *Avonmore* was wrecked near Bude. The Second Officer and six other members of the crew were drowned.

Wm. Simpson took the rocket apparatus from Bude and with it saved nine of the crew, but six men still lay jammed amongst the debris on the wreck, one of them with a broken limb.

Although the ship was expected to break up at any moment, Simpson determined to reach the deck himself if possible by means of the gear. When being hauled to the wreck the line became fast in the block and the gear was for a time rendered useless. Simpson was hauled through the water under the stern of the ship amongst floating wreck, and at great risk succeeded in reaching the deck unaided.

The ship was on her beam ends, masts had gone by the board, the decks were swept by the sea, and the leeside was under water. When on board the wreck Simpson saw that the gear, which had become choked by drift oakum, must at once be cleared. He did so with his teeth whilst he held on to the wreck with his hands.

When the rocket gear was restored to working order and got clear of all obstacles, four other volunteers were hauled on board from the shore to assist; under Simpson's direction the injured man was extricated from the debris, and the six remaining members of the crew saved. Simpson was the last to leave the wreck. (7.2.70)

Heroism at Karachi

EDWARD GILES, Captain, Indian Navy, Master Attendant, Karachi

The barque *Alicia*, of Greenock, was driven upon the bar of Karachi Harbour on the 20th June 1868 in very heavy weather, and at the height of a south-west monsoon. The sea at once washed boats and everything else from the ship's decks, and obliging the crew to take to the mizen rigging.

Capt. Giles, the Master Attendant, and Mr. Robert Henry Mason, Senior Pilot, made attempts to reach the stranded vessel in two boats, 25 feet long, fitted as life-boats and manned by natives.

Capt. Giles's boat on entering the breakers was swept back half-filled, but was carried into comparatively smooth water. By great exertion, however, he brought her within 50 feet of the vessel, the confused mass of surging wreck threatening instant destruction if he approached nearer.

The shipwrecked crew were at first too frightened to attempt to leave their vessel, but eventually, upon a light line being successfully flung on board of her, two seamen and the pilot hauled themselves by means of it through the water, and were got into the boat. The boat up to this time had been kept clear by bailing, but now, being half-filled by a heavy sea which struck her, was compelled at once to return, and the three men were transferred to another boat waiting in smooth water.

A little before sunset Capt. Giles was again by the wreck, passing through the midst of broken spars and all kinds of wreckage. Having rescued six more men, he was taking them ashore when a wave rolled over the boat and filled her, breaking her rudder and six oars, and sweeping three of her crew overboard. The following roller fortunately carried these men into smooth water, where they were picked up.

Both the station life-boats were now disabled; but as some of the crew still remained on board the *Alicia* Capt. Giles determined upon a further attempt in the boat of the tug *Dagmar*. This boat was fitted with cork floats but was heavy. After great exertion the wreck was reached, and the remaining men, with the exception of the master, were got into the boat, when she was carried away half-filled.

The master of the *Alicia*, who had jumped overboard with a plank, was carried in the direction of the waiting boats and ultimately picked up.

The Commissioner of Sind bore testimony to the conspicuous bravery of Capt. Giles in thus rescuing fourteen persons during a strong gale of wind and in a very high sea, over a period of three hours, at any moment of which the boats in the surf ran risk of being swamped. (30.11.70)

Naval officer rescues ship's boy

WILLIAM BALFOUR FORBES,
Lieutenant R.N., H.M.S. Rapid

On the night of 17th September 1870 a boy fell from the main yard-arm of H.M.S. *Rapid*, proceeding from Tarragona to Gibraltar, and in his fall struck his head against the gunwale of one of the boats.

Forbes at once jumped overboard, seized the unconscious boy, and held him up. When the ship's boat reached them he was quite exhausted and, with the boy, was under water. Had the boat arrived a minute later both would have been drowned. (7.3.71)

British heroism in Formosa

AUGUSTUS RAYMOND MARGARY,
Assistant, H.M. Consular Service, China
JOHN DODD,
British Merchant, Ke-lung, Formosa

During a very violent typhoon, which burst over the north coast of Formosa on the 9th August 1871, the schooner *Anne*, of Hong Kong, and the French barque *Adèle* were amongst the vessels blown from their anchorage and driven on the rocky shore of Ke-lung Harbour. The night was dark, with blinding rain, and great quantities of wreckage were floating in the water and being washed ashore in the surf, but, by the aid of the brilliant light of burning camphor, the position of the ships was made out from the shore.

Mr. Augustus Raymond Margary and Mr. John Dodd had ropes fastened to them and went into the surf to aid the crew of the *Anne*, the nearest ship that could be discerned. They waded and then swam a distance of some 30 or 40 yards through the surf. The rope proving to be too short, they threw it off and reached the ship by swimming. They then tried to reach the shore with a rope from the ship and, after making an unsuccessful effort to do this, persuaded two volunteers to lower a small boat in which Messrs. Margary and Dodd tried to row back with a rope. Their efforts were frustrated. The boat was turned completely over and Mr. Margary was for a few moments underneath her. They were, however, thrown bruised on shore. The ship was rocking violently from side to side when they left her, but by the advice of the Captain, who then appeared confident of his ship, they desisted from further efforts as there were more distressing cases calling for assistance farther off. Timber was strewn on the beach and was beating amongst the rocks in such a way that little hope could be entertained of any living thing yet remaining; but an occasional wail of the sufferers in the sea induced Messrs. Margary and Dodd to persevere for several hours. They then with difficulty, effort, and danger, and in the dark, crawled over rugged sandstone rocks, amidst breakers and wreck, until they got close to the remains of the *Adèle*, and by swimming they were able to get a rope to her.

Mr. Dodd swam to seize the buoy which the Frenchmen threw over, while Mr. Margary swam to meet him with the shore rope. They joined the two and immediately gained the shattered deck. With the aid of the rope the greater part of the crew passed safely to shore, when Mr. Dodd and Mr. Margary discovered the boatswain lying half under water, with a broken leg. They raised him and carried him on shore by swimming. They then made repeated efforts to cross the broken back of the ship, to save four helpless men there. They succeeded in the end, but were both washed down by a heavy sea, which caused much injury to Mr. Dodd.

The last thing which left the ship was a black cat which clung to Mr. Margary's shoulder in spite of the heavy surf. When they left the ship she was actually breaking up beneath their feet. (28.10.72)

One man's courage saves a boat's crew from murder and annihilation

DAVID WEBSTER, *late Second Mate, barque* Arracan, *Broughty Ferry*

Whilst the barque *Arracan* was on a voyage from Shields to Bombay, her cargo of coal took fire from spontaneous combustion, and on the 17th February was abandoned by her crew, who took to boats and endeavoured to make for the Maldive Islands. The boats kept company till the 20th, when, finding the currents too strong, it was agreed to separate after dividing the provisions. The master in command of the long-boat then made for Cochin, the mate in charge of the gig, and the second mate, Mr. David Webster, in charge of the pinnace with four of the crew, viz. three men and one boy, made for the Maldive Islands.

After two days Mr. David Webster's boat was injured by a heavy sea and could not keep up with the gig, and lost sight of her. From this time the pinnace was kept working to windward until the 9th March, by which day the provisions and water had been consumed.

Shortly afterwards the crew cast lots to decide who should be first killed to be eaten, and the lot fell upon the ship's boy Horner, but Webster, who had been asleep, awoke in time to save the boy's life. After dark an attempt was made to kill Webster himself, but the boy

Horner awoke him in time. On the following day Webster fell asleep, but was awakened by the struggles of the crew for the possession of his gun, with which to shoot him. Two hours later the crew attempted to take Horner's life again, but were prevented by the determined conduct of Webster, who threatened to shoot and throw overboard the first man who laid hands on the boy.

The next day one of the crew attempted to sink the boat, but Webster mastered him and prevented further mischief. Two days later the same member of the crew again tried to sink the boat, and expressed his determination to take the boy's life. For this he would have been shot by Webster had not the cap on the gun missed fire. Putting a fresh cap on his gun, Webster shot a bird which flew over the boat soon after. It was at once seized and devoured by the crew, even to the bones and feathers. During the next five days the crew were quieter, subsisting on barnacles which attached themselves to the bottom of the boat and on sea blubber for which they dived. Next day some of the men became delirious. One of them lay down exhausted, when another struck him several blows on the head with an iron belaying-pin, cutting him badly. The blood which flowed was caught in a tin and drunk by the man himself and two other men. Afterwards they fought and hit one another, and only left off when completely exhausted, to recommence as soon as they were able; the boy Horner during the time keeping watch with Webster.

On the 31st day in the boat they were picked up 600 miles from land by the *City of Manchester*, Hardie, master, by whom they were brought to Calcutta. Webster by his conduct was the means of saving the lives of all in the boat. (10.7.74)

Naval officer rescues ship's corporal

THE HON. FRANCIS ROBERT SANDILANDS, Lieutenant, H.M.S. Audacious

At 1 a.m. on the 1st January 1875, the ship being under steam, in the Indian Ocean off the Arabian coast, it being at the time dark, and the weather fine and clear, Frederick Cowd, ship's corporal of the 1st class, fell overboard from the top-gallant forecastle, and passed aft, apparently unable to help himself.

Sandilands, who had had the first watch and was at the time on the bridge in conversation with the officer of the middle watch, sprang after him, swam to him, and kept him above water. Owing to part of the slipping apparatus having been carried away, some delay was occasioned in getting the life-boat clear of the slings, but Lt. Sandilands never ceased his efforts to keep the man above water. Both were eventually picked up, the ship's corporal being insensible, and dying soon after being got on board the ship. Lt. Sandilands was unable to reach the lifebuoys which had been let go, and he supported the man in the water from 12 to 18 minutes, never quitting him until he was taken into the boat. (14.3.75)

A gallant deed at Stanley Harbour in Falkland Islands

ALFRED CARPENTER, *Lieutenant, H.M.S. Challenger* At 10.30 p.m. on the 31st January 1876 while the *Challenger* was at anchor in Stanley Harbour, Falkland Islands, in five fathoms of water, distant a quarter of a mile from the shore, Thomas Bush, an able seaman, fell overboard from the steam pinnace, which was coming alongside, and sank without uttering a cry. The night was dark, the weather boisterous and raining; there was a short chopping sea (which rendered swimming extremely difficult) and an outsetting current.

Lt. Carpenter jumped from the gangway and swam towards the spot where the man disappeared, which was some 20 feet from the ship, and touched him with his feet under water. He then dived, seized hold of Bush, and brought him to the surface, and supported him from 3 to 5 minutes; but Bush, being a very heavy man, and encumbered with thick waterproof clothing and, moreover, being quite insensible, Lt. Carpenter, as he got exhausted with his exertions, was obliged to let him slip down. He supported him with his legs for a few moments, and then they were both hauled into the pinnace, and taken on board. When picked up, they were between 40 and 50 yards from the ship's stern, which distance they were drifted by the current and wind. Every effort was at once made by the medical officers to restore Bush, but without success.

There were several patches of floating kelp round the ship, amongst which the strongest swimmer would be helpless, which materially increased the risk incurred.

From the unusual and strange fact that the man was not seen from the time of his falling overboard until brought to the surface by Lt. Carpenter, no boat but for his prompt action could have attempted to save the man with any chance of success. (20.6.76)

A Peterhead man saves six lives

JOHN SKELTON SUMMERS, *Master, Fishing-boat Flying Scud of Peterhead* On the 3rd August 1876 Summers was riding by his nets, 35 miles ESE. from Buchan-ness, and broke adrift about noon in the height of a violent gale, with a dangerous cross-sea running accompanied by heavy rain. About 15 minutes after getting his close-reefed foresail set, to make for the land, he observed a boat on his weather bow, about a quarter of a mile off, with sail down and making signals of distress. He hauled up for her at once and, on nearing, observed she was swamped, and her mast lying to leeward at an angle of about 45°, rendering great caution necessary in approaching her, for fear of carrying away his own mast as she rolled so heavily in the trough of the sea.

At the first sweep, close on her port quarter, Summers picked off two men with lines; but he had to wear round and come up to her again five times before he succeeded in getting off the third man; nothing daunted, he repeated his manœuvre nearly twenty times before he got off the last man, who was the master and much exhausted.

Summers first observed the distressed vessel at about 12.30 and it was 4 p.m. before the last man was dragged on board. In consequence of the violence of the gale he did not reach Peterhead until 4 next morning.

The total number of men rescued was six; and there is little doubt that this could not have been effected if Summers had not displayed great coolness and intrepidity, combined with very skilful handling of his boat.
(14.11.76)

A gallant resuce off Cape Horn

ERNEST WILLIAM OWENS, *Second Mate of the* Com-*padre of Liverpool*

On the morning of the 28th August 1875, the *Compadre* being off Cape Horn, in a very severe gale, a heavy sea struck the ship and washed overboard Duncan McKay, an apprentice. Mr. Owens, seeing McKay in the sea bleeding and fainting, immediately jumped overboard to his assistance, notwithstanding that he was very heavily clothed, and had on his oilskins and sea boots.

A rope was thrown to them from the ship, which Mr. Owens caught with his right hand, and wound round McKay's body, which he was supporting with his left hand. His hands, however, were so benumbed with cold that he could not make the rope fast, but winding it several times round his own wrist, he held on to it with all his power. Difficulty was experienced in getting them on board, as McKay was quite helpless, and both wore oilskins and sea boots, besides heavy clothing which was saturated with water. After several efforts they were taken on board, having been in the water about 15 to 20 minutes.
(29.12.76)

Gallantry of a Naval Officer

ROBERT JAMES ARCHIBALD MONTGOMERIE *Acting Sub-Lieutenant,* H.M.S. Immortalité

At 3.10 on the morning of the 6th April 1877, the *Immortalité* being under all plain sail, moving 4½ knots with the wind, the port gangway look-out reported a man overboard. Mr. Montgomerie, who was on the bridge, working at the chart table, ran over to the lee-side, and jumped after him. He made for Hocken, asking him if he could swim; Hocken replied 'Yes, Sir,' but did not seem to be moving vigorously. Mr. Montgomerie then got hold of him, hauled him on to his back, and towed him to where he (Montgomerie) supposed the lifebuoy would be, but seeing no relief he told Hocken to keep himself afloat while he took his clothes off. While he was in the act of doing so Hocken, evidently sinking, caught hold of him by the legs, and dragged him down a considerable depth. Mr. Montgomerie, however, succeeded in getting clear and swam to the surface, bringing the drowning man with him. Hocken was now insensible and too great a weight to support any longer; and finding that his only chance of saving himself was to leave Hocken, Mr. Montgomerie reluctantly gave up the hope of saving him and struck out for the ship. In the meantime the ship's course was stopped and two boats were lowered, by one of which Mr. Montgomerie was picked up. The sea was shark-infested, and sufficiently disturbed to render small objects, even boats, difficult to discern. Had not Mr. Montgomerie been a most powerful swimmer he would have had little chance of life. (15.6.77)

Heroism in tidal waves and earthquakes off Chile

JOHN MITCHELL, *Carpenter*
WILLIAM STEWART, *Sailmaker*
CHARLES WILSON, *A.B.*, *all seamen of the* Conference, *of Bristol*

On the 9th May 1877, the *Conference*, the *Avonmore*, and 25 or 30 other vessels were lying at anchor off Huanillos (Chile), loading guano. The village itself stands on a ledge of the mountains, about 30 feet above sea-level; the mountains rise precipitously to a height of 5,000 feet. Capt. George Williams,[1] the late Master of the *Conference*, reported that at about 8.30 p.m., the weather being dark and gloomy, with a calm sea, a severe shock of an earthquake was felt. The ship trembled so much that the masts and yards seemed to be coming down, and the stern-moorings parted. The noise of the earthquake as it shook the mountains was very great. Large boulders were rolled down the side of the mountains and striking against each other emitted sparks of fire, while the cries of the guano-diggers on the mountains, who were in danger of their lives, increased the terror of the scene. The earthquake was followed by three distinct tidal waves, which rolled in from seawards at intervals of about 10 minutes, rising about 50 feet as seen by the marks on the shore, causing many vessels to break their moorings or drag their anchors, and submerging the

[1] The Board of Trade recognized the great bravery and presence of mind shown by Capt. Williams, of the *Conference*, by a gift of plate.

village of Huanillos. The first tidal wave drove two vessels across the bows of the *Conference* and carried away her bowsprit and jib-boom. The second tidal wave carried away her starboard bower-chains; and at the same time the American vessel *Geneva* was driven against the fore-rigging of the *Conference*, damaging her severely. She then commenced to drift towards the rocks. The *Geneva* was then carried back, and again driven against the *Conference*, cutting the latter down amidships, four or five planks below the covering-board. The *Avonmore* was seen for a moment as she was driven at a furious rate across the bows of the *Conference*. Almost immediately her anchor-light disappeared, and the cries of drowning people were heard. At this moment, when 'everything was calculated to destroy the strongest nerves', when ships out of control were ranging about in all directions, the sea confused and turbulent, and the *Conference* herself badly damaged, the Master called for volunteers from his crew to man the jolly-boat. John Mitchell, William Stewart, and Charles Wilson volunteered and rowed into a darkness so great that objects at only a ship's-length distance were invisible, and after some time found and rescued the master of the *Avonmore* with his child, the second and third officers, and an A.B. Fortunately there was no further tidal wave, and when the boat returned to the *Conference* the disturbance of the sea had considerably abated, but the rest of the crew were about to abandon the *Conference* in their other boat as she was then close on the rocks with her stern and bows knocked in. Both boats then rowed out to sea. Four vessels, including the *Avonmore* and the *Conference*, were totally wrecked that night at Huanillos, five were uninjured from being moored outside of the others, and all the rest were more or less damaged. Numerous lives were lost. (26.2.78)

A lunatic rescued from drowning

ANTHONY GERRIGHTY, *Private, Royal Marines*
On the 27th July 1878, at 10 p.m., a lunatic, on his way home in the transport *Baron Colonsay*, of Greenock, off the coast of N. Africa, broke away from the sentry in the sick-berth and climbed to the fore top-gallant yard. Men were sent aloft to try to prevent his falling, but on their approach he struck one of them on the head. After remaining aloft all night, calling 'Murder', &c., he came down about 5 a.m. on the 28th. The sentries that were placed to watch over him then tried to secure him, but he jumped overboard. Gerrighty instantly jumped after him and, though struck at with a knife which Field had in his hand, succeeded in rescuing him.

The ship was making eight knots and a fresh breeze was blowing. (29.11.78)

A hero of the China Sea

WILLIAM BUYERS,
Second Mate of the
Harlaw *of Aberdeen*

On the 31st July 1878 the *Harlaw*, from Sydney to Shanghai, was wrecked on the Tung Sha Bank. Buyers was ordered into the dinghy, which was to remain by the ship. The steward, four seamen, one of whom was Thomas Lawrie, A.B., and three apprentices got into the boat, in addition to the second mate, making nine in all. Owing to the strong tide that was running and the heavy sea, the boat was loosed from the ship and kept near it head to wind. One other boat was seen to leave the ship and run before the wind; then the ship was shut out from the sight of those in the dinghy by squalls of wind and rain.

When the ship was again seen from the dinghy the two other boats had left her, and she was swinging round; and before the dinghy reached her she fell over. A box of Indian cornflour was picked up, and the second mate swam on board the wreck, cut the jib-sheet adrift, and brought it back to the boat.

The dinghy was then run before the wind, and at sundown the Gutzlaff Lightship was sighted but they failed to reach it. In attempting to keep the boat's head to sea, and towards the light, during the night she shipped two heavy seas and capsized. The crew in their efforts to clamber up on the bottom of the boat caused her to turn round like a cask, and one by one the men and boys dropped off her. The second mate was seized by the steward, but managed to extricate himself after being dragged down some depth. When he again reached the boat he found Lawrie alone. Early in the morning Lawrie was washed off, when Buyers at great risk to his life swam to his assistance, and with difficulty brought him back to the boat. They then managed to right the boat and got inside her. Lawrie was, however, washed out of the boat by a heavy sea, but Buyers again saved his life and pulled him back into the boat by means of one of the boards at the bottom of the boat. Soon after, when close to the light, the two survivors were picked up by a junk and landed at Shanghai. (6.12.78)

Through fire and water off Bayonne

PETER SHARP,
Captain
JOHN MCINTOSH,
A.B., of the Annabella
Clark *of Ardrossan*

On the 20th November 1878 a fire suddenly broke out on board the French ship *Mélanie* which was lying in the River Adour at Boucan, near Bayonne, loaded with 500 barrels of petroleum of which forty were on deck. A mass of flame shot up from the main hatch and the ship quivered all over from the explosion of some of the barrels. The ship's seams opened at once, and the petroleum, pouring through, spread a belt of flame around the ship. The master and a seaman then jumped overboard, but the mate remained to try to save his son, who was lying helpless under some heavy objects which had fallen on him. Captain Peter Sharp, master of the *Annabella Clark* which was lying close by in the river, accompanied by John McIntosh came at once to his assistance. They rowed their boat through the flames, picked up the seaman who had jumped overboard and took the mate from the blazing vessel. Capt. Sharp and McIntosh both sustained very severe injuries. It was feared at first that Capt. Sharp would lose the sight of one eye, and McIntosh the use of his hands. (1.4.79)

The unselfish captain of a fishing-smack

ALEXANDER CHRISTIE, *Captain, fishing-smack* Expert *of Stonehaven*

On the 24th January 1879 the *Expert* was run down by the S.S. *Countess of Durham* off Dunnottar Castle, Kincardineshire. The *Expert* at once sank and three members of the crew were drowned. Capt. Christie got a buoy, by which he supported himself, and a boat put off from the steamer to his assistance. Although he had been in the water a quarter of an hour, and the cold was so great that the spray turned to ice, he refused to be taken into the boat until one of his crew, George Main, who was lying some two or three boats' lengths off in a state of insensibility, had been picked up. (15.5.79)

An attempted rescue in the Bay of San Francisco

E. D. THORNBURGH CROPPER, *Captain, West Kent Militia*

At 11 a.m. on the 6th August 1878, as the S.S. *Idaho* was crossing the bar of San Francisco Bay, outward bound, about two miles from the shore, Thomas Nolan, a coloured waiter, threw himself overboard. Captain Cropper, a passenger, instantly jumped overboard and made a most gallant attempt to reach the drowning man who, however, sank before he was reached. Captain Cropper was subsequently picked up by the steamer's life-boat, after being in the water 25 minutes. The steamship was going 8 knots at the time, and there was a high sea running with a westerly wind. (5.6.79)

Explosion on H.M.S. Thunderer

WILLIAM J. BRIDGES, *Quartermaster, H.M.S. Thunderer*

On the occasion of the recent explosion which took place on board the *Thunderer*, Bridges was at his station in the shell-room. When the explosion occurred the shell-room was immediately filled with smoke and many burning fragments of clothing, &c., were blown down into it. The magazine was also filled with smoke and reported to be on fire. All lights were put out, and the cries of the wounded were distracting. The prevailing impression seems to have been that one of the filled common shells had exploded, and the men stationed in the room made their escape as speedily as possible, with the exception of Bridges who, taking off his woollen comforter, wrapped it round the burning fragments and brought them up on the flats.

Bridges afterwards went down again to make further search for any smouldering material amongst the projectiles. (6.6.79)

Gallant rescues on the Gold Coast

HENRY WESLEY,[1] Agent at Addah for Messrs. Miller Bros., Glasgow
On the 3rd August 1879 the brigantine *Harriet* of London, whilst on a voyage from Cape Coast Castle to Jellah Coffee, was wrecked on the bar of the River Volta, about 5 miles east of Addah. Owing to the heavy surf the crew were unable to launch any of their small boats, as they would have been swamped, and the men once in the water would have fallen a prey to sharks.

The perilous position of the crew was noticed from the shore and a surf-boat was launched, but was capsized and had to return. The boat then put out again, being in charge of Mr. Henry Wesley and manned by thirteen Krooboys, but, owing to the roughness of the surf, she had to go round the vessel six times before the distressed crew could be rescued. They were at length all saved by jumping into the boat as she came under the bulwarks. The risk being so great, Mr. Wesley had great difficulty in persuading the Krooboys to man the boat. (24.2.80)

A gallant Royal Naval Reservist

GEORGE OATLEY, R.N., Gunner's mate, and Drill Instructor, R.N.R., Peterhead
On Monday, 16th February 1880, during a very heavy gale, the Swedish schooner *Augusta* was observed by the coast-guard at Peterhead showing signals of distress and labouring heavily in the trough of the sea.

On reaching the opening of the Peterhead South Bay the vessel headed for the land. As it was clear that she would come ashore, the life-saving apparatus was at once started, but by the time it reached the beach the vessel had struck on the rocks near Boddam, about 4 miles south of Peterhead, and drifted towards the shore, where she lay exposed to all the fury of the gale. Two rockets were fired and the second carried the line over the stern of the ship, but the crew were quite ignorant of the working of the apparatus, and were unable to avail themselves of the assistance. Oatley thereupon took off his clothes and, swimming through the breakers and broken water, reached the smooth water between the ship and the rocks and was pulled on board by a rope

[1] The medal awarded to Wesley is in the House of Commons Collection.

thrown to him. He then proceeded to haul in the line and fix it to the rigging, after which the crew, five in number, were one by one drawn ashore. Oatley, who contrary to the captain's wishes was the last to leave the ship, was landed benumbed with cold and fatigue, and cut and bleeding from contact with the rocks. Oatley is not of a strong constitution and was invalided five years ago for phthisis. (26.4.80)

A gallant coast-guard

GEORGE WILLIAMS, Boatman, Uzon Station of the Coast-guard

On Sunday morning, the 6th March 1881, during a heavy gale accompanied by blinding snow and sleet, the Norwegian brig *Ranger*, of Fredrikshald, was wrecked at Marywells, on the Uzon Guards, when Williams saved the four survivors of the crew, the master and mate having been washed overboard when the vessel struck on the rocks.

The rocket apparatus threw a line to the wreck, but the crew did not know how to use it, so Williams got into the breeches buoy and hauled himself out hand over hand. On getting within about 20 yards of the wreck and finding he was making no headway, he dropped from the buoy on to the rocks and made his way over them and through the wreckage to the wreck, on reaching which he found the crew quite helpless. By dint of great exertion he got on board and secured the hawser, but the whip (the endless rope by which the breeches buoy is hauled backwards and forwards by the party on shore) was foul among the wreckage. In endeavouring to clear it the whip carried away, leaving one end on board, the other on shore. Williams then sent one man on shore but, in hauling off, the whip again got foul of the wreckage and was cleared with great difficulty. Then two more men were landed. One man was then left, with whom Williams himself intended going ashore, but before he could get into the buoy it was hauled away from him. The lines again got foul and the man was in great danger of being drowned in the breakers, when Williams jumped from the wreck, swam to the breeches buoy, and cleared it. They were then both hauled ashore much exhausted and severely bruised. Williams suffered severely from exposure and shock. (4.5.81)

A gallant chief officer

FRANCIS PITTS, Chief Officer, S.S. Pleiades, of Liverpool

At about 7 a.m. on the 30th May 1881, while the *Pleiades* was running before a very heavy south-west gale, an able seaman was washed overboard. Three life-buoys were at once thrown to him, and the engines slowed. Soon after the look-out man reported him to be on the starboard beam, but owing to the tremendous sea that was running the master dared not lower a boat or imperil the ship by turning her.

The master then, knowing Mr. Pitts to be a fair swimmer, called upon him to attempt the rescue of the man by swimming to him with a line. Without a moment's hesitation Mr. Pitts jumped overboard with the line, but after going about 300 yards he was obliged to let go the line and swim towards the ship. So great was the force of the waves that he was carried past the ship and was not rescued without much difficulty. When taken out of the sea he was quite exhausted. (2.1.82)

Heroism of Newfoundland men

ARTHUR MCKEE, *Mate*
JOHN ADAMS,
WILLIAM ROLLESTON,
Seamen of the barque Low Wood *of St. John, New Brunswick*

The *Low Wood* when off the Newfoundland coast on the 20th October 1881 fell in with the barquentine *Bend Or* in a disabled and sinking condition, and showing signals of distress. The weather was very bad and the sea very high, but the *Low Wood* rounded to, and sent a boat manned by five men to her assistance. Half-way between the two vessels the boat was capsized in a violent squall and all her crew were drowned.

The *Low Wood* stayed by the wreck till the 23rd, and at about 1 p.m. on that day a second boat, manned by the men named, was lowered and proceeded to the rescue. The sea was then as high as ever, and the risk greater. The smaller size of the boat made it necessary to make two trips to the wreck, and on the second it was almost swamped. (10.2.82)

A Northumberland hero

HENRY HOOD, *Coxswain, R.N.L.I. Life-boat, Seaton Carew*

For saving life at the imminent risk of his own, on the occasion of the wreck of the Norwegian schooner *Atlas* on the Long Scar Rocks, on the 11th March 1883. (17.5.83)

Heroism off the Fiji Islands

WILLIAM MACGREGOR, M.D., C.M.G., *Chief Medical Officer and Receiver-General, Fiji*

The *Syria*, from Calcutta to the Fiji Islands, with 494 coolie emigrants, stranded on the evening of the 11th May 1884 upon the Nasalai Reef, some 25 miles to the eastward of Suva, Fiji. This reef is exposed to the full force of the south-east trade winds, which were blowing with great force: also to the long roll of the sea from the South Pacific. Owing to the peculiar set of the tides over the reef, the shipwrecked emigrants who tried to swim ashore were swept out into the surf, which was breaking 30 feet high over the edge of the reef.

The captain did not leave the wreck until he believed that all the people were out of it; he then started bringing with him a half-drunken Indian woman. He was leading her across a broken mast at a slight incline across the gap between the two portions of the hull, when both were knocked over.

An official at the risk of his own life dashed to their rescue, but he too was thrown down and all three were being rolled along to destruction when Dr. MacGregor, who was standing by the fallen mainmast directing the removal of the struggling Indians, seized a line that was floating by, and taking two or three turns with it round his wrist plunged into the surf, grasped the struggling bodies of the drifting people, and dragged them back into shallow water.

But for him, the loss of life, which was great, 59 in all, would have been even greater. (17.10.84)

Another rescue at South Shields

JOHN HENRY WOOD, *South Shields Volunteer Life Brigade* — Awarded for his gallantry, at the imminent risk of his own life, in rescuing a boy washed off the pier at South Shields during a gale on the 24th October 1885. (21.5.86)

Heroism off Cape Horn and in Sydney Harbour

THOMAS AVERETT WHISTLER, *First Mate of the* Ennerdale *of Liverpool* — On the 17th December 1885, as the *Ennerdale* was rounding Cape Horn, an apprentice named Duncan McCallum fell from aloft into the sea, striking the rigging in his fall. Immediately Harry Pochin,[1] an A.B., leapt overboard after McCallum, who sank before Pochin could reach him. Pochin, afraid of being seized with cramp before a boat could come to his assistance, asked for a life-buoy to be thrown to him, and at the same moment the master called all hands to man a boat. Whistler, who was 24 years old, had been asleep in his berth. He ran on deck and heard Pochin's hail; calling to the boatswain to heave him a life-buoy, he sprang overboard, secured the life-buoy thrown to him, and succeeded in reaching Pochin. The latter was already on the point of sinking, but with the help of the life-buoy Whistler was able to keep him up. The water was bitterly cold; an albatross hovered round the two men ready to attack them.

Meanwhile considerable delay had occurred in the dispatch of the boat, her lashings had been secured extra firmly for the passage round Cape Horn and, when at last launched, so many men crowded into her that she capsized. When righted and re-launched she rescued Whistler

[1] See next page for award to Pochin.

and Pochin, who were now entirely exhausted after 40 minutes in the water. The albatross had to be driven off with a boat-hook. Directly they were lifted into the boat both men became insensible, and Whistler was delirious for some time afterwards.

About a year later, on 13th December 1886, while the *Ennerdale* was in Sydney Harbour an apprentice named James F. Beattie was taking the captain's gig from the starboard to the port side of the vessel when the boat sheered off and he was thrown into the water.

Whistler immediately dived, fully dressed, from the poop, but reached the water too close to the boy, who caught him from behind, put his arms around his waist, and locked his legs in his. They both sank, and whilst under water Whistler cleared himself from Beattie's grasp, caught him by the shoulder, and struck out for a life-buoy which had been thrown overboard. Before it could be reached, both sank a second time, and Whistler, who was by this time thoroughly exhausted, was obliged to let go his hold of the boy. The body was afterwards found floating in another part of the harbour. (27.7.87)

HARRY SALISBURY POCHIN,
Seaman of the Ennerdale *of*
Liverpool } See foregoing item. (5.7.89)

A rescue from ice-covered sea

ROBERT GRAY, On the 28th April 1888, about 10 p.m., the *Eclipse*
Seaman, S.S. was in the North Atlantic when a seaman named
Eclipse *of* George Pressley fell overboard. A life-buoy and lines
Peterhead were immediately thrown to him and the ship's boat
was cleared as soon as possible. Pressley got hold of a line and was being dragged along under water when another seaman, Robert Gray, jumped into the sea with a line round his arm, got hold of Pressley, and kept him up as well as he could until both of them were rescued by the ship's boat.

The sea was intensely cold and covered with ice, and the high waves caused the vessel, which was making considerable headway, to raise the men out of the water and then dip them under for some time, and both were very much exhausted when picked up. (20.2.89)

A wreck off the South American Coast

WILLIAM CARTER, The *Gettysburg*, from Monte Video to Pensacola,
A.B. of the barque was lost by striking on the Morant Cays, W.
Gettysburg Indies, on the night of 31st March/1st April
of Aberdeen 1889, seven of her crew being drowned.
The sea during the night washed over the remaining nine of the crew, who hung on to the wreck until daylight,

when William Carter and seven men reached a rock above water 500 yards away.

The master tried to follow, but was injured; the sea was so strong that he was knocked down and would have been drowned had not Carter returned and carried him to the rock.

Carter afterwards swam out and secured part of the topmast and yard, lashed them together, and with assistance brought them ashore, where they were formed into a raft.

The nine men left got on the raft and paddled to the nearest island, $1\frac{1}{2}$ miles distant, Carter and another seaman at times swimming alongside, and directing the raft, which was frequently turned off its course and sometimes upset by the heavy sea. He and six others later swam to a larger island a quarter of a mile distant, Carter returning the next day to assist the master and a seaman, who were seriously injured, to reach it.

The survivors remained on the larger island till the 21st April, when they made a larger raft, on which two of the crew sailed to Jamaica, a distance of 32 miles, in two days, whereby the rescue of all the men was ultimately effected. (22.8.89)

A Wreck at Barrow

JOHN DINNEEN,
Chief Mate, S.S.
Albatross *of London*

On the 4th November 1888 the schooner *Isabella Hall* of Barrow stranded on the Tongue Sand, and the crew having lost their boat in a heavy sea were obliged to take to the rigging.

Next morning two boats went to their relief but could not get near the wreck owing to heavy seas, and the shipwrecked crew were in danger of losing their lives, when the *Albatross*, which was passing up channel, sent a boat manned by John Dinneen and four seamen, who despite warnings rowed close to the wreck and after nearly an hour's struggle threw a line on board and rescued one of the crew. He had scarcely been lifted into the boat when a heavy sea nearly swamped her and washed Dinneen and three seamen out of her, but they regained the boat, and bailing her out proceeded with their task, finally succeeding in rescuing the rest. (24.7.89)

Repeated rescues at East London, Natal

RONALD MACLEAN,
East London,
Cape Colony

In 1872 a man, while suffering from delirium tremens, jumped off the pierhead at East London and was carried out to sea. Maclean swam out, and brought him ashore.

On the 25th September 1872 the brig *Wild Rose* stranded near Buffalo River in a strong gale. The crew were rescued by Maclean and five other men in a whale-boat. Two days later a man working on board the wreck of the vessel fell overboard and would have been drowned had not Maclean jumped in after him and rescued him.

On the 27th November 1872 the barque *Crixea* stranded on the coast in a heavy gale. Maclean went far into the surf and assisted out of the breeches buoy the crew who were being saved by the rocket apparatus. A day or two later a drunken man employed on board the wreck of the vessel jumped into the sea; Maclean swam through a heavy surf and at very great personal risk brought him ashore.

On the 28th October 1873 the brig *Lord of the Isles* went ashore on the East Bank. Maclean swam out to the vessel for a rope. The sea was extremely high, and he was several times thrown back bruised and bleeding on the rocks. Persevering, however, he at last succeeded in reaching the vessel, and returned with a rope, by means of which the crew were safely rescued. While landing, one of the crew fell out of the breeches buoy. Maclean, injured as he was, plunged into the surf and reached him. The man, who could not swim, caught Maclean by the throat, and both would have been drowned had not assistance been rendered from shore. Maclean's injuries were so serious that his life was for some time despaired of.

At midnight on the 1st November 1876 the *Elise* stranded in a heavy gale and high sea. The rocket apparatus being engaged on the wreck of another vessel, Maclean swam out to the *Elise* for a rope. He succeeded in reaching her but was unable to make his presence known to the crew, and returned ashore. He renewed the attempt, and after some time a rope was thrown to him by means of which the crew were saved.

On the 11th November 1882 two lighters were capsized in a heavy sea in the river. Maclean flung himself into the breakers, and succeeded in rescuing three of the crew.

On various occasions during the years 1874–83 Maclean rendered most valuable assistance in working the rocket apparatus at wrecks, and helping the crews ashore, and was in consequence selected to take charge of the local Volunteer Rocket Brigade. (18.6.90)

Rescues at Gibraltar

WILLIAM SEED, *Chief of Police, Gibraltar*
WILLIAM McQUE, *Corporal, 3rd Bn., King's Royal Rifles*

When the S.S. *Utopia* sank through collision off Gibraltar on the 17th March 1891, with a loss of 551 lives, a number of boats were put out by the vessels of the Channel Squadron to the assistance of the shipwrecked persons.

The launch of H.M.S. *Immortalité* while engaged in rescue fouled her screw, became uncontrollable, and was wrecked on the shore near the breakwater. Two of her crew were drowned, two others swam safely ashore, and the remainder, with eight emigrants from the *Utopia*, were rescued in an exhausted condition by officers and men of the Port Department and of the King's Royal Rifles, among whom William Seed, Chief of Police, and Corporal William McQue, of the Rifles, particularly distinguished themselves.

Although the night was dark, with a strong gale blowing and a strong current and heavy sea dashing on the breakwater—a low line of jagged rocks, giving no foothold outside the wall of the fortifications—they plunged into the waves with ropes, and although washed back on the rocks, renewed their attempt until they succeeded in reaching the launch, which was 80 yards off shore, when the rescue was effected. (22.6.91)

A fishing-smack wrecked at Scarfskerry

JAMES WOOD SMITH, *Master, Fishing Boat* Lady Matheson *of Macduff, Scotland*

The fishing-smack *Lady Matheson*, manned by three men, Smith (Master), Morrison, and McKay, stranded about midnight on the 1st March 1891, in a north-west gale and snow-storm, among rocks in 20 feet of water, 100 yards from a dangerous part of the coast at Scarfskerry, Caithness, Scotland.

Smith swam ashore, but finding that the others were unable to follow him, he swam back to the boat for a line, with which he again returned ashore. Morrison, while preparing to make use of the line, was washed off the boat by the waves, and was only saved from drowning by Smith, who rushed into the surf and pulled him out. Smith then called to McKay, but the latter replying that he had lost hold of the line, Smith again swam out to the boat with the line round his waist, and finding McKay unable to use it, fastened him on to himself, and both were hauled ashore by Morrison. Smith was disabled by his efforts. (9.7.91)

Life-saving in the Indian Ocean

ALFRED JOHN COOPER, *Fourth Officer, S.S.* Massilia *of Greenock*

On the morning of 8th April 1890, when the *Massilia* was some 500 miles from Aden, in the Indian Ocean, an Indian seaman fell from the rigging into the water. Cooper at once ran up on deck, jumped fully clothed overboard into shark-infested waters, swam to the man, and kept him afloat until they were picked up by the ship's boat. (9.9.91)

Life-saving off Sydney, New South Wales

WILLIAM BORLAND, *Sapper, Submarine Mining Corps, Sydney, N.S.W.*

On the 3rd April 1891 a boat containing twelve men and two officers was engaged in submarine mining operations about half a mile from the shore at Middle Head, Sydney, N.S.W. By the accidental explosion of a 100 lb. gun-cotton mine, the after part of the boat was blown to pieces, and the two officers and two of the men were instantly killed, while the others were all more or less severely injured.

Borland jumped overboard in order to lighten the boat, and whilst holding on to the gunwale, supported Sapper Brentnall, who was semi-conscious. Another of the crew, named Adams, in the excitement of the moment, jumped overboard, but when some yards away called out for help, as he was unable to swim. Borland at once swam to his assistance, and supported him until a boat arrived from the shore.

Borland was nearest to the explosion of any of the crew, and received severe wounds. He was in hospital several weeks, and could not follow his ordinary work for some months. (16.11.92)

Rescue in the Red Sea

SPENCER W. SCRASE-DICKINS, *Captain, 2nd Highland Light Infantry*

While the S.S. *Peshawur* was passing through the Red Sea on 27th April 1893 a Lascar fell overboard. Captain Scrase-Dickins, who had been invalided home and was lying half-asleep in a chair on deck, immediately jumped overboard, and swimming to the Lascar kept him afloat until they were both picked up by the ship's boat a mile and a half away from the vessel. The sea was high and infested with sharks. (17.8.93)

Attempted rescue of a suicide

CHARLES WOOD ROBINSON, *Sub-Lieutenant R.N.R., Third Officer of the R.M.S. Teutonic of Liverpool*

While the R.M.S. *Teutonic* was steaming at the rate of about 21 knots in St. George's Channel on 17th April 1895, at 6.30 a.m., when few people were about the deck, Mr. Robinson noticed a passenger climbing on the rail of the ship with the evident intention of jumping overboard. He made an ineffectual attempt to prevent him and then dived fully clothed after the man from a height of 25 feet above the water, and only about 30 feet forward of the propellers of the vessel.

His efforts at rescue were met with violent resistance, and in the end the man succeeded in drowning himself.

Mr. Robinson ran great risk of being drawn under the propellers, and when picked up was in a very exhausted condition. (21.6.95)

A brother's heroism at Newcastle, New South Wales

HEREWARD HEWISON, *Newcastle, N.S.W.*

While a number of men were bathing on the sea beach at Newcastle, N.S.W., on 28th November 1894, the cry of 'Shark!' was suddenly raised. Everyone made for the shore save Horace Hewison, who cried out that the shark had seized him, and disappeared. Hereward Hewison promptly turned and, swimming to the spot, found that the shark had seized his elder brother's right arm.

He at once grasped his brother round the body, and the two fought the shark until the complete severance of the arm, just below the elbow-joint, released Horace Hewison, who reached the shore with his brother's assistance. (8.7.95)

A master faces death to rescue a fireman

WILLIAM JOHN NUTMAN, *Master, S.S.* Aidar *of Liverpool*

At 2 a.m. on the 19th January 1896, signals of distress were observed from the S.S. *Aidar*, of Liverpool; the *Staffordshire*, from Marseilles to Port Said, immediately went to her assistance. As the *Aidar* was found to be sinking fast, three of the *Staffordshire*'s life-boats were at once launched and with great difficulty, owing to the darkness and heavy sea, succeeded in rescuing the passengers and crew, twenty-nine in number.

At 6 a.m. the only persons left on the *Aidar* were Mr. Nutman (the master) and an injured fireman, whom he refused to abandon.

The steamer was now rapidly settling down, and as it was no longer safe to remain near her, the officer in charge of the rescuing boat asked Mr. Nutman for a final answer. He still persisted in remaining with the injured man. The men in the boat were obliged to pull away, and immediately afterwards, at 6.15 a.m., the *Aidar* gave one or two lurches and foundered.

After she disappeared Mr. Nutman was seen on the bottom of an upturned boat still holding the fireman. Half an hour elapsed before the rescuing boat could approach, but eventually Mr. Nutman and the fireman were picked up and taken on board the *Staffordshire*, where the injured man was with difficulty restored by the ship's surgeon. (8.4.96)

A passenger tries to rescue a fireman

HERBERT C. FRENCH, *Captain, R.A.M.C.*

While H.M.T. *Wakool* was steaming through the Straits of Malacca, on 17th November 1902, a native fireman jumped overboard. Capt. French dived from 36 feet. The man disappeared before he could be reached and Capt. French was obliged to make for a life-buoy as he was exhausted with the weight of his clothing. Subsequently both were rescued by the ship's life-boat.

Capt. French incurred considerable risk as a strong current was running at the time, and he might have been drawn under the propellers of the ship. He was also in danger of sharks and water snakes. (9.3.03)

The Russian Baltic Fleet attack British fishing-fleet

WILLIAM SMITH, *Mate*, ARTHUR REA, *Second Engineer*, both of the steam trawler Crane of Hull
CHARLES BEER, *Mate*, HARRY SMIRK, *Chief Engineer*, EDWIN COSTELLO, *Boatswain*, all of the steam trawler Gull *of Hull*

The steam trawler *Crane* was so badly damaged by the gunfire of the Russian Baltic Fleet in the North Sea, on the night of the 21st October and the morning of the 22nd October 1904, that she began to sink. The skipper and the third hand of the vessel had been killed, and all but one of the crew wounded.

William Smith was severely wounded while on his way to help the boatswain, and when he found that the skipper was killed, took charge of the sinking vessel. He subsequently signalled for assistance and when the boat from the steam trawler *Gull* arrived he got the wounded and the bodies of the dead into the boat, and was the last to leave the *Crane* before she sank.

As the chief engineer had been rendered insensible soon after the firing began, the second engineer, Arthur Rea (22 years of age), took charge of the engines, and although the lights had been extinguished he went into the stokehold to discover the cause of a loud report and an escape of steam. He was knocked down by a shot on his way but went on, and finding the stokehold more than a foot deep in water and steam, looked at the gauge-glass, and pumping additional cold water into the boiler partially drew the fires to avert an explosion. He also set the pumps of the vessel working and, after reporting that the vessel was sinking, went again into the darkened engine-room and stopped the engines. Although wounded he did not stop working till he left the ship.

In answer to signals of distress from the *Crane* the men named, after the firing, which had been heavy and sustained, went in a boat from the *Gull* to the *Crane*, and succeeded with great difficulty in rescuing the wounded from the sinking ship, and in bringing away the bodies of the killed. (13.5.05)

Gallantry of a Yarmouth Skipper

ARTHUR JAMES DYE, Skipper, Steam Drifter Marie *of Yarmouth*

The Steam Drifter *Marie*, when about 65 miles NE. by N. of Haisborough Lightship, North Sea, at 10 p.m. on the 30th September 1911, shipped a heavy sea which broke the skylight, flooded the cabin, and extinguished the cabin light. The mate, who was in his berth asleep, was awakened by the sudden inrush of water and, finding the cabin in darkness, lit a match. Immediately the gas from a tin of carbide of calcium exploded and the cabin was set on fire.

The skipper, Arthur James Dye, hurried below from the wheelhouse, seized the burning tin in his hands and threw it into the galley, from which it was rolled on to the deck. Dye seized it again and tried to push it overboard. It rolled inboard at the first attempt, but he again took hold of it, and ultimately managed to throw it overboard.

In rendering these services Dye's left hand and his face were badly burnt, and on arrival in port he had to receive treatment at the hospital. A gale was blowing at the time, with a heavy sea. (8.12.11)

Men and shark at Sydney, New South Wales

ALFRED BARLOW, WILLIAM D. McKAY, *both of Sydney, N.S.W.*

While James Edward Morgan was bathing at Lane Cove, Sydney, N.S.W., on the 26th of January 1912, he was attacked by a shark.

In response to his cries the men named, who were in the water, went to him, and brought him to land. While doing so, the shark made a second attack on Morgan, and inflicted injuries from which he died. (10.9.12)

A gallant leading stoker of Royal Indian Marine

SHAIK MUHI-UD-DIN, *Tindal of Stokers, Royal Indian Marine*

On the 14th April 1913 the Shatt-al-Arab Outer Bar gas-buoy in the Persian Gulf was being charged with acetylene gas from the R.I.M.S. *Lawrence*, and as the carbide, soaked in crude oil, was being passed down a canvas chute to the buoy, an explosion occurred. Shaik Muhammad, who was inside the cage of the buoy tending the chute, was knocked senseless, and as the chute caught fire both inside and outside the cage, enveloping the manhole in flames, his life was in extreme danger. Shaik Muhi-ud-Din saw the accident, jumped on to the buoy, dashed through the high flames, knocked the burning chute aside and dragged Shaik Muhammad out of the cage. He then put him in the water and held him up till a boat came. (31.10.13)

A gallant ship's engineer during the Great War

JOSEPH CONOLLY, *Third Engineer, S.S. Vanellus of Cork*

On the 1st October 1916 the S.S. *Vanellus* struck a mine in Havre Roads and the vessel, which was laden with petrol, immediately burst into flames.

The flames spread so quickly that it was impossible to clear away the boats, and most of the crew jumped overboard, with a loss of three lives.

Although the engine-room telegraph was broken by the explosion Mr. Conolly remained in the engine-room until every one else had left the ship. He kept the engines working astern, and thus made it possible for a life-boat to be lowered on the port side; thus saving many lives.

Before leaving the ship he again went below and stopped the engines. He was badly burnt. (30.1.17)

A heroic second officer

PETER THOMSON, *Second Officer, S.S. Polpedn of London*

On the 14th November 1916 the S.S. *Polpedn* was torpedoed in the English Channel, and began to sink. The crew had just time to get into the starboard life-boat and cut the painter when the life-line was found to be fast coiled round Mr. Thomson's leg. Realizing the danger of the boat being capsized Mr. Thomson at once jumped overboard, thus freeing the boat, and allowing her to be pushed away as the vessel foundered. While under water he freed his leg from the life-line, and he was afterwards picked up by those in the boat.

Mr. Thomson ran the greatest possible risk of losing his life; his self-sacrifice prevented serious loss of life. (23.3.17)

Acts of gallantry at Archangel

JAMES CAMPBELL HURRY, *Master, S.S.* Earl of Forfar *of Glasgow*

On the 8th November 1916, while the S.S. *Earl of Forfar* was lying at Archangel, a fire broke out on a Russian steamship and spread to the *Earl of Forfar* which was lying immediately ahead. Capt. Hurry attempted to return to his vessel but, being unable to do so, went to help other vessels which were in danger of being burnt. While doing so he heard voices coming from his own ship which was burning and exploding furiously. Calling for volunteers, he led them on board and rescued seven injured men, some of whom he personally carried to a tug.

While thus engaged he had to lift several live shells from the deck of the vessel in order to get at the wounded. Within ten minutes of the last man being rescued the deck blew up. (7.9.17)

Heroism at Archangel

EDGAR TWIDLE, *Master*, WILLIAM FRANCIS GORDON MARTIN, *Chief Officer, both of S.S.* Bayropea *of London*, ROBERT MACBRYDE, *Admiralty clerk, temporary Commodore's Secretary*

On the 26th January 1917 a series of fires and explosions occurred at the port of Archangel. When Capt. Twidle arrived on the scene his ship was burning fiercely.

On being informed that the chief engineer was alive, Capt. Twidle climbed on board but found him dead. He then examined the other rooms and found a dazed Chinese sailor.

With the assistance of the men named this man was got over the ship's side across the ice, and eventually to the Red Cross station. A few minutes later the vessel blew up. (7.9.17)

Munitions ship on fire

JOHN DAVID BULMER, *Boatswain, S.S.* Rhydwen *of Cardiff*
JOHN EDWARD BROWN, *Private, R.M.L.I.*

On the 31st January 1917, while the S.S. *Rhydwen* was lying at Genoa, a fire broke out in the ship's magazine. A fire signal was immediately hoisted, but before assistance arrived Bulmer and Brown went below at great personal risk, unlocked the door of the magazine, and got the hose at the seat of the fire.

Water was then played on the magazine and the ammunition was taken out on deck, and owing to the prompt action of the ship's crew the fire was extinguished. (7.9.17)

Another munitions ship on fire

ALEXANDER MCINTYRE SPENCE, *Master, S.S.* Shuna *of Glasgow*

On the 3rd July 1917, while the S.S. *Shuna* was anchored in the River Seine, a fire broke out among some cases of grenades which formed part of the deck cargo.

Spence hurried to the scene, but by the time he reached the spot the cases were well alight. With a few buckets of water he succeeded at great personal risk in extinguishing the fire before the fire-hose could be started, and then removed the charred cases. Others caught alight, but the fire was got under by means of the hose.

His prompt action undoubtedly saved many lives. (30.10.17)

Fire on a French troopship

JAMES WILLIAM BROWN, *Acting-Q.M.S., R.A.M.C.* WILLIAM SEYMOUR, *Sergeant, Northumberland Fusiliers,* ARTHUR DUFF HADDEN ALLAN, *Private, R.A.M.C. (T.),* JAMES CUTHBERTSON, *Private, R.A.M.C. (T.)*

On the morning of the 5th February 1917 a serious explosion occurred in the French troopship *St. Laurent* at Malta, followed by a fire which cut off three men in the forepart of the ship, where the flames were fiercest.

None of the boats near would approach the ship owing to the heat and danger of a further explosion until Acting-Q.M.S. Brown persuaded a labourer to row him out; but when within 30 yards of the ship the labourer refused to go any farther.

Brown returned, and was then joined by the men named. They rowed to the forepart of the ship, the sides of which were by this time red hot, while the plates were falling into the sea.

When they were within a few yards of the ship two of the three men in the forepart jumped into the sea and were rescued; the third, who had climbed up the mast, was saved later when the mast fell. (8.11.17)

A hospital ship sunk in Havre Roads

SAMUEL ARNOLD BODSWORTH, *Private, R.A.M.C.*

On the 10th April 1917 H.M. Hospital Ship *Salta* was sunk in Havre Roads. H.M.S. *Druid* proceeded to render assistance and got alongside a swamped boat of the *Salta*. All the occupants of the boat were rescued except a Hospital Sister and Bodsworth. The former was so exhausted that she was unable to hold the ropes thrown to her, and eventually became unconscious.

Although he might have been rescued, Bodsworth remained in the boat with the Sister, and after she had fallen overboard and been hauled back again, he finally got a line round her body, by means of which she was hauled on board. (11.1.18)

A steamer torpedoed during the Great War

ALFRED WILLIAM FURNEAUX, *Chief Steward, Mercantile Marine*

In April 1917 the steamship in which Mr. Furneaux was serving was torpedoed by the enemy, and a Lascar who was on the spot where certain deck plates had buckled and broken, had his legs so firmly caught between the plates that he would have gone down with the ship. Mr. Furneaux, at imminent danger to his own life, got one leg out, but the other was nearly severed above the knee. Finding it impossible to pull this leg out Mr. Furneaux amputated it with an ordinary clasp-knife and then carried the man to a boat. When in the boat he dressed the wound as well as possible, and gave the life-belt he was wearing to the wounded man. Mr. Furneaux also rendered first aid in the boat to another Lascar who was badly scalded. (21.1.18)

Gallantry of a New Zealander on a sinking transport during the Great War

JAMES WERNER MAG-NUSSON, *Trooper, New Zealand Mounted Rifles*

Awarded in recognition of Magnusson's gallant action in saving life on the occasion of the loss of a transport.

He was on the deck of the transport *Transylvania*, when he saw an injured soldier struggling in the water, and immediately dived overboard into a very rough sea, swam to his assistance, and got him into a boat. Magnusson then returned to the sinking ship and rejoined his unit. His life was lost. (7.3.18)

A steamer torpedoed during the Great War

ROBERT COULSON, *Second Engineer, Mercantile Marine*

The steamship in which Mr. Coulson was serving (the *Luis* of Hartlepool) was struck by a torpedo in the stokehold. The engine-room became full of escaping steam, and Coulson and the fourth engineer were seriously scalded. Instead of making for safety, however, Coulson, in spite of his injuries, carried the fourth engineer, who was in a helpless condition, up the engine-room ladders to the top platform out of immediate danger of steam and the inrush of water, and he then himself became exhausted.

The chief engineer, who had run to the engine-room from the bridge, assisted both the injured men out of the engine-room, and with help managed to get them into a life-boat. After being landed they were taken to hospital, where both succumbed to their injuries. (26.8.18)

Heroism on a munitions transport

REGINALD CURTIS CLAYTON, *Apprentice, Mercantile Marine*

In March 1918 the steamship in which Clayton was serving (the *War Knight* of London) was in collision, and a serious fire broke out on board. He was aft, where the accommodation for the crew was situated. It was his fire-station duty to stand by the flood-valve of the magazine, and in spite of the whole of the deck being in flames, he groped his way through the fire, found the valve, and turned it on to 'flood'. He died in hospital four days later.

Those of the crew who survived no doubt owed their lives to the flooding of the magazine. (27.8.18)

Heroism on an oil tanker

CHARLES MCKENZIE, *Chief Officer, Mercantile Marine*

A violent explosion, followed by fire, occurred in one of the holds of the steamship in which Mr. McKenzie was serving, which had a cargo of petroleum. Four men in the hold received serious injuries.

Mr. McKenzie went down, found the ship's carpenter and assisted him to a sling, by means of which the man was hauled up on deck. He then searched the hold again, and rescued another seaman. Both men, however, subsequently died. Mr. McKenzie also found the third man, who was badly burned, and assisted him to mount the ladder. The fourth man managed to escape by his own exertions. (28.8.18)

Heroism on a torpedoed steamer

MAURICE LISTER, *Assistant Butcher, Mercantile Marine, of S.S.* Ausonia *of Liverpool*

The *Ausonia* was torpedoed and disappeared within twenty minutes of being struck. Lister and a pantry boy, both on their first voyage, were below, and both received serious injuries.

When Lister regained consciousness he found that both his ankles were broken. He made his way to the top of the stairs but found the door jammed. There was, however, a hatchway opening overhead, and Lister placed some of the planking which had been blown up against this opening in order to clamber up the planking and escape, but hearing cries of distress returned and searched the chamber on his hands and knees until he found the other boy with both legs broken, and managed to get him up the planking to the steps leading to the deck. Other members of the crew then assisted both boys into the boats which were picked up after several days. The pantry boy died later. (15.10.18)

Fire on a munitions transport at Sunderland

CHRISTOPHER FEETHAM, *Fireman, S.S.* Hornsey *of London*

On the 10th November 1918, while the S.S. *Hornsey* was lying at Sunderland, a fire broke out in the mess-room and adjoining saloon. A quantity of ammunition was on board which, had it exploded, would have caused widespread loss of life.

The whole of the ship's company behaved admirably in the emergency. The decisive factor, however, in extinguishing the fire was the heroism of Feetham. He volunteered to be let down into the cabin, and there, waist-high in water, directed his hose on to that part of the fire which would have exploded the ammunition in a very short time.

As it was, some of the ammunition cases were already scorched. His courage saved many lives. (18.3.19)

Heroism in fire after collision at sea

DAVID FALCONER, *Chief Engineer, S.S. War Knight of London*

On the 24th March 1918 the S.S. *War Knight* was proceeding up Channel in convoy, in company with the U.S. Oil Carrier *O.B. Jennings*. About 2.30 a.m. the *War Knight* struck the other vessel on the starboard side abreast the bridge. Flames and fumes of naphtha appear to have spurted out of the *O.B. Jennings*, rushed the whole length of the *War Knight* and set her on fire. The after part of the *O.B. Jennings* was also soon burning furiously and the ships swung together, the *War Knight*, being to leeward of the *O.B. Jennings* and consequently completely enveloped in the smoke, fumes, and flames from the weather ship.

Immediately after the collision flames swept across the top of the engine-room through the open skylight. Mr. Falconer stood in the flames and shut the skylight down to prevent the fire from entering the engine-room.

Later on, when the third engineer and a fireman, who had remained below, made their way on deck, the former was severely burned and gassed, and Mr. Falconer dragged both men to a place where there were less flames and fumes, and then put them into the engineers' mess-room with others whom he had collected from their bunks, and by breaking the skylight he assisted them all to get on to the boat deck.

Finally, although he could not swim, he took off his own life-belt and put it on the third engineer, and did not leave the ship until he was satisfied that there were no others in need of assistance.

Mr. Falconer died in hospital. (25.3.19)

Heroism in the North Atlantic

HUGH BROWN, *Boatswain, S.S. Orissa of Liverpool*

On the 25th June 1918 this ship was torpedoed and sunk in the North Atlantic Ocean, six lives being lost.

The explosion took place about 20 feet from the store-room, where some members of the crew, including Brown and his son, who was the steward's boy, were receiving their tobacco issue. The store-room was immediately flooded, but the boatswain and his son were able to fight their way to the stairway leading to the weather deck, the bottom stairs of which were blown away.

The boy reached the weather deck, but Brown then heard the

store-keeper calling for help. Brown wished his son farewell and, though he could probably have saved himself together with his son, turned back to help the store-keeper, though he must have been aware that he had very little chance of being able to win his way to the deck a second time.

The ship sank not long after, and neither the boatswain nor the store-keeper was seen again. (23.5.19)

An Indian cavalryman rescues a Turkish and British soldier

MANGAL SAIN, *Trumpeter, 2nd Lancers, Indian Army*

On the 15th March 1919, while Turkish prisoners-of-war were bathing at Beirut under a British guard, one of them got into difficulties. Two of the escort went to his assistance but failed to rescue him. Mangal Sain then swam out through the surf and with great difficulty brought him ashore.

Shortly afterwards two British soldiers who were bathing were caught in a current and in danger of drowning. Mangal Sain, although exhausted by his rescue of the first man, again swam out and brought one man ashore. Although exhausted he started to rescue the other soldier but was called back, as the man had drifted so far out that it was impossible to save him.

Both men who were rescued were in the last state of collapse and must inevitably have been drowned but for Mangal Sain. (11.7.19)

Fire at Archangel

SAMUEL JAMES HAINES, *Junior Officer M.M.R., attached Up-River Transport Service*

On the 17th June 1919 a fire occurred on a Russian motor-launch in the harbour of Archangel, and a Russian tug and a picket boat from an American man-of-war proceeded to render assistance, Haines going in the tug.

Just before the tug reached the launch an explosion took place on board the latter. Immediately the tug got alongside, the crew of the launch abandoned her. Haines at once went on board the launch and endeavoured to extinguish the fire, and being unable to do so, he ordered the other boats to lay off, while he went down into the magazine and brought up on deck a quantity of ammunition and a large quantity of gasoline and some rifles. Then, calling the picket boat alongside, he passed these stores aboard her.

Had the fire reached the magazine an explosion would undoubtedly have occurred, and Mr. Haines would have had no chance of saving his life. (12.12.19)

Fire on a munitions transport

THOMAS STRATFORD KNILL, *Master S.S. War Pike of London*

At Novorossisk on the 14th October 1919, when the S.S. *War Pike*, laden with stores and several hundred tons of explosives, took fire, Knill, although deserted by most of his crew and in spite of the intense heat and frequent explosions, remained on board the ship, casting off hawsers from the quay and making others fast to a tug, only abandoning ship by order of the captain of H.M.S. *Grafton* as his vessel was being towed out of the entrance of the harbour. He then boarded a tug, stood by his ship after she had grounded; and later, though the bridge, boats, and starboard coal bunkers were a mass of flames, boarded her and assisted in getting hoses to work, successfully preventing the fire from spreading aft, where there were still large quantities of explosives. The vessel was then grounded in shallow water. (26.4.20)

Heroes of the engine-room

DAVID FRASER, *Chief Engineer*
AARON EDWARD HIGGINS, *Third Engineer*,
S.S. Melville Dollar *of Vancouver, B.C.*

On the 27th August 1919, when the S.S. *Melville Dollar* was in the North Pacific Ocean, the main steam pipe burst, killing the second engineer and five Chinese firemen.

Attempts were immediately made to get down into the engine-room to rescue the injured and to shut off steam from the boilers. The chief engineer, Mr. David Fraser, tried first but was not able to get beyond the fiddley door, being badly scalded about the arms, throat, and face. The master and mates then fitted up two tarpaulins as wind-sails, in order to force as much air as possible down the skylights into the engine- and boiler-rooms.

Meanwhile Higgins, having wrapped himself in coverings as a protection against the still escaping steam, made several attempts to get to the valves, but he was driven back each time by high-pressure steam. The master then descended with him and put a bowline around him as a life-line, and Higgins made another attempt, this time reaching the burst part of the steam pipe, but he became exhausted and found it impossible to get to the valves and had to be pulled back by the life-line.

It was not until $1\frac{1}{2}$ hours after the explosion that the pressure in the boilers fell sufficiently to permit a descent, when the bodies were removed, the fires drawn, and the steam shut off, which was done by Higgins.

Both officers incurred great risk in rendering the services, as the engine-room was filled with super-heated steam, and Fraser received serious injuries. (6.8.20)

Man and shark in New South Wales

JACK CHALMERS, *Sydney, N.S.W.* On the 4th February 1922 Milton Coughlan was swimming just outside the breakers of Coogee Beach, Sydney, N.S.W., when he was attacked by a shark which bit deeply into his left forearm. Freeing himself, he fought and drove away the shark which, however, returned and succeeded in establishing a hold on his right arm, but the grip was again broken.

Observing what had happened, Chalmers had a line tied round his waist, and dashed to the rescue, and although he slipped and fell and was momentarily stunned, he quickly recovered, plunged into the water, and swam out to Coughlan, who was floating helpless. Chalmers caught hold of him and held him until they were both hauled in to the rocks. The injured bather's arms were practically bitten through and the flesh torn from them, and he died in hospital.

Chalmers fully realized the risk he was incurring and showed extraordinary gallantry. (7.7.22)

GORDON LEES, *Newcastle, N.S.W.* A youth named Jack Canning was attacked by a shark when bathing, on the 12th March 1925. A rush was made to launch the surf boat, but before this could be done Gordon Lees, employed by the City Council to patrol the beach and assist surf bathers in difficulties, put on a belt with a life-line attached and swam out alone to Canning's assistance. Canning had been attacked three times by the shark and was terribly injured, and Lees reached him just as he appeared to abandon all further effort to save himself. The shark was then only a few yards away from rescuer and rescued. Lees lifted Canning up when he was almost submerged and the two were then immediately hauled in to the beach by the life-line.

The rescued man died later. (29.9.25)

Heroes of the engine-room

GEORGE HENRY WHITE, *Second Engineer, S.S.* Paul Beau *of Hong Kong* On the 4th May 1925 the *Paul Beau* was steaming from Hong Kong to Canton when a tube blew out in the starboard boiler, projecting a stream of boiling water and steam 35 feet long into the after end of the boiler-room and engine-room. Two men, Hau Foong and So Hau,[1] were on duty on the boilers

[1] So Hau was awarded the Board of Trade Bronze Medal for Gallantry in Saving Life at Sea.

and two others on the engines. Hau Foong was immediately overcome and collapsed, and So Hau at once went to his assistance and at the risk of his own life managed to drag him clear of the scalding water before making his way on deck where he collapsed also. Meanwhile the other two men sought refuge in the tunnel way.

Observing a thick cloud of steam rising from the engine- and boiler-rooms to the level of the promenade deck, White, wrapping his face in wet towelling, made his way through the steam along the top of the boilers and shut off the valves connecting the boilers to the engines, and the valve connecting the two boilers. The three men in the engine- and boiler-rooms were reached as soon as the steam had cleared away and were removed unconscious to the upper deck. But for White they would have been suffocated by the escaping steam.

White ran a very grave risk since he had to grope about in the scalding steam fog, blinded by the covering on his head, in his endeavour to shut the stop-valves on the boilers, and he might have encountered the full force of the issuing steam, in which case the result would have been fatal. In spite of being badly scalded he took charge, and having effected the necessary repairs raised steam again, thus enabling the vessel to be brought safely to the wharf at Canton. (17.11.25)

Man and shark in New South Wales

STANLEY GIBBS, *Sydney, N.S.W.* On the 3rd January 1927 at Port Hacking, near Sydney, a youth named Mervyn Allum was swimming a short distance from the shore when he was attacked by a large shark. It was at first thought that he was drowning, and Stanley Gibbs, who was standing on the nose of a launch he was driving, ready to give assistance to Allum, observed that he was being attacked by the shark. Gibbs dived from the launch and fought the shark with his hands and feet and eventually succeeded in getting Allum, who was very badly injured, from the jaws of the shark, and with the assistance of a man named Macdonald placed him in a rowing boat. Allum died later. (7.2.27)

Heroism at Newport, Mon.

FRANK HOPKINS, *Newport, Mon.* On the night of the 18th August 1927 the S.S. *Cambrian Baroness* was lying ready to sail in South Lock at Newport, Mon., with a space of 2 or 3 feet between her side and the quay wall. At the last moment a fireman returning to the ship began to climb the pilot ladder, but lost his hold and fell into the lock between the vessel and the dock wall. The ladder was lowered to the water and the man caught hold of it, but as the ladder was being hauled up he fell back.

Seeing the accident Hopkins, an unemployed seaman, went down the ladder to the water level, 15 feet below. By the light of an electric torch from the ship's deck he caught hold of the unconscious fireman, and began to carry him up the ladder: his progress was necessarily slow. As he struggled up the ladder the vessel began to move towards the quay wall and some one shouted to Hopkins to let the man go and save himself. Hopkins replied, 'I have got him now and will bring him up.' As soon as the fireman was within reach of men standing on the quay they hauled him into safety; Hopkins had barely managed himself to get up to the quay when the vessel closed with the wall. A few seconds later he and the man he rescued would have been crushed to death. Hopkins could have made sure of his own safety if he had given up his hold of the fireman. He knew quite well the risk he was running, and knowing it, saved the man. (3.11.27)

Man and shark in South Africa

ANDRIES MULLER HEYNS, *George, Cape Province, South Africa*

On the 28th December 1927, at Little Brak Beach, Mossel Bay, a youth named Ockardus Heyns, aged 17, was bathing when he was attacked by a shark, which carried him some distance out to sea and bit off his left leg above the knee.

Andries Muller Heyns immediately went out to the assistance of his nephew. The shark meanwhile had returned and gripped Ockardus Heyns by the right ankle. Andries Heyns got hold of his nephew and tried to free him from the shark. Nevertheless the foot and ankle of Ockardus Heyns were severely crushed.

Andries Heyns succeeded in reaching the shore with his nephew, who died later. (3.10.29)

They died to save a town

ALEXANDER JOHNSTON, *Chief Engineer*,
WILLIAM HALL, *Second Engineer*,
S.S. Tritonia *of Glasgow*

The S.S. *Tritonia*, with a general cargo on board and a quantity of explosives in No. 3 hold, arrived at Buenaventura, Colombia, on the 27th February, 1929. The discharging of the cargo began next day. During the afternoon a fire was discovered among cases of dynamite; the alarm was at once given and the shore gang, with most of the crew, left the ship.

The master, officers, and a few members of the crew who remained on board tried without success to control the fire and the ship had to be abandoned owing to the intense heat and dense smoke, as well as the danger of explosion.

Upon reaching the shore the master, after consultation with the Port Authorities, decided to try to sink the *Tritonia* because of the danger of serious damage to persons and property in the port if the explosives on the ship blew up. Accordingly the master and the men named went back to the burning ship. The two engineer officers went on board for the purpose of opening the sea-cocks. The launch drew off and waited until it was seen that they were approaching the ship's side in readiness to leave again. The launch was about to be sent to the *Tritonia* to take off the two officers when the ship blew up and both were killed.

The launch was severely damaged and those on board were taken off and put on another launch which cruised about for some time in a vain search for the missing engineers before returning to the shore.

The two engineers sacrificed their lives in a heroic attempt to prevent the explosion. (26.2.30)

Man and shark in New South Wales

ROBERT MURRAY KAVANAUGH, *Darlinghurst, N.S.W.*

On the evening of the 12th January 1929 Colin J. Stewart, a boy of 14 years of age, was bathing at Bondi Beach, N.S.W., 50 yards from the shore, when he was attacked by a shark. Kavanaugh, aged 22 years, who was bathing a few yards from Stewart, swam to his aid and had almost reached him when the shark made a second attack on Stewart. Undeterred by the danger Kavanaugh secured hold of Stewart and struggled with him towards the shore. He had gone a considerable distance when he was met by two other men and together they got him to the beach. Stewart died next morning. (16.10.30)

Heroism on an ice-floe

WILLIAM GEORGE JOHNSON, *First Master Watch, British sealing steamer* Viking *of St. John's, Newfoundland*

On the night of 15th March 1931 the *Viking* was in the ice some 9 miles from Horse Islands, White Bay, Newfoundland, when an explosion occurred in the magazine, tearing away a large part of the stern, and setting the ship on fire. The men in the cabin, galley, and engine-room and on the bridge were either killed or badly injured, but the majority of the crew, whose quarters were forward, were able to get out on the ice, and after the first shock to return to the ship and provide themselves with clothing and some food. The *Viking* carried a crew of 153 men all told, and of these 27 lost their lives. The great majority of those saved were able to reach Horse Islands and were eventually taken off by a relief ship.

After the explosion Johnson started for the land with a party of about 20 men hauling a dory containing the mate of the *Viking* and a passenger, both seriously injured. The party proceeded, hauling the dory through 'marshy' ice until 4 p.m. next day, when Johnson sent all the men in the party, except three, to Horse Islands for assistance.

At daylight on 17th March no assistance had arrived. Johnson and the men with him had then been for a day and two nights without food or water, and they were still several miles from land. No vessel was in sight, nor was there any sign of assistance, and they were in field ice which at any moment with a change of weather conditions might become a mass of disintegrating pans. Johnson persuaded the three uninjured men remaining with him to make for the land, but refused himself to leave the injured men.

That afternoon seven men from Horse Islands, bringing food with them, reached the dory, but it was so badly damaged that they were unable to drag it over the ice and they returned to Horse Islands. Johnston remained standing by the two injured men. Two hours later he saw the smoke of the S.S. *Beothic* searching for survivors. A party of men were landed from the vessel on to the ice, but darkness overtook them before they could reach Johnson and they were compelled to return to the ship. At daylight next morning a rescue party was again landed from the *Beothic*, and this party, finding it impossible to convoy the injured men across the ice in the damaged dory, returned to the ship for another dory, and eventually succeeded in getting Johnson and the two injured men on board the *Beothic* at 11 a.m. on the 18th March.

The ice conditions prevailing at the time were very treacherous, and the ice was of the type which has very little stability in fog, rain, or snow, and might break up rapidly. A sudden change of wind from an off-shore direction would probably have loosened all the pack ice very quickly and sent it out to sea, and Johnson, with his knowledge of ice and weather conditions, must have realized the grave risk he was running in remaining with the injured men. (23.4.32)

A hero of the boiler-room

HENRY HARTLEY WADSWORTH, *Sixth Engineer, S.S.* City of Cairo *of Liverpool*

On the 5th November 1933, an explosion occurred in the boiler-room of the S.S. *City of Cairo* while she was in the Mediterranean Sea.

The second engineer, and Mr. Wadsworth, the sixth engineer, were in charge of the watch, and immediately the explosion occurred the second engineer rushed out of the stokehold and informed the first engineer, who was off duty, of the mishap.

The first engineer and the second engineer then went below. The second engineer went through the engine-room and opened the door of the stokehold, but scalding steam drove him back. In returning he passed Wadsworth making his way towards the stokehold where it was known that some Lascar firemen had been trapped at the time of the explosion. Wadsworth went into the stokehold; and when the steam had cleared away he was found dead in the port wing, close to the Lascar firemen whom he had tried to rescue.

Wadsworth must have known that in entering the steam-filled stokehold in an endeavour to save the Lascar firemen he was running a very great risk of losing his own life. (17.12.34)

Heroism in the North Atlantic

THOMAS GIBSON,
Cook, S.S. Usworth
of Newcastle

In December 1934 the S.S. *Usworth* was in distress in the North Atlantic Ocean while on a voyage from Montreal to Queenstown with a cargo of grain. Attempts were made to save the vessel, but at about midnight on 13th/14th December it became clear that she would have to be abandoned by her crew. Very gallant efforts were then made by the Belgian S.S. *Jean Jadot* and the S.S. *Ascania* of Liverpool[1] to take off the crew. In the course of these efforts the *Ascania* manœuvred as close as was possible to the *Usworth*, and about 2 p.m. on 14th December sent away a life-boat to her. There had been a whole gale from the west-north-west which at this time had slightly moderated, but there were still heavy squalls and high seas: oil was being pumped on the sea. The life-boat from the *Ascania* got under the lee of the *Usworth* about 15 feet away from her, with the crew ready to pull away as the *Usworth* drifted down on to the life-boat.

Those on the *Usworth* were told to jump one at a time into the life-boat, but in the excitement three members of the *Usworth*'s crew jumped into the water together. One of the men who jumped was the cook, T. Gibson. He was a strong swimmer and would probably have reached the *Ascania*'s life-boat in another two or three strokes, but the mess-room boy, L. Jones, who had got into difficulties, shouted for help and Gibson was seen to tread water and then to turn back. Unfortunately he was unable, in the oil-coated sea, to swim with the boy to the *Ascania*'s life-boat, and notwithstanding attempts made to save them by those remaining on the *Usworth* they were swept under the *Usworth*'s stern and both were drowned.

There is no doubt that Mr. Gibson sacrificed his life in attempting to save the mess-room boy. (24.6.35)

[1] For awards of Board of Trade Medal for Sea Gallantry, *v.* p. 382.

CHAPTER XIX

AWARDS OF BOARD OF TRADE MEDALS FOR GALLANTRY IN SAVING LIFE AT SEA (S.G.M.), 1854–1921

> Be well assured that on our side
>   The abiding oceans fight,
> Though headlong wind and heaping tide
>   Make us their sport to-night.
>
> . . . . .
>
> Be well assured, 'though wave and wind
>   Have weightier blows in store,
> That we who keep the watch assigned
>   Must stand to it the more.
>
> . . . . .
>
> Be well assured, though in our power
>   Is nothing left to give
> But chance and place to meet the hour,
>   And leave to strive to live,
>
> . . . . .
>
> Then welcome Fate's discourtesy
>   Whereby it is made clear,
>   How in all time of our distress,
>   And in our triumph too,
>   The game is more than the player of the game,
>   And the ship is more than the crew!
>
>   KIPLING, *A Song in Storm.*
>   From '*The Years Between*'

AS stated in Chapter V of this work (p. 59), the Sea Gallantry Medal (S.G.M.), in silver and bronze, was the first official decoration of its kind for which British subjects, or foreigners serving in British ships, were eligible. Though awards are made in the name of His Majesty by the President of the Board of Trade, the basis of awards is not a Royal Warrant but a section of one of the Merchant Shipping Acts. The riband is scarlet with two narrow white stripes.

The precise relationship between the Sea Gallantry Medal and the Albert Medal, which was instituted twelve years later, has never been defined, and in some respects the S.G.M. overlaps both with Albert and Edward Medals. The class of medal awarded, viz. silver or bronze, depends upon the degree of risk deemed to have been involved, and the measure of gallantry displayed by the recipient.

UNREWARDED ACTS OF HEROISM

The small number of silver medals issued show how high is the standard. Indeed, the average number in either class is lower over a period of ten years than the number of promotions to knighthood in many of the orders of chivalry.

There is no record of the numbers issued previous to 1887; the relative papers have been destroyed and the register cannot be traced: it seems to have been no one's business to preserve for posterity a recital of deeds as noble as any in the annals of our race. No account of the awards is published in *The London Gazette*. From 1887 to 1921 a list of names, with a bald summary of the occasion for which the medal was awarded, is available and is here reproduced.

From January 1922 onwards a full record is available and is here reproduced, in summarized form.

The record does not, of course, include more than a small proportion of gallant deeds performed at sea. Many go unreported, and when a ship is lost with all hands the evidence of heroism perishes with the crew.

One such case may here be recorded. On 29th September 1938 the steam trawler *St. Sebastian* of Hull, Skipper T. Weightman, with 16 hands on board, was stranded at Kobbekuta on the north coast of Bear Island and sent out by radio telephony to all ships in the vicinity the message 'We've run ashore. Require immediate assistance'. This was at 8.15 p.m. At 8.43 p.m. came the message 'Urgent but not last resource'; at 9.20, 'Ship bumping'. Just after midnight on 29/30th September, 'We fear seas will wash bridge away'. At 12.20 a.m., 'Lights are failing. Compasses unreliable. Do not try to come in too near. Life-belts on. Men preparing to leave.' At 12.52 a.m., 'Lights have gone out.' 1.35 a.m., the wireless operator, F. W. Keates, aged 19, on his third voyage, telephoned: 'Have had to leave the chart-room. Motor will soon be submerged and useless. Bridge is now broken in.' This was his last message.

The owners wrote of him: 'He courageously stuck to his job in the chart-room under the shattered bridge until the rising water put the motor out of action. Not only did he continue to send out messages, but in his telephone conversation with other vessels he was cheerful and his voice firm and clear to the last, even to the extent of making jocular references to the terrible plight of his ship, when he must have known that his life was drawing very near its close.'

Soon after he had sent his last message the cold waters of the Arctic must have overwhelmed the crew. None survived and no bodies were found.

Every effort was made by other trawlers, notably the *Cape Duner* and the *Davy*, to rescue any survivors who might have been cast on Bear Island. After several unsuccessful attempts they landed a party on the dangerous east coast, in spite of darkness and a strong tide, and with the aid of a Norwegian operator from Bear Island radio station made their way to the wreck, which they reached at 2 p.m. on 30th September. There was no sign of life on her nor on the shore and cliffs near by. The landing party divided into two groups to search the Island, but without avail. They finally returned exhausted to the radio station having had no food for 24 hours and their boots were worn through. In the words of the official report:

'Skipper A. Wilson of the *Davy*, and Skipper J. Myers of the *Cape Duner* were stubbornly determined to do all in their power to save the crew of the *St. Sebastian* and stuck to it as long as hope remained. The former is an experienced man. Myers is only 22: he acquitted himself with great credit, showing resource and leadership beyond his years and a willingness to take responsibility which augurs well for his future.'

In the following pages, a recipient's name in capitals indicates that the Medal was awarded in silver.

The date in parentheses is that of the incident, so far as ascertainable from the records.

The serial order is that of the Board of Trade manuscript register.

When the services rendered were to another vessel, the name is added in brackets. Unless otherwise stated, the ships named are steamships.

1st JAN. 1887–31st DEC. 1909

PATRICK PICOT, coast-guard boatman at Scrabster (*Flower of Obrig* and *James*). (31.3.87)

L. G. STAR, master, T. EASTAWAY, 2nd mate, J. English, J. Dyer, T. Pike, J. Layis, A.B.s, of *Juno* (*George Moore* of Glasgow). (21.5.87)

W. REID, chief officer of *Santa Rosa* (two members of crew). (5.6.87)

W. H. Bullock, 2nd mate of barque *Athelstone* of Liverpool. (5.12.86)

J. R. MEAD, master, F. E. MICHELL, 2nd mate, F. Snell, A. George, F. Miller, G. Sanderson, of *Gwalia* (*Serpho* of Sunderland). (24.11.87)

W. TURNBULL, master, W. BROWN, mate, K. FINLAYSON, bo'sun, of *Brackley*. R. JONES, carpenter of *Douro* (*Douro* of Liverpool). (16–20.11.87)

J. Williamson rescued crew of a fishing boat off Shetlands. (9.12.87)

J. McNicol, commissioned coast-guard boatman at Port Logan (Schooner *Rhoda* of Coleraine). (4.1.87)

W. LAWSON, skipper, M. GANGER, J. THOMPSON, C. HICKFORD, crew, of *Lena* (*Tyne Queen* of Hull). (1888)

J. H. GRIFFIN, coast-guard boatman at Drummore, Greenock (*Glagorm Castle* of Belfast). (13.3.80)

T. E. Crocker, commissioned boatman, R. Pavlovsky, boatman (Schooner *Marjorie Johnson* of Dublin), H. SMITH, H. Norton, H. Norton, coast-guards (Volunteer Lifeboat *Refuge*). (9.11.87)

W. DYER, master of *Ben Voirlich* (*Blackwatch* of Cardiff). (11.11.88)

W. MURRAY, commissioned boatman at Portpatrick (Barque *Roseneath* of Glasgow). (2.2.89)

J. GREEN, 2nd mate, A. McDonald, L. Davies, C. Bristowe, of *Rose* of Cardiff. (17.2.89)

W. KING, H. FEDDER, R. LACY, A. OAKLEY, O.S., of *Albatross* (Schooner *Isabella Hall* of Barrow). (4.11.88)

A. Wares, of Wick Life-Saving Company (Brig *Helmik* of Norway). (10.5.89)

T. POTTS, 2nd mate, J. Welch, O. Bugge, F. Boos, J. Smith, O.S., of *Napier* (*Domingo* of Sunderland). (27.11.88).

J. MORRIS (Barque *Tenby Castle* of Liverpool). (17.12.89)

W. Ross, master of *East Lothian* (Barque *Bellaport* of Workington). (12.8.89)

W. E. Murray, Q. A. Rhodes, apprentices of *Northbrook* of London. (3.3.89)

R. ELLIS, master of barque *Isobel* (*Sophia* of London). (23.8.89)

J. WATSON, skipper, J. Kilby, 2nd hand, W. G. Payne, deck hand, of S.T. *Heron* (Barque *Latona* of Liverpool). (18.1.90)

W. H. Parker, 3rd officer of *Colonist* (Schooner *Hebe* of Greenock). (22.2.90)

T. BATH, English engineer at Algiers (*Minerva*). (13.7.90)

F. Vitto, A.B., of barque *Claudine* of Barnstaple. (19.11.90)

J. R. Simpson of *Urania* of Grimsby. (14.12.90)

F. M. BURKE, Lloyd's Agent at Algiers (*Arbib Brothers* of London). (8.1.91)

E. J. DUFFY, master, W. NASH, chief mate, H. Graham, bo'sun, J. Green, F. Nicholson, J. Dyer, A.B.s, of *Nepthis* (Ship *Great Victoria* of Liverpool). (30.1.91)

J. R. SIMPSON, 2nd hand of S.T. *Rector* of Grimsby. (29.3.91)

G. W. DAVID, master, D. M. HENDERSON, chief mate, A. Nichols, bo'sun, W. Thomas, H. Martin, B. Reynolds, J. Butler, A.B.s, of *Mosser* (Schooner *Nordkap* of Fowey). (13.3.91)

W. REYNOLDS, commissioned coast-guard boatman at Ballygally (*Dungonnell* of Belfast). (3.4.91)

J. Mugford, 3rd hand of smack *Dazzler* of Brixham. (3.3.91)

H. C. Rhodes, master of fishing smack *Star of Hope* of Grimsby. (17.4.91)

R. P. LAWSON, 1st mate, S. BASS, 3rd mate, H. Moreau, E. Wilcox, J. Spenser, A. Lace, W. Robinson, A.B.s, of *Engineer* (*Fearnought* of Liverpool). (10.10.90)

W. FISHER, J. LEWIS, coast-guards, W. BARKER, volunteer at Coverack (*Bay of Panama* of London). (10.3.91)

H. WHEELER, 2nd mate, F. Loosemore, J. Turl, S. Southcott, O.S., of cutter *Resolute*. W. UNDERY, boarding officer, P. ERAO, coxswain, C. NILE, J. CHAPPERY, J. ROMOGNIN, A.B.s, F. CORREA, engine-driver, F. STAGNO, fireman, W. G. Adair (*Utopia* and H.M.S. *Rodney*). (17.3.91)

W. Pike, coast-guard chief boatman at Scarborough (*Halcyon* of Lowestoft). (6.8.91)

J. PARK, master, H. SMITH, 2nd mate, G. Cross, 4th mate, A. McLennon, R. Cameron, J. Scott, D. Patterson, J. McLeod, A.B.s, of *Siberian* (Schooner *Little Wonder* of Fowey). (24.9.91)

T. H. PARRY, master of *Mangalore* of Liverpool. (7.7.91)

W. CHRISTIE, master, W. WHITE, chief officer, M. McDonald, R. Campbell, J. Noble, W. T. Carter, J. McDonald, J. McSwain, K. Mathieson, A. McLachlan, A. McLennan, N. McDonald, W. McNeil, J. Rennie, C. Stephens, J. Sinclair, M. Macaulay, O.S., of *Norwegian* (*Devonshire* of London). (9.10.91)

T. SEED, master, G. LOFTHOUSE, coxswain, G. Orford, H. Owen, R. Jones, J. Salthouse, H. Sheridan, O.S., of *Bickerstaffe* (Schooner *Gefion* of Norway). (26.8.91)

N. ALLEN, 2nd officer, T. Evans, J. Williams, Q.M.s, T. A. Jawoodeen, 2nd Tindal of Lascars, of *Knight Commander* (Schooner *John Smith* of Ardrossan). (4.11.91)

T. J. WATSON, skipper, W. BURTON, 2nd hand, E. HURLE, 3rd hand, of smack *Britain's Pride*. W. P. Seaton, master, A. Chafer, 2nd mate, of *Ashton* (S.V. *Enterkin* of Glasgow). (12.12.91)

W. Heard, Skipper, J. Howe, 2nd hand, of fishing-smack *Vineta* (Fishing-smack *Snipe* of Grimsby). (12.11.91)

D. Oprey, E. Clarke, H. Taylor, R. Taylor, T. West, fishermen of Killough, Co. Down (Fishing-boat *Alexander* of Belfast). (17.12.91)

P. Rooney, master of fishing-boat *Bonnie Jane* (Fishing-boat *St. Patrick* of Newry). (15.2.92)

F. W. MACDONALD, mate, D. McDIARMID, 2nd mate, T. WILKIE, extra 2nd mate, G. Tocher, J. Nick, A.B.s, of barque *Forfarshire* (Barque *Mountain Laurel* of Liverpool). (6.7.91)

C. Sullivan, J. Pearce, coast-guardsmen of Orford Haven (*Ariel* of Goole). (1892)

J. L. HEMEON, 1st mate, D. Keefe, F. Sullivan, A.B.s, T. Cleary (or O'Leary) of Sailing-ship *Arlington* (Barque *Countess of Dufferin* of Londonderry). (30.12.91)

J. F. NUNN, skipper, J. Day, 3rd hand, of smack *Prima Donna* (Brig *Contest* of Guernsey). (13.12.91)

D. Regan, P. Regan, C. Regan, M. Driscoll. H. Driscoll, fishermen of Calf Island, Co. Cork (Schooner *Petrel* of Montrose). (21.1.92)

W. PETERSON, 2nd mate, E. Gundersen, M. Karreman, A.B.s, D. De Jong, carpenter, of *Mendelssohn* (Barque *Invertrossachs* of Dundee). (28.2.92)

T. COLE, chief boatman, W. WRIGHT, boatman, of Kilmore (Barque *Vaar* of Norway and Schooner *Esther* of Fleetwood). (21.2.92)

D. S. TURNER, 2nd mate of barque *Aikshaw* of Maryport. (24.12.91)

W. Parnell, skipper, J. Huckstep, 2nd hand, C. Pottle, 3rd hand, of smack *British Queen* (Brigantine *Caroline* of Faversham). (11.12.91)

F. HARNDEN, master, W. P. BROWNLESS, 1st mate, A Sidotti, bo'sun, S. Diego, L. Sabatini, G. Chindemi, B. Foca, A.B.s, of *Peconic* (Barquentine *Venture* of Banff). (3.3.92)

Alexr. MacCuish, Senior, Alexr. McCuish, Junior, Alick MacCuish, M. MacCuish, D. MacIntosh, A. MacDonald, M. MacDonald, D. E. MacDonald, A. Ferguson, N. Laing, fishermen of Heisker Is., Hebrides (Barque *Columbus* of Norway). (4.4.92)

P. H. MILLAR, 5th officer, J. Orman, Q.M., of *Moselle* of London. (29.10.91)

G. THOMAS, fisherman of Lundy Island (*Tunisei* of France). (19.2.92)

J. BROOKE, skipper, C. BALLARD, 2nd hand, H. Timms, 3rd hand, W. Tottle, deck hand, of steam trawler *Magneta* (Schooner *June and Alice* of Carnarvon). (19.2.92)

T. Smallcombe, chief officer of coast-guard at Norris Castle (*Violante* of Cardiff). (23.2.92)

F. D. Pengelly, E. W. Nickells, master of barque *Stanmore* (*Viscount Castlereagh* of Sunderland). (22.10.92)

R. ROER, master, H. Helders, J. Gill, J. Jensen, J. Betts, A.B.s of yawl *Result* (*Viscount* of Liverpool). (16.3.92)

W. H. BULLOCK, chief officer of *Floridian* of Liverpool. (31.7.92)

G. Watts, chief officer, C. Boyle, chief boatman, of Donna Nook Coast-guard Station (Barque *Albert* of Russia). (14.10.92)

C. JONES, chief mate, H. Kennedy, lamp-trimmer, W. Copeland, E. Gulterio, O.S., of *Euclid* (Schooner *Maggie W. Smith* of Ardrossan). (11.11.92)

A. PETERSON, mate, J. B. Elder, C. McK. Pow, L. Scott, A.B.s, E. L. Grey, apprentice, L. Warrins, stowaway, of *Herschel* (*Città di Messina* of London). (27.11.92)

C. EVANS, of Norfolk Islands, rescued a man who was pitched overboard from a Whaler off Norfolk Is. (1892)

J. BURGOYNE, skipper of smack *Catherine McKilvie* of Rothesay. (17.2.93)

R. KEANE, Station officer, L. Brinkworth, W. Parker, commissioned boatmen, H. Warren, W. Chamberlain, C. Hawkins, boatmen, of Helens Bay Coast-guard Station (Schooner *Clano* of Chester). (26.2.93)

G. GREEN, 2nd hand, J. S. BARTLETT, 3rd hand, of smack *British Queen* (Smack *Columbus* of Hull). (1.1.93)

P. McGraw, B. McGraw, beachmen of Dundrum, rescued a man from a boat which had capsized off Dundrum. (28.3.93)

W. Brown, skipper of fishing-boat *Helen Brown* (Fishing-boat *Lady Margaret* of Dunbar). (14.2.93)

W. MARTIN, commissioned boatman of Fraserburgh Coast-guard (Schooner *Sophia and Frances* of London). (15.3.93)

C. HUNTER, 1st mate, C. Halgren, A. Blom, G. Ferraro, G. Grillo, O.S., of *Eglantine* (Barquentine *Chislehurst* of Swansea). (27.2.93)

F. MUNROE, mate, J. Reagan, bo'sun, W. Elliott, R. Hewis, W. Halloran, A.B.s, of *Abendana* (*Austin Friars* of London). (22.2.93)

J. MACKRILL, C. ROWSTON, J. ROBINSON, R. ROBINSON, J. GRANT, J. YOUNG, A. APPLEYARD, A. Priestley, W. Priestley, fishermen of Cleethorpes (Brig *Oswy* of Whitby and Brig *Agricola* of Aberdeen). (18.11.93)

H. ROBERTS, 1st mate, R. H. LLOYD, 2nd mate, R. Harris, 3rd mate, W. Williams, 4th engineer, J. Murphy, W. Thomas, R. Balderson, D. Jones, A.B.s, J. Hindmarsh, fireman, of *North Gwalia* (*Provincia* of Glasgow). (18.11.93)

C. BROWN, F. BROWN, R. PURVIS, J. H. USHER, T. CLARKE, fishermen of Bridlington Quay (Schooner *Victoria* of Aberdeen). (19.11.93)

C. MAHONEY, commissioned coast-guard boatman at Gardenstown, near Banff (Barquentine *Betty* of Norway). (17.11.93)

R. MAJOR, W. MAINPRIZE, R. STEPHENSON, fishermen of Flamborough (Fishing coble, name unknown). (18.11.93)

J. M. CRUICKSHANK, advocate, W. KINNIN, fisherman, W. QUIRK, W. Joughin, farmers, F. Brew, bank clerk, W. H. Kneale, outfitter, W. G. Cowin, railway guard, E. Corkish, porter, J. White, P. Knight, fishermen, J. Brew, butcher, J. C. Duggan, boat-builder, T. Teare, draper, W. T. Cubban, tobacconist, J. K. Kneen, mate, of Ramsey, Isle of Man (Brig *Geir* of Norway). (10.12.93)

T. DAWES, commissioned coast-guard boatman of Ramsey, Isle of Man (Brig *Cormorant* of Norway). (10.12.93)

J. Gloyn, J. Kirkpatrick, W. Harper, eoast-guard boatmen of Staithes (Brig *Middleton* of West Hartlepool). (18.11.93)

J. CAIN, coast-guard boatman at Reculvers Stations, Kent (Ketch *Glenrosa* of Harwich). (20.11.93)

F. KENT, chief officer, C. Huxstep, commissioned boatman, J. Kelcher, J. Goble, E. W. Smith, boatmen, of Sandwich Coast-guard Station (Cutter *Eclipse* of Ramsgate). (19.11.93)

A. EMPTAGE, E. WHITEHEAD, A. TWYMAN, J. TAYLOR, G. SANDWELL, J. COX, beachmen of Margate (Brigantine *Druide* of Cardiff). (19.11.93)

C. Hambly, of Cornwall (Barque *Iota* of Italy). (20.12.93)

W. FOLEY, of Co. Down, A. MOORE, coast-guard of Co. Down (Fishing boat *Mary of Doonfeeney* of Westport). (20.2.94)

A. Hulow, 2nd hand, R. Wilson, 3rd hand, A. Holmes, 4th hand, of smack *Mercury* (Smack *Majestic* of London). (12.2.94)

W. Cooper, commissioned coast-guard boatman of Morthoe, Devonshire (Brig *A.C.L.* of Nantes). (25.1.94)

J. McLEAN, mate, G. J. Andersen, I. E. Andersen, F. Lawson, J. Jeffery, O.S., of *Ferraro* (Ketch *Bluejacket* of Yarmouth). (11.2.94)

J. WEEKS, E. MODIN, C. LUCHT, J. ROSIN, A.B.s of barque *George Thompson* (Barque *Girvan* of Ayr). (12.6.93)

J. GOVE, mate, J. Wishart, bo'sun, G. Rumsby, A. Opsahl, O.S., of *Garnet* (*Ashburne* of Sunderland). (5.5.94)

T. W. Vale, commissioned boatman of Buckie (Fishing luggers *Endeavour* and *Evening Train* of Banff). (15.10.94)

R. CROME, J. WILSON, L. JONNSON, O. E. MADSEN, O.S., of barque *Dee* (Barque *Cambrian Chieftain* of Liverpool). (16.4.94)

W. J. JONES, chief officer, T. E. Costain, F. Faragher, T. Rex, O.S., of *Vigilant* (Schooner *Mariner* of Carnarvon). (9.12.94)

H. Hunt, coast-guard boatman, W. R. Jones, O.S., of Holyhead (Barque *Kirkmichael* of Liverpool). (22.12.94)

F. Norie, commisssioned boatman of coast-guard at Bude (Schooner *Elter Water* of Dublin). (22.12.94)

J. MORRIS, commissioned boatman of coast-guard at Sandgate (Ketch *Northern Belle* of London). (13.1.95)

D. CLARKE, 3rd hand, J. MILLS, 4th hand, of fishing-smack *Duke* (Fishing-smack *Phocea* of Yarmouth). (23.12.94)

S. Tansley, chief boatman, J. Hynes, commissioned boatman, H. Pitman, T. Stinner, J. Carr, boatmen, of Goodwick Coast-guard Station, Fishguard, and J. Owen, fisherman (Schooner *Ceres* of Carnarvon and Schooner *Pansilippo* of Ramsey). (12.1.95)

F. P. WHITEHEAD, chief officer of *Norham Castle*, R. P. G. FERRIES, apprentice of barque *Fascadale* of Glasgow. (7.2.95)

H. W. WILLIS, skipper, T. HEWETT, 3rd hand, E. SAUNDERSEN, 4th hand, of fishing-smack *Amy* (Fishing smack *Edward and Sarah* of Yarmouth). (8.12.95)

A. W. Simpson, 2nd officer, of *Clan Mackenzie* (*Topaz* of Glasgow). (5.12.95)

R. Woodgate, 2nd hand, T. Gardiner, bo'sun, of S.T. *Datura* (Schooner *John Williams* of Carnarvon). (24.12.95)

W. JOHNSTON, mate, M. H. Jockem, A. T. Lund, T. Manson, J. Zieboldt, O.S., of *Tortona* (Fishing-smack *Invincible* of Hull). (8.12.95)

G. Webster, J. Harrison, fishermen, of fishing-coble *Sarah* (Fishing-coble *Edward Camble* of Whitby). (14.3.96)

T. Verrill, J. Crispin, R. Longster, fishermen, of fishing-coble *Mary and Jane* (Fishing-coble *Phyllis* of Whitby). (14.3.96)

M. BEASLEY, chief officer, A. B. CROSSE, 2nd mate, E. ROBIN, 3rd mate, T. POUND, L. W. ILEFF, Q.M.s, T. RAILTON, R. BELL, A. JACOBS, S. PEMBERTON, C. HAGGES, E. ROHRER, W. EDWARDS, J. HINES, R. WOOLLEY, stewards, A. D. BUN, tindal, L. ALLEE, D. SOMEER, J. EBRAHIM, A. MAHOMED, Lascars, of *Staffordshire* (*Aidar* of Liverpool). (19.1.96)

C. Porossinan, of fishing lugger *Meteor* of Tralee. (8.5.96)

J. T. SPIERS, chief officer, R. PHILLIPS, J. C. POOLEY, R. H. JAGO, A. PAULSEN, C. TAPSTER, A.B.s of *Batanga* (Barquentine *Indian Chief* of Banff). (23.12.95)

H. Cowling, coast-guard boatman of Rosslare (Pilot schooner *No. 1* of Wexford). (25.9.96)

T. Herkes, of the Dunbar life-boat (*Poderosa* of Sunderland). (28.11.96)

R. HOOPER, 2nd hand, J. NIXON, 3rd hand, W. J. WOOD, bo'sun, of S.T. *Circe* (Schooner *Boreas* of Bristol). (28.11.96)

W. Witten, commissioned coast-guard boatman of Aldborough (*Euphrates* of Yarmouth). (8.1.97)

A. PHILLIPS, 2nd mate, E. TACK, carpenter, W. LARGE, P. LECKIE, W. GIBSON, O.S., of *Damara* (Brig *Victoria* of Fowey). (6.12.96)

C. R. COWIE, E. H. HUTCHINSON, passengers on *Staffordshire* (*Aidar* of Liverpool). (19.1.96)

W. H. SANDERS, 1st mate, J. A. Henwood, bo'sun, O. Olsen, T. Denehey, A. Smith, J. D. Bordessa, A. Lewis, O.S., of *Ontario* (Sailing-ship *Androsa* of Liverpool). (8.3.97)

S. PRIOR, 3rd mate of sailing-ship *Khyber* of Liverpool. (27.4.97)

W. Hodge, chief boatman, Coast-guard Station, Sunderland (Schooner *Resolve* of Inverness). (29.11.97)

R. PAGE, skipper, C. THURSTON, 3rd hand, of fishing-smack *Problem* (Fishing-smack *Olive* of Yarmouth). (29.11.97)

A. E. THOMAS, 1st mate, W. RAMSEY, bo'sun, C. TURNER, cook, J. H. STALEY, C. BAKER, W. SVENSON, O.S., H. ELSMORE, fireman, of *Nellie*, W. O. DIVER, 3rd mate, S. PERRY, bo'sun, R. SEAMAN, S. GRASSOM, C. SMITH, O.S., of *Lisbon* (*Newminster* of Newcastle). (29.11.97)

G. H. DODD, 1st mate, H. W. BROADBENT, extra 2nd mate, D. GARSTER, bo'sun's mate, J. Henderson, master-at-arms, J. HAYES, Q.M., R. COLLINS, J. MURPHY, T. CALLIGAN, F. W. YOUNG, O.S., of *Etruria* (*Millfield* of Whitby). (11.12.97)

G. Adolphus, G. J. Bewey, fishermen, of Guernsey (*Channel Queen* of Guernsey). (1.2.98)

L. E. FITZCLARKE, 2nd hand, J. BARRETT, O.S., of steam cutter *Europe* (Fishing-smack *Primrose* of Hull). (17.2.98)

S. J. Payne, of Volunteer Life Brigade, Sunderland (Schooner *Resolve* of Inverness). (29.11.97)

P. DWYER, J. L. SAVELL, C. T. BROWN, boatmen, of Coast-guard Station, Sandlemere (Brig *Oscar* of Norway). (27.3.98)

J. Wilson, R. Paterson, T. Carnie, J. Flucker, W. Paterson, A. Wilson, pilots, of Methil (Brig. *Thetis* of Norway). (23.11.98)

W. Adams, C. P. Field, commissioned boatmen of Blyth Haven Coast-guard Station (Sloop *Fremad* of Norway). (16.10.98)

T. Keightley, commissioned boatman of Muchalls Coast-guard Station (Barquentine *Felix* of Sweden). (20.10.98)

J. W. H. JUDDERY, Q.M. of *Mohegan* of Hull. (14.10.98)

J. C. HOOD, master, F. Webb, mate, W. Baldock, engineer, G. Wells, W. Maltby, O.S., S. Perry, C. Jeffrey, F. Funnell, stokers, E. Cullis, cook, of tug *Simla* (Barque *Blengfell* of Liverpool). (17.10.98)

J. DORAN, 1st mate, E. N. HOBBS, 2nd mate, J. CASSIDY, W. MASON, P. McLAUGHLIN, J. COLLINS, R. R. MOORE, A. GARNER, W. MOUAT, A.B.s, of *Vedamore*, R. P. GITTINS, 2nd mate, A. E. TONGE, F. LEMSKE, A.B.s, of *Londonian* of Hull. (25–7.11.98)

C. H. BATE, 1st mate, J. BICKFORD, steward, W. LAKEMAN, J. DIAMOND, H. M. YOUNG, G. STILLIANO, A.B.s, of *Charing Cross*, H. W. HAM, 1st mate, G. CAPON, T. R. JONES, C. GALLANT, E. HUTNER, G. FIDAN, A.B.s of *Kanawha* (*Gallina* of West Hartlepool). (4–5.1.99)

R. J. GREEN, A.B. of *Olive* (*Fitzjames* of London). (24.11.98)

J. B. STODDEN, 1st mate, B. LISLEY, bo'sun, of *Tregurno*, W. J. JONES, 1st mate, J. KINNON, 2nd mate, of *William Connal* of Glasgow. (14.2.99)

F. J. LIVERSAGE, 2nd mate, C. ANDERSON, bo'sun, H. OLSEN, A. ANDERSEN, A. BRUN, O.S., of *Trojan* (*Rossmore* of Liverpool). (6.2.99)

S. J. LANGUEDOE, 2nd mate, F. W. LAZELL, 3rd mate, S. WARREN, carpenter, J. W. HOPKINS, carpenter's mate, G. WATSON, bo'sun's mate, C. HOLM, J. SEGAR, Q.M.s, C. H. WOODWARD, saloon steward, W. A. DYKE, mess steward, W. E. CLAY, P. E. PETERSEN, J. GORDON, O. FUHREA, M. de CORIA, A.B.s, G. FOX, O.S., of *Menominee* (*Glendower* of Leith). (12.1.99)

W. Allard, E. Forster, T. H. Fuller, W. J. Godbolt, crew of *Dudgeon* Lightship (Fishing-smack *Lord Brougham* of Grimsby). (13.1.99)

J. D. PORTEOUS, 1st mate, S. BRUCE, bo'sun, J. OLSEN, C. LINDHOLM, A.B.s of *King David* (Schooner *Silver Spray* of Stornoway). (5.2.99)

K. KASCH, A.B. of *Incharran* of Liverpool. (22.4.99)

A. SWANGER, O.S., of *Oroya* of Liverpool. (29.4.99)

J. W. McGRATH, master of *Beverley* of Glasgow. (11.6.99)

J. Brown, of Aberdeen (Fishing-boat *Diadem* of Banff). (16.8.99)

J. PASCHO, G. H. SKELTON, T. STADDON, Trinity Pilots, W. SKELTON, R. FROOD, O.S., of pilot-cutter *Drift* (Hulk *Shamrock*). (3.11.99)

J. W. GOTTWALL, 1st mate, B. HORSBURGH, fireman of *Orkla* (*Borghese* of London). (29.12.99)

W. Hennen, coast-guard at Sunderland (*Maliano* of Spain). (23.3.00)

G. W. HILLIARD, apprentice of barque *Principality* of Liverpool. (19.11.99)

J. Diver, fisherman, of Moville, Ireland (Fishing-boat *Rose* of Londonderry). (4.10.00)

J. M. HOWSAGORE, 2nd officer, J. A. STOTE, bo'sun, P. PAUL, steward, J. HILL, G. GIFOROS, J. BALLMAR, A.B.s of *Glengoil*, W. QUINN, sailmaker, F. DOWNIE, A. ROBINSON, A.B.s, of sailing-ship *Nonpareil* of London. (22.9.00)

R. CHANDLER, skipper, R. BUSHELL, 2nd hand, D. McDONALD, 3rd hand, A. AGUTTER, apprentice, of fishing-smack *Florence* (Barque *Lanarkshire* of Glasgow). (28.1.01)

G. W. King, chief boatman in charge, A. Argent, J. Hopkins, commissioned boatmen, T. Trevett, boatman, of Coast-guard, Felixstowe, T. G. Meadows, W. J. Meadows, civilian boatmen, of Felixstowe (Schooner *Rose* of Ipswich). (30.3.01)

C. Spencer, commissioned boatman at Doohooma Coast-guard Station (Cutter *St. Patrick* of Westport). (1901)

W. Grainger, member of Middleton Volunteer Life Saving Company (Barque *Trio* of Sweden). (13.11.01)

J. Simmons, commissioned coast-guard boatman, Skinningrove (Barque *Erato* of Norway). (14.11.01)

J. A. PHILIPSEN, 2nd mate, W. BURMAN, bo'sun, A. E. LANE, B. HOGAN, S. KELLY, B. COE, A.B.s, J. DOHERTY, fireman, of *Planet Neptune* (Brigantine *Lilian* of Liverpool). (16.12.01)

A. Chapman, of Seaton Carew Life Saving Apparatus Company (*Trefusis* of St. Ives). (14.12.01)

W. G. TUDOR, chief officer, J. CAMPBELL, A. KELLNER, P. CULLEN, K. E. OLSEN, A.B.s, of *Askehall* (Ketch *Lord Salisbury* of Leith). (3.2.02)

Lance-Corporal F. J. TAYLOR, R.E. (Fishing-smack *Lottie* of Ramsgate). (1.2.02)

T. MELGUIN, cook of S.T. *Honoria* of Hull. (19.2.02)

C. Pettersen, O.S., of barque *Dalblair* of Glasgow. (5.2.02)

R. J. Jones, bo'sun of *Cymric* of Liverpool (member of crew of *Cymric*). (5.2.02)

H. GRAY, mate, A. Wenke, T. Murphy, A. Erikson, M. Pulliner, O.S., of sailing-ship *Vanduara* of Swansea. (25.6.02)

J. Hampson, of Maryport (Schooner *Wild Rose* of Liverpool). (3.9.02)

W. Costello, T. Fitzpatrick, T. Flaherty, M. Conneely, fishermen, of Galway (Fishing canoe *Lively Lass* of Galway). (6.2.03)

W. Cay, T. Gray, A. Cay, A. Hay, J. Hay, Junior, G. Hay, J. R. Hay, A. Morgan, A. J. Heeland, C. Cay, fishermen, of Aberdeen (*Xenia* of Copenhagen). (1.2.03)

T. Sherwin, coast-guard boatman at Whitburn (*Chamois* of London). (10.1.03)

D. Price, J. Hewitt, pilots, of pilot cutter *Lavinia* (Schooner *Corby Castle* of Beaumaris). (16.3.03)

G. F. Figgins, chief boatman, W. T. Vincest, A. E. Cowley, commissioned boatmen, R. Sullivan, E. Holland, C. Livermore, boatmen, of Coast-guard Station, Kingston, Dublin (Ketch *Confido* of Faversham). (16.3.03)

D. F. SHERET, master of *Chelsea* of London. (1903)

J. J. R. Dick, commissioned boatman, F. E. Aers, boatman of coast-guard, Portland. W. C. Norris, bo'sun of H.M.S. *Agincourt* (*Patria* of Norway). (25.10.03)

H. Plant, coast-guard boatman of Portreath (Ketch *Wheat Ear* of Poole). (20.11.03)

G. STRENG, O.S., J. WEST, apprentice, of *Laurelwood* of Middlesbrough. (1904)

J. Gargett, mate, A. Alege, O.S., of Schooner *Red Tail* (Ketch *Rhoda* of Padstow). (17.9.04)

J. O'CONNOR, 1st mate, C. LARSEN, carpenter, J. REID, E. R. MORRISON, F. GRADIKE, O.S., of sailing-ship *Lonsdale* (Barque *Eivion* of Carnarvon). (3.10.04)

I. WILLIAMS, 2nd mate, J. GRAYSON, bo'sun, W. HILL, F. D. HEFFERMAN, W. ROGERS, W. J. BROWN, W. HALLER, O.S., of *Dunstan* (Sailing-ship *Godiva* of Liverpool). (16.12.04)

E. Hyatt, commissioned boatman-in-charge, T. Baker, W. Mahoney, boatmen of coast-guard, Sheephaven (Lugger *Williamina* of Fraserburgh). (22.11.04)

J. West, 2nd hand, E. J. Wells, 3rd hand, of fishing-smack *Satanita* (Brigantine *Lizzie Lee* of Goole). (21.2.05)

T. H. WEBBER, mate of *Chicklade* of West Hartlepool. (14.1.05)

A. S. A. CAMPBELL, 4th officer, of *Rippingham Grange* of London. (25.9.04)

D. PEARCE, bedroom steward of R.M.S. *Rimutaka* of Plymouth. (16.4.05)

A. Chalmers, of the Drummore L.S.A. Company (*Gorgon* of Glasgow). (19.8.05)

G. B. Fleet, 2nd hand, C. Harvey, 3rd hand of S.T. *Alderney* (S.T. *Shetland* of Hull). (6.10.05)

A. GROAT, W. HUME, fishermen, of Papa Westray, Orkneys (Trawler *City of Lincoln* of Grimsby). (30.9.05)

A. G. Cheshire, commissioned coast-guard boatman, of Jury's Gap (Schooner *Marie Christine* of Hennebon). (14.2.06)

G. CALDER, commissioned boatman, T. Grills, boatman, of coast-guard, Flimstone (Schooner *Annie Park* of Barrow. (2.1.06)

W. BROWN, 1st mate, S. A. CORNWELL, 2nd mate, J. NELSON, bo'sun, A. McEWEN, chief steward, J. SIMEY, bo'sun's mate, W. GIBSON, O. BOWDEN, E. COLLARD, W. WHITEHOUSE, J. H. GALBRAITH, J. E. FITZ GERALD, H. McMANUS, C. WOODS, O.S., of *Bostonian* (*British King* of Liverpool). (11.3.06)

C. Davison, 2nd hand of S.T. *Southcoates* of Hull. (14.2.06)

W. Windows, commissioned coast-guard boatman, Essex Hill, Alderney (Schooner *Le Petit Raymond* of Nantes). (18.9.06)

J. Miller, of Scrabster (Sailing-ketch *Elizabeth Miller* of Whitby). (19.7.06)

S. SYDENHAM, chief officer of *Alleghany* of West Hartlepool. (16.11.06)

H. Ditter, O.S., of *Alnmere*. T. Welcome, cook of *Wearside* of Sunderland. (7.1.07)

E. H. GRAINGER, 1st mate, A. Harvey, 2nd engineer, of *Heung Shan* of Hong Kong. (18.9.06)

E. Purslow, chief boatman of Bolt Head Coast-guard Station, R. Hayter, commissioned boatman of Hope Cove Coast-guard Station, I. Jarvis, J. Argent, civilians, W. S. Day, Customs officer (*Jebba* of London). (18.3.07)

F. Fearnley, 2nd hand of S.T. *Swan* of Hull. (10.8.07)

P. M. Price, coast-guard boatman of Tenby (Ketch *Lady of the Isles* of Milford). (19.10.07)

G. W. Brown, 4th hand of S.T. *Terrier* of Hull. (11.1.08)

P. Holbert, chief boatman of coast-guard, Amble, A. Barton, Police Sergeant, of Amble, J. Helm, police constable of Warkworth (*Ina Mactavish* of Glasgow). (17.10.07)

W. Adams, commissioned boatman, of Sandgate (Sailing-barge *Astriald* of London. (25.11.07)

Lieut. J. STIVEY, R.N.R., chief officer, R. J. JONES, bo'sun, R. MATTHEWS, J. REDMOND, Q.M.s, H. WILSON, W. HARPER, M. BLAKE, J. RUSSELL, O.S., of *Cymric* (*St. Cuthbert* of Liverpool). (3.2.08)

J. R. DENTON, of Leeds (*Arzila* of Liverpool). (24.2.08)

W. Smith, T. Lennard, coast-guards of Ballygeary, T. Murphy, R.N.R., mate of schooner *Ocean Maid* of Wexford. (6.3.08)

M. Cahill, T. Cahill, J. Cahill, P. Donoghue, P. Connell, T. Connell, J. Connell, D. Connell, J. Connell, P. Connell, J. Connell, P. Donoghue, J. Sugrue, P. Sugrue,

C. Shea, M. Falvey, M. Keating, T. Lee, fishermen of Knightstown, Valencia Island, Co. Kerry (Fishing-boats *Aughlass* and *Skelligs* of Tralee). (14.9.08)

A. WARMAN, A. Laccohee, coast-guard boatmen, Ballingall, Co. Kerry, P. J. Connor, J. M. Kennedy, civilians (Barquentine *Orient* of Riga). (9.9.08)

A. Lee, 2nd officer of *Ennisbrook* of Glasgow. (18.10.08)

W. Tyson, chief officer, E. Hobbs, chief boatman, E. Hayman, J. Cole, commissioned boatmen, W. C. Cock, G. Cluett, J. Lander, boatmen, of Gorran Haven Coastguard (Fowey Division), W. H. Mitchell, civilian (Brigantine *Try Again* of Padstow). (6.10.08)

T. L. S. POPHAM, chief officer, D. Flynn, bo'sun's mate, J. FLEMING, J. COLE, Q.M.s, J. McMAHON, A. HILL, J. MORAHAN, A.B.s, of *Canadian* (Barquentine *Sunbeam* of St. John's, Newfoundland). (21.1.08)

K. GILMOUR, stewardess of *Sardinia* of Liverpool. (25.11.08)

W. BURGAR, J. HARCUS, J. GROAT, J. DREVER, R. REID, fishermen of Pharay Island, Orkney (S.T. *Hope* of Peterhead). (29.12.08)

W. Hodge, chief officer, J. House, chief coast-guard boatman, Bridge of Don (*Luddick* of Aberdeen). (25.3.08)

M. Verrill, of the National Lifeboat Institution's life-boat at Staithes, Yorkshire. R. PORRITT, of the Volunteer L.S.A. Company at Staithes (Schooner *Eliso* of Sweden). (11.2.09)

J. GUNNS, commissioned coast-guard boatman, Caister (Barge *Ernest Piper* of London). (10.12.08)

H. O. WELCH, coast-guard boatman, Kildonan (Greenock) Division (Schooner *Bessie Arnold* of Whitehaven). (28.12.08)

W. J. Shickley, commissioned boatman, A. M. Bird, boatman, of coast-guard, Inniscrone. W. Connolly, constable R.I.C., Inniscrone (Fishing-boat *Mary Jane* of Inniscrone), (12.8.09)

R. Gilham, skipper, J. G. Barber, hawseman, of fishing-boat *Our Boys* of Great Yarmouth. (27.10.09)

R. E. TROUT, 3rd officer, T. A. H. BROADBENT, pantryman of *Fantee*. J. R. SMITH, carpenter of *Sierra Leone* (*Fantee* of London). (23.9.09)

M. Miller, commissioned coast-guard boatman, Lydden Spout (Brigantine *Osprey* of Waterford). (7.10.09)

1910–1921

R. J. Hewitt, 2nd hand, E. M. Downes, deck hand of S.T. *Oldham* (S.T. *Gothic* of Hull). (25–26.1.10)

R. FORSTER, chief officer, O. M. JOHANSEN, bo'sun, A. RAND, H. H. BALDERSON, O.S., S. MOTTRAM, fireman, of *Carham* (*Trevorian* of St. Ives). (25.1.10)

J. R. Lascelles, chief officer of *Elswick Hall* of Newcastle. (12.9.10)

A. S. GEMPTON, skipper, J. H. TIDMARSH, 3rd hand, of ketch *Gratitude* (Fishing-ketch *Friendship* of Brixham). (17.12.10)

A. Watt, deck hand of steam drifter *Speedwell IV* (Ketch *Egremont* of Hull). (31.10.10)

S. W. MORTIMER, fisherman, S. GUPPY, S. HUSK, petty officers of coast-guard, St. Davids (*Gem* of St. Davids (life-boat belonging to R.N.L. Institution) and ketch *Democrat* of Barnstaple). (13.10.10)

W. Hall, leading coast-guard boatman, Leysdown (Barge *Cecil Rhodes* of Faversham). (12.1.11)

A. Hughes, coast-guard boatman, St. Margarets (Sailing-ship *Preussen* of Hamburg). (6.11.10)

C. Sisman, leading coast-guard boatman, Corton (Barge *Pioneer* of Rochester). (12.1.11)

D. DOWNEY, coast-guard boatman, Arklow (Fishing-yawl *Mary Immaculate* of Dublin). (15.12.10)

G. H. Hitchcock, G. Budden, leading coast-guard boatmen, Arklow (Fishing-boat *Fisher Lad* of Dublin). (15.12.10)

Rev. JOHN O'SHEA, Catholic curate, R. BARRY, coast-guard 2nd class petty officer, A. NEAL, coast-guard, D. LAWTON, constable R.I.C., J. O'BRIEN, Volunteer L.S.A. Company, P. Power, W. HARRIS, hotel-keeper, C. O'BRIEN, all of Ardmore, Co. Waterford (Schooner *Teaser* of Montrose). (18.3.11)

W. J. CHRISTIE, 1st mate of *British Sun* of Liverpool. (26.5.11)

J. L. DAVIES, 3rd engineer of *Konakry* of Liverpool. (4.7.11)

A. Brenner, A.B., of *Penpol* of Falmouth. (20.7.11)

T. W. Dunn, R.N.R., mate of barge *Flower of Essex* of Harwich. (23.8.11)

G. E. JOHNSON, 2nd mate, J. R. MARKHAM, J. W. HILL, E. J. TOTHAM, T. McKESSACK, A.B.s, of *Rievaulx Abbey* (Fishing-ketch *Hope* of Lowestoft). (1.10.11)

B. FREEMAN, apprentice of fishing-ketch *Alfred* (Fishing-dandy *Gratitude* of Lowestoft). (2.10.11)

F. P. HORSFALL, 2nd officer, A. LENYGON, F. W. SHEPHERD, N. G. JOHNSON, B. L. ALLINGTON, A.B.s, G. F. BAKER, C. BOLTON, firemen, of *Wrexham* (*Edward Dawson* of Middlesbrough). (1.10.11)

C. B. HUMBLE, captain of Brentford Troop of Boy Scouts, rescued some of his troop who were bathing off Hardelot Plage, France. (28.8.11)

R. ROBSON, 2nd hand, J. R. SCOTT, bo'sun, J. COWELL, deck hand, of S.T. *Lucerne* (Ketch *Good Templar* of Bridgwater). (13.11.11)

H. Green, chief coast-guard officer, Blatchington (Spritsail barge *Speranza* of London). (29.10.11)

T. E. PUCKEY, 1st mate, J. ROSS, O.S., of *Lincairn* (*Guillemot* of London). (21.12.11)

G. H. Warren, 2nd mate, J. Shorland, steward, D. Owen, S. Thomas, R Laurie, A.B.s, of *Milo* (Ketch *Rival* of Rye). (8.12.11)

L. C. Standford, leading boatman, R. M. Murphy, boatman, of coast-guard, Balbriggan (Trawler *Rosebud* of Balbriggan). (15.10.11)

F. G. Gowen, bo'sun, F. Clayton, 3rd hand, of S.T. *Pigeon* (S.T. *Bassein* of Hull). (6.11.11)

W. H. Sedgeman, of Perranuthnoe, T. L. Row, of Penzance (Norwegian barque *Suluto* of Christiansand). (14.12.11)

T. WATKINS, 3rd mate of *Devonshire* (*Hughenden* of Sunderland). (21.12.11)

Lt. W. CREAGH DOWNING, Royal Garrison Artillery, Rear-Admiral SIR CHRISTOPHER GEORGE FRANCIS MAURICE CRADOCK, K.C.V.O., C.B., Atlantic Fleet, Lt. CHRISTOPHER JOHN FREDERICK WOOD, H.M.S. *Black Prince*, Lt. NOEL MARCUS FRANCIS CORBETT, H.M.S. *London*, Lt. MAX KENNEDY HORTON, H.M.S. *Duke of Edinburgh*, Lt. GEORGE EDWARD CUMMING, H.M.S. *London*, Mr. SAMUEL CHARLES ARTHUR

SMITH, Gunner, H.M.S. *London*, Cmdr. WILLIAM HENRY NILES, R.D., R.N.R., Captain of the Port, Gibraltar, William Charles Undery, 1st boarding officer, Port Dept., Gibraltar, James Scott Noble, 3rd boarding officer, Port Dept., Gibraltar, Lt. Robert Russell Gossett, H.M.S. *Duke of Edinburgh*, Harry Penfold, petty officer 1st class, H.M.S. *Duke of Edinburgh*, Reginald Tatterson, Herbert J. Rogers, Alfred H. Jacob, Fredk. Butterfield, Albert E. Dean, Herbert W. Pullen, Percival Stephen Rowland, Alfred Knight, Joseph Margarison, Austen S. Batty, Robert Bath, Fredk. Lovell, James H. Wainscott, Chas. A. Chapman, Geo. C. Parker, Sidney E. Symes, A.B.s of H.M.S. *Prince of Wales*, Herbert Charles Presley, leading signalman, H.M.S. *Duke of Edinburgh*, Harry Cross, signalman, H.M.S. *London*, James Cheetham, signalman, H.M.S. *Duke of Edinburgh*, Horace Richard Mason, leading signalman, H.M.S. *Black Prince*, Ernest Davey, A.B., H.M.S. *London*, Fredk. Lancaster, leading seaman, H.M.S. *Duke of Edinburgh*, Geo. Henry Spencer, Jas. Barton Wyatt, Leo. Thompson, Ernest Lane, Cecil Haden, Jas. Edward Chappell, Jas. Harvey Clark, Wm. Francis Nash, Chas. Edward Allen, Oates Allen, Ernest Wm. Allright, William Wylde, A.B.s of H.M.S. *Duke of Edinburgh* (*Delhi* of Greenock). (13.12.11)

A. Third, A. May, volunteers, of Cairnbulg Rocket L.S.A. Company (S.T. *Clio* of Dundee). (14.1.12)

T. C. COKER, coast-guard boatman, Holmton (S.T. *Crux* of Grimsby). (10.1.12)

W. Sinclair, W. Wards, fishermen, J. Cruickshank, constable, A. H. Wards, Receiver of Wreck (Norwegian barque *Adel* of Brevik). (19.1.12)

E. Davies, chief officer, A. Haslar, leading boatman of coast-guard, J. Gillings, assistant, L.S.A. Company (Norwegian barque *Idun* of Christiansand). (17.1.12)

M. Georgeson, H. Rendall, R. Robertson, A. Pearson, C. G. Gilbertson, G. McWhirter, R. Peterson, G. Georgeson, fishermen of Lunnasting, Shetlands (S.T. *Rapid* of Peterhead). (17.1.12)

F. Pearson, labourer, of Scarborough (S.T. *Lark* of Hull). (13.12.11)

H. J. TULL, leading coast-guard boatman, Newquay (Schooner *Bessie* of Truro). (5.3.12)

C. M. Redhead, chief officer, J. C. Kilroy, A.B., *Caledonia* of Greenock. (10.4.12)

J. C. PITTENDRIGH, Apprentice of *Lincairn* (*Guillemot* of London). (21.12.11)

Midshipman E. F. Fanning, H.M.S. *Duke of Edinburgh*, Midshipman E. Scott Williams, W. Beaumont, Leading Seaman, W. T. Leggate, A. A. Dunk, L. H. Davies, A. W. Stratton, A. Johnson, P. West, G. W. Garlinge, E. Roberts, J. Beaumont, J. W. Brockman, S. G. B. Cutmore, F. Borras, C. H. Rednall, A.B.s of H.M.S. *London* (*Delhi* of Greenock). (13.12.11)

J. REES, 2nd mate, A. NISFOLK, bo'sun, S. W. MUIR, A. NORDLUND, A. McLLELAN, A.B.s, of *Ruabon* (Schooner *Mary Jane* of Lancaster). (12.11.11)

G. W. JUSTICE, coxswain, G. W. KRUEGER, driver, C. McARTNEY, deck hand, of S. Australia Marine Board Motor Boat *President*, T. S. HUGHES, coxswain, R. S. JUSTICE, driver, of S. Australia Marine Board Motor Boat *Controller* (*South Africa* of Melbourne). (21.8.10)

T. SARGENT, 3rd hand, T. G. C. PLANNER, deck hand, of S.T. *Xenia* (Schooner *Uzziah* of Salcombe). (25.11.12)

T. R. LEWIS, 1st mate, W. ERIKSON, carpenter and A.B., E. REISON, lamp-trimmer and A.B., A. J. SPENCE, A.B., J. INGLIS, fireman, of *Hockwold* (Schooner *Richard and Emily* of Goole). (27.11.12)

T. RILEY, sergeant, S. McNEIL, lance-corporal, H. SIMONS, J. B. COX, C. J. PHILLIP, constables in Harbour Constabulary, San Fernando, Trinidad, C. ETIENNE, civilian of San Fernando (Flat *Clyde* of San Fernando, and also a fishing-boat). (9.11.12)

C. HEIGHTON, leading coast-guard boatman, Cove Bay, Kincardineshire, A. CRAIG, civilian, of Torry, Aberdeenshire (*G. Koch* of Odensee, Denmark). (12.1.13)

W. H. HARMER, leading coast-guard boatman, Seaton Sluice, J. Ingram, C. W. Major, volunteers of L.S.A. Company (Russian barque *California* of Mariehamn). (15.1.13)

W. MARSDEN, leading coast-guard boatman, Blyth Haven, P. Gibney, E. G. M. Kelsey, A. Robertson, G. E. Scott, members of North Blyth Volunteer L.S.A. Company, E. Archbold, fisherman, G. Beading, labourer, W. Brown, R. Macarthy, hoppermen, A. Nixon, coxswain of Cambois life-boat (*Dunelm* of Sunderland). (11.1.13)

W. B. Wheeler, A.B., of *Brescia* of Liverpool. (22.2.13)

Lt. D. BLAIR, R.N.R., 1st officer of *Majestic* of Liverpool. (6.5.13)

E. V. Hugo, chief officer, E. R. Williams, 2nd officer, F. Martin, bo'sun, W. Jay, G. Jacob, A.B.s, of *Veronese* of Liverpool. (16.1.13)

P. Beard, leading coast-guard boatman, Bangor, T. Price, fisherman, Bangor, R. Jones, boatman to University College, Bangor (a small row boat (pleasure boat)). (30.5.13)

B. Dorsey, 2nd hand of *Warrior*, steam liner of Grimsby. (26.8.13)

J. Gallagher, 2nd officer, G. Anson, C. Bremer, E. Dahlquist, A.B.s, T. Smith, lamp-trimmer and A.B. of *Thornley* (Steam drifter *Scots Greys* of Banff). (19.11.13)

W. CAIRNS, chief officer, J. T. MUIR, 2nd officer, A. E. DUHRIN, carpenter, of *Baron Erskine* of Ardrossan. (10.7.13)

A. HALL, chief mate, M. RIORDAN, bo'sun, G. LINNGVIST, bo'sun's mate, J. ALLEN, F. W. BARLOW, J. McALLISTER, O.S., R. HUNT, apprentice, of *Asian*. F. J. R. GARDNER, 1st officer, J. WISE, H. PAYNE, G. O. THOMPSON, stewards, J. DONOGHUE, S. SMITH, W. TURTON, M. MURRAY, W. H. DONKING, T. TITCHEN, E. J. HEIGHWAY, A.B.s, of *Carmania*. T. STEELE, chief mate, T. B. KNIGHT, 1st mate, W. H. BAKER, 2nd mate, J. SOUTER, 5th engineer, J. NAVARRO, bo'sun, F. J. BAILEY, bo'sun's mate, W. H. FLETCHER, J. BROWN, J. ROSSITER, L. O'NEILL, Q.M.s, W. WALSH, lamp-trimmer, A. HAZLEWOOD, W. A. REED, E. D. CUNNINGHAM, W. BROWN, W. POTTER, C. WOODS, A.B.s, J. H. PRICE, O.S., of *Devonian*. W. ROBISON, 1st officer, P. J. LEWIS, 3rd officer, J. M. COATES, 4th officer, T. GARVEY, WALTER ELSE, G. W. MADAMS, F. W. STEPHENS, G. LEONARD, W. LIESEN, W. CRAWLEY, G. J. HORTON, S. GASKELL, F. R. PITTS, J. A. ROGERS, J. C. LAWRENCE, W. H. COWARD, J. KENDALL, W. HONEYMAN, G. SHAW, V. BOTTERILL, R. POTTER, A.B.s, of *Minneapolis*. J. B. JOHNSON, chief officer, J. E. NOTON, 2nd officer, W. E. CLEMENTS, bo'sun, F. WINTERFIELD, M. JOLLIVET, F. STAGG, F. THOMPSON, W. WILSON, A. CIVILL, H. C. P. GIBSON, A.B.s, T. MACKENZIE, C. L. COOPER, apprentices, of *Narragansett*. J. O. DAVIES, chief officer, J. BARKER, bo'sun, G. OLAFSEN, carpenter, H. HARGAN, W. BLACK, S. WAYGOOD, A. STEWART, J. BELL, O.S., W. PYNE, donkeyman, of *Rappahannock* (*Volturno* of London). (9.10.13)

H. LINKLATER, chief officer, R. SHARP, Q.M., J. FLETT, lamp-trimmer, B. GREEN, O.S., E. NEWHAM, S. SEARING, S. TRIMINGHAM, A.B.s, of *Cawdor Castle* (Schooner *Lucie* of Mauritius). (30.1.13)

W. J. Richardson, 3rd engineer, of *Sir Garnet Wolseley* of Newcastle. (26.12.13)

W. RUSSELL, chief officer, D. McPHEE, 3rd officer, F. BRADSHAW, bo'sun, W. JONES, carpenter, J. T. CRADDOCK, J. HAMILTON, A.B.s, J. Hull, O.S., J. PICKER, greaser, of *Monmouth* (Brig *Evelyn* of Carnarvon). (30.11.13)

W. HUGHES, chief officer, R. WILLIAMS, bo'sun, R. HUGHES, petty officer, A. WILLIAMS, Q.M., E. KEYS, J. HAYWARD, A.B.s of *Cornishman* (Schooner *Banshee* of Barnstaple). (17.1.14)

A. W. Adcock, 2nd officer of *Indrabarah* of Liverpool. (10–13.5.13)

A. M. SOUTER, chief officer, J. FLYNN, E. GRUNDSTROM, F. WILKING, A.B.s, G. FOOT, of *Invergyle* (Brig *Evelyn* of Carnarvon). (27.11.13)

W. F. Vowles, assistant scoutmaster, Port of London Sea Scouts (Ketch *Mirror* of Dartmouth). (25.10.13)

A. ODDY, chief petty officer of coast-guard, Sennen Cove, B. SWORN, leading boatman of coast-guard, Penzance (Swedish barque *Trifolium* of Gothenburg). (15.3.14)

A. W. Ladner, volunteer, Rocket L.S.A. Company, Cornwall (Trawler *Condor* of Brixham). (1.5.14)

J. F. Howlett, skipper of S.D. *Datum* (S.D. *Achievable* of Lowestoft). (9.5.14)

C. FULLER, W. Hughes, of Avonport, Nova Scotia (Tug *Chester* of Windsor, N.S.). (4.10.13)

T. N. PHILLIPS, skipper of trawler *Coriander*, G. E. JACOBS, skipper of trawler *J.G.C.* (H.M. ships *Aboukir*, *Cressy*, *Hogue*). (22.9.14)

J. COLLIN, skipper of S.D. *Faithful* (H.M. submarine *D.5*). (3.11.14)

W. PILLAR, skipper, W. G. E. CARTER, 2nd hand, J. J. CLARKE, 3rd hand, D. TAYLOR, apprentice, of trawler *Provident* (Launch of H.M.S. *Formidable*). (1.1.15)

J. STOCKLEY, police sergeant, Lyme Regis (Sailing pinnace of H.M.S. *Formidable*). (1.1.15)

Capt. C. T. M. Fuller, R.N., Comdr. H. C. V. B. Cheetham, R.N.R., Lt. C. J. Webb, R.N.R., Acting Lt. H. S. Daniel, R.N.R., Lt. A. B. Clough, R.E., S. G. Odam, artificer 3rd class, F. H. Grant, mechanician, P. J. Farrell, acting leading stoker, F. Davis, stoker, 1st class (boat of Nigerian Government Yacht *Ivy*). (21.10.14)

J. W. BENNETT, master, W. LORAM, O.S., of Sunk Lightship *Argo*. (28.12.14)

A. E. FISHER, skipper of S.T. *Euripides*, F. WOLLASTON, skipper of S.T. *Cameo*, W. ILETT, skipper of S.T. *Silanion*, H. WICKS, skipper of S.T. *Straton*, M. HOWARD, skipper of S.T. *Prince Victor* (*Runo* of Hull). (5.9.14)

W. WHITEHEAD, leading seaman, H.M.S. *Essex* (*Empress of Ireland* of Liverpool). (21.6.14)

D. L. H. Hoare, Apprentice of *Empress* of Cardiff. (14.2.15)

S. Robinson, 2nd engineer of *Oakley* of West Hartlepool. (23.2.15)

A. JENNER, skipper of S.D. *Homeland* (H.M. Submarine *D.5*). (3.11.14)

L. N. MORTON, J. Barry, O.S., of *Lusitania* of Liverpool. (7.5.15)

A. R. Ness, apprentice of *Verdala* of Glasgow. (11.8.15)

C. Hetherington, apprentice of *Jacona* of Dundee. (12.8.15)

T. ALEXANDER, 2nd officer of *Stanislas* of Liverpool. (1.11.15)

T. H. Weatherstone, saloon steward of *Corinthian* of Glasgow. (2.12.15)

W. F. Dark, chief mate of *Ellerslie* of Cardiff. (25.10.15)

W. J. Terlour, A.B., of H.M.S. *Lord Nelson* (Steam pinnace *No. 183*). (21.12.15)

H. A. White, leading coast-guard boatman, Blyth Haven (S.T. *Naval Prince* of N. Shields). (10.12.15)

H. B. Thomas, C. Dibben, engine-driver, H. Bell, turner and mechanic, E. P. Lester, civil engineer, C. Ripoll, foreman, J. Ribillard, pilot, F. H. Booth, clerk, T. Dearling, fitter fireman, of Les Falaises, Algeria (*Glenroy* of West Hartlepool). (10.2.16)

J. A. COVERLEY, master of *Virginia* of Glasgow. (16.7.16)

Rev. R. J. P. Peyton-Burbery, M.A., Chaplain, R.N., of H.M.S. *Suffolk* (*Pollokshields* of Sunderland). (8.9.15)

J. R. DAVIS, bo'sun's mate of *Corinthian* of Glasgow. (7.9.16)

J. J. SELBY, chief officer, R. WOOD, carpenter's mate, G. CAIN, lamp-trimmer, of *Devonian* of Liverpool. (2.11.16)

W. F. Yeo, civilian, of Sidmouth (*Grindon Hall* of London). (5.11.16)

H. Johnston, coast-guard boatman, Rattray Head (*Kiev* of Russia). (28.10.16)

C. KINCH, 2nd hand, E. H. OUTHOUSE, 3rd hand, W. BLACKMORE, W. WELDRICK, deck hands, of S.T. *Exeter* (Ketch *Frieda* of London (*C.S. 83*)). (20.11.16)

J. RONAYNE, A.B., of War Department Vessel *Cambridge*. (27.10.16)

J. J. Brandon, coast-guard petty officer, Peterhead (S.T. *Deeside* of Aberdeen). (21.1.17)

M. PURCELL, J. PHILLIPS, O.S., of *Clackmannanshire* of Glasgow. (25.1.17)

Lt. E. G. N. RUSHBROOKE, F. S. NICOLL, A.B., of H.M.S. *Sharpshooter* (*Kittiwake* of Cork). (9.4.17)

W. T. Watson, H. Holmes, Corporals of 19th Reserve Battalion Royal Irish Rifles (Schooner *Fulvia* of Svendborg). (18.11.16)

Capt. E. D. Gairdner, D.S.O., Royal Army Medical Corps (T.), L.-Corp. H. F. Crandall, West Kent Yeomanry, Pte. H. H. H. Jackson, 6th Battalion Highland Light Infantry (H.M. Transport *Ivernia*). (1.1.17)

Major T. H. BARCLAY, Surrey Yeomanry, Capt. R. A. HILL, Royal Irish Regiment (H.M. Transport *Transylvania* of Glasgow). (4.5.17)

G. AINSLIE, O.S. (acting leading seaman), R.N.R., H.M. Transport *Cape Transport*. (18.8.17)

Lt.-Comdr. C. K. Sergent, R.N.R. (retired), S. C. Pearson, O.S., examination vessel *Southern Prince*, J. Cox, gunner, Royal Garrison Artillery (*Rio Colorado* of London). (22.3.17)

S. G. L. Martin, leading seaman H.M. Torpedo Boat *No. 95* (*Clan Ferguson* of Glasgow). (7.9.17)

G. C. MACDONALD, chief officer, F. R. WILKIN, 2nd officer, J. BRYMER, chief engineer, K. AHMED, 2nd tindal, of *Chilka* of Glasgow. (1.7.17)

R. BURTON, Q.M., R. Davis, J. Mouat, O.S., of *Colonia* of Newcastle-on-Tyne. (21.10.17)

J. WHITELEY, chief officer of *Colorado* of Hull. (20.10.17)

R. T. Nichols, chief coast-guard officer (retired), St. Dogmaels (fishing-smack *Emrys* of Aberystwyth). (13.9.17)

Flight Sub-Lt. J. L. GORDON, R.N., Flight Sub-Lt. G. R. HODGSON, R.N., S. F. ANDERSON, leading mechanic (E), B. H. MILLICHAMP, wireless telegraphist (A.M. II) (a waterlogged seaplane float). (29.5.17)

G. F. W. Burr, leading coast-guard boatman, Sennen Cove (*Port Colborne* of Newcastle-upon-Tyne). (16.10.17)

Capt. W. L. COCKCROFT, Royal Army Medical Corps (H.M. Transport *Royal Edward* of Toronto). (13.8.15)
C. COLIN, chief officer of *Lapwing* of London. (11.11.17)
R. McBURNIE, chief officer of H.M. Transport *Cameronia* (?) (15.4.17)
G. RHODES, acting C.S.M., F. E. POLLARD, Sergeant, A. E. REA, acting Sergeant, H. J. BUTLER, F. TAPLIN, H. WADLOW, Privates, 9th Battalion Royal Warwickshire Regiment. H. BENNELL, Corporal, 1st Battalion Manchester Regiment, A. W. ANDREW, J. BIRD, Privates, Manchester Regiment. L. CROSSLEY, acting Corporal, W. RINGLAND, Private, 1st Battalion Highland Light Infantry. G. CHRISTISON, J. C. JENKINS, D. M. LLEWELLYN, A. RICHARDSON, Privates 9th Battalion Worcestershire Regiment. W. MUNDAY, Private, 7th Battalion Gloucestershire Regiment, P. FISHER, Private, 2nd Battalion Royal Highlanders. W. JONES, Private, Royal Welsh Fusiliers (H.M. Transport *Coronia*). (May 1917)
G. Healey, 2nd mate of *New Pioneer* (*Cork* of Dublin). (26.1.18)
J. S. GRUNDLEY, 2nd engineer of *Ellerslie* of Cardiff. (20.10.17)
G. H. Morton, O.S., R.N.R., H.M. Trawler *Elm*. (1.3.18)
W. RUSSELL, chief engineer, *Clan Macphee* of Glasgow. (2.4.18)
S. A. HEADON, A.B., of *Dalewood* of London. (26.2.18)
W. H. Quiggin, master of yacht *Armistice* (*Torbay* of Beaumaris). (15.3.18)
T. Handley, chief steward of *Saldanha* of N. Shields. (18.3.18)
Lt. T. P. Ryan, R.N.R., Surgeon E. A. Fiddian, R.N., G. Colman, A. Nocks, leading deck hands, R.N.R., of H.M.T. *Daniel Henley* (*Glodale* of Cardiff). (3.1.18)
Temporary Lt. J. COOK, General List, attached Inland Water Transport (H.M. Transport *Coronia*). (May 1917)
A. S. ANDERSON, chief officer, J. W. WHITE, 2nd engineer, T. CASSIDY, bo'sun, W. BROWN, O.S., of *War Bittern* of London. (7.5.18)
H. PARTINGTON, master of *Scholar* of Liverpool. (18.5.18)
J. WALTON, chief engineer of *Ayuthia* of London. (7.2.18)
Engineer-Lt. J. HEGGIE, R.N.R., Lt. O. BATEMAN, R.N.R., S. G. BIRKS, senior 2nd engineer, A. SUTHERLAND, 2nd engineer, W. BOOTH, junior 2nd engineer, R. WILSON, 3rd engineer. W. CLARK, boilermaker, R. JONES, greaser, H. FOULKES, trimmer, P. COONEY, J. GARNER, greasers, of H.M. Transport *Caronia*. (May 1917)
T. W. MORRIS, Q.M., of *Oranian* of Liverpool. (26.4.18)
W. BARNES, chief officer of *Betwa* of London. (7.2.18)
R. S. Willard, bo'sun, W. H. West, O.S., of *Mirlo* of London. (16.8.18)
E. Chatters, leading seaman R.N.R. (*Kiev* of Russia). (28.10.16)
L. F. REYBOULD, 3rd engineer of *Innisfallen* of Cork. (23.5.18)
E. J. HOLL, D.S.C., master of *Leasowe Castle* of London. (26.5.18)
Acting Capt. G. F. F. S. ELLIS, R.N. (*Islanda* of Glasgow). (10.12.17)
H. C. FLEMING, assistant 3rd engineer, W. HOMER, senior 5th engineer, of *Justicia* of Liverpool. (19.7.18)
H. A. FOREMAN, master, A. BERESFORD, chief engineer, of tug *Torfrida* (two of H.M. ships). (15.8.18)
Lt. E. S. F. FEGEN, R.N., P. DRISCOLL, R.N., chief petty officer, of H.M.S. *Garland* (U.S. oil carrier *O.B. Jennings*). (24.3.18)

H. Jardine, A.B., R.N.V.R., member of gun's crew of *Paragon* of Dublin. (8.11.18)

W. J. LAPPER, assistant engineer, Marine Department, Nigeria (Government steam barge *Gallwey*). (9.12.16)

J. NICOL, chief engineer, of *Themistocles* of Aberdeen. (6.4.17)

A. ELSOME, D.S.M., R.N.R., 2nd hand, J. Ansley, Newfoundland, R.N.R., leading seaman, H. Curman, R.N.R., deck hand, of H.M. trawler *Crucis* (*Lord Charlemont* of Belfast). (19.4.18)

Lt. J. C. ORR, Royal Irish Rifles (*Burutu* of Liverpool). (3.10.18)

H. CLOUTER, A.B., C. W. PENNEY, R.N.R., A. MOREY, R.N.R., O.S., M. DALTON, R.N.R., temporary skipper, D. RALPH, R.N.R., M. WHELAN, R.N.R., O.S., E. C. PERRY, master of *Gordon C.*, M. Shanahan, P. Gallagher, G. Westcott, A.B.s, R. Pierson, chief engineer, J. Budden, O.S. (*Florizel* of Liverpool). (26.2.18)

W. H. RITCHIE, chief engineer of *Ben Nevis* of Glasgow. (1.10.17)

J. McQUARRIE, 2nd engineer of *Clan Ross* of Glasgow. (5.5.18)

K. MORRISON, chief officer of *Sunik* of London. (9.4.18)

R. H. JAMES, 3rd officer, C. Fielding, 2nd officer, of *Polgowan* of London. (27.5.19)

J. S. Bastian, chief officer, C. Flynn, A.B., of *Trevanion* of St. Ives. (27.5.19)

W. FRASER, 2nd engineer, H. GUNTER, 3rd engineer, of *Sydney* of London. (26.11.19)

S. WILKINSON, chief officer, O. WILLIAMS, 2nd officer, N. WATSON, 3rd officer, A. MALABAR, 3rd engineer, J. T. OWEN, chief steward, G. W. BRISCOE, bo'sun, J. UNTHANK, bo'sun's mate, R. A. FULTON, G. O'GORMAN, H. OWEN, P. RODGER, Q.M.s, J. STEELE, lamp-trimmer, J. FITZGERALD, J. OWENS, H. SHELDON, J. C. SIMMS, P. STARKEY, O.S., of *Oxonian* (*Bradboyne* of Bideford). (6.2.20)

D. WELLS, donkeyman, of *Servian Prince* of Newcastle-upon-Tyne. (29.3.20)

G. H. FLAVEL, chief officer of Post office cable ship *Alert* (February 1920).

W. BRIGGS, skipper, H. BROWN, mate, S. G. SAYER, J. DYER, H. J. WARD, W. S. COLLETT, F. DYER, O. E. EASEY, J. McCARTHY, W. PRICE, members of the crew of S.D. *Sentinel Star* (S.D. *Dorothy Rose* of Lowestoft). (18.10.20)

J. Moriarty, skipper, E. Moriarty, 2nd hand, C. Brosnan, D. Devans, C. Gearen, members of crew of M.T. *Mairead* (Motor fishing-vessel *Spree* of Tralee). (11–12.10.20)

W. Harold, divisional chief coast-guard officer, Stornoway (Danish schooner *Ada*). (3.1.21)

Capt. E. R. G. R. EVANS, C.B., D.S.O., R.N., Lt.-Comdr. J. B. B. TOWER, D.S.C., R.N., Gunner J. G. DEWAR, D.S.C., R.N., W. G. Eldrett, leading seaman, A. E. Whitehead, A.B., of H.M.S. *Carlisle* (*Hong Moh* of Singapore). (3.3.21)

J. K. Watson, 2nd mate, H. Peterson, J. Spoore, S. Mathison, M. Bonett, A. O. Elkman, O.S., T. E. Noble, donkeyman, of *Heronspool* (Schooner *Elsie L. Corkum* of St. John's, Newfoundland). (26.12.20)

J. A. Cleeve, 2nd officer, R. J. Back, chief officer, of *Pentakota*, Lt. H. A. S. Scott, Second Lt. J. C. Farmer, Second Lt. A. G. Hedger, of Inland Water Transport, Royal Engineers (Native dhow *Kalyan Passa*). (14.6.20)

R. REVERS, bo'sun, G. REED, J. R. KITCHEN, O.S., W. BROWN, fireman, of *Stonewall* (Schooner *Donald T* of Lunenburg, N.S.). (15.1.21)

W. Gourlay, ship's carpenter of H.M.T. *Field Marshal*. (9.8.20)

CHAPTER XX

AWARDS OF THE BOARD OF TRADE SEA GALLANTRY MEDAL, 1922–1938

> One service more we dare to ask.
> Pray for us, heroes, pray,
> That when Fate lays on us our task
> We do not shame the Day!
>
> KIPLING, *The Veterans*, 1907.

Timely action of H.M.S. Cherwell

Lt. GEORGE GRIFFITHS, R.N.,[1] *Leading Seamen* WALTER G. BINDON, *and* REGINALD HONEY, *Able Seaman* ALBERT E. B. COOMBE, *all of* H.M.S. *Cherwell*

On the 22nd November 1921, the Schooner *Faithful* of Chester from Plymouth to Preston grounded on a shingle bank in the South Shear entrance to Wexford Bay. The vessel got off undamaged but, not answering her helm, again stranded on Catrick Rock, close by, and remained fast. The sea was so rough that the ship's boat could not be launched, and signals of distress were lighted, and, in addition, the crew's bedding was set alight to attract attention.

In response to a signal from the Irish Lights Vessel *Ierne*, H.M.S. *Cherwell*, at anchor at Rosslare, proceeded at 8.25 p.m. to render assistance, but as the night was very dark the correct position could not be ascertained, and, owing to the high sea and strong tide, H.M.S. *Cherwell* anchored to the northward of Catrick Rock and it was decided to try to reach the *Faithful* by boat.

The Skiff *Julia* under the command of Lt. Griffiths, Commanding Officer of H.M.S. *Cherwell*, and manned by Leading Seamen Bindon and Honey, and Able Seaman Coombe, was launched, and after much difficulty was able to get alongside the lee quarter of the *Faithful* which was just clear of the *Perch* on Catrick Rock, and succeeded in taking off the crew of five hands.

The rescue services occupied about an hour, and were attended by considerable risk to the boat's crew, who broke four oars on their way, and were in great peril in getting clear of the breakers on Catrick Rock. (15.3.22)

---

[1] Also awarded binoculars.

A North Sea rescue

ROBERT SPENCER,[1] *Second Officer*, MARTIN WENNERBURG, *Boatswain*, AUGUST HELLMAN *and* ARTHUR EDWARD CLERK, *Able Seamen*, HENRY FUDGE, *Donkeyman, all of S.S.* Dalton *of Newcastle-upon-Tyne*

On the 12th January 1922, the S.S. *Tidal* of Cardiff, laden with coal, was in distress about 8 miles off the Corton Lightship, near Lowestoft, the vessel having shipped tremendous seas, which caused her to take a heavy and increasing list.

In response to signals of distress the S.S. *Dalton* of Newcastle-upon-Tyne came to her assistance, and although the weather conditions were very bad the master of the *Dalton* decided to try to launch a boat.

Volunteers were called for, and after the *Dalton* had been manœuvred about 50 yards to the windward of the *Tidal* a life-boat, in charge of Mr. Robert Spencer and manned by the seamen mentioned, was launched and succeeded in rescuing the crew and passengers consisting of ten men, two women, and three children, and safely transferred them to the *Dalton*.

The rescuing boat had only gone some 30 yards on the return journey when the *Tidal* foundered. (6.4.22)

Gallantry in the Mid-Atlantic

James Corrigan, *Second Engineer of S.S.* Adriatic

On the 11th August 1922, during a voyage from Liverpool to New York, a violent explosion occurred in No. 3 lower hold of the *Adriatic* of Liverpool, as a result of which a number of seamen lost their lives.

On learning that some of his men were still below, Mr. Corrigan groped his way through smoke and fumes into the hold, where he found the water from the deck fire-hose coming through breaks in the hatch cover. He had the water turned off and went to search for his men.

On his return to the engine-room, Mr. Corrigan proceeded to call the roll, and, finding three men still unaccounted for, he went back at great personal risk from gas fumes and wreckage to the hold and carried out a further systematic search amongst the wreckage, which resulted in the discovery of one man lying dead under some debris. The body was extricated with much difficulty. (2.1.23)

---

[1] A piece of plate was awarded to Capt. James Joseph Shaw, master of the *Dalton*, and binoculars to Mr. R. Spencer.

Rescues from a gas-filled hold

Donald Macdonald, *Chief Officer,* George Archibald, James Joseph Lyon, John Foster, Harold Norris, Laurence Fauchelle,[1] *Seamen, all of S.S.* Tahiti *of London*

On the 28th February 1922, the S.S. *Tahiti* was sealed at San Francisco for fumigation with hydrocyanic acid gas. At 1.30 p.m., the fumigation having been completed, the seals were broken, and at 4.45 p.m. the steamer was considered free from gas and given clearance.

John Newton, ship's carpenter, arrived on board about 5.10 p.m. and was instructed by the chief officer to thaw out No. 1 lower hold by means of steam, and see to the drain-cocks of the chain locker. At 5.30 p.m. groans were heard in No. 1 hold. Newton, who had evidently tried to regain the deck, fell off the ladder on to his head, which caused it to bleed profusely. Chief Officer D. Macdonald immediately went down to Newton's assistance, but, feeling himself overcome, reclimbed the ladder, and managed to regain the deck. A seaman named George Archibald then went down, but was at once overcome by the fumes, as also was Fauchelle who followed. Lyon and Norris also went down, followed in a second attempt by the chief officer, whose efforts were again unsuccessful, and he had to be hauled up on deck in a state of collapse. Lyon and Norris also managed to regain the deck, where they also collapsed.

On the arrival of the San Francisco Fire Dept. fire-boat *Dennis T. Sullivan,* three men were still lying unconscious down in the hold, viz. Newton, Archibald, and Fauchelle, and Capt. John F. Kearney of the fire-boat put on a Gibbs gas-mask, and went down to their assistance. He managed to put slings around each man, but had to come up on deck for fresh air after each operation, as the gas mask was defective.

The Gold Medal for Foreign Service was awarded to J. F. Kearney for his gallantry on this occasion. (17.1.23)

Forty-two lives saved

George Ernest Lobb, *Boatswain,* **Samuel Fox, John Patrick Golding,** *Able Seamen, of S.S.* Tuscan Prince *of Newcastle-upon-Tyne*

The S.S. *Tuscan Prince,* whilst on a voyage from Middlesbrough to Puget Sound, was wrecked off Village I., W. of Vancouver, in a snowstorm in the early morning of the 15th February 1923. The vessel remained hard and fast upon the rocks and the only means of saving the lives of the crew was by getting on to the rocks.

Samuel Fox attempted to swim ashore with a line, but was unsuc-

---

[1] Awarded posthumously, as he lost his life in endeavouring to save his comrades.

cessful, and had to be hauled back on board. A boat was then lowered and manned by George Lobb, Boatswain, and J. P. Golding, with ropes fastened to them, but the boat swung round on to the rocks and was broken up. Golding was hauled back on board, but Lobb succeeded in scrambling ashore, where he made a line fast, and by this means the entire crew of forty-two made their way ashore. (31.7.23)

An officer's brave act at Muscat

MAJOR WILLOUGHBY LUGARD HOGG, D.S.O., *Late 3rd Brahmans, Indian Army*

On the 10th May 1918 Major Hogg, who was in command of a detachment at Muscat in the Persian Gulf, received a message from the Acting Consul, reporting that the S.S. *Oruro* was on fire in Muscat harbour and asking for assistance.

Major Hogg at once boarded the vessel with 100 men of his regiment and found that owing to the absence of adequate appliances the fire was rapidly gaining ground.

During the operations which followed, Major Hogg and a lascar were standing on a wood hatchway when the main beam collapsed, precipitating them both into the hold below. The officer managed to climb up the steel perpendicular ladder, which was very hot, and regained the deck, calling to the lascar to follow, but he failed to do so. Thereupon Major Hogg sat astride the coaming of the hatchway, and, bending down, succeeded with difficulty in hauling the lascar up from below into safety.

It was mainly due to Major Hogg's skill in directing the salvage operations that no loss of life ensued. (18.10.23)

Rescues from a sinking vessel

FREDERICK COOK, *Chief Officer*,[1] MICHAEL MAHONEY, JOHN COLLINS, GEORGE ELLIOT, RICHARD LESLIE DAVIES, *Seamen*, JOSEPH GRAY REID, *Carpenter, all of S.S.* Hollinside *of Newcastle-upon-Tyne*

The *Gay Gordon*, of St. John's, Newfoundland, from Oporto to Newfoundland, was in distress on the 21st April 1923 in the North Atlantic, and in response to her signals the S.S. *Hollinside* of Newcastle-upon-Tyne, proceeded to her assistance. At about 8.30 p.m. the crew of *The Gay Gordon* shouted to be taken off as their vessel was sinking, and after considerable difficulty the port life-boat of the *Hollinside* was launched in charge of Mr. Frederick Cook, chief

---

[1] The High Commissioner of Newfoundland presented Capt. A. Blakey, master of S.S. *Hollinside*, with plate, and awarded binoculars to Mr. Cook and £3 to each of the seamen concerned.

officer, and manned by the above-mentioned seamen, and succeeded in rescuing, in spite of darkness, strong winds, and rain the crew of six hands belonging to the Newfoundland schooner.

By skilful manœuvring the master of the *Hollinside* succeeded in getting to the leeward of the sinking vessel, and after about 1¼ hours' work rescuers and rescued were safely got on board. (21.11.23)

Rescue in Rangoon River

OSCAR EDWARD EMERY, *Chief Officer*,[1] JOHN MALCOLM GORDON EDWARDS, *Third Officer*, ALI AKBAR, AZIZUL HAQQ, AMIN ULLAH, KALA MIAH, NUR AHMAD, NUR-UL- HAQQ, *Lascar Seamen of S.S.* Lady Blake

On the 10th December 1922 the Burmese schooner *Ba La Aung*, with a crew of five hands, went aground on the western sands below Elephant Point off the mouth of the Rangoon River, and her signals of distress were observed by the *Lady Blake*.

A life-boat was launched in charge of Chief Officer O. E. Emery, and manned by Edwards and the above-mentioned lascar seamen, and pulled down, with an ebb stream and a tide running at about three knots, towards the *Ba La Aung*.

When ahead of the schooner the boat's anchor was dropped, and the life-boat slacked down alongside the vessel in distress, but the ship-wrecked crew refused to jump overboard and swim to the rescuing boat. A heaving-line was then passed to the wrecked vessel and the life-boat hauled closely alongside, when the crew jumped into her.

The boat's anchor was then hauled in; a mast was erected and sail set, but the mast was soon carried away by the force of the wind; ultimately the *Lady Blake* was reached in safety, and the rescued transferred on board. (12.12.23)

Rescue by night in North Atlantic

John Thompson Baker, *Chief Officer*,[2] Edmund Smith, *Carpenter*, Robert Inglis, William Stewart, David Gimblett, *Seamen, all of the S.S.* Cairnmona *of Newcastle-upon-Tyne*

On the 28th December 1923 the barquentine *Czarina* of St. John's, Newfoundland, was in distress in the North Atlantic in a heavy gale with hurricane force; her signals of distress were observed and answered about 10 p.m. by the *Cairnmona*, whose master manœuvred as closely as possible to the *Czarina*, and upon hailing the distressed

[1] The Government of Burma also awarded a watch to Capt. O'Kimber, master, and binoculars to Mr. Emery.

[2] In addition, the Government of Newfoundland awarded plate to Capt. John T. Berlin, master of the *Cairnmona*, binoculars to Mr. Baker, and a money gratuity to the men who manned the rescuing boat.

crew ascertained that the only life-boat had been smashed, and lost overboard, together with all the sails and various spars.

In spite of the very dark night and heavy seas which were running, a life-boat was got away from the *Cairnmona* in charge of Mr. Baker and manned by the men named, proceeded with great difficulty to the shipwrecked vessel, which was rolling very heavily, and succeeded in taking off the crew of eight hands. (17.7.24)

Rescues in Hong Kong typhoon

John Cropper, *Chief Officer*, **George Owen Reginald Jenkins**, *Third Officer*, **Bond Huggins**, *Apprentice*, **Won Jak, Hong Kam, Lam Pow,** and **Leong Yoe**, *Seamen, of the S.S.* Bowes Castle; **Thomas Lloyd Williams**, *Chief Officer*, **Kenneth Henry Stuart**, *Second Officer*, **Harold Wainwright, George Arthur Parker, Stanley Leonard Garrett, John Edward Snaith**, *Apprentices*, **Ge Ling Low**, *Quartermaster*, **Sing Yung Sang**, *Boatswain*, **Ching Chin Fong, Lin Ah Yok, Lee Van Chan, Chang Chin Pan, Chang Pan Fah,** and **Ying Ah Pan**, *Seamen of the S.S.* Egremont Castle; **A. Lexow**, *Chief Officer*, **Rolf Fredrik Moltzau**, *Second Officer*, **G. Dakserhoff**, *Third Officer*, **Chee Ah Kun**, *Boatswain's Mate*, **Han Fat Sang, Tse Tor,** and **Lin Chang Chin**, *Quartermasters, fireman, and the Chinese cabin boy who formed part of the boat's crew from the S.S.* Hwah Ping

On the 18th August 1923, when the colony of Hong Kong was struck by a typhoon, the S.S. *Loong Sang* of London, lying in Kowloon harbour, dragged her anchors, and being without steam (her main engines had been opened up for survey), after colliding with another vessel, she foundered.

Whilst the typhoon was at its height men were seen from the S.S. *Bowes Castle* floating by clinging to wreckage, and a life-boat was got away from that vessel in charge of Mr. Cropper and manned by Messrs. Jenkins, Huggins, and the Chinese seamen, Won Jak, Hong Kam, Lam Pow, and Leong Yoe. After about $5\frac{1}{2}$ hours' work in the raging sea and blinding rain two survivors were picked up.

On the *Egremont Castle* both life-boats were swung out in readiness for launching when a boat from another steamer, the Chinese S.S. *Hwah Ping*, came alongside, in charge of Mr. Lexow, and manned by Messrs. Moltzau, Dakserhoff, Chee Ah Kun, Han Fat Sang, Tse Tor, Lin Chang Chin, also a fireman and a cabin boy, who had picked up a survivor from the water, and rescuers and rescued were taken on board the *Egremont Castle*. Later, this life-boat was sent away, manned by a crew from the latter vessel, consisting of Mr. Williams (in charge) and Sing Yung Sang, **Ching Chin** Fong, Lin Ah

Yok, Lee Van Chan, Chang Chin Pan, Chang Pan Fah, and Ying Ah Pan, in an attempt to rescue further survivors of the *Loong Sang* who were observed floating by, struggling in the water. The boat being partly full of water, little progress could be made owing to the high sea and violent wind and rain, and the crew were unable to effect any rescues. They drifted and finally brought up alongside another vessel.

Shortly afterwards, the starboard life-boat of the *Egremont Castle* was launched in charge of Mr. Stuart and manned by Messrs. Wainwright, Parker, Garrett, Snaith, and Ge Ling Low of that vessel, and Messrs. Lexow, Moltzau, Dakserhoff, Han Fat Sang, Tse Tor, and Lin Chang Chin of the *Hwah Ping*, and succeeded in picking up another survivor of the *Loong Sang*.

Very great risk was incurred in rendering these services owing to the high sea, violent wind, and blinding rain. (3.1.25)

Gallantry of a 73-year-old fisherman

George Craig[1]
Fisherman

Early morning on 26th November 1924, the steam drifter *Press Home* of Buckie went ashore to the south of Portlethen village during heavy weather and a thick mist. The crew of eight hands endeavoured to gain the rocks, but five unfortunately were swept away by the surging seas and drowned; the remaining three, however, succeeded in reaching a high rock between 30 and 40 feet from the shore. Several attempts were made to reach them with lines, but another large rock which intervened made this impossible.

The tide was rising, and the position of the three men was becoming more and more dangerous, when Craig, who said that he knew of certain submerged boulders which could be used as stepping stones, volunteered to go to their assistance. With a rope fastened round his waist he forced his way over these submerged boulders, through the rough sea, in which he was at times immersed up to the neck, and gained the intervening boulder; from this position he was able to throw the rope to the survivors and to draw them one by one through the water to the rock upon which he stood. Then the rescued and the rescuer were hauled ashore by willing helpers on the beach.

In effecting these rescues, owing to the darkness, the submerged rocks, and the rough sea, Craig ran a great risk of being carried away or dashed against the rocks, and his action called for considerable skill and endurance on his part, he being 73 years of age. (16.1.25)

[1] A pecuniary award of £10 was also made.

Breeches-buoy rescue off Devon coast

WILLIAM HARRISON THURLBECK
WILLIAM ISAAC ARNOLD
JOHN JARVIS[1]

The steam-tug *Joffre* went ashore on the rocks under a cliff about 400 feet high at Bolt Head, Devon, about 2.20 a.m. on the 27th May last, during a gale accompanied by fog and rain.

Attempts were made to establish a connexion with the vessel by means of rockets, but the first two fired failed to reach her. The master was dangerously ill, and Mr. Thurlbeck, the mate, who had taken charge, called for volunteers to go and fetch the line which had fallen short. The crew being exhausted, there was no response, so Mr. Thurlbeck went alone in the ship's boat, which was connected to the tug with a line: he pulled inshore among the rocks, and succeeded in grasping the line. He was hauled back to his vessel, and made the line fast, but the boat was smashed. In the meantime, the Life Saving Apparatus Company had descended the cliff farther and succeeded in establishing connexion with the vessel with a third rocket.

As there was no means of securing the third rocket line to the cliffs, the shore end had to be held firmly by members of the Life Saving Apparatus Company on a ledge 70 feet up the cliff, and the line thus took up a steep sagging position. For this reason and owing to there being a large intervening rock between the vessel and the foot of the cliff, the breeches buoy could not be hauled ashore and it was necessary to send assistance on to the rocks below in order to bring the shipwrecked crew safely to land.

Before the breeches buoy had been hauled out to the *Joffre* a member of her crew came ashore by means of the line and would in all probability have lost his life had not John Jarvis, Francis Jarvis, and Arthur Thornton waded out on to the rocks and helped him ashore. The remaining ten members of the crew of the tug then came ashore in the breeches buoy, being assisted over the rocks by E. D. Lancey and Coast-guards Robert Richards and James Manning under the leadership of District Officer Arnold and John Jarvis.

This work was very dangerous as the tide was rising, the wind was blowing from 30 to 45 miles per hour, and the sea was breaking violently over the slippery rocks. During the rescue District Officer Arnold and Coast-guard Richards were washed off the rocks and had to be rescued by other members of the party, and Lancey was injured by falling rock. (23.9.25)

[1] In addition the Board of Trade awarded plate to Mr. Arnold, and £5 each to John Jarvis, Francis Jarvis, Arthur Thornton, Ernest Diplock Lancey, assistants of the L.S.A. Company, and Coast-guards Robert Richards and James Manning.

Explosion in China waters

So Hau, *Fireman of S.S. Paul Beau*   For details of this award see entry on p. 376, relating to George Henry White. (17.11.25)

Engineer's brave action

George Wilson   On the 13th December 1924, whilst the *Clan Macvicar* was lying in harbour at Brooklyn, New York, Mr. D. McLean, Fourth Engineer, opened up the main stop-valve cover on the port boiler by mistake: the cover blew off and he was very badly scalded.

Hearing the escape of steam, Mr. Wilson immediately went to investigate the cause. He could see nothing for steam, but thought that the auxiliary steam pipe connected with the starboard boiler had burst. Knowing that other engineers were working in the compartment, he rushed through the steam across the boiler tops and shut off the stop-valve of the starboard boiler, and, in so doing, was seriously scalded.

While closing the valve, Mr. Wilson caught sight of Mr. McLean, who spoke to him, but Mr. Wilson was almost choked by steam and was unable to reply. He managed, however, to escape from the boiler-room, being followed shortly afterwards by Mr. McLean; both were taken to hospital where Mr. McLean died next day.

The starboard boiler was under high pressure and in the belief that the auxiliary steam pipe connected with this boiler had burst, Mr. Wilson was right in going to close the stop valve and, had the conditions been as he thought them, his action would have involved him in very grave risk of losing his own life. (4.1.26)

Cliff rescue at South Shields

James Darling
WILLIAM HENRY WHITE

About 7.45 a.m. on the 27th November 1925 the ex-Admiralty vessel *P.C. 71*, with two men on board, under tow to Charlestown, Fife, for breaking up, stranded on the Trow Rocks, South Shields, during a heavy north-east gale accompanied by a hailstorm.

While the Life Saving Apparatus was being brought to the spot, Police Constable Darling, of the South Shields Borough Police, went with others to the top of the cliff overlooking the wreck and was lowered a distance of about 40 feet down the face of the cliff by means of a life-belt with line attached. He was immersed up to his waist in water. He endeavoured to reach the two men with another line, but failed to do so. A line was then thrown from the ship which he caught and fastened to the other life-belt and line, and these were then hauled on board the ship. By this means the constable was able to haul one man after the other to the place where he was standing at the foot of the cliff.

By this time the Life Saving Apparatus had arrived, and the breeches buoy was then lowered from the top of the cliff and one of the survivors was hauled up the cliff; but when the apparatus was lowered again, the constable and the other man were so exhausted that the constable had to signal for assistance. Station Officer White of H.M. Coast-guard, South Shields, then slid down the rope into the sea and assisted first the other survivor and afterwards the constable into the breeches buoy. These were successively brought to safety, Station Officer White using another rope to steady the breeches buoy and prevent the men from being dashed against the cliff. White himself was then hauled up, at considerable risk to his life. (8.4.26)

Rescue from a schooner

GEORGE SMALL MATTHEW, *Chief Officer*, JOHN DICK WILSON, *Second Officer*, ROBERT COLVILLE THOMSON BAILLIE, *Third Officer*, NORMAN ALLAN RICHARDSON, *Fourth Engineer*, WILLIAM IGNATIUS COSTELLOE, *Wireless Operator*, *two Chinese seamen (names not ascertained), all of S.S.* Benvorlich *of Leith*

The schooner *Nancy Lee* of St. John's, Newfoundland, of 188 tons gross, from Emily Harbour, Labrador, to Seville, with a crew of six, encountered a succession of gales from the 3rd October until the 18th October 1925. By this date she was leaking badly owing to straining in the gales, and from the 18th to the 21st October the vessel was hove to. At midnight on the 22nd October a heavy sea struck the vessel and carried away about 25 feet of bulwarks, rails, stanchions, &c., the latter breaking off below the deck. The vessel's life-boat was also smashed.

The storm abated somewhat, and at 10 p.m. on the 23rd October the lights of the S.S. *Benvorlich* were sighted, and signals of distress made. At midnight the S.S. *Benvorlich* closed with the schooner, but could not render immediate assistance, so she stood by until daylight, when the master of the steamer sent to the rescue a boat in charge of Mr. Matthew and manned by the men named, and two Chinese seamen whose names have not yet been ascertained. They succeeded in rescuing the crew of the *Nancy Lee*, and in so doing incurred considerable risk owing to the heavy sea and high wind. (22.4.26)

Gallantry on Spanish coast

Frederick Charles Reece

About 3 a.m. on the 17th January 1926, the S.S. *Clovelly* stranded near Barra de Ortigueira on the coast of Spain and, despite all efforts to refloat her, remained hard and fast. The weather was dark and misty, with heavy rain and a very rough sea. About 9 a.m. a boat was launched with a crew of five hands in charge of the second officer, for the purpose of taking soundings and running out a kedge anchor, but the boat on leaving the ship was overturned and the occupants were thrown into the water. All regained the upturned boat with the exception of the second officer and a Malay seaman, who were carried away.

Observing them in difficulties, Reece dived overboard from the *Clovelly* into the rough sea in an endeavour to place a life-buoy within reach of the second officer, who, however, disappeared before Reece could reach him.

The remaining four members of the boat's crew, and Reece himself, were rescued by means of lines. (3.6.26)

Thirty-seven persons rescued in North Atlantic

HERBERT ALONZO STROWGER, *Chief Officer*,[1] THOMAS FISHWICK, *Boatswain*, ISAAC JEWELL, RICHARD HARVEY WILLIAMS, SAMUEL BATE, EDWARD JOHN READY, BENJAMIN ORCHARD, *Seamen, of S.S.* Shirvan *of London*

The S.S. *Laleham* of London with a crew of thirty-seven hands, bound from Chile to this country, was in the North Atlantic Ocean on the 29th March 1926 when she encountered very severe weather with a violent wind, hail squalls, and high seas. Conditions grew worse, and during the next two days damage was done on deck and the two life-boats were smashed. Water poured in below, and the vessel took a list which increased to such an extent that it became clear the vessel could not survive. On the 31st March a wireless distress call was sent out.

In answer to this call the S.S. *Shirvan* arrived near the *Laleham* about 5.45 p.m. Shortly after 6 p.m. a life-boat was launched in charge of Mr. Strowger and manned by Fishwick, Jewell, Williams, Bate, Ready, and Orchard. Owing to the heavy swell it was not possible to go alongside the *Laleham*; but twenty members of her crew were rescued by being drawn through the water from the ship to the life-boat by means of a line with life-buoy attached. They were transferred from the boat to the *Shirvan* in the same way. The boat then returned

---

[1] The Board of Trade also awarded plate to Captain Goodricke, master of the *Shirvan*, binoculars to Mr. Strowger, and £2 to each of the other men named.

to the *Laleham* and the operation was successfully repeated, thus rescuing the remaining seventeen members of her crew. The rescue was completed by 10.30 p.m.

The services were hazardous owing to the high seas. Darkness added to the risk and the second part of the rescue had to be carried out in the light of burning oil barrels on the *Laleham*. (24.6.26)

Skilful rescue in Australian Bight

ARTHUR HUGH DYER, *Fifth Officer*, JOSEPH BLACK, FRANK ROBERT STANNARD, WILLIAM WILSON, LESLIE MAYNARD CLARK, *Seamen, of S.S.* Orvieto, *of Belfast*

On the 14th February 1926, whilst the *Orvieto* was crossing the Australian Bight, Sidney Dawson, deck boy, was washed overboard from the forecastle head. A fresh gale was blowing with heavy squalls and a very high sea. The vessel was immediately manœuvred into a position favourable for picking up the boy. The starboard accident boat in charge of Mr. Dyer and manned by Black, Stannard, Wilson, and Clark was lowered and sent away. After skilful manœuvring Dawson was picked up and the boat returned safely to the *Orvieto*.

The rescue was attended with considerable risk, especially when the boat was leaving and returning to the ship's side, as it was impossible to afford her efficient lee protection. It was only the expert handling of the boat which prevented her from being swamped. (1.7.26)

Rescue from a gas-filled tank

Captain Niels Marius Nielson
JOHN THOMSON MATTHEW

The S.S. *Bloomfield*, a British oil tanker, was proceeding in ballast to Beaumont, Texas, on the 18th October 1926, when the second Engineer collapsed, overcome by benzol gas fumes, while engaged in repairing a pump in one of the ship's tanks; the accident was reported to Mr. Matthew, Chief Engineer, who immediately went into the tank to the assistance of the Second Engineer and had just got hold of him when he himself collapsed.

The Chief Officer had rigged a block and tackle over the tank and had sent for gas helmets, when Nielsen appeared and went down into the tank with the object of rescuing the two men lying there, but he was overcome by the gas before reaching the bottom of the ladder.

All three officers were got up on deck within 10 minutes by other members of the crew, using gas helmets. The Chief and Second Engineers revived after artificial respiration, but Captain Nielson died. (8.2.27)

Volunteer life-boatmen's gallantry

LESTER NEWMAN, *Second Officer*,[1] THOMAS MCCULLOCH MCLEAN, DAVID STUART SORBY, ROBERT KENNEDY, *Able Seamen*, CHARLES RESIDE, *Sailor*, ARTHUR WILLIAMS, *Donkeyman*, *of Royal Fleet Auxiliary* War Diwan *of London*

The schooner *Cecil Junior* of St. John's, Newfoundland, from Seville to St. John's, in March 1926, encountered a succession of gales with heavy seas, and on the 18th March the schooner's rudder was carried away, causing the vessel to leak badly; other damage was also sustained.

The crew managed to keep the water down by pumping until the 22nd March, when, just before darkness set in, the attention of the S.S. *War Diwan* was attracted by distress flares. The *War Diwan* stood by while the crew of the schooner attempted to abandon ship in their own boat, but this boat was smashed by the heavy seas as soon as an attempt was made to launch it.

The master of the *War Diwan* then decided to send his own lifeboat, and in response to his call for volunteers, Mr. Newman, with a boat's crew consisting of McLean, Sorby, Kennedy, Reside, and Williams, proceeded to the *Cecil Junior* and took off the master and the five members of the crew. A very rough and high sea was running, and the boat's crew from the *War Diwan* ran considerable risk in getting alongside the schooner, and saving the lives of those on board. (9.6.27)

Trawler-hands' brave attempt

𝕮𝖍𝖆𝖗𝖑𝖊𝖘 𝕯𝖔𝖜𝖓, *Second Hand*[2] 𝕾𝖊𝖑𝖜𝖞𝖓 𝕰𝖗𝖓𝖊𝖘𝖙 𝕲𝖎𝖑𝖑, *Deck Hand*

The steam trawler *Oku*, of Milford, was in distress on the fishing-grounds off the south-west coast of Ireland early in the morning of the 11th February, having been damaged by heavy seas which caused a serious inrush of water. Signals of distress were made, and these were answered by the steam trawler *Limeslade*.

The *Limeslade* stood by from 4 a.m. until 8.30 a.m. Her skipper then sent away the small boat with a line attached, manned by Down and Gill, to try to reach the *Oku*. After battling for nearly an hour against the hurricane and the raging sea, they had to give up their attempt owing to exhaustion, and the boat was pulled back to the *Limeslade*.

---

[1] The Government of Newfoundland also awarded binoculars to Mr. Newman and £3 to each of the others named.

[2] The Board of Trade also awarded plate to James Gale, D.S.C., skipper of the *Limeslade* and £3 each to Down and Gill.

A dan-cast was then fastened to the line, and Down and Gill later made another attempt to reach the *Oku*. Again they had to give up.

The skipper of the *Limeslade* then decided to try to get the empty boat alongside the *Oku*. A longer line was fastened to the boat, the *Limeslade* was manœuvred into a favourable position, and the boat was drifted down to the *Oku* and secured by means of a grapnel. After the ten members of the crew of the *Oku* had got into the boat it was pulled through the water to the *Limeslade*, and they were helped on board.

Although Down and Gill failed in their attempts to reach the *Oku* they displayed great gallantry and ran grave risk. (16.4.28)

A hero of the boiler-room

John Whyte On the 29th September 1927 the *King George V* was waiting to enter Irvine Harbour when an explosion in one of the high-pressure water-tube boilers forced open the furnace doors. Two firemen on duty were very seriously injured by the escaping steam and burning coal. The explosion also blew out the lid of the man-hole in the port alleyway, and the upper part of the engine-room and the alleyway were filled with steam.

Mr. Whyte, Chief Engineer, and the Third Engineer, who were on duty in the engine-room, immediately took steps to clear away the steam from the boiler-room, to reduce the steam pressure, and by extinguishing the fires to stop the generation of steam. Mr. Whyte helped one of the firemen from the boiler-room into the alleyway and was then lowered through the open man-hole to the assistance of the other fireman, but the intense heat made it impossible for him to stay down. Shortly after Mr. Whyte had been hauled up, the second fireman was seen through the manhole, and, on being called, managed to climb the ladder and was assisted out of the man-hole. Both he and the other fireman died of their injuries after admission to hospital.

In trying to go to the assistance of the fireman Mr. Whyte took a very great risk; although steps had been taken to disperse the steam, the high-pressure steam from both the boilers of the vessel was still escaping into the boiler-room. There was a great danger of Mr. Whyte being fatally injured through inhaling hot, dry steam. (14.5.28)

Rescue of four men from a drifting barge

HAROLD WALWIN CLARKE The concrete barge *Cretetree*, with a crew of four hands, left Lerwick on the 28th March in tow for Stornoway. The vessels ran into a gale, and during the night of the 29th/30th March the tow-rope parted and the barge's rudder was broken. The tug endeavoured to get another line on board, but the gale and the rough seas made this impossible; the vessels became separated and lost sight of one another. The barge was helpless and was becoming swamped, the crew having to resort to the pumps and baling to keep the water down. Rockets were fired, and at daybreak on the 30th March signals of distress were sent up.

During the afternoon the steam trawler *Liberia* of Grimsby sighted the signals, and went to the assistance of the *Cretetree*, which was then 35 miles north by west of the Orkney Islands. A wire rope was got on board and towing began, but the rope soon parted. An attempt was made to get another line with a chain on board, but there was no wire on the barge with which to connect them up. The crew of the *Cretetree* tried to get away in their boat, but it was smashed.

An attempt was next made to launch the *Liberia*'s boat, but it also was stove in. The *Liberia* was then manœuvred close to the stern of the barge and a heaving-line was thrown, and secured on board the trawler. One of the crew of the *Cretetree*, after fastening the other end of the line to himself, jumped overboard, and was pulled through the water to the *Liberia*. The *Liberia* then took up a position to windward of the *Cretetree*; a line attached to a life-buoy was drifted to the barge, and another of the crew jumped overboard and was hauled aboard the *Liberia* by the line.

The two remaining men on the barge were too exhausted to be rescued in this way, and Harold Walwin Clarke, a deck-hand of the *Liberia*, volunteered to swim with a line to the barge. When the *Liberia* had approached within 20 yards of the *Cretetree*, Clarke jumped overboard and actually reached the barge, but it was feared that he would be injured when attempting to get on board, and he was pulled back to his ship. The *Liberia* was then manœuvred to windward and brought stem on to the *Cretetree*, and a line with a life-buoy was thrown on board; the two men remaining jumped overboard with the life-buoy and were safely transferred to the *Liberia*. (27.7.28)

Rescues in the St. George's Channel

WILFRED OSBORNE STANLEY,[1] *Mate*, ROBERT JAMES GEORGE, *Whaleman*, ALBERT EDWARD STOCKTON, *Net-stower*, *of the Steam Drifter* George Albert *of Great Yarmouth*

The *Guiding Star* of Runcorn, a small wooden schooner with a crew of four hands, was badly damaged on the night of 14th April in the St. George's Channel by shipping heavy seas. Distress signals were hoisted at noon on 15th April and were answered next morning at 8 a.m. by the steam drifter *George Albert*, when the *Guiding Star* was in a sinking condition.

[1] Also awarded binoculars by the Board of Trade.

The small boat of the schooner had been smashed by the seas and was useless, and the life-boat of the drifter, manned by Stanley, George, and Stockton, was sent away to effect a rescue. Although the weather conditions had moderated somewhat, there was still a strong wind blowing and heavy sea running, and the work of approaching the schooner was difficult and dangerous. The boat was swamped and had three planks stove in when alongside the *Guiding Star*. But she was kept afloat by skilful handling, and the men on the schooner were safely taken off and transferred to the *George Albert*. (8.8.28)

Life-boatmen's bravery

JOHN WILLIAM HARRIS, *First Mate*, STEPHEN CORNER STEPHENSON TAWS, *Second Mate*, REGINALD THISTLE FOSTER, *Quartermaster*, PERCY ARTHUR WALKER, *and* WILLIAM ROUSE, *Able Seamen, of the* City of Lahore *of Liverpool*

The *Selma Creaser* of St. John's, Newfoundland, was in distress in a sinking condition in the Atlantic on the 30th October 1927, and at 5.25 a.m. on that day the *City of Lahore* sighted a distress flare and went to her assistance. After pouring oil on to the sea the *City of Lahore* stood by until 6.30 a.m., when the master sent away a life-boat in charge of Mr. Harris and manned by the second mate and the other men named. The wind was still blowing at storm force with a heavy swell running and it required skilful handling by Mr. Harris to prevent the life-boat from being thrown against the side of the schooner or capsized. The master and the five members of the crew of the *Selma Creaser* were safely transferred to the life-boat; one of them fell into the water between the schooner and the life-boat, but he was got into the boat uninjured.

The rescue was completed by 7.35 a.m. and the *City of Lahore* continued her voyage. (5.1.29)

A hero of the boiler-room

𝔚illiam 𝔄rthur 𝔍ames

On the 12th October 1928 a fire broke out in the stokehold of the *Trojanstar*, at about 6.30 p.m., when the vessel was off the Pacific Coast of the United States. This was caused by the failure of a joint in one of the heaters which was being used to supply oil fuel to a boiler, and a stream of hot oil was projected across the stokehold in the direction of a coal-burning furnace, some of the oil falling on burning coal which lay on the floor plates of the stokehold.

Several members of the crew who were in the stokehold succeeded in escaping into the engine-room, but the Second Engineer and two firemen were unable to do so, being trapped by the flames. James was in another part of the stokehold and could himself have escaped, but ran to, and closed, the door leading to the pump-room, in which there were some 40 tons of oil. This compartment was close to the heater from which the hot oil was escaping, and James ran considerable risk of coming into contact with the blazing oil and of being burned to death. After closing the door he joined the other men in the port wing. Later, one of the firemen was so overcome by the conditions that he rushed through the flames into the engine-room and then on deck, but he was so severely burned that he died soon afterwards.

The fire was subdued soon after 9 p.m., when the remaining three men were rescued from the stokehold.

By his action in closing the door of the pump-room James undoubtedly prevented the fire extending to the compartment containing the oil fuel. (11.3.29)

Another hero of the boiler-room

𝕳𝖚𝖌𝖍 𝕻𝖊𝖓𝖓𝖞, *Second Officer* The S.S. *Trentwood* of Middlesbrough, from Ghent to Middlesbrough, was off Whitby on the 16th March when an explosion occurred in the boiler; the engine-room quickly filled with steam. As the boiler was fast losing water, the Second Engineer, Mr. R. Buckley, who was on watch at the time, made his way to the rear of the engines to start the feed-tank pump, which is situated close to the boiler, and while he was engaged in this work another, but more violent, explosion occurred, and he was rendered unconscious.

After giving orders for the fires to be withdrawn the Chief Engineer went from the stokehold to the engine-room to find Mr. Buckley but was unsuccessful; he then opened the engines out in order to take the steam off the boiler. The Master also tried to enter the engine-room but was prevented by escaping steam, and, returning to the bridge in order to haul the ship in as close as possible to land, he told Penny to see if he could help in the engine-room. Mr. Penny went down to the stokehold and finally reached the engine-room through the engine-room grating, then, getting on to the engine platform by a ladder, found Mr. Buckley unconscious and with great difficulty carried him through the engine-room and then on to the deck. After the application of artificial respiration, Mr. Buckley recovered and later returned to duty in the engine-room. (24.10.29)

Gallant life-boat rescue

WILLIAM DYNHAND CONGDON, *Chief Officer*,[1] H. HANSEN, F. BERTELSEN, T. FINKELENBERG, K. J. BEEK, P. PEDERSIN, S. ERIKSEN, CHARLES J. E. OEHLERS, HANS OLAY HANSEN, *Seamen, of S.S.* Manistee *of Liverpool*

The Canadian auxiliary-motor schooner *Quaco Queen* of St. John, New Brunswick, was in distress in a strong westerly gale and heavy swell in the Atlantic Ocean on the 30th January 1929; she was waterlogged, her rudder had been carried away, and seas were sweeping over her.

Her signals of distress were sighted during the afternoon by the S.S. *Manistee* of Liverpool. The Master altered the ship's course and went to the assistance of the schooner and, as there were indications that the weather conditions would become worse, arrangements were made to send a boat away from the *Manistee*. The ship was manoeuvred into a position to windward of the schooner in order to make a lee for a life-boat and, after oil had been discharged on to the rough sea, a life-boat was sent away in charge of Mr. W. D. Congdon, Chief Officer, with a crew consisting of the seamen named.

The boat's crew were in considerable risk owing to the heavy gale and rough sea before they reached the schooner and took off the nine members of her crew, and Mr. Congdon exercised great skill in preventing his boat from being capsized and in getting the rescued men safely on board the *Manistee*. (11.10.29)

Rescue in Mid-Atlantic

William Henry Downing, *Second Mate*,[2] Ernest William Espley, *Third Mate*, John Bromage, John Manin, Harold James Stringer, Patrick Kearns, John Arthur Chidlow, *Able Seamen, and* R. P. Ziegler, *a passenger, of S.S.* Manchester Regiment *of Manchester*

On the 8th December 1929, the British S.S. *Volumnia* of Glasgow was in distress in very bad weather in the Atlantic Ocean; in response to distress signals the S.S. *Manchester Regiment* went to her assistance, and, having approached, waited for a lull in the storm before attempting a rescue. Shortly after 9 o'clock, despite the very dangerous sea running, the Master of the *Manchester Regiment* decided to attempt a rescue, and a boat was

---

[1] The Canadian Government also awarded plate to Capt. James Pengelly, master of the *Manistee*, binoculars to Mr. Congdon, and £3 to each of the above-named seamen.

[2] The Board of Trade also awarded plate to Capt. Philip Linton, master of the S.S. *Manchester Regiment*, binoculars each to Mr. Downing and Mr. Espley, and monetary awards to the men mentioned above.

launched, in charge of the Second Mate, Mr. Downing, with a crew consisting of Mr. Espley, Third Mate, Bromage, Manin, Stringer, Kearns, Chidlow, and Mr. Ziegler. Very great difficulty was experienced in keeping the boat afloat, but by skilful manœuvring Mr. Downing, though badly injured in the hand in the launching of the boat, made two trips to the *Volumnia* and the entire forty-five members of the crew of that vessel were eventually taken off. The rescuing boat was badly damaged and abandoned. (30.1.30)

Gallant rescue off Durban

EDWARD GEORGE FULLICK, *Fourth Officer*, ERNEST ALEXANDER IRWIN, *Boatswain's Mate*, FRANK RICHARD DOMINEES, HARRY HENBEST, ALBERT NOTLERS, HENRY JAMES PARNELL, LESLIE THOMAS PATTINSON, JOSEPH EDWARD PARKISS, GEORGE STEWART, WILLIAM ALBERT TAYLOR, NORMAN WARD, RICHARD WALTER WALTON, HERBERT THOMAS MARK WILLOCK, *Able Seamen*, and HENRY LEALE, *Lamp-trimmer, of the S.S.* Armadale Castle

The fishing-vessel *Bluff* of Capetown left Durban on the 8th June 1929 for the fishing-grounds off North Sands and on the same day ran into squally weather. Early next day the wind had increased to gale force and a heavy sea swept the vessel, smashing the fishing-gear. Shortly afterwards, heavy seas washed three of the crew overboard; two succeeded in regaining the vessel and the other managed to cling to a raft which had broken adrift and was picked up later on the beach. A course was then set for Durban, but mooring wire fouled the propeller and stopped the engines. The crew were unable to clear the obstruction. The starboard anchor was let go, but lost. After drifting for awhile, the *Bluff* let go the port anchor and succeeded in anchoring some two and a half miles from the shore.

About 7.30 a.m. the *Armadale Castle, en route* from East London to Durban, was attracted by signals of distress made by the *Bluff*. Heavy seas were still running, but the *Armadale Castle* was manœuvred into such a position that a life-boat could be sent away. This boat was in command of Mr. Fullick, Fourth Officer, and the men named. Approach to the wreck was very difficult, but Mr. Fullick succeeded in getting alongside and took off seventeen of the crew of the *Bluff* before he was compelled to return to the *Armadale Castle*, as the life-boat had shipped so much water as to be in danger of sinking. On return to the *Armadale Castle*, the life-boat was taken on board and the steamer was manœuvred to a more favourable position in the hope of making a further trip to the *Bluff*, as there were five men still on board that vessel. Mr. Fullick again took charge of the boat, which was manned by the men named. By skilful seamanship, Mr. Fullick took the boat a second time alongside the *Bluff* and rescued the remainder of the crew. (7.2.30)

Gallantry in Mid-Atlantic

ALFRED HENDER, *Chief Officer*,[1] PATRICK CRAINE, *Boatswain*, NORMAN CODY, WILLIAM HEAPS, WILLIAM JAMES HEMMINGS, GEORGE SAUNDERSON, EDWARD DOUGLAS THORKILSON, *Seamen, of the S.S.* Nova Scotia, *of Liverpool*

The Newfoundland fishing-schooner *Janie E. Blackwood* left St. John's on 29th November 1929 for the northern part of the island, but owing to bad weather conditions she was driven out into the Atlantic Ocean.

The vessel continued to encounter severe weather conditions which carried away the boats, and on 12th December 1929 she had become unseaworthy and signals of distress had to be made. At 10.30 p.m. on that date the S.S. *Nova Scotia* observed distress flares on the schooner and proceeded to her assistance. The S.S. *Lord Antrim* also stood by to render help if required.

At 11 p.m. a life-boat was sent away from the *Nova Scotia* in charge of Mr. A. Hender, Chief Officer, manned by the men named.

After some difficulty this boat succeeded in reaching the *Janie E. Blackwood* and took off ten members of the crew.

Weather conditions were so severe that the life-boat could not be recovered. (25.2.30)

Rescue off Land's End

WILLIAM STOKES, *Carpenter*

The *Frances Duncan* sailed from Barry on 4th December 1929, with coal for Rouen, carrying a crew of twenty-one hands and ran into bad weather. Next morning the wind was blowing at storm force and a high confused sea was running from the south-west. At about 11.50 a.m., when a mile and a half from the Longships Lighthouse, Land's End, she was struck by a tremendous sea which shook the whole ship and caused her to take a dangerous list to port

The list increased and the crew were ordered to abandon ship. Within a few minutes the *Frances Duncan* was on her beam ends, and soon afterwards turned turtle.

The *Alice Marie*[2] was near and tried to give assistance. Despite the

---

[1] Also awarded binoculars by the Government of Newfoundland.
[2] The Board of Trade also awarded plate to Capt. Charles Blaylock, master of the *Alice Marie*, in recognition of his action.

violence of the wind and the very rough seas, the Master of the *Alice Marie* began to search for survivors and soon saw five men clinging to an upturned boat. The *Alice Marie* was manœuvred close to this boat and one man was got on board by means of a line. The boat drifted away, but the *Alice Marie* managed once again to get alongside and three more survivors were rescued. The remaining man had died from exposure.

By this time the *Frances Duncan* had sunk, but the search was continued and two more survivors were seen floating on pieces of wreckage. Unfortunately, when the *Alice Marie* reached the wreckage it was found that one of the two men had disappeared. A rope was thrown to the remaining man but he was too exhausted to make use of it. Stokes then lashed a rope round his waist, went over the side at very great risk to himself down a rope ladder, and made a rope fast to the man in the water, who was thus safely taken on board.

The rescue of the survivors, carried out under most difficult conditions, called for skilful seamanship on the part of the Master of the *Alice Marie*, Captain Blaylock, owing to the severe weather and the close proximity of rocks. During the operations the *Alice Marie* had, of necessity, to approach very near to the cliffs, and as it was impossible for her to turn, she had to be manœuvred out of danger stern first. (27.2.30)

Rescue in Mid-Atlantic

JOHN HOLLAND WALKER, *Third Mate*, JOHN FITZGERALD, *Boatswain's Mate*, JOHN BOYLAN, *Chief Petty Officer*, JOHN WHELAN, *Storekeeper, and* PETER CODD *and* WILLIAM HENRY WILLIAMS, *Quartermasters*, ALBERT EDWARD COLE, GEORGE DELAHAY, GEORGE AUGUSTUS RILEY, *Able Seamen, and* JOHN ROBERTS. *Sailor, of the S.S.* Baltic

The schooner *Northern Light* of St. John's, Newfoundland, was in distress in the Atlantic Ocean on the 6th December 1929 and the *Baltic* went to her assistance. A very strong westerly gale was blowing and a heavy sea was running. After the *Baltic* had been manœuvred into position at windward, oil was forced overboard to facilitate the launching of a life-boat. It was only with difficulty that the boat was got away in charge of Mr. Walker and manned by the men named. The boat approached near enough to the *Northern Light* to enable a line attached to a piece of wood which had been floated from the schooner to be secured and made fast to the boat. By means of this line the schooner's crew then succeeded one by one in reaching the life-boat, except one man who was drowned owing to the line being dragged from his grasp by the pitch of the boat in the heavy seas.

The risk was great and the life-boat had great difficulty in returning to the *Baltic*, where rescued and rescuers had to be got on board by means of lines, and the boat abandoned. (9.2.31)

A Newfoundland schooner's crew saved

FRANK JOHN GOODCHILD, *First Mate*,
HARRY JAMES SMITH, *Boatswain*,
HAROLD BERNARD AMMONSEN
PETER CHARLES DONOVAN
JOHN ALBERT KILVERT
WALTER SKEGGS
JAMES SKELLY, *Able Seamen*

The Newfoundland schooner *Dorothy Baird* of St. John's, with a crew of seven hands, was in distress in the Atlantic in January–February 1930. Owing to stress of weather, her main and mizen topmasts had been carried away and she had sprung a leak. The pumps were started, but they became choked and the water gradually gained on the vessel. For fifteen days the schooner drifted in this condition until on the 10th February she was sighted flying a distress signal by the S.S. *British Valour* of London, which went at once to her assistance.

At the time the sea was very rough with a heavy swell and a strong wind was blowing. Despite these difficult conditions a steel life-boat was launched from the *British Valour* in charge of Mr. F. J. Goodchild, Chief Officer, with a crew consisting of the men named, and the crew of the *Dorothy Baird* were transferred to the steamship.

During the operations the life-boat was severely damaged. (10.3.31)

A hero of the engine-room

Robert McGregor Forth, *Second Engineer*

On the 30th January 1931 the *Lumina* was in the N. Atlantic when it was discovered that the plates in the pump-room were awash with benzine.

Mr. Forth went down to the lower grating of the pump-room and reported that the gas in the compartment was strong. The Chief Engineer then put on a gas helmet, descended into the port side of the pump-room and opened up the valves to allow the benzine to be cleared. He returned to the top deck and after a rest was lowered down the starboard side of the pump-room, a 'boatswain's chair' being used for the purpose, as there were no ladders on that side.

The Chief Engineer was seen to open up certain valves on the starboard side when the air-pipe connected with the gas helmet as well as the safety-line became fastened round one of the pipes in the pump-room. Although advised against such a course, Mr. Forth immediately rushed down the ladders on the port side to the assistance of his Chief, and, having apparently freed the air-pipe and the life-line, called for the Chief Engineer to be pulled up on deck. When about 10 feet from the bottom of the pump-room, the Chief Engineer grasped a pipe, pulling himself out of the 'boatswain's chair', and fell to the bottom of the compartment.

By this time Mr. Forth was seen to reach the upper platform of the pump-room, when, either through slipping or having been rendered semi-conscious by the power of the gas, he fell to the bottom.

The 'boatswain's chair' had been pulled up on deck and Mr. Meikle, the boatswain, with a sweat-rag round his mouth, was secured to the 'chair' and lowered to the assistance of the Chief Engineer. He succeeded in fastening a line to the Chief Engineer, when he himself became unconscious and both were pulled up by members of the crew. The body of the Second Engineer was soon recovered by grappling, but it was found that Mr. Forth had been killed by the fall. There was a wound at the back of his head and his right arm was broken.

The boatswain recovered, but all efforts to restore the Chief Engineer were unsuccessful. (18.5.31)

Rescues from a sinking yacht

ROBERT REYNOLDS, *Third hand*,
WALTER HARCOURT BURGESS, *Boatswain*[1]

The *Maitenes II*, with a crew of nine hands, left Cowes on the 11th August on a race to the Fastnet Rock and back to Plymouth. Owing to bad weather she anchored for shelter at St. Ives soon after midnight on the 13th August, but went on her way at 6 a.m. next day.

After rounding Fastnet on the 15th the yacht had to be hove to in consequence of the increasing wind and sea. She remained hove to until 11.45 a.m. on the 16th August when she was overpowered by tremendous squalls and lay on her beam ends shipping heavy seas. At midday the yacht was put before the wind under bare poles; soon afterwards a man fell overboard and was drowned.

The conditions gradually became worse. During the afternoon the trawler *Dunraven Castle* was sighted and was requested to stand by until the weather moderated. Warning had, however, been received of another gale; and, as the seas and wind were still increasing and the crew were exhausted, it was decided to abandon the yacht.

At 4 p.m. the trawler's dinghy, manned by the men named, was

[1] Harold Wood, skipper of the *Dunraven Castle*, was also awarded plate by the Board of Trade.

launched with a warp made fast; the trawler then went ahead paying out the warp to allow the yacht to come up with the dinghy. This manœuvre failed at the first attempt but succeeded on being repeated, and the eight persons on the yacht entered the dinghy and were safely transferred to the trawler. (21.10.31)

Gallantry of Scottish Coast-guardsmen

WILLIAM RAYMOND SMAILES,[1]
FRANK SHELLEY,
THOMAS WALKER,
JOHN HENDERSON
JOHN ROBERTSON

The steam trawler *Nairn* of Aberdeen, with a crew of ten hands, went ashore at Broadhaven, near Collieston, soon after 10 p.m. on 2nd December 1931 during a south-easterly gale. The Collieston Life-saving Apparatus Company, with life-saving gear, reached the top of a cliff, about 150 feet high, abreast of the *Nairn* at 11.20 p.m. and fired four rockets, but failed to establish communication with the wreck.

W. R. Smailes, District Officer of Coast-guard, Peterhead, then proceeded down the cliff to a ledge where he was joined by F. Shelley, Coast-guardsman, and T. Walker, J. Henderson, and J. Robertson, members of the Life-saving Company, with the rocket gear and a powerful acetylene lamp. Great difficulty was experienced in setting up the gear on the ledge owing to the limited space; but eventually communication with the *Nairn* was effected by means of a rocket.

While the life-saving gear was being hauled out to the wrecked vessel by her crew, Smailes, Walker, Henderson, and Robertson climbed on to some intervening rocks to prevent the gear becoming fouled. On three occasions, however, the gear was caught in the rocks; and each time it was cleared by Smailes, who was assisted down to a lower outer ledge and supported by Walker and Henderson, these operations being facilitated by the light from the lamp which Robertson had carried, through seas, to an outer rock. The life-saving gear was then secured on board the *Nairn* and her crew were safely landed by the Company by about 3.15 a.m.

In clearing the fouled gear, Smailes, Walker, Henderson, and Robertson incurred considerable risk, as the rocks over which they climbed were very slippery and were being swept by violent seas, while the strong wind and the darkness added to the difficulties. Coast-guardsman Shelley also incurred grave risk in climbing, alone, up and down the cliff to convey messages between the party on the rocks and the remainder of the Life-saving Company on the cliff top. (17.2.32)

[1] Also awarded plate by the Board of Trade.

1932   BOARD OF TRADE SEA GALLANTRY MEDAL   425

Rescue of schooner crew stranded in the Thames

Captain FREDERICK WILLIAM NOYON,[1] *Master*, HENRY STEPHEN FALLA, *Able Seaman*, HENRY CHARLES BISSON

The auxiliary motor schooner *Mary Jones* of Bideford, with a crew of four hands, stranded on the Tongue Shoal, at the mouth of the Thames, at about 6.30 p.m. on the 20th February 1932. A strong wind was blowing from the north-east and a heavy north-easterly sea was running. After she had been ashore an hour, the vessel showed signs of breaking up. An attempt was made to launch the schooner's boat, but as soon as it touched the water it was thrown against the side of the vessel and rendered useless.

Distress signals were then sent up; and in response the *Foam Queen* approached and, at about 8.30 p.m., anchored about half a mile away, which was as near to the wreck as was prudent. The master of the *Foam Queen*, Captain F. Noyon, considered that in the prevailing conditions an ordinary ship's life-boat would have been unmanageable; he decided, therefore, to attempt a rescue by means of his small boat, in which he, with two of his crew, H. Falla, A.B., and H. Bisson, O.S., reached the *Mary Jones*, although only after considerable difficulty.

Two of the shipwrecked men—the small boat would not hold more —were then transferred to the *Foam Queen*, and a second trip was made to rescue the two remaining members of the *Mary Jones* crew. As on the first occasion, great difficulty was experienced in reaching the wrecked vessel, the boat almost being capsized. The rescue was completed at about 10 p.m., and shortly afterwards the *Mary Jones* disappeared. (3.6.32)

Trawler wrecked on Bear Island

GEORGE HARMER, ERNEST HUNTER, GEORGE WILLIAM SMITH, *Deck Hands* of *Hull and Grimsby*[2]

On the early morning of the 19th November 1931 the *Howe*, with a crew of fifteen hands, stranded on the west coast of Bear Island, between Spitzbergen and Norway. The vessel rapidly filled with water, and heavy seas which swept over the stern made it impossible for the crew to leave by means of her boats, which were eventually washed overboard.

---

[1] The Board of Trade also awarded plate to Capt. Noyon and £2 each to the men named.

[2] In addition, the Board of Trade awarded pieces of silver plate to Thorlaf Johansen and Egil Lindberg, Wireless Operators, Bear Island, and to Skipper E. Drinkall of the s.t. *Elf King* of Grimsby; binoculars to Skipper T. Worthington of the s.t. *Imperialist* of Hull; and other inscribed souvenirs to Francis Frith, First Engineman, William W.

Wireless calls for assistance were acknowledged by several trawlers and by the wireless station situated near the north-east coast of the island, of which the two wireless operators and their families were the only inhabitants. The *Howe* sent out messages that she was ashore near Cape Bull, a point at the southern extremity of the island, and that, owing to the conditions of weather and sea, her crew could not be rescued from the seaward side.

Having satisfied themselves that trawlers were approaching the island, the two wireless operators, Norwegians named Thorlaf Johansen and Egil Lindberg, set out for the reported position of the wreck. They made their way in the darkness (which in winter is almost perpetual on the island) across eight miles of rough, frozen ground, hampered by dangerous boulders and crevices to Cape Bull and, finding no trace of the wreck, returned to the station, where they arrived late at night, footsore and exhausted.

Meanwhile several British trawlers had anchored off the north-east coast near the wireless station, and on the following morning Mantripp, Walker, Crawford, Thornton, Millener, Wallace, Hodgson, Hattan, Rumsey, and Rogers, without food or equipment, attempted to cross the island in an endeavour to locate the wreck. These men were unaware of the difficulties to be encountered; they became exhausted and had to return to the wireless station, which was reached at about 8.30 p.m.

During the same day other trawlers had located the wreck on the west coast and had communicated its true position to the trawlers on the other side of the island; but heavy surf and breakers rendered a near approach to the wreck out of the question.

The *Howe*'s boats had now been washed away by seas and, in order to secure a means of rescue for his shipmates, Harmer made two gallant attempts to swim with a line through the surf from the wreck to the shore, 40 yards away. On each occasion he was overwhelmed by the heavy surf, and he had to be hauled back on board the wreck.

On the morning of the next day, the 21st November, the conditions had improved and Skipper T. Worthington of the *Imperialist* endeavoured to manoeuvre his vessel towards the wreck. The *Imperialist*, however, grounded slightly and had to return to deeper water.

Mantripp, second hand, Henry P. Walker, deck hand, William Coulbeck and Frank R. Crawford, trimmers, and Frederick A. Thornton, deck-hand fireman, of the s.t. *Elf King* of Grimsby; to Robert W. Millener, second hand, George Burrell, third hand, Charles A. Wallace, boatswain, Robert W. Glentworth, cook, and Lester Brooks, Thomas W. Giles, and Thomas Hodgson, spare hands, of the s.t. *Cape Spartivento* of Hull; and to Harold Osbourn, second hand, Walter Rumsey, third hand, William A. Hattan, boatswain, W. L. Rust, deck hand, and Arthur Rogers, John W. Walton, and R. Palmer, spare hands, of the s.t. *Pennine* of Hull.

A small boat then went away from the *Thomas Hardy* with a Carley float in tow and anchored near the edge of the surf. Hunter and Smith then entered the float, which was veered into the breakers to within 20 yards of the wreck. They could get no nearer owing to the surf and the rocks and both men were thrown into the surf. Smith succeeded in climbing back into the float, but Hunter, whose hand was injured, could only hold on to the float while it was being hauled back to the small boat.

Meanwhile, Skipper E. Drinkall of the *Elf King* had determined to cross the island with a new party to the actual position of the wreck. This party, which included Johansen to act as guide, Frith, Coulbeck, Osbourn, Rust, Walton, Burrell, Glentworth, Brooks, and Giles, set off at 7 a.m., taking with them compasses, lights, food, and a buoy-line. Impeded by rough ground, boulders, quicksands, and lakes, some of the party were unable to keep up with the leaders. The others pressed on as it was realized that the position of the shipwrecked men was becoming very serious. Guided by the compass, and by signals from the *Imperialist* and other trawlers near the wreck, Drinkall, Johansen, Burrell, and Coulbeck located the wreck beneath a cliff at about 1.30 p.m. when darkness was approaching. After several efforts had been made to throw a buoy-line on board the *Howe*, the slack end of the line was thrown from the cliff top into the surf which carried it towards the wreck where it was secured by a grappling hook. With the buoy-line and the *Howe*'s life-buoys, the shipwrecked men improvised a breeches buoy by means of which they were safely landed. Rust joined the party on the cliff while this operation was in progress and assisted in bringing the shipwrecked men to safety.

The return to the wireless station was necessarily very slow owing to the exhausted condition of the rescued men who were suffering severely as the result of their exposure, two of them having to be carried. The latter part of the journey was made easier by the assistance of scattered groups of a large party of men who had been landed from other trawlers. At the wireless station all were given food and hot coffee by the wives and maidservant of the Norwegian wireless operators.

The crew of the *Howe* were later taken on board the *Elf King* which left Bear Island for the mainland on the 22nd November.

Owing to the heavy surf and breakers and to the rocks which surrounded the wreck, the gallant attempts of Harmer to effect communication with the shore, and of Hunter and Smith to reach the wreck in a Carley float, involved grave risk to their lives; while the services of the others named, performed under difficult conditions, called for qualities of great determination and endurance. (3.6.32)

Rescue off Halifax

HENRY STUART KNIGHT, *Second Officer*,[1] WALTER DOYLE, *Boatswain*, WILLIAM THOMAS HUGHES, *Quartermaster*, HORACE ADDICOTT, *Storekeeper*, JOHN PETER SMYTH, *Lamp-trimmer*, JOHN CARR, WILLIAM JOHN LAWRY, LESLIE JOHN PAGE, HENRY PEARCE, *Able Seaman*, of *S.S.* Metcalfe *of Liverpool*

On the 12th March 1932 the steam tug *Reindeer I* of Halifax, Nova Scotia, carrying a crew of thirty hands, had been at sea off Halifax for several hours in a heavy gale and huge seas. She was leaking badly and her pumps were choked; her crew were becoming exhausted by their efforts to keep down the water, and wireless distress signals were sent out. These were answered by the S.S. *Montcalm* of Liverpool, then about 45 miles away.

The *Montcalm* arrived about three hours later. The *Reindeer I* was then low in the water, and her captain decided that she must be abandoned without delay. Owing to the violent rolling of the tug, a life-boat could not be launched from her and preparations were made to launch a life-boat from the *Montcalm*, which took up a position as near to the distressed vessel as was prudent. Considerable difficulty was experienced in launching a boat which, although damaged, was eventually sent away soon after 6 p.m. This boat was in charge of Mr. Henry S. Knight, the Second Officer of the *Montcalm*, and manned by the men named.

At first, the life-boat was unable to get close to the tug as she was drifting before the gale. Later, however, the engineer of the *Reindeer I* was able to put the engines astern for a few minutes in order to check the drifting, and the crew of the life-boat succeeded in securing lines which had been thrown overboard from the tug and so brought their boat alongside.

Meanwhile, the *Montcalm* had been pouring oil on the water to make the work of rescue easier, but in spite of this the life-boat was continually ranging back and forth and moving up and down the side of the tug, the crew of which had to jump into the life-boat as opportunity offered.

By 7 p.m., the crew of the *Reindeer I* were all in the life-boat. As it was damaged and heavily laden, it took nearly three-quarters of an hour to reach the *Montcalm*. The boat's crew and the crew of the tug were taken on board by a rope ladder, but the boat had to be abandoned. (8.12.32)

[1] His Majesty's Government in Canada also awarded plate to Arthur Rothwell, the master of the *Montcalm*, binoculars to Mr. Knight, and monetary awards to the men named.

One man saves thirty-seven lives off Nova Scotia

Herbert Mant,
Second Officer of S.S. Watford of London

The S.S. *Watford*, carrying a crew of forty, stranded at Cape Percy, Nova Scotia, on the 10th September 1932 in a hurricane, with mountainous seas and heavy rain squalls, and became a total loss. After lowering and manning a ship's life-boat from the vessel, which lay about 500 feet from the shore, the master came to the conclusion that it was too dangerous to attempt this method and he ordered the crew back on board. He then decided to try to effect communication with the shore by means of a line fired from a line-throwing pistol. There was, however, no one in sight to take a line and H. Mant, Second Officer, volunteered to swim ashore and make fast the end of a line with the object of rigging up hawser communication between the ship and shore by which the crew could be landed.

Mant entered the sea with a light life-line round him, but while he was swimming towards shore the line sagged to leeward, and men on board, fearing that he was getting into difficulties, let go the line. Mant, after struggling for some time, managed to scramble on to the rocks in an exhausted condition.

Soon after, three men appeared on the cliffs and assisted Mant to drag ashore, and secure to a tree, a hawser attached to a line fired from the ship. A hauling-line was got ashore by means of the line-throwing pistol and a 'boatswain's chair' was rigged. By these means, all but two of the remaining thirty-nine members of the crew were saved. One man had died from exposure, and one fell from the 'boatswain's chair' and was drowned. (20.12.32)

An attempted rescue on the Tyne

PETER THOMSON,
Asst. Engineer Supt., River Tyne

The S.S. *Oregon Star* caught fire in the Tyne on the 13th November 1932, and was seriously damaged. Mr. A. V. Hamilton, the Chief Officer, wearing a life-line and a breathing apparatus, containing 25 minutes' supply of oxygen, went down into the shelter 'tween deck in order to locate the seat of the fire, which was accompanied by dense smoke. About 5 minutes after descending it appeared that Hamilton was about to return, as the life-line became slack and could be hauled and it was feared that Hamilton was in difficulties. The line was hauled in until owing to some obstruction it broke. Mr. Peter Thomson, Ship's Superintendent, wearing a smoke helmet with hose attachment, then went down into the 'tween decks and found Hamilton, whom he dragged to a place near the ladder-way. Thomson then returned to the deck for a line which he fastened round the body. On Thomson's second return to the deck he was exhausted.

Efforts were made to haul Hamilton up to the deck, but they were unfortunately unsuccessful. (27.3.33)

An attempted rescue on the Tyne

JAMES WILLIAM SCOTT, *First Mate of motor mission vessel* Southern Cross

The motor vessel *Southern Cross* belonging to the Melanesia Mission, with a crew of eight Europeans and fifteen Solomon Islanders, while on passage from Auckland to the New Hebrides, encountered overcast and squally weather. During a sudden squall the vessel struck, at about 3.15 a.m. on the 31st October 1932, a reef off Aneityum Island, and was immediately thrown broadside on to it. The engine-room was quickly flooded, and a heavy sea swept over the bridge, smashing a boat which the crew were attempting to launch. The angle at which the ship lay prevented the launch of the second boat.

The vessel, which was pounding heavily on the reef, was several hundred yards from the beach and about sixty yards from where it was possible for a man to touch bottom, but the position of the ship in relation to the beach and shallow water was not known until later. Mr. J. W. Scott, the First Mate, although suffering from a severe blow on the head, undertook to attempt to swim ashore through the surf in darkness and adverse weather conditions, without knowing all the difficulties to be faced, but with a full knowledge of the dangers from sharks. After reaching the beach with a life-line Mr. Scott was able to haul the Second Engineer ashore before the life-line was cut by the coral. The rest of the crew reached the shore by their own efforts. (14.6.33)

Two daring swimmers

Ernest Hay Halliday, *Chief Officer*,
Antonio M. Viana, *Boatswain*

The S.S. *Newbrough* stranded, in heavy weather, on the South-East Morant Cay, West Indies, on the 24th December 1932. Mr. Halliday reached the Cay in the *Newbrough*'s life-boat and then endeavoured to effect communication by swimming to the *Norseman*'s life-boat, which had anchored outside the line of the surf of the leeward side of the Cay, from which a rescue party from the *Norseman* was unable to land owing to the surf. Later Mr. Halliday swam out on the windward side of the Cay and found an opening in the reef through which a second life-boat from the *Newbrough* could reach the Cay. When Mr. Halliday was unsuccessful in reaching the *Norseman*'s life-boat, Mr. Viana swam from the life-boat to the Cay through the surf and was successful in establishing communication with the Cay. Those on the Cay were subsequently transferred to the *Norseman* by the *Norseman*'s life-boat. (28.6.33)

Rescues in North Atlantic

DAVID MARION BURTON BAKER, *First Mate*, ROBERT WILLIAMS, *Carpenter*, JOHN HELMER KJELLBERG, *Boatswain*, FREDERICK JOHN COLLINS, *Quartermaster*, GEORGE WILLIAM BUCHLEY, *Chief Cook*, AUSTIN PATRICK YOUNG, *Second Cook*, GEORGE SCOTT BRUCE and GEORGE NEWBOLD, *Assistant Stewards, of S.S. Aztec of Bristol*

On the night of the 16th November 1931, the Newfoundland schooner *Ria* of St. John's was in distress in the North Atlantic Ocean. For several days the vessel had encountered stormy weather, which had carried away the sails, and by 16th November the *Ria* was leaking badly.

Her signals of distress were observed about 9.30 p.m. by the S.S. *Aztec* of Bristol, which altered course towards her. A rough sea, with a high confused swell, was running and the wind was blowing at gale force; and in view of the unfavourable conditions, the Master of the schooner did not expect a rescue to be attempted before daylight. The *Aztec*, however, at once took up a position to windward in order to launch a life-boat. Difficulty was experienced and several oars were lost or broken in sending away a life-boat in charge of Mr. Baker, and manned by the men named. Further difficulty was encountered in getting the boat alongside the *Ria*, but the distressed crew of six hands were eventually taken off and transferred in safety to the *Aztec*. (28.6.33)

Rescue from a drifter

DAVID WILLIAM ELLIS, *Seaman, of steam drifter Olivae*

About 3 a.m. on the 3rd May 1933, the steam drifter *Olivae* was in a position about 70 miles west by north from St. Anne's Head, Pembrokeshire, and was hauling her nets. The wind at the time was strong with a heavy sea and thunderstorm. While the operation was in progress Reginald Muskett, a member of the crew, was knocked overboard by a rope. A line was thrown over him from the drifter, but as Muskett was only semi-conscious he was unable to grasp it. Muskett had sunk twice when David William Ellis threw off his oilskin and jumped overboard to rescue him. Ellis, wearing his ordinary clothes, including sea-boots which reached to his thigh, managed to catch hold of Muskett when he was sinking for the third time, and swam with him to the net rope in which both men became entangled. Fortunately, the crew were able to haul the net and the two men back on board the trawler. In effecting the rescue Ellis was hampered, not only by the rough sea and the darkness, but also by his clothing and sea-boots; he was pulled on board the drifter in an exhausted condition. (25.8.33)

Rescues off Jaffa by Palestinian Arabs

AHMAD BAJAWI,
MUHAMMAD DABABISH,
Boatmen of Jaffa

The British S.S. *Bilbeis*, carrying a crew of fifty-six and eight passengers, stranded off Jaffa at about 5.45 a.m. on the 5th March 1934, when there was a moderate breeze accompanied by a moderate swell, and a dust haze over the coast.

Shortly after the stranding the wind increased considerably and the sea rose rapidly. It seemed likely that the conditions would get worse.

In view of the threatening weather the Master arranged for the passengers and the stewardess to be taken ashore by a Government launch.

By 10.30 a.m. a strong westerly gale was blowing and the Master decided to land some of his crew by means of the ship's life-boats. The first boat, under the charge of the Second Officer, successfully negotiated the surf, and her occupants, aided by local boatmen, landed safely. An attempt was made to send back some of the crew who had landed so that they might help to disembark the remainder of the crew, but the attempt failed; the boat was swamped, overturned, and smashed up by the heavy surf against the rocks, fortunately without loss of life.

At about 11.40 a.m. a second boat was launched from the *Bilbeis* under charge of the Third Officer, but this boat was not so successful as the first and one member of her crew in endeavouring to get ashore was carried away by the seas. Ahmad Bajawi, a local boatman, courageously swam out to the rescue, but he himself got into difficulties.

Muhammad Dababish, a lighterman, then gallantly swam out to the rescue of the two men who were in danger, and after great difficulty succeeded in bringing them to shore with the aid of a life-buoy flung to him. (10.9.34)

Anglo-Belgian co-operation in Mid-Atlantic

Ernest James Rigby Pollitt, *Junior Third Officer*; Donald Brodie, *Lamp-trimmer and A.B.*; Kenneth Campbell, *A.B. and Look-out*; Robert Walter Beckett, James Brawn, Robert Charles William Brown, James William Mortimore, William Skinner, Harry Victor Julius Ward, Alan Williams, *A.B.s*, and George James Bowles, *Sailor*, of S.S. Ascania.

For heroic services in saving life of the member of the crew of S.S. *Usworth*[1] (see p. 38).

[1] The Board of Trade Medal for 'Foreign Services' in silver was awarded on the same occasion, in recognition of services rendered to s.s. *Usworth*, to Jules Leblanc, second officer; Paul Lambert, fourth officer; Jean Schroyens, cadet; George De Plecker, Alphonse Dobbelaere, Alfred Spreutels, sailors; Lodewyk De Jongh, donkeyman-greaser; Gaston Vanhests, Henri Hermans, and Henri Beeldens, firemen, of the Belgian S.S. *Jean Jadot*. In the case of Lambert and De Jongh the awards were posthumous as both men lost their lives while rendering the service.

APPENDIX I

Medals Granted by Special Act or Resolution of U.S.A. Congress

(Medals of Gold and Presented by the President except as Otherwise Noted)

List furnished by the courtesy of the Chief Reference Librarian, Library of Congress, Washington, U.S.A. (12th Sept. 1938)

Date of Act or Resolution	Citation	Recipient	Reason for Granting
March 29, 1800	2 Stat. 87 (IV)	Captain Thomas Truxton.	Action with the *Vengeance*.
March 3, 1805	2 Stat. 346 (II)	Commodore Edward Preble.	Conduct in attack on Tripoli.
Jan. 29, 1813	2 Stat. 830 (I)	Captains Isaac Hull, Stephen Decatur, and Jacob Jones (silver medals to officers, including nearest male relatives of two).	Capture of the *Guerrière*, the *Macedonian*, and the *Frolic*.
March 3, 1813	2 Stat. 831 (III)	Captain William Bainbridge (silver medals to officers).	Capture of the *Java*.
Jan. 6, 1814	3 Stat. 141 (II)	Captains Oliver Hazard Perry and Jesse D. Elliott (silver medals to commissioned officers, including nearest male relative of Lieutenant John Brooks).	Conduct in battle of Lake Erie.
Jan. 6, 1814	3 Stat. 141 (III)	Lieutenants William Burrows (i.e. his nearest male relative) and Edward R. McCall (silver medals to officers).	Capture of the *Boxer*.
Jan. 11, 1814	3 Stat. 142 (IV)	Captain James Lawrence (i.e. his nearest male relative), silver medals to officers.	Capture of the *Peacock*.
Oct. 20, 1814	3 Stat. 245 (I)	Captains Thomas Macdonough and Robert Henley, and Lieutenant Stephen Cassin (silver medals to officers, including nearest male relatives of two).	Conduct in battle of Lake Champlain.
Oct. 21, 1814	3 Stat. 246 (II)	Captain Lewis Warrington (silver medals to officers).	Capture of the *Épervier*.
Nov. 3, 1814	3 Stat. 246 (IV)	Captain Johnston Blakely (silver medals to officers).	Capture of the *Reindeer*.
Nov. 3, 1814	3 Stat. 247 (V)	Major-Generals Brown, Scott, Gaines, Macomb, and Porter, and Brigadier-Generals Ripley and Miller.	Conduct in victories of Chippewa, Niagara, and Erie.
Feb. 27, 1815	3 Stat. 249 (X)	Major-General Andrew Jackson.	Conduct in battle of New Orleans.
Feb. 22, 1816	3 Stat. 341 (III)	Captain Charles Stewart (silver medals to commissioned officers).	Capture of the *Cyare* and the *Levant*.

Date of Act or Resolution	Citation	Recipient	Reason for Granting
Feb. 22, 1816	3 Stat. 341 (IV)	Captain James Biddle (silver medals to officers).	Capture of the *Penguin*.
April 4, 1818	3 Stat. 476 (XII)	Major-General William Henry Harrison and Ex-Governor Isaac Shelby.	Conduct in victory of the Thames (Canada).
Feb. 13, 1835	4 Stat. 792 (II)	Colonel George Croghan.	Defence of Fort Stephenson.
July 16, 1846	9 Stat. 111, No. 11	Major-General Zachary Taylor.	Conduct in operations on the Rio Grande.
March 2, 1847	9 Stat. 206, No. 5	Major-General Zachary Taylor.	Taking of Monterey.
March 9, 1848	9 Stat. 333, No. 2	Major-General Winfield Scott.	Conduct in Mexican Campaign of 1847.
May 9, 1848	9 Stat. 334, No. 7	Major-General Zachary Taylor.	Conduct in battle of Buena Viata.
*Aug. 4, 1854	10 Stat. 594, No. 24	Commander Duncan N. Ingraham.	Rescue of Martin Koszta from Austrian brig *Hussar*.
*March 3, 1857	11 Stat. 255, No. 15	Dr. Kane, his officers and men.	'Their merits and services' (Arctic exploration).
May 11, 1858	11 Stat. 369, No. 10	Assistant-Surgeon Fred A. Rose, British Navy.	Services in care of yellow-fever patients on U.S.S. *Susquehanna*.
Dec. 17, 1863	13 Stat. 399, No. 1	Major-General Ulysses S. Grant, to be presented 'in the name of the people of the U.S.'	Conduct in various battles.
Jan. 28, 1864	13 Stat. 401, No. 10	Cornelius Vanderbilt	Gift of steamship to United States during Civil War.
March 2, 1867	14 Stat. 574, No. 57	Cyrus W. Field, to be presented 'in the name of the people of the U.S.'	Laying of Atlantic cable.
March 16, 1867	15 Stat. 20, No. 3	George Peabody, 'in the name of the people of the U.S.'	Gift for education in southern and southwestern states.
March 1, 1871	16 Stat. 704, No. 46	George F. Robinson.	Saving life of Secretary Seward.
Feb. 24, 1873	17 Stat. 638, No. 4	Jared S. Crandall, William Nash,† and others, of Westerly, R.I.	Life-saving, wreck of *Metis*.
June 20, 1874	18 Stat. 573, c. 359	John Horn, Jr.	Life-saving on Detroit river.
Feb. 5, 1883	22 Stat. 636, No. 7	John F. Slater, 'in the name of the people of the U.S.'	Gift for education of negroes in southern states.
July 19, 1886	24 Stat. 146, c. 776	Thomas Sampson, medal of honour.	Distinguished service in saving lives from the sea.

* Medal not specified.

† By Resolution of March 3, 1876 (19 Stat. 497, No. 2), the medal awarded William Nash was authorized to be presented to his widow.

Date of Act or Resolution	Citation	Recipient	Reason for Granting
May 14, 1888	25 Stat. 140, c. 247	Captain Thomas Sampson, gold medal of the first class.	Bravery in rescuing five boys from drowning.
Aug. 27, 1888	25 Stat. 1249, No. 40	Joseph Francis.	Perfection of life-saving appliances.
Sept. 30, 1890	26 Stat. 553, c. 1128, § 3	Members of Jeannette Arctic Expedition and heirs.	'For service in said expedition.'
June 3, 1898	30 Stat. 746, No. 42	Officers and men under Commodore George Dewey, bronze medals (by Secretary of the Navy).	Battle of Manila Bay.
Feb. 27, 1899	30 Stat. 1589, No. 19	Michael F. Barry (by Secretary of the Treasury).	Life-saving medal for rescuing people from drowning.
March 2, 1897	29 Stat. 837, No. 22	Danial E. Lynn (gold life-saving medal).	Heroic services in attempt to rescue crew of schooner *William Shupe*, May 19, 1894.
May 3, 1900	31 Stat. 716, No. 24	Lieutenant Frank Newcomb and command, Revenue-Cutter Service, gold, silver, and bronze (by Secretary of the Treasury).	Rescue of torpedo boat *Winslow*.
Feb. 7, 1901	31 Stat. 1809, No. 6	Lieutenant Fidelio S. Carter, U.S.N. (life-saving medal of first class).	Services in saving lives of two persons from drowning off Fort Monroe, Va., April 24, 1898.
March 3, 1901	31 Stat. 1465, No. 18	Officers and men of Navy and Marine Corps participating, bronze medals (by Secretary of the Navy).	Naval engagements, &c., in Spanish War.
June 28, 1902	32 Stat. 492, c. 1311	Lieutenants David H. Jarvis and Ellsworth P. Bertholf, Dr. Samuel J. Call, Revenue-Cutter Service (by Secretary of the Treasury), Medal of Honour to each.	Overland expedition for relief of whaling fleet in Arctic regions, 1897-8.
Jan. 25, 1907	34 Stat. 1420, No. 8	Corp. Roe Reisinger, Pa. Vol. Inf., 'Congressional Medal of Honour', by Secretary of War.	Conduct at battle of Gettysburg.
March 4, 1909	35 Stat. 1627, No. 30	Orville and Wilbur Wright (by Secretary of War).	Services to science of aerial navigation.
July 6, 1912	37 Stat. 639, No. 32	Captain Arthur Rostron of *Carpathia*.	*Titanic* relief.
March 19, 1914	38 Stat. 769, No. 8	Officers and crew of *Kroonland* (by Secretary of Commerce), gold, silver, and bronze.	Relief of *Volturno*.
March 4, 1915	38 Stat. 1228, No. 17	Señors de Gama, Naón, and Suárez.	Mediation between U.S. and warring parties in Mexico.
March 4, 1915	38 Stat. 1593, c. 221	Major John O. Skinner, 'Medal of Honour'.	Gallantry during Modoc Indian Campaign of 1873.

Date of Act or Resolution	Citation	Recipient	Reason for Granting
*June 5, 1920	41 Stat. 977, c. 240	City of Verdun, France, Medal of Honour.	Valour of City's defenders.
March 4, 1921	41 Stat. 1367, c. 160	'Unidentified' British and French soldiers, in Westminster Abbey and Arc de Triomphe, 'Congressional Medal of Honour'.	—
Feb. 1, 1921	41 Stat. 1526, c. 32	Robert Edward Cox, Chief Gunner, U.S.N., 'Medal of Honour'.	Heroism at accident on U.S.S. *Missouri*, 1904
Aug. 24, 1921	42 Stat. 191, c. 87	Unidentified American soldier in Arlington Cemetery, 'Congressional Medal of Honour' and 'Distinguished Service Cross'.	—
Oct. 12, 1921	42 Stat. 203, c. 103	Unidentified Italian soldier in Rome, 'Medal of Honour'.	—
Feb. 25, 1925	43 Stat. 979, c. 322	Army world flyers, Major Fred L. Martin, Captain Lowell Smith, and Lieutenants Leigh Wade, Leslie Arnold, and Erick Nelson, 'Distinguished Service Medals'.	Round-the-world flight by aeroplane.
Jan. 5, 1927	44 Stat. 933, c. 23.	Richard E. Byrd, Lieut.-Commander U.S.N., retired, 'Medal of Honour', in the name of Congress.	North Pole flight by aeroplane.
Jan. 5, 1927	44 Stat. 933, c. 24	Floyd Bennett, aviation pilot, U.S.N., 'Medal of Honour', in the name of Congress.	Services in Byrd Arctic expedition.
Dec. 14, 1927	45 Stat. 1, c. 1	Colonel Charles A. Lindbergh, U.S.A.A.C.R., 'Medal of Honour', in the name of Congress.	New York–Paris flight.
April 20, 1928	45 Stat. 1722, c. 391	Lieut.-Col. William J. Sperry, duplicate Congressional Medal of Honour (by Secretary of War).	Distinguished gallantry at Petersburg, Va., April 2, 1865.
May 2, 1928	45 Stat. 482, c. 480	Distinguished Flying Cross to Colonel de Pinedo, to Costes and Le Brix, and to von Huenefeld, Fitzmaurice, and Koehl.	Several aircraft flights.
May 4, 1928	45 Stat. 490, c. 503	Colonel Charles A. Lindbergh (by Secretary of the Treasury).	In recognition of achievements.
May 29, 1928	45 Stat. 1012, c. 919	Thomas A. Edison (by Secretary of the Treasury).	In recognition of achievements.
May 29, 1928	45 Stat. 2026, c. 981	Lincoln Ellsworth, Roald Amundsen, and Umberto Nobile. Gold Medal to Ellsworth and gold medals of honour to Amundsen and Nobile.	Trans-polar flight of 1926.

* Metal not specified.

Date of Act or Resolution	Citation	Recipient	Reason for Granting
Dec. 18, 1928	45 Stat. 2036, c. 38	Orville Wright and Wilbur Wright, Distinguished Flying Cross.	Pioneering in aviation.
Feb. 9, 1929	45 Stat. 1158, c. 167	Commander John Towers, and crew of NC-4, 'in the name of Congress'.	Trans-Atlantic flight of 1919.
Feb. 28, 1929	45 Stat. 1409, c. 381	Walter Reed, James Carroll, and twenty others* (or their representatives designated by the Secretary) (by Secretary of the Treasury).	Services in yellow-fever investigations in Cuba.
March 1, 1929	45 Stat. 2342, c. 461	Captain Benjamin Mendez, Distinguished Flying Cross.	Seaplane flight from U.S. to Colombia.
May 23, 1930	46 Stat. 379, c. 318	Rear-Admiral Richard E. Byrd, and officers and men of his expedition, gold, silver, and bronze medals (by Secretary of the Navy).	Antarctic explorations.
June 9, 1930	46 Stat. 530, c. 421	Lieutenants Wallace M. Dillon, Richard F. Whitehead, and Eugene F. Burkett, Radio Electrician Claude G. Alexander, Chief Aviation Pilot Thomas G. Reid, Patrick A. McDonough, chief photographer, and William J. Murtha, photographer, first class, waiver of two years' limit on award of Distinguished Flying Cross.	Not specified.
July 2, 1932	47 Stat. 571, c. 396	Amelia Earhart Putnam, Distinguished Flying Cross.	Non-stop flight from Newfoundland to Ireland.
July 11, 1932	47 Stat. 655, c. 470	Russell N. Boardman, John L. Polando, Wiley Post, and Harold Gatty, Distinguished Flying Cross to each.	Trans-Altantic and round the world flight.
Feb. 6, 1933	47 Stat. 1717, c. 36	Eugene B. Ely, posthumous award of Distinguished Flying Cross.	Contribution to development of aviation.
Feb. 9, 1933	47 Stat. 1719, c. 47	Henry Clay Dexter and George Robert Cholister, posthumous award of 'Medal of Honour'.	Heroic endeavour to submerge charge of powder to prevent explosion.
Feb. 14, 1933	47 Stat. 1720, c. 68	Richmond Pearson Hobson, 'Medal of Honour'.	Sinking of *Merrimac*, June 3, 1898.
March 1, 1933	47 Stat. 1738, c. 178	Glen H. Curtiss, posthumous award of Distinguished Flying Cross.	Distinguished service in development of aviation.

* By Act of June 25, 1930 (46 Stat. 809, c. 605), the name of 'John H. Andrus' was substituted for 'James A. Andrus'.

Date of Act or Resolution	Citation	Recipient	Reason for Granting
June 6, 1934	48 Stat. 1373, c. 417	Private Harry H. Horton, recommendation for award of decoration to be considered.	Distinguished conduct near Malancourt, France, about Oct. 12, 1918.
June 18, 1934	48 Stat. 1412, c. 647	Emory B. Bronte, Distinguished Flying Cross.	Airplane flight from California to Hawaii.
March 21, 1935	49 Stat. 2048, c. 38	Major-General Adolphus Washington Greely, 'Medal of Honour'.	For life of splendid public service.
April 10, 1935	49 Stat. 152, c. 56	Air Marshal Italo Balbo and General Aldo Pellegrini of Royal Italian Air Force, Distinguished Flying Cross.	Transatlantic formation flight of twenty-four seaplanes.
Feb. 25, 1936	49 Stat. 2224, c. 84	Lieutenant-Colonel Francis T. Evans, U.S. Marine Corps, Distinguished Flying Cross.	Extraordinary achievement in aerial flight.
April 17, 1936	49 Stat. 1214, c. 232	Commander Percy Todd, Distinguished Service Medal, and Lt.-Commander Charles A. de W. Kitcat, British Navy, Navy Cross.	Heroism at burning of U.S.S. *Fulton* in 1934.
*May 15, 1936	49 Stat. 2293, c. 408	Lt.-Commander Johannes F. Jensen, Naval Reserve.	Saving of U.S.S. *Finland* after it was torpedoed.
May 21, 1936	49 Stat. 2302, c. 442	Brigadier-General Robert H. Dunlap, Marine Corps (posthumously), Navy Cross.	Extraordinary courage in trying to save life of French peasant woman.
June 2, 1936	49 Stat. 1395, c. 479	Personnel of Second Byrd Antarctic Expedition (silver medals: President not mentioned).	Polar exploration.
June 5, 1936	49 Stat. 1487, c. 534	Major-General Clarence Ransom Edwards (posthumously), Distinguished Service Medal.	Command of 26th Division at the Front.
June 16, 1936	49 Stat. 2324, c. 590	Lincoln Ellsworth.	Exploratory aviation in Arctic and Antarctic.
June 20, 1936	49 Stat. 2342, c. 687	J. Harold Arnold, Marine Corps drummer, Navy Cross.	Risk of life beyond call of duty in actual conflict.
June 29, 1936	49 Stat. 2370, c. 876	George M. Cohan.	Composition of 'Over There' and 'A Grand Old Flag'.
June 18, 1937	50 Stat. 997, c. 365	Major John W. Thomason and Gunnery Sergeant Robert Slover, Navy Cross.	Extraordinary heroism in the battle of Soissons, July 18, 1918.
Aug. 23, 1937	50 Stat. 1071, c. 740	Private Acors Rathbone Thompson (President 'authorized to cause the recommendation for the award of a decoration').	Distinguished service at Jaulny and Mont Blanc Ridge, France.

* Medal not specified.

Date of Act or Resolution	Citation	Recipient	Reason for Granting
June 7, 1938	52 Stat. 625, c. 324	British Officers: Rear Admiral Reginald Vesey Holt and Captain George Eric Maxia O'Donnell, Distinguished Service Medal; Vice Admiral Lewis Gonne Eyre Crabbe and Lieutenant Commander Harry Douglas Barlow, Navy Cross.	Assistance in recovery of survivors of U.S.S. *Panay*.
June 20, 1938	52 Stat. 1365, c. 552 [Private No. 644]	Mrs. Richard Aldrich, *née* Margaret Livingston Chanler, and posthumously to Anna Bouligny.	Service to Army of U.S. in establishment of hospitals for care and treatment of military patients in Puerto Rico during war with Spain.

APPENDIX II

Correspondence relating to the institution of the Distinguished Service Order, from the Windsor Archives, here printed with the approval of the Keeper of the King's Archives

I

5 April 1886,
War Office.

Dear Sir Henry Ponsonby,

There is a matter which I find has been for some time under consideration here, but only in a vague and general way, and regarding which, before taking any step towards a definite proposal or submission, I should greatly desire to know how you think Her Majesty would regard it.

The greatest difficulty has been found in suitably recognizing good service rendered in the field, and especially in the smaller expeditions or operations of which we have lately had so many. Officers are mentioned as having distinguished themselves, and the only rewards available are the C.B., and Brevet promotion. But the former is limited, and the latter gives rise to great inconvenience. Resort has also been had to the C.M.G., in the case of Colonial wars especially, but this is essentially irregular, and is not a proper destination of that order.

H.R.H. therefore is of opinion that the difficulty can best be met by the institution of an Order of Merit, which would enable officers of all ranks, Senior and Junior, to receive some recognition without the difficulties and inconvenience incurred under existing arrangements. I think my predecessor was favourable to the idea. But before putting it even into a definite form for consideration I am anxious to know whether the proposal would, on a general view, commend itself to the Queen's approval.

H.R.H. has, I know, been in communication with you on the cognate question of the Bath.

Believe me,
Yours very truly,
H. Campbell-Bannerman.

Minuted by Sir Henry Ponsonby on April 7.

Mr. W. H. Smith originated the proposal that a new Decoration should be established to meet the great number of claims for reward, and he left it with the Duke of Cambridge, who has now urged it on Mr. Campbell-Bannerman.

H. P.

Minuted by Her Majesty.

The Queen quite agrees—but wishes there sh^d be a Civil branch attached to it—w^h w^d enable the Queen to confer it on people like Max Müller and other distinguished men. It might be for g^t literary merit—and artistic merit and devoted services to the Sovereign.

It is strange that the Queen was just thinking of this Civil branch today and meant to propose . . . .

Memorandum to Sir H. Campbell-Bannerman from Sir H. Ponsonby on April 9.

Q. approves of inst. of new decoration but thinks there should be civil side as well as military.

H. P(onsonby).

II

16 May 1886,
War Office.

Dear Sir Henry Ponsonby,

I hope very shortly to make a submission to Her Majesty with regard to the new order. It will be rather a decoration than an order: my idea is that it may be a cross or medal for Distinguished Service in the Field—thus carrying into the Commissioned ranks a somewhat similar reward to that which exists in the ranks below. But as soon as the particulars are agreed upon (in which of course the Admiralty has to join) I will submit the proposal definitely for the Queen's judgment and approval.

In writing about it before, you mentioned that the Queen hoped that the Civil Service would be included, but perhaps you would be good enough to submit to Her Majesty that the present available honour of the Bath is open to all ranks of the Civil Service; whereas the difficulty which we are now desirous to meet arises from the fact that no one under Field rank can receive the C.B., and that thus we are reduced to the inconvenient alternative of Brevet Promotion for all junior officers whose services deserve recognition.

It will also be confined to service in the Field.

I will, however, explain all this when it becomes my duty to make the submission to the Queen—in a very few days.

I shall also be able immediately to submit names for promotion in, and appointment to, the Bath on Her Majesty's Birthday.

Yours very sincerely,
H. Campbell-Bannerman.

THE DISTINGUISHED SERVICE ORDER

III

July 7, 1886.

Mr. Campbell-Bannerman, with his humble duty to Your Majesty, has the honour to submit a draft Warrant for the institution of a new Naval and Military Decoration.

It has been brought to Your Majesty's notice that on many recent occasions great difficulty has been found in suitably recognizing the claims of Officers who have rendered distinguished service in active operations in the field, but who owing to their junior rank were not eligible for the honour of the Bath. Recourse has been had, in such cases, to Brevet promotion, either conferred immediately or postponed until the rank of the Officer entitled him even to this honour, and the consequences have been most inconvenient, as a too great extension of Brevet promotion causes much confusion, and, occasionally, considerable unfairness.

It has therefore appeared to His Royal Highness the Field Marshal Commanding in Chief, and Mr. Campbell-Bannerman agrees in the opinion, that it would be greatly in the interest of the Service if Your Majesty would be graciously pleased to institute a decoration which would furnish the means of fitly recognizing the exemplary discharge of duty in the Field on the part of Officers of Your Navy and Army. The Board of Admiralty and the Secretary of State for India have been consulted, and acquiesce both in the general idea and in the particular conditions suggested in the enclosed draft: and Mr. Campbell-Bannerman humbly lays it before Your Majesty in the hope that Your Majesty will be pleased to approve it.

IV

July 7. 86.
Windsor Castle.

Minute by Her Majesty.

The Queen cannot say she much likes the proposal.

It ought to be an *Order*—and not a sort of secondary Victoria Cross. 1^{stly} It sh^d not be worn as a cross—nor called so.—It sh^d be worn round the neck (without a star)—w^h is constantly the case abroad.

2^{ly} The ribbon sh^d be the same for both Services—red, edged with blue, or red.—

3^{ly} I think the 5th Clause sh^d be omitted.

It sh^d be quite unlike the Victoria Cross—as it is not at all intended to supplement that—but rather the Bath.—

The Queen is *quite* decided on these points and feels sure the Duke of Connaught w^d agree. He stops at Plymouth till Saturday—Would

Sir Henry send the proposals with the Queen's remarks thereon to him by Post tomorrow? Does not Sir Henry agree with her?

V

July 9 1886
Windsor Castle

General Sir Henry Ponsonby presents his humble duty to Your Majesty.

He wrote yesterday to the Duke of Connaught about the new decoration as proposed for the lower commissioned ranks of the Army.

Sir Henry Ponsonby thinks it should certainly not be a Cross.

What is proposed by the Duke of Cambridge and Mr. Bannerman is really an extended Distinguished Service Medal and not in any way an order.

Sir Henry Ponsonby does not well see how the actions rewarded will be distinguished from those that earn the Victoria Cross. There is already this difficulty as regards the Privates and this will be increased by this decoration unless some limits are defined.

It would almost be better to have a 5th class (Military) of the Bath.

Minute by Her Majesty on the same day.

There w^d be no harm in a 5th Class of the Bath if one knew where to make it?

V.R.

VI

July 10th /86
Royal Yacht Osborne
off the Lands End

My dear Ponsonby,

Many thanks for your letter and the enclosures which I herewith return. It is very difficult to give an answer with regard to the proposed new order. I think the Queen is quite right in objecting to have a *cross* which would be a mixture of the Victoria Cross and the good conduct medal. If it is considered necessary to have an order which could be given to Capts. and Subalterns for good service in the Field, in the place of Brevet promotion, it almost appears to me to be better to add a fourth class to the Bath, to be designated the '*Assistant*' or 'Lieutenant' of the Bath (I can't think of any other designation). The star might be of silver instead of gold and to be worn without a buckle. We have already so many orders that it seems a pity to have another and I can't say that I at all fancy the name 'distinguished service cross'. The question of course is a difficult one and what I write is merely my own suggestion. The positions of officers of the Army and **Navy** are different, to the former *Brevet* promotion is given for service in the field, to the latter *positive* promotion.

The number of such promotions in the Navy is generally very small and is very highly valued and I hope for the Naval officers' sake that it is not intended to abolish these few promotions which are a great help to those that receive them.

Brevet promotions in the Army frequently place officers in an invidious position, often placing Majors and sometimes even Capts. senior in the Army to their Col.

I hope the matter may be most carefully considered before a new order is founded. I think it would be as well if the Prince of Wales and the Duke of Edinburgh were asked *privately* their opinions.

Believe me
Yours very sincerely

Arthur
July 13 1886
Windsor Castle

Minute by Sir Henry Ponsonby.

General Sir Henry Ponsonby humbly thinks it would be better to have a fourth class (Military) of the order of the Bath than to create a new order which would be of an inferior grade.

Minute by Her Majesty.

Entirely agree with you and Arthur.

V.R.

VII

July 14 1886
Windsor Castle

Dear Mr. Campbell Bannerman

The Queen does not at all like the proposed decoration.

It will interfere with the Victoria Cross both in name and object—it will be regarded as a class of the D.C. Medal and esteemed accordingly and it will only afford a temporary relief from the claims of postulants for honours as all will expect another more distinguished order later.

The Queen thinks it would be better to create a 4th class Military (only) of the Order of the Bath to meet the requirements you refer to.

(S^d) H. Ponsonby.

VIII

19 July 1886
War Office

My dear Sir Henry Ponsonby,

There will be no danger of the evil which the Queen dreads as likely to arise from the new Order being limited to Officers mentioned in despatches. Such mention will give no right, but will only be a condition of eligibility, as it is, in fact, at present in the case of the C.B. The selection of actual recipients of the honour would therefore rest precisely where it does now for either promotion or the other Orders.

I do not understand whether Her Majesty has definitely determined upon the particular name of the Order? I hope I may be permitted to say that 'Service' would be much preferable to 'Conduct'. It would mark the special occasion of the Order, and would avoid any confusion with what is ordinarily known as Good Conduct. H.R.H. is at Aldershot today, but I know that he would entirely agree as to this.

Yours very truly,
H. Campbell-Bannerman

Minute by Sir H. Ponsonby.
(Very well—G. Service.)

IX

August 8 /86.
Royal Yacht Osborne
Cowes

My dear Ponsonby,

The enclosed letter from A. Ellis and Drawings speak for themselves. Will you kindly submit them to the Queen. I am most strongly of opinion that the Order should be called 'For Merit' instead of 'For distinguished Service' and trust the Queen may be of the same opinion. I think Ellis's coloured drawing Nr. I is by far the best. Nr. II is also pretty—and both are simple—Garrards' designs are I think hideous. I suggested the ribbon to be the Waterloo one—as if it were plain red it would look like the Bath.

Ellis has taken some trouble in the matter—and I hope the Queen will approve of Nr. I or Nr. II. You might bring me back the enclosures when you come to dinner tonight.

I am,
Yours very sincerely
Albert Edward

X

6. viii. 86
29 Portland Place W.

Sir,

In obedience to Y.R.H.'s expressed wish, and the Duke of Cambridge's request I have had some designs made for the Order. The D. of Cam. said it was 'For Merit'. The draft of the memo from W. Office says 'For distinguished service'. I venture to suggest that the former shorter title is the simplest and certainly easier introduced on to the cross.

No. I. A. is my first design and it is to my idea the best. In shape not unlike the Austrian M. Theresian cross—and very much like the Italian order of the crown, it has the merit of simplicity.

No. II. B. is another treatment of the same character. The fault is that the cross is lying on top of the wreath.

No. III. C. The colour (red) of the enamel cross clashes with the crimson of the riband—and it is too gothic to please me entirely.

No. IV. has the same fault in colour and the shape—square end of the cross savours too much of the Geneva surgical and medical convention.

In all cases I have introduced the Bar with chased laurels on it.

When Mr. Garrard, (as Crown Jeweller) was first consulted by the W. Office he was limited to 5£ as the cost of each decoration.

The C.B. is worth 17£—and for 5£ it wd. be manifestly impossible to obtain anything suitable.

The tracings enclosed are the designs at the cheaper price submitted by Mr. Garrard to the W. Office. I understand that the cost price has now been raised and probably as much as 12£ or 13£ will be allowed per cross.

For this price something may be made.

The drawings are actual proposed size—and *smaller* than C.B.

Tracings

No. 1 is too like Vict. Cross in design.

No. 2 is much the same as mine only without laurel.

No. 3 is like No. III without laurel—and like Geneva Badge absolutely.

No. 4 is *too* like a garter star at first sight.

No. 5 wh. is made up of Vs looks like a papal decoration!!

No. 6 might be mistaken for the Brigade of Guards Badge of the Guards' Club.

If Y.R.H. thinks any of these worth submitting to the Queen, it would be well to remember that the coloured sketches *of the tracings* will be submitted by the War Minister.

I am leaving England on Tuesday night for Salzburg in the Lungau valley—the rest of the men have been there all this week and I have missed this much of what I believe is very good sport.

I have the honour to be, Sir
Y.R.H.'s very faithful servant
Arthur Ellis

XI

August 11. 1886
War Office

My dear Sir Henry,

I am in some difficulty as to the badges to be worn for 'Distinguished Service'. My predecessor received the Queen's Commands to procure designs and submit them for H.M.'s approval. The Prince of Wales also communicated with the Messrs. Garrard, and other designs were made and supplied to H.R.H.

I had conferred with the Duke of Cambridge respecting them and we had agreed together to submit that No. 4 in the list would be a becoming and suitable decoration—the price being with a plain back £8. 15.

Last evening Mr. Garrard came to H.R.H. the Duke of Cambridge with a letter from Colonel Ellis enclosing one from you intimating that the Queen had chosen the design No. 1 A the cost of which will be £13. 15.—but nothing is said as to whether the reverse 'For Merit' is to be adopted.

If I might be permitted a suggestion it would be that this should not be added, as it has something of a schoolboy or a good boy air about it: and as a matter of course 'merit' is assumed in granting the decoration.

If the Queen has seen all these drawings and prefers A No. 1 I do not wish to ask for any re-consideration although I am afraid the Treasury may kick at the cost, but if it has not been, I should be very glad if the question of the reverse 'For Merit' could be considered from the point of view I have suggested.

Yours very truly,
W. H. Smith

Lt.-Gen. Sir Henry Ponsonby, K.C.B.

XII

August 11. 1886
War Office

Mr. W. H. Smith presents his humble duty to Your Majesty and he begs to submit a draft of the Statutes for the new Naval and Military Order of distinction for Your Majesty's approval.

The tenth article in the Statutes will be filled in so soon as Your Majesty has been pleased to declare Your pleasure as to the specific decoration to be worn.

Minute by Her Majesty.

Osborne. Aug. 14. 1886

The Queen agrees that the *words* Mr. Smith objects to sh^d be omitted but w^d like to keep to No. 1 A.

(ENCLOSURE) *(Draft)*

Victoria, by the Grace of God, of the United Kingdom of Great Britain and Ireland, Queen, Defender of the Faith, Empress of India, to all to whom these presents shall come, greeting:

Whereas We have taken into Our Royal consideration that the means of adequately rewarding the distinguished services of Officers in Our Naval and Military Services who have been honourably mentioned in despatches are limited to the numbers fixed by the statutes of Our Most Honourable Order of the Bath, and that the Third Class of that Order is limited to the higher ranks of both services; now for the purpose of attaining an end so desirable as that of rewarding individual instances of meritorious or distinguished service in war, We have instituted and created and by these presents, for Us, Our Heirs and Successors, do institute and create a new Naval and Military Decoration—to be designated as hereinafter described—which We are desirous should be highly prized and eagerly sought after by the Officers of Our Naval and Military Services, and We are graciously pleased to make, ordain, and establish the following rules and ordinances for the government of the same, which shall henceforth be inviolably observed and kept:

Firstly. It is ordained, that the distinction shall be styled and designated the 'Distinguished Service Cross', and shall consist of . . .

Secondly. It is ordained that the decoration shall be suspended from the left breast by a blue ribbon for the Navy, and by a red riband for the Army.

Thirdly. It is ordained that the names of those upon whom We may be pleased to confer the decoration shall be published in the *London Gazette*, and a registry thereof kept in the Office of Our Secretary of State for War.

Fourthly. It is ordained that no person shall be eligible for this decoration who does not actually hold, at the time of his nomination, a Commission in Our Navy, in Our Land Forces, or Marines, or in Our Indian or Colonial Naval or Military Forces, or a Commission in one of the Departments of our Navy or Army, the holder of which is entitled to Honorary or relative Navy or Army rank, nor shall any person be nominated unless his services shall have been marked by the especial mention of his name, by the Commander-in-Chief of the Forces in the Field, in despatches for meritorious or distinguished service in the Field, or before the enemy.

Fifthly. It is ordained, in order to make such additional provision as shall effectually preserve pure this honourable distinction, that if any person upon whom such distinction shall have been conferred, be found guilty of any act derogatory to his honour as an Officer or a gentleman, his name shall be erased, by an order under Our Sign Manual, from the register of those upon whom the said decoration shall have been conferred.

And it is hereby declared that We, Our Heirs and Successors, shall be the sole judge of the conduct which may require the erasure from the register of the name of the offending person, and that it shall at all times be competent for Us, Our Heirs and Successors, to restore the name if such restoration should be justified by the circumstances of the case.

Given at Our Court at   this   day of   , in the forty-ninth year of Our Reign, and in the year of Our Lord one thousand eight hundred and eighty six.

By Her Majesty's Command.

XIII

August 14 1886
Osborne

Dear Mr. Smith

The Queen quite agrees in your remarks on the sentence 'For Merit' and wishes those words to be omitted from the decoration for the D.S. Order, but hopes that the Insignia A No. 1 will be adhered to.

XIV

August 19 1886
War Office

Mr. Smith with his humble duty to Your Majesty ventures to submit an addition to the Statutes of the Distinguished Service Order in order to authorize the inclusion of Foreign Officers.

It has frequently happened that such officers have been associated with Your Majesty's troops in Military operations and the only distinction that could be conferred upon them has been the Order of St. Michael and St. George which is not in all respects a suitable reward for Services in the Field in a Foreign Country.

Mr. Smith has given directions that the design for the decoration marked No. 1 A of which Your Majesty graciously approved shall be forthwith adopted.

Minute by Sir H. Ponsonby.

August 20 1886
Holyrood

General Sir Henry Ponsonby humbly thinks this Clause should certainly be added to include foreign officers associated with Your Majesty's troops.

XV

8 November 1886
War Office

Mr. Smith with his humble duty to Your Majesty ventures to submit for final approval the Cross and ribbon, the design of which was approved by Your Majesty for the Distinguished Service Order.

Minute by Sir H. Ponsonby.

Approved and kept by The Queen.

Nov. 10 1886

XVI

December 13 1886
Windsor Castle

General Sir Henry Ponsonby presents his humble duty to Your Majesty.

The Prince of Wales was very much pleased at Your Majesty wishing him to be present at the inauguration of the Distinguished Service Order and His Royal Highness will therefore be here for luncheon on Friday next.

The Prince of Wales regretted that Your Majesty's suggestion of having a civil side to the Order had not been adopted.

He thought it would be most useful and would check other demands for new Orders.

INDEX

Part I. NAMES
Part II. PLACES
Part III. GENERAL

Abbreviations used include the following:

A.B.	Able Seaman.
App.	Apprentice.
A.S.C.	Army Service Corps.
Ch.	Chief.
Cox.	Coxswain.
Eng.	Engineer.
I.A.	Indian Army.
I.M.D.	Indian Medical Department.
Insp.	Inspector.
L.A./C.	Leading Aircraftsman, R.A.F.
L./C.	Lance-Corporal.
L./N.	Lance-Naik.
Ldg.	Leading (Seaman, &c.).
O.S.	Ordinary Seaman.
Q.M.	Quartermaster.
P.C.	Police Constable.
P.O.	Petty Officer.
P.S.	Police Sergeant.

Explanations:

Havildar.	Indian Army Sergeant.
Nafar.	Police Constable.
Naik.	Indian Army Corporal.
Lascar.	Indian Ordinary Seaman.
Shawish.	Police Sergeant.

PART I
INDEX OF NAMES

Aaron, diamond miner, Kimberley, 123.
Abang Ahmad, 42.
Abang Haji Khalil, Datu Imam, 42.
Abbott, Edmund Geoffrey, Lt. R.N., 329.
Abbott, George F. P., deck hand, 165, 319.
Abdus Samad Golandaz, Bombay, 302.
Ablett, George, collier, 92.
Ackred, William, steel worker, 143.
Ackred, Mrs., 143.
Adair, W. G., 385.
Adams, John, seaman, 358.
Adams, Wm., Q.M. Mate, 4.
Adams, W., boatman, 390.
Adams, W., commissioned boatman, 392.
Adamson, George John, insp. police, 307.
Adamson, Hugh, gasworks manager, 118.
Adcock, A. H., Canadian railwayman, 131.
Adcock, A. W., 2nd off., 397.
Addicott, Horace, storekeeper, 428.
Addy, Mark, waterman, 93.
Adolphus, G., 389.
Aers, F. E., 391.
Agutter, A., 390.
Ahmad Bajawi, boatman, 432.
Ahmad Yar, Havildar R.A., 287.
Ahmad, K., tindal, 398.
Ahom, Gurzie, workman, 145.
Aimansing Pun, Gurkha Rifles, 217.
Ainslie, G., O.S., 398.
Aitken, Thomas, waterworks foreman, 149.
Akers, John Thomas, miner, 261.
Alder, Thomas Edward, L.-Sergt., 287.
Alderson, George, L./C., 157.
Alege, A., O.S., 391.
Alexander, T., 2nd off., 397.
Ali Akbar, lascar, 405.
Allan, Arthur D. H., Pte., 370.
Allan, John, donkeyman, 324.
Allard, W., 390.
Allee, L., 389.
Allen, C. E., A.B., 395.
Allen, Ernest Charles, munition worker, 201.
Allen, Florence Alice, nurse, 220.
Allen, J., app., 396.
Allen, N., 386.
Allen, Oates, A.B., 395.
Allington, B. L., A.B., 394.
Allport, Ernest, collier, 265.
Allright, E. W., 395.
Ambury, Arthur H. (Mt. Egmont), 181.

Amin Eff. Hemeida, Yuzbashi, Sudan Force, 290.
Amin Ullah, lascar, 405.
Ammonsen, Harold Bernard, A.B., 422.
Andersen, A., 390.
Andersen, G. J., 388.
Andersen, I. E., 388.
Anderson, Alexander, A.S.C., 160.
Anderson, A. S., Ch. Off., 399.
Anderson, C., 390.
Anderson, Charles Alexander, Maj.-Gen., 113.
Anderson, Charles Henry, L./C., 161.
Anderson, S. F., Ldg. mechan., 398.
Anderson, Thomas, dock hand, 200.
Anderson, Walter, Flying Off. R.A.F., 284.
Andrew, A. W., Pte., 399.
Andrews, H. J., Temp. Capt., I.M.S., 11.
Angel, Andrea, Dr., 195.
Annis, Percy F., Corpl. Canadian Inf., 170.
Ansley, J., Ldg. seaman, 400.
Anson, G., A.B., 396.
Appleyard, A., 387.
Archbold, E., fisherman, 396.
Argent, A., commissioned boatman, 391.
Argent, J., civilian, 392.
Armytage, Reginald William, Lt. R.N., 331.
Arnold, Walter, L.A./C. R.A.F., 284.
Arnold, William Isaac, District Off., 408.
Artis, Joseph, collier, 134.
Ashburnham, D., aged 11 (Vancouver), 163.
Ashley, Charles (Faversham), 197.
Ashraf-un-Nisa Begum, purdah lady, 308.
Aspinall, Harry, miner, 235.
Asquith, Percy, collier, 134.
Aston, Harold, 49.
Atkinson, E. L., Surg. Lt.-Cmdr., 328.
Ayres, Alice, 77, 79.
Azizul Haqq, lascar, 405.

Babu Bhupendra Narayen Singh, 303.
Babu Lakham Ram, rly. employee, 252.
Babu Ranjit Singh, Revenue Off., 304.
Back, R. J., Ch. Off., 400.
Badenoch, Ian Forbes Clark, Lt. R. Fus., 171.
Bagnall, George, steel worker, 143.
Bagnall, Mrs., 143.
Bagot, Arthur Gerald, Sub-Lt., D.S.C., 324.
Bailey, Albert Victor, stoker P.O., 330.
Bailey, F. J., bo'sun's mate, 396.
Baillie, Robert C. T., 3rd off., 410.
Bain-Smith, George Stewart, 217.

INDEX OF NAMES

Baird, David, miner, 197.
Baird, Q.M. (of transport *Sea Horse*), 6.
Baker, C., 389.
Baker, David Marion Burton, 1st mate, 431.
Baker, G. F., fireman, 394.
Baker, John Thomas, pit lad, 253.
Baker, John Thompson, Ch. Off., 405.
Baker, Paling, miner, 239.
Baker, T., 391.
Baker, W. H., 2nd mate, 396.
Balder Singh, sub-insp. police, 300.
Balderson, H. H., O.S., 393.
Balderson, R., 387.
Baldock, W., 390.
Ball, Horace, workman, 227.
Ball, William, pitman, 126.
Ballard, C., 386.
Ballmar, J., 390.
Bamber, Joshua, docker, 49.
Bangley, L. W., employee gold mines, 274.
Banks, Thomas, pitman, 126.
Bannister, James, 79.
Baptista, Joseph, excise constable, 300.
Barber, John, A.B., 311.
Barber, seaman, 110.
Barber, J. G., 393.
Barclay, T. H., Maj., 398.
Barkat Singh, Naik I.A., 292.
Barker, J., bo'sun, 396.
Barker, T. G., colliery asst. manager, 276.
Barker, Thomas, cotton spinner, 137.
Barker, W., 385.
Barlow, Alfred (N.S. Wales), 367.
Barlow, F. W., app., 396.
Barnard, Capt., 83.
Barnard, Isaac, miner, 228.
Barnard, John, miner, 228.
Barnes, James Brack, diamond miner, 123.
Barnes, W., Ch. Off., 399.
Barnett, William, L./C., 291.
Barraclough, Arnold, Sergt., India, 285.
Barrett, J., O.S., 389.
Barry, J., O.S., 397.
Barry, R., coast-guard, 394.
Bartlett, Charles E. C., Lt., bombing off., 157.
Bartlett, Christopher, fisherman, 84.
Bartlett, J. S., 387.
Barton, A., P.S., 392.
Bass, S., 385.
Baster, Norman, colliery agent, 271.
Bastian, J. S., Ch. Off., 400.
Bate, C. H., 390.
Bate, Samuel, seaman, 411.
Bateman, O., Lt., 399.
Bath, Robert, A.B., 395.
Bath, T., 385.
Batist, John, coastguardsman, 85, 309, 340.

Batt, Alice, V.A.D., 183.
Batty, Austen S., A.B., 395.
Batty, John, pitman, 126.
Battye, Basil Condon, Capt., 113.
Bauri, Ram Lal, shunting porter, 130.
Bayley, Cyril Anthony, Trooper, India, 286.
Baynham, Charles, collier, 92.
Beach, Urbane Charles (Faversham), 197.
Beading, G., labourer, 396.
Beaman, George William, collier, 271.
Beard, Edward S., R.N. Canadian V.R., 327.
Beard, P., Ldg. coast-guard boatman, 396.
Beard, Walter Richard, L./C., R.E., 181.
Bearne, Lewis C., D.S.O., Maj. A.S.C. 166.
Beasley, M., Ch. Off., 389.
Beattie, John (Durham), 299.
Beaumont, J., A.B., 395.
Beaumont, W., Ldg. seaman, 395.
Becker, William, A.B., 321.
Beckett, Robert Walter, A.B., 432.
Beeldens, Henri, fireman, 432.
Beek, K. J., seaman, 418.
Beer, Charles, mate, 366.
Behari Dome, rly. porter, 237.
Beith, William (Tynewydd Colliery), 92.
Belben, George Devereux, Lt., D.S.C., 326.
Bell, Edward, Canadian Copper Co., 114.
Bell, Edward W. D. (Battle of Alma), 11.
Bell, H., turner, 398.
Bell, J., O.S., 396.
Bell, John Frederick, gold-mine manager, 299.
Bell, R., 389.
Benn, Daniel, pitman, 126.
Bennell, H., Corpl., 399.
Bennett, George, Pte., 178.
Bennett, George E., cinema proprietor, 116.
Bennett, J. W., master, 397.
Bennett, Rowland, colliery manager, 269.
Bennetts, Harry, gold-miner, 125.
Benning, Ernest, compositor, 77.
Benstead, Albert, smelter, 144.
Benton, Henry, miner, 122.
Beresford, A., Ch. Eng., 399.
Beresford, James, collier, 235.
Bertelsen, F., seaman, 418.
Bethnell, William E. (Faversham), 197.
Betts, J., 386.
Bevan, George Parker, Capt. R.N., 323.
Bewey, G. J., 389.
Bhattu, ferryman, 62.
Bhikam Sirdar, colliery contractor, 246.
Bhim Singh, sub-insp. police, 300.
Bhudu Kol, coal-miner, 202.
Bickford, J., 390.
Bigland, John Edward, L./C. driver, 176.
Biloca, Giovanni, dockyard labourer, 97.
Bindan, Walter G., Ldg. seaman, 401.

INDEX OF NAMES

Binns, Jack, wireless operator, 57.
Birch, William, miner, 133.
Bird, A. M., 393.
Bird, J., Pte., 399.
Birkett, Thomas, pitman, 126.
Birks, John, washerman, 264.
Birks, S. G., 2nd eng., 399.
Birnie, Samuel, pitman, 126.
Bishop, Douglas H. O., colliery manager, 269.
Bisson, Henry Charles, O.S., 425.
Black, Joseph, seaman, 412.
Black, W., O.S., 396.
Blackburn, Richard, Pte., 290.
Blackmore, W., deck hand, 398.
Blair, D., Lt. R.N.R., 1st off., 396.
Blair, Robert Richmond, pitman, 126.
Blake, Edward, 78.
Blake, M., 392.
Blakemore, Arthur Torr, diamond miner, 123.
Bland, George Hubert, M.C., Capt., 214.
Blencowe, George, 77.
Blogg, Henry George, Cox. life-boat, 296.
Blom, A., 387.
Bodsworth, Samuel A., Pte. R.A.M.C., 370.
Bolton, boy of training-ship *Goliath*, 52.
Bolton, C., fireman, 394.
Boner, Eric W., Flt.-Sergt. R.A.F.R., 301.
Bonett, M., O.S., 400.
Bonnici, Paolo, Maltese labourer, 105.
Booker, David Noel, collier, 275.
Booker, Samuel, collier, 275.
Boos, F., 385.
Boot, Frank, foreman, 248.
Booth, F. H., clerk, 398.
Booth, James Frederick, colliery surveyor, 138.
Booth, W., 2nd eng., 399.
Booth, Wilby, collier, 199.
Bordessa, J. D., 389.
Borland, William, sapper, submarine, 364.
Borras, F., A.B., 395.
Botterill, V., A.B., 396.
Bourton, Thomas, steelworker, 250.
Bowden, O., 392.
Bower, John Thomas, miner, 267.
Bowles, George James, sailor, 432.
Bowman, Joseph, dockyard workman, 211.
Boxall, Elizabeth, 78.
Boylan, John, Ch. P.O., 421.
Boyle, C., 387.
Boyle, John, miner, 197.
Bradford, Mr. L. (Anne Port), 38.
Bradshaw, F., bo'sun, 397.
Branch, G. R., Pilot Off., Aux.A.F., 292.
Brandon, J. J., coast-guard P.O., 398.
Brandon, William, sewer worker, 136.
Brawn, James, A.B., 432.
Breadon, Norman George, L.A./C. R.A.F., 287.

Bremer, C., A.B., 396.
Brenner, A., A.B., 394.
Brett, D. A., M.C., Maj. I.A., 286.
Brew, F., bank clerk, 387.
Brew, J., butcher, 387.
Bridges, William J., Q.M., 355.
Briggs, Herbert, gasman, 152.
Briggs, W., skipper, 400.
Brinkworth, L., 387.
Briscoe, G. W., bo'sun, 400.
Bristow, Henry James, 78.
Bristowe, Arthur H., works manager, 205.
Bristowe, C., 385.
Broadbent, H. W., 389.
Broadbent, T. A. H., 393.
Broadhurst, Geo., Corpl., 159.
Brockman, J. W., A.B., 395.
Brodie, Donald, A.B., 432.
Bromage, John, A.B., 418.
Brooke, J., 386.
Brookes, Richard, fitter, 141.
Brookfield Fox, Charles James, Dr., 261.
Brooks, Arthur, Pte., 288.
Brooks, Victor, Sergt. Canadian Cav., 180.
Broomhall, William, workman, 154.
Brosnan, C., seaman, 400.
Brown, Alexander Stewart, Surgeon, 78.
Brown, C., fisherman, 387.
Brown, C. T., boatman, 389.
Brown, Donald A., arsenal foreman, 229.
Brown, F., fisherman, 387.
Brown, G. W., 392.
Brown, H., mate, 400.
Brown, Hugh, bo'sun, 373.
Brown, J., Q.M., 396.
Brown, J. (Aberdeen), 390.
Brown, James William, Act. Q.M.S., 370.
Brown, John Borland, collier, 242.
Brown, John Edward, Pte., 369.
Brown, Richard Leslie, Lt., 170.
Brown, Robert Charles William, A.B., 432.
Brown, Thomas William, fireman, 212.
Brown, W., mate, 384.
Brown, W., skipper, 387.
Brown, W., 1st mate, 392.
Brown, W., hopperman, 396.
Brown, W., A.B., 396.
Brown, W., O.S., 399.
Brown, W., fireman, 400.
Brown, W. J., O.S., 391.
Brown, Walter Russell, Vice-Consul, 118.
Brownless, W. P., 386.
Bruce, George Scott, asst. steward, 431.
Bruce, S., 390.
Brun, A., O.S., 390.
Bryer, Benjamin, gunner H.M.S. *Torbay*, 2.
Brymer, J., Ch. Eng., 398.

INDEX OF NAMES

Bryson, Oliver Campbell, Lt., Air Pilot, 161.
Buchley, George William, chief cook, 431.
Buckle, Henry, Off. H.M.S. *Tiger*, 330.
Buckley, Thomas, miner, 261.
Budden, G., Ldg. coast-guard, 394.
Budden, J., O.S., 400.
Bugg, Rupert Walter, Ldg. deck-hand, 322.
Bugge, O., 385.
Bullock, W. H., 2nd mate, 384.
Bullock, W. H., Ch. Off., 386.
Bulmer, John David, bo'sun, 369.
Bun, A. D., 389.
Burgar, W., 393.
Burgess, Walter Harcourt, bo'sun, 423.
Burgoyne, J., 387.
Burke, F. M., 385.
Burke, James (Manchester), 298.
Burman, W., 391.
Burr, G. F. W., coast-guard boatman, 398.
Burt, Alfred, D.S.O., Brig.-Gen., 180.
Burt, James, Sergt., 191.
Burt, Thomas L., factory Ch. of Police, 195.
Burt, William Henry, 94.
Burton, Archibald, miner, 251.
Burton, H. E., Maj. Supdt. Life Boat, 296.
Burton, Kenneth, Asst. Manager Oil Co., 145.
Burton, R., Q.M., 398.
Burton, W., 386.
Bushell, R., 390.
Buswell, R. W., Capt. attached R.A.F., 176.
Butcher, Henry, munition worker, 201.
Butler, H. J., Pte., 399.
Butler, J., 385.
Butterfield, Frederick, A.B., 395.
Butterfield, Henry, miner, 251.
Buyers, William, 2nd mate, 354.
Bywater, Christopher, gasman, 152.

Cahill, J., fisherman, 392.
Cahill, M., fisherman, 392.
Cahill, T., fisherman, 392.
Cain, G., lamp-trimmer, 398.
Cain, J., coast-guard boatman, 387.
Cairns, John, miner, 148.
Cairns, W., Ch. Off., 396.
Calder, G., 392.
Calladine, Thomas, miner, 232.
Calligan, T., 389.
Calthrop, Walter H., Cmdr. R.N., 324.
Calverley, Frank Herbert, Lt. R.E., 179.
Cameron, R., 385.
Camp, Bernardino, Capt. brig. *Emilio*, 65.
Campbell, A. S. A., 392.
Campbell, J., 391.
Campbell, John Pitts, Lt. R.F.A., 162.
Campbell, Joseph, colliery fireman, 151.
Campbell, Kenneth, A.B., 432.

Campbell, Malcolm S. C., Maj., 113.
Campbell, Matthew James, sewerman, 241.
Campbell, R., 385.
Campbell, William, pitman, 126.
Canavan, John, 43.
Cannell, Ernest, steel worker, 143.
Cannon, Horace, Flt. Sergt., 172.
Cannon, James, mine chargeman, 134.
Cannon, Thomas, pitman, 126.
Capon, G., 390.
Carlin, G. W., T.F. Nursing Service, 182.
Carne, Charles John, rly. goods insp., 165.
Carney, James, railwayman, 95.
Carnie, T., 389.
Carpenter, Alfred, Lt., 310, 350.
Carr, J., 388.
Carr, John, A.B., 428.
Carter, Herbert, sewerman, 136.
Carter, James Julian, brakesman, 118.
Carter, William, A.B., 360.
Carter, W. G. E., 2nd hand, 397.
Carter, W. T., O.S., 385.
Cartwright, A., colliery under-manager, 127.
Cassidy, J., 390.
Cassidy, T., bo'sun, 399.
Cawley, Mr. K. (Anne Port), 38.
Cay, A., fisherman, 391.
Cay, C., fisherman, 391.
Cay, R. B., Cmdr., 309.
Cay, W., fisherman, 391.
Cazaly, Herbert Peter, clerk, 78.
Chafer, A., 386.
Chalmers, A., 392.
Chalmers, Jack (Sydney, N.S.W.), 376.
Chalmers, Robert Mills, P.O. R.N., 283.
Chamberlain, W., 387.
Chambers, J. E., colliery manager, 146.
Chandler, Francis, miner, 120.
Chandler, R., 390.
Chang Chin Pan, seaman, 406.
Chang Pan Fah, seaman, 406.
Chant, Frederick, Pte., 283.
Chapman, A., 391.
Chapman, Charles (N. Zealand), 215.
Chapman, Charles A., A.B., 395.
Chapman, J. K., docks works manager, 103.
Chappell, J. E., A.B., 395.
Chappery, J., 385.
Chapple, Henry, fireman, 46.
Chardin, Geoffrey Walter, eng., 238.
Charlie the Gunner, *see* Fitzpatrick, C.
Chatters, E., Ldg. seaman, 399.
Chatterton, Thomas, loader, 147.
Chavasse, N., Capt. R.A.M.C., 11.
Chee Ah Kun, bo'sun's mate, 406.
Cheetham, H. C. V. B., Cmdr., 397.
Cheetham, James, signalman, 395.

INDEX OF NAMES 457

Cheshire, A. G., 392.
Cheshire, William Donald, Capt., 163.
Chetwynd, Charles, collier, 95.
Chetwynd, Joseph, collier, 95.
Chidley, Joseph Thomas, miner, 231.
Chidlow, John Arthur, A.B., 418.
Chindemi, G., 386.
Ching Chin Fong, seaman, 406.
Chitrabahadur, Gurung, L./N., I.A., 288.
Christie, Alexander, Capt. fishing-smack, 355.
Christie, George Shearer, miner, 197.
Christie, W., 385.
Christie, W. J., 1st mate, 394.
Christison, G., Pte., 399.
Christmas, Jesse, P.C., 173.
Civill, A., A.B., 396.
Clark, Alexander, Dr., 219.
Clark, Ambrose, foreman sinker, 97.
Clark, J. Harvey, A.B., 395.
Clark, Leslie Maynard, seaman, 412.
Clark, W., boilermaker, 399.
Clarke, Azariah, pitman, 277.
Clarke, D., 388.
Clarke, E., 386.
Clarke, Harold Walwin, deck hand, 414.
Clarke, Hugh, Capt., 113.
Clarke, J. J., 3rd hand, 397.
Clarke, T., 387.
Clay, W. E., 390.
Clayton, F., 3rd hand, 394.
Clayton, Reginald Curtis, app., 371.
Cleall, Walter, soldier, 186.
Cleary, T. (or O'Leary), 386.
Cleeve, J. A., 2nd off., 400.
Clements, W. E., bo'sun, 396.
Clerk, Arthur Edward, A.B., 402.
Clifford, Walter, miner, 121.
Clinton, John (aged 10), 78.
Close, Gerald C. N., Pilot Off. R.A.F., 291.
Clough, A. B., Lt., 397.
Clouter, H., A.B., 400.
Cluett, G., 393.
Coates, J. M., 4th off., 396.
Cobb, The Reverend Charles, 85, 340.
Cobham, Anthony J., midshipman R.N., 283.
Cock, W. C., 393.
Cockcroft, W. L., Capt. R.A.M.C., 399.
Coco, diamond miner, 123.
Codd, Peter, Q.M., 421.
Cody, Norman, seaman, 420.
Coe, B., A.B., 391.
Coghlam, Elizabeth, 79.
Coker, T. C., coast-guard, 395.
Cole, Albert Edward, A.B., 421.
Cole, George, station-master, 130.
Cole, J., boatman, 393.
Cole, J., Q.M., 393.

Cole, T., chief boatman, 386.
Cole, William, P.C., 96.
Coleman, George, ambulance man, 246.
Colin, C., Ch. Off., 399.
Collard, E., 392.
Collett, W. S., seaman, 400.
Collin, J., skipper, 397.
Collingwood, James, collier, 239.
Collins, Frederick John, Q.M., 431.
Collins, J., A.B., 390.
Collins, James, Pte. R.A.M.C., 166.
Collins, John, seaman, 404.
Collins, R., 389.
Collis, Capt., fireship *Duke* (St. Tropez 1742), 2.
Colman, G., deck hand, 399.
Colwell, Edward, steeple-jack, 204.
Congdon, William Dynhand, Ch. Off., 418.
Conneely, M., 391.
Connell, D., fisherman, 392.
Connell, J., fisherman (1), 392.
Connell, J., fisherman (2), 392.
Connell, J., fisherman (3), 392.
Connell, P., fisherman (1), 392.
Connell, P., fisherman (2), 392.
Connell, T., fisherman, 392.
Connolly, W., Constable R.I.C., 393.
Connor, P. J., civilian, 393.
Conolly, Joseph, 3rd eng., 368.
Cook, Frederick, Ch. Off., 404.
Cook, J., Lt., 399.
Cook, Joseph, miner, 154.
Cook, Percy Edwin, P.C., 79.
Coombe, E. B., A.B., 401.
Cooney, P., greaser, 399.
Cooper, A. H., colliery under-manager, 147.
Cooper, Alfred John, 4th off., 363.
Cooper, C. L., app., 396.
Cooper, W., 388.
Copeland, W., 387.
Coppard, Thomas, munition worker, 201.
Corbett, N. M. F., Lt., 394.
Cordey, John George, miner, 246.
Cordy, Frederick Raymond, miner, 267.
Corea, M. de, 390.
Corkish, E., 387.
Cornwell, Jack, boy H.M.S. *Chester*, 47.
Cornwell, S. A., 2nd mate, 392.
Correa, F., 385.
Corrigan, James, 2nd eng., 402.
Costain, T. E., 388.
Costello, Edwin, bo'sun, 366.
Costello, W., 391.
Costelloe, William I., wireless operator, 410.
Cotton, Arthur Stedman, Col., 211.
Coulson, Robert, 2nd eng., 371.
Coulson, William (Hartley Coll.), 53.
Coulthard, James, pitman, 126.

INDEX OF NAMES

Couth, 84.
Coverley, J. A., master, 398.
Cowan, Joseph, pitman, 126.
Coward, W. H., A.B., 396.
Cowell, J., deck hand, 394.
Cowie, C. R., s.s. passenger, 389.
Cowin, W. G., ry. guard, 387.
Cowley, A. E., 391.
Cowley, John Guise, Lt. R.E., 220.
Cowling, H., 389.
Cowper, Lt., 6.
Cox, J., beachman, 388.
Cox, J., gunner, 398.
Cox, J. B., P.C., 396.
Cox, Philip, miner, 261.
Coyne, David Emmitt, Sergt. A.I.F., 178.
Craddock, J. T., A.B., 397.
Cradock, Sir C. G. F. M., 394.
Craig, A., civilian, 396.
Craig, Bert, miner, 236.
Craig, George, fisherman, 107.
Craine, Patrick, bo'sun, 420.
Crandall, H. F., L./C., 398.
Crane, Mr., 84.
Cranmer, John, clerk, 78.
Cranswick, James, miner, 121.
Crawley, W., A.B., 396.
Crean, Thomas, P.O., 116, 315.
Crispen, J., 389.
Crocker, T. E., 384.
Croft, Frederick Alfred, insp., 77.
Crofts, Samuel, deputy miner, 256.
Crome, R., 388.
Crompton, James, eng., 265.
Crook, John, mine manager, 96.
Cropper, E. D. T., Capt., 355.
Cropper, John, Ch. Off., 406.
Crosby, Bertie Frederick, aged 16, 250.
Cross, G., 385.
Cross, Harry, signalman, 395.
Crosse, A. B., 2nd mate, 389.
Crossley, E., Adm. Dockyard foreman, 305.
Crossley, L., Corpl., 399.
Crowden, James, Ch. Off., 309, 344.
Cruickshank, J., P.C., 395.
Cruickshank, J. M., 387.
Crumpton, James, eng., 50.
Cubban, W. T., 387.
Cudbird, Charles S. V., stationmaster, 136.
Cullen, P., 391.
Cullen, Walter, miner, 136.
Cullinan, Patrick, railwayman, 99.
Cullis, E., 390.
Cumming, George E., Lt., 394.
Cummings, Peter, collier, 202.
Cunningham, E. D., A.B., 396.
Curman, H., deck hand, 400.

Cutfield, H. E., Dist. Off., 42.
Cuthbertson, James, Pte. R.A.M.C., 370.
Cutmore, S. G. B., A.B., 395.

Dahlquist, E., A.B., 396.
Dakserhoff, G., 3rd off., 406.
Dally, James, workman, 189.
Dalton, M., R.N.R., 400.
Dando, Edwin Arthur, Dr., 127.
Daniel, H. S., Lt., 397.
Dann, Elisha, bo'sun H.M.S. *Torbay*, 2.
Darby, Arthur, smelter, 142.
Dark, W. F., Ch. mate, 397.
Darker, Richard Edward, collier, 265.
Darley, Charles Curtis, Flt. Lt. R.A.F., 214.
Darling, James, P.C., 409.
Dart, John, miner, 261.
Davey, Ernest, A.B., 395.
David, Edward, collier, 92.
David, G. W., 385.
Davies, Mr., 84.
Davies, David, colliery owner, 92.
Davies, E., Ch. Off., 395.
Davies, Edmund, colliery fireman, 125.
Davies, Fred, fireman, 49.
Davies, Henry (Abercarn Coll.), 93.
Davies, J. L., 3rd eng., 394.
Davies, J. O., Ch. Off., 396.
Davies, L., 385.
Davies, L. H., A.B., 395.
Davies, Richard Leslie, seaman, 404.
Davies, Thomas G., colliery manager, 92.
Davies, William, diver, 262.
Davis, David, 16th Lancers, 96.
Davis, Edward P. M., Flt. Lt. R.N.A.S., 319.
Davis, F., stoker, 397.
Davis, J. R., bo'sun's mate, 398.
Davis, Joseph, gold miner, 124.
Davis, Pioneer David T., 97.
Davis, R., O.S., 398.
Davis, Thomas N., Ldg. seaman, 321.
Davison, C., 392.
Dawes, Nicholas B. E., Capt. R.E., 107.
Dawes, T., 387.
Dawson, Albert Henry Fowler, miner, 235.
Day, Charles, collier, 95.
Day, Henry M. A., Act. Lt., 326.
Day, J., 386.
Day, W. S., 392.
Dean, Albert F., A.B., 395.
Dean, Harry, fireman, 78.
Dearling, T., fitter, 398.
Dee, James, P.C., 95.
Deedes, Richard, Capt., 286.
Delahay, George, A.B., 421.
Denehey, T., 389.
Denman, Alice Maud, 79.

INDEX OF NAMES

Denny, Harry, foundryman, 207.
Denton, Arthur, works fitter, 231.
Denton, J. R., 392.
Devans, D., seaman, 400.
Devenport, Christopher, miner, 193.
Devine, David, pitman, 126.
Dewar, J. G., D.S.C., R.N., 400.
Diamond, Frank, asylum attendant, 109.
Diamond, J., 390.
Dibben, C., eng. driver, 398.
Dick, J. J. R., 391.
Dickson, Sydney, gas worker, 138.
Dickson, Thomas Johnstone, Lt., 169.
Dickson, William, miner, 122.
Diego, S., 386.
Dingli, Antonio, Maltese labourer, 105.
Dinneen, John, Ch. mate, 361.
Ditter, H., O.S., 392.
Diver, J., fisherman, 390.
Diver, W. O., 3rd mate, 389.
Dixon, Thomas, miner, 261.
Dobbelaere, Alphonse, sailor, 432.
Dobinson, Herbert, explosives worker, 139.
Dodd, G. H., 389.
Dodd, John, merchant, 347.
Dodd, William, pit under-manager, 97.
Doherty, J., 391.
Dominees, Frank Richard, A.B., 419.
Donald, Thomas, pitman, 126.
Donald, William, clerk, 77.
Donking, W. H., A.B., 396.
Donoghue, J., A.B., 396.
Donoghue, P., fisherman (1), 392.
Donoghue, P., fisherman (2), 392.
Donovan, Charles Creaghe, Capt., 113.
Donovan, Ellen, 77.
Donovan, John, Ch. boatman, 85, 310, 341.
Donovan, Peter Charles, A.B., 422.
Doran, J., 390.
Dorsey, B., 2nd hand, 396.
Douglas, Maj., 6.
Douglas, Robert Ewing, L.A./C. R.A.F., 285.
Dow, Robert Dunn (Ferozepore), 113.
Down, Charles, 2nd hand, 413.
Downes, E. M., 393.
Downey, D., 394.
Downie, F., 390.
Downing, W. Creagh, Lt. R.G.A., 394.
Downing, William Henry, 2nd mate, 418.
Doyle, Walter, bo'sun, 428.
Drabble, Robert, sinker, 97.
Drake, William, 76.
Drever, J., 393.
Driscoll, H., fisherman, 386.
Driscoll, M., fisherman, 386.
Driscoll, P., Ch. P.O., 399.
Dryburgh, George, miner, 121.

Dryburgh, James, miner, 121.
Duffin, Charles Godfrey, diver, 306.
Duffy, E. J., 385.
Dugdale, Bert (Faversham), 197.
Duggan, J. C., 387.
Duhrin, A. E., carptr., 396.
Duller, Frank, miner, 206.
Dunbar, Robert, miner, 153.
Dunk, A. A., A.B., 395.
Dunlop, James, pitman, 126.
Dunn, James, Pte., 177.
Dunn, T. W., R.N.R., mate, 394.
Durrant, Robert, worker, 78.
Dwyer, P., boatman, 389.
Dye, Arthur James, skipper, 367.
Dyer, Arthur Hugh, 5th off., 412.
Dyer, F., seaman, 400.
Dyer, J., A.B., 384.
Dyer, J., A.B., 385.
Dyer, J., seaman, 400.
Dyer, W., master, 385.
Dyke, W. A., steward, 390.

Eastaway, T., 384.
Easton, David, collier, 151.
Eavey, O. E., seaman, 400.
Ebrahim, J., 389.
Eccleshall, Arthur, rly. porter, 103.
Edgelow, Frederick H., mining insp., 134.
Edwards, Arthur Frederick (Faversham), 197.
Edwards, George, collier, 140.
Edwards, John Malcolm Gordon, 3rd off., 405.
Edwards, W., 389.
Edwardson, Herbert (St. Ouen's Bay), 38.
Elder, J. B., 387.
Eldrett, W. G., Ldg. seaman, 400.
Elias, diamond miner, 123.
Elkman, A. O., O.S., 400.
Ellaya, Subadar-Maj., 213.
Elliot, George, seaman, 404.
Elliott, George, workman, 78.
Elliott, Thomas W., colliery manager, 228.
Elliott, W., 387.
Ellis, Bernard George, Lt., 185.
Ellis, David William, seaman, 431.
Ellis, G. F. F. S., Act. Capt. R.N., 399.
Ellis, R., master, 385.
Else, Walter, A.B., 396.
Elsmore, H., 389.
Elsome, A., R.N.R., 400.
Elston, Ernest Mathew, Pte., 288.
Elwick, Vincent, miner, 240.
Emery, Edmund, 77.
Emery, Oscar Edward, Ch. Off., 405.
Emmett, Mrs., station-master's wife, 212.
Emptage, A., 388.
English, J., 384.

INDEX OF NAMES

Erao, P., Cox., 385.
Eriksen, S., seaman, 418.
Erikson, A., O.S., 391.
Erikson, W., carptr. and A.B., 395.
Erskine, James, miner, 197.
Espley, Ernest William, 3rd mate, 418.
Etienne, C., civilian, 396.
Evans, C., 387.
Evans, David, colliery manager, 92.
Evans, David Hywel, Sub-Lt., 326.
Evans, E. R. G. R., Capt. (later Adm. Sir), 66, 116, 400.
Evans, Henry, colliery manager, 129.
Evans, John, engine-driver, 131.
Evans, T., 386.
Evans, Thomas, steel worker, 143.
Evans, Thomas Phillip, steel worker, 250.
Evans, William, pit carptr., 125.
Evans, Wyndham, pit overman, 258.
Everson, Henry, miner, 120.
Evetts, George (Faversham), 197.
Ewington, Herbert F., Metrop. Ry., 117.

Fairclough, John, gunner R.A., 218.
Falconer, David, Ch. Eng., 373.
Falla, Henry Stephen, A.B., 425.
Falvey, M., 393.
Fanning, E. F., midshipman, 395.
Farabani, Seedie Tindal, H.M.S. *Wild Swan*, 310.
Faragher, F., 388.
Farmer, J. C., 2nd Lt., 400.
Farquharson, Alexander, miner, 151.
Farrell, P. J., stoker, 397.
Farren, Joseph Collington, sapper, 176.
Farrer, Anthony, aged 8 (Vancouver), 163.
Farrington, Robert, mine under-manager, 201.
Fauchelle, Laurence, seaman, 403.
Fearnley, F., 2nd hand, 392.
Fearon, John, pitman, 126.
Fedder, H., 385.
Feetham, Christopher, fireman, 372.
Fegen, E. S. F., Lt. R.N., 399.
Feldwick, Corpl., 162.
Ferguson, A., 386.
Ferraro, O., O.S., 387.
Ferries, R. P. G., 388.
Ferris, Richard, labourer, 77.
Ferryman, Thomas, pitman, 126.
Fidan, G., A.B., 390.
Fiddian, E. A., Surgeon, 399.
Field, C. P., 390.
Figgins, G. F., 391.
Finch, Richard E., colliery manager, 206.
Finkelenberg, T., seaman, 418.
Finlayson, K., 384.
Firoze Khan, L./N., 220.

Fish, William, miner, 198.
Fisher, A. E., skipper, 397.
Fisher, G., colliery deputy, 146.
Fisher, P., Pte., 399.
Fisher, W., coast-guard, 385.
Fisher, William, 77.
Fishwick, Thomas, bo'sun, 411.
Fiske, Charles William, Capt., 171.
Fitzclarke, L. E., 2nd hand, 389.
Fitzgerald, J., O.S., 400.
Fitzgerald, John, bo'sun's mate, 421.
FitzGerald, J. E., 392.
Fitzherbert, Thos. Charles, Capt., 166.
Fitzpatrick, Charles (Bill Quay), 53.
Fitzpatrick, Patrick John, Staff Sergt., 113.
Fitzpatrick, T., fisherman, 391.
Fitzsimmons, Harry, Pte., 221.
Flaherty, T., 391.
Flavel, G. H., Ch. Off., 400.
Fleet, G. B., 392.
Fleming, H. C., 3rd eng., 399.
Fleming, J., 393.
Fleming, Thomas Pearson, charge hand, 257.
Fleming, William George, Cox. life-boat, 297.
Fletcher, Donald, miner, 244.
Fletcher, Geoffrey, miner, 227.
Fletcher, James, bus-insp., 50.
Fletcher, W. H., Q.M., 396.
Flett, J., lamp trimmer, 396.
Flucker, J., 389.
Flynn, C., A.B., 400.
Flynn, D., 393.
Flynn, J., A.B., 397.
Foca, B., A.B., 386.
Fogarty, Michael, miner, 206.
Foley, Richard, driver R.F.A., 159.
Foley, W. (co. Down), 388.
Foot, G., 397.
Forbes, Robert John, fireman, 161.
Forbes, William Balfour, Lt. R.N., 309, 347.
Ford, Albert, Sergt., 163.
Ford, Joseph Andrew, fireman, 76.
Foreman, H. A., master, 399.
Forrester, William, tram-driver, 49.
Forster, E., 390.
Forster, R., Ch. Off., 393.
Forth, Robert McGregor, 2nd eng., 422.
Foster, Henry, collier, 201.
Foster, John, seaman, 403.
Foster, Reginald Thistle, Q.M., 416.
Foster, William Henry, Pte., 219.
Foulds, Daniel, miner, 198.
Foulkes, H., trimmer, 399.
Fox, G., O.S., 390.
Fox, Samuel, A.B., 403.
Foy, Clifford, Lt., 171.
Francis, Alfred, diamond miner, 123.

INDEX OF NAMES

Frank, George Herbert, works manager, 260.
Frankland, Arthur (Ardeer explosion), 191.
Franklin, Charles Benjamin, miner, 192.
Fraser, David, Ch. Eng., 375.
Fraser, Harriet Elizabeth, staff nurse, 182.
Fraser, W., 2nd eng., 400.
Frazer, Edgar H., H.M. Insp. Mines, 265.
Freeman, B., app., 394.
French, Herbert C., Capt. R.A.M.C., 366.
Frood, R., O.S., 390.
Fudge, Henry, donkeyman, 402.
Fuhrea, O., steward, 390.
Fuller, C. (Nova Scotia), 397.
Fuller, C. T. M., Capt., 397.
Fuller, T. H., 390.
Fullick, Edward George, 4th off., 419.
Fulton, R. A., Q.M., 400.
Funnell, F., stoker, 390.
Funnell, George Stephen, P.C., 78.
Furlonger, Alfred H., D.C.M., sapper, 176.
Furneaux, Alfred William, Ch. steward, 370.

Gairdner, E. D., D.S.O., Capt., 398.
Galaman, Solomon, aged 11, 79.
Galbraith, Ian William, M.C., Lt., 213.
Galbraith, J. H., O.S., 392.
Gale, George, dockhand, 200.
Gallagher, J., 2nd off., 396.
Gallagher, P., A.B., 400.
Gallant, C., A.B., 390.
Ganger, M., 384.
Gardiner, Alfred, driver, 49.
Gardiner, T., bo'sun, 388.
Gardner, F. J. R., 1st off., 396.
Gargett, J., 391.
Garlinge, G. W., A.B., 395.
Garner, A., A.B., 390.
Garner, J., greaser, 399.
Garner, John, stoker, 202.
Garnish, The Reverend G., 77.
Garrett, Stanley Leonard, app., 406.
Garster, D., 389.
Garvey, T., A.B., 396.
Gaskell, S., A.B., 396.
Gaunt, George, shaft-sinker foreman, 247.
Geake, William H. G., Lt. A.I.F., 180.
Gearen, C., seaman, 400.
Ge Ling Low, Q.M., 406.
Gempton, A. S., skipper, 393.
George, A., 384.
George, Archibald, seaman, 403.
George, Robert James, whaleman, 415.
Georgeson, G., fisherman, 395.
Georgeson, M., fisherman, 395.
Gerrighty, Anthony, Pte., 353.
Gharib Shah, waterman, 211.
Ghulam Mohi-ud-Din, Sub-Insp. Police, 300.

Gibbs, Stanley (Sydney, N.S.W.), 377.
Gibney, P., volunteer, 396.
Gibson, Alexander, Sergt., 184.
Gibson, Charles, pitman, 126.
Gibson, H. C. P., A.B., 396.
Gibson, Thomas, ship's cook, 381.
Gibson, W., O.S., 389.
Gibson, W., O.S., 392.
Giforos, G., A.B., 390.
Gilber, Henry, master H.M.S. *Torbay*, 2.
Gilbertson, C. G., fisherman, 395.
Giles, Edward, Capt. I.N., 346.
Gilham, George (Faversham), 197.
Gilham, R., skipper, 393.
Gill, J., A.B., 386.
Gill, Selwyn Ernest, deck hand, 413.
Gillings, J., assistant boatman, 395.
Gillmour, Kate, stewardess, 66, 393.
Gimble, Edward, Pte., 156.
Gimblett, David, seaman, 405.
Ginbey, William, pitman, 126.
Gittins, R. P., 390.
Gleave, Harold, ry. porter, 276.
Glendenning, Robert, colliery overman, 253.
Gloyn, P., 387.
Goble, J., boatman, 388.
Goff, William Edward, aged 16, 268.
Golding, John Patrick, A.B., 403.
Golledge, Herbert John, pitman, 196.
Godbolt, W. J., 390.
Goodchild, Frank John, 1st mate, 422.
Goodhart, Francis H. H., Comdr., 320.
Goodrum, William, signalman, 77.
Gordon, J., A.B., 390.
Gordon, J. L., Flt. Sub-Lt., 398.
Gossett, R. R., Lt., 395.
Gottwall, J. W., 390.
Gough, John Ingram, miner, 256.
Gourlay, W., ship's carptr., 400.
Gove, J., mate, 388.
Gowen, F. G., bo'sun, 394.
Gradike, F., O.S., 391.
Graham, Abraham C., munition worker, 201.
Graham, H., bo'sun, 385.
Graham, Isaac, pitman, 126.
Graham, John, pitman, 126.
Graham, Samuel, miner, 246.
Graham, Thomas, pitman, 126.
Graham, Wilson, pitman, 126.
Grainger, E. H., 1st mate, 392.
Grainger, W., volunteer (life-saving), 391.
Grant, F. H., mechanician, 397.
Grant, J., fisherman, 387.
Grassom, S., 389.
Graves, Mr., 84.
Gray, H., mate, 391.
Gray, Reginald H. M., 301.

INDEX OF NAMES

Gray, Robert, seaman, 360.
Gray, T., fisherman, 391.
Grayson, J., 391.
Green, Lt. (at St. Tropez 1742), 2.
Green, B., O.S., 396.
Green, Charles W. T., Eng. P.W.D., 303.
Green, G., 2nd hand, 387.
Green, H., Ch. coastguard, 394.
Green, J., 2nd mate, 385.
Green, J., A.B., 385.
Green, James, foreman miner, 140.
Green, Mrs., 140.
Green, R. J., A.B., 390.
Greenless, Robert, explosive worker, 140.
Greenoff, Edward George Brown, P.C., 79.
Gregory, Christopher, pitman, 126.
Gregory, Harold, miner, 192.
Grey, E. L., app., 387.
Grier, Henry, Surgeon, 93.
Grieu, Paul (Frenchman), 306.
Griffen, J. H., 384.
Griffen, Thomas, fitter's labourer, 78.
Griffiths, gold miner (Johannesburg), 122.
Griffiths, Alexander, miner, 144.
Griffiths, George, Lt. R.N., 401.
Grillo, G., O.S., 387.
Grills, T., boatman, 392.
Groat, A., fisherman, 392.
Groat, J., fisherman, 393.
Groves, George, ammonia worker, 137.
Groves, Mrs., 138.
Grundley, J. S., 2nd eng., 399.
Grundstrom, E., A.B., 397.
Gulterio, E., O.S., 387.
Gundersen, E., 386.
Gunner, Walter George, Pte., 172.
Gunns, J., coastguard boatman, 393.
Gunter, H., 3rd eng., 400.
Guppy, S., P.O., 393.

Habib Khan, L./N., S. & M., 97.
Haddon, James, miner, 198.
Haden, Cecil, A.B., 395.
Hagges, C., steward, 389.
Haines, Samuel James, jun. off., 374.
Halfpenny, Frank, miner, 229.
Halgren, C., 387.
Hall, A., Ch. mate, 396.
Hall, W., coastguard boatman, 394.
Haller, W., O.S., 391.
Halliday, Ernest Hay, Ch. Off., 430.
Halloran, W., 387.
Halstead, Arthur, M.C., Lt., 165.
Ham, H. W., 390.
Hamblin, Henry Charles, collier, 253.
Hambly, C., 388.
Hamilton, Alfred, munition worker, 201.

Hamilton, J., A.B., 397.
Hampson, J., 391.
Hampson, John, pitman, 126.
Hand, William George, M.M., Sergt., 283.
Handford, Robert, miner, 233.
Handley, Frederick, Capt., 113.
Handley, T., Ch. steward, 399.
Hankey, Thomas Barnard, 2nd Lt., 158.
Hanlon, John, pitman, 126.
Hansen, H., seaman, 418.
Hansen, Hans Clay, seaman, 418.
Hanson, Arthur, on Yangtze R., 115.
Harcus, J., 393.
Hardiment, Arthur, rly. crossing-keeper, 102.
Hardman, John, miner, 135.
Hardwick, Albert Victor (Finsbury, Pk.), 98.
Hargan, H., O.S., 396.
Harkbir Thapa, Gurkha Rifles, Rifleman, 221.
Harmer, George, deck hand, 425.
Harmer, W. H., Ldg. coastguard boatman, 396.
Harnden, F., 386.
Harold, W., coastguard off., 400.
Harper, Leonard, Lt., 178.
Harper, Thomas, collier, 203.
Harper, W., coastguard boatman, 387.
Harper, W., O.S., 392.
Harris, Charles Joshua Joseph, Dr., 126.
Harris, Charles Thomas (Faversham), 197.
Harris, John, mason (Abercarn), 93.
Harris, John William, 1st mate, 416.
Harris, Lewis, (Abercarn), 93.
Harris, R., 3rd mate, 387.
Harris, W., hotel-keeper, 394.
Harrison, George Willet, A.B., R.N., 284.
Harrison, J., fisherman, 388.
Harrison, John (Faversham), 197, 201.
Harrison, Joseph, miner, 232.
Hartley, James, miner, 135.
Harvey, A., 2nd eng., 392.
Harvey, C., 3rd hand, 392.
Harvey, William Fryer, Surg. Lt. R.N., 325.
Harwood, Harrie Stephen, R.F.C., 157.
Hasil, of Chitral, 101.
Haslar, A., boatman, 395.
Hatcher, Arthur, miner, 235.
Hau Fat Sang, Q.M., 406.
Havercroft, Percy Roberts, collier, 195.
Hawkins, C., boatman, 387.
Hawkins, Henry Morley, clerk, 133.
Hawthorn, Archbold, colliery overman, 257.
Hay, A., fisherman, 391.
Hay, G., fisherman, 391.
Hay, J., jun., fisherman, 391.
Hay, J. R., fisherman, 391.
Hayes, J., Q.M., 389.
Hayman, E., 393.
Hayter, R., 392.

INDEX OF NAMES

Hayward, J., A.B., 397.
Hayward, Victor George, R.N., 215; 331.
Hazlewood, A., A.B., 396.
Headon, S. A., A.B., 399.
Healey, G., 2nd mate, 399.
Healy, Michael, D.C.M., M.M., Sergt., 168.
Heaps, William, seaman, 420.
Heard, W., skipper, 386.
Hearne, diver, 101.
Hearne, Henry, Corpl. R.F.C., 157.
Heathcote, William, miner, 198.
Hedger, A. G., 2nd Lt., 400.
Heeland, A. J., 391.
van Heerden, Jacobus Lowies, miner, 231.
Hefferman, F. D., 391.
Heggie, J., Eng. Lt., 399.
Helm, J., P.C., 392.
Heighton, C., Ldg. coastguard boatman, 396.
Heighway, E. J., A.B., 396.
Helders, H., A.B., 386.
Hellman, August, A.B., 402.
Hemcon, J. L., 386.
Hemmings, William James, seaman, 420.
Henbest, Harry, A.B., 419.
Hendon, Alfred, Ch. Off., 420.
Henderson, D. M., 385.
Henderson, George Stuart, Capt., 12.
Henderson, Herbert Reuben (London), 299.
Henderson, J., Master-at-arms, 389.
Henderson, John, coastguardsman, 424.
Henderson, John William, Colour-Sergt., 115.
Henderson, Robert, collier, 151.
Hendry, James C. S., mechanic R.N.A.S., 315.
Hennen, W., 390.
Hennessey, Lawrence, life-boat Cox., 311.
Henney, John Alfred, factory hand, 196.
Henry, George, pitman, 126.
Henry, James, pitman, 126.
Henry, James Dixon, A.B., 323.
Henry, William John, pitman, 126.
Henshaw, George, L./C., 289.
Henwood, J. A., 389.
Hepburn, John, mine worker, 151.
Herbert, Thomas, (Abercarn Coll.), 93.
Herkes, T., life-boatman, 389.
Hermans, Henri, fireman, 432.
Herring, John, miner, 135.
Heslop, George C., mine manager, 272.
Hetherington, C., app., 397.
Hewers, James, 77.
Hewett, T., 388.
Hewis, R., A.B., 387.
Hewison, Hereward (Newcastle, N.S.W.), 365.
Hewitt, Arthur Bernard, colliery manager, 147.
Hewitt, J., pilot, 391.
Hewitt, Jack, schoolboy (Goole), 112.
Hewitt, R. J., 2nd hand, 393.

Heyns, George Andries Muller, youth, 378.
Hickford, C., 384.
Higgins, Aaron Edward, 3rd eng., 375.
Higgs, Henry Joseph, Lt. of bombers, 160.
Higson, George, fireman, 96.
Hill, A., A.B., 393.
Hill, J., A.B., 390.
Hill, J. W., A.B., 394.
Hill, R. A., Capt., 398.
Hill, W., O.S., 391.
Hilliard, G. W., app., 390.
Hilliard, Matthew, miner, 121.
Hilton, John, miner, 135.
Hindley, George, blacksmith, 96.
Hindmarsh, J., 387.
Hines, J., 389.
Hinge, John George, plumber, 188.
Hinton, William, Revenue Off., 94.
Hitchcock, G. H., 394.
Hoare, D. L. H., app., 397.
Hoare, George, boatman, C.G. station, 311.
Hoare, Robin Keith, Lt., 324.
Hobbs, E., Ch. boatman, 393.
Hobbs, E. N., 2nd mate, 390.
Hodge, W., Ch. boatman, 389.
Hodge, W., Ch. boatman, 393.
Hodges, Isaac, 128.
Hodgson, G. R., Flt. Sub-Lt., 398.
Hogan, B., fireman, 391.
Hogg, Willoughby Lugard, Maj., 404.
Holbert, P., 392.
Holdway, Frederick, collier, 203.
Holl, E. J., D.S.C., master, 399.
Holland, E., 391.
Holley, Elizabeth, nurse, 115.
Holliday, Allan, brewery worker, 148.
Holm, C., Q.M., 390.
Holmes, A., 4th hand, 388.
Holmes, H., Corpl., 398.
Homer, W., 5th eng., 399.
Honey, Reginald, A.B., 401.
Honeyman, W., A.B., 396.
Hong Kam, seaman, 406.
Hood, Henry, Cox. R.N.L.I. life-boat, 358.
Hood, J. C., master, 390.
Hood, Mr., 83.
Hooper, R., 2nd hand, 389.
Hopkins, Frank, seaman, 377.
Hopkins, J., boatman, 391.
Hopkins, J. W., carpenter's mate, 390.
Hopkins, Richard, collier, 92.
Hopwood, James, miner, 121.
Horn, Alfred, miner, 205.
Horne, Alfred, driver A.S.C., 180.
Horsburgh, B., 390.
Horsfall, F. P., 2nd off., 394.
Horton, G. J., A.B., 396.

INDEX OF NAMES

Horton, M. K., Lt., 394.
Hosey, James, miner, 128.
Hoskin, William, pitman, 126.
Hoskyn, Charles R., Capt. R.A.M.C., 167.
Hostler, Harold H., distillery vat man, 263.
Houghton, Frederick Leonard, Lt., 168.
House, J., Ch. coastguard, 393.
van Hove, Camiel, 303.
Howard, M., skipper, 397.
Howe, J., 386.
Howell, John W. (Tynewydd Colliery), 92.
Howells, John, ex-Cox. life-boat, 297.
Howells, Llewellyn, collier, 142.
Howells, Morgan, boy, 121.
Howells, Richards, collier, 92.
Howlett, J. F., skipper, 397.
Howsagore, J. M., 2nd off., 390.
Hoyle, George, mill boy of 14, 207.
Huckstep, J., 386.
Hudson, Charles William, miner, 192.
Hudson, James, app., 342.
Huggins, Bond, app., 406.
Hughes, A., coastguard boatman, 394.
Hughes, Arianfryn, miner, 267.
Hughes, Caroline (Hove), 106.
Hughes, Frank, diver (Australia), 101.
Hughes, Hugh Thomas, district surveyor, 130.
Hughes, J. R., (Port Talbot), 50.
Hughes, R., P.O., 397.
Hughes, T. S., Cox., 395.
Hughes, W., Ch. Off., 397.
Hughes, W. (Avonport), 397.
Hughes, William Thomas, Q.M., 428.
Hughff, Samuel, hewer, 253.
Hugill, Hannah, farm worker, 125.
Hugo, E. V., Ch. Off., 396.
Hukam Dad, L./N. Punjab Regt., 222.
Hull, J., O.S., 397.
Hulley, H., colliery deputy, 146.
Hulow, A., 388.
Humble, C. B., Capt. Boy Scouts, 394.
Hume, W., fisherman, 392.
Humphrey, David, rly. porter, 188.
Humphreys, Patrick Noel, Lt. R.N., 291.
Humphries, William, miner, 233.
Hunt, Alfred, pottery worker, 103.
Hunt, H., coastguard boatman, 388.
Hunt, R., app., 396.
Hunter, C., 387.
Hunter, Ernest, deck hand, 425.
Hurle, E., 3rd hand, 386.
Hurry, James Campbell, master, 368.
Husk, S., coastguard, 393.
Hutchinson, Albert, Sergt. M.L.I., 170.
Hutchinson, E. H., 389.
Hutner, E., 390.
Huxstep, C., 388.

Hyatt, E., 391.
Hynes, J., 388.

Ileff, L. W., Q.M., 389.
Ilett, W., skipper, 397.
Ince, Llewellyn, smelter, 142.
Inglis, J., fireman, 395.
Inglis, Robert, seaman, 405.
Ingram, J., volunteer, 396.
Irish, George Frederick (Redditch), 117.
Irwin, Ernest Alexander, bo'sun's mate, 419.
Isaac, diamond miner, 123.
Ishar Singh, Sepoy, Punjabis, 12.

Jackson, H. H. H., Pte., 398.
Jackson, Shadrach, smelter, 142.
Jackson, Mrs., 142.
Jackson, William (Swindon), 49.
Jacob, Alfred H., A.B., 395.
Jacob, G., A.B., 396.
Jacobs, A., steward, 389.
Jacobs, G. E., skipper, 397.
Jacques, Amy M., farmer's daughter, 110.
Jaggers, F. G. W., coastguard boatman, 310.
Jago, R. H., 389.
Jais, juragan of m.l. *Anne*, 42.
Jak Taha, Shawish Khartoum Police, 298.
James, Miss, (Anne Port), 38.
James, R. H., 3rd off., 400.
James, William Arthur, stoker, 416.
Jamieson, William, gold mine shift supt., 305.
Jardine, H., A.B., 400.
Jarvis, I., civilian boatman, 392.
Jarvis, John, Dist. Off., 408.
Jawoodeen, T. A., 386.
Jay, W., A.B., 396.
Jeffells, William, collier, 199.
Jeffery, J., O.S., 388.
Jeffrey, C., stoker, 390.
Jemat, sub-insp. police, 43.
Jenkins, George O. R., 3rd off., 406.
Jenkins, J. C., Pte., 399.
Jenner, A., skipper, 397.
Jensen, J., 386.
Jewell, Isaac, seaman, 411.
Jockem, M. H., O.S., 388.
Johansen, O. M., 393.
Johnson, A., A.B., 395.
Johnson, Arthur, Pte. A.S.C., 180.
Johnson, Ernest, labourer, 50.
Johnson, G. E., 2nd mate, 394.
Johnson, John, miner, 204.
Johnson, J. B., Ch. Off., 396.
Johnson, N. G., A.B., 394.
Johnson, William George, master watch, 379.
Johnston, Alexander, Ch. Eng., 378.
Johnston, George Edward, sapper, 176.

INDEX OF NAMES

Johnston, H., coastguard, 398.
Johnston, James, mine overseer, 245.
Johnston, Robert, miner, 261.
Johnston, W., 388.
Jollivet, M., A.B., 396.
Jones, Alfred, miner, 128.
Jones, Ben Littler, quarry worker, 278.
Jones, C., Ch. mate, 387.
Jones, D., A.B., 387.
Jones, David, colliery manager, 92.
Jones, F. D., worker, 78.
Jones, George, fireman, 137.
Jones, Gomer, asst. examiner, 129.
Jones, James, workman, 145.
Jones, John, miner (Monmouth), 117.
Jones, John, wharfinger, 237.
Jones, John, collier (Natal), 122.
Jones, John, gold miner (Joh'burg), 122.
Jones, R., carptr., 384.
Jones, R., O.S., 386.
Jones, R., boatman, 396.
Jones, R., greaser, 399.
Jones, R. J., bo'sun, 391.
Jones, R. J., bo'sun of *Cymric*, 392.
Jones, Thomas, colliery owner, 92.
Jones, Thomas, collier, 201.
Jones, T. R., A.B., 390.
Jones, W., carptr., 397.
Jones, W., Pte., 399.
Jones, W. J., Ch. Off., 388.
Jones, W. J., 1st mate, 390.
Jones, W. R., O.S., 388.
de Jong, D., carpenter, 386.
de Jongh, Lodewyk, donkeyman-greaser, 432.
Jonghin, W., 387.
Jonnson, L., 388.
Joyce, Ernest E. M., R.N., 215, 331.
Joyce, Michael, eng. rm. artif., 317.
Juddery, J. W. H., 390.
Jumari, nakoda, 42.
Justice, G. W., cox., 395.
Justice, R. S., driver motor-boat, 395.

Kabul Singh, L./N., 222.
Kala Miah, lascar, 405.
Kallan Khan, sapper, 97.
Karreman, M., 386.
Kasch, K., 390.
Kavanagh, Robert Murray (N.S.W.), 379.
Keane, R., 387.
Kearney, J. F., seaman, 403.
Kearns, Patrick, A.B., 418.
Keating, M., 393.
Keefe, D., 386.
Keightley, T., 390.
Kelcher, J., 388.

Kellner, A., 391.
Kelly, Benjamin, diamond miner, 123.
Kelly, Cecil Francis, river surveyor, 307.
Kelly, Fred, Lt., 172.
Kelly, S., A.B., 391.
Kelsey, E. G. M., volunteer, 396.
Kemp, Henry, Supt. Police, 95.
Kemp, William, miner, 139.
Kempster, Albert Joseph, Sergt. Maj., 108.
Kendall, J., A.B., 396.
Kennedy, Amelia, 76.
Kennedy, H., lamp-trimmer, 387.
Kennedy, James, miner, 154.
Kennedy, J. M., civilian, 393.
Kennedy, Robert, A.B., 413.
Kenny, John, hewer, 253.
Kenny, William David, Lt. I.A., 11.
Kent, Ernest William, pile worker, 279.
Kent, F., Ch. Off., 388.
Kent, James, miner, 261.
Keogh, M. S., Ch. P.O., 156, 316.
Keys, E., A.B., 397.
Khudadad, Sepoy, 11.
Kilby, J., 385.
Kilroy, J. C., A.B., 395.
Kilvert, John Albert, A.B., 422.
Kimber, Walter, Stoker P.O., 317.
Kinch, C., 2nd hand, 398.
King, G. W., 391.
King, Richard Henry, miner, 261.
King, Victor, miner, 261.
King, W., O.S., 385.
King, William, still-worker, 234.
Kinnin, W., fisherman, 387.
Kinnon, J., 2nd mate, 390.
Kipli, sailor, 42.
Kipling, James, mine under-manager, 245.
Kirkham, Robert J., munitions examiner, 195.
Kirkpatrick, J., 387.
Kitchen, J. R., O.S., 400.
Kjellberg, John Helmer, bo'sun, 431.
Klee, Gilbert Thomas, labourer, 50.
Kneale, W. H., outfitter, 387.
Kneen, J. K., mate, 387.
Knight, Alfred, A.B., 395.
Knight, Henry Stuart, 2nd off., 428.
Knight, P., fisherman, 387.
Knight, T. B., 1st mate, 396.
Knill, Thomas Stratford, master, 375.
Knollys, Robert W. E., Capt., 100.
Knoulton, Richard, O.S., 165, 319.
Knox, G. T., master s.s. *Nubia*, 62.
Knox, James, pitman, 126.
Knox, John Simpson (at battle of Alma), 11.
Krueger, G. W., driver, 395.
Krishna, Parbati, workman, 205.
Kristo Kamar, collier sirdar, 246.

INDEX OF NAMES

Krull, John, miner, 241.
Kushaba, Newarti, coolie, 197.

Lace, A., A.B., 385.
Lacy, R., O.S., 385.
Ladner, A. W., 397.
Laing, N., 386.
Lake, Samuel, Bombay Reclamation Co., 85, 339.
Lakeman, W., 390.
Lamb, George Huddleston, miner, 120.
Lambert, Paul, 4th off., 432.
Lam Pow, seaman, 406.
Lancaster, F., Ldg. seaman, 395.
Lander, J., 393.
Lane, A. E., A.B., 391.
Lane, Ernest, A.B., 395.
Langton, Ethel, lighthouse keeper, 67.
Languedoe, S. J., 390.
Lapper, W. J., asst. eng., 400.
Large, W., 389.
Larsen, C., 391.
Lascelles, J. R., 393.
Lashley, William, Ch. stoker, 116, 315.
Latham, Lt. (at Albuera), 4–5.
Lau Khiok Kang, Chinese, 42.
Laurie, R., A.B., 394.
Lavan, Michael, docker, 49.
Laver, George Henry, collier, 203.
Lawrence, J. C., A.B., 396.
Lawrence, Joseph Thomas, A.S.C., 160.
Lawrence, Mr., 84.
Lawry, William John, A.B., 425.
Lawson, Charles, mine manager, 135.
Lawson, F., O.S., 388.
Lawson, R. P., 1st mate, 385.
Lawson, W., skipper, 384.
Lawton, D., Constable R.I.C., 394.
Layang, dayak, 43.
Layis, J., 384.
Lazell, F. W., 390.
Leach, Grey de Leche, Lt., 164.
Leach, James Joseph, collier, 142.
Leake, A. Martin, Lt. R.A.M.C., 11.
Leale, Henry, lamp-trimmer, 419.
Leblanc, Jules, 2nd off., 432.
Leckie, P., 389.
Lecky, Halton Stirling, Lt. R.N., 312.
Lee, A., 2nd off., 393.
Lee, George, fireman, 77.
Lee, T., fisherman, 393.
Lee Van Chan, seaman, 406.
Lee, William H., benzol works labourer, 237.
Leech, Henry James, A.F.M. R 101, 219.
Lees, Gordon (Newcastle, N.S.W.), 376.
Lees, Joseph, miner, 261.
Leggate, W. T., A.B., 395.
Lemske, F., 390.

Lennard, T., 392.
Lenygon, A., A.B., 394.
Leonard, G., A.B., 396.
Leong Yoe, seaman, 406.
Lester, E. P., Civ. Eng., 398.
Lewin, Arthur William (Lincoln), 252.
Lewis, A., O.S., 389.
Lewis, Capt., 84.
Lewis, Alwyn, collier, 258.
Lewis, Henry, colliery manager, 92.
Lewis, J., coast-guard, 385.
Lewis, P. J., 3rd off., 396.
Lewis, Thomas, boy, 105.
Lewis, T. R., 1st mate, 395.
Lexow, A., Ch. Off., 406.
Liesen, W., A.B., 396.
Lin Ah Yok, seaman, 406.
Lin Chang Chin, cabin boy, 406.
Lindholm, C., 390.
Lindley, Frederick, steeplejack, 204.
Lindsay, Robert J. (Lord Wantage), 10, 11.
Lindsay, Robert Leiper, eng., 164.
Linklater, H., Ch. Off., 396.
Linngvist, G., bo'sun's mate, 396.
Lisley, B., 390.
Lister, Maurice, asst. butcher, 372.
Lithgow, Hughes Lancaster, Maj., 104.
Littlewood, James, pitman, 126.
de Livera, Albert Rienzi, Police Insp., 304.
Livermore, C., boatman, 391.
Livermore, G., disabled ex-service man, 236.
Liversage, F. J., 390.
Llewellyn, D. M., Pte., 399.
Lloyd, R. H., 2nd mate, 387.
Lloyd, William, sub-foreman, 248.
Lobb, George Ernest, bo'sun, 403.
Locke, George, steel erector, 244.
Lodge, John, collier, 189.
Lofthouse, G., Cox., 386.
Lofthouse, George, pitman, 188.
Longster, R., 389.
Loosemore, F., 385.
Loram, W., O.S., 397.
Lovell, Fredk., A.B., 395.
Lowdell, Samuel, bargeman, 78.
Lowry, Arthur Cole, Lt. R.N., 312.
Lowson, David, Dr., 94.
Lucas, Charles David, mate, 10.
Lucas, Joseph, pitman, 126.
Lucas, William Freer, Surgeon, 78.
Lucht, C., A.B., 388.
Lund, A. T., O.S., 388.
Lungley, Alfred, Bombardier R.A., 289.
Lyell, Walter Howden, Lt., 159.
Lyon, James Joseph, seaman, 403.
Lyons, Michael, gold miner, 123.
Lys, Mr. (St. Helier), 51.

INDEX OF NAMES

McAllister, John, pitman, 126.
McAllister, J., O.S., 396.
McAloney, William S., aircraftsman, 223.
McArtney, C., deck hand, 395.
MacBride, Robert, Admiralty clerk, 369.
McBurnie, R., Ch. Off., 399.
McCabe, John, colliery boy, 206.
McCafferty, Edward, miner, 197.
McCarthy, E., M.M., Pte. R. Canadians, 185.
McCarthy, J., seaman, 400.
McCarthy, James, Corpl., 174.
Macarthy, R., hopperman, 396.
Macaulay, M., O.S., 385.
McClean, J., mate, 388.
McClelland, William, steeplejack, 124.
McCombie, Thomas G. F., Capt., 296.
McCormack, Thomas, workman, 103.
McCreath, Andrew Berghans, Lt., 167.
MacCuish, Alexr., sen., fisherman, 386.
MacCuish, Alexr., jun., fisherman, 386.
MacCuish, Alick, fisherman, 386.
MacCuish, M., fisherman, 386.
McDiarmid, D., 2nd mate, 386.
McDonald, A. (Cardiff), 385.
MacDonald, A., fisherman, 386.
MacDonald, D. E., fisherman, 386.
McDonald, D., 3rd hand, 390.
Macdonald, Donald, Ch. Off., 403.
MacDonald, F. W., mate, 386.
Macdonald, G. C., Ch. Off., 398.
McDonald, J., O.S., 385.
McDonald, John Roderick, 190.
McDonald, M., O.S., 385.
MacDonald, M., fisherman, 386.
McDonald, N., O.S., 385.
McDonald, Robert, pitman, 126.
Macdonald, Ronald Hume, R.E., 97.
McEwen, A., Ch. steward, 392.
McFall, William, eng. driver, 136.
McFall, Mrs., 136.
Macfarlane, Thomas, miner, 136.
McGrath, J. W., master, 390.
McGraw, B., beachman, 387.
McGraw, P., beachman, 387.
MacGregor, Capt., 6.
MacGregor, William, M.D., 358.
MacIntosh, D., fisherman, 386.
McIntosh, John, A.B., 354.
McKessack, T., A.B., 394.
McKay, William D. (N.S.W.), 367.
McKechnie, James (at battle of Alma), 11.
McKechnie, W. N., Flt. Cadet R.A.F., 284.
McKee, Adam, pitman, 126.
McKee, Arthur, mate, 358.
McKenzie, Charles, Ch. Off., 372.
McKenzie, Edward, sen., pitman, 126.
McKenzie, Edward, jun., pitman, 126.
McKenzie, Hugh, pitman, 126.
McKenzie, James, pitman, 126.
Mackenzie, T., app., 396.
Mackinnon, Neil, Lt., 160.
Mackrill, J., 387.
McLachlan, A., 385.
McLaughlin, James, Pte., 179.
McLaughlin, P., A.B., 390.
Maclean, Ronald (East London), 361.
McLean, Thomas McCulloch, A.B., 413.
McLennan, A., O.S., 385.
McLennon, A., A.B., 385.
McLeod, J., A.B., 385.
McLlelan, A., A.B., 395.
McMahon, J., A.B., 393.
MacMahon, Maurice, Lt.-Cmdr. R.N.R., 319.
McManus, H., O.S., 392.
MacMillan, David Atkinson, supt., 185.
McNab, Kenneth, asst. foreman fitter, 131.
McNeil, S., L./C., 396.
McNeil, W., O.S., 385.
McNicol, J., coastguard boatman, 384.
MacOnoghu, Herbert, schoolboy aged 13, 77.
McPhee, D., 3rd off., 397.
MacPherson, Lt., 6.
McPolland, Duncan, Pte., 191.
McQuarrie, 2nd eng., 400.
McQue, William, Corpl. 362.
McSwain, J., O.S., 385.
McTeague, T. P., D.C.M., Corpl. R.A.F., 284.
McWhirter, David, steeplejack, 124.
McWhirter, G., fisherman, 395.
Madams, G. W., A.B., 396.
Maddox, James Edward, Lt., 183.
Madsen, O. E., 388.
Magnusson, James Werner, trooper, 371.
Mahabir Dubey, rly. gateman, 255.
Mahoney, C., coastguard boatman, 387.
Mahoney, H. J., R.N., stoker P.O., 283.
Mahoney, Michael, seaman, 404.
Mahoney, W., coastguard boatman, 391.
Mainprize, W., 387.
Major, C. W., volunteer, 396.
Major, R., fisherman, 387.
Makbul Khan, watchman, 42.
Makepiece, H. R. (Hamstead), 53.
Malabar, A., 3rd eng., 400.
Malcolm, Pulteney, Lt. Gurkhas, 96.
Maley, Albert, collier, 269.
Maltby, Reginald Harry, Staff Sgt., 298.
Maltby, W., O.S., 390.
Mamba, P.C., 42.
Mangal Sain, trumpeter, 374.
Manin, John, A.B., 418.
Manley, Aaron, pit carpenter, 96.

INDEX OF NAMES

Mann, Algernon Edward, ship eng., 111.
Mann, James Rogerson, fireman, 227.
Manson, T., 388.
March, Edward B., Vice-Consul, 343.
March, Frederick Hamilton, chauffeur, 297.
Margarison, Joseph, A.B., 395.
Margary, A. R., Asst. Consul, 347.
Markham, J. R., 394.
Markland, William, miner, 135.
Marron, James, founder, 249.
Marsden, W., Ldg. coastguard boatman, 396.
Marsh, F. S., colliery manager, 95.
Marshall, F. George, mechanician, 315.
Martin, F., bo'sun, 396.
Martin, H., A.B., 385.
Martin, S. G. L., Ldg. seaman, 398.
Martin, W., boatman, 387.
Martin, William F. G., Ch. Off., 369.
Martinus, diamond miner, 123.
Maruti Vithoba, workman, 205.
Mason, George Forster, miner, 261.
Mason, Horace R., Ldg. signalman, 395.
Mason, Joseph, miner, 235.
Mason, W., A.B., 390.
Mata Din, L./N. I.A., 289.
Matelot, Madame, lighthouse keeper, 66.
Mather, John Thomas, pitman, 126.
Mathers, Allison, pitman, 126.
Mathieson, K., 385.
Mathison, S., O.S., 400.
Matthew, George Small, Ch. Off., 410.
Matthew, John Thomson, Ch. Eng., 412.
Matthew, R. M., dockyard workman, 211.
Matthews, R., Q.M., 392.
Mathias, J. S., pumping-station worker, 269.
Mattison, A. C., R.N.Can.V.R., 327.
Maxwell-Hyslop, A. H., Lt.-Cmdr. R.N., 333.
May, A., Volunteer Rocket Co., 395.
Mbuzimaceba, native (Natal), 151.
Mead, J. R., 384.
Meadows, A. J., asst. storekeeper, 263.
Meadows, T. G., boatman, 391.
Meadows, W. J., boatman, 391.
Mears, John Henry, sewer worker, 278.
Melguin, T., cook, 391.
Mellon, Percy Hope, lock-keeper, 110.
Melly, A. J. M., M.C., F.R.C.S., 222.
Melton, Robert, P.C., 173.
Ment, Herbert, 2nd off., 429.
Menzies, Thomas, diamond miner, 123.
Meredith, William Herbert, L./C., 182.
Merritt, Henry, collier, 139.
Meynell, Godfrey, M.C., Capt. I.A., 13.
Millar, Andrew, pitman, 126.
Millar, P. H., 5th off., 386.
Miller, F. (Sunderland), 384.
Miller, J. (Whitby), 392.
Miller, Lewis, docker, 247.
Miller, M., coast-guard, 393.
Miller, Thomas, Pte., 283.
Millett, W. H., 3rd off., 85, 339.
Millichamp, B. H., wireless teleg., 398.
Mills, Frederick, sewer-man, 78.
Mills, J., 4th hand, 388.
Mirghany Ahmad Muhammad, 301.
Michell, F. E., 2nd mate, 384.
Mitchell, John, carptr., 352.
Mitchell, John, miner, 140.
Mitchell, W. H., civilian boatman, 393.
Modin, E., 388.
Moir, William, foreman cooper, 133.
Moltzau, Rolf Fredrik, 2nd off., 406.
Montgomerie, R. J. A., Act. Sub-Lt., 310, 351.
Moodie, Hugh Frederick, collier, 242.
Moore, A., coast-guard, 388.
Moore, Albert, miner, 128.
Moore, R. F., A.B., 390.
Moore, Richard Walker, pitman, 126.
Morahan, J., A.B., 393.
Moreau, H., A.B., 385.
Morey, A., R.N.R., 400.
Morgan, A., fisherman, 391.
Morgan, Charles (Abercarn), 93.
Morgan, William, collier, 92.
Morgan, William Marychurch, Lt., 158.
Moriarty, E., 2nd hand, 400.
Moriarty, J., skipper, 400.
Morris, Arthur, miner, 199.
Morris, Edward, aged 10, 78.
Morris, Ernest Alfred, foreman, 238.
Morris, J. (Liverpool), 385.
Morris, J., boatman, 388.
Morris, T. W., Q.M., 399.
Morris, William, collier, 95.
Morrison, E. R., O.S., 391.
Morrison, K., Ch. Off., 400.
Morrison, W. A., explosives worker, 194.
Morteshed, F. A., Const. R.Ulst.Constab., 295.
Mortimer, S. W., fisherman, 393.
Mortimore, James William, A.B., 432.
Morton, G. H., O.S., 399.
Morton, L. N., O.S., 397.
Moseley, Miles (Abercarn), 93.
Moss, James, miner, 135.
Mott, Joseph Edward, Pte., 292.
Mottram, S., fireman, 393.
Mottram, Thomas H., colliery manager, 95.
Mouat, J., O.S., 398.
Mouat, W., A.B., 390.
Moulder, James, farmer, 112.
Mugford, J., 385.
Muhammad, A., lascar, 389.
Muhammad Abdulla, Khartoum Pol., 298.

INDEX OF NAMES

Muhammad Ali of Dir, 101.
Muhammad Dababish, boatman, 432.
Muhammad Khalifa, Shawish Berber Pol., 298.
Muir, J. T., 2nd off., 396.
Muir, S. W., A.B., 395.
Muir, William Nicol, inspector, 122.
Muir, Mrs., 122.
Mulholland, William James, pitman, 126.
Mullen, James, founder, 249.
Munday, W., Pte., 399.
Munian, Indian (Natal), 151.
Munro, Robert, road labourer, 100.
Munroe, F., mate, 387.
Murdoch, Allan, bargeman, 149.
Murphy, J., A.B., 387.
Murphy, J., O.S., 389.
Murphy, R. M., boatman, 394.
Murphy, T., O.S., 391.
Murphy, T., R.N.R., 392.
Murray, M., A.B., 396.
Murray, W., boatman, 385.
Murray, W. E., app., 385.
Mwene (Bulawayo), 231.

Nancollas, George, miner, 261.
Nani Khan, timber-drawer, 245.
Nash, W., Ch. mate, 385.
Nash, Wm. Francis, A.B., 395.
Nandlal Thapa, Naik I.A., 289.
Naughton, Frank, Pte., 291.
Navarro, J., bo'sun, 396.
Naylor, Edward, workman, 227.
Neal, A., coast-guard, 394.
Neale, John, Lt. R.N.V.R., 171, 319.
'Neighbour' (Australian aboriginal), 115.
Nelson, J., bo'sun, 392.
Neilson, William, Capt., bombing off., 175.
Ness, A. R., app., 397.
Nevin, John Joseph, miner, 205.
Nevitt, Albert, M.C., Lt., 169.
Newall, Cyril Louis Norton, Maj., 157.
Newbold, George, asst. steward, 431.
Newham, E., A.B., 396.
Newman, Alfred William, act. mate R.N., 320.
Newman, Lester, 2nd off., 413.
Nicholl, Thomas, Flt.-Sergt. R.F.C., 174.
Nicholls, Edward, miner, 98.
Nichols, A., bo'sun, 385.
Nichols, R. T., coastguard off., 398.
Nicholson, F., A.B., 385.
Nicholson, G. M., distillery manager, 78.
Nick, J., A.B., 386.
Nickells, E. W., 386.
Nicol, J., Ch. Eng., 400.
Nicoll, F. S., A.B., 398.
Nielson, Niels Marius, Capt., 412.
Nile, C., A.B., 385.

Niles, William Henry, Cmdr., 395.
Nisfolk, A., bo'sun, 395.
Niven, George Paterson, R.N., A.B., 283.
Nixon, A., Cox., 396.
Nixon, J., 3rd hand, 389.
Noble, J., O.S., 385.
Noble, J. Scott, 3rd bdg. off., 395.
Noble, T. E., donkeyman, 400.
Nocks, A., deck hand, 399.
Nordlund, A., A.B., 395.
Norie, F., boatman, 388.
Norris, Harold, seaman, 403.
Norris, W. C., bo'sun, 391.
Norton, H. (*a*), coast-guard, 384.
Norton, H. (*b*), coast-guard, 384.
Norwood, Percy, railwayman, 153.
Notlers, Albert, A.B., 419.
Noton, J. E., 2nd off., 396.
Noyon, Frederick William, Capt., master, 425.
Nugent, Nicholas, A., app., 49.
Nunn, Edward, seaman H.M.S. *Glatton*, 326.
Nunn, J. F., skipper, 386.
Nur Ahmad, seaman lascar, 405.
Nur ul Haqq, seaman lascar, 405.
Nurse, Edward, miner, 192.
Nutman, William John, master, 365.

Oakley, A., O.S., 385.
Oatley, George, gunner's mate, 310, 356.
Oatridge, Charles, collier, 92.
O'Brien, C. (Ardmore), 394.
O'Brien, J., volunteer, 394.
O'Connor, J., 1st mate, 391.
O'Connor, Luke (at battle of Alma), 11.
Odam, S. G., artificer, 397.
Oddy, A., Ch. P.O., 397.
Oehlers, J. E., seaman, 418.
O'Gorman, G., Q.M., 400.
O'Hea, Timothy, Pte., 8.
Olafsen, G., carptr., 396.
Oliver, Dick, Ldg. seaman, 331.
Oliver, Frederick, foreman miner, 241.
Olsen, H., O.S., 390.
Olsen, J., A.B., 390.
Olsen, K. E., A.B., 391.
Olsen, O., O.S., 389.
Omara, Edward (Uganda), 304.
O'Neill, L., Q.M., 396.
Ong Kee Poh, Chinese, 43.
Onslow, Joseph William, lighterman, 77.
Opie, Albert, miner, 139.
Oprey, D., 386.
Opsahl, A., O.S., 388.
Orchard, Benjamin, seaman, 411.
Orman, J., 386.
Orr, J. C., Lt., 400.
Orr, Samuel, Const. R. Ulster Const., 295.

O'Shea, Rev. John, 394.
O'Shea, Rev. John Michael, 296.
Oswald, Ernest William, pitman, 126.
Outhouse, E. H., 3rd hand, 398.
Outram, Joseph, miner, 121.
Owen, gold miner (Johannesburg), 122.
Owen, D., A.B., 394.
Owen, Evan, colliery under-manager, 125.
Owen, H., O.S., 386.
Owen, H., Q.M., 400.
Owen, J., fisherman, 388.
Owen, J. T., ch. steward, 400.
Owens, Ernest William, 2nd mate, 351.
Owens, J., O.S., 400.
Oxenham, William Thomas, skipman, 131.
Orford, G., 386.

Paddock, Robert Edward, miner, 231.
Padfield, Sydney William, miner, 260.
Paffett, Frederick, Ch. stoker, 313.
Page, Leslie John, A.B., 428.
Page, R., skipper, 389.
Pargiter, Henry, 113.
Park, J., master, 385.
Parker, George Arthur, app., 406.
Parker, George C., A.B., 395.
Parker, John Henry, pitman, 126.
Parker, W., boatman, 387.
Parker, W. H., 3rd off., 385.
Parkin, James, miner, 235.
Parkinson, Charles, fireman, 96.
Parkiss, Joseph Edward, A.B., 419.
Parnell, Henry James, A.B., 419.
Parnell, W., skipper, 386.
Parry, T. H., master, 385.
Parsons, Harry, steelworker, 143.
Partington, H., master, 399.
Pascho, T., pilot, 390.
Paterson, R., pilot, 389.
Paterson, W., pilot, 389.
Patterson, D., A.B., 385.
Pattinson, Leslie Thomas, A.B., 419.
Pattinson, Robert, miner, 121.
Paul, P., steward, 390.
Paulsen, A., A.B., 389.
Pavlovsky, R., boatman, 384.
Payne, H., steward, 396.
Payne, S. J., Volunteer Life Brig., 389.
Payne, W. G., deck hand, 385.
Pearce, D., steward, 392.
Pearce, Henry, A.B., 428.
Pearce, J., coastguardsman, 386.
Pearce, William Henry, railwayman, 101.
Pearse, William, 55.
Pearson, A., fisherman, 395.
Pearson, F., labourer, 395.
Pearson, John, pitman, 126.

Pearson, Robert, labourer, 243.
Pearson, S. C., O.S., 398.
Peart, Walter, driver, 78.
Peat, Joseph, miner, 191.
Pedersin, P., seaman, 418.
Pegge, J. (St. Ouen's Bay), 38.
Pemberton, Daniel, rly. foreman, 79.
Pemberton, Leonard (Livingstone), 219.
Pemberton, S., steward, 389.
Penfold, H., P.O., 395.
Pengelly, F. D., master, 386.
Penney, C. W., R.N.R., 400.
Penny, Hugh, 2nd off., 417.
Perkins, John Henry, shaft-sinker, 247.
Perry, E. C., master, 400.
Perry, S., bo'sun, 389.
Perry, S., stoker, 390.
Peters, Samuel, miner, 232.
Petersen, P. E., A.B., 390.
Peterson, A., mate, 387.
Peterson, H., O.S., 400.
Peterson, R., fisherman, 395.
Peterson, W., 2nd mate, 386.
Pettersen, C., O.S., 391.
Peyto, Lilian, Mrs., flock-worker, 242.
Peyton-Burberry, Rev. R. J. P., 398.
Philipsen, J. A., 2nd mate, 391.
Phillip, C. J., P.C., 396.
Phillips, A., 2nd mate, 389.
Phillips, J., O.S., 398.
Phillips, R., A.B., 389.
Phillips, T. N., skipper, 397.
Picker, J., greaser, 397.
Pickering, Thomas, jigger, 201.
Pickering, William, collier, 95.
Pickering, William Henry, Insp. of Mines, 128.
Pickersgill, Henry, Colour-Sergt., 97.
Pickersgill, Herbert, collier, 134.
Picot, Patrick, coastguard boatman, 384.
Piercey, William, porter, 130.
Pierson, R., Ch. eng., 400.
Pike, T., A.B., 384.
Pike, W., coastguard boatman, 385.
Pilgrim, George Edward, rly. porter, 230.
Pillar, W., skipper, 397.
Pinnington, Thomas, docker, 49.
Pitman, H., boatman, 388.
Pitman, Thomas C. (Drakewalls Mine), 96.
Pittendrigh, J. C., app., 395.
Pitts, Francis, Ch. Off., 357.
Pitts, F. R., A.B., 396.
Place, Alfred, P.O. R.N., 166, 318.
Planner, T. G. C., deck hand, 395.
Plant, H., coastguard boatman, 391.
Platt, Frank, labourer, 230.
de Plecker, George, sailor, 432.
Pochin, Harry Salisbury, seaman, 359.

INDEX OF NAMES

Pollard, F. E., Sergt., 399.
Polley, James Henry, miner, 135.
Pollitt, Ernest J. R., jun. 3rd off., 432.
Pollitt, James, collier, 271.
Ponteney, soldier (St. Helier), 51.
Pooley, Ernest A., motor mechanic, 318.
Pooley, J. C., A.B., 389.
Popham, T. L. S., Ch. Off., 393.
Popplestone, Samuel, farmer, 84, 339.
Porossinan, C., fisherman, 389.
Porritt, R., Volunteer L.S.A., 393.
Porteous, J. D., 1st mate, 390.
Porter, James Frederick, dye worker, 238.
Potter, R., A.B., 396.
Potter, W., A.B., 396.
Pottle, C., 3rd hand, 386.
Potts, T., 2nd mate, 385.
Pound, T., Q.M., 389.
Pow, C. McK., 387.
Powell, Ernest Reid, managing director, 270.
Powell, Leo Patrick (Alberta), 190.
Powley, Herbert, deck hand, 318.
Preen, Charles (Abercarn), 93.
Presley, H. C., signalman, 395.
Price, D., pilot, 391.
Price, J. H., O.S., 396.
Price, P. M., coastguard boatman, 392.
Price, T., fisherman, 396.
Price, W., seaman, 400.
Pride, Isaac (Tynewydd Colliery), 92.
Priestley, A., fisherman, 387.
Priestley, W., fisherman, 387.
Prince, W. H., contractor, 146.
Prior, S., 3rd mate, 389.
Protheroe, William R., under-manager, 129.
Puckey, T. E., 1st mate, 394.
Pullen, H. W., A.B., 395.
Pulliner, M., O.S., 391.
Purcell, M., O.S., 398.
Purkis, A. E., Indian Ordnance Corps, 112.
Purser, Eli, miner, 200.
Purslow, E., Ch. boatman, 392.
Purvis, James Sydney, pit boy, 253.
Purvis, R., fisherman, 387.
Pyne, W., donkeyman, 396.
Pysden, Edmund J., artificer eng. R.N., 318.

Quayle, John, pitman, 126.
Quiggin, W. H., master, 399.
Quinn, W., sailmaker, 390.
Quirk, W., farmer, 387.

Rabbeth, Samuel, Med. Off., 77.
Rackham, Geoffrey, Lt. A.S.C., 181.
Raghu Nandan Singh, Sepoy, 213.
Railton, T., steward, 389.
Ralph, D., R.N.R., 400.

Ramsay, John, A.B., 102, 315.
Ramsey, W., bo'sun, 389.
Rand, A., O.S., 393.
Ransom, Capt., 57.
Rath, Nicholas, seaman R.N.R., 165, 319.
Rathbone, William L. C., 2nd Lt., 162.
Rea, A. E., Act. Sergt., 399.
Rea, Arthur, 2nd eng., 366.
Ready, Edward John, seaman, 411.
Reagan, J., bo'sun, 387.
Redhead, C. M., Ch. Off., 395.
Redmond, J., Q.M., 392.
Rednall, C. H., A.B., 395.
Reece, Frederick Charles, 411.
Reed, G., O.S., 400.
Reed, James Vivian, 2nd mate, 104.
Reed, Robert, mine under-manager, 261.
Reed, W. A., A.B., 396.
Reekie, Stanley Martin, 2nd Lt., 179.
Rees, David, collier, 92.
Rees, J., 2nd mate, 395.
Regan, C., fisherman, 386.
Regan, D., fisherman, 386.
Regan, P., fisherman, 386.
Regelous, Arthur, carman, 79.
Reid, J., O.S., 391.
Reid, Joseph Gray, carptr., 404.
Reid, R., fisherman, 393.
Reid, W., Ch. Off., 384.
Reison, E., A.B., lamp-trimmer, 395.
Rendall, H., fisherman, 395.
Reneuf, Mr. (Anne Port), 38.
Rennie, J., O.S., 385.
Reside, Charles, sailor, 413.
Revers, R., bo'sun, 400.
Rew, Thomas, munition worker, 201.
Rex, T., O.S., 388.
Reybould, L. F., 3rd eng., 399.
Reynolds, B., A.B., 385.
Reynolds, Robert, 3rd hand, 423.
Reynolds, Thomas, conductor C.P.R., 106.
Reynolds, W., coastguard boatman, 385.
Reynolds, William, at battle of Alma, 11.
Rhoades, William Ernest, Sergt., 168.
Rhodes, G., C.S.M., 399.
Rhodes, George Henry, gas worker, 138.
Rhodes, H. C., master, 385.
Rhodes, Q. A., app., 385.
Rhodes-Moorhouse, W. B., 2nd Lt., airman, 11.
Rian, Pte., 42.
Ribillard, J., pilot, 398.
Richards, Albert Ernest, Marine, 332.
Richards, Richard Walter, R.N., 215.
Richards, Stephen, collier, 235.
Richards, William Rayment, 331.
Richardson, A., Pte., 399.
Richardson, Edward Henry, A.B., 323.

Richardson, Norman Allen, 4th eng., 410.
Richardson, Joseph G., diamond miner, 123.
Richardson, W. J., 3rd eng., 397.
Ricketts, Harold Frank, P.C., 79.
Ricketts, John, Ldg. seaman, 309, 343.
Ridling, Randolph Gordon, Lt. N.Z., 186.
Riley, George Augustus, A.B., 421.
Riley, T., sergt., 396.
Rimmer, Reginald, P.S., 299.
Ringland, W., Pte., 399.
Riordan, M., bo'sun, 396.
Ripoll, C., foreman, 398.
Ritchie, W. H., Ch. eng., 400.
Roberts, E., A.B., 395.
Roberts, H., 1st mate, 387.
Roberts, Hugh, timberman, 137.
Roberts, John, sailor, 421.
Roberts, Robert, miner, 135.
Roberts, William, quarryman, 239.
Robertson, A., volunteer, 396.
Robertson, John, coastguardsman, 424.
Robertson, P. D., R.N.A.S., 175, 322.
Robertson, R., fisherman, 395.
Robin, E., 3rd mate, 389.
Robins, Rev. C. A. W., 67.
Robinson, A., A.B., 390.
Robinson, Arthur James (Ferozepore), 113.
Robinson, Charles W., Sub-Lt. R.N.R., 364.
Robinson, Harold V., air mechanic, 173, 320.
Robinson, J., fisherman, 387.
Robinson, John, steel worker, 143.
Robinson, R., fisherman, 387.
Robinson, S., 2nd eng., 397.
Robinson, W., A.B., 385.
Robison, W., 1st off., 396.
Robson, R., 2nd hand, 394.
Rodger, P., Q.M., 400.
Rodriques, George David, I.M.D., 283.
Roer, R., master, 386.
Rogers, Herbert J., A.B., 395.
Rogers, J. A., A.B., 396.
Rogers, Mary, stewardess, 78.
Rogers, W., O.S., 391.
Rohrer, E., steward, 389.
Rolleston, William, seaman, 358.
Romognin, J., A.B., 385.
Ronayne, J., A.B., 398.
Rooney, P., master, 386.
Root, J. W., fireman, 44–5.
Rosbotham, Hannah, schoolmistress, 94.
Rosin, J., A.B., 388.
Rospiri, Capt. s.s. *Florida*, 57.
Ross, Eglintoune Frederick, Capt., 113.
Ross, J., O.S., 394.
Ross, W., master, 385.
Rosser, Evan, pit fireman, 258.
Rossiter, J., Q.M., 396.

Rothery, John, pitman, 126.
Rourke, Bombardier, 83.
Rouse, William, A.B., 416.
Row, T. L. (Penzance), 394.
Rowland, P. S., A.B., 395.
Rowlands, George Thomas, Corpl., 182.
Rowlandson, Sidney Albert, Lt. A.S.C., 160.
Rowston, C., fisherman, 387.
Rubythorn, Steven A., munition worker, 201.
Rudd, William James, charge hand, 262.
Rumsby, G., O.S., 388.
Rupai, Kol, coal-miner, 202.
Rur Singh, Havildar-Maj., 214.
Rushbrooke, E. G. N., Lt., 398.
Russell, J., O.S., 392.
Russell, W., Ch. Off., 397.
Russell, W., Ch. Eng., 399.
Rutland, Frederick Joseph, Lt. R.N., 316.
Rutter, A., sewage worker, 78.
Ryan, T. P., Lt. R.N.R., 399.

Sabatini, L., A.B., 386.
Salmon, 84.
Salthouse, J., O.S., 386.
Samuels, John Edwards, collier, 273.
Sandilands, Hon. Francis R., Lt., 310, 349.
Sandwell, G., beachman, 388.
Sang, George, explosives worker, 194.
d'Santos, Joseph John, chargeman, 241.
Sargent, T., 3rd hand, 395.
Sanders, W. H., 1st mate, 389.
Sanderson, G. (Sunderland), 384.
Saunders, Henry, miner, 144.
Saunders, Robert Benjamin, Dr., 274.
Saundersen, E., 4th hand, 388.
Saunderson, George, seaman, 420.
de Sausmarez, L. A., Sub-Lt., 309, 344.
Savell, J. L., boatman, 389.
Sayer, S. G., seaman, 400.
Scawcroft, James, pitman, 126.
Schofield, Albert, loader, 147.
Schroyens, Jean, cadet, 432.
Scott, Andrew, miner, 197.
Scott, G. E., volunteer, 396.
Scott, H. A. S., Lt., 400.
Scott, J., A.B., 385.
Scott, J. R., bo'sun, 394.
Scott, James William, 1st mate, 430.
Scott, L., A.B., 387.
Scott, Richard James R., Lt.-Cmdr., 329.
Scott, Walter Robert, mine manager, 261.
Scrase-Dickens, Spencer W., Capt., 364.
Scullion, Edward, chemical worker, 96.
Scurfield, B. G., Lt.-Cmdr., 335.
Seaman, R., O.S., 389.
Searing, S., A.B., 396.
Sears, John (Faversham explosion), 197.

Seaton, W. P., master, 386.
Sedgeman, W. H., 394.
Seed, T., master, 386.
Seed, William, Ch. of Police, 362.
Segar, J., Q.M., 390.
Selby, J. J., Ch.Off., 398.
Sellars, Charles, collier, 203.
Selves, David, 77.
Sergent, C. K., Lt.-Cmdr., 398.
Sewell, Herbert William, Lt. R.E., 169.
Seymour, William, Sergt., 370.
Shacklady, Eric Arnold, Lt., 167.
Shanahan, M., A.B., 400.
Sharp, Peter, Capt., 354.
Sharp, R., Q.M., 396.
Shaw, G., A.B., 396.
Shea, C., fisherman, 393.
Sheikh Abdul Samand, sapper, 97.
Sheikh Mohi ud Din, stoker, 367.
Sheldon, H., O.S., 400.
Sheldrake, Walter Henry, miner, 261.
Shelley, Frank, coastguardsman, 424.
Shepherd, F. W., A.B., 394.
Shepherd, John W. H., workman, 254.
Sheret, D. F., master, 391.
Sheridan, H., O.S., 386.
Sherwin, T., coastguard boatman, 391.
Shickley, W. J., boatman, 393.
Shields, John, gold miner, 123.
Shields, John, miner, 233.
Shippey, J. W., fisherman, 49.
Shorland, J., steward, 394.
Shooter, William, Sergt.-Maj., 170.
Short, James, miner, 198.
Shuttleworth, A. T., forest conservator, 342.
Sidotti, A., bo'sun, 386.
Silkstone, George Handle, miner, 128, 134.
Simey, J., bo'sun's mate, 392.
Simmons, Edward Arthur, Lt., 183.
Simmons, J., coastguard boatman, 391.
Simmons, Walter Charles, rly. station man, 143.
Simms, Alfred Edward, air mechanic, 157.
Simms, J. C., O.S., 400.
Simonds, George Frederick, 77.
Simons, H., P.C., 396.
Simons, William (Abercarn), 93.
Simpson, A. W., 2nd off., 388.
Simpson, James, miner, 203.
Simpson, J. R., 2nd hand, 385.
Simpson, J. R. (Grimsby), 385.
Simpson, Thomas, 77.
Simpson, William, Ch. boatman, 309, 345.
Sinclair, J., O.S., 385.
Sinclair, W., fisherman, 395.
Sing Yung Sang, bo'sun, 406.
Singh, Bhupendra Narayen, Mr., 303.
Sirdar Bideshi Kol, coal-miner, 202.

Sisley, Harry, aged 10, 77.
Sisman, C., 394.
Skeggs, Walter, A.B., 422.
Skelly, James, A.B., 422.
Skelton, G. H., pilot, 390.
Skelton, W., O.S., 390.
Skinner, William, A.B., 432.
Slack, Charles, miner, 194.
Slade, John, Pte., 79.
Slater, Samuel, miner, 127.
Sloss, Joseph, docker, 49.
Smail, James, P.O. R.N., 291.
Smailes, William R., coastguardsman, 424.
Smallcombe, T., Ch. Off., coast-guard, 386.
Smallman, Reuben, mining eng., 95.
Smirk, Harry, Ch. Eng., 366.
Smith, A., O.S., 389.
Smith, Albert Edward, miner, 229.
Smith, Alfred, miner, 198.
Smith, Alfred, P.C., 79.
Smith, C., O.S., 389.
Smith, E. W., boatman, 388.
Smith, Edmund, carptr., 405.
Smith, Frank, foreman labourer, 132.
Smith, Frederick Stuart, Lt., 168.
Smith, George (Ferozepore), 113.
Smith, George, miner, 233.
Smith, George Henry, workman, 103.
Smith, George William, deck hand, 425.
Smith, H., coast-guard, 384.
Smith, H., 2nd mate, 385.
Smith, Harry, Eng. R.N., 330.
Smith, Harry James, bo'sun, 422.
Smith, Henry, A.B., 104.
Smith, J., O.S., 385.
Smith, J., Corp. Mil. Mounted Police, 184.
Smith, James Wood, master fishing-boat, 363.
Smith, John (Sheffield), 96.
Smith, John, pitman, 126.
Smith, John Edward, app., 406.
Smith, J. R., carpenter, 393.
Smith, Robert, Cox. life-boat, 296.
Smith, Robert Sydney Steele, R.N.V.R., 318.
Smith, S., A.B., 396.
Smith, Sarah, actress, 76.
Smith, S. C. A., gunner, 395.
Smith, T., A.B., lamp-trimmer, 396.
Smith, Thomas, miner, 192.
Smith, William, collier, 239.
Smith, W., coast-guard, 392.
Smith, William, mate, 366.
Smith, William R., M.C., Maj. R.F.A., 184.
Smyth, John Peter, lamp-trimmer, 428.
Snell, F., 384.
So Han, boilerman, 376, 409.
Sol Ibrahim Negib, Khartoum Police, 298.
Soper, William John, miner, 132.

INDEX OF NAMES

Sorby, David Stuart, A.B., 413.
Soulsby, Oliver, collier, 265.
Someer, D., lascar, 389.
Souter, A. M., Ch. Off., 397.
Souter, J., 5th eng., 396.
Southcott, S., O.S., 385.
Spalding, Edward Thomas, A.B., 327.
Spawi, sailor, 42.
Speke, Shadrach, smelter, 142.
Spence, A. J., A.B., 395.
Spence, Alexander McIntyre, master, 369.
Spencer, C., boatman, 391.
Spencer, G. H., A.B., 395.
Spencer, Robert, 2nd off., 402.
Spenser, J., A.B., 385.
Spicer, Eric Dennis (St. Ouen's Bay), 38.
Spiers, J. T., Ch. Off., 389.
Spoore, J., O.S., 400.
Spoors, Robert, Pte., 222.
Spowf, Otto Reinhold, mate, 66.
Sprankling, Charles, boatman, 84, 210, 241.
Spreutels, Alfred, sailor, 432.
Spring, James, Pte., 96.
Spruce, Samuel, mining eng., 95.
Staddon, T., pilot, 390.
Stagg, F., A.B., 396.
Stagno, F., fireman, 385.
Staley, J. H., O.S., 389.
Standford, L. C., boatman, 394.
Stanley, Wilfred Osborne, mate, 415.
Stannard, Frank Robert, seaman, 412.
Stanners, John George, deck hand, 322.
Star, L. G., master, 384.
Starkey, P., O.S., 400.
Starr, Mrs., missionary, 33.
Startin, James, K.C.B., Admiral, 323.
Startin, Robert Arthur, Lt. R.N., 316.
Stebbings, John Morley, (Faversham), 197.
Steel, Robert, pitman, 126.
Steele, J., lamp-trimmer, 400.
Steele, T., Ch. mate, 396.
Steele, Mr., 84.
Steere, Eric, boy air mechanic, 173, 320.
Stephens, C., O.S., 385.
Stephens, Charles, Sergt.-Maj., 104.
Stephens, F. G., colliery under-manager, 191.
Stephens, F. W., A.B., 396.
Stephenson, R., fisherman, 387.
Stewart, A., O.S., 396.
Stewart, Alexander James, fireman, 107.
Stewart, George, A.B., 419.
Stewart, James Ernest, Lt.-Col. R.E., 299.
Stewart, William, sailmaker, 352.
Stewart, William, seaman, 405.
Stickley, Alfred, Ch. stoker, 97, 314.
Still, James, of A.P.O.C., 164.
Stilliano, G., 390.

Stinner, T., 388.
Stivey, J., Lt. R.N.R., 392.
Stockley, J., P.S., 397.
Stockton, Albert Edward, net-stower, 415.
Stodden, J. B., 390.
Stoker, Albert Ernest, P.O., 326.
Stoker, Ralph, miner, 272.
Stokes, Thomas, collier, 139.
Stokes, Mrs., 140.
Stokes, Thomas, miner, 200.
Stokes, William, carptr., 420.
Stones, Robert, A.B., 321.
Stoppard, Samuel, miner, 190.
Stote, J. A., bo'sun, 390.
Stoves, John, prison officer, 299.
van Straate, Coert Hattingh, gold miner, 248.
Strange, Arthur, carman, 79.
Stratton, A. W., A.B., 395.
Streams, Albert Edward, marine, 333.
Streng, G., O.S., 391.
Stringer, Harold James, A.B., 418.
Stroud, Albert Edward, guard, 145.
Strowger, Herbert Alonzo, Ch. Off., 411.
Stuart, Kenneth Henry, 2nd off., 406.
Sugrue, J., fisherman, 392.
Sugrue, P., fisherman, 392.
Suku Kol, coal-miner, 202.
Sullivan, C., coastguardsman, 386.
Sullivan, F., A.B., 386.
Sullivan, John, Ch. stoker, 315.
Sullivan, R., boatman, 391.
Summers, John S., master fishing-boat, 350.
Summerton, John (Hamstead,) 53.
Sutherland, A., 2nd eng., 399.
Sutherland, James, Ldg. stoker, 314.
Sutton, A. H., eng. driver, 49.
Sutton, J. W., bus driver, 50.
Svenson, W., O.S., 389.
Swainston, Albert, app. plumber, 111.
Swan, John T., ex-Cox. motor life-boat, 297.
Swanger, A., O.S., 390.
Swinburne, Thomas, pitman, 126.
Sworn, B., coastguard boatman, 397.
Sydenham, S., Ch. Off., 392.
Sykes, Frank, collier, 265.
Symes, Sydney E., A.B., 395.
Synge, Rev. A. H., 67.

Tack, E., carptr., 389.
Taha Idris, Sergt. Sudan Police, 300.
Tallant, Michael, 2nd off., 67.
Tanguy, Julien, 306.
Tanner, Bertie, hydraulic packer, 50, 245.
Tansley, S., Ch. boatman, 388.
Taplin, F., Pte., 399.
Tapster, C., 389.
Tarn, John George, miner, 261.

INDEX OF NAMES

Tattersall, H. G., wireless operator, 57.
Tattersall, Thomas, munition worker, 201.
Tatterson, Reginald, A.B., 395.
Taws, Stephen C. S., 2nd mate, 416.
Taylor, D., app., 397.
Taylor, F. J., L./C. R.E., 391.
Taylor, George Henry, miner, 200.
Taylor, H., fisherman, 386.
Taylor, J., beachman, 388.
Taylor, James, pitman, 126.
Taylor, John Thomas, shaft sinker 247.
Taylor, Patrick Gordon, Capt. R.A.F., 308.
Taylor, R., fisherman, 386.
Taylor, Robert, boy, galley *Mary*, 2.
Taylor, W., crane driver, 50.
Taylor, William Albert, A.B., 419.
Teare, T., draper, 387.
Teasdale, T., miner, 122.
Tehan, Alfred George, Pte., 159.
Temperley, S. J., colliery surveyor, 265.
Terlour, W. J., A.B., 397.
Thackeray, Ernest, blast-furnace worker, 143.
Third, A., volunteer, 395.
Thom, Archibald, jun., pitman, 126.
Thomas, diamond miner, 123.
Thomas, Arthur Devere, rly. flagman, 259.
Thomas, A. E., 1st mate, 389.
Thomas, Daniel (Tynewydd), 86, 92.
Thomas, Dorothy Louise, hospital sister, 302.
Thomas, Edmund, colliery manager, 92.
Thomas, G., fisherman, 386.
Thomas, H. B., eng. driver, 398.
Thomas, Isaiah, colliery manager, 92.
Thomas, Rees, miner, 234.
Thomas, Rees, fireman, 92.
Thomas, S., A.B., 394.
Thomas, Thomas, colliery manager, 92.
Thomas, Thomas, colliery mechanic, 150.
Thomas, Thomas, miner, 268.
Thomas, W., A.B., 385.
Thomas, W., A.B., 387.
Thomas, William, colliery manager, 92.
Thompson, Edward, hewer, 49.
Thompson, Edward C., Surgeon, 96.
Thompson, F., A.B., 396.
Thompson, George, workman, 147.
Thompson, G. O., steward, 396.
Thompson, J., seaman, 384.
Thompson, Leo, A.B., 395.
Thompson, Malcolm, A.B., 323.
Thompson, Thomas, collier, 147.
Thomson, John, collier, 202.
Thomson, John Wardrop, postman, 99.
Thomson, Peter, 2nd off., 368.
Thomson, Peter, assist. eng. supt., 429.
Thorkilson, Edward Douglas, seaman, 420.
Thorne, John Henry, miner, 121.

Thorne, J. H., pitman (Whitehaven), 126.
Thorner, Harry, Lt., 174.
Thorpe, George Edward, shaft sinker, 247.
Thurlbeck, William Harrison, mate, 408.
Thurston, C., 3rd hand, 389.
Tidmarsh, J. H., 393.
Tierney, James Edward, dock hand, 200.
Timme, Frederick W., 97.
Timms, H., 3rd hand, 386.
Titchen, T., A.B., 396.
Tocher, G., A.B., 386.
Tolson, George, works fireman, 259.
Toman, Richard Wright, eng., 312.
Tomlinson, Albert Henry, collier, 195.
Tomlinson, C., lorry driver, 50.
Tomlinson, Mark, 79.
Tonge, A. E., A.B., 390.
Tonge, Alfred Joseph, miner, 135.
Torley, Patrick, workman, 268.
Totham, E. J., A.B., 394.
Tottle, W., deck hand, 386.
Touzel, Edward (St. Helier), 51.
Tower, J. B. B., D.S.C., R.N., 400.
Townsend, Emma José (Portlemouth), 301.
Trapman, Adrian S. G. R., Vice-Consul, Addis Ababa, 307.
Trevett, T., boatman, 391.
Triggs, Tom Kenneth, Cmdr., 321.
Trimingham, S., A.B., 396.
Troake, Frederick Henry, Pte., 283.
Trout, R. E., 3rd off., 393.
Troy, Patrick, shipyard worker, 50.
Tse Tor, fireman, 406.
Tudor, W. G., Ch. Off., 391.
Tull, H. J., coastguard boatman, 395.
Tunn, John Patrick, 2nd Lt. A.I.F., 179.
Tupper, Henry de Beauvoir, Cmdr., 327.
Turl, J., O.S., 385.
Turnbull, W., master, 384.
Turner, C., cook, 389.
Turner, D. S., 2nd mate, 386.
Turner, Joseph, cordite factory hand, 256.
Turner, Samuel, pitman, 126.
Turner, William Wagner, Dr., 125.
Turton, W., A.B., 396.
Tutton, Cyril James, prison officer, 298.
Twidle, Edgar, master, 369.
Twyman, A., beachman, 388.
Tyler, Albert, workman, 255.
Tyson, W., Ch. Off., 393.

Underhill, Robert, workman, 78.
Undery, W., Bdg. Off., 385.
Undery, W. C., Bdg. Off., 395.
Unthank, J., bo'sun's mate, 400.
Uren, Thomas Henry, miner, 261.
Urquhart, Leslie, Consul (Baku), 99.

INDEX OF NAMES

Usher, Albert Edward, Pte. A.S.C., 166.
Usher, J. H., fisherman, 387.
Usop bin Daud (Melanau), 42.

Vaisey, Guy Maddison, Lt., 175.
Vale, T. W., boatman, 388.
Vanhests, Gaston, fireman, 432.
Veitch, Mr., 84.
Veladi, Sammai, shikari, 216.
Venter, Joseph Johannes, miner, 193.
Verrill, M., of N.L. Inst., 393.
Verrill, T., fisherman, 389.
Viana, Antonio M., bo'sun, 430.
Vincest, W. T., boatman, 391.
Vinters, Thomas, gasman, 152.
Villaverde, Mr., mate, 65.
Vitto, F., A.B., 385.
Vowles, W. F., scoutmaster, 397.

Waddams, Arthur Richard, Lt. I.A., 176.
Wade, Charles Herbert, Lt. Lab. Comp., 168.
Wadlow, H., Pte., 399.
Wadsworth, Henry Hartley, 6th eng., 380.
Wagenaar, James, miner, 189.
Wagner, Charles, driver, 107.
Wagstaff, Thomas, brewery worker, 148.
Wainscott, J. H., A.B., 395.
Wainwright, David, Lt. R.N., 328.
Wainwright, Harold, app., 406.
Walker, Isaiah, miner, 127.
Walker, John, collier, 195.
Walker, John Holland, 3rd mate, 421.
Walker, Percy Arthur, A.B., 416.
Walker, Thomas, coastguardsman, 424.
Walker, William, miner, 193.
Wallace, William (Faversham), 197.
Walsh, James, eng. driver, 232.
Walsh, Martin, master, 66.
Walsh, Matthew, pitman, 126.
Walsh, W., lamp-trimmer, 396.
Walters, William (Abercarn), 93.
Walton, J., Ch. eng., 399.
Walton, Richard Walter, A.B., 419.
Walton, Thomas Michael, A.S.C., 160.
Wan Bujang, Police Sub-Insp., 43.
Wapplington, John, labourer, 132.
Ward, H. J., seaman, 400.
Ward, Harry Victor Julius, A.B., 432.
Ward, John, colliery pony driver, 265.
Ward, Norman, A.B., 419.
Ward, Robert, workman, 145.
Warden, Arthur R. S., Lt.-Comdr., 156, 316.
Wards, A. H., receiver, 395.
Wards, W., fisherman, 395.
Wares, A., Life Saving Co., 385.
Warman, A., coast-guard, 393.
Warne, Albert Edgar, Flt.-Sergt., 172.

Warren, G. H., 2nd mate, 394.
Warren, H., boatman, 387.
Warren, S., carpenter, 390.
Warrins, L., stowaway, 387.
Warwick, Percy, L./C., 159.
Wastie, Glanville Charles, farmer, 256.
Waterfield, Albert, park keeper, 295.
Watkins, T., 3rd mate, 394.
Watson, Christopher, A.B., 323.
Watson, G., bo'sun's mate, 390.
Watson, J., skipper, 385.
Watson, J. K., 2nd mate, 400.
Watson, N., 3rd off., 400.
Watson, T. J., skipper, 386.
Watson, Victor A., R.N., Flt.-Lt., 173, 320.
Watson, W. T., Corpl., 398.
Watt, A., deck hand, 393.
Watts, Frederick, miner, 123.
Watts, G., Ch. Off., 387.
Waugh, William, miner, 261.
Waygood, S., O.S., 396.
Weatherstone, T. H., steward, 397.
Webb, C. J., Lt., 397.
Webb, F., mate, 390.
Webb, James, Corpl. R.A.M.C., 159.
Webber, T. H., 392.
Webster, David, 2nd mate, 348.
Webster, G., fisherman, 388.
Weeks, Frederick W., Act. Lt. R.N.R., 317.
Weeks, J., A.B., 388.
Welch, H. O., coastguard boatman, 393.
Welch, J., O.S., 385.
Welcome, T., cook, 392.
Welding, Alfred, steel worker, 244.
Weldrick, W., deck hand, 398.
Wells, D., donkeyman, 400.
Wells, E. J., 3rd hand, 392.
Wells, G., mate, 390.
Welsby, John, miner, 121.
Welsby, Mrs., 121.
Wenborne, George, 195.
Wenke, A., O.S., 391.
Wennerburg, Martin, bo'sun, 402.
Wesley, Henry, Mr., 87.
Wesley, Henry, agent, 356.
West, Harold, miner, 232.
West, J., 2nd hand, 392.
West, P., A.B., 395.
West, J., app., 391.
West, T., fisherman, 386.
Westcott, G., A.B., 400.
Westoe, Wilfrid, miner, 237.
Wheal, David, gate rly. porter, 141.
Wheeler, H., 2nd mate, 385.
Wheeler, W. B., A.B., 396.
Whelan, John, storekeeper, 421.
Whelan, M., R.N.R., 400.

INDEX OF NAMES

Whelpton, Charles, workman, 227.
Whiffen, Cecil Herbert, coal-miner, 202.
Whillans, John, pitman, 126.
Whistler, Thomas Ancrett, 1st mate, 359.
White, George Henry, 2nd eng., 376.
White, Gladys, Brit. Red Cross Soc., 182.
White, H. A., coastguardsman, 398.
White, J., fisherman, 387.
White, J. W., 2nd eng., 399.
White, John, Ch. eng., 414.
White, Thomas James, miner, 200.
White, W., Ch. Off., 385.
White, William Henry, coastguard off., 409.
Whitehead, A. E., A.B., 400.
Whitehead, E., beachman, 388.
Whitehead, F. P., Ch. Off., 388.
Whitehead, Nicholas, painter's labourer, 257.
Whitehead, Thomas A., still-worker, 234.
Whitehead, W., Ldg. seaman, 397.
Whitehead, William, L./C., 184.
Whitehouse, W., O.S., 392.
Whiteley, J., Ch. Off., 398.
Whittingham, James, miner, 121.
Wicks, H., skipper, 397.
Wilcox, E., A.B., 385.
Wild, Harry Ernest, R.N., 215–16, 331.
Wild, Robert (Rochdale), 298.
Wilkie, T., extra 2nd hand, 386.
Wilkin, F. R., 2nd off., 398.
Wilking, F., A.B., 397.
Wilkinson, S., Ch. Off., 400.
Willard, R. S., bo'sun, 399.
Willets, Anthony, miner, 127.
William, Henry William, Q.M., 421.
Williams, A., Q.M., 397.
Williams, Alan, A.B., 432.
Williams, Arthur, donkeyman, 413.
Williams, E. R., 2nd off., 396.
Williams, E. Scott, midshipman, 395.
Williams, George, boatman, 357.
Williams, I., 2nd mate, 391.
Williams, J., Q.M., 386.
Williams, John, collier, 92.
Williams, Llewellyn, miner, 135.
Williams, O., 2nd off., 400.
Williams, Osmond, foreman (Sierra Leone), 267.
Williams, R., bo'sun, 397.
Williams, Richard Harvey, seaman, 411.
Williams, Robert, carptr., 431.
Williams, Robert Ralph, schoolmaster, 108.
Williams, Sidney, L./C., 177.
Williams, Thomas, stationmaster, 184.
Williams, Thomas Lloyd, Ch. Off., 406.
Williams, W., 4th eng., 387.
Williams, William, quarry worker, 278.
Williamson, Herbert, mech. eng., 146.
Williamson, J. (off Shetlands), 384.

Willis, H. W., skipper, 388.
Willis, Patrick Henry, P.O. R.N., 334.
Willock, Herbert Thomas Mark, A.B., 419.
Willoughby, James B., Capt., 309, 345.
Wilson, A., pilot, 389.
Wilson, Archibald, chargeman, 103.
Wilson, Charles, A.B., 352.
Wilson, George, eng., 409.
Wilson, George, miner, 240.
Wilson, H., O.S., 392.
Wilson, Harry, miner, 239.
Wilson, Mrs. Isabelle, 104.
Wilson, J., O.S., 388.
Wilson, J., pilot, 389.
Wilson, John Dick, 2nd off., 410.
Wilson, John, pitman, 126.
Wilson, Joseph, miner, 254.
Wilson, Matthew, pitman, 126.
Wilson, R., 3rd hand, 388.
Wilson, R., 3rd eng., 399.
Wilson, W., A.B., 396.
Wilson, William, Col.-Sergt., 97.
Wilson, William, seaman, 412.
Wiltshire, S. N., Pilot Off. R.A.F., 285.
Wiltshire, William James (Faversham), 197.
Winborn, Arthur Thomas, collier, 142.
Windows, W., coastguard boatman, 392.
Wingfield, Edward, collier, 195.
Winterfield, F., A.B., 396.
Wise, J., steward, 396.
Wiseman, Laurence, collier, 203.
Wishart, J., bo'sun, 388.
Withers, Matthew, colliery deputy, 150.
Witten, W., coastguard boatman, 389.
Wollaston, F., skipper, 397.
Wolsey, Hilda Elizabeth, nurse, 111.
Won Jak, seaman, 406.
Wood, Archibald C., Corpl. R.A.F., 222.
Wood, C. J. F., Lt., 394.
Wood, Douglas, Lt., 162.
Wood, Herbert, gas worker, 138.
Wood, J. H., volunteer, Life Brigade, 359.
Wood, R., carptr., 398.
Wood, W. J., bo'sun, 389.
Woodgate, R., 2nd hand, 388.
Woodhouse, Arthur, miner, 191.
Woodman, Thomas Henry, sapper, 176.
Woods, C., O.S., 392.
Woods, C., A.B., 396.
Woodward, C. H., steward, 390.
Wooley, William Downing, collier, 142.
Woolley, R., steward, 389.
Worrall, Thomas, under-looker, 96.
Wren, James, pitman, 126.
Wright, Douglas William, Lt., 186.
Wright, Frances Maude, carman's wife, 109.
Wright, Frederick, Police Insp., 173.

Wright, James A., gold miner, 141.
Wright, John, workman, 274.
Wright, Robert, P.C., 78.
Wright, W., boatman, 386.
Wright, William, seaman, 2.
Wyatt, J. B., A.B., 395.
Wylde, W., A.B., 395.

Yaldwyn, William E., accountant, 96.
Yarman, Mrs., 78.
Yates, Phillip William, collier, 265.
Yehia-el-Imam, P.C. (Khartoum), 300.
Yeo, W. F., civilian (Sidmouth), 398.

Ying Ah Pan, seaman, 406.
York, David, miner, 267.
Young, Archibald, explosives worker, 194.
Young, Austen Patrick, 2nd cook, 431.
Young, David Coley, Maj., 113.
Young, F. W., O.S., 389.
Young, Fletcher, pitman, 126.
Young, H. M., A.B., 390.
Young, J., fisherman, 387.

Zammit, Giuseppe, dockyard labourer, 97.
Zieboldt, J., O.S., 388.
Ziegler, R. P., steamship passenger, 418.

PART II
INDEX OF PLACES

Aberavon Colliery, Port Talbot, Glam., 191.
Abercarn Colliery, Mon., 93.
Aberdeenshire, *see* Boddam, Broadhaven, Peterhead, Scatraw Creek.
Abyssinia, *see* Addis Ababa, Ethiopia.
Ackton Hall Colliery, Featherstone, Yorks., 203.
Adarowfie, *see* Wadi Adarowfie.
Addis Ababa, Abyssinia, 222, 307.
Aden, 363.
Adilang, Uganda, 304.
Agecroft Colliery, Lancs., 96.
Aix Roads (naval engagement), 4.
Ajiabampo, Mexico, 343.
Alcran Shoal, G. of Mexico, 65.
Aldersgate Str. Station, Met. Ry., London, 117.
Aldershot, Surrey, 96.
Alexandra Dock, Newport, Mon., 105.
Alexandria, Egypt, 345.
Alibagh, Bombay (Chaul Kadu Reef), 342.
Almería, Spain, 291, 335.
Ambala, India, 218.
Amble, N.E.R., Northumberland, 131.
Anne Port, Jersey, 38.
Annesley Colliery, nr. Nottingham, 150.
Antarctic, *see* Ross Is., Ross Sea, Weddel Sea.
Arabia, *see* Jeddah.
Archangel, Russia, 368–9, 374.
Archangel (Bakaritsa), Russia, 319, 323.
Ardeer, Ayrshire, Nobel's Explosives Factory, 131, 191.
Ardmore, co. Waterford, 296.
Ariston Gold Mine, *see* Prestea.
Arran Is., *see* Lamlash.
Armour Pt., Labrador, 311.
Ashanti, *see* Côte d'Or, Obuassi.
Askern Colliery, Doncaster, Yorks., 200.
Assam, *see* Digboi, Tikak.
Audley Colliery, Staffs., 97.
Australia, 242, 308. *See* Bendigo, Charleville, Hamilton, Kalgoorlie, Roper R., Westralia. *See also* New South Wales, Queensland, Victoria.
Australian Bight, 412.
Ayrshire, *see* Ardeer, Irvine Harbour.

Backford, Cheshire, Pump Farm, 268.
Baddesley Colliery, Staffs., 95.
Bakaritsa, *see* Archangel.

Baku, Caspian Sea, 99.
Baltic Sea, 329.
Baluchistan, 220 ff., 287 ff. *See also* Quetta.
Bamfurlong Mine, Wigan, Lancs., 140.
Banbridge (Gas Works), co. Down, 118.
Banffshire, *see* Buckie.
Bantry Bay, Ireland, 1, 63.
Barnsley, Yorks., 50.
Barnsley Main Colliery, Yorks., 235.
Barra de Ortigueira, Spain, 411.
Barrow, Hematite Steel Co., Lancs., 143.
Barry, Docks, Glam., 50, 245.
Barton, England, 301.
Barton Moss, nr. Manchester, 112.
Batang Lupar R., Sarawak, 42.
Bear Is., 425. *See also* Kobbekuta.
Beaumont, Texas, 412.
Beauvais, France, 219.
Bechuanaland, *see* N'gamiland.
Bedfordshire, *see* Luton, Woburn Sands.
Beirut, Syria, 374.
Belfast (fire at 2 Amelia Str.), 270.
Belfast (office robbery), 295.
Belgium, *see* Courtrai, Rousbrugge, Ruysselede, St. Pietersveld, Zonnebecke.
Bendigo Gold Mine, Australia, 124.
Bengal Province, *see* Chittagong, Darjeeling, Delhi Fort.
Bentley Colliery, Yorks., 265.
Berkshire, *see* Pangbourne, Tilehurst.
Bhagalpur, *see* Bihar.
Bhutan (State), India, 10.
Bihar, India, 303.
Billingham, nr. Stockton-on-Tees, Synthet. Ammon. Ltd., 259.
Bill Quay, Gateshead, co. Durham, 54–5.
Bintulu R., Sarawak, 43.
Bishop Auckland Collieries, co. Durham, 49.
Blackhouse Colliery, Durham, 154.
Blandford, Dorset, 166.
Blaydon-on-Tyne, Ottovale Works, co. Durham, 274.
Blue Nile Province, Sudan, 302.
Boddam, nr. Peterhead, Aberdeenshire, 356.
Bolckow, Vaughan & Co.'s Steel Works, 144.
Bolt Hd., Devon, 408.
Bolton (Cotton Mill), Lancs., 227.
Bombay, India, 299, 300, 339, 348.
— Province, *see* Alibagh, Sholapur, Tapti R.
— Reclamation Works, 85.

INDEX OF PLACES

Bombay, India, Sewage Works, 197.
— Simplex Mills, 205.
Boucan, nr. Bayonne, 354.
Boulogne, France, 156.
Bournemouth Station, S.R., 143.
Bow R., Calgary, Alberta, 190.
Box Station, Wilts., 115.
Bracciano, Lake, north of Rome, 214.
Bradford, Yorks., 50.
Braysdown Colliery, nr. Bath, 196.
Bretby Colliery, S. Derbyshire, 256.
Bridlington, Yorks., 49.
Bristol, City Docks, 247. *See also* Hanham, Temple Meads Stn.
Brithwynydd Colliery, 92.
Broadhaven, nr. Collieston, Aberdeens.
Brockton Camp, Brockton, Stafford, 186.
Brodie Burn, Co. Elgin, 100.
Brooklyn, New York, 409.
Brownston Hd., Bay of Tramore, co. Waterford, 5.
Brynamman Colliery, Glam., 268.
Bryncethin Colliery, nr. Bridgend, Glam., 140.
Buchan-ness, 350.
Buckie, Banffs., 407.
Buckinghamshire, *see* Slough.
Bude, Cornwall, 345.
Buenaventura, Colombia, 378.
Buffalo R., Natal, 361.
Bukhtiarpur Station, East India Ry., 145.
Bulawayo, Lonely Mine, 231.
Bulthy Mine, Shropshire, 231.
Burley Colliery, Apedale, Staffs., 251.
Burma, *see* Rangoon.
Burnham Green, Welwyn, Herts., 255.
Burnopfield, co. Durham, 49.
Burton Coastguard Station, 85, 341.
Burton-on-Trent, Charrington's Brewery, 141.
— Burton Brewery Company's Works, 148.
Bushbury, Staffs., 103.
Bwlffa Dare Colliery, nr. Aberdare, S. Wales, 129.

Cadder Colliery, Lanarks., 153.
Cadeby Colliery, Warwicks., 122.
Cadeby Main Colliery, Doncaster, 146.
Cairo, Egypt, 297.
Caithness, *see* Scarfskerry.
Calais, France, 169.
Calcutta, India, 339, 349.
— *see* Hugli R.
California, *see* San Francisco.
Camborne, Cornwall, 139.
Cambrai, France, 3.
Cambuslang, *see* Loanend Colliery.

Camden Town, London (Gilbey's Distillery), 263.
Canada, *see* Bow R., Montreal, Ontario, South Porcupine, Strathcona.
Cannock Chase Colliery, Staffs., 139.
Canton, China, 376.
Canvery R., Krishnarajkatte, Mysore, 107.
Cape Colony, *see* Capetown, Danger Point.
Cape Horn, 351, 359.
Cape Percy, Nova Scotia, 429.
Capetown, Cape Colony, 61.
Cardiff (National Benzol Co.), 237.
— (Royal Hotel fire), 186.
— *see also* Darran Colliery, Monmouthshire.
Carmarthenshire, *see* Castle Colliery, Llanelly, Ponthenry.
Carnarvonshire, *see* Dorothea Quarry, Llysfaen.
Castle Colliery, Llanelly, Carmarthens., 234.
Castleford, Yorks., 260.
Castleton, Derbys. (Man Farm), 130.
Ceylon, *see* Mount Lavinia.
Channel Is., *see* Jersey.
Charlestown, Fifes., 409.
Charleville, Queensland, Australia, 96.
Charlton (Eng. Works of Johnson & Phillips), 241.
Chatham Dockyard, Kent, 305.
Chaul Kadu Reef, *see* Alibagh.
Cheshire, *see* Backford, Stockport.
Chieveley Station, Natal, 107.
Chile, *see* Huanillos.
Chilwell (Filling Factory), 205.
China, 283, 285, 287, 299. *See also* Canton, Chungking, Hankow, Hong Kong, Kowloon, Peking, Szechuan, Tung Sha, Yangtze R.
Chittagong, Bengal, 62, 285.
Christinehaven, Sweden, 296.
Chua District, *see* Uganda.
Chungking, China, 118.
Cicely Colliery, Tonyrefail, Glam., 258.
Città Vecchia, Italy, 3.
Claybury, Essex, 109.
Clay Cross, nr. Chesterfield, Derbys., 154, 190.
Cleethorpes, Lincs., 167.
Cliffe, Kent (Explosives Factory), 139.
Clifton Hall Colliery, Lancs., 96.
Clonmany, Co. Donegal, 182.
Clydach Vale, Glam., 108.
Cochin, Madras, 348.
Coleorton Mine, nr. Ashby-de-la-Zouch, Leics., 133.
Colombia, *see* Buenaventura.
Coltness Iron Works, Newmains, Lanarks., 124.
Congo R., Banana Creek, 344.

INDEX OF PLACES

Coppice Colliery, Derby, 235.
Cornwall, see Bude, Camborne, Drakewalls Mine, East Pool, Falmouth, St. Ives.
Corton Lightship, Lowestoft, 402.
Côte d'Or Mine, see Obuassi.
Courtrai, Belgium, 11.
Courtmacsherry Bay, co. Cork, 341.
Cowdenbeath Colliery, Fife, 197-8.
Cowichan Lake, Vancouver I., 163.
Cranwell Aerodrome, Lincs., 284.
Cresswell Colliery, Derbys., 244.
Cromer, Norfolk, 294.
Crumlin Viaduct, G.W.R., Mon., 189.
Curragh Camp, co. Kildare, 170.
Cumberland, see Frizington, Roachburn, Townhead Mine, Wellington Pit, Whitehaven, Workington.
Cwmcarn Pit, Mon., 93.
Cwm Cynon Colliery, Glam., 201.
Cymmer Colliery, Rhondda Valley, Glam., 92.
Cymmer Valley, Rhondda, Glam., 92.

Dagenham Dock, Essex, 262.
Dalhousie, India, 96.
Danger Point, Simon's Bay, C. Col., 6.
Darjeeling, Bengal, India, 97.
Darjeeling (Lebong Race Course), Bengal, India, 303.
Darlaston Green Furnaces, Staffs., 142.
Darlinghurst, N.S.W., 378.
Darngavil Colliery, Lanarks., 233.
Darran Colliery, Deri, Cardiff, 125.
Delhi Fort, India, 115.
Denbighshire, see Gresford Colliery, Old Conway.
Derbyshire, see Bretby, Castleton, Clay Cross, Coppice, Cresswell, Holmewood, Ireland Coll., Langwith, Marcham, Wood Lane.
Devizes, Market-place, Wilts., 94.
Devon, see Bolt Hd., Kingsbridge, Plymouth, Portlemouth, Start Pt.
Digboi, Assam Oil Co., India, 145.
Digby Aerodrome, Lincs., 284.
Dinapur, India, 95.
Dinas Isaf Colliery, Glam., 92.
Dinnington Main Colliery, Newcastle-upon-Tyne, 229.
Dir, Peshawar, India, 100.
Dorothea Slate Quarry, Carnarvons., 239.
Dorset, see Blandford.
Dover, Kent, 172.
— Harbour, 326, 328.
Drakewalls Mine, Calstock, Cornwall, 96.
Dublin Bay, see Kingstown, Eire.
Dunkerton Colliery, Somerset, 189.
Dunkirk, France, 2.
Dunnottar Castle, Kincardines., 355.

Durban, S. Africa, 419.
Durham, co., see Billingham, Bill Quay, Bishop Auckland, Blackhouse, Blaydon-on-Tyne, Burnopfield, Eppleton, Felling, Hartlepool, Hedley Pit, Jarrow, Murton, North Biddick, Pelaw Main, Pelton, S. Garesfield, S. Shields, Sunderland, Trindon Grange, Wardley, Wingate, Woodland.
Dymchurch, Kent, 85, 340.

Earnoch Colliery, Lanark, 154.
East Greenwich, Standard Ammonia Works, 137.
East India Ry. Co., India, 130.
East London, Natal, 361.
East Markham, Notts., 132.
East Pool and Agar Mines, see Camborne.
Ebbw Vale, Mon., 250.
Egypt, see Alexandria, Cairo, Port Said.
Eire, see Ireland.
Elgin, co., 100. See also Brodie Burn.
Emily Harbour, Labrador, 410.
Energlyn Colliery, Fife, 92.
English Chan., 368.
Enham Village Centre, Andover, Hants., 236.
Ennis, Eire, 99.
Eppleton Colliery, co. Durham, 272.
Esher, Surrey, 171.
Essex, see Claybury, Dagenham, George Lane, Romford.
Ethiopia, see Addis Ababa.

Falkland Is., see Stanley Harbour.
Falmouth, 342.
Fastnet Rock, Coast of Cork, Eire, 423.
Faversham, Kent, 197.
Felling Colliery, Durham, 138.
Feltham, Borstal Inst., Middx., 188.
Ferndale, Rhondda, Glam., 92.
Ferozepore, Punjab, 113, 300.
Fifeshire, see Charlestown, Cowden Beath, Glencraig, Lockhead, Rosyth.
Finsbury Park Station, London, 98.
Firhill Bridge, see Forth and Clyde Canal.
Fishguard, Needle Rock, Pembrokeshire, 297.
Fiji, see Suva.
Flanders, 176.
Flintshire, see Main Coal Colliery.
Formosa I., see Kee-lung.
Forth and Clyde Canal (Firhill Bridge), 43.
France, 177-9. See also Beauvais, Boucan, Boulogne, Calais, Cambrai, Dunkirk, Gorre, Guillemont, Le Cateau, Le Havre, Marseilles, Meuse R., Molène, Neuve Chapelle, St. Pol, Ushant, Warley, Wizernes.
Frickley Colliery, Yorks., 239.

INDEX OF PLACES

Frizington (Margaret Iron Ore Mine), Cumberland, 205.
Frodingham Iron & Steel Co., *see* Scunthorpe.

Genoa, Italy, 369.
George Lane, Epping, 136.
Germiston, Transvaal, 131.
Gibraltar, 3, 347, 362.
Giffnock Colliery, Glasgow, 202.
Gilfach Goch, Glam., Llewellyn Sinking Pit, 150.
Glamorganshire, *see* Aberavon, Barry, Brynamman, Bryncethin, Bwlffa Dare, Cicely Coll., Clydach Vale, Cwm Cynon, Cymmer, Cymmer Valley, Dinas Isaf, Ferndale, Gilfach Goch, Llanbradach, Llwyncelyn, Llwynpia, Mountain Ash, Neath, Nixon's Coll., Penriwfer, Pontypridd, Port Talbot, Resolven, Rhondda, Swansea, Tonypandy, Tynewydd, Tylacoch, Ynishir.
Glasgow, *see* Giffnock, Loanend.
Glencoe Colliery, Natal, 122.
Glencraig Colliery, Fife, 203.
Glynvase, *see* Falmouth.
Gold Coast, *see* Prestea, Volta R.
Good Hope, C. of, S. Africa, 6.
Goole, R. Ouse, Yorks., 112.
Gorangdih Colliery, India, 202.
Gorleston, *see* Lowestoft.
Gorre, France, 163.
Great Busby, Court House Farm, 125.
Greenwich, London, 247.
Gresford Colliery, Denbigh, 273.
Grimthorpe Colliery, Barnsley, Yorks., 203.
Guillemont, France, 11.

Hackney Wick Stadium, London, 279.
Haidari Kach, Waziristan, 12.
Haifa, Palestine, 292.
Haisborough Lightship, North Sea, 367.
Halesowen, Staffs., 94.
Halifax, Nahum's Mills Co., Yorks., 207.
Halifax, Nova Scotia, 321, 428.
Hamilton, Victoria, 223.
Hampshire, *see* Bournemouth, Enham Village, Liss, Lyndhurst Road, Southampton.
Hamstead Colliery, nr. Birmingham, 53, 121.
Hanham Colliery, Bristol, Somerset, 123.
Hankow, China, 287.
Hanley Deep Colliery, N. Staffs., 269.
Hanwell Asylum, Middx., 111.
Harod Colliery, 92.
Harriseahead Colliery, Staffs., 239.
Hartford Mine, Northumberland, 198.
Hartlepool, Durham, 371.
Hartley, Northumberland, 52.
Harton Colliery, Durham, 193.

Harwich, Essex, 314, 316.
Hatting Spruit, Natal, 151.
Hedley Pit, South Moor, co. Durham, 261.
Hertfordshire, *see* Burnham Green, Watford.
Hewarth Parish, 53.
Hickleton Main Mine, nr. Thurnscoe, Yorks., 235.
Hilla, *see* Iraq.
Himalayas (Mt. Everest Expdn.), 217.
Holditch Colliery, N. Staffs., 277.
Holmewood Colliery, nr. Chesterfield, 232.
Holton Heath, R.N. Cordite Factory, Worcestershire, 256.
Hong Kong, 57, 376.
Horse I., Newfoundland, 379.
Hotton-le-Hole, *see* Lyons Colliery.
Hove, Sussex, 106.
Hoyland Silkstone Colliery, Barnsley, Yorks., 120.
Huanillos, Chile, 352.
Hucknall Colliery, Notts., 228.
Huddersfield, Yorks., 94.
Hugli R., India, 307.
Hull, St. Andrew's Dock, 96.
Hulton Colliery, nr. Atherton, Lancs., 135.
Hunza Nagar, NW. India, 10.
Hythe, Kent, 311.
Hyderabad, Deccan, India, Cordite Magazine, 112.
——— Moti Mahal Cinema, 308.

Iffley Lock, nr. Oxford, 110.
Imbros Aerodrome, Aegean Sea, 156.
India, *see* Alibagh, Bhutan, Bihar, Bukhtiarpur, Calcutta, Canvery R., Chaul Kadu Reef, Dalhousie, Dinapur, Dir, East Ind. Ry., Gorangdih, Himalayas, Hugli R., Hunza Nagar, Hyderabad, Indrayani, Jamalpur, Jharwan, Karachi, Keonjhar, Kirkee, Kohat, Kustore, Lahore, Lowari Pass, Luskai, Madras, Malabar, Manipur, Maringhat, Meerut, Moghal Kot, Mohpani, Moshi, Najibabad, Nariana, Nayadih, Nidhauli, Orissa, Pahartali, Peshawar, Piaza Raghza, Punjab, Rander, Sabathu, South Chanda, Surat, Umbeyla, Waziristan.
Indian Ocean, 349.
Indrayani R., nr. Moshi, India, 291.
Invergordon, Ross-shire, 329.
Iraq, 12, 176. *See also* Hilla, Shahraban.
Ireland, *see* Ardmore, Banbridge, Bantry Bay, Belfast, Brownston Hd., Clonmany, Courtmacsherry, Curragh, Ennis, Fastnet Rock, Kingston (Eire), Kinsale, Queenstown, Tramore, Waterford, Wexford.
Ireland Colliery, Staveley, Derbys., 192.
Irvine Harbour, Ayrs., 414.

INDEX OF PLACES

Irwell R., Salford, Lancs., 93.
Italy, see Bracciano, Cività Vecchia, Genoa.

Jaffa, Palestine, 432.
Jamalpur, E. Indian Ry., 241.
Jarrow, Palmer's Shipbuilding Co., co. Durham, 254.
— Docks, 103.
Jeddah, Arabia, 339.
Jersey (Channel Is.), 157. See Anne Port, Pontac, St. Heliers, St. Peter's Barracks.
Jharwan, Saharanpur Distr., United Provinces, India, 304.
Jullundur, Punjab, 300.

Kakamega, Kenya, Kimingini Co. goldmines, 274.
Kalgoorlie, 101. See Lake View.
Karachi, India, 346.
Kasauli, Punjab, 290.
Ke-lung, Formosa, 347.
Kent, see Chatham, Cliffe, Dover, Dymchurch, Faversham, Hythe, Leysdown, Margate, Tilmanstone, Wouldham, Wye.
Kenya, see Kakamega.
Keonjhar, State of Keonjhar, India, 185.
Kerdonis Lighthouse, Malta, 66.
Khajuri Post, Waziristan, 11.
Khartoum, Sudan, 298, 300.
Kimberley Diamond Mine, S. Africa, 123.
Kincardineshire, see Dunnottar Castle.
Kingsbridge (Portlemouth), S. Devon, 301.
King's Cross Met. Ry. Station, London, 259.
Kingstown, Eire, 296.
Kinsale Coast-Guard Station, co. Cork, 85.
Kinsale, Old Head of, co. Cork, 6, 341.
Kirkee, India, 104.
Kobbekuta, Bear Is., nr. Spitzbergen, 383.
Kohat, India, 222, 285.
Kosi Bay, Delagoa Bay, 312.
Kot Kai, Waziristan, 11.
Kowloon, China, 406.
Krugersdorp, Randfontein Gold Mine, S. Africa, 125, 248.
Kustore Colliery, Bihar, India, 276.

Labrador, see Armour Pt., Emily Harb.
La Hogue (Normandy Coast), 1.
Lahore, India, 296.
Lake View Consul Mine, Kalgoorlie, W. Australia, 98.
Lamlash, Brodick, Is. of Arran, 97, 314.
Lanarkshire, see Cadder, Coltness, Darngavil, Earnoch, Glasgow, Stanriffe, Swinhill.

Lancashire, see Barrow, Barton Moss, Bolton, Irwell R., Miles Platting, Oldham, Park Lane, Rochdale, St. Helen's, Salford, Shaw, Smedley Bridge, Warrington, Widnes.
Langwith Colliery, Derbys., 269.
Le Cateau, France, 181.
Leeds, see Water Haigh.
Le Havre, France, 304, 306.
Le Havre Roads, 368.
Leicestershire, see Coleorton.
Lerwick, Shetlands, 414.
Lewis I., see Stornoway.
Leven, R., Scotland, 37.
Leysdown, Sheerness, 284.
Lincoln, Pelham Str. Level Crossing, 252.
Lincolnshire, see Cleethorpes, Cranwell, Digby Aerodrome, Scunthorpe, Sleaford.
Liss, S.R., Hants., 153.
Littleton Colliery, S. Staffs., 275.
Liverpool, Lancs., 49.
— Harrington Dock, 149.
Livingstone, Zambesi R., N. Rhodesia, 219.
Llanbradach Colliery, Glam., 233.
Llanelly Copper Works, Carmarthens., 49. See also Castle Colliery.
Llanhilleth Mine, Mon., 199.
Llwyncelyn Colliery, Rhondda, Glam., 92.
Llwynpia Colliery, Tonypandy, Glam., 267.
Llysfaen, Carnarvons., 278.
Loanend Colliery, Cambuslang, Glasgow, 136.
Lockhead Colliery, Fife, 121.
Lodge Mill Colliery, Lepton, Huddersfield, 147.
Loftus Ironstone Mine, Yorks., 272.
Lomond, Loch, 37.
London, 173, 299.
— Middlesex Hospital, 302.
— Oxford Street (Bourne & Hollingsworth), 244.
— (film fire), 297.
— Redhill Street, Regent's Park, 250.
— See also Aldersgate, Camden Town, East Greenwich, Finsbury Pk. Stn., Greenwich, Hackney Wick, King's Cross, Pentonville Prison, Plumstead, Richmond Pk., Silvertown, Stratford Stn., Wandsworth, Wellington Barracks, Westminster Hall, Woolwich.
Lonely Mine, see Bulawayo.
Long Scar Rocks, Northumberland, 358.
Loos, see Rutoire Plain.
Lowari Pass, Chitral, 97, 100.
Lower Wortley, Leeds, 152.
Lowestoft, 297. See also Corton Lightship.
Low Moor (Munition Company), Yorks., 161.
Luskai, NE. India, 10.
Luton, Sewage Farm, Beds., 136.

INDEX OF PLACES

Lyndhurst Road Station, S.R., 130.
Longships Lighthouse, Land's End, 420.
Lyons Colliery, Hotton-le-Hole, 135.

Madras, St. Thomas's Mount Arsenal, 213. *See also* Cochin.
Main Coal Colliery, Northop, nr. Flint, 137.
Malabar, India, 283.
Malacca, Str. of, 366.
Maldive Is., Indian Ocean, 348.
Malta, 97, 312, 331, 370. *See also* Kerdonis Lighthouse, Zabbar.
Manchester, Lancs., 55, 264, 298. *See also* Walkden.
Manipur, NE. India, 10.
Margaret Iron Ore Mine, *see* Frizington.
Margate, Kent, 171.
Maringhat, on Ganges, India, 62.
Marcham Colliery, Staveley, Derbys., 147.
Markham Colliery, Tredegar, Mon., 142.
Marseilles, France, 365.
Mediterranean Sea, 380.
Meerut, India, 292.
Mells Colliery, Somerset, 253.
Mersey, R., Docks, 49.
Mesopotamia, *see* Iraq.
Messel Bay, Cape Prov., S. Africa, 378.
Messina, Sicily, 104.
Meuse, R., France–Belgium, 184.
Mexico, *see* Ajiabampo, Alcran.
Middlesbrough, Yorks., 403.
— Acklam Iron Works, 249, 417.
Middlesex, *see* Feltham, Hanwell.
Middlesex Hospital, *see* London.
Midlothian, *see* Roslin.
Miles Platting, Manchester, 278.
Milford, Pembrokeshire, 413.
Modderfontein, S. Africa, B.S. Afr. Explosives Works, 140.
—— Consolidated Mine, 193.
Moghal Kot, India, 214.
Mohpani Colliery, G.I.P. Ry., India, 245.
Molène, France, 61.
Monmouthshire, *see* Abercarn, Cardiff, Crumlin Viaduct, Cwm Carn, Ebbw Vale, Llanhilleth, Markham, Newport, North Celynen, Penallta, Ponytpool, Staveley, Usk R., West Elliot.
Montreal, Canada, 381.
Morant Cays, W. Indies, 360, 430.
Moshi, India, *see* Indrayani R.
Mountain Ash, Glam., 236.
Mt. Egmont, Taranaki, N.Z., 181.
Mt. Lavinia, Ceylon, 304.
Mt. Morgan Mine, Brisbane, Queensland, 123, 206.

Murton Colliery, South Hetton, Durham, 240, 254.
Murton Ry. Station, 188.
Muscat, Persian Gulf, 404.

Nanga Meluan, Sarawak, 43.
Najibabad Station, Indian Rys., 252.
Nariana, R. Beas, India, 211.
Natal, S. Africa, 61. *See also* Buffalo R., Chieveley, East London, Glencoe, Hatting Spruit.
National Shell Filling Factory, 201.
Nayadih, E. Ind. Ry., 237.
Neath Colliery, Glam., 121.
Neuve Chapelle, France, 163.
Newark-on-Trent, Notts., 160, 248.
New Brunswick, *see* St. John.
Newcastle, N.S. Wales, 101, 365, 376.
Newcastle-upon-Tyne, 50, 120, 212. *See also* Dinnington.
Newdigate Colliery, Nuneaton, Warwicks., 204.
Newfoundland, 358, 420. *See also* Horse I., St. John's.
Newmains, *see* Coltness.
Newmarket, Suff., 179.
Newport, Mon., 377. *See also* Alexandra Dock.
New South Wales, *see* Darlinghurst, Newcastle, Port Hacking, Sydney. *See also* Australia.
New Zealand, 308. *See also* Mt. Egmont, Paparoa.
N'gamiland, Bechuanaland, 301.
Nidhauli, India, 222.
Nile, R., *see* Khartoum.
Nixon's Colliery, Mountain Ash, Glam., 236.
Norfolk, *see* Cromer, Scroby Sands, Tivetshall.
North Biddick Colliery, Washington, co. Durham, 257.
North Celynen Colliery, Mon., 246.
North Gawber Colliery, Yorks., 199.
North Leigh, Witney, Oxon., 256.
Northop, *see* Main Coal Colliery.
Northumberland, *see* Amble, Hartford, Hartley, Long Scar Rocks, Seaton Carew, Shields, Tynemouth, Tyneside.
North Wakefield, Can. Pacific Ry., 136.
Nottinghamshire, *see* Annesley, East Markham, Hucknall, Newark-on-Trent, Pye Hill.
Nova Scotia, *see* Cape Percy, Halifax.
Novorossisk, S. Russia, 211, 375.
Nuneaton, *see* Newdigate Colliery.

Obuassi, Ashanti, 238.
—— Côte d'Or Mine, 132.
Oldham, Lancs., 36.

INDEX OF PLACES

Old Colwyn, Denbigh, 145.
Omdurman, Sudan, 290.
Ontario, *see* South Porcupine, Sudbury, Tweed, Wilton R. *See also* Canada.
Orissa, India, 303.
Oulton, *see* Water Haigh Colliery.
Oxfordshire, *see* Iffley, North Leigh.

Pahartali Power House, Assam–Bengal Ry., India, 286.
Palestine, 174, 291. *See also* Haifa, Jaffa.
Pangbourne, *see* Tilehurst.
Paparoa township, N.Z., 215.
Parkhurst Prison, I. of Wight, 298.
Park Lane Colliery, Wigan, Lancs., 206.
Passaro, C. of., I. of Sicily, 2.
Peking, *see* China.
Pelaw Main Colliery, Bill Quay, co. Durham, 53.
Pelton Colliery, Pelton Fell, co. Durham, 267.
Pembrokeshire, *see* St. Anne's Hd., Fishguard.
Pembroke Dock, 325.
— Station, G.W.R., 184.
Penallta Colliery, Mon., 120.
Penriwfer, Rhondda, Glam., 92.
Pentonville Prison, London, 299.
Persia, *see* Tembi.
Persian Gulf, *see* Muscat, Shatt al Arab.
Peshawar, India, 100, 212.
Peterhead, Aberdeens., 360, 424.
Piaza Raghza, NW. Frontier, India, 213.
Plumstead, London (White Hart Lane), 242.
Plymouth, Devon, 423.
Podmore Hall Colliery, Staffs., 229.
Pontac, Jersey, 108.
Ponthenry Colliery, Carmarthens., 251.
Pontypridd Colliery, Glam., 92.
Pontypool Rd. Station, Mon., 117.
Port Hacking, nr. Sydney, 377.
Portlemouth, *see* Kingsbridge.
Port Said, Egypt, 324, 365.
Portsmouth Dockyard, 284, 306.
— Harbour, 313.
Port Talbot, Glam., 50.
Prestea, Gold Coast, Ariston Gold Mine, 299, 305.
Psyche Mine, S. Rhodesia, 134.
Pulau Bulong, Sarawak, 42.
Punjab, 300. *See also* Ferozepore, India, Jullundur, Kasauli.
Pye Hill Colliery, Notts., 198.

Queensland, *see* Mt. Morgan.
Queenstown, Eire, 381.
Quetta, Baluchistan, 32, 221, 287 ff.

Ramsgate, Kent, 5.
Rand Clip Mine, Bocksburg, S. Africa, 141.

Rander, India, 302.
Randfontein, *see* Krugersdorp.
Rangoon, Burma, 111, 405.
Redditch, Worcs., 117.
Red Sea, 364.
Resolven, nr. Neath, Glam., 92.
Rhodesia, *see* Livingstone, Psyche Mine, Salisbury, Tebekwe.
Rhondda Valley, *see* Llwyncelyn Colliery.
Richmond Park (Spanker Hill Plantation), London, 295.
Roachburn Colliery, Cumberland, 121.
Rochdale, Lancs., 298.
Romford (Brewery), Essex, 133.
Roper, R., Australia, 115.
Roslin Explosives Factory, Midlothian, 194.
Ross I., Antarctic, 331.
Ross-shire, *see* Invergordon.
Rosslare, Wexford, 401.
Ross Sea, Antarctic, 215, 331.
Rosyth, Fife, 211.
Rotherham, Yorks., 55.
Rotherham Main Mine, Yorks., 97.
Rousbrugge (Clearing Station), Belgium, 183.
Rugby (Thomson-Houston Co.), Warwicks., 202.
Russell Colliery, Dudley, Staffs., 127.
Russia, *see* Archangel, Baku, Novorossisk.
Rutoire Plain, nr. Loos, France, 162.
Ruysselede, Belgium, 303.

Sabathu, Simla Hills, India, 219.
St. Anne's Hd., Pembrokes., 431.
St. George's Chan., 364, 415.
St. Helena I., 332.
St. Helen's Collieries, Lancs., 201.
St. Helen's Fort Lighthouse, I. of Wight, 67.
St. Heliers, Jersey, 51.
St. Ives, Cornwall, 423.
St. John, New Brunswick, 131, 418.
St. John's, Newfoundland, 413, 420, 431.
St. Margaret's Station, G.E.R., Herts., 141.
St. Peter's Barracks, Jersey, 157.
St. Pietersveld Wyngene, Belgium, 303.
St. Pol, France, 186.
Salford, *see* Irwell, R.
Salisbury, Rhodesia, *see* Tebekwe.
Samarahan R., Sarawak, 42.
Sandgate, Kent, 311.
San Francisco, California, 355, 403.
San Sebastian, Spain, 343.
Sarawak, *see* Batang, Bintulu, Nanga Meluan, Pulau Bulong, Samarahan, Sebangan, Sibu, Simanggang.
Scarfskerry, Caithness, 363.
Scatraw Creek, S. of Aberdeen, 344.
Scroby Sands, Gorleston, Norfolk, 295.

INDEX OF PLACES

Scunthorpe, Fordingham Iron & Steel Co., Lincs., 143.
Seabrook, 311.
Seaton Carew, Northumberland, 358.
Sebangan, Sarawak, 42.
Seine, R., France, 369.
Shahraban, Iraq, 185.
Shapur Tangi, Waziristan, 214.
Shatt al Arab, Persian Gulf, 367.
Shaw, Lancs., Hawk Cotton Spinning Factory, 137.
Shaw, Oak Mills, nr. Oldham, Lancs., 230.
Sheffield, Atlas Works, 227.
— Don River Works (Vickers'), 49.
— Gas Company, Effingham Str., 138.
— Norfolk Works, 96.
— *See also* Vickers' Works.
Shetlands, *see* Lerwick.
Shields, Northumberland, 348.
Sholapur District, Bombay, 300.
Shropshire, *see* Bulthy.
Sibu, Sarawak, 43.
Sierra Leone, W. Africa, 267.
Silkstone Colliery, Yorks., *see* Hoyland.
Silvertown (Chemical Works), E. London, 195.
Simanggang, Sarawak, 43.
Simmer & Jack Mine, *see* Germiston.
Sleaford, Lincs., 285.
Slough (Empire Cinema), 116.
Smedley Bridge Dye Works, nr. Manchester, 238.
Somerset, *see* Braysdown, Dunkerton, Mells.
South Africa, *see* Durban, Kimberley, Kosi Bay, Krugersdorp, Messell Bay, Modderfontein, Rand Clip Mine, Randfontein, Vlakfontein, Wesselton.
Southampton, Hants, 49.
South Chanda, Central Prov., India, 216.
South Garesfield Colliery, co. Durham, 237, 253, 271.
South Hetton, *see* Murton.
South Kirby Colliery, Yorks., 233, 271.
South Porcupine, Ontario, 114.
South Shields (Coast Guard), co. Durham, 310, 359, 409.
Spain, *see* Almería, Barra di Ortigueira, San Sebastian, Tarragona, Vigo.
Spitzbergen, *see* Bear Is.
Spurn Point, Yorks., 49.
Stanley Harbour, Falkland Is., 350.
Stanriffe Colliery, Airdrie, Lanarks., 206.
Start Point, Devon, 339.
Staveley, *see* Markham Colliery, Ireland Colliery.
Staffordshire, *see* Audley, Baddesley, Brockton, Burley, Burton-on-Trent, Bushbury, Cannock Chase, Darlaston Green, Halesowen, Hamstead, Hanley, Harriseahead, Holditch, Littleton, Podmore Hall, Russell, Stoke-on-Trent, Tunstall, West Bromwich.
Stirling, Stirlingshire, Scotland, 99.
Stockingford Station, M.R., 130.
Stockport, Cheshire, 50.
Stockport (H. Marsland, Ltd.), Cheshire, 243.
Stoke-on-Trent, Staffs., 50.
Stornoway, I. of Lewis, 414.
Stratford Station, G.E.R., 230.
Strathcona, Alberta, Canada, 120.
Sudan, *see* Adarowfie, Blue Nile, Khartoum, Omdurman, Wadi Adarowfie.
Sudbury, Ontario, 106.
Suffolk, *see* Newmarket.
Sunderland, co. Durham, 219, 234, 372.
Surat, India, 302.
Surrey, *see* Aldershot, Esher.
Sussex, *see* Hove.
Sutton, 94.
Suva, Fiji Is., Pacific Ocean, 352.
Swansea, Glam., 95.
— Queen's Dock, 269.
Swindon, nr. Doncaster, L.M.S., 49.
Swinhill Colliery, Larkhall, Lanarks., 151.
Swinton Common Colliery, Yorks., 147.
Sydney, N.S. Wales, 241, 360, 364, 367, 376.
Syria, *see* Beirut.
Szechuan, Yangtze R., China, 115.

Tapti R., *see* Bombay.
Tarragona, Spain, 347.
Tebekwe Mine, Salisbury, S. Rhodesia, 274.
Tees, R., Durham–Yorks., 111.
Tembi, Pumping Station (A.P.O.C.), Persia, 164.
Temple Meads Station, Bristol, 102, 315.
Texas, *see* Beaumont.
Thames, R., *see* Tongue Shoal.
Tikak Colliery, Assam, 246.
Tilehurst–Pangbourne Water Co., Berks., 149.
Tilmanstone Colliery, Kent, 260.
Tivetshall Ry. Crossing, Norfolk, 102.
Tongue Sand, 361.
— Shoal, Thames Estuary, 425.
Tonypandy, Glam., *see* Llwynpia Coll.
Townhead Iron Ore Mine, Egremont, Cumberland, 148.
Tramore, Waterford Bay, 5–6.
Transvaal, *see* Germiston, Witwatersrand.
Trimdon Grange Mine, Durham, 299.
Tung Sha Bank, China Sea, 354.
Tunstall, Staffs., 103.
Tweed, Ontario, 118.
Tylacoch, Rhondda, Glam., 92.
Tyne, R., Northumb.–Durham, 429.

INDEX OF PLACES 487

Tynemouth, Northumberland, 68, 296, 311.
Tyneside, 85.
Tynewydd Colliery, Rhondda Valley, Glam., 92.
Tyrone, Ulster, 96. *See also* Ulster.

Uganda, Chua District, 304. *See also* Adilang.
Ulster, 295. *See also* Tyrone.
Umbeyla, NW. India, 10.
United States, *see* Brooklyn.
Upavon, Wilts., 292.
Ushant, France, 61.
Usk, R., Newport, Mon., 237.
Uzon Guards, Marywells, 357.

Vancouver I., B.C., 375. *See also* Cowichan Lake.
— Village I., 403.
Vickers' Works, Sheffield, 49.
Victoria, Australia, *see* Hamilton.
Vigo, Spain, 2.
Vlakfontein, S. Africa, 11.
Volta, R., Gold Coast, 356.

Wadi Adarowfie, Berber Prov., Sudan, 298.
Walkden, nr. Manchester (Farnworth Cotton-Spin. Co.), 50, 265.
Waleswood Colliery, nr. Sheffield, 195.
Wandsworth, London (Metal Powder Works), 231.
Wardley Colliery, *see* Pelaw.
Warley, France, 162.
Warrington, Bank Quay Station, Lancs., 276.
— White Cross Co. Works, 262.
Warwickshire, *see* Cadeby, Newdigate, Rugby.
Waterford, Eire, 5.
Water Haigh Colliery, Oulton, nr. Leeds, 128, 134.
Watford, Explosives Factory, Herts., 195.
Waziristan, NW. India, 291. *See also* Haidari Kach, Khajuri, Kot Kai, Shapur Tangi.
Weddell Sea, Antarctic, 215, 331.
Wellington Barracks, London, 97.
Wellington Pit, *see* Whitehaven.
Wermels-Kirchen, Rhineland, 185.
Wesselton Mine, Kimberley, 228.

West Bromwich, Guest & Sons' Foundry, Staffs., 207.
West Elliot Colliery, Mon., 227.
West Indies, *see* Morant Cays.
Westralia & East Extension Mine, Australia, 101.
Westminster Hall (explosion), London, 96.
Wexford Bay, Catrick Rock, 401.
Whitby, Yorks., 296, 417.
Whitehaven, Wellington Pit, Cumberland, 126.
Whittington Moor, 34.
Widnes, Lancs., 244.
Wilton, River, Ontario, 115.
Wiltshire, *see* Box Station, Devizes, Upavon, Yatesbury.
Wingate, co. Durham, 189.
Witwatersrand Gold Mine, Johannesburg, 122.
— City Deep Gold Mine, 189.
Wizernes, France, 184.
Woburn Sands Brick Works, Beds., 103.
Woodland Colliery, Durham, 194.
Wood Lane Colliery, Horsley, nr. Derby, 191.
Woolwich, R.N. Ord. Depot, 229.
Worcestershire, *see* Redditch.
Workington, Derwent Works, Cumberland, 257.
— United Steel Co. Works, Cumberland, 268.
Wouldham, Kent, 183.
Wye Aerodrome, Kent, 161.

Yangtze R., China, 287. *See also* Szechuan.
Yatesbury, Wilts., 176.
Ynishir Colliery, Glam., 92.
Yorkshire, *see* Askern, Barnsley, Bentley Bradford, Bridlington, Castleford, Frickley Goole, Grimthorpe, Halifax, Hickleton Main, Hoyland, Huddersfield, Hull, Leeds Lodge Mill, Loftus Mine, Lower Wortley Low Moor, Middlesbrough, North Gawber Oulton, Rotherham, Sheffield, Silkstone, South Kirby, Swindon, Swinton, Waleswood, Whitby.

Zabbar, Malta, 105.
Zonnebecke, Belgium, 11.

PART III
GENERAL INDEX

Aboriginal's bravery, 115.
Abyssinia campaign, 10, 222, 305.
Adèle, Fr. barque, 347.
Admiralty, xii, 2, 338, 441; Board of, 309; Register, xii, 309; *see also* War Office.
Adriatic, s.s., 402.
Aerodromes, 168.
Aeroplanes, 156.
Afghanistan campaign, 9.
Afonwen, s.s., 104.
Afridi, 33.
Aidar, s.s., 365.
Air Force Cross (A.F.C.), 14; eligibility for and number, 16; number of awards, 21.
Air Force Medal, x, 20; number of awards, 21; *see also* Royal Air Force.
Air Raids, *see* Flying incidents.
Airship R 101: wreck of, 219.
Albatross, s.s.
Albert Medal, x–xii, 61–2, 65, 91, 382; correspondence, 82–6; first awards, 85–6; description, 86–7; awards in gold, 86–7; for Sea service, 87, 336 ff.; criterion of award, 87; awards to *1938*, 87; awards *1915–19*, 156 ff.; awards *1920–38*, 211 ff.; summary of awards, 119, 309; for Land service, 337.
Albert and Edward Medals, 21, 26–7, 32, 51, 61, 62, 65, 82 ff.
Albuera, *see* Peninsular War.
Algeria, 26.
Alice Marie, s.s., 420–1.
Alicia, barque, 346.
Alicia, schooner, 66.
Alma, battle of, recipients of V.C., 10–11.
Ambrose Lightship, 56–7.
Ambulance Service, 34.
Andaman I., Little, campaign, 9.
Anderson, Sir John, attempted murder of, 301.
Anglo-Persian Oil Co., 164.
Annabella Clark, s.s., 355.
Anne, Queen, gold medals sent by, 2.
Anne, schooner, 347.
Antarctic Expdn., *see* Scott.
Antinoe, s.s., disaster, 67.
Apollo, Imp. Airways aircraft, 303.
Arbeitsfront, German symbol for, 88.
Arctic, barge, 149.
Armada Medal, 1.
Armadale Castle, s.s., 419–20.

Armenia, massacres, 27.
Arracan, barque, 348.
Ascania, s.s., 381.
Ashanti campaign, 9, 10.
Associations: National Fire Brigades, 47; London Private Fire Brigade, 47; Boy Scouts, 47; Girl Guides, 47; *see also* Societies.
Atkinson, E. L., of Scott's Expdn., 116.
Atlantic, Norwegian schooner, 310.
Audacious, H.M.S., 349.
Augusta, schooner, 356.
Augustus Caesar, medal of, 66.
Aurora, Antarctic Expdn., 215, 331.
Aurora, H.M.S., 396.
Ausonia, s.s., 372.
Australia, 35, 96, 98; *see* Humane Society.
Australia–N. Zealand Air Mail, 306.
Avalanche, 101.
Avonmore, vessel, 345, 352.
Awards for Civil Gallantry: Foreign Countries, 26 ff.; Gt. Britain and Europe—on land, 32 ff.;—at sea, 59 ff.
Aztec, s.s., 431.

Bacon, Lord Chancellor, quoted, vii.
Baden, ex-German battleship, 329.
Badges, Forlorn Hope, 1; of Elizabeth and James I, 1; of military merit (U.S.), 25.
Ba La Aung, Burmese schooner, 405.
Baltic campaign, 9.
Baltic, R.M.S., 56–7.
Baltic, s.s., 421.
Baluchistan, 10; earthquake in, 285–8; *see also* Earthquakes.
Bantry Bay, engagement by French fleet, 1.
Baron Colonsay, transport, 353.
Baron Driesen, s.s., 323.
Bastia, capture of, 3.
Basutoland campaign, 9.
Bath, *see* Humane Society.
Bath, *see* Order of.
B.B.C., xii, 89.
Beaconsfield, Lord, correspondence of, 86.
Bean, Rev. Canon W. S., 40.
Belgium: decorations, 26; Carnegie Trust, 69.
Bell, Mr. R., of Hewarth, letter of, 54.
Bend Or, barquentine, 358.
Beothic, s.s., 380.
Bengal, 62; disturbances in, 283–5.
Benvorlich, s.s., 410.

GENERAL INDEX

Beowulf, cited, viii.
Berwickshire, s.s., 342-3.
Biddulph, Sir Thos., 84.
Bilbeis, s.s., 432.
Birkenhead, H.M. Transport, loss of, 6-7; Yule's poem, 7.
Birmingham, Soho Foundry, 4.
Blake, Admiral, Armada medal awarded to, 1.
Blake, s.s., 62.
Bloomfield, oil tanker, 412.
Bluff, fishing-vessel, 419.
Board of Admiralty, *see* Admiralty.
Board of Trade, xii; Medals, 32, 59, 61, 85-6, 309, 382; awards of medals, 307 ff.
Board of Trade Gold and Silver Medals for Foreign Service, 59; awards, 59-60, 337, 382 ff.
Board of Trade Medal for Saving Life at Sea (Sea Gallantry) (S.G.M.), xi, 32, 61, 82, 91, 310, 336, 381 ff., 401 ff.
Board of Trade, awards of plate, &c., 401-2, 404-5, 408, 411, 413, 415, 418, 420, 423-8.
Bolton Humane Soc., 38.
Bomb throwing, 158 ff.
Boulton, Mr. (of Soho Foundry), 1, 3-4.
Bowcher, Frank, medal designer, 58.
Bowen, Canon, 184-5.
Bowes Castle, s.s., 406.
Boy Scouts Association, *see* Associations; Cornwell Scout Badge.
Bradford City Fire Brigade, 161.
Brady, A. N., Memorial fund, 30.
Bramley-Moore Medal (Gold) awards, 65.
Brevet Promotion, 441, 443-4.
Brigade Grenade School, France, 175.
Brigade of Guards Badge, 446.
Brilliant, s.s., 67.
Bristol, *see* Humane Society.
Britannia, H.M.S., 326.
British Empire Medal, *see* Medal of Order of.
British Empire, Order of, *see* Order of B.E.
British Hero Trust Fund, *see* Carnegie Dunfermline Trust.
British King, s.s., 67.
British Legion in Spain, 5.
British Mercantile Marine, *see* Mercantile Mar.
British Possessions in India, 35.
British Seamen's Union, 337-8; Havelock Wilson, 337.
British Valour, s.s., 422.
Bronte, D. of, *see* Nelson.
Bronze Medallion, *see* Carnegie Trust.
Bronze Medals, 3, 25-6, 55: Victoria Cross, 8; Italian, 29; U. States, 30-1; St. John of Jerusalem, 33-4; Roy. Hum. Soc., 34-5, 93; Jersey, 38; Canada, 40; N. Zealand, 41; Fire Brigade, 45-7; Boy Scouts Med. and Cross, 47; Prevention of Cruelty to Animals, 48; Albert and Edward, 51; H.M.S. *Goliath*, 53; B. of Trade, 59-60; Gallantry and Humanity, 61; Govt. of Bengal, 62; Unofficial, 62 ff.; Liverpool Shipwreck and Humane, 64-5; Lloyds, 66-7; Carnegie Medallion, 72, 75; Albert, 86-7; Edward, 89; Congress, Awards of, 309.
Brooke, Raja, *see* Sarawak.
Bubonic plague, Hong Kong, 57.
Buffs, 3rd Foot, 4.
Bulgaria, s.s., 67.
Bulls, attacks by, 110, 125, 130-1.
Burdwan, Maharaja of: medal, 51; letter to *The Times*, 51-2; medal described, 32; successor of, 52.
Burma campaign, 10, 62.
Byng, Adm. Sir George, 2.

Cairnmona, s.s., 405.
Cambrai, attack near, in 1798, 3.
Cambrian Baroness, s.s., 377.
Cambridge, Duke of, 440 f.
Cambridge, s.s., 314.
Camp and Villaverde Medal, 64-5.
Camp, Capt. Bernardino, 65.
Campbell-Bannerman, H., 440 ff.
Canada: campaign, 10; Humane Soc., 35; rare medals, 39-40; Roy. Canadian Humane Assoc., 40; Carnegie awards, 75.
Canton, plague at, 57.
Cape Duner, trawler, 383.
Carlisle, H.M.S., 66.
Carlyle, Thos., quoted, vii.
Carnegie, Andrew: quoted, 69; his explanatory letter, 70-1.
Carnegie Dunfermline Trust (Bequest), 69-70.
Carnegie Hero Trust Fund, 27, 30, 37, 69 ff.; countries in which established, 69-70; Act, 69; constitution of, 70-1; investigation for award, 71-2; types of cases, 72; Roll of, 72-4; awards, 72-3; annuitants, 73; finance of, 73-4; Annual Report for 1936, 74-5; bronze medallion, 75.
Casmona, s.s., 67.
Cecil Junior, schooner, 413.
Central Chancery, xii.
Certificate of Honour (Order of St. John), 33.
Challenger, H.M.S., 350.
Charity Commissioners, 46.
Charles I at Edgehill, 1.
'Charlie the Gunner', *see* Fitzpatrick.
Cherwell, H.M.S., 401.
Chester, H.M.S., 47.
China: medals awarded in, x; campaigns, 9-10; disturbances in, 285.

Chinese and plague, 57.
Chitral campaign, 10.
Christchurch, N.Z., 40.
Christian martyrs, viii.
City of Cairo, s.s., 380.
City of Lahore, s.s., 416.
City of Manchester, s.s., 349.
Civil awards, xi.
Civil Contingencies Fund, 60.
Civil Gallantry, 1-2; awards in Gt. Britain and Empire—on land, 32 ff.;—at sea, 59 ff.
Clan Macvicar, s.s., 409.
Clio, H.M.S., 343.
Clovelly, s.s., 411.
Coast-guards, H.M., 61.
Coburg, Duke of, 27.
Collections of medals: National Maritime Mus., Greenwich, 4; British Museum, 35, 38-9, 51-3, 55, 62, 67; Château de Ramezay, 39, 40; H. of Commons, 39-40, 43, 46, 52-3, 67-8, 87, 356; Canada, 62; *see also* Museum.
Collett, Capt. C. H., at Imbros Aerodrome, 156.
Collieries, *see* Index of Places.
Colonies, 63; *see also* Dominions.
Columbia, District of, 30.
Comet, H.M.S., 327.
'Common Employment, Doctrine of', 50.
'Common Good' Fund, Glasgow Corporation, 43.
Compadre, of Liverpool, 35.
Companionate of Honour, xi.
Conference, vessel, 352.
Congress, U.S., *see* Medals granted by.
Connaught, Duke of, 442 ff.
Conspicuous Gallantry Cross, suggested name, x.
Conspicuous Gallantry Medal (Navy) (C.G.M.), x, 19-20; annuities, 19; awards of, to 1920, 20.
Conspicuous Service Cross (C.S.C.), *see* Distinguished S.C. (D.S.C.).
Conway, H.M.S., 68.
Cornwell Scout Badge, conditions and awards, 47.
Coronation, The (1937), invitation of medallists to, 88.
Corsica, I., attack on, 3.
Count de Mercy, inscription on tomb, 76.
Courage, definition of, vii, viii, ix.
Courier de Dieppe, lugger, 340.
C Q D signal, *see* S O S.
Crane, steam trawler, 366.
Crete campaign, 10.
Cretetree, barge, 414.
Crimean War, 8-9, 19.
Crixea, barque, 362.
Crocodiles, 42.

Croix de Guerre, 23.
Croix du Combattant, 23.
Cross of Honour, Iron (German), 24-5.
Cruz de Beneficencia (Spanish), 30.
Czarina, barquentine, 405.

Dagmar, tug, 346.
Daily Herald Order of Industrial Heroism, 48; awards, 49, 50.
Dalton, s.s., 402.
Daring, H.M.S., 313.
Davison, Mr. (Nelson's prize agent), medals presented by, 1, 3.
Davy, trawler, 383.
Dayaks, 42-3.
Decorations, conditions of award of, 1 ff., 441; *see* specific Medals and Orders.
Décoration Civique, 26.
Denmark: compensation to workers, 26; Carnegie Trust, 69.
Dennis T. Sullivan, fire-boat, 103.
Devonshire, H.M.S., 283, 333.
De Zelada, Cardinal, *see* Pius VI.
Diamond, pilgrim ship, 339.
Dienstauszeichnung (Service Medal), 25.
Di Vernon, s.s., 343.
Dilke, Adm., squadron of, 2.
Disasters: colliery, 92, 126; at sea, 61, 67.
Distinguished Conduct Medal (D.C.M.), *see* Medal for.
Distinguished Flying Cross (D.F.C.), x, 16, 437 f.; number of awards to 1938, 21.
Distinguished Flying Medal (D.F.M.), x, 20; number of awards, 21.
Distinguished Service Cross (D.S.C.), x, 14, 448; eligibility for and awards, 16; replaces C.S.C., 16; grounds for amalgamation with M.C., 16.
Distinguished Service Medal (D.S.M.), x, 443; table, 18; eligibility for, 20.
Distinguished Service Medal, Indian (I.D.S.M.), 14, 18; eligibility for, 20.
Distinguished Service Order (D.S.O.), x, 9, 14; table of awards during Gt. War, 15; complete record since 1886, 15; gratuity, 15-16; counterparts, 17; specific holders of, 156, 166, 180, 211; correspondence *re*, 440-50.
Dolon incident (*Iliad*), viii.
Dominions, 16, 62, 88; *see* Colonies.
Donegal, H.M.S., 102, 315.
Dorothy Baird, schooner, 422.
Dragoons, *see* Light Dragoons.
Drake, Sir Francis, 1.
Druid, H.M.S., 370.
Drummond Castle, s.s., disaster 1896, medals, 61.

GENERAL INDEX

Dryden, quoted, 23.
Dudley, Earl of, 33–4.
Duke, fire-ship, 2.
Dunraven Castle, trawler, 423.

Earl of Forfar, s.s., 319–20, 323, 368.
Earthquakes: Quetta, 32–3, 221–2; Baluchistan, 220 ff.; Messina, 29, 104; Chile, 352–3.
Eastcote House, *see* British Seamen's Union.
East India Company medals, 1, 18, 59.
Ecclesiasticus quoted, vii, 336–7.
Eclipse, s.s., 360.
Edgehill, battle of, 1.
Edinburgh, Duke of, 444.
Edward VII, 69; Royal Warrant of, 87–8.
Edward Medal (E.M.), xi–xiii, 62, 65, 87 ff., 382; awards to 1937, 88; awards to date, 89; pecuniary grants, 88–9; extended scope of, 91; individual awards, 120–155; *1920–38*, 226–78.
Egremont Castle, s.s., 406.
Egypt: campaign, 10; murder of Sir L. Stack, 295.
Ehrenzeichen (Mark of Honour), 28.
Eider, French schooner, 311.
Elf King, trawler, 427.
Eliott, Gen., and defence of Gibraltar, 3.
Elise, s.s., 362.
Elizabeth, Queen, honorary badges, 1.
Ellis, Arthur, Col., correspondence, 445 ff.
Ellis, Miss, missionary, 33.
Emeu, P. & O. s.s., 85, 340.
Emerson quoted, vii.
'Emile Robin' Trust, terms of, 64.
Emilio, brig, 64.
Empire Gallantry Medal (E.G.M.), *see* Medal of Order of British Empire, Civil Division, for Gallantry; *and* Medal of Order of British Empire, Military Division, for Gallantry.
Endymion, s.s., 247–8.
Engadine, H.M.S., 316.
England, number of Carnegie awards, 75.
Ennerdale, of Liverpool, 359.
Ethiopia, *see* Abyssinia.
Euryalus, H.M.S., 10.
Évadés (Escaped Prisoners') Medal, 23.
Evans, Capt. E. R. G. R. (Adm. Sir), 66, 116.
Evans, Gen. de Lacy, in Spain, 5.
Expert, fishing-smack, 355.
Explosions: Ferozepore, 113–14; Silvertown, 195; Faversham, 197.
Explosives, 194 ff.

Faithful, schooner, 401.
Fenian outrage, Westminster Hall, 96.
Fenian Raid, Canada, 8.

Fernebo, s.s., of Christinehaven, 296–7.
Ferozepore, *see* Explosions.
Firdausi cited, viii.
Firemen, awards to, 40, 46, 90.
Fire Brigades: New York, 30; Report of Committee on (L.C.C.), 44–5; West Ham Corporation, 46; National Assocn. of, 46; London Assocn. of Private, 46; *see also* London County Council.
Fire Brigade Medals: King's, xi; German, 28; District of Columbia, 30; New York, 30; L.C.C. silver, 33, 43–5; Montreal, 39; London Private F. Brig. Assocn., 44; Metropolitan, 44–5; bronze, 46; Liverpool Shipwreck and Humane, 64; *see also* London County Council.
Fitzpatrick, Charles: 'Charlie the Gunner', career of, 54–5.
Florida, Italian s.s., collision, 56–7.
Flying incidents, 172 f.
Flying Scud, fishing-boat, 350.
Foam, H.M.S., 312.
Foam Queen, river-boat, 425.
Foch, Marshal, *Méd. Militaire*, 23.
Foreign Orders: military, 23–5; civil, 26–31.
Forlorn Hope Badge of Charles I, 1.
France, 23; decorations and medals, 26–7; Carnegie Trust, 69; War incidents in, 161 ff.
Frances Duncan, collier, 420.
Fraser, Sir Andrew, Lt.-Gov. Bengal, 52.
Frontier Force, India, 17.
Führer Service Med., 25.

Gallantry, Civil: foreign countries, 26 ff.; Gt. Britain and Empire, 32 ff.; notice to press about King's Medals, 91.
Gallantry, Military: Gt. Britain and Empire, 1 ff.; foreign, 23 ff.
Gallantry at sea, 59 ff., 91, 309 ff.
Gallina, s.s., 67.
Gambia campaign, 10.
Garrard, Mr. (Crown Jeweller), designs of medals, 445 ff.
Garter, *see* Order of.
Gay Gordon, s.s., 404.
Geneva, American vessel, 353.
Geneva Badge, 446.
George I, early silver medal, 2.
George II, 2, 66.
George III, 1, 3; medal and gold chain awarded by, 4; and Joseph Hanson, 56.
George V, 32, 63.
George Albert, drifter, 415.
German seamen, 337.
Germany: military crosses, 24–5; civil decorations, 27; Carnegie Trust, 69.
Germany, Emperor of, gold medal of 1798, 3.

Gettysburg, barque, 360.
Gibraltar, defence of, 3.
Gibson, Mr. Milner, 82–3.
Girl Guides Association, awards of, 47.
Gladstone, Mr. Herbert, Home Sec., 88.
Glanusk Park, Crickhowell, Hemy's picture at, 7.
Glasgow Corporation: medals of, xii, 43; 'Bravery Medal', 43; *see also* Humane Society; 'Common Good' Fund.
Glasgow Bravery Medal, *see* Glasgow.
Glasgow, s.s., 66.
Glatton, H.M.S., 326–8.
Glendower, s.s., 67.
Gold Medals: Charles I to Robert Welsh, 1; Queen Anne, 2; to Capt. Collis, 2; Pope Pius VI, 3; Emp. Germany, 3; Bat. of Nile, 3; Geo. III, 4; Albuera, 4–5, 25, 26; Italian, 29; Swedish, 30; U. States, 30–1; Kaisar-i-Hind, 33; St. John of Jerusalem, 33–4; Stanhope, 35–6; Jersey Hum. Soc., 38; Roy. Canadian Hum. Ass., 40; N. Zealand, 41, 51, 53, 54–5, 57, 60; Board of Trade, 59–60, 61; unofficial awards, 62–3; Liverpool Shipwreck, 64–5; Lloyds, 1921, 66; Albert, 86–7; suggestion for Edward, 89; Salford Hum. Soc., 93; R.N. Life-Boat Inst., 296–7; Congress awards of, 307–13; for foreign service, 403.
Goliath, training-ship, destruction by fire, 51–2; *see* Burdwan, Maharaja of.
Grafton, H.M.S., 375.
Grantham, Mr. Justice, 55.
Gratuities, *see* Monetary Awards.
Great City, s.s., salvage operations, 200–1.
Great War, 10, 21–2, 23–4, 88, 337, 368, 370; awards, 14, 15, 16; awards *1914–18*, 156.
Greece, Ancient, vii, viii.
Green, Lt., monetary award to, 2.
Greenwich National Mar. Mus., *see* Museum.
Grenades, 178–9.
Grey, General, 82–3.
Grey, Lord, 59.
Guiding Star, schooner, 415.
Gull, steam trawler, 366.
Gustavus Adolphus IV of Sweden, medal, 30.

Hammonia, s.s., 67.
Hamstead Colliery fire, 53.
Hannen Swaffer, *see Daily Herald*.
Hanoverian Brigade, 3.
Hanson, Joseph, 'Weavers' Friend', account of, 55–6.
Hardy, Capt., Medal, 1, 4.
Harlaw, of Aberdeen, 354.
Harriet, brigantine, 356.
Harriet, s.s., 87.

Hartley colliery disaster, special medals, 52–3.
Havelock Wilson, *see* British Seamen's Union.
Hawes, Dr., and resuscitation, 34.
Health Insurance, 338.
Hecla, H.M.S., 10.
Hemy, Thos. M. M., painter, 7.
Henry VIII, 120.
Herald newspaper, Montreal, fire at, 39.
Hermina, motor schooner, 297.
Herodotus quoted, 76.
Highflyer, H.M.S., 321–2.
Himalaya Expdn., 217–18.
Hindenburg, President von, 24, 27.
Hollinside, s.s., 404.
Holmes Safety Awards, U.S., 30–1.
Holyrood, 450.
Home Office, xii, 50, 95; awards, 315.
Home Secretary, 86, 88–9, 309.
Hong Kong Plague Medal, 57–8.
Hong Kong typhoon, 406–7.
Hong Moh, s.s., 66.
Honorary badges, *see* Elizabeth; James I.
Hood, H.M.S., 284.
Hope, H.M.S., 315.
Hopelyn, s.s., 297.
Horace quoted, 82.
Hornsey, s.s., 372.
House of Commons, *see* Collections.
Howe, trawler, wreck of, 425–7.
Hull, *see* Humane Society.
Humane Societies, list of, 38–9.
Humane Society, Bath, 37.
— — Bristol, 35–6.
— — Glasgow, 33, 36–7, 73.
— — Hull, 38.
— — Jersey, 38; awards, 38.
— — Liverpool Shipwreck and, 33, 64; awards, 65.
— — Royal, xi, 33 ff., 55, 93; medals of, 34; offices of, 34; awards, 35; report of and list of Societies, 38–9.
— — Royal, Australia (Australasia), 35–6, 40.
— — Royal, Canada, 35–6, 40; *see also* Canada.
— — Royal, New Zealand, 35–6, 40–1.
— — Rym Lynter and Tavy, 38.
— —, for Salford Hundred, 36.
— — Southampton, 37.
— — Vale of Leven, Scotland, 37–8.
Hunter, H.M.S., 291, 335.
Hwah Ping, Chinese s.s., 406.

Idaho, s.s., 355.
Ierne, lights vessel, 401.
Iliad quoted, viii.
Ida, ketch, 310.
Imanol, s.s., 237.

GENERAL INDEX

Immortalité, H.M.S., 351, 362.
Imo, Norwegian s.s., 321, 327.
Imperial Airways, 301.
Imperialist, vessel, 426.
India: NW. Frontier, 9; Naga Hills, 10, 35, 62, 63.
India, Viceroy of, *see* Viceroy.
Indian Distinguished Service Medal (I.D.S.M.), *see* Distinguished Serv. Med., Indian.
Indian Order of Merit (I.O.M.), *see* Order of Merit, Indian.
Indian Police Medal, *see* Police Medal.
Individual Medal, *see* Burdwan.
Insigne des blessés et réformés, 23.
Ireland, 5; Carnegie awards, 75.
Iron Cross, *see* Cross of Honour.
Iron Medal, *see* Hardy.
Isabella Hall, schooner, 361.
Italy: decorations, 29; Carnegie Trust, 69.
Italy, King of, special medal, 29.

Jacques La Blonde, privateer, 2.
James I, honorary badges, 1.
Janie E. Blackwood, fishing schooner, 420.
Japan: campaign awards, 10; Medal, 29.
Jean Jadot, Belgian s.s., 381.
Jennings, U.S. oil carrier, 373.
Jericho, 'Garden of roses' symbol, 48.
Jersey, *see* Humane Society.
Jerusalem, *see* Order of St. John of.
Joffre, Marshal, *Méd. Militaire*, 23.
Joffre, steam tug, 408.
Johnson, Dr., quoted, ix.
Joyce, John, Pres. N.Z. Hum. Soc., 40.
Jutland, battle of, 47, 316.

Kaffir War awards, 10.
Kaisar-i-Hind Gold Medal, 33.
Kassala campaign awards, 10.
Keates, F. W., wireless operator, bravery of, 383.
Kersal Moor, *see* Hanson, Joseph.
Khartoum awards, 10.
Kian, s.s., 285.
Kiatung, s.s., 287.
King George V, H.M.S., 414.
Kingsford-Smith, Sir Charles, Air Mail flight, 306.
Kingstown (Dublin) Motor Life-Boat, 63
Kinloss, schooner, 344.
Kipling quoted, 382.
Kitchener, Lord, and D.S.C., 16.

Labour Gazette, Ministry of, 89.
Laches quoted, viii.
Lady Blake, s.s., 62, 405.

Lady Mathieson, fishing-smack, 363.
Laleham, s.s., 411.
Lancashire Life-Saving Society, 39.
Lansbury, Mr. George, 49.
Lawrence, R.I.M.S., 367.
Laws, The, quoted, viii.
Lechmere, Sir E., and Ambulance, 33–4.
Lee, lighter, 322.
Légion d'Honneur, 23.
Leicestershire, s.s., Bibby L., 111.
Leven, Vale of, *see* Humane Soc.
Lewis, Matthew, school teacher, bravery of, 109.
Liberia, steam trawler, 415.
Life-Boat Institution, Royal National, xi, 62–3, 73, 296–7; medals and awards of, 62–3.
Life-boat service, 194–5.
Life-saving Medal (Order of St. John), 33.
Light Dragoons, *see* Bastia.
Lily, H.M.S., 311.
Limesdale, steam trawler, 413.
Liverpool Shipwreck and Humane Soc., *see* Societies; Bramley-Moore Medal.
Lloyds Medal: for Saving Life at Sea, 65–7; for Services to Lloyds, 67; for Meritorious Service, 67.
London County Council, xii; Silver Medal, 33; Fire Brigade Medal, 43–5; Report of Fire Brigade, 44–5; *see also* Fire Brigades.
London deeds of gallantry by Londoners, 76–9; *see* Watts, G. F.
London, Corporation of City of, xiii.
Londoners, *see* London deeds.
London Gazette, xii, 59, 89, 95, 337, 383, 448.
London Private Fire Brigade Association, *see* Associations.
Loonsang, s.s., 406.
Lord Antrim, s.s., 420.
Lord of the Isles, brig, 362.
Lord Melville, transport, wreck of, 6.
Low Wood, barque, 358.
Luis, s.s., 371.
Lumina, s.s., 422.
Lusitania, sinking of, 7.
Lygden, Russian s.s., 66.

Mahsuds, 11.
Maid of Orleans, s.s., 342.
Maine, s.s., ammunition ship, 156.
Maitenes II, yacht, 423.
Malabar, insurrection in, 281.
Malta, s.s. *Sardinia* on fire off, 66.
Maltese, 15, 16, 19.
Manchester, 36, 50, 55; Corporation Medal, xii, 46.
Manchester Regiment, s.s., 418.
Mandated Territories, x.

494 GENERAL INDEX

Man-eating tiger, 216.
Manipur (NE. India) campaign, 10.
Manistee, s.s., 418.
Margaret Wheatley Cross (R.S.P.C.A.), 48.
Margerie, M. de, gold medal to, 27.
Maria Theresian Cross, 446.
Marie, steam drifter, 367.
Marmion, of N. Shields, 342.
Martyrs, *see* Christian.
Mary, *see* William III.
Mary, galley, 2.
Mary Jones, motor schooner, 425.
Massilia, s.s., 363.
Matabeleland campaign, 10.
Max Müller, 441.
McMurdo Sound, *see* Shackleton Expdn.
Médaille des Épidémies, 26.
Médaille Militaire, 23.
Médaille de la Reconnaissance Française, 23.
Médaille de Sauvetage ou de Dévouement, 26.
Medal for Deeds of Valour (Sweden), 30.
Medal for Distinguished Conduct in the Field (D.C.M.), x, 20, 168, 444; table of, 18; eligibility and awards during Gt. War, 19.
Medal for Escaped Prisoners (*Évadés*), 23.
Medal for Foreign Services (1839), 60–2.
Medal for Gallantry and Humanity, 60–1.
Medal of India Total Abstinence Association, 35.
Medal for Life Saving (Poland), 29.
Medal for Meritorious Service (1845), *see* Meritorious Service Medal.
Medalha de Merito (Portuguese), 30.
Medal of Order of British Empire, Civil Div., for Gallantry (E.G.M.), x, xi, 8, 14, 21–2, 26, 32–3, 51, 61–2; individual awards down to 1938, 293–306.
Medal of Order of British Empire, Military Div., for Gallantry (E.G.M.), x, xi, 8, 14, 21–2, 32–3, 61–2; individual awards 1923–38, 281–90.
Medal of Order of British Empire, Civil Div., for Meritorious Service (B.E.M.), 18, 32–3.
Medal of Order of British Empire, Military Div., for Meritorious Service, 14, 21–2, 32–3.
Medal with Red Riband (Japan), 29.
Medals: table of, 18; special Messina, 29; classes of, 60–1; *see also* Gold Medals, Silver M., Bronze M.
Medals granted by Congress, 25; Appendix I, 433–9.
Mediator, H.M.S., Medal to officers of, 4.
Mélanie, French s.s., 354.
Melpomene, H.M.S., 316.

Melville Dollar, s.s., 375.
Memorial plaques, *see* St. Botolph's Churchyard.
Mercantile Marine Fund, 84, 86; Service Association, 67.
Merchant Shipping Acts, 59, 84, 338, 382.
Mercy, Count de, *see* Count de.
Merit, *see* Order of Merit.
Meritorious Service Medal (1845), xi, 19, 22; annuity, 22; number of recipients, 22.
Messina: special medal, 29; earthquake, 104.
Metropolitan Fire Brigade Bill, 45–6.
Military Cross (M.C.), x, 15, 156; gratuities, 15–16; awards during Gt. War, 16; monetary rewards, 21.
Military Medal (M.M.), x, 32, 168, 179, 185, 281; eligibility of women, 14; table, 18; awards during Gt. War, 20; awards since May 1920, 20.
Militia, 17.
Miners, eligibility, 22; Welfare Fund, 29.
Mines, Mining, 30–1; Royal Commission on, 88.
Ministry of Labour Gazette, *see Labour Gaz.*
Mint, Royal, 59; care of dies, 60.
Mixol, R.F.A., 324.
Mohmand tribesmen, 13.
Monarch, s.s., 149–50.
Monetary awards, x, 1–2, 14–16, 22, 65, 407; Victoria Cross, 8, 21.
Monk, General, Armada Medal to, 1.
Mont Blanc, French s.s., 321, 327.
Montcalm, s.s., 428.
Monthyon, Baron de, Prizes, 27.
Montreal: Corporation of, 39; Champ de Mars, 40.
Morin, Monsieur Victor, 39.
Morris, Major, Ch. Off. Fire Brig., 45.
Motor Life-boat, *see* Life-boat.
Mottoes of Orders, 14–15.
Munition factories, fire at, 161, 194.
Museum, National Maritime, Greenwich, 4; American, of Safety, 30; *see* Collections.
Musquash, tug, 321–2.
Mutiny, Indian, Medal, 1; awards, 9–10.
Myrmidon, H.M.S., 344.
Myrtle, H.M.S., 329.

Nairn, steam trawler, 424.
Nancy Lee, schooner, 410.
Napoleon I: surrender on H.M.S. *Bellerophon*, 5; wars, 7.
National Fire Brigades Association, medal of, 47.
Naval Court Martial, 6–7.
Naval General Service Medal, 4.

GENERAL INDEX

Naval and Military Decoration, *see* Victoria Cross.
Nelson, Adm. Lord, 3–4, 63.
Newbrough, s.s., 430.
Newcastle and Gateshead Chemical Company, 96.
Newton, Isaac, Master of Mint, 2.
New York, 57; Fire Department, 30; Police Department, 30; Electric Inst., 30.
New Zealand, 9; Carnegie Awards, 75; *see* Humane Society, Royal, New Zealand.
Nicias, in *Laches*, viii.
Nigeria campaign, 10.
Nile: battle of, 3–4; campaign, 10; flood, 299.
Niobe, H.M.C.S., 321, 327.
Nördlinger, battle of, 76.
Nore, mutiny at, 3.
Norfolk Humane Soc., 38.
Norseman, s.s., 430.
Norsemen, religion of, vii.
Northcote, Sir Stafford, 83–4.
Northern Light, schooner, 421.
Norway: Carnegie Trust, 69; Norwegian wireless operators, 427.
Nouveau Caboteur, French ship, 343.
Nova Scotia, s.s., 420.
Nubia, s.s., rescue of crew of, 62.
Numismatic Society of Canada, 39.
Nurses, nursing sisters, 13–14, 57.

Odyssey, quoted, 66.
Oku, steam trawler, 413.
Olivae, steam drifter, 431.
Omdurman campaign, 10.
O'Moore Creagh, Sir N. (C.-in-C. India), 8, 15; *see also* Bibliography.
Ontario, *see* Tornado.
Order of the Bath, 440 ff.
Order of British Empire (O.B.E.), 8, 32.
Order of British Empire, Civil and Military Divisions, for Gallantry (E.G.M.), *see* Medal of Order, &c.
Order of British Empire, Civil and Military Divisions for Meritorious Service (B.E.M.), *see* Medal of Order, &c.
Order of British India (O.B.I.), 17; additional pay, 17; number of living holders, 17.
Order of Garter, 337, 440.
Order of Industrial Heroism, *see Daily Herald*.
Order of Merit (O.M.), xi, 15, 440.
Order of Merit, Indian (I.O.M.), 1; classes, 13; record and number of awards, 17–18.
Order of St. John of Jerusalem, *see* St. John of, &c.
Order of St. Michael and St. George, 449.
Order of St. Patrick, 337.
Order of the Thistle, 337.

Orders of Knighthood, vii, xii; list of British, 1 ff.; table of, 14; foreign, 23 ff.; *see* specific Order; Mottoes.
Oregon Star, s.s., 429.
Oruro, s.s., 404.
Orvieto, s.s., 412.
Osborne, Royal Yacht, 443 f.

Palestine, operations in, 289–90.
Palme, barque, 296.
Parliament, orders given by, 1.
Passfield, Lord, 50.
Passmore Edwards, Mr., and Watts, G. F., 80.
Paul Beau, s.s., 376.
Pecuniary awards, *see* Monetary.
Peggy, schooner, 311.
Penarth, H.M.S., 328.
Peninsular War, 4–5.
Pennsylvania Railroad, medals of, 30.
Perak campaign, 10.
Persia campaign, 10.
Peshawar, s.s., 364.
Pétain, Marshal, *Méd. Militaire*, 23.
Phillips, Col., *see* Hanson, Jos.
Phillips, Mr., of Cockspur Str., and preparation of medals, 85.
Phipps, Sir Charles, 82–3.
Picton, General, medal struck by, 3.
Pistrucci, Benedetto, engraver, 60.
Pit fires, 126–7.
Pittsburgh, U.S.A., and Carnegie Trust, 69.
Pius VI, Pope, gold medals of, 3.
Plague Medal, *see* Hong Kong.
Pleiades, s.s., 357.
Plato cited, viii.
Plutarch quoted, vii.
Poland, *see* Medal for Life Saving.
Police Force, *see* Police Medals.
———, Indian, 297–8.
Police Medals: Columbia, 30; King's (old), 32, 82 ff.; Indian, 32; King's, xi–xiii, 82, 89–90; awards down to 1938, 90; conditions of award, 90–1.
Polpedn, s.s., 368.
Ponsonby, Sir Henry, 440 ff.
Poor Law Institutions, 52.
Portugal, Decoration of, 30.
Poseidon, H.M. Subm., 334.
Power, Eileen, quoted, 120.
'Postmen's Park', *see* St. Botolph's.
Poulsen mast, 165.
Press Home, steam drifter, 407.
Prevention of Cruelty to Animals, Royal Society for, *see* Societies.
Prince Consort, Field-Marshal, Royal Warrant of, 8, 82, 86.
Prince of Wales, *see* Albert and Edward Medals.

GENERAL INDEX

Prisoner of War, 162.
Prix de Vertu, 27.
Prizes, *see* Monthyon, Baron de.
Protection of Life from Fire, Society for, *see* Societies.
Proton, s.s., 324.
Prussia, *see* Germany.
Public recognition, lack of, xiii.
Punjabis, 28th, 12–13.

Quaco Queen, motor schooner, 418.
Quarrymen, eligibility of, 88.
Quetta, *see* Earthquakes.

Raja of Sarawak, *see* Sarawak.
Ranger, brig, 357.
Rapid, H.M.S., 347.
Red Cross Association (German), 27.
Red Cross Decoration (German), 27.
Red Labour Banner (U.S.S.R.), Order of, 31.
Redoubtable, Fr. ship (Trafalgar), metal from, for medals, 4.
Regiment, 91st, 6–7.
Registers of various Orders, xii; B. of Trade MS. register, 384.
Reichsfeuerwehrabzeichen (Fire Brigade Med.), 27–8.
Reichsgrubenabzeichen (Mining Med.), 27–9.
Reindeer I, steam tug, 428.
Republic, R.M.S., collision and sinking of, 56–7.
Resuscitation of drowned, 34.
Rettungsmedaillen (Life Saving Med.), 27–8.
Rhydwen, s.s., 369.
Ria, schooner, 431.
Ribands, 8, 9.
Richmond, Sir W., R.A., 81.
Robin, Emile, *see* 'Emile Robin' Trust.
Rob Roy, T.B.D., 330.
Rocket Life Saving Apparatus medals, 61.
Rohilla, Govt. Hosp. steamer, rescues from, 296.
Rome, Ancient, viii.
Ross Sea, *see* Shackleton Expdn.
Royal Air Force: 14, 20; gallantry in, 282–3; *see also* Air Force Medal; Royal Flying Corps.
Royal Commission on Mines, *see* Mines, Mining.
Royal Cypher, 59.
Royal Engineers and Hong Kong plague, 57.
Royal Flying Corps, 157–8.
Royal Humane Society, *see* Humane Society, Royal.
Royal Marines, 5, 19, 86.
Royal Mint, 59–60; *see* Wyon.

Royal National Life-Boat Inst., *see* Life-Boat Inst.
Royal Navy, 2, 16, 19, 20, 86, 443–4, 448; gallantry in, 281–2.
Royal Red Cross (R.R.C.), 13; awards during Gt. War, 14.
Royal Warrants: *1813*, 4; *1856*, 8; *1898 and 1920*, 8; *1931*, 9; texts of, 14; *1916*, 15; and D.S.O., 15; and C.S.C. *1901*, 16, 19, 59; I.D.S.M., 20; of Q. Victoria *1894*, 40; *1866*, 82, 87, 337; *1909*, 89–90.
R.S.P.C.A., *see* Margaret Wheatley; Societies.
Russell, victory at La Hogue, 1.
Russell, William Howard, correspondent of *The Times*, 8.
Russian Baltic Fleet incident, 1904, 366–7.
Rym Lynter and Tavy Humane Society, *see* Humane Society.

St. Botolph's Churchyard, Aldersgate, xiii; Watts Memorial, 76; list of plaques in, 76–9, 89; *see* Watts, G. F.
St. Christopher, Legend of, 48.
St. Francis of Assisi, 120.
St. George and Dragon (on coinage), 60.
St. John of Jerusalem, Order of, 33–4, 67, 73; Grand Prior of, 33; Report of Chapter-General, 34; Offices of, 33.
St. Laurent, French troopship, 370.
St. Patrick, *see* Order of.
St. Sebastian, steam trawler, loss of, 383–4.
St. Tropez naval action, 2.
St. Vincent, Adm. Earl, 3.
Salford, Hundred of, *see* Humane Soc.
Salmon, T.B.D., 314.
Salta, H.M.Hosp.S., 370.
Sanderson, P.S., *see* Bell, Mr. R.
Sandwich, Lord, gift of medals to Nat. Mar. Museum, 4.
Sarawak Medal for Conspicuous Bravery, 41–2; award names, 42–3.
Sardinia, s.s., on fire, 66.
Scandinavian sagas, viii.
Scotland, Carnegie awards, 75.
Scott, Lt., *see Sea Horse*.
Scott's Antarctic Expedition, 116, 315.
Sea Gallantry Medal (S.G.M.), xii, xiii, 59 ff., 382 ff.; awards *1920–38*, 60; *1854–1921*, 382; *1922–38*, 401.
Sea Horse, transport, wreck of, 5–6.
Sealby, Capt., *see Republic*, R.M.S.
Seaplanes, 165.
Selection for Medals, principle of, 2–3.
Selma Creaser, s.s., 416.
Seneca quoted, 1.

GENERAL INDEX

Shackleton Trans-Antarctic Expedition, 215-16, 331.
Serbian Army, 166.
Shah-in-Shah, brig, 62.
Shipwrecked Fishermen and Mariners' Society, *see* Societies.
Shirvan, s.s., 411.
Shropshire Light Infantry and Hong Kong Plague, 57.
Shuna, s.s., 369.
Sidney, Sir Philip, ix.
Silver Crosses: Boy Scouts, 47; Girl Guides, 47.
Silver Medals: Anne, 2; George I, 2; Nore, 3; to Hanoverian Brigade at Gibraltar, 3; Mr. Davison, 3; E.G.M., 21, 32 ff.; Germ. Service Medal, 25; Méd. de Sauvetage, 26; Italian, 29; Japan, 29; U.S. and Congress, 30-1, App. I; Sweden, 30; St. John of Jerusalem, 33-4, 67; Humane Societies, 34 ff., 93; Canada, 39; New Zealand, 41; Sarawak, 41; L.C.C. Fire Brigade, 44-6; London Private Fire Brig. Assoc., 47; S.P.C.A., 48; Albert, 51; Edward, 51, 88; Burdwan, 51; Hartley Colliery, 53; Hamstead Colliery, 53; Hong Kong Plague, 57; Gallantry at Sea, 59 ff.; Liverpool Shipwreck, table of awards, 65; Lloyds, 66-7; King's Police, 89-90.
Silver Spray, s.s., 67.
Silvertown disaster, 46.
Silver plate, gifts of, 402, 404-5, 408, 411, 413, 418, 420, 423, 424-5, 428.
Silver watches, gifts of, 46, 72.
Sirius, German brig, 67.
Smillie, Robert, 88.
Smith, Mr. W. H., 440 ff.
Societies: Protection of Life from Fire (London), 45-6, 73; Royal, for Prevention of Cruelty to Animals, 47; Shipwrecked Fishermen and Mariners', 63; Liverpool Shipwreck and Humane, 33, 64-5, 73; *see also* Associations.
Soho, fire in, 44.
Soho Foundry (Birmingham), 4.
Solomon, Wisdom of, quoted, 26.
Somaliland campaign, 9.
S O S signal, 57.
South African War, 9, 107.
Southampton Charitable Dispensary, 37, 49-50; *see also* Humane Society.
Southern Cross, motor vessel, 430.
Spain: decorations of, 30; non-intervention incident, 291.
Spaniards, action with, off C. Passaro, 2.
Spanish River, Ontario, 106.
Spartans, viii.
Special Medals: Messina, 29; 52; 61.

Spirit of the Ocean, barque, 339.
Stack, Sir Lee, murder of, 297.
Staffordshire, s.s., 365.
Stanhope, Capt. C. S. S., 35.
Stanhope Gold Medal, 35.
Star and jewel to Sir F. Drake, 1.
Success, H.M.S., 97, 314.
Sudan: campaign, 10; 297.
Sunderland, tug, 323.
Sutlej Campaign Medal, 83.
Sweden: medal of, 30; Carnegie Trust, 69.
Swinburne quoted, 337.
Switzerland, Carnegie Trust, 69.
Syria, emigrant ship, 358.

Tahiti, s.s., 403.
Taurus, H.M.S., 283.
Tavy, *see* Rym Lynter.
Tayleur, emigrant ship, wreck of, 63.
Tayleur Fund, 63.
Tearaght, s.s., 294.
Teaser, schooner, 296.
Terzah, ship, 343.
Teutonic, R.M.S., 364.
Thermopylae, viii.
Thetis, barque, 341.
Thistle, *see* Order of the.
Thomas Hardy, s.s., 427.
Thunderer, H.M.S., 355-6.
Tibet campaign, 10.
Tidal, s.s., 402.
Tiger, H.M.S., 211, 330.
Times, The, quoted, xiii, 45-6, 52, 61; Watts's letter to, 79-80.
Torbay, H.M.S., at Vigo, 2.
Tornado in Ontario, 114.
Total Abstinence Association, India, 35.
Trafalgar, battle of, and medal, 3-4.
Transylvania, transport, 371.
Travessa, s.s., 67.
Trentwood, s.s., 417.
Treasury, the, xii.
Trenches, bravery in, 161-2.
Tritonia, s.s., 378.
Trojanstar, vessel, 416.
Tudor Prince, s.s., 67.
Tuscan Prince, s.s., 403.
Tweed, R.M.S., 65.

U-boats, 24.
Umbeyla, NW. India, campaign 1863, 10.
U.S.S.R., *see* Red Labour Banner.
Unemployment Insurance, 338.
United States: medals of, 25, 30-1; citizen, 67; and Carnegie Hero Trust, 69; *see* Congress.
Unofficial agencies for award of medals, list of, 33.

Unofficial awards for gallantry, 62 ff.
Usworth, s.s., 67, 381, 432.
Utopia, s.s., 362.

Vail, Theodore N., Fund, 30.
Valhalla, Municipal, *see* St. Botolph's.
Vanellus, s.s., 368.
Vengeance, H.M.S., 315.
Verwundeten-Abzeichen (Medal of Wounded), 25.
Viceroy of India, 17, 20.
Victoria Cross, x, xii, xiii, 1, 9, 14–15, 18, 80, 82, 86, 88, 156, 442, 444, 446; institution of, and annuity, 8; extension to Indian troops, 8; warrant and amended warrant, 8–9; analysis of awards 1856–1914, 9–10; awards during Gt. War 1914–20, 10; awards since 1920, 11; not an 'Order', 15; monetary rewards, 21; living holders of, 51.
Victoria, Queen, letters of, 9, 15, 40, 45, 59, 61, 82 ff., 95, 336.
Victory, H.M.S., 3–4.
Viking, sealer, 379.
Villaverde Medal, *see* Camp.
Ville de Paris, flagship, 3.
Vindobala, s.s., disaster, 67.
Virgil quoted, ix, 23.
Vivid, H.M.S., 102.
Volturno, s.s., disaster, 67.
Volumnia, s.s., disaster, 67, 418.

Wakool, H.M.T., 366.
Wales, Carnegie awards, 75.
Walsh, Ensign, at Albuera, 4.
Walter, John H., executors of, 4.
Wantage, Lord, *see* Lindsay.
War Diwan, Roy. Fleet Auxiliary, 413.
War Knight, s.s., 371, 373.
War Office and Admiralty, x, xii, 16, 446; *see* Admiralty.

War Pike, s.s., 211, 375.
Warrior, H.M.S., 316.
Warspite, H.M.S., 331.
Washington, *see* United States.
Waterloo, 1, 3; ribbon, 445.
Watford, s.s., 429.
Watts, G. F., xiii, 76; quoted, 32; letter to *The Times*, 79–80; memorial to, 81; *see* St. Botolph's Churchyard.
Watts, Mrs. M. S., 79–81.
Waziristan, *see* Index of Places.
Weekly Dispatch and Chas. Fitzpatrick, 54–5.
Welch, Robert, knighted, 1.
Wellesley, training ship, 55.
Wellington, Duke of, and principle of selection of medals, 2–3.
West Ham Corporation, xii; awards of medals, 46.
Widgeon, H.M.S., 312.
Wild Rose, brig, 361.
Wild Swan, H.M.S., 310.
William I, Emperor of Germany, 25.
William III and Mary, recognition of bravery, 1–2.
Windsor Castle, 60; archives of, 82, 440 ff.
Wireless: C Q D message, 56; S O S message, 57; compulsory use of, 57.
Women, eligibility of, for decorations, 14.
Wooldridge, Capt. James, in Aix Roads, 4.
Wright, Capt., *see Birkenhead*, H.M.S.
Wuhu, s.s., 287.
Wyon, A., engraver, 58 ff., 63; family, 66; *see also* Wyon, W.
Wyon, W., engraver, 60, 66.

Yule's poem *The Birkenhead*, 7.

Zeppelin incendiary bomb, 45.
Zulu, H.M.S., 317.
Zululand campaign, 9.

www.ingramcontent.com/pod-product-compliance
Lightning Source LLC
Chambersburg PA
CBHW060313230426
43663CB00009B/1681